C#

Software Solutions

FOUNDATIONS OF **PROGRAM DESIGN**

C#
Software Solutions
FOUNDATIONS OF **PROGRAM DESIGN**

John Lewis
Villanova University

PEARSON

Addison
Wesley

Boston San Francisco New York
London Toronto Sydney Tokyo Singapore Madrid
Mexico City Munich Paris Cape Town Hong Kong Montreal

Publisher	Greg Tobin
Senior Acquisitions Editor	Michael Hirsch
Editorial Assistant	Lindsey Triebel
Cover Designer	Joyce Cosentino Wells
Supplements Supervisor	Marianne Groth
Marketing Manager	Michelle Brown
Marketing Assistant	Dana Lopreato
Senior Manufacturing Buyer	Carol Melville
Project Management	Argosy Publishing
Copyeditor	William McManus
Proofreader	Cara Anderson
Indexer	Larry Sweazy
Composition and Art	Argosy Publishing

Access the latest information about Addison-Wesley titles from our World Wide Web site:
http://www.aw-bc.com/computing

Many of the designations used by manufacturers and sellers to distinguish their products are claimed as trademarks. Where those designations appear in this book, and Addison-Wesley was aware of a trademark claim, the designations have been printed in initial caps or all caps.

The programs and applications presented in this book have been included for their instructional value. They have been tested with care but are not guaranteed for any particular purpose. The publisher does not offer any warranties or representations, nor does it accept any liabilities with respect to the programs or applications.

Library of Congress Cataloging-in-Publication Data

Lewis, John, 1963-
   C# software solutions / John Lewis. -- 1st ed.
     p. cm.
   Includes index.
   ISBN 0-321-26716-8
   1. C# (Computer program language) 2. Computer software
--Development.   I. Title.
   QA76.73.C154L38 2006
   005.13'3--dc22

                  2005035820

ISBN 0-321-26716-8
1 2 3 4 5 6 7 8 9 10—CRS—09 08 07 06

Preface

Welcome to C# *Software Solutions*. This book is designed for a first course in computer programming using Microsoft's Visual C#. It is written for those with no previous programming experience, but even those who know another programming language will enjoy the presentation of material in this book.

Cornerstones of the Text

This text is based on the following basic ideas that we believe make for a sound introductory text for computer science, business, information technology, and information systems students:

> **True object-orientation.** A text that really teaches a solid object-oriented approach must use what we call object-speak. That is, all processing should be discussed in object-oriented terms. That does not mean, however, that the first program a student sees must discuss the writing of multiple classes and methods. A student should learn to use objects before learning to write them. This text uses a natural progression that culminates in the ability to design real object-oriented solutions.

> **Sound programming practices.** Students should not be taught how to program; they should be taught how to write good software. There's a difference. Writing software is not a set of cookbook actions, and a good program is more than a collection of statements. This text integrates practices that serve as the foundation of good programming skills. These practices are used in all examples and are reinforced in the discussions. Students learn how to solve problems as well as how to implement solutions. We introduce and integrate basic software engineering techniques throughout the text.

> **Examples.** Students learn by example. This text is filled with fully implemented examples that demonstrate specific concepts. We have intertwined small, readily understandable examples with larger, more realistic ones. In addition, some extra fairly complex examples that are filled with comments are available as supplementary material. See "Supplements" section of this Preface.

> **Windows Applications.** Graphical User Interfaces (GUIs) and writing windows-based applications can be a great motivator for students, and their use can serve as excellent examples of object-orientation. As such, we use them throughout the text in a well-defined set of sections that we call the Windows Track. This coverage includes the use of Visual Studio Interactive Development Environment (IDE), GUI design and use of controls, event processing and drawing graphics. Students learn to build windows applications in the appropriate way by using a natural progression of topics. The Windows Track can be avoided entirely for those who choose to teach programming principles using only console applications.

Chapter Breakdown

Chapter 1 (Introduction) introduces computer systems in general, including basic architecture and hardware, networking, programming, and language translation. C# is introduced in this chapter, and the basics of general program development, as well as object-oriented programming, are discussed. This chapter contains broad introductory material that can be covered while students become familiar with their development environment.

Chapter 2 (Data and Expressions) explores some of the basic types of data used in a C# program and the use of expressions to perform calculations. It discusses the conversion of data from one type to another, and how to read input interactively from the user. The Windows Track (Graphics Device Interface or GDI) describes several of the methods for drawing text and lines plus filling various shapes.

Chapter 3 (Using Classes and Objects) explores the use of predefined classes in the .NET architecture and the objects that can be created from them. Classes and objects are used to manipulate character strings, produce random numbers, perform complex calculations, and format output. Enumerated types are also discussed. The Windows Track (Components and Containers, Pens, Images) details the creation, design, layout and loading of forms, including adding and configuring controls on the form. It also introduces the concept of pens, C# enumeration use as well as drawing stored images on the form and other controls.

Chapter 4 (Writing Classes) explores the basic issues related to writing classes and methods. Topics include instance data, visibility, scope, method parameters, and return types. Encapsulation and constructors are covered as well. Some of the more involved topics are deferred to or revisited in Chapter 6. The Windows Track (Events, Buttons, Text Boxes, Brushes, and Tab Stops) extends the concepts of classes into drawing graphical images. The concept of events is incorporated into a fairly detailed description of text boxes, brushes, and buttons.

Chapter 5 (Conditionals and Loops) covers the use of boolean expressions to make decisions. All related statements for conditionals and loops are discussed. The Windows Track (Drawing with Loops, Event Sources, Dialog Boxes, Check Boxes, Radio Buttons) incorporates loops in the windows-form environment while describing creation and use of dialog boxes. Also included is a description of the system message box tool, check boxes, and radio buttons. Finally, input validation is described, along with infinite loops in GUIs.

Chapter 6 (Object-Oriented Design) reinforces and extends the coverage of issues related to the design of classes. Techniques for identifying the classes and objects needed for a problem and the relationships among them are discussed. This chapter also covers static class members, interfaces, and the design of enumerated type classes. Method design issues and method overloading are also discussed. The Windows Track (GUI Design, Panels, Picture Boxes, Tab Control) teaches design methodologies for GUIs using panels, picture boxes and the tab control.

Chapter 7 (Arrays) contains extensive coverage of arrays and array processing. Topics include command-line arguments, variable-length parameter lists, and multidimensional arrays. The `ArrayList` class and its use as a generic type are explored as well. The Windows Track (Polygons, Events Extended) expands on the concept of arrays through drawing of polygons and tracking multiple data points using some predefined system classes. Also included is a detailed description of mouse and key events along with special form events.

Chapter 8 (Inheritance) covers class derivations and associated concepts such as class hierarchies, overriding, and visibility. Strong emphasis is put on the proper use of inheritance and its role in software design. The Windows Track (Overriding Event Handlers, Extending Components, Timer Class) delves into a few advanced topics, including overriding the standard behavior of event handlers as well as extending existing controls and even creating custom controls. Also included is how to create simple animation with the `Timer` class.

Chapter 9 (Polymorphism) explores the concept of binding and how it relates to polymorphism. Then we examine how polymorphic references can be accomplished using either inheritance or interfaces. Sorting is used as an example of polymorphism. Design issues related to polymorphism are examined as well. The Windows Track (System Dialog Boxes, Sliders, System Registry Access) describes some of the .NET framework tools for doing many necessary functions (opening files, selecting colors, etc.). Also described is how to save configuration information in the Window's system registry.

Chapter 10 (Exceptions) explores the class hierarchy from the .NET architecture used to define exceptions, as well as the ability to define our own exception objects. We discuss the use of exceptions when dealing with input and output, and examine an example that writes a text file. Also described are creating and throwing custom exceptions. The Windows Track (Scroll Panes, Scrolling Text Boxes, Split Panes) details use of some advanced controls for showing larger amounts of information in a limited space. This chapter also lists some of the extra programs on the CD.

Chapter 11 (Recursion) covers the concept, implementation, and proper use of recursion. Several examples from various domains are used to demonstrate how recursive techniques make certain types of processing elegant. The Windows Track (Recursion in

Graphics, Fractals, Printing) extends the discussion of recursion into the graphics arena as well as detailing how to create printed reports.

Chapter 12 (Collections and Link Lists) introduces two advanced data structures. Abstraction is revisited in this context; in conjunction with a discussion of these classic data structures, this can serve as an introduction to a CS2 course.

Appendices

A: Number Systems

B: Unicode Character Set

C: C# Coding Guidelines

D: Visual Studio Installation Guide

E: Glossary

F: C# Operators

G: C# Modifiers

Appendices E through G are available at www.aw.com/cssupport under "Author: Lewis."

Debugging

In addition to the programming concepts and Windows Track content, several of the chapters have special sections that describe how to get the most from the Visual Studio development environment. Most of these special sections cover debugging an application:

Chapter 1:	Starting and single-stepping an application
Chapter 2:	Breakpoints and viewing content of intrinsic variables
Chapter 4:	Viewing the content of object variables; step in, step out, and step over
Chapter 5:	The Watch and Command windows
Chapter 6:	Module level testing and changing program order; tracing problems and writing to the output window

Supplements

The CD that accompanies this book includes a copy of Microsoft Visual C# Express.

A variety of supplemental materials are available for this text. The following resources are available for all students at www.aw.com/cssupport:

> Source code for all the programs in the text

> Appendices E through G

In addition, the following supplements are available to qualified instructors at Addison-Wesley's Instructor Resource Center www.aw.com/irc. Please contact your Addison-Wesley sales representative, or send e-mail to computing@aw.com, for information on how to access them:

> PowerPoint slides

> Solutions to many exercises and programming projects

Acknowledgements

This book would not have happened without the hard work of Ken Culp, who took our Java book and adapted it for C#, and who wrote the Windows Track as well as most of the Windows-based applications. Ken is an expert on Microsoft's Visual Studio and the C# language. Ken currently teaches computer classes for the Department of Mathematics and Computer Science at Northern Michigan University as well as CIS courses for NMU's College of Business. Prior to his teaching career, Ken spent several years running a dental software company and as a consultant to small businesses. He holds an M.B.A. from the University of Houston and a double major in electrical engineering and mathematics from The University of Texas.

We'd also like to thank the team at Addison-Wesley. They include Michael Hirsch, Lindsey Triebel, Patty Mahtani, Joyce Wells, Michelle Brown, and Dana Lopreato. In addition, Megan Schwenke and Edalin Michael at Argosy Publishing were amazing at their work on composition. We thank all of these people for ensuring that this book met the highest quality standards.

Contents

Introduction

CHAPTER OBJECTIVES

> Describe the relationship between hardware and software.

> Define various types of software and how they are used.

> Identify the core hardware components of a computer and explain their roles.

> Explain how the hardware components interact to execute programs and manage data.

> Describe how computers are connected into networks to share information.

> Introduce the C# programming language.

> Describe the steps involved in program compilation and execution.

> Present an overview of object-oriented principles.

This book is about writing well-designed software. To understand software, we must first have a fundamental understanding of its role in a computer system. Hardware and software cooperate in a computer system to accomplish complex tasks. Establishing the basic role of various hardware components, and the way those components are connected into networks, are important prerequisites to the study of software development. This chapter first discusses basic computer processing, and then begins our exploration of software development by introducing the C# programming language and the principles of object-oriented programming.

1.1   COMPUTER PROCESSING

We begin our exploration of computer systems with an overview of computer processing, including definitions of some fundamental terminology and details about how the key pieces of a computer system interact.

A computer system is made up of hardware and software. The *hardware* components of a computer system are the physical, tangible pieces that support the computing effort. They include chips, boxes, wires, keyboards, speakers, disks, cables, plugs, printers, mice, monitors, and so on. If you can physically touch it and it can be considered part of a computer system, then it is computer hardware.

The hardware components of a computer are essentially useless without instructions to tell them what to do. A *program* is a series of instructions that the hardware executes one after another. *Software* consists of programs and the data those programs use. Software is the intangible counterpart to the physical hardware components. Together they form a tool that we can use to solve problems.

The key hardware components in a computer system are:

> central processing unit (CPU)

> input/output (I/O) devices

> main memory

> secondary memory devices

Each of these hardware components is described in detail in the next section. For now, let's simply examine their basic roles. The *central processing unit* (CPU) is the device that executes the individual commands of a program. *Input/output* (I/O) *devices*, such as the keyboard, mouse, and monitor, allow a human being to interact with the computer.

Programs and data are held in storage devices called memory, which fall into two categories: main memory and secondary memory. *Main memory* is the storage device that holds the software while it is being processed by the CPU. *Secondary memory* devices store software in a relatively permanent manner. The most important secondary memory device of a typical computer system is the hard disk that resides inside the main computer box. A floppy disk is similar to a hard disk, but it cannot store nearly as much information as a hard disk. Floppy disks have the advantage of portability; they can be removed temporarily or moved from computer to computer as needed. Other portable secondary memory devices include flash drives and compact discs (CDs).

Figure 1.1 shows how information moves among the basic hardware components of a computer. Suppose you have an executable program you wish to run. The program is stored on some secondary memory device, such as a hard disk. When you instruct the computer to execute your program, a copy of the program is brought in from secondary memory and stored in main memory. The CPU reads the individual program instructions from main memory. The CPU then executes the instructions one at a time until the program ends. The data that the instructions use, such as two numbers that will be added together, is also stored in main memory. The data is either brought in from secondary memory or read from an

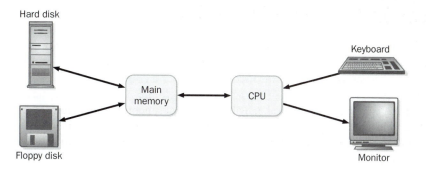

FIGURE 1.1 A simplified view of a computer system

input device such as the keyboard. During execution, the program may display information to an output device such as a monitor.

The process of executing a program is fundamental to the operation of a computer. All computer systems basically work in the same way.

> **Key Concept**
>
> The CPU reads the program instructions from main memory, executing them one at a time until the program ends.

Software Categories

Software can be classified into many categories using various criteria. At this point we will simply differentiate between operating systems and applications.

The *operating system* is the core software of a computer. It performs two important functions. First, it provides a *user interface* that allows the user to interact with the machine. Second, it manages computer resources such as the CPU and main memory; it determines when programs are allowed to run, where they are loaded into memory, and how hardware devices communicate. The operating system's job is to make the computer easy to use and to ensure that it runs efficiently.

Several popular operating systems are in use today. Windows 2000 and Windows XP are two versions of the operating system developed by Microsoft Corporation for personal computers. Various versions of the Unix operating system are also quite popular, especially in larger computer systems. A version of Unix called Linux was developed as an open source project, which means that many people contributed to its development and that its code is freely available. Because it is open source, Linux has become a particular favorite among some users. Mac OS is the operating system used for computing systems developed by Apple Computer Corporation.

> **Key Concept**
>
> The operating system provides a user interface and manages computer resources.

Application is a generic term for just about any software other than the operating system. Word processors, missile control systems, database managers, Web browsers, and games can all be considered applications. Each application has its own user interface that allows the user to interact with that particular program.

The user interface for most modern operating systems and applications is a *graphical user interface* (GUI), which, as the name implies, uses graphical screen elements. These elements include:

> *windows,* which are used to separate the screen into distinct work areas

> *icons,* which are small images that represent computer resources, such as a file

> *pull-down menus,* which provide the user with lists of options

> *scroll bars,* which allow the user to move up and down in a particular window

> *buttons,* which can be "pushed" with a mouse click to indicate a user selection

The mouse is the primary input device used with GUIs; thus, GUIs are sometimes called *point-and-click interfaces.* The screen shot in Figure 1.2 shows an example of a GUI.

The interface to an application or operating system is an important part of the software because it is the only part of the program with which the user directly interacts. To the user, the interface *is* the program. Throughout this book we discuss the design and implementation of GUIs.

Key Concept

As far as the user is concerned, the interface is the program.

The focus of this book is the development of high-quality applications. We explore how to design and write software that will perform calculations, make decisions, and control graphics. We use the C# programming language throughout the text to demonstrate various computing concepts.

Digital Computers

Two fundamental technologies are used to store and manage information: analog and digital. *Analog* information is continuous, in direct proportion to the source of the information.

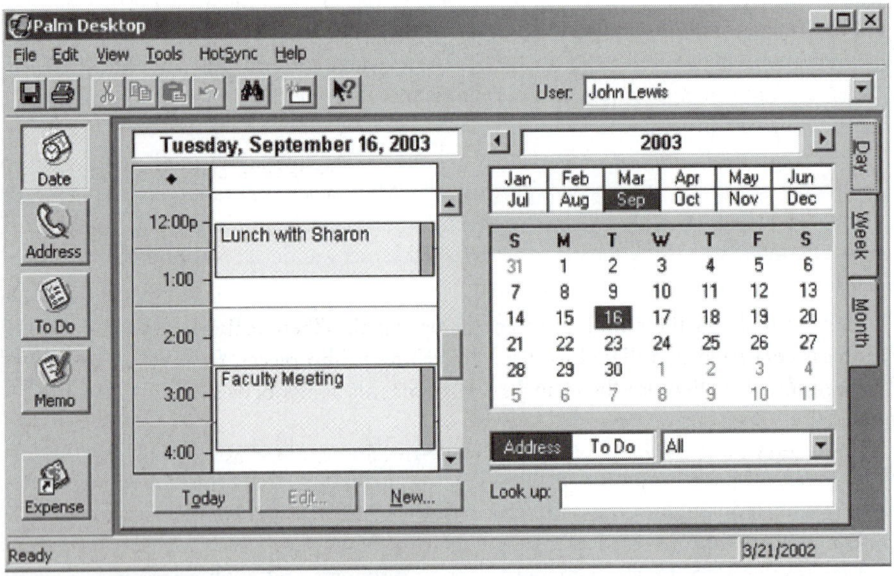

FIGURE 1.2   An example of a graphical user interface (GUI)
(Palm Desktop™ Courtesy of 3Com Corporation)

For example, a mercury thermometer is an analog device for measuring temperature. The mercury rises in a tube in direct proportion to the temperature outside the tube. Another example of analog information is an electronic signal used to represent the vibrations of a sound wave. The signal's voltage varies in direct proportion to the original sound wave. A stereo amplifier sends this kind of electronic signal to its speakers, which vibrate to reproduce the sound. We use the term analog because the signal is directly analogous to the information it represents. Figure 1.3 graphically depicts a sound wave captured by a microphone and represented as an electronic signal.

Digital technology breaks information into discrete pieces and represents those pieces as numbers. The music on a compact disc is stored digitally, as a series of numbers. Each number represents the voltage level of one specific instance of the recording. Many of these measurements are taken in a short period of time, perhaps 40,000 measurements every second. The number of measurements per second is called the *sampling rate*. If samples are taken often enough, the discrete voltage measurements can be used to generate a continuous analog signal that is "close enough" to the original. In most cases, the goal is to create a reproduction of the original signal that is good enough to satisfy the human senses.

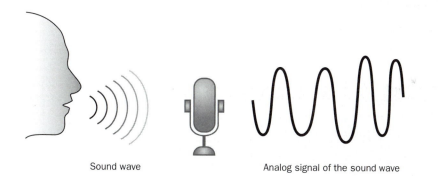

Sound wave   Analog signal of the sound wave

FIGURE 1.3   A sound wave and an electronic analog signal that represents the wave

Figure 1.4 shows the sampling of an analog signal. When analog information is converted to a digital format by breaking it into pieces, we say it has been *digitized*. Because the changes that occur in a signal between samples are lost, the sampling rate must be sufficiently fast.

Production note: Generally the figures should be positioned as close to the first reference as the lay out allows.

Sampling is only one way to digitize information. For example, a sentence of text is stored on a computer as a series of numbers, where each number represents a single character in the sentence. Every letter, digit, and punctuation symbol has been assigned a number. Even the space character is assigned a number. Consider the following sentence:

> **Key Concept**
>
> Digital computers store information by breaking it into pieces and representing each piece as a number.

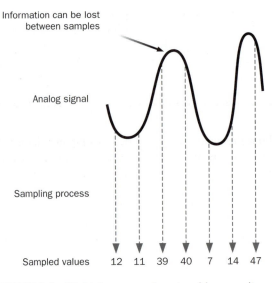

Information can be lost between samples

Analog signal

Sampling process

Sampled values   12   11   39   40   7   14   47

FIGURE 1.4   Digitizing an analog signal by sampling

Hi, Heather.

The characters of the sentence are represented as a series of 12 numbers, as shown in Figure 1.5. When a character is repeated, such as the uppercase 'H', the same representation number is used. Note that the uppercase version of a letter is stored as a different number than the number stored for the lowercase version, such as the 'H' and 'h' in the word Heather. They are considered separate and distinct characters.

Modern electronic computers are digital. Every kind of information, including text, images, numbers, audio, video, and even program instructions, is broken into pieces. Each piece is represented as a number. The information is stored by storing those numbers.

Binary Numbers

A digital computer stores information as numbers, but those numbers are not stored as *decimal* values. All information in a computer is stored and managed as *binary* values. Unlike the decimal system, which has 10 digits (0 through 9), the binary number system has only 2 digits (0 and 1). A single binary digit is called a *bit*.

All number systems work according to the same rules. The *base value* of a number system dictates how many digits we have to work with and indicates the place value of each digit in a number. The decimal number system is base 10, whereas the binary number system is base 2. Appendix A contains a detailed discussion of number systems.

Modern computers use binary numbers because the devices that store and move information are less expensive and more reliable if they have to represent only one of two possible values. Other than this characteristic, there is

> **Key Concept**
>
> Binary is used to store information in a computer because the devices that store and manipulate binary data are inexpensive and reliable.

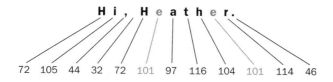

FIGURE 1.5 Text is stored by mapping each character to a number

nothing special about the binary number system. Computers have been created that use other number systems to store information, but they aren't as convenient.

Some computer memory devices, such as hard drives, are magnetic in nature. Magnetic material can be polarized easily to one extreme or the other, but intermediate levels are difficult to distinguish. Therefore, magnetic devices can be used to represent binary values quite efficiently-a magnetized area represents a binary 1 and a demagnetized area represents a binary 0. Other computer memory devices are made up of tiny electrical circuits. These devices are easier to create and are less likely to fail if they have to switch between only two states. We're better off reproducing millions of these simple devices than creating fewer, more complicated ones.

Binary values and digital electronic signals go hand in hand. They improve our ability to transmit information reliably along a wire. As we've seen, an analog signal has continuously varying voltage, but a digital signal is *discrete,* which means the voltage changes dramatically between one extreme (such as +5 volts) and the other (such as -5 volts). At any point, the voltage of a digital signal is considered to be either "high," which represents a binary 1, or "low," which represents a binary 0. Figure 1.6 compares these two types of signals.

As a signal moves down a wire, it gets weaker and degrades due to environmental conditions. That is, the voltage levels of the original signal change slightly. The trouble with an analog signal is that as it fluctuates, it loses its original information. Since the information is directly analogous to the signal, any change in the signal changes the information. The changes in an analog signal cannot be recovered because the degraded signal is just as valid as the original. A digital signal degrades just as an analog signal does, but because the digital signal is originally at one of two extremes, it can be reinforced before any information is

Analog signal   Digital signal

FIGURE 1.6 An analog signal vs. a digital signal

lost. The voltage may change slightly from its original value, but it still can be interpreted as either high or low.

The number of bits we use in any given situation determines the number of unique items we can represent. A single bit has two possible values, 0 and 1, and therefore can represent two possible items or situations. If we want to represent the state of a light bulb (off or on), 1 bit will suffice, because we can interpret 0 as the light bulb being off and 1 as the light bulb being on. If we want to represent more than two things, we need more than 1 bit.

Two bits, taken together, can represent four possible items because there are exactly four permutations of 2 bits: 00, 01, 10, and 11. Suppose we want to represent the gear that a car is in (park, drive, reverse, or neutral). We would need only 2 bits, and could set up a mapping between the bit permutations and the gears. For instance, we could say that 00 represents park, 01 represents drive, 10 represents reverse, and 11 represents neutral. In this case, it wouldn't matter if we switched that mapping around, though in some cases the relationships between the bit permutations and what they represent is important.

> **Key Concept**
>
> There are exactly 2^N permutations of N bits. Therefore, N bits can represent up to 2^N unique items.

Three bits can represent eight unique items, because there are eight permutations of 3 bits. Similarly, 4 bits can represent 16 items, 5 bits can represent 32 items, and so on. Figure 1.7 shows the relationship between the number of bits used and the number of items they can represent. In general, N bits can represent 2^N unique items. For every bit added, the number of items that can be represented doubles.

We've seen how a sentence of text is stored on a computer by mapping characters to numeric values. Those numeric values are stored as binary numbers. Suppose we want to represent character strings in a language that contains 256 characters and symbols. We would need to use 8 bits to store each character because there are 256 unique permutations of 8 bits (2^8 equals 256). Each bit permutation, or binary value, is mapped to a specific character.

Ultimately, representing information on a computer boils down to the number of items there are to represent and determining the way those items are mapped to binary values.

1.2   HARDWARE COMPONENTS

Let's examine the hardware components of a computer system in more detail. Consider the computer described in Figure 1.8. What does it all mean? Is the system capable of running the software you want it to? How does it compare to other systems? These terms are explained throughout this section.

Computer Architecture

The architecture of a house defines its structure. Similarly, we use the term *computer architecture* to describe how the hardware components of a computer are put together. Figure 1.9 illustrates the basic architecture of a generic computer system. Information travels between components across a group of wires called a *bus*.

1 bit 2 items	2 bits 4 items	3 bits 8 items	4 bits 16 items	5 bits 32 items	
0	00	000	0000	00000	10000
1	01	001	0001	00001	10001
	10	010	0010	00010	10010
	11	011	0011	00011	10011
		100	0100	00100	10100
		101	0101	00101	10101
		110	0110	00110	10110
		111	0111	00111	10111
			1000	01000	11000
			1001	01001	11001
			1010	01010	11010
			1011	01011	11011
			1100	01100	11100
			1101	01101	11101
			1110	01110	11110
			1111	01111	11111

FIGURE 1.7   The number of bits used determines the number
of items that can be represented

The CPU and the main memory make up the core of a computer. As we mentioned earlier, main memory stores programs and data that are in active use, and the CPU methodically executes program instructions one at a time.

Suppose we have a program that computes the average of a list of numbers. The program and the numbers must reside in main memory while the program runs. The CPU reads one

- 2.8 GHz Intel Pentium 4 processor

- 512 MB RAM

- 160 GB Hard Drive

- 48x CD-RW / DVD-ROM Combo Drive

- 17" Flat Screen Video Display with
  1280 × 1024 resolution

- 56 Kb/s Modem

FIGURE 1.8   The hardware specification of a particular computer

program instruction from main memory and executes it. If an instruction needs data, such as a number in the list, to perform its task, the CPU reads that information as well. This process repeats until the program ends. The average, when computed, is stored in main memory to await further processing or long-term storage in secondary memory.

Almost all devices in a computer system other than the CPU and main memory are called *peripherals*; they operate at the periphery, or outer edges, of the system (although they may be in the same box). Users don't interact directly with the CPU or main memory. Although they form the essence of the machine, the CPU and main memory would not be useful without peripheral devices.

Controllers are devices that coordinate the activities of specific peripherals. Every device has its own particular way of formatting and communicating data, and part of the controller's role is to handle these idiosyncrasies and isolate them from the rest of the computer hardware. Furthermore, the controller often handles much of the actual transmission of information, allowing the CPU to focus on other activities.

Input/output (I/O) devices and secondary memory devices are considered peripherals. Another category of peripherals includes *data transfer devices,* which allow information to be sent and received between computers. The computer specified in Figure 1.8 includes a data transfer device called a *modem,* which allows information to be sent across a telephone line. The modem in the example can transfer data at a maximum rate of 56 *kilobits* (Kb) per second, or approximately 56,000 *bits per second* (bps).

In some ways, secondary memory devices and data transfer devices can be thought of as I/O devices because they represent a source of information (input) and a place to send infor-

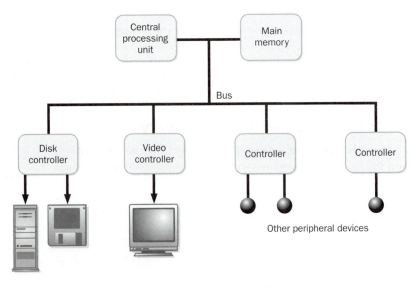

FIGURE 1.9   Basic computer architecture

mation (output). For our discussion, however, we define I/O devices as those devices that allow the user to interact with the computer.

Input/Output Devices

Let's examine some I/O devices in more detail. The most common input devices are the keyboard and the mouse. Others include:

> *bar code readers,* such as the ones used at a grocery store checkout

> *joysticks,* often used for games and advanced graphical applications

> *microphones,* used by voice recognition systems that interpret simple voice commands

> *virtual reality devices,* such as gloves that interpret the movement of the user's hand

> *scanners,* which convert text, photographs, and graphics into machine-readable form

Monitors and printers are the most common output devices. Others include:

> *plotters,* which move pens across large sheets of paper (or vice versa)

> *speakers,* for audio output

> *goggles,* for virtual reality display

Some devices can provide both input and output capabilities. A *touch screen* system can detect the user touching the screen at a particular place. Software can then use the screen to display text and graphics in response to the user's touch. Touch screens are particularly useful in situations where the interface to the machine must be simple, such as at an information booth.

The computer described in Figure 1.8 includes a monitor with a 17-inch diagonal display area. It is a flat screen, which uses newer liquid crystal display (LCD) technology rather than the older cathode ray tube (CRT) technology found in traditional monitors that take up much more space on a desk. A picture is represented in a computer by breaking it up into separate picture elements, or *pixels.* The monitor can display a grid of 1280 by 1024 pixels. Representing and managing graphical data is discussed in more detail in Chapter 2.

Main Memory and Secondary Memory

Main memory is made up of a series of small, consecutive *memory locations,* as shown in Figure 1.10. Associated with each memory location is a unique number called an *address.*

When data is stored in a memory location, it overwrites and destroys any information that was previously stored at that location. However, data is read from a memory location without affecting it.

> **Key Concept**
>
> An address is a unique number associated with each memory location.

On many computers, each memory location consists of 8 bits, or 1 *byte,* of information. If we need to store a value that cannot be represented in a single byte, such as a large number, then multiple, consecutive bytes are used to store the data.

The *storage capacity* of a device such as main memory is the total number of bytes it can hold. Devices can store thousands or millions of bytes, so you should become familiar with larger units of measure. Because computer memory is based on the binary number system, all units of storage are powers of two. A *kilobyte* (KB) is 1024, or 2^{10}, bytes. Some larger units of storage are a *megabyte* (MB), a *gigabyte* (GB), and a *terabyte* (TB), as listed in Figure 1.11. It's usually easier to think about these capacities by rounding them off. For example, most computer users think of a kilobyte as approximately 1000 bytes, a megabyte as approximately 1 million bytes, and so forth.

Many personal computers have 256 or 512 MB of main memory, or RAM, such as the system described in Figure 1.8 (we discuss RAM in more detail later in this chapter). A large main memory allows large programs, or multiple programs, to run efficiently because they don't have to retrieve information from secondary memory as often.

Main memory is usually *volatile,* meaning that the information stored in it will be lost if its electric power supply is turned off. When you are working on a computer, you should often save your work onto a secondary memory device such as a disk in case the power goes out. Secondary memory devices are usually *nonvolatile*; the information is retained even if the power supply is turned off.

Key Concept

Main memory is volatile, meaning the stored information is maintained only as long as electric power is supplied.

The most common secondary storage devices are hard disks and floppy disks. A high-density floppy disk can store 1.44 MB of information. The storage capacities of hard drives vary, but on personal computers, capacities typically range between 40 and 120 GB, such as in the system described in Figure 1.8.

A disk is a magnetic medium on which bits are represented as magnetized particles. A read/write head passes over the spinning disk, reading or writing information as appropriate. A hard disk drive might actually contain several disks in a vertical column with several read/write heads, such as the one shown in Figure 1.12.

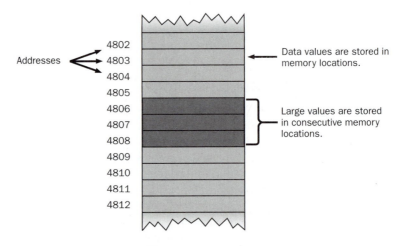

FIGURE 1.10   Memory locations

Unit	Symbol	Number of Bytes
byte		$2^0 = 1$
kilobyte	KB	$2^{10} = 1024$
megabyte	MB	$2^{20} = 1,048,576$
gigabyte	GB	$2^{30} = 1,073,741,824$
terabyte	TB	$2^{40} = 1,099,511,627,776$

FIGURE 1.11   Units of binary storage

To get an intuitive feel for how much information these devices can store, consider that all the information in this book, including pictures and formatting, requires about 7 MB of storage.

Magnetic tapes are also used as secondary storage but are considerably slower than disks because of the way information is accessed. A disk is a *direct access device* since the read/write head can move, in general, directly to the information needed. The terms direct access and *random access* are often used interchangeably. However, information on a tape can be accessed only after first getting past the intervening data. A tape must be rewound or fast-forwarded to get to the appropriate position. A tape is therefore considered a *sequential access device.* Tapes are usually used only to store information when it is no longer used frequently, or to provide a backup copy of the information on a disk.

Two other terms are used to describe memory devices: *random access memory* (RAM) and *read-only memory* (ROM). It's important to understand these terms because they are used often, and their names can be misleading. The terms RAM and main memory are basically

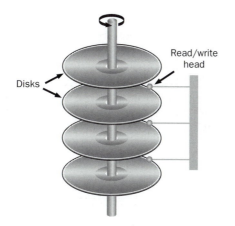

FIGURE 1.12   A hard disk drive with multiple disks and read/write heads

interchangeable. When contrasted with ROM, however, the term RAM seems to imply something it shouldn't. Both RAM and ROM are direct (or random) access devices. RAM should probably be called read-write memory, since data can be both written to it and read from it. This feature distinguishes it from ROM. After information is stored on ROM, it cannot be altered (as the term "read-only" implies). ROM chips are often embedded into the main circuit board of a computer and used to provide the preliminary instructions needed when the computer is initially turned on.

A *CD-ROM* is a portable secondary memory device. CD stands for compact disc. It is accurately called ROM because information is stored permanently when the CD is created and cannot be changed. Like its musical CD counterpart, a CD-ROM stores information in binary format. When the CD is initially created, a microscopic pit is pressed into the disc to represent a binary 1, and the disc is left smooth to represent a binary 0. The bits are read by shining a low-intensity laser beam onto the spinning disc. The laser beam reflects strongly from a smooth area on the disc but weakly from a pitted area. A sensor receiving the reflection determines whether each bit is a 1 or a 0 accordingly. A typical CD-ROM's storage capacity is approximately 650 MB.

> **Key Concept**
>
> The surface of a CD has both smooth areas and small pits. A pit represents a binary 1 and a smooth area represents a binary 0.

Variations on basic CD technology have emerged quickly. It is now common for a home computer to be equipped with a *CD-Recordable* (CD-R) drive. A CD-R can be used to create a CD for music or for general computer storage. Once created, you can use a CD-R disc in a standard CD player, but you can't change the information on a CD-R disc once it has been "burned." Music CDs that you buy in a store are pressed from a mold, whereas CD-Rs are burned with a laser.

> **Key Concept**
>
> A rewritable CD simulates the pits and smooth areas of a regular CD by using a coating that can be made amorphous or crystalline as needed.

A *CD-Rewritable* (CD-RW) disc can be erased and reused. CD-RW discs can be reused because the pits and flat surfaces of a normal CD are simulated on a CD-RW by coating the surface of the disc with a material that becomes amorphous (and therefore nonreflective) when heated to one temperature and becomes crystalline (and therefore reflective) when heated to a different temperature. The CD-RW media doesn't work in all players, but CD-RW drives can create both CD-R and CD-RW discs.

CDs were initially a popular format for music; they later evolved to be used as a general computer storage device. Similarly, the *DVD* format was originally created for video and is now making headway as a general format for computer data. DVD once stood for digital video disc or digital versatile disc, but now the acronym generally stands on its own. A DVD has a tighter format (more bits per square inch) than a CD and can therefore store much more information. It is likely that DVD-ROMs eventually will replace CD-ROMs completely because there is a compatible migration path, meaning that a DVD drive can read a CD-ROM. Similar to CD-R and CD-RW, there are DVD-R and DVD-RW discs. The drive listed in Figure 1.8 allows the user to read and write CD-RW discs and read DVD-ROMs. This, of course, includes the ability to play music CDs and watch DVD videos.

The speed of a CD or DVD drive is expressed in multiples of x, which represents a data transfer speed of 153,600 bytes of data per second. The drive described in Figure 1.8 has a maximum data access speed of 48x, though it probably writes data at much slower speeds.

The capacity of storage devices changes continually as technology improves. A general rule in the computer industry suggests that storage capacity approximately doubles every 18 months. However, this progress eventually will slow down as capacities approach absolute physical limits.

The Central Processing Unit

The central processing unit (CPU) interacts with main memory to perform all fundamental processing in a computer. The CPU interprets and executes instructions, one after another, in a continuous cycle. It is made up of three important components, as shown in Figure 1.13. The *control unit* coordinates the processing steps, the *registers* provide a small amount of storage space in the CPU itself, and the *arithmetic/logic unit* performs calculations and makes decisions.

The control unit coordinates the transfer of data and instructions between main memory and the registers in the CPU. It also coordinates the execution of the circuitry in the arithmetic/logic unit to perform operations on data stored in particular registers.

In most CPUs, some registers are reserved for special purposes. For example, the *instruction register* holds the current instruction being executed. The *program counter* is a register that holds the address of the next instruction to be executed. In addition to these and other special-purpose registers, the CPU also contains a set of general-purpose registers that are used for temporary storage of values as needed.

The concept of storing both program instructions and data together in main memory is the underlying principle of the *von Neumann architecture* of computer design, named after John von Neumann, who first advanced this programming concept in 1945. These computers continually follow the *fetch-decode-execute* cycle depicted in Figure 1.14. An instruction is fetched from main memory at the address stored in the program counter and is put into the instruction register. The program counter is incremented at this

Key Concept

The fetch-decode-execute cycle forms the foundation of computer processing.

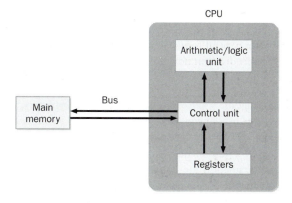

FIGURE 1.13   CPU components and main memory

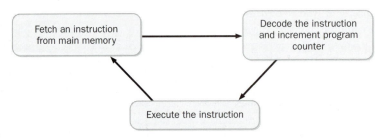

FIGURE 1.14 The continuous fetch-decode-execute cycle

point to prepare for the next cycle. Then the instruction is decoded electronically to determine which operation to carry out. Finally, the control unit activates the correct circuitry to execute the instruction, which may load a data value into a register or add two values together, for example.

The CPU is constructed on a chip called a *microprocessor*, a device that is part of the main circuit board of the computer. This board also contains ROM chips and communication sockets to which device controllers, such as the controller that manages the video display, can be connected.

Another crucial component of the main circuit board is the *system clock*. The clock generates at regular intervals an electronic pulse that synchronizes the events of the CPU. The rate at which the pulses occur is called the *clock speed*, and it varies depending on the processor. The computer described in Figure 1.8 includes a Pentium 4 processor that runs at a clock speed of 2.8 gigahertz (GHz), or approximately 2.8 billion pulses per second. The speed of the system clock provides a rough measure of how fast the CPU executes instructions. Similar to storage capacities, the speed of processors is constantly increasing with advances in technology.

1.3 NETWORKS

A single computer can accomplish a great deal, but connecting several computers together into a network can dramatically increase productivity and facilitate the sharing of information. A *network* is two or more computers connected together so that they can exchange information. Using networks has become the normal mode of commercial computer operation. New technologies are emerging every day to capitalize on the connected environments of modern computer systems.

Key Concept

A network consists of two or more computers connected together so that they can exchange information.

Figure 1.15 shows a simple computer network. One of the devices on the network is a printer, which allows any computer connected to the network to print a document. One of the computers on the network is designated as a *file server*, which is dedicated to storing programs and data that are needed by many network users. A file server usually has a large amount of secondary memory. When a network has a file server, each individual computer doesn't need its own copy of a program.

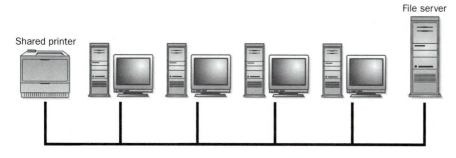

FIGURE 1.15   A simple computer network

Network Connections

If two computers are directly connected, they can communicate in basically the same way that information moves across wires inside a single machine. Connecting two geographically close computers works well and is called a *point-to-point connection.* However, consider the task of connecting many computers together across large distances. If point-to-point connections were used, every computer would have to be directly connected by a wire to every other computer in the network. This is not a workable solution, because every time a new computer needed to be added to the network, a new communication line would have to be installed for each computer already in the network. Furthermore, a single computer can handle only a small number of direct connections.

Figure 1.16 shows multiple point-to-point connections. Consider the number of communication lines that would be needed if two or three additional computers were added to the network.

Compare the diagrams in Figure 1.15 and Figure 1.16. All of the computers shown in Figure 1.15 share a single communication line. Each computer on the network has its own *network address,* which uniquely identifies it. These addresses are similar in concept to the addresses in main memory except that they identify individual computers on a network instead of individual memory locations inside a single computer. A message is sent across

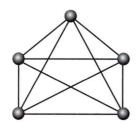

FIGURE 1.16   Point-to-point connections

the line from one computer to another by specifying the network address of the computer for which it is intended.

Sharing a communication line is cost effective and makes adding new computers to the network relatively easy. However, a shared line introduces delays. The computers on the network cannot use the communication line at the same time. They have to take turns sending information, which means they have to wait when the line is busy.

One technique to improve network delays is to divide large messages into segments, called *packets,* and then send the individual packets across the network intermixed with pieces of other messages sent by other users. The packets are collected at the destination and reassembled into the original message. This situation is similar to a group of people using a conveyor belt to move a set of boxes from one place to another. If only one person were allowed to use the conveyor belt at a time, and that person had a large number of boxes to move, the others would be waiting a long time before they could use it. By taking turns, each person can put one box on at a time, and they all can get their work done. It's not as fast as having a conveyor belt of your own, but it's not as slow as having to wait until everyone else is finished.

Local-Area Networks and Wide-Area Networks

A *local-area network* (LAN) is designed to span short distances and connect a relatively small number of computers. Usually a LAN connects the machines in only one building or in a single room. LANs are convenient to install and manage and are highly reliable. As computers became increasingly small and versatile, LANs became an inexpensive way to share information throughout an organization. However, having a LAN is like having a telephone system that allows you to call only the people in your own town. We need to be able to share information across longer distances.

A *wide-area network* (WAN) connects two or more LANs, often across long distances. Usually one computer on each LAN is dedicated to handling the communication across a WAN. This technique relieves the other computers in a LAN from having to perform the details of long-distance communication. Figure 1.17 shows several LANs connected into a WAN. The LANs connected by a WAN are often owned by different companies or organizations, and might even be located in different countries.

The impact of networks on computer systems has been dramatic. Computing resources can now be shared among many users, and computer-based communication across the entire world is now possible. In fact, the use of networks is now so pervasive that some computers require network resources in order to operate.

The Internet

Throughout the 1970s, a United States government organization called the Advanced Research Projects Agency (ARPA) funded several projects to explore network technology. One result of these efforts was the ARPANET, a WAN that eventually became known as the

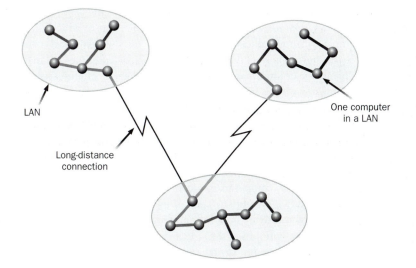

FIGURE 1.17 LANs connected into a WAN

Internet. The *Internet* is a network of networks. The term Internet comes from the WAN concept of *internetworking*-connecting many smaller networks together.

Key Concept

The Internet is a wide-area network (WAN) that spans the globe.

From the mid 1980s through the present day, the Internet has grown incredibly. In 1983, there were fewer than 600 computers connected to the Internet. By the year 2000, that number had reached over 10 million. As more and more computers connect to the Internet, the task of keeping up with the larger number of users and heavier traffic has been difficult. New technologies have replaced the ARPANET several times since the initial development, each time providing more capacity and faster processing.

A *protocol* is a set of rules that governs how two things communicate. The software that controls the movement of messages across the Internet must conform to a set of protocols called TCP/IP (pronounced by spelling out the letters, T-C-P-I-P). TCP stands for *Transmission Control Protocol,* and IP stands for *Internet Protocol.* The IP software defines how information is formatted and transferred from the source to the destination. The TCP software handles problems such as pieces of information arriving out of their original order or information getting lost, which can happen if too much information converges at one location at the same time.

Every computer connected to the Internet has an *IP address* that uniquely identifies it among all other computers on the Internet. An example of an IP address is 204.192.116.2. Fortunately, the users of the Internet rarely have to deal with IP addresses. The Internet allows each computer to be given a name. Like IP addresses, the names must be unique. The Internet name of a computer is often referred to as its *Internet address.* Two examples of Internet addresses are spencer.villanova.edu and kant.gestalt-llc.com.

Key Concept

Every computer connected to the Internet has an IP address that uniquely identifies it.

The first part of an Internet address is the local name of a specific computer. The rest of the address is the *domain name,* which indicates the organization to which the computer belongs. For example, villanova.edu is the domain name for the network of computers at Villanova University, and spencer is the name of a particular computer on that campus. Because domain names are unique, many organizations can have a computer named spencer without causing confusion on the Internet. Individual departments might be assigned *subdomains* that are added to the basic domain name to uniquely distinguish their set of computers within the larger organization. For example, the csc.villanova.edu subdomain is devoted to the Department of Computing Sciences at Villanova University.

The last part of each domain name, called a *top-level domain* (TLD), usually indicates the type of organization to which the computer belongs. The TLD .edu indicates an educational institution. The TLD .com refers to a commercial business. For example, gestalt-llc.com refers to Gestalt, LLC, a company specializing in software technologies. Another common TLD is .org, used mostly by nonprofit organizations. Many computers, especially those outside of the United States, use a TLD that denotes the country of origin, such as .uk for the United Kingdom or .au for Australia. Recently, in response to a diminishing supply of domain names, some new top-level domain names have been created, such as .biz, .info, and .name.

When an Internet address is referenced, it gets translated to its corresponding IP address, which is used from that point on. The software that does this translation is called the *Domain Name System* (DNS). Each organization connected to the Internet operates a *domain server* that maintains a list of all computers at that organization and their IP addresses. It works somewhat like telephone directory assistance in that you provide the name, and the domain server gives back a number. If the local domain server does not have the IP address for the name, it contacts another domain server that does.

The Internet has revolutionized computer processing. Initially, the primary use of interconnected computers was to send electronic mail, but Internet capabilities continue to improve. One of the most significant uses of the Internet is the World Wide Web.

The World Wide Web

The Internet gives us the capability to exchange information. The *World Wide Web* (also known as WWW or simply the Web) makes the exchange of information easy. Web software provides a common user interface through which many different types of information can be accessed with the click of a mouse.

> **Key Concept**
>
> The World Wide Web is software that makes sharing information across a network easy.

The Web is based on the concepts of hypertext and hypermedia. The term *hypertext* was first used in 1965 to describe a way to organize information so that the flow of ideas is not constrained to a linear progression. In fact, that concept was entertained as a way to manage large amounts of information as early as the 1940s. Researchers on the Manhattan Project, who were developing the first atomic bomb, envisioned such an approach. The underlying idea is that documents can be linked at various points according to natural relationships so that the reader can jump from one document to another, following the appropriate path for that reader's needs. When other media components are incorporated, such as graphics, sound, animations, and video, the resulting organization is called *hypermedia.*

The terms Internet and World Wide Web are sometimes used interchangeably, but there are important differences between the two. The Internet makes it possible to communicate via computers around the world. The Web makes that communication a straightforward and enjoyable activity. The Web is essentially a distributed information service and is based on a set of software applications. It is not a network. Although it is used effectively with the Internet, it is not inherently bound to it. The Web can be used on a LAN that is not connected to any other network or even on a single machine to display HTML documents.

A *browser* is a software tool that loads and formats Web documents for viewing. *Mosaic,* the first graphical interface browser for the Web, was released in 1993. The designer of a Web document defines *links* to other Web information that might be anywhere on the Internet. Some of the people who developed Mosaic went on to found the Netscape Communications Corporation and create the Netscape Navigator browser. It is currently one of the most popular systems for accessing information on the Web. Microsoft's Internet Explorer is another popular browser.

A computer dedicated to providing access to Web documents is called a *Web server.* Browsers load and interpret documents provided by a Web server. Many such documents are formatted using the *HyperText Markup Language* (HTML). In the past, the Java programming language was the primary language for use with Web processing because links to Java programs could be embedded in HTML documents and executed through Web browsers. However, Microsoft's C# language can now be used for Web programming and can be accessed from within Web browsers. Unfortunately, Web programming with C# is beyond the scope of this book.

Uniform Resource Locators

Information on the Web is found by identifying a *Uniform Resource Locator* (URL). A URL uniquely specifies documents and other information for a browser to obtain and display. The following is an example URL:

> http://www.google.com

The Web site at this particular URL is a popular *search engine,* which enables you to search the Web for information using particular words or phrases.

A URL contains several pieces of information. The first piece is a protocol, which determines the way the browser transmits and processes information. The second piece is the Internet address of the machine on which the document is stored. The third piece is the file name of interest. If no file name is given, as is the case with the Google URL, the Web server usually provides a default page (such as index.html).

Let's look at another example URL:

> http://www.gestalt-llc.com/vision.html

In this URL, the protocol is http, which stands for *HyperText Transfer Protocol.* The machine referenced is www (a typical reference to a Web server), found at domain gestalt-llc.com.

> **Key Concept**
>
> A URL uniquely specifies documents and other information found on the Web for a browser to obtain and display.

Finally, vision.html is a file to be transferred to the browser for viewing. Many other forms for URLs exist, but this form is the most common.

1.4   THE C# PROGRAMMING LANGUAGE

Let's now turn our attention to the software that makes a computer system useful. A program is written in a particular *programming language* that uses specific words and symbols to express the problem solution. A programming language defines a set of rules that determines exactly how a programmer can combine the words and symbols of the language into *programming statements,* which are the instructions that are carried out when the program is executed.

Since the inception of computers, many programming languages have been created. We use the C# language in this book to demonstrate various programming concepts and techniques. Although our main goal is to learn these underlying software development concepts, an important side effect will be to become proficient in the development of C# programs.

C# is a recent addition to the world of programming that was developed by Microsoft for use in both Web-based and stand-alone applications. Microsoft incorporated into C# the latest features in the object-oriented technology from its C++ language and the ease-of-use features of its Visual Basic language.

The syntax of C# and its object-oriented nature also resembles the Java language developed by Sun Microsystems. Since Java and C++ were modeled on C, the C# language retains much of the structure of these earlier languages. This enables programmers who are familiar with Java, C, or C++ to feel comfortable with C# quite quickly.

C# is an *object-oriented programming language.* Objects are the fundamental elements that make up a program. The principles of object-oriented software development are the cornerstone of this book. We explore object-oriented programming concepts later in this chapter and throughout the rest of the book.

> **Key Concept**
>
> This book focuses on the principles of object-oriented programming.

The C# language and the .NET platform expose a wide variety of functions and facilities for developing programs. This software, referred to as *namespaces,* provides the ability to create graphics, communicate over networks, interact with databases, and many other features. Since the level of functionality available in .NET is so extensive, we will be able to cover only a portion of the features, primarily those that are needed in the development of the programs covered in this book. For information on facilities not covered in this book, use the help system in .NET (see Appendix D).

C# is now appearing in many commercial environments all over the world. It is one of the fastest growing programming technologies of all time. So not only is it a good language in which to learn programming concepts, it is also a practical language that will serve you well in the future.

A C# Program

Let's begin by creating a simple but complete C# program. Open Visual Studio and select File/New/Project. This opens the New Project dialog box, shown in Figure 1.18. Click the Console Application icon in the Templates window, type a name of Lincoln, select a directory in the Location box, and click OK.

Visual Studio creates the application for you and fills in a lot of the code, as shown in Listing 1.1. It then places a comment line where your code is to be placed (// TODO: Add code to start application here). In a moment, you will type your code in this window so that it matches the code shown in Listing 1.1. For now, let's take a moment to examine all this code that C# has created for us.

Listing 1.1

```
using System;
System.Collections.Generic;
System.Text

namespace Lincoln
{
  class Program
  {
    static void Main(string[] args)
    {
    }
  }
}
```

Brief Analysis of System-Generated Code for Console Applications

At this time, we will only highlight the code that Visual Studio produces when you create a console application. We will elaborate on this code in Chapter 2 when we examine the additional code Visual Studio creates for a Windows application.

The first three lines, **using** System;, at the top of the form make available to the program those services commonly needed for a simple console application. To simplify your access to these services and to minimize typing, Visual Studio has assumed that you will be using these libraries in your console application You should not remove these lines, because your console application will not compile if you do.

The next line, **namespace** Lincoln, tells Visual Studio that you are creating your own application library called Lincoln. Namespaces will be discussed in greater detail in Chapter 3, with additional information available in the help files.

The line that begins with class defines a container for your program. Classes will be described in Chapters 3 and 4. For now, recognize that all programs within C# are classes within namespaces.

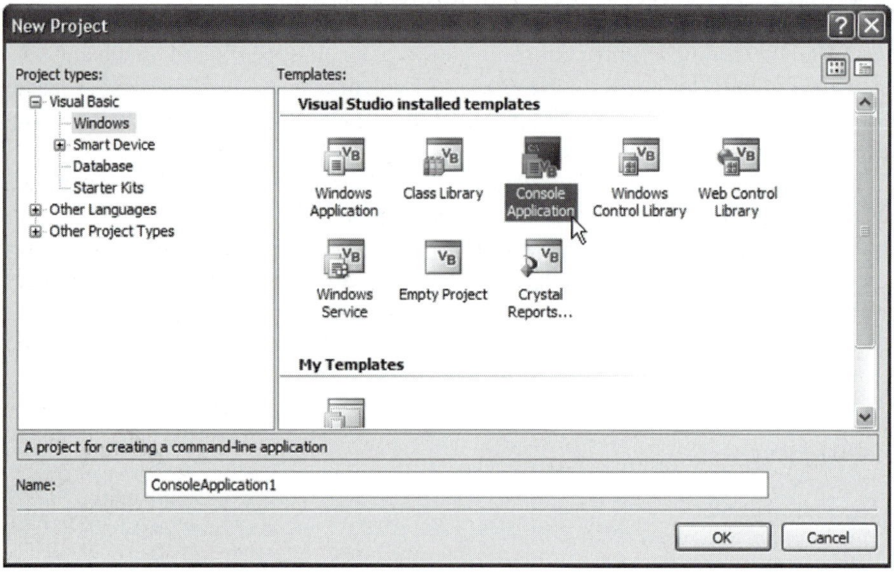

FIGURE 1.18 New Project dialog box for console application

The line that begins with `static void Main` defines the entry point to your program. Immediately following this line is where you will type your application. For our example, you will type code in this space to write two sentences to the screen.

Now let's create a working program. Open a blank line between the opening and closing braces after the `main` statement. The easiest way is to place the cursor after the opening brace using the mouse and then press the Enter key. Type the lines of code so that your program looks like Listing 1.1 (except for Visual Studio supplied comments):

```
//----------------------------------------------------------
//  Prints a presidential quote.
//----------------------------------------------------------
Console.Out.WriteLine("A quote by Abraham Lincoln2:");
Console.Out.WriteLine("Whatever you are, be a good one.");

Console.In.ReadLine(); // Wait for enter key
```

The last line of this program, which has the `ReadLine` in it, is added to the end of all console applications so that you have time to view the results of the program. This line is included because Visual Studio opens the command window when the program starts and closes it when the program completes. Thus, when the last `WriteLine` is issued, the program would go away and you would have to look fast to see your results. When this line is added, you have to press the Enter key to terminate the application.

Debugging: Starting and Single Stepping Through the Program

Once the program is typed in, we need to run it to see how it works. To start the application inside Visual Studio, select the Debug/Start menu item. This menu item normally maps to the F5 key, so just press F5 any time you want to run your program. F5 runs the program without stopping until user input is needed (pressing the Enter key in this example), the program terminates, or an error is encountered.

As an alternative to just letting the program run to completion, you can see the program run one step at a time. In this case, select the Debug/Step Into menu item, which usually maps to the F8 key but may map to F11 on some installations. Each time you press the F8 key, the program will advance to the next statement, highlighting the next statement with a yellow bar and a yellow arrow, as shown in Figure 1.19.

Additional details on debugging and single stepping through applications is given in Chapter 6. You will want to consult that material if you are having difficulty finding problems with your program.

Program Structure

All C# applications have a similar basic structure. Despite its small size and simple purpose, this program contains several important features. Let's carefully dissect it and examine its pieces.

The first few lines of the program are comments, which start with the // symbols and continue to the end of the line. Comments don't affect what the program does but are included to make the program easier to understand by humans. Programmers can and should include comments as needed throughout a program to clearly identify the purpose of the program and describe any special processing. Any written comments or documents, including a user's guide and technical references, are called *documentation.* Comments included in a program are called *inline documentation.*

The rest of the program is a *class definition.* This class is called Lincoln, though we could have named it just about anything we wished. The class definition runs from the first opening brace ({) to the final closing brace (}) on the last line of the program. All C# programs are defined using class definitions.

```
Console.Out.WriteLine("A quote by Abraham Lincoln2:");
Console.Out.WriteLine("Whatever you are, be a good one.");

Console.In.ReadLine();  // Wait for enter key
```

FIGURE 1.19   Single-step display

```
//***********************************************************
//  Lincoln.cs        C#:  Ken Culp
//  Demonstrates the basic structure of a C# application
//***********************************************************
using System;
namespace Lincoln
{
  class Lincoln
  {
    public static void Main(string[] args)
    {
      //-------------------------------------------------
      //  Prints a presidential quote.
      //-------------------------------------------------
      Console.Out.WriteLine("A quote by Abraham Lincoln2:");
      Console.Out.WriteLine("Whatever you are, be a good one.");

      Console.In.ReadLine();  // Wait for enter key
    }
  }
}
```

Output

```
A quote by Abraham Lincoln:
Whatever you are, be a good one.
```

Key Concept

Comments do not affect a program's processing; instead, they serve to facilitate human comprehension.

Inside the class definition are some more comments describing the purpose of the Main method, which is defined directly below the comments. A *method* is a group of programming statements that is given a name. In this case, the name of the method is Main and it contains only two programming statements. Like a class definition, a method is also delimited by braces.

All C# applications have a Main method, which is where processing begins. Each programming statement in the current Main method is executed, one at a time in order, until the end of the method is reached. Then the program ends, or *terminates*. The Main method definition in a C# program is always preceded by the words static and void, which we examine later in the text. The use of string and args does not come into play in this particular program. We describe these later also.

The two lines of code in the Main method invoke another method, called WriteLine. We *invoke,* or *call,* a method when we want it to execute. The WriteLine method prints the specified characters to the screen. The characters to be printed are represented as a *character string,* enclosed in double quote characters ("). When the program is executed, it calls the WriteLine method to print the first statement, calls it again to print the second statement, and then, because that is the last line in the Main method, the program terminates.

The code executed when the WriteLine method is invoked is not defined in this program. The WriteLine method is part of the Console.Out object, which is part of the C#

standard class library. It's not technically part of the C# language, but is always available for use in any C# program. We explore the WriteLine method in more detail in Chapter 2.

Comments

Let's examine comments in more detail. Comments are the only language feature that allows programmers to compose and communicate their thoughts independent of the code. Comments should provide insight into the programmer's original intent. A program is often used for many years, and often many modifications are made to it over time. The original programmer often will not remember the details of a particular program when, at some point in the future, modifications are required. Furthermore, the original programmer is not always available to make the changes; thus, someone completely unfamiliar with the program will need to understand it. Good documentation is therefore essential.

As far as the C# programming language is concerned, the content of comments can be any text whatsoever. Comments are ignored by the computer; they do not affect how the program executes.

The comments in the Lincoln program represent one of two types of comments allowed in C#. The comments in Lincoln take the following form:

```
// This is a comment.
```

This type of comment begins with a double slash (//) and continues to the end of the line. You cannot have any characters between the two slashes. The computer ignores any text after the double slash to the end of the line. A comment can follow code on the same line to document that particular line, as in the following example:

```
Console.Out.WriteLine ("Monthly Report"); // use this title
```

The second form a C# comment may have is the following:

```
/*  This is another comment.  */
```

This comment type does not use the end of a line to indicate the end of the comment. Anything between the initiating slash-asterisk (/*) and the terminating asterisk-slash (*/) is part of the comment, including the invisible *newline* character that represents the end of a line. Therefore, this type of comment can extend over multiple lines. No space can be included between the slash and the asterisk.

The two basic comment types can be used to create various documentation styles, such as:

```
// This is a comment on a single line.
//-------------------------------------------------------
// Some comments such as those above methods or classes
// deserve to be blocked off to focus special attention
// on a particular aspect of your code.  Note that each
// of these lines is technically a separate comment.
//-------------------------------------------------------
```

```
/*
    This is one comment
    that spans several lines.
*/
```

Programmers often concentrate so much on writing code that they focus too little on documentation. You should develop good commenting practices and follow them habitually. Comments should be well written, often in complete sentences. They should not belabor the obvious but should provide appropriate insight into the intent of the code. The following examples are *not* good comments:

> **Key Concept**
>
> Inline documentation should provide insight into your code. It should not be ambiguous or belabor the obvious.

```
Console.Out.WriteLine ("hello");   // prints hello
Console.Out.WriteLine ("test");    // change this later
```

The first comment paraphrases the obvious purpose of the line and does not add any value to the statement. It is better to have no comment than a useless one. The second comment is ambiguous. What should be changed later? When is later? Why should it be changed?

Identifiers and Reserved Words

The various words used when writing programs are called *identifiers*. The identifiers in the `Lincoln` program are `class`, `Lincoln`, `public`, `string`, `static`, `void`, `Main`, `string`, `args`, `Console`, `out`, and `WriteLine`. These fall into three categories:

> words that we make up when writing a program (`Lincoln` and `args`)

> words that another programmer chose (`Console`, `out`, `WriteLine`, and `main`)

> words that are reserved for special purposes in the language (`string`, `class`, `public`, `static`, and `void`)

While writing the program, we simply chose to name the class `Lincoln`, but we could have used one of many other possibilities. For example, we could have called it `Quote`, or `Abe`, or `GoodOne`. The identifier `args` (which is short for arguments) is often used in the way we use it in `Lincoln`, but we could have used just about any other identifier in its place.

The identifiers `Console`, `Out`, and `WriteLine` were chosen by other programmers. These words are not part of the C# language. They are part of the C# standard library of predefined code, a set of classes and methods that someone has already written for us. The authors of that code chose the identifiers in that code-we're just making use of them.

Reserved words are identifiers that have a special meaning in a programming language and can only be used in predefined ways. A reserved word cannot be used for any other purpose, such as naming a class or method. In the `Lincoln` program, the reserved words used are `class`, `public`, `static`, and `void`. Throughout the book, we show C# reserved words in bold type. Figure 1.20 lists all of the C# reserved words in alphabetical order. The keyword `goto` should not be used in C# because their use would create a poorly constructed program.

An identifier that we make up for use in a program can be composed of any combination of letters, digits, and the underscore character (_), but it cannot begin with a digit. Identifiers may be of any length. Therefore, `total`, `label7`, `nextStockItem`, and `NUM_BOXES` are all valid identifiers, but `4th_word` and `coin#value` are not valid.

1.5   C# IDENTIFIERS

An identifier is a letter followed by zero or more letters and digits.

A C# letter can be any of the 26 English alphabetic characters in both uppercase and lowercase and the _ (underscore) character, as well as alphabetic characters from other languages. A C# digit includes the digits 0 though 9.

Examples:

> total
> MAX_HEIGHT
> num1
> Keyboard
> System

Both uppercase and lowercase letters can be used in an identifier, and the difference is important. C# is *case sensitive,* which means that two identifier names that differ only in the case of their letters are considered to be different identifiers. Therefore, `total`, `Total`, `ToTaL`, and `TOTAL` are all different identifiers. As you can imagine, it is not a good idea to use multiple identifiers that differ only in their case, because they can be easily confused.

Although the C# language doesn't require it, using a consistent case format for each kind of identifier makes your identifiers easier to understand. There are various C# conventions regarding identifiers that should be followed, though technically they don't have to be. For example, we use *title case*

(uppercase for the first letter of each word) for class names. Throughout the text, we describe the preferred case style for each type of identifier when it is first encountered and summarize all of them in the Coding Standards Appendix.

While an identifier can be of any length, you should choose your names carefully. They should be descriptive but not verbose. You should avoid meaningless names such as `a` or `x`. An exception to this rule can be made if the short name is actually descriptive, such as using `x` and `y` to represent (*x, y*) coordinates on a two-dimensional grid. Likewise, you should not use unnecessarily long names, such as the identifier `theCurrentItemBeingProcessed`. The name `currentItem` or even `CurItem` would serve. As you might imagine, the use of verbose identifiers is a much less prevalent problem than the use of names that are not descriptive.

You should always strive to make your programs as readable as possible. Therefore, you should always be careful when abbreviating words. You might think `curStVal` is a good name to represent the current stock value, but another person trying to understand the code

abstract	event	long	sizeof
as	explicit	namespace	stackalloc
base	extern	new	static
bool	false	null	string
break	finally	object	struct
byte	fixed	operator	switch
case	float	out	this
catch	for	override	throw
char	foreach	params	true
checked	get	partial	try
class	goto*	private	type of
char	if	protected	uint
const	implicit	public	ulong
continue	implements	readonly	unchecked
decimal	in	ref	ushort
default	int	return	using
do	interface	sbyte	value
double	internal	sealed	virtual
else	is	set	void
enum	lock	short	while

FIGURE 1.20   C# reserved words

> **Key Concept**
>
> Identifier names should be descriptive and readable.

may have trouble figuring out what you meant. It might not even be clear to you two months after writing it.

A *name* in C# is a series of identifiers separated by the dot (period) character. The name `Console.Out` is the way we designate the object through which we invoked the `WriteLine` method. Names appear quite regularly in C# programs.

White Space

All C# programs use *white space* to separate the words and symbols used in a program. White space consists of blanks, tabs, and newline characters. The phrase "white space" refers to the fact that, on a white sheet of paper with black printing, the space between the words and symbols is white. The way a programmer uses white space is important because it can be used to emphasize parts of the code and can make a program easier to read.

Except when it's used to separate words, the computer ignores white space. It does not affect the execution of a program. This fact gives programmers a great deal of flexibility in how they format a program. The lines of a program should be divided in logical places and certain lines should be indented and aligned so that the program's underlying structure is clear.

Because white space is ignored, we can write a program in many different ways. For example, taking white space to one extreme, we could put as many words as possible on each line. The code in Listing 1.2, the `Lincoln2` program, is formatted quite differently from `Lincoln` but prints the same message.

Taking white space to the other extreme, we could write almost every word and symbol on a different line with varying amounts of spaces, such as `Lincoln3`, shown in Listing 1.3.

All three versions of `Lincoln` are technically valid and will execute in the same way, but they are radically different from a reader's point of view. Both of the latter examples show poor style and make the program difficult to understand. You may be asked to adhere to particular guidelines when you write your programs. A software development company often has a programming style policy that it requires its programmers to follow. In any case, you should adopt and consistently use a set of style guidelines that increases the readability of your code.

Listing 1.2

```
//*************************************************************
//   Lincoln2.cs          C#:   Ken Culp
//
//   Demonstrates a poorly formatted, though valid program.
//*************************************************************
using System; namespace Lincoln2{
class Lincoln2 { static void Main(string[] args)  {
Console.Out.WriteLine("A quote by Abraham Lincoln:");
Console.Out.WriteLine("Whatever you are, be a good one.");
Console.In.ReadLine();}}}
```

Output

```
A quote by Abraham Lincoln:
Whatever you are, be a good one.
```

Listing 1.3

```
//*************************************************************
//   Lincoln3.cs          C#:   Ken Culp
//
//Demonstrates another valid program that is poorly formatted.
//*************************************************************
using System;

namespace Lincoln3 {
```

Listing 1.3   continued

```
        public           class
    Lincoln3
  {
                  public
    static
        void
  Main
        (
String
          []
    args                        )
  {
  Console.Out.WriteLine         (
"A quote by Abraham Lincoln:"             )
    ;        Console.Out.WriteLine
              (
      "Whatever you are, be a good one."
        )
    ;
    Console.In.ReadLine(
                                  );
  }
          }
  }
```

Output

```
A quote by Abraham Lincoln:
Whatever you are, be a good one.
```

1.6   PROGRAM DEVELOPMENT

The process of getting a program running involves various activities. The program has to be written in the appropriate programming language, such as C#. That program has to be translated into a form that the computer can execute. Errors can occur at various stages of this process and must be fixed. Various software tools can be used to help with all parts of the development process as well. Let's explore these issues in more detail.

Programming Language Levels

Suppose a particular person is giving travel directions to a friend. That person might explain those directions in any one of several languages, such as English, Russian, or Italian. The directions are the same no matter which language is used to explain them, but the manner in which the directions are expressed is different. The friend must be able understand the language being used in order to follow the directions.

Similarly, a problem can be solved by writing a program in one of many programming languages, such as Java, Ada, C, C++, C#, Pascal, or Smalltalk. The purpose of the program is essentially the same no matter which language is used, but the particular statements used to express the instructions, and the overall organization of those instructions, vary with each language. A computer must be able to understand the instructions in order to carry them out.

Programming languages can be categorized into the following four groups. These groups basically reflect the historical development of computer languages.

> > machine language
>
> > assembly language
>
> > high-level languages
>
> > fourth-generation languages

In order for a program to run on a computer, it must be expressed in that computer's *machine language.* Each type of CPU has its own language. For that reason, we can't run a program specifically written for a Sun Workstation, with its SPARC processor, on a Dell PC, with its Intel processor.

Each machine language instruction can accomplish only a simple task. For example, a single machine language instruction might copy a value into a register or compare a value to zero. It might take four separate machine language instructions to add two numbers together and to store the result. However, a computer can do millions of these instructions in a second, and therefore many simple commands can be executed quickly to accomplish complex tasks.

Machine language code is expressed as a series of binary digits and is extremely difficult for humans to read and write. Originally, programs were entered into the computer by using switches or some similarly tedious method. Early programmers found these techniques to be time consuming and error prone.

These problems gave rise to the use of *assembly language,* which replaced binary digits with *mnemonics,* short English-like words that represent commands or data. It is much easier for programmers to deal with words than with binary digits. However, an assembly language program cannot be executed directly on a computer. It must first be translated into machine language.

> **Key Concept**
>
> All programs must be translated to a particular CPU's machine language in order to be executed.

Generally, each assembly language instruction corresponds to an equivalent machine language instruction. Therefore, similar to machine language, each assembly language instruction accomplishes only a simple operation. Although assembly language is an improvement over machine code from a programmer's perspective, it is still tedious to use. Both assembly language and machine language are considered *low-level languages.*

Today, most programmers use a *high-level language* to write software. A high-level language is expressed in English-like phrases, and thus is easier for programmers to read and write. A single high-level language programming statement can accomplish the equivalent of many-perhaps hundreds-of machine language instructions. The term high-level refers to the fact that the programming statements are expressed in a way that is far removed from the machine language that is ultimately executed. C# is a high-level language, as are Ada, C++, Smalltalk, and many others.

Figure 1.21 shows equivalent expressions in a high-level language, assembly language, and machine language. The expressions add two numbers together. The assembly language and machine language in this example are specific to a SPARC processor.

The high-level language expression in Figure 1.21 is readable and intuitive for programmers. It is similar to an algebraic expression. The equivalent assembly language code is somewhat readable, but it is more verbose and less intuitive. The machine language is basically unreadable and much longer. In fact, only a small portion of the binary machine code to add two numbers together is shown in Figure 1.21. The complete machine language code for this particular expression is over 400 bits long.

A high-level language insulates programmers from needing to know the underlying machine language for the processor on which they are working. But high-level language code must be translated into machine language in order to be executed.

Key Concept

High-level languages allow a programmer to ignore the underlying details of machine language.

Some programming languages are considered to operate at an even higher level than high-level languages. They might include special facilities for automatic report generation or interaction with a database. These languages are called *fourth-generation languages,* or simply 4GLs, because they followed the first three generations of computer programming: machine, assembly, and high-level.

Editors, Compilers, and Interpreters

Several special-purpose programs are needed to help with the process of developing new programs. They are sometimes called software tools because they are used to build programs. Examples of basic software tools include an editor, a compiler, and an interpreter.

High-Level Language	Assembly Language	Machine Language
a + b	ld [%fp-20], %o0	...
	ld [%fp-24], %o1	1101 0000 0000 0111
	add %o0, %o1, %o0	1011 1111 1110 1000
		1101 0010 0000 0111
		1011 1111 1110 1000
		1001 0000 0000 0000
		...

FIGURE 1.21   A high-level expression and its assembly language and machine language equivalent

Initially, you use an *editor* as you type a program into a computer and store it in a file. There are many different editors with many different features. You should become familiar with the editor you will use regularly, because proper use of it can dramatically affect the speed at which you enter and modify your programs.

Figure 1.22 shows a very basic view of the program development process. After editing and saving your program, you attempt to translate it from high-level code into a form that can be executed. That translation may result in errors, in which case you return to the editor to make changes to the code to fix the problems. Once the translation occurs successfully, you can execute the program and evaluate the results. If the results are not what you want, or if you want to enhance your existing program, you again return to the editor to make changes.

The translation of source code into (ultimately) machine language for a particular type of CPU can occur in a variety of ways. A *compiler* is a program that translates code in one language to equivalent code in another language. The original code is called *source code*, and the language into which it is translated is called the *target language*. For many traditional compilers, the source code is translated directly into a particular machine language. In that case, the translation process occurs once (for a given version of the program), and the resulting executable program can be run whenever needed.

An *interpreter* is similar to a compiler but has an important difference. An interpreter interweaves the translation and execution activities. A small part of the source code, such as one statement, is translated and executed. Then another statement is translated and executed, and so on. One advantage of this technique is that it eliminates the need for a separate compilation phase. However, the program generally runs more slowly because the translation process occurs during each execution.

The process generally used to translate and execute C# programs combines the use of a compiler and an interpreter. This process is pictured in Figure 1.23. The C# compiler translates C# source code into C# intermediate language (IL), which is a representation of the program in a low-level form similar to machine language code. The C# interpreter reads C# IL and executes it on a specific machine. Another compiler could translate the IL into a particular machine language for efficient execution on that machine.

The difference between C# IL and true machine language code is that C# IL is not tied to any particular processor type. This approach has the distinct advantage of making C# *architecture neutral*, and therefore easily portable from one machine type to another. The

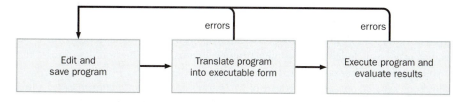

FIGURE 1.22   Editing and running a program

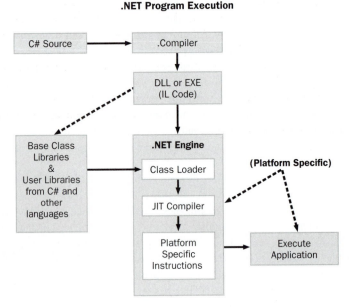

.NET Program Execution

FIGURE 1.23   The C# translation and execution process

only restriction is that there must be an IL interpreter or an IL compiler for each processor type on which the C# IL is to be executed.

Since the compilation process translates the high-level C# source code into a low-level representation, the interpretation process is more efficient than interpreting high-level code directly. IL is then converted to machine code by the Just-In-Time compiler (JIT). As a result, performance equals that of native code produced by other languages.

Development Environments

A software *development environment* is the set of tools used to create, test, and modify a program. Some development environments are available for free while others, which may have advanced features, must be purchased. Some environments are referred to as *integrated development environments* (IDEs) because they integrate various tools into one software program.

Any development environment will contain certain key tools, such as a C# compiler and interpreter. Some will include a *debugger*, which helps you find errors in a program. Other tools that may be included are documentation generators, archiving tools, and tools that help you visualize your program structure.

This book is based on the 2003 release of Microsoft's development platform called Visual Studio .NET (read as "dot net"). This development platform, also called the IDE, is included with this book and is needed for the exercises included in this book. For instructions on installing or using this platform, see Appendix D. Note that you could create the applications shown in this book by using the 2000, 2002, or 2003 releases of Visual Studio .NET.

Various key aspects of the IDE will be presented as part of the examples and problems. The IDE will greatly simplify your development process and speed the process of producing working programs. We recommend that you spend a fair amount of time becoming comfortable with the Visual Studio .NET IDE, because the more you learn, the faster you will be able to program. Use the help system when you cannot find answers in this text (see Appendix D for how to use the help system).

Syntax and Semantics

Each programming language has its own unique *syntax*. The syntax rules of a language dictate exactly how the vocabulary elements of the language can be combined to form statements. These rules must be followed in order to create a program. We've already discussed several C# syntax rules. For instance, the fact that an identifier cannot begin with a digit is a syntax rule. The fact that braces are used to begin and end classes and methods is also a syntax rule.

During compilation, all syntax rules are checked. If a program is not syntactically correct, the compiler will issue error messages and will not produce IL. C# has a similar syntax to the programming languages Java, C, and C++, and therefore the look and feel of the code is familiar to people with a background in those languages.

The *semantics* of a statement in a programming language define what will happen when that statement is executed. Programming languages are generally unambiguous, which means the semantics of a program are well defined. That is, there is one and only one interpretation for each statement. On the other hand, the *natural languages* that humans use to communicate, such as English and Italian, are full of ambiguities. A sentence can often have two or more different meanings. For example, consider the following sentence:

> Time flies like an arrow.

The average human is likely to interpret this sentence as a general observation: that time moves quickly in the same way that an arrow moves quickly. However, if we interpret the word *time* as a verb (as in "run the 50-yard dash and I'll time you") and the word *flies* as a noun (the plural of fly), the interpretation changes completely. We know that arrows don't time things, so we wouldn't normally interpret the sentence that way, but it is a valid interpretation of the words in the sentence. A computer would have a difficult time trying to determine which meaning is intended. Moreover, this sentence could describe the preferences of an unusual insect known as a "time fly," which might be found near an archery range. After all, fruit flies like a banana.

> **Key Concept**
>
> Syntax rules dictate the form of a program. Semantics dictate the meaning of the program statements.

The point is that one specific English sentence can have multiple valid meanings. A computer language cannot allow such ambiguities to exist. If a programming language instruction could have two different meanings, a computer would not be able to determine which one should be carried out.

Errors

Several different kinds of problems can occur in software, particularly during program development. The term computer error is often misused and varies in meaning depending on the situation. From a user's point of view, anything that goes awry when interacting with a machine can be called a computer error. For example, suppose you charged a $23 item to your credit card, but when you received the bill, the item was listed at $230. After you have

> **Key Concept**
>
> The programmer is responsible for the accuracy and reliability of a program.

the problem fixed, the credit card company apologizes for the "computer error." Did the computer arbitrarily add a zero to the end of the number, or did it perhaps multiply the value by 10? Of course not. A computer follows the commands we give it and operates on the data we provide. If our programs are wrong or our data is inaccurate, then we cannot expect the results to be correct. A common phrase used to describe this situation is "garbage in, garbage out."

You will encounter three kinds of errors as you develop programs:

> > compile-time errors
>
> > run-time errors
>
> > logical errors

The compiler checks to make sure you are using the correct syntax. If you have any statements that do not conform to the syntactic rules of the language, the compiler will produce a *syntax error*. The compiler also tries to find other problems, such as the use of incompatible types of data. The syntax might be technically correct, but you may be attempting to do something that the language doesn't semantically allow. Any error identified by the compiler is called a *compile-time error*. If a compile-time error occurs, an executable version of the program is not created.

The second kind of problem occurs during program execution. It is called a *run-time error* and causes the program to terminate abnormally. For example, if we attempt to divide by zero, the program will "crash" and halt execution at that point. Because the requested

> **Key Concept**
>
> A C# program must be syntactically correct or the compiler will not produce IL output.

operation is undefined, the system simply abandons its attempt to continue processing your program. The best programs are *robust*; that is, they avoid as many run-time errors as possible. For example, the program code could guard against the possibility of dividing by zero and handle the situation appropriately if it arises. In C#, many run-time problems are called *exceptions* that can be caught and dealt with accordingly.

The third kind of software problem is a *logical error*. In this case, the software compiles and executes without complaint, but it produces incorrect results. For example, a logical error occurs when a value is calculated incorrectly or when a graphical button does not appear in the correct place. A programmer must test the program thoroughly, comparing the expected results to those that actually occur. When defects are found, they must be traced back to the source of the problem in the code and corrected. The process of finding and correcting defects in a program is called *debugging*. Logical errors can manifest themselves in many ways, and the actual root cause might be difficult to discover.

1.7 OBJECT-ORIENTED PROGRAMMING

As we stated earlier in this chapter, C# is an object-oriented language. As the name implies, an *object* is a fundamental entity in a C# program. This book is focused on the idea of developing software by defining objects that interact with each other.

The principles of object-oriented software development have been around for many years, essentially as long as high-level programming languages have been used. The programming language Simula, developed in the 1960s, had many characteristics that define the modern object-oriented approach to software development. In the 1980s and 1990s, object-oriented programming became wildly popular, due in large part to the development of programming languages like C++ and Java. It is now the dominant approach used in commercial software development.

One of the most attractive characteristics of the object-oriented approach is the fact that objects can be used quite effectively to represent real-world entities. We can use a software object to represent an employee in a company, for instance. We'd create one object per employee, each with behaviors and characteristics that we need to represent. In this way, object-oriented programming allows us to map our programs to the real situations that the programs represent. That is, the object-oriented approach makes it easier to solve problems, which is the point of writing a program in the first place.

> **Key Concept**
>
> Object-oriented programming helps us solve problems, which is the purpose of writing a program.

Let's discuss the general issues related to problem solving, then explore the specific characteristics of the object-oriented approach that help us solve those problems.

Problem Solving

In general, problem solving consists of multiple steps:

1. Understanding the problem.
2. Designing a solution.
3. Considering alternatives to the solution and refining the solution.
4. Implementing the solution.
5. Testing the solution and fixing any problems that exist.

Although this approach applies to any kind of problem solving, it works particularly well when developing software. These steps aren't purely linear. That is, some of the activities will overlap others. But at some point, all of these steps should be carefully addressed.

The first step, understanding the problem, may sound obvious, but a lack of attention to this step has been the cause of many misguided software development efforts. If we attempt to solve a problem that we don't completely understand, we often end up solving the wrong problem or at least going off on improper tangents. Each problem has a *problem domain,* the real-world issues that are key to its solution. For example, if we are going to write a program to score a bowling match, then the problem domain includes the rules of bowling. To develop a good solution, we must thoroughly understand the problem domain.

The key to designing a problem solution is breaking it down into manageable pieces. A solution to any problem can rarely be expressed as one big task. Instead, it is a series of small cooperating tasks that interact to perform a larger task. When developing software, we don't write one big program. We design separate pieces that are responsible for certain parts of the solution, then integrate them with the other parts.

Our first inclination toward a solution may not be the best one. We must always consider alternatives and refine the solution as necessary. The earlier we consider alternatives, the easier it is to modify our approach.

Implementing the solution is the act of taking the design and putting it in a usable form. When developing a software solution to a problem, the implementation stage is the process of actually writing the program. Too often programming is thought of as writing code. But in most cases, the act of designing the program should be far more interesting and creative than the process of implementing the design in a particular programming language.

Key Concept

Program design involves breaking a solution down into manageable pieces.

At many points in the development process, we should test our solution to find any errors that exist, so that we can fix them. Testing cannot guarantee that there aren't still problems yet to be discovered, but it can raise our confidence that we have a viable solution.

Throughout this text we explore techniques that allow us to design and implement elegant programs. Although we will often get immersed in these details, we should never forget that our primary goal is to solve problems.

Object-Oriented Software Principles

Object-oriented programming ultimately requires a solid understanding of the following terms:

> object

> attribute

> method

> class

> encapsulation

> inheritance

> polymorphism

In addition to these terms, there are many associated concepts that allow us to tailor our solutions in innumerable ways. This book is designed to help you evolve your understanding of these concepts gradually and naturally. This section provides an overview of these ideas at a high level to establish some terminology and provide the big picture.

We mentioned earlier that an *object* is a fundamental element in a program. A software object often represents a real object in our problem domain, such as a bank account. Every object has a *state* and a set of *behaviors*. By "state" we mean state of being-fundamental characteristics that currently define the object. For example, part of a bank account's state is its current balance. The behaviors of an object are the activities associated with the object. Behaviors associated with a bank account probably include the ability to make deposits and withdrawals.

In addition to objects, a C# program also manages primitive data. *Primitive data* includes fundamental values such as numbers and characters. Objects usually represent more interesting or complex entities.

An object's *attributes* are the values it stores internally, which may be represented as primitive data or as other objects. For example, a bank account object may store a floating point number (a primitive value) that represents the balance of the account. It may contain other attributes, such as the name of the account owner. Collectively, the values of an object's attributes define its current state.

As mentioned earlier in this chapter, a *method* is a group of programming statements that is given a name. When a method is invoked, its statements are executed. A set of methods is associated with an object. The methods of an object define its potential behaviors. To define the ability to make a deposit into a bank account, we define a method containing programming statements that will update the account balance accordingly.

> **Key Concept**
>
> Each object has a state, defined by its attributes, and a set of behaviors, defined by its methods.

An object is defined by a *class*. A class is the model or blueprint from which an object is created. Consider the blueprint created by an architect when designing a house. The blueprint defines the important characteristics of the house-its walls, windows, doors, electrical outlets, and so on. Once the blueprint is created, several houses can be built using it, as depicted in Figure 1.24.

In one sense, the houses built from the blueprint are different. They are in different locations, have different addresses, contain different furniture, and are inhabited by different people. Yet in many ways they are the "same" house. The layout of the rooms and other crucial characteristics are the same in each. To create a different house, we would need a different blueprint.

A class is a blueprint of an object. It establishes the kind of data an object of that type will hold and defines the methods that represent the behavior of such objects. However, a class is not an object any more than a blueprint is a house. In general, a class contains no space to store data. Each object has space for its own data, which is why each object can have its own state.

Once a class has been defined, multiple objects can be created from that class. For example, once we define a class to represent the concept of a bank account, we can create multiple objects that represent specific, individual bank accounts. Each bank account object would keep track of its own balance.

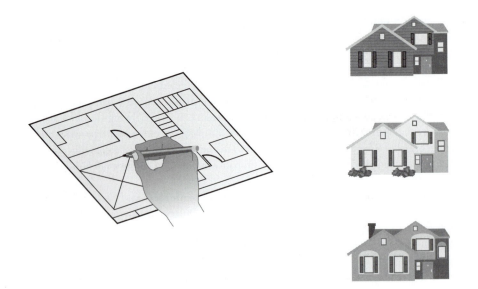

FIGURE 1.24   A house blueprint and three houses created from it

An object should be *encapsulated,* which means that it protects and manages its own information. That is, an object should be self-governing. The only changes made to the state of the object should be accomplished by that object's methods. We should design objects so that other objects cannot "reach in" and change its state.

Classes can be created from other classes by using *inheritance.* That is, the definition of one class can be based on another class that already exists. Inheritance is a form of *software reuse,* capitalizing on the similarities between various kinds of classes that we may want to create. One class can be used to derive several new classes. Derived classes can then be used to derive even more classes. This creates a hierarchy of classes, where the attributes and methods defined in one class are inherited by its children, which in turn pass them on to their children, and so on. For example, we might create a hierarchy of classes that represent various types of accounts. Common characteristics are defined in high-level classes, and specific differences are defined in derived classes.

> **Key Concept**
>
> A class is a blueprint of an object. Multiple objects can be created from one class definition.

Polymorphism is the idea that we can refer to multiple types of related objects over time in consistent ways. It gives us the ability to design powerful and elegant solutions to problems that deal with multiple objects.

Some of the core object-oriented concepts are depicted in Figure 1.25. We don't expect you to understand these ideas fully at this point. Most of this book is designed to flesh out these ideas. This overview is intended only to set the stage.

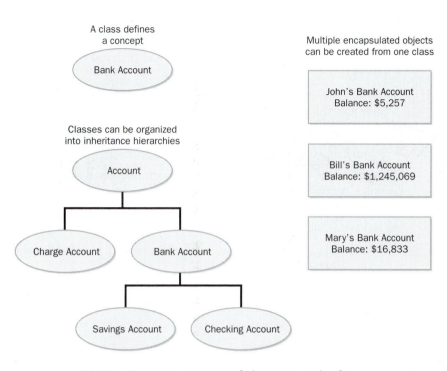

FIGURE 1.25   Various aspects of object-oriented software

Summary of Key Concepts

> A computer system consists of hardware and software that work in concert to help us solve problems.

> The CPU reads the program instructions from main memory, executing them one at a time until the program ends.

> The operating system provides a user interface and manages computer resources.

> As far as the user is concerned, the interface *is* the program.

> Digital computers store information by breaking it into pieces and representing each piece as a number.

> Binary is used to store information in a computer because the devices that store and manipulate binary data are inexpensive and reliable.

> There are exactly 2^N permutations of N bits. Therefore, N bits can represent up to 2^N unique items.

> The core of a computer is made up of main memory, which stores programs and data, and the CPU, which executes program instructions one at a time.

> An address is a unique number associated with each memory location.

> Main memory is volatile, meaning the stored information is maintained only as long as electric power is supplied.

> The surface of a CD has both smooth areas and small pits. A pit represents a binary 1 and a smooth area represents a binary 0.

> A rewritable CD simulates the pits and smooth areas of a regular CD by using a coating that can be made amorphous or crystalline as needed.

> The fetch-decode-execute cycle forms the foundation of computer processing.

> A network consists of two or more computers connected together so that they can exchange information.

> Sharing a communication line creates delays, but it is cost effective and simplifies adding new computers to the network.

> A local-area network (LAN) is an effective way to share information and resources throughout an organization.

> The Internet is a wide-area network (WAN) that spans the globe.

> Every computer connected to the Internet has an IP address that uniquely identifies it.

> The World Wide Web is software that makes sharing information across a network easy.

> A URL uniquely specifies documents and other information found on the Web for a browser to obtain and display.

> This book focuses on the principles of object-oriented programming.

> Comments do not affect a program's processing; instead, they serve to facilitate human comprehension.

> Inline documentation should provide insight into your code. It should not be ambiguous or belabor the obvious.

> C# is case sensitive. The uppercase and lowercase versions of a letter are distinct.

> Identifier names should be descriptive and readable.

> Appropriate use of white space makes a program easier to read and understand.

> You should adhere to a set of guidelines that establishes the way you format and document your programs.

> All programs must be translated to a particular CPU's machine language in order to be executed.

> High-level languages allow a programmer to ignore the underlying details of machine language.

> A C# compiler translates C# source code into Microsoft intermediate language (IL), a low-level, architecture-neutral representation of the program.

> Syntax rules dictate the form of a program. Semantics dictate the meaning of the program statements.

> The programmer is responsible for the accuracy and reliability of a program.

> A C# program must be syntactically correct or the compiler will not produce IL output.

> Object-oriented programming helps us solve problems, which is the purpose of writing a program.

> Program design involves breaking a solution down into manageable pieces.

> Each object has a state, defined by its attributes, and a set of behaviors, defined by its methods.

> A class is a blueprint of an object. Multiple objects can be created from one class definition.

Self-Review Questions

1.1   What is hardware? What is software?

1.2   What are the two primary functions of an operating system?

1.3   What happens to information when it is stored digitally?

1.4   How many unique items can be represented with the following?

    a. 2 bits

    b. 4 bits

    c. 5 bits

    d. 7 bits

1.5 How many bits are there in each of the following?

    a. 8 bytes

    b. 2 KB

    c. 4 MB

1.6 What are the two primary hardware components in a computer? How do they interact?

1.7 What is a memory address?

1.8 What does volatile mean? Which memory devices are volatile and which are nonvolatile?

1.9 What is a file server?

1.10 What is the total number of communication lines needed for a fully connected point-to-point network of five computers? Six computers?

1.11 What is the origin of the word Internet?

1.12 Explain the parts of the following URLs:

    a. duke.csc.villanova.edu/jss/examples.html

    b. java.sun.com/products/index.html

1.13 What is the relationship between a high-level language and machine language?

1.14 What is Microsoft intermediate language (IL)?

1.15 What is white space? How does it affect program execution? How does it affect program readability?

1.16 Which of the following are not valid C# identifiers? Why?

    a. `RESULT`

    b. `result`

    c. `12345`

    d. `x12345y`

    e. `black&white`

    f. `answer_7`

1.17 What do we mean by the syntax and semantics of a programming language?

1.18 What are the primary concepts that support object-oriented programming?

Exercises

1.1   Describe the hardware components of your personal computer or of a computer in a lab to which you have access. Include the processor type and speed, storage capacities of main and secondary memory, and types of I/O devices. Explain how you determined your answers.

1.2   Why do we use the binary number system to store information on a computer?

1.3   How many unique items can be represented with each of the following?

   a. 1 bit

   b. 3 bits

   c. 6 bits

   d. 8 bits

   e. 10 bits

   f. 16 bits

1.4   If a picture is made up of 128 possible colors, how many bits would be needed to store each pixel of the picture? Why?

1.5   If a language uses 240 unique letters and symbols, how many bits would be needed to store each character of a document? Why?

1.6   How many bits are there in each of the following? How many bytes are there in each?

   a. 12 KB

   b. 5 MB

   c. 3 GB

   d. 2 TB

1.7   Explain the difference between random access memory (RAM) and read-only memory (ROM).

1.8   A disk is a random-access device but it is not RAM. Explain.

1.9   Determine how your computer, or a computer in a lab to which you have access, is connected to others across a network. Is it linked to the Internet? Draw a diagram to show the basic connections in your environment.

1.10   Explain the differences between a local-area network (LAN) and a wide-area network (WAN). What is the relationship between them?

1.11   What is the total number of communication lines needed for a fully connected point-to-point network of eight computers? Nine computers? Ten computers? What is a general formula for determining this result?

1.12   Explain the difference between the Internet and the World Wide Web.

1.13 List and explain the parts of the URLs for:

    a. your school

    b. the Computer Science department of your school

    c. your instructor's Web page

1.14 Use a Web browser to access information through the Web about the following topics. For each one, explain the process you used to find the information and record the specific URLs you found.

    a. the Philadelphia Phillies baseball team

    b. wine production in California

    c. the subway systems in two major cities

    d. vacation opportunities in the Caribbean

1.15 Give examples of the two types of C# comments and explain the differences between them.

1.16 Which of the following are not valid C# identifiers? Why?

    a. `Factorial`

    b. `anExtremelyLongIdentifierIfYouAskMe`

    c. `2ndLevel`

    d. `level2`

    e. `MAX_SIZE`

    f. `highest$`

    g. `hook&ladder`

1.17 Why are the following valid C# identifiers not considered good identifiers?

    a. `q`

    b. `totVal`

    c. `theNextValueInTheList`

1.18 C# is case sensitive. What does that mean?

1.19 What do we mean when we say that the English language is ambiguous? Give two examples of English ambiguity (other than the example used in this chapter) and explain the ambiguity. Why is ambiguity a problem for programming languages?

1.20 Categorize each of the following situations as a compile-time error, run-time error, or logical error.

    a. multiplying two numbers when you meant to add them

    b. dividing by zero

    c. forgetting a semicolon at the end of a programming statement

d. spelling a word wrong in the output

e. producing inaccurate results

f. typing a { when you should have typed (

Programming Projects

1.1 Create a new console application called Test and enter the code shown after the `Main` specification. Select File/New/Project, select C# Projects, and select Console Application. Type the name Test in the directory of your choosing. Your complete application should look like the following::

```
public class Test
{
    public static void Main (string[] args)
    {
        Console.Out.WriteLine ("An Emergency Broadcast");
    }
}
```

1.2 Introduce the following errors, one at a time, to the program from Programming Project 1.1. Record any error messages that the compiler produces. Fix the previous error each time before you introduce a new one. If no error messages are produced, explain why. Try to predict what will happen before you make each change.

a. change `Test` to `test`

b. change `Emergency` to `emergency`

c. remove the first quotation mark in the string

d. remove the last quotation mark in the string

e. change `main` to `man`

f. change `WriteLine` to `bogus`

g. remove the semicolon at the end of the `WriteLine` statement

h. remove the last brace in the program

1.3 Write an application that prints, on separate lines, your name, your birthday, your hobbies, your favorite book, and your favorite movie. Label each piece of information in the output.

1.4 Write an application that prints the phrase `Knowledge is Power`:

a. on one line

b. on three lines, one word per line, with the words centered relative to each other

c. inside a box made up of the characters = and |

1.5 Write an application that prints the following diamond shape. Don't print any unneeded characters. (That is, don't make any character string longer than it has to be.)

```
       *
      ***
     *****
    *******
   *********
    *******
     *****
      ***
       *
```

1.6 Write an application that displays your initials in large block letters. Make each large letter out of the corresponding regular character. For example:

```
JJJJJJJJJJJJJJJ    AAAAAAAAA      LLLL
JJJJJJJJJJJJJJJ    AAAAAAAAAAA    LLLL
          JJJJ     AAA     AAA    LLLL
          JJJJ     AAA     AAA    LLLL
          JJJJ     AAAAAAAAAAA    LLLL
J         JJJJ     AAAAAAAAAAA    LLLL
JJ        JJJJ     AAA     AAA    LLLL
 JJJJJJJJJJJJ      AAA     AAA    LLLLLLLLLLLLLL
  JJJJJJJJJJ       AAA     AAA    LLLLLLLLLLLLLL
```

Answers to Self-Review Questions

1.1 The hardware of a computer system consists of its physical components such as a circuit board, monitor, or keyboard. Computer software refers to the programs that are executed by the hardware and the data that those programs use. Hardware is tangible, whereas software is intangible. In order to be useful, hardware requires software and software requires hardware.

1.2 The operating system provides a user interface and efficiently coordinates the use of resources such as main memory and the CPU.

1.3 The information is broken into pieces, and those pieces are represented as numbers.

1.4 In general, N bits can represent 2^N unique items. Therefore:

a. 2 bits can represent 4 items because $2^2 = 4$.

b. 4 bits can represent 16 items because $2^4 = 16$.

c. 5 bits can represent 32 items because $2^5 = 32$.

d. 7 bits can represent 128 items because $2^7 = 128$.

1.5 There are 8 bits in a byte. Therefore:

a. 8 bytes = 8 * 8 bits = 64 bits

b. 2 KB = 2 * 1024 bytes = 2048 bytes = 2048 * 8 bits = 16,384 bits

c. 4 MB = 4 * 1,048,576 bytes = 4,194,304 bytes = 4,194,304 * 8 bits = 33,554,432 bits

1.6 The two primary hardware components are main memory and the CPU. Main memory holds the currently active programs and data. The CPU retrieves individual program instructions from main memory, one at a time, and executes them.

1.7 A memory address is a number that uniquely identifies a particular memory location in which a value is stored.

1.8 Main memory is volatile, which means the information that is stored in it will be lost if the power supply to the computer is turned off. Secondary memory devices are nonvolatile; therefore, the information that is stored on them is retained even if the power goes off.

1.9 A file server is a network computer that is dedicated to storing and providing programs and data that are needed by many network users.

1.10 Counting the number of unique connections in Figure 1.16, there are 10 communication lines needed to fully connect a point-to-point network of five computers. Adding a sixth computer to the network will require that it be connected to the original five computers, bringing the total number of communication lines to 15.

1.11 The word Internet comes from the word internetworking, a concept related to wide-area networks (WANs). An internetwork connects one network to another. The Internet is a WAN.

1.12 Breaking down the parts of each URL:

a. `duke` is the name of a computer within the `csc` subdomain (the Department of Computing Sciences) of the `villanova.edu` domain, which represents Villanova University. The `edu` top-level domain indicates that it is an educational organization. This URL is requesting a file called `examples.html` from within a subdirectory called `jss`.

b. `java` is the name of a computer (Web server) at the `sun.com` domain, which represents Sun Microsystems, Inc. The `com` top-level domain indicates that it is a commercial business. This URL is requesting a file called `index.html` from within a subdirectory called `products`.

1.13 High-level languages allow a programmer to express a series of program instructions in English-like terms that are relatively easy to read and use. However, in order to execute, a program must be expressed in a particular computer's machine language, which consists of a series of bits that is basically unreadable by humans. A high-level language program must be translated into machine language before it can be run.

1.14 C# IL is a low-level representation of a C# source code program. The C# compiler translates the source code into IL, which can then be executed using the C# interpreter.

1.15 White space is a term that refers to the spaces, tabs, and newline characters that separate words and symbols in a program. The compiler ignores extra white space; therefore, it doesn't affect execution. However, it is crucial to use white space appropriately to make a program readable to humans.

1.16 All of the identifiers shown are valid except `12345` (since an identifier cannot begin with a digit) and `black&white` (since an identifier cannot contain the character &). The identifiers `RESULT` and `result` are both valid, but should not be used together in a program because they differ only by case. The underscore character (as in `answer_7`) is a valid part of an identifier.

1.17 Syntax rules define how the symbols and words of a programming language can be put together. The semantics of a programming language instruction determine what will happen when that instruction is executed.

1.18 The primary elements that support object-oriented programming are objects, classes, encapsulation, and inheritance. An object is defined by a class, which contains methods that define the operations on those objects (the services that they perform). Objects are encapsulated such that they store and manage their own data. Inheritance is a reuse technique in which one class can be derived from another.

Data and Expressions

2

CHAPTER OBJECTIVES

> Discuss the use of character strings, concatenation, and escape sequences.

> Explore the declaration and use of variables.

> Describe the C# primitive data types.

> Discuss the syntax and processing of expressions.

> Define the types of data conversions and the mechanisms for accomplishing them.

> Introduce the Console class to create interactive console programs.

> Explore basic graphics concepts and the techniques for drawing shapes.

This chapter explores some of the basic types of data used in a C# program and the use of expressions to perform calculations. It discusses the conversion of data from one type to another, and how to read input interactively from the user running a program. This chapter also begins the Windows Track for the book, in which we introduce the concepts of graphical programming and delve into C#'s abilities to manipulate color and draw shapes.

2.1   CHARACTER STRINGS

In Chapter 1 we discussed the basic structure of a C# program, including the use of comments, identifiers, and white space, using the `Lincoln` program as an example. Chapter 1 also included an overview of the various concepts involved in object-oriented programming, such as objects, classes, and methods. Take a moment to review these ideas if necessary.

A character string is an object in C#, defined by the class `string`. Because strings are so fundamental to computer programming, C# provides the ability to use a *string literal*, delimited by double quotation characters, as we've seen in previous examples. We explore the `String` class and its methods in more detail in Chapter 3. For now, let's explore the use of string literals in more detail.

The following are all examples of valid string literals:

```
"The quick brown fox jumped over the lazy dog."
"602 Greenbriar Court, Chalfont PA 18914"
"x"
""
```

A string literal can contain any valid characters, including numeric digits, punctuation, and other special characters. The last example in the list above contains no characters at all.

The `Write` and `WriteLine` Methods

In the `Lincoln` program in Chapter 1, we invoked the `WriteLine` method as follows:

```
Console.Out.WriteLine ("Whatever you are, be a good one.");
```

This statement demonstrates the use of objects. The `Console.Out` object represents an output device or file, which by default is the monitor screen. To be more precise, the object's name is `Out` and it is stored in the `Console` class. We explore that relationship in more detail later in the text.

The `WriteLine` method is a service that the `Console.Out` object performs for us. Whenever we request it, the object will print a character string to the screen. We can say that we send the `WriteLine` message to the `Console.Out` object to request that some text be printed.

Each piece of data that we send to a method is called a *parameter*. In this case, the `WriteLine` method takes only one parameter: the string of characters to be printed.

The `Console.Out` object also provides another service we can use: the `Write` method. The difference between `Write` and `WriteLine` is small but important. The `WriteLine` method prints the information sent to it, then moves to the beginning of the next line. The `Write` method is similar to `WriteLine`, but does not advance to the next line when completed.

Key Concept

The `Write` and `WriteLine` methods represent two services provided by the `Console.Out` object.

The program shown in Listing 2.1 is called Countdown, and it invokes both the Write and WriteLine methods.

Listing 2.1

```
//***************************************************************
//  Countdown.cs          C#:  Ken Culp
//
//  Demonstrates the difference between Write and WriteLine.
//***************************************************************
using System;

namespace Countdown
{
  public class Countdown
  {
    //--------------------------------------------------------
    //  Prints 2 lines of output representing a rocket countdown.
    //--------------------------------------------------------
    static void Main(string[] args)
    {
      Console.Out.Write("Three... ");
      Console.Out.Write("Two... ");
      Console.Out.Write("One... ");
      Console.Out.Write("Zero... ");

      Console.Out.WriteLine("Liftoff!"); // on first line out

      Console.Out.WriteLine("Houston, we have a problem.");
      Console.In.ReadLine();
    }
  }
}
```

Output

```
Three... Two... One... Zero... Liftoff!
Houston, we have a problem.
```

Carefully compare the output of the Countdown program, shown at the bottom of the program listing, to the program code. Note that the word Liftoff is printed on the same line as the first few words, even though it is printed using the WriteLine method. Remember that the WriteLine method moves to the beginning of the next line *after* the information passed to it is printed.

String Concatenation

A string literal cannot span multiple lines in a program. The following program statement is improper syntax and would produce an error when attempting to compile:

```
// The following statement will not compile
Console.Out.WriteLine ("The only stupid question is
the one that's not asked.");
```

When we want to print a string that is too long to fit on one line in a program, we can rely on *string concatenation* to append one string to the end of another. The string concatenation operator is the plus sign (+). The following expression concatenates one character string to another, producing one long string:

```
"The only stupid question is " + "the one that's not asked."
```

The program called `Facts` shown in Listing 2.2 contains several `WriteLine` statements. The first one prints a sentence that is somewhat long and will not fit on one line of the program. Since a character literal cannot span two lines in a program, we split the string into two and use string concatenation to append them. Therefore, the string concatenation operation in the first `WriteLine` statement results in one large string that is passed to the method to be printed.

Note that we don't have to pass any information to the `WriteLine` method, as shown in the second line of the `Facts` program. This call does not print any visible characters, but it does move to the next line of output. So, in this case, calling `WriteLine` with no parameters has the effect of printing a blank line.

The last three calls to `WriteLine` in the `Facts` program demonstrate another interesting thing about string concatenation: strings can be concatenated with numbers. Note that the numbers in those lines are not enclosed in double quotes and are therefore not character strings. In these cases, the number is automatically converted to a string, and then the two strings are concatenated.

Listing 2.2

```
//****************************************************************
//  Facts.cs        C#:  Ken Culp
//
//  Demonstrates the use of the string concatenation operator and
//  the automatic conversion of an integer to a string.
//****************************************************************
using System;

namespace Facts
{
  class Facts
```

Listing 2.2   continued

```
{
  static void Main(string[] args)
  {
    // Strings can be concatenated into one long string
    Console.Out.WriteLine(
      "We present the following facts for your " +
      "extracurricular edification:");
    Console.Out.WriteLine();

    // A string can contain numeric digits
    Console.Out.WriteLine(
      "Letters in the Hawaiian alphabet: 12");

    // A numeric value can be concatenated to a string
    Console.Out.WriteLine(
      "Dialing code for Antarctica: " + 672);

    Console.Out.WriteLine(
      "Year in which Leonardo da Vinci invented " +
      "the parachute: " + 1515);

    Console.Out.WriteLine("Speed of ketchup: " + 40 +
      " km per year");
    Console.In.ReadLine();  // Wait for enter key
  }
}
}
```

Output

```
We present the following facts for your extracurricular
edification:
Letters in the Hawaiian alphabet: 12
Dialing code for Antarctica: 672
Year in which Leonardo da Vinci invented the parachute: 1515
Speed of ketchup: 40 km per year
```

Because we are printing particular values, we simply could have included the numeric value as part of the string literal, such as:

```
"Speed of ketchup: 40 km per year"
```

Digits are characters and can be included in strings as needed. We separate them in the Facts program to demonstrate the ability to concatenate a string and a number. This technique will be useful in upcoming examples.

As you can imagine, the + operator is also used for arithmetic addition. Therefore, what the + operator does depends on the types of data on which it operates. If either or both of the operands of the + operator are strings, then string concatenation is performed.

The `Addition` program, shown in Listing 2.3, demonstrates the distinction between string concatenation and arithmetic addition. The `Addition` program uses the + operator four times. In the first call to `WriteLine`, both + operations perform string concatenation, because the operators are executed left to right. The first operator concatenates the string with the first number (24), creating a larger string. Then that string is concatenated with the second number (45), creating an even larger string, which gets printed.

In the second call to `WriteLine`, we use parentheses to group the + operation with the two numeric operands. This forces that operation to happen first. Because both operands are numbers, the numbers are added in the arithmetic sense, producing the result 69. That number is then concatenated with the string, producing a larger string that gets printed.

We revisit this type of situation later in this chapter when we formalize the precedence rules that define the order in which operators get evaluated.

Escape Sequences

Key Concept

An escape sequence can be used to represent a character that would otherwise cause compilation problems.

Because the double quotation character (") is used in the C# language to indicate the beginning and end of a string, we must use a special technique to print the quotation character. If we simply put it in a string ("""), the compiler gets confused because it thinks the second quotation character is the end of the string and doesn't know what to do with the third one. This results in a compile-time error.

To overcome this problem, C# defines several *escape sequences* to represent special characters. An escape sequence begins with the backslash character (\), which indicates that the character or characters that follow should be interpreted in a special way. Figure 2.1 lists the C# escape sequences.

Escape Sequence	Meaning
\b	backspace
\t	tab
\n	newline
\r	carriage return
\"	double quote
\'	single quote
\\	backslash

FIGURE 2.1   C# escape sequences

Listing 2.3

```
//*****************************************************************
//  Addition.cs           C#:   Ken Culp
//
//  Demonstrates the difference between the addition and string
//  concatenation operators.
//*****************************************************************
using System;

namespace Addition
{
  class Addition
  {
    static void Main(string[] args)
    {
      Console.Out.WriteLine("24 and 45 concatenated: " + 24 +45);
      Console.Out.WriteLine("24 and 45 added: " + (24 + 45));
      Console.In.ReadLine();
    }
  }
}
```

Output

```
24 and 45 concatenated: 2445
24 and 45 added: 69
```

The program in Listing 2.4, called Roses, prints some text resembling a poem. It uses only one WriteLine statement to do so, despite the fact that the poem is several lines long. Note the escape sequences used throughout the string. The \n escape sequence forces the output to a new line, and the \t escape sequence represents a tab character. The \" escape sequence ensures that the quote character is treated as part of the string, not the termination of it, which enables it to be printed as part of the output.

Listing 2.4

```
//*****************************************************************
//  Roses.cs             C#:   Ken Culp
//
//  Demonstrates the use of escape sequences.
//*****************************************************************
using System;

namespace Roses
```

Listing 2.4   continued

```
{
  class Roses
  {
    static void Main(string[] args)
    {
      Console.Out.WriteLine(
        "Roses are red,\n\tViolets are blue,\n" +
        "Sugar is sweet,\n\tBut I have " +
        "\"commitment issues\",\n\t" +
        "So I'd rather just be friends\n\t" +
        "At this point in our relationship.");
      Console.In.ReadLine();
    }
  }
}
```

Output

```
Roses are red,
        Violets are blue,
Sugar is sweet,
        But I have "commitment issues",
        So I'd rather just be friends
        At this point in our relationship.
```

2.2 VARIABLES AND ASSIGNMENT

Most of the information we manage in a program is represented by variables. Let's examine how we declare and use them in a program.

Variables

A *variable* is a name for a location in memory used to hold a data value. A variable declaration instructs the compiler to reserve a portion of main memory space large enough to hold a particular type of value and indicates the name by which we refer to that location.

> **Key Concept**
>
> A variable is a name for a memory location used to hold a value of a particular data type.

Consider the program PianoKeys, shown in Listing 2.5. The first line of the main method is the declaration of a variable named keys that holds an integer (int) value. The declaration also gives keys an initial value of 88. If an initial value is not specified for a variable, the value is undefined. Most C# compilers give errors or warnings if you attempt to use a variable before you've explicitly given it a value.

The keys variable, with its value, could be pictured as follows:

keys   88

In the PianoKeys program, two pieces of information are used in the call to the WriteLine method. The first is a string, and the second is the variable keys. When a variable is referenced, the value currently stored in it is used. Therefore, when the call to WriteLine is executed, the value of keys, which is 88, is obtained. Because that value is an integer, it is automatically converted to a string and concatenated with the initial string. The concatenated string is passed to WriteLine and printed.

A variable declaration can have multiple variables of the same type declared on one line. Each variable on the line can be declared with or without an initializing value. For example:

```
int count, minimum = 0, result;
```

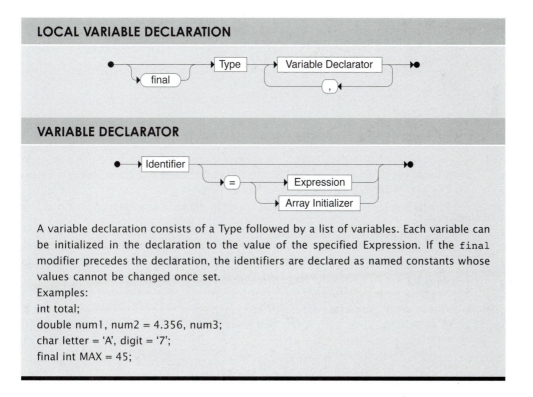

LOCAL VARIABLE DECLARATION

final

Type → Variable Declarator → ,

VARIABLE DECLARATOR

Identifier

= → Expression

→ Array Initializer

A variable declaration consists of a Type followed by a list of variables. Each variable can be initialized in the declaration to the value of the specified Expression. If the final modifier precedes the declaration, the identifiers are declared as named constants whose values cannot be changed once set.
Examples:
int total;
double num1, num2 = 4.356, num3;
char letter = 'A', digit = '7';
final int MAX = 45;

Listing 2.5

```
//****************************************************************
//  PianoKeys.cs         C#:  Ken Culp
//
//  Demonstrates the declaration, initialization, and use of an
//  integer variable.
//****************************************************************
using System;

namespace PianoKeys
{
  class PianoKeys
  {
    static void Main(string[] args)
    {
      int keys = 88;

      Console.Out.WriteLine("A piano has " + keys + " keys.");
      Console.In.ReadLine();
    }
  }
}
```

Output

```
A piano has 88 keys.
```

The Assignment Statement

Let's examine a program that changes the value of a variable. Listing 2.6 shows a program called `Geometry`. This program first declares an integer variable called `sides` and initializes it to 7. It then prints out the current value of `sides`.

The next line in `main` changes the value stored in the variable `sides`:

```
sides = 10;
```

Listing 2.6

```
//****************************************************************
//  Geometry.cs         C#:  Ken Culp
//
//  Demonstrates the use of an assignment statement to change the
//  value stored in a variable.
//****************************************************************
using System;
```

Listing 2.6   continued

```
namespace Geometry
{
  class Geometry
  {
    //-----------------------------------------------------------
    //  Prints the number of sides of several geometric shapes.
    //-----------------------------------------------------------
    static void Main(string[] args)
    {
      int sides = 7;   // declaration with initialization
      Console.Out.WriteLine("A heptagon has " +
        sides + " sides.");
      sides = 10;   // assignment statement
      Console.Out.WriteLine("A decagon has " +
        sides + " sides.");
      sides = 12;
      Console.Out.WriteLine("A dodecagon has " +
        sides + " sides.");
      Console.In.ReadLine();   // Wait for enter key
    }
  }
}
```

Output

```
A heptagon has 7 sides.
A decagon has 10 sides.
A dodecagon has 12 sides.
```

This is called an `assignment statement` because it assigns a value to a variable. When executed, the expression on the right-hand side of the assignment operator (=) is evaluated, and the result is stored in the memory location indicated by the variable on the left-hand side. In this example, the expression is simply a number, 10. We discuss expressions that are more involved than this in the next section.

A variable can store only one value of its declared type. A new value overwrites the old one. In this case, when the value 10 is assigned to sides, the original value 7 is overwritten and lost forever, as follows:

After initialization: sides | 7 |

After first assignment: sides | 10 |

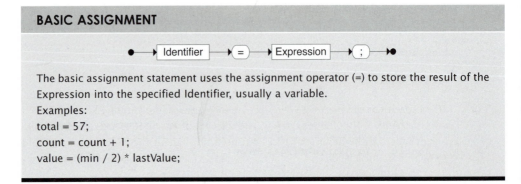

BASIC ASSIGNMENT

Identifier → = → Expression → ;

The basic assignment statement uses the assignment operator (=) to store the result of the Expression into the specified Identifier, usually a variable.
Examples:
total = 57;
count = count + 1;
value = (min / 2) * lastValue;

> **Key Concept**
>
> Accessing data leaves it intact in memory, but an assignment statement overwrites the old data.

When a reference is made to a variable, such as when it is printed, the value of the variable is not changed. This is the nature of computer memory: accessing (reading) data leaves the values in memory intact, but writing data replaces the old data with the new.

The C# language is strongly typed, meaning that we are not allowed to assign a value to a variable that is inconsistent with its declared type. Trying to combine incompatible types will generate an error when you attempt to compile the program. Therefore, the expression on the right-hand side of an assignment statement must evaluate to a value compatible with the type of the variable on the left-hand side.

Constants

Sometimes we use data that is constant throughout a program. For instance, we might write a program that deals with a theater that can hold no more than 427 people. It is often helpful to give a constant value a name, such as MAX_OCCUPANCY, instead of using a literal value, such as 427, throughout the code. The purpose and meaning of literal values such as 427 is often confusing to someone reading the code. By giving the value a name, you help explain its role in the program.

Constants are identifiers and are similar to variables except that they hold a particular value for the duration of their existence. Constants are, to use the English meaning of the words, not variable. Their value doesn't change.

> **Key Concept**
>
> Constants hold a particular value for the duration of their existence.

In C#, if you precede a declaration with the reserved word const, the identifier is made a constant. By convention, uppercase letters are used when naming constants to distinguish them from regular variables, and individual words are separated using the underscore character. For example, the constant describing the maximum occupancy of a theater could be declared as follows:

```
const int MAX_OCCUPANCY = 427;
```

The compiler will produce an error message if you attempt to change the value of a constant once it has been given its initial value. This is another good reason to use constants. Constants prevent inadvertent coding errors because the only valid place to change their value is in the initial assignment.

There is a third good reason to use constants. If a constant is used throughout a program and its value needs to be modified, then you have to change it in only one place. For example, if the capacity of the theater changes (because of a renovation) from 427 to 535, then you have to change only one declaration, and all uses of MAX_OCCUPANCY automatically reflect the change. If the literal 427 had been used throughout the code, each use would have to be found and changed. If you were to miss any uses of the literal value, problems would surely arise.

2.3   PRIMITIVE DATA TYPES

There are 13 *simple data types* in C#: eight subsets of integers, two subsets of floating point numbers, a character data type, a boolean data type, and a decimal data type. Everything else is represented using objects. Note, however, that although the type string is treated as a simple data type, it mostly exhibits the characteristics of objects, so it will not be discussed at this point. Actually, as we shall see later, every simple data type in C# is really an object with methods and properties. For now, however, let's examine these 13 *simple* data types in more detail.

Integers and Floating Points

C# has two basic kinds of numeric values: integers, which have no fractional part, and floating points, which do. There are eight integer data types (**byte**, **sbyte**, **short**, **ushort**, **int**, **uint**, **long**, and **ulong**) and two floating point data types (**float** and **double**). All of the numeric types differ by the amount of memory space used to store a value of that type, which determines the range of values that can be represented. The size of each data type is the same for all hardware platforms. All numeric types are *signed*, meaning that both positive and negative values can be stored in them. Figure 2.2 summarizes the numeric primitive types.

> **Key Concept**
>
> C# has two kinds of numeric values: integer and floating point. There are eight integer data types and two floating point data types.

Recall from our discussion in Chapter 1 that a bit can be either a 1 or a 0. Because each bit can represent two different states, a string of N bits can be used to represent 2^N different values. Appendix A describes number systems and these kinds of relationships in more detail.

When designing programs, we sometimes need to be careful about picking variables of appropriate size so that memory space is not wasted. This occurs in situations where memory space is particularly restricted, such as a program that runs on a personal data assistant (PDA). In such cases, we can choose a variable's data type accordingly. For example, if the value of a particular variable will not vary outside of a range of 1 to 1000, then a 2-byte

Reserved Word	Aliased Type	Storage	Min Value	Max Value
sbyte	System.SByte	8 bits	−128	127
byte	System.Byte	8 bits	0	255
short	System.Int16	16 bits	−32,768	32,767
ushort	System.UInt16	16 bits	0	65,535
int	System.Int32	32 bits	−2,147,483,648	2,147,483,647
uint	System.UInt32	32 bits	0	4,294,967,295
long	System.Int64	64 bits	−9,223,372,036,854,775,808	9,223,372,036,854,775,807
ulong	System.UInt64	64 bits	0	18,446,744,073,709,551,615
float	System.Single	32 bits	1.5_10^{-45}	3.4_10^{38}
double	System.Double	64 bits	5.0_10^{-324}	1.7_10^{308}
decimal	System.Decimal	96 bits	1.0_10^{-28}	7.9_10^{28}

FIGURE 2.2   C# numeric primitive types

integer (**short**) is large enough to accommodate it. On the other hand, when it's not clear what the range of a particular variable will be, we should provide a reasonable, even generous, amount of space. In most situations, memory space is not a serious restriction, and we can usually afford generous assumptions.

Note that even though a **float** value supports very large (and very small) numbers, it has only seven significant digits. Therefore, if it is important to accurately maintain a value such as 50341.2077, we need to use a **double**.

As we've already discussed, a *literal* is an explicit data value used in a program. The various numbers used in programs such as Facts, Addition, and PianoKeys are all integer literals. C# assumes that all integer literals are of type **int**, unless an L or l is appended to the end of the value to indicate that it should be considered a literal of type **long**, such as 45L.

Signed and Unsigned Integers

C# supports the use of both signed and unsigned integers. Signed integers are used where both positive and negative numbers are needed. However, when a simple counter is involved, you can use an unsigned integer. This might allow you to use a smaller amount of storage for a number. For example, if you need a counter whose maximum value is 200, you could use a **byte**, but the **sbyte** type would not work because it is limited to a maximum value of 127.

In Figure 2.2, the simple data types are shown in pairs as signed and then unsigned. There is a corresponding unsigned type for each signed integer type. For a signed integer to take both positive and negative values, one of the bits is used to indicate the sign (more precisely, signed integers are stored in a two's complement form). Therefore, their positive (or negative) range is limited by one less bit than the actual length. For example, consider **short** in Figure 2.2. A **short** is 16 bits long, so its value ranges from -32,768 to 32,767 ($2^{15} = 32,768$). The unsigned companion to **short** is **ushort**, which is also

DECIMAL INTEGER LITERAL

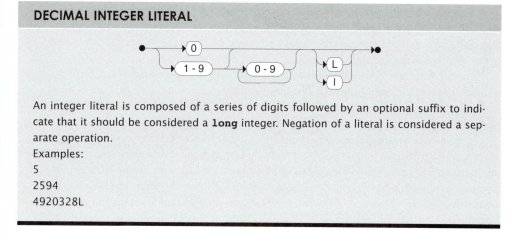

An integer literal is composed of a series of digits followed by an optional suffix to indicate that it should be considered a **long** integer. Negation of a literal is considered a separate operation.

Examples:

5

2594

4920328L

16 bits long. However, all 16 bits are used for the number, so it ranges from 0 to 65,535 (2^{16} = 65,536).

As a final note, you should be aware that other languages in the Visual Studio package might not support some of the unsigned data types. You should consult the Microsoft documentation before using these types.

Likewise, C# assumes that all floating point literals are of type **double**. If we need to treat a floating point literal as a **float**, we append an F or f to the end of the value, as in 2.718F or 123.45f. Numeric literals of type **double** can be followed by a D or d if desired.

The following are examples of numeric variable declarations in C#:

```
int answer = 42;
byte smallNumber1, smallNumber2;
long countedStars = 86827263927L;
float ratio = 0.2363F;
double delta = 453.523311903;
```

The Decimal Data Type

C# also supports a decimal data type that uses 128-bit data bits in storage. Compared to floating point types, the decimal type has a greater precision and a smaller range, which makes it suitable for financial and monetary calculations. The approximate range and precision for the decimal type are shown in Figure 2.2.

Characters

Characters are another fundamental type of data used and managed on a computer. Individual characters can be treated as separate data items, and, as we've seen in several examples, they can be combined to form character strings.

A `character literal` is expressed in a C# program with single quotes, such as `'b'` or `'J'` or `';'`. You will recall that `string literals` are delineated using double quotation marks, and that the `String` type is not a primitive data type in C#, but rather is a class name. We discuss the `String` class in detail in the next chapter.

Note the difference between a digit as a character (or part of a string) and a digit as a number (or part of a larger number). The number `602` is a numeric value that can be used in an arithmetic calculation. But in the string `"602 Greenbriar Court"` the 6, 0, and 2 are characters, just like the rest of the characters that make up the string.

The characters we can manage are defined by a `character set`, which is simply a list of characters in a particular order. Each programming language supports a particular character set that defines the valid values for a character variable in that language. Several character sets have been proposed, but only a few have been used regularly over the years. The *ASCII character set* is a popular choice. ASCII stands for the American Standard Code for Information Interchange. The basic ASCII set uses 7 bits per character, providing room to support 128 different characters, including:

> uppercase letters, such as `'A'`, `'B'`, and `'C'`

> lowercase letters, such as `'a'`, `'b'`, and `'c'`

> punctuation, such as the period (`'.'`), semicolon (`';'`), and comma (`','`)

> the digits `'0'` through `'9'`

> the space character, `' '`

> special symbols, such as the ampersand (`'&'`), vertical bar (`'|'`), and backslash (`'\'`)

> control characters, such as the carriage return, null, and end-of-text marks

The `control characters` are sometimes called nonprinting or invisible characters because they do not have a specific symbol that represents them. Yet they are as valid as any other character and can be stored and used in the same ways. Many control characters have special meaning to certain software applications.

As computing became a worldwide endeavor, users demanded a more flexible character set containing other language alphabets. ASCII was extended to use 8 bits per character, and the number of characters in the set doubled to 256. The extended ASCII contains many accented and diacritical characters used in languages other than English.

Key Concept

C# supports several character encoding methods, including the 16-bit Unicode (UTF-16) character set to represent character data.

However, even with 256 characters, the ASCII character set cannot represent the world's alphabets, especially given the various Asian alphabets and their many thousands of ideograms. Therefore, the C# programming language supports the `Unicode character set`, which uses 16 bits per character, supporting 65,536 unique characters. This will appear in the documentation as UTF-16 encoding. The characters and symbols from many languages are included in the Unicode definition. ASCII is a subset of the Unicode character set. Appendix B discusses the Unicode character set in more detail.

A character set assigns a particular number to each character, so by definition the characters are in a particular order. This is referred to as lexicographic order. In the ASCII and Unicode ordering, the digit characters `'0'` through `'9'` are continuous (no other characters intervene) and in order. Similarly, the lowercase alphabetic characters `'a'` through `'z'` are continuous and in order, as are the uppercase alphabetic characters `'A'` through `'Z'`. These characteristics make it relatively easy to keep things in alphabetical order.

In C#, the data type **char** represents a single character. The following are some examples of character variable declarations in C# :

```
char topGrade = 'A';
char symbol1, symbol2, symbol3;
char terminator = ';', separator = ' ';
```

Booleans

A boolean value, defined in C# using the reserved word **bool**, has only two valid values: **true** and **false**. A boolean variable is usually used to indicate whether a particular condition is true, but it can also be used to represent any situation that has two states, such as a light bulb being on or off.

A boolean value cannot be converted to any other data type, nor can any other data type be converted to a boolean value. The words **true** and **false** are reserved in C# as boolean literals and cannot be used outside of this context.

The following are some examples of boolean variable declarations in C#:

```
bool flag = true;
bool tooHigh, tooSmall, tooRough;
bool done = false;
```

2.4   EXPRESSIONS

An `expression` is a combination of one or more operators and operands that usually performs a calculation. The value calculated does not have to be a number, but often is. The operands used in the operations might be literals, constants, variables, or other sources of data. The manner in which expressions are evaluated and used is fundamental to programming. For now we will focus on arithmetic expressions that use numeric operands and produce numeric results.

> **Key Concept**
>
> Expressions are combinations of operators and operands used to perform a calculation.

Arithmetic Operators

The usual arithmetic operations are defined for both integer and floating point numeric types, including addition (+), subtraction (–), multiplication (*), and division (/). C# also has another arithmetic operation: the remainder *operator* (%) returns the remainder after dividing the second operand into the first. The remainder operator is sometimes called the modulus operator. The sign of the result of a remainder operation is the sign of the numerator. Therefore:

17%4 equals 1
–20%3 equals -2
10%-5 equals 0
3%8 equals 3

As you might expect, if either or both operands to any numeric operator are floating point values, the result is a floating point value. However, the division operator produces results that are less intuitive, depending on the types of the operands. If both operands are integers, the / operator performs *integer division*, meaning that any fractional part of the result is discarded. If one or the other or both operands are floating point values, the / operator performs *floating point division*, and the fractional part of the result is kept. For example, the result of 10/4 is 2, but the results of 10.0/4 and 10/4.0 and 10.0/4.0 are all 2.5.

A unary operator has only one operand, while a binary operator has two. The + and – arithmetic operators can be either unary or binary. The binary versions accomplish addition and subtraction, and the unary versions represent positive and negative numbers. For example, –1 is an example of using the unary negation operator to make the value negative. The unary + operator is rarely used.

C# does not have a built-in operator for raising a value to an exponent. However, the Math class provides methods that perform exponentiation and many other mathematical functions. The Math class is discussed in Chapter 3.

Operator Precedence

Operators can be combined to create more complex expressions. For example, consider the following assignment statement:

```
result = 14 + 8 / 2;
```

The entire right-hand side of the assignment is evaluated, and then the result is stored in the variable. But what is the result? If the addition is performed first, the result is 11; if the division operation is performed first, the result is 18. The order of operator evaluation makes a big difference. In this case, the division is performed before the addition, yielding a result of 18.

Note that in this and subsequent examples, we use literal values rather than variables, to simplify the expression. The order of operator evaluation is the same if the operands are variables or any other source of data.

> **Key Concept**
>
> C# follows a well-defined set of precedence rules that governs the order in which operators will be evaluated in an expression.

All expressions are evaluated according to an operator precedence hierarchy that establishes the rules that govern the order in which operations are evaluated. The arithmetic operators generally follow the same rules you learned in algebra. Multiplication, division, and the remainder operator all have equal precedence and are performed before (have higher precedence than) addition and subtraction. Addition and subtraction have equal precedence.

Any arithmetic operators at the same level of precedence are performed left to right. Therefore, we say the arithmetic operators have a left-to-right association.

Precedence, however, can be forced in an expression by using parentheses. For instance, if we really wanted the addition to be performed first in the previous example, we could write the expression as follows:

```
result = (14 + 8) / 2;
```

Any expression in parentheses is evaluated first. In complicated expressions, it is good practice to use parentheses even when it is not strictly necessary, to make it clear how the expression is evaluated.

Parentheses can be nested, and the innermost nested expressions are evaluated first. Consider the following expression:

```
result = 3 * ((18 - 4) / 2);
```

In this example, the result is 21. First, the subtraction is performed, forced by the inner parentheses. Then, even though multiplication and division are at the same level of precedence and usually would be evaluated left to right, the division is performed before multiplication because of the outer parentheses. Finally, the multiplication is performed.

After the arithmetic operations are complete, the computed result is stored in the variable on the left-hand side of the assignment operator (=). In other words, the assignment operator has a lower precedence than any of the arithmetic operators.

The evaluation of a particular expression can be shown using an *expression tree*, such as the one in Figure 2.3. The operators are executed from the bottom up, creating values that are used in the rest of the expression. Therefore, the operations lower in the tree have a higher precedence than those above, or they are forced to be executed earlier using parentheses.

The parentheses used in expressions are actually operators themselves. Parentheses have a higher precedence than almost any other operator. Figure 2.4 shows a precedence table with the relationships between the arithmetic operators, parentheses, and the assignment operator. Appendix F includes a full precedence table showing all C# operators.

For an expression to be syntactically correct, the number of left parentheses must match the number of right parentheses and they must be properly nested. The following examples are not valid expressions:

```
result = ((19 + 8) % 3) - 4);   // not valid
result = (19 (+ 8 %) 3 - 4);    // not valid
```

Keep in mind that when a variable is referenced in an expression, its current value is used to perform the calculation. In the following assignment statement, the current value of the

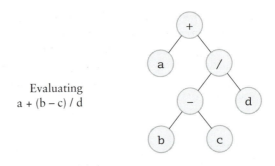

Evaluating
a + (b − c) / d

FIGURE 2.3 An expression tree

Precedence Level	Operator	Operation	Associates
1	+	unary plus	R to L
	−	unary minus	
2	*	multiplication	L to R
	/	division	
	%	remainder	
3	+	addition	L to R
	−	subtraction	
	+	string concatenation	
4	=	assignment	R to L

FIGURE 2.4 Precedence among some of the C# operators

variable `count` is added to the current value of the variable `total`, and the result is stored in the variable `sum`:

```
sum = count + total;
```

The original value contained in `sum` before this assignment is overwritten by the calculated value. The values stored in `count` and `total` are not changed.

The same variable can appear on both the left-hand side and the right-hand side of an assignment statement. Suppose the current value of a variable called `count` is 15 when the following assignment statement is executed:

```
count = count + 1;
```

Because the right-hand expression is evaluated first, the original value of `count` is obtained and the value 1 is added to it, producing the result 16. That result is then stored in the variable count, overwriting the original value of 15 with the new value of 16. Therefore, this assignment statement increments, or adds 1 to, the variable count.

Let's look at another example of expression processing. The program in Listing 2.7, called TempConverter, converts a particular Celsius temperature value to its equivalent Fahrenheit value using an expression that computes the following formula:

$$\text{Fahrenheit} = \frac{9}{5}\text{Celsius} + 32$$

Note that in the temperature conversion program, the operands to the division operation are floating point literals, to ensure that the fractional part of the number is kept. The precedence rules dictate that the multiplication happens before the addition in the final conversion computation.

Listing 2.7

```
//*************************************************************
//   TempConverter.java        C#:   Ken Culp
//
//   Illustrates primitive data types and arithmetic expressions.
//*************************************************************
using System;

namespace TempConverter
{
  class TempConverter
  {
    //-----------------------------------------------------------
    //   Computes the Fahrenheit equivalent of a specific Celsius
    //   value using the formula F = (9/5)C + 32.
    //-----------------------------------------------------------
    static void Main(string[] args)
    {
      const int BASE = 32;
      const double CONVERSION_FACTOR = 9.0 / 5.0;

      int celsiusTemp = 24;   // value to convert
      double fahrenheitTemp;
      fahrenheitTemp = celsiusTemp * CONVERSION_FACTOR + BASE;

      Console.Out.WriteLine(
        "Celsius Temperature: " + celsiusTemp);
      Console.Out.WriteLine(
        "Fahrenheit Equivalent: " + fahrenheitTemp);
      Console.In.ReadLine();
    }
  }
}
```

Listing 2.7 continued

Output

```
Celsius Temperature: 24
Fahrenheit Equivalent: 75.2
```

The `TempConverter` program is not very useful because it converts only one data value that we included in the program as a constant (24 degrees Celsius). Every time the program is run, it produces the same result. A far more useful version of the program would obtain the value to be converted from the user each time the program is executed. Interactive programs that read user input are discussed later in this chapter.

Increment and Decrement Operators

There are two other useful arithmetic operators. The `increment operator` (++) adds 1 to any integer or floating point value. The two plus signs that make up the operator cannot be separated by white space. The `decrement operator` (--) is similar except that it subtracts 1 from the value. They are both unary operators because they operate on only one operand. The following statement causes the value of `count` to be incremented:

```
count++;
```

The result is stored back into the variable `count`. Therefore, it is functionally equivalent to the following statement, which we discussed in the previous section:

```
count = count + 1;
```

The increment and decrement operators can be applied after the variable (such as `count++` or `count--`), creating what is called the `postfix form` of the operator. They can also be applied before the variable (such as `++count` or `--count`), in what is called the `prefix form`. When used alone in a statement, the prefix and postfix forms are functionally equivalent. That is, it doesn't matter if you write

```
count++;
```

or

```
++count;
```

However, when such a form is written as a statement by itself, it is usually written in its postfix form.

When the increment or decrement operator is used in a larger expression, it can yield different results depending on the form used. For example, if the variable `count` currently contains the value 15, the following statement assigns the value 15 to total and the value 16 to count:

```
total = count++;
```

However, the following statement assigns the value 16 to both total and count:

```
total = ++count;
```

The value of count is incremented in both situations, but the value used in the larger expression depends on whether a prefix or postfix form of the increment operator is used.

Because of the subtle differences between the prefix and postfix forms of the increment and decrement operators, they should be used with care. As always, favor the side of readability.

Assignment Operators

As a convenience, several assignment operators have been defined in C# that combine a basic operation with assignment. For example, the += operator can be used as follows:

```
total += 5;
```

This performs the same operation as the following statement:

```
total = total + 5;
```

The right-hand side of the assignment operator can be a full expression. The expression on the right-hand side of the operator is evaluated, then that result is added to the current value of the variable on the left-hand side, and that value is stored in the variable. Therefore, the following statement:

```
total += (sum - 12) / count;
```

is equivalent to:

```
total = total + ((sum - 12) / count);
```

Many similar assignment operators are defined in C#, including those that perform subtraction (-=), multiplication (*=), division (/=), and remainder (%=). The entire set of C# operators is discussed in Appendix F.

All of the assignment operators evaluate the entire expression on the right-hand side first, then use the result as the right operand of the other operation. Therefore, the following statement:

```
result *= count1 + count2;
```

is equivalent to:

```
result = result * (count1 + count2);
```

Likewise, the following statement:

```
result %= (highest - 40) / 2;
```

is equivalent to:

```
result = result % ((highest - 40) / 2);
```

Some assignment operators perform particular functions depending on the types of the operands, just as their corresponding regular operators do. For example, if the operands to the += operator are strings, then the assignment operator performs string concatenation.

2.5   DATA CONVERSION

Because C# is a strongly typed language, each data value is associated with a particular type. It is sometimes helpful or necessary to convert a data value of one type to another type, but we must be careful that we don't lose important information in the process. For example, suppose a **short** variable that holds the number 1000 is converted to a **byte** value. Because a **byte** does not have enough bits to represent the value 1000, some bits would be lost in the conversion, and the number represented in the **byte** would not keep its original value.

A conversion between one primitive type and another falls into one of two categories: widening conversions and narrowing conversions. Widening conversions are the safest because they usually do not lose information. They are called widening conversions because they go from one data type to another type that uses an equal or greater amount of space to store the value. Figure 2.5 lists the C# widening conversions.

For example, it is safe to convert from a **byte** to a **short** because a **byte** is stored in 8 bits and a **short** is stored in 16 bits. There is no loss of information. All widening conversions that go from an integer type to another integer type, or from a floating point type to another floating point type, preserve the numeric value exactly.

> **Key Concept**
>
> Narrowing conversions should be avoided because they can lose information.

Although widening conversions do not lose any information about the magnitude of a value, the widening conversions that result in a floating point value can lose precision. When converting from an **int** or a **long** to a **float**, or from a **long** to a **double**, some of the least significant digits may be lost. In this case, the resulting floating point value will be a rounded version of the integer value, following the rounding techniques defined in the IEEE 754 floating point standard.

Narrowing conversions are more likely to lose information than widening conversions are. They often go from one type to a type that uses less space to store a value, and therefore some of the information may be compromised. Narrowing conversions can lose both numeric magnitude and precision. Therefore, in general, they should be avoided. Figure 2.6 lists the C# narrowing conversions.

Note that we have items of the same bit size listed as narrowing conversions (**sbyte** to **byte**, **long** to **ulong**, etc.). These are still considered narrowing conversions because the sign bit is incorporated into one of the numbers and not into the other. As a result, it is possible that the value from one type would not fit in the other. For example, a valid byte value of 200 would not fit in an **sbyte**, which can take a maximum positive value of 127. It is possible that these conversions will work (a byte value of 100 would fit in **sbyte**), but

From	To
sbyte	short, ushort, int, uint, long, ulong, float
byte	short, ushort, int, uint, long, ulong, float
short	int, uint, long, ulong, float
ushort	int, uint, long, ulong, float
int	long, ulong, float
uint	long, ulong, float
long	double
ulong	double
float	double

FIGURE 2.5   C# widening conversions

From	To
sbyte	byte, char
byte	sbyte, char
short	byte, sbyte, char, ushort
ushort	byte, sbyte, char, short
int	byte, sbyte, char, short, ushort, uint
uint	byte, sbyte, char, short, ushort, int
long	byte, sbyte, char, short, ushort, int, uint, ulong
ulong	byte, sbyte, char, short, ushort, int, uint, long
float	byte, sbyte, char, short, ushort, int, uint, long, ulong

FIGURE 2.6   C# narrowing conversions

the compiler issues an error if these are attempted. Although, as discussed in the next section, we can force the compiler to take these by using a cast, by default it will not accept them.

Note that **bool** values are not mentioned in either widening or narrowing conversions. A bool value cannot be converted to any other primitive type and vice versa.

Conversion Techniques

In C#, conversions can occur in three ways:

> assignment conversion

> promotion

> casting

`Assignment conversion` occurs when a value of one type is assigned to a variable of another type during which the value is converted to the new type. Only widening conversions can be accomplished through assignment. For example, if money is a **float** variable and dollars is an **int** variable, then the following assignment statement automatically converts the value in dollars to a **float**:

```
money = dollars;
```

Therefore, if dollars contains the value 25, after the assignment, money contains the value 25.0. However, if we attempt to assign money to dollars, the compiler will issue an error message alerting us to the fact that we are attempting a narrowing conversion that could lose information. If we really want to do this assignment, we have to make the conversion explicit by using a cast.

Conversion via promotion occurs automatically when certain operators need to modify their operands in order to perform the operation. For example, when a floating point value called sum is divided by an integer value called count, the value of count is promoted to a floating point value automatically, before the division takes place, producing a floating point result:

```
result = sum / count;
```

A similar conversion takes place when a number is concatenated with a string. The number is first converted (promoted) to a string, then the two strings are concatenated.

`Casting` is the most general form of conversion in C#. If a conversion can be accomplished at all in a C# program, it can be accomplished using a cast. A cast is a C# operator that is specified by a type name in parentheses. It is placed in front of the value to be converted. For example, to convert money to an integer value, we could put a cast in front of it:

```
dollars = (int) money;
```

The cast returns the value in `money`, truncating any fractional part. If `money` contained the value `84.69`, then after the assignment, `dollars` would contain the value `84`. Note, however, that the cast does not change the value in `money`. After the assignment operation is complete, `money` still contains the value `84.69`.

Casts are helpful in many situations where we need to treat a value temporarily as another type. For example, if we want to divide the integer value `total` by the integer value `count` and get a floating point result, we could do it as follows:

```
result = (float) total / count;
```

First, the cast operator returns a floating point version of the value in `total`. This operation does not change the value in `total`. Then, `count` is treated as a floating point value via arithmetic promotion. Now the division operator will perform floating point division and produce the intended result. If the cast had not been included, the operation would have performed integer division and truncated the answer before assigning it to `result`. Also note that because the cast operator has a higher precedence than the division operator, the cast operates on the value of `total`, not on the result of the division.

2.6   INTERACTIVE PROGRAMS

It is often useful to design a program to read data from the user interactively during execution. That way, new results can be computed each time the program is run, depending on the data that is entered.

Listing 2.8

```csharp
//********************************************************************
//   Echo.cs        C#:   Ken Culp
//
//   Demonstrates the use of the ReadLine method of the
//   Console.In class.
//********************************************************************
using System;
using CS1;

namespace Echo
{
  class Echo
  {
    //-----------------------------------------------------------
    //  Reads a character string from the user and prints it.
    //-----------------------------------------------------------
    static void Main(string[] args)
    {
```

Listing 2.8   continued

```
    String message;

    Console.Out.WriteLine("Enter a line of text:");

    message = Console.In.ReadLine();
    Console.Out.WriteLine("You entered: \"" + message + "\"");

    Console.In.ReadLine();
  }
 }
}
```

Output

```
Enter a line of text:
Set your laser printer on stun!
You entered: "Set your laser printer on stun!"
```

Note in the output of the Echo program that the user is prompted for a line of text and then the program waits on that input. In this case, whatever the user types is placed in the string variable message and then that variable is written back out with a Console. Out.WriteLine.

Let's now turn our attention to an interactive program that requires numeric information to be typed at the keyboard. Since ReadLine() always returns a string, we have to add an additional step to move the data from a string form to the appropriate numeric form. For example, the user would type "123.45" as a string. However, the program needs that information as a double.

To convert from the string form to another form, we use the Parse static method associated with the type of data we require. In the following code example, we convert from myString, which has "123.45", to a double that contains 123.45:

```
    myDouble = double.Parse(myString);
```

Every numeric data type in Figure 2.2 includes a Parse method for converting from strings to the type of data required. If the data is in the proper format, this function works fine as written above. If, however, you type improper data, like "n.xx", the conversion will fail and will throw an exception, as shown in Figure 2.7

Handling exceptions will be covered later, in Chapter 10. For now, recognize that you must use the proper format for the numbers or else your program will be terminated. Do not worry, however, that this exception might cause any problems on your computer. When encountering the error now, just fix the error and restart the program with the F5 key to try again.

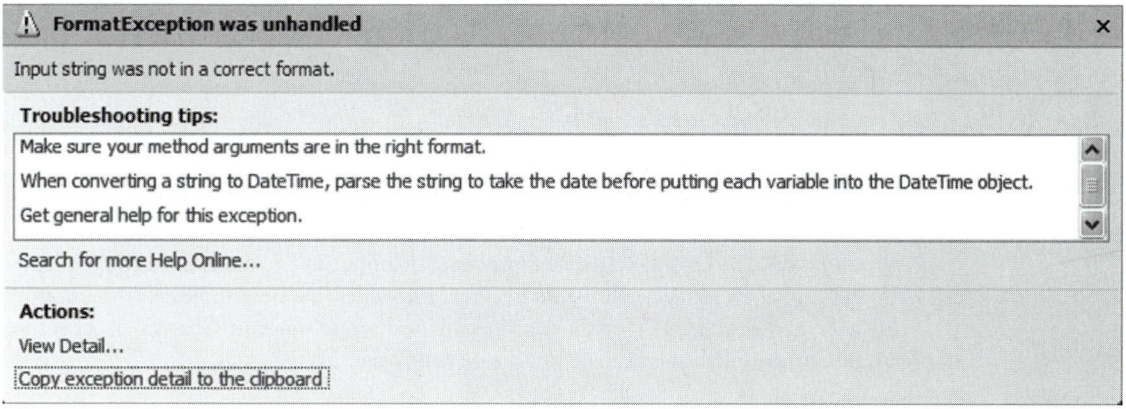

FormatException was unhandled   ✕

Input string was not in a correct format.

Troubleshooting tips:

Make sure your method arguments are in the right format.

When converting a string to DateTime, parse the string to take the date before putting each variable into the DateTime object.

Get general help for this exception.

Search for more Help Online...

Actions:

View Detail...

Copy exception detail to the clipboard

FIGURE 2.7   Exception caused by trying to convert invalid numeric data

Listing 2.9

```csharp
//***************************************************************
//  GasMileage.cs          C#:  Ken Culp
//
//  Demonstrates the use of the Console.In.ReadLine method to
//  read the keyboard and then parse the input into variables.
//***************************************************************
using System;
using System;
namespace GasMileage
{
  class GasMileage
  {
    static void Main(string[] args)
    {
      int miles;
      double gallons, mpg;
      Console.Out.Write("Enter the Number of Miles: ");
      miles = int.Parse(Console.In.ReadLine());

      Console.Out.Write(
        "Enter the gallons of fuel used: ");
      gallons = double.Parse(Console.In.ReadLine());

      mpg = miles / gallons;

      Console.Out.WriteLine("Miles Per Gallon: " +
        mpg.ToString("0.0"));
      Console.In.ReadLine();
    }
  }
}
```

Listing 2.9 continued

Output

```
Enter the number of miles: 328
Enter the gallons of fuel used: 11.2
Miles Per Gallon: 29.28571428571429
```

A `System.In.ReadLine` method processes the input one token at a time, one per line. If multiple values are to be placed on one line, the values first need to be extracted from the list and then processed. We will describe this technique more in Chapter 5. This more advanced functionality is included in the **string** class.

Debugging: Breakpoints and Viewing Contents of Variables

In addition to single stepping through an application, as described in Chapter 1, you can set the application to run freely until it reaches a point where you would like it to stop. Telling an application where to stop is called *setting breakpoints*. When the program reaches a breakpoint, it pauses and Visual Studio switches from the application (command window or form) back to Visual Studio with focus in the code window.

To set a breakpoint, move the cursor on to the tan vertical bar to the left of the code window and click at the line at which you wish to stop. Figure 2.8 illustrates setting a breakpoint in our `GasMileage` application just after the `miles` variable was read in.

If you start the application, the console window is displayed and you are prompted to enter the number of miles. Once you type the number of miles and press Enter, Visual Studio pops up with the application stopped at the breakpoint. The window now looks as shown in Figure 2.9.

Once your application is paused at a breakpoint or during single stepping, you can view the contents of primitive data type variables by moving the mouse cursor over the variable name. Visual Studio shows the variable's contents as illustrated in Figure 2.10, in which the cursor is over the variable `miles`.

To remove a breakpoint, simply click again on the same line that has a breakpoint and the breakpoint will be removed. Alternately, you can select Debug/Clear All Breakpoints to remove all breakpoints.

When the application is stopped at a breakpoint, you can resume the application by selecting Debug/Continue (F5) or Debug/Step Into (F11). Selecting Debug/Step Out will

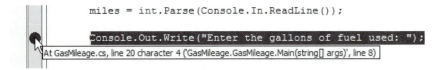

FIGURE 2.8 Setting a breakpoint

```
miles = int.Parse(Console.In.ReadLine());

Console.Out.Write("Enter the gallons of fuel used: ");
gallons = double.Parse(Console.In.ReadLine());
```

FIGURE 2.9   Application stopped at a breakpoint

```
miles = int.Parse(Console.In.ReadLine());
     miles = 678
Console.Out.Write("Enter the gallons of fuel used: ");
gallons = double.Parse(Console.In.ReadLine());
```

FIGURE 2.10   Primitive data type variable preview

be covered in a later debugging topic. Note that multiple breakpoints can be set and the F5 key can be used to step between them.

2.7 WINDOWS-BASED APPLICATIONS

A variety of program types can be created with Visual Studio. So far, we have looked at what are called "console applications," because the interaction takes place at the primitive level of the DOS command prompt. We now look at a second type of application, called a "Windows application." To understand Windows applications, it is necessary to have a basic grasp of event-based programming and the concept of a graphical user interface (GUI).

Event-Based Programming

The applications we have been reviewing up to this point interact with the user at the console level, requesting data and writing data one line at a time. If you review the `GasMileage` example, you will note that the program is in control of the user. That is, when the program starts, it requests the number of miles driven and the gallons used and then prints the results. The only choice the user at the console has it to enter the data as requested or to not run the program.

Although more complex console applications might present the user with various choices, the application program is still in control because the program decides what choices to offer to the user.

Conversely, when you use a Windows-based application (like Microsoft Word or Visual Studio), you see menus and buttons and have a wide variety of choices. These programs are said to be *event driven,* because nothing happens in the application until the user requests something. When something is requested by the user, this creates what is called an *event*.

Events occur in many places. For example, a key is typed at the keyboard, data is typed into a field, the mouse is moved or clicked, time expires on a timer, etc. Thus, every interaction with a Windows application generates a need for service from the application. Throughout the book we will describe ways the application processes events and interacts with the user.

The event model affords a great deal of flexibility and power in configuring applications. In fact, this model enables the application to do multiple things at the same time. For example, you can print a document in Word while you are editing another document. The distinction between procedural and event-based programs is illustrated in Figure 2.11.

In Figure 2.11, procedural programs are in control of the user, telling the user what to do and then processing what the user types in. In the event-based model, the program relinquishes control to the user, so the user decides what needs to be done and when it needs to be done. In fact, this event model allows the user to request a time-consuming function to be performed that the program initiates. However, the program continues to respond to user events, so the user could request other services from the program. Thus, multiple things can be done at one time using the event model.

All interactions with a GUI program generate a request in the form of an event (sometimes referred to as a message) to which the program responds. Thus the user controls the program instead of the other way around as with procedural applications. As you can imagine, this change in orientation has a substantial effect on the way applications are developed. Therefore, most of the code associated with user interaction in the event model centers on handling events. In fact, much of our discussion on developing Windows form-based applications centers on the handling of events.

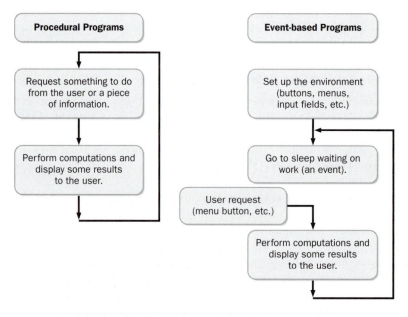

FIGURE 2.11   Procedural and event-based programs

Throughout the book, we will finish each chapter with a discussion of that chapter's contents as related to the event architecture. This material will also cover step-by-step procedures on creating Windows-based applications. In this chapter, we will illustrate a couple of simple GUI applications.

Handling Events

Internally, events could be considered as messages that are sent to the application for further distribution to the appropriate part of the program that can service the events. To understand the concept, consider email messages. These messages are sent to different people who will do different things with the messages.

In a Windows program, different events, or messages, are automatically distributed to the appropriate part of the program for processing. Some of these messages are handled by C# for you, while others must be handled by code that you write. For example, every tiny move of the mouse generates a mouse event. If you don't care where the mouse is but only need to know when a button is clicked, then you do not need to write any code to handle the mouse `Move` event. You can just allow the system to handle it for you. For this reason, code that processes events is called an *event handler*. The code *handles* the event.

For another way to consider the handling of messages, consider the decision of sending something by UPS or Federal Express. Both accept parcels for shipment but each one is specialized to handle them in a different way. So it is with your code in that each different event typically takes special processing. In summary, much of Windows programming involves writing event handlers.

Graphical User Interface (GUI)

The GUI is what you see when you use a Windows-based program on a PC or on a Mac. It is the collection of buttons, instructions, menus, input areas, and graphical images that make up the complete interface when you use the application. It may consist of many different windows (called *dialog boxes*), or only one simple window, as in the example we will create shortly.

2.8   THE GRAPHICS MODEL

Graphics and the event model play a crucial role in computer systems. Throughout this book we explore various aspects of graphics and discuss how they are accomplished. We refer to this as the `Windows Track` throughout the book. The manner in which these sections are presented enables you to skip them without losing continuity through the rest of the text, read them as part of the regular flow of the chapters, or explore them together as a group. In this chapter, we look at simple code examples that draw some lines, text, and simple graphical images on the screen. Therefore, let's start by looking at how images are drawn on a form.

> **Key Concept**
>
> Graphical data is represented by dividing it into many small pieces called pixels.

A picture, like all other information stored on a computer, must be digitized by breaking the information into pieces and representing those pieces as numbers. In the case of pictures, we break the picture into `pixels` (picture elements). A pixel is a tiny region that represents a very small piece of the picture. The complete picture is stored by storing the color of each individual pixel.

A digitized picture can be reproduced when needed by reassembling its pixels. The more pixels used to represent a picture, the more realistic it looks when it is reproduced. The number of pixels used to represent a picture is called the `picture resolution`. The number of pixels that can be displayed by a monitor is called the `monitor resolution`.

A black and white picture can be stored by representing each pixel using a single bit. If the bit is 0, that pixel is white; if the bit is 1, it is black. Figure 2.12 shows a black and white picture that has been stored digitally and an enlargement of a portion of that picture, which shows the individual pixels.

Coordinate Systems

Visual Studio and C# present the user with a variety of coordinate systems. You have a choice of units of measurement (Display, Document, Inch, Millimeter, Pixel, and Point) as well as the origin of the system and the positive direction for each axis. For simplicity at this point, we will work only with the default units of pixels and a coordinate system as described below. If you would like to use a different coordinate system, check the online help files. Also note that conversions are available between coordinate systems.

When drawn, each pixel of a picture is mapped to a pixel on the monitor screen. Each computer system and programming language defines a coordinate system so that we can refer to particular pixels (or other units of measure). Note that the number of pixels per inch on the screen is a function of the resolution selected for the screen (640×480, 800×600,

FIGURE 2.12 Digitized picture with a small portion magnified

1024×768, etc.). Therefore, the physical location of a pixel offset will vary by screen resolution.

A traditional two-dimensional Cartesian coordinate system has two axes that meet at the origin. Values on either axis can be negative or positive. In the default C# coordinate system, all of the visible coordinates are positive. Figure 2.13 compares a traditional coordinate system to the C# coordinate system.

Each point in the C# coordinate system is represented using an (x,y) pair of values. The top-left corner of any C# drawing area has coordinates (0, 0). The x-axis coordinates get larger as you move to the right, and the y-axis coordinates get larger as you move down.

Key Concept

The C# coordinate system has the origin in the upper-left corner and all visible coordinates are positive.

As we've seen in previous examples, a C# program does not have to be graphical in nature. However, once we add the graphical component, the program has its own coordinate system, with the origin (0, 0) in the top-left corner. This consistent approach makes it relatively easy to manage various graphical elements. For example, a coordinate of (200, 300) would be a point 200 pixels from the left edge of the graphical component's work surface and 300 pixels down from the top of the drawing surface.

Note that the origin of the graphical surface of a component might not be located at the upper-left edge of the component. Windows forms always have a banner on top (with the name of the form and the Minimize, Maximize, and Close buttons). For these forms, the y origin starts below this banner. Similarly, adding a menu bar to a form moves the y origin down further. Thus, you need to check the documentation for each component to determine where the origin of the graphics surface is located.

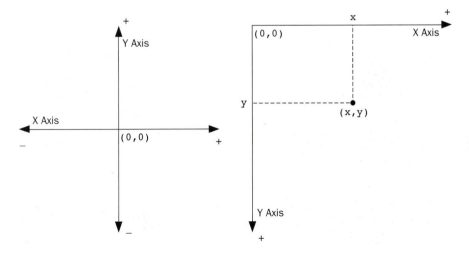

FIGURE 2.13   A traditional coordinate system and the C# coordinate system

Representing Color

Color pictures are divided into pixels, just as black and white pictures are. However, because each pixel can be one of many possible colors, it is not sufficient to represent each pixel using only one bit. There are various ways to represent the color of a pixel. Let's briefly discuss the method used by Visual Studio .NET.

Every color can be represented as a mix of three primary colors: red, green, and blue. In Visual Studio, as in many other computer languages, colors are specified by three numbers that are collectively referred to as an RGB value. RGB stands for Red-Green-Blue. Each number represents the contribution of a primary color. Using 1 byte (8 bits) to store each of the three numbers, the numbers can range from 0 to 255. The level of each primary

AliceBlue	DarkOrange	Khaki	MediumSpringGreen	SaddleBrown
AntiqueWhite	DarkOrchid	Lavender	MediumTurquoise	Salmon
Aqua	DarkRed	LavenderBlush	MediumVioletRed	SandyBrown
Aquamarine	DarkSalmon	LawnGreen	MidnightBlue	SeaGreen
Azure	DarkSeaGreen	LemonChiffon	MintCream	SeaShell
Beige	DarkSlateBlue	LightBlue	MistyRose	Sienna
Bisque	DarkSlateGray	LightCoral	Moccasin	Silver
Black	DarkTurquoise	LightCyan	NavajoWhite	SkyBlue
BlanchedAlmond	DarkViolet	LightGoldenrodYellow	Navy	SlateBlue
Blue	DeepPink	LightGray	OldLace	SlateGray
BlueViolet	DeepSkyBlue	LightGreen	Olive	Snow
Brown	DimGray	LightPink	OliveDrab	SpringGreen
BurlyWood	DodgerBlue	LightSalmon	Orange	SteelBlue
CadetBlue	Firebrick	LightSeaGreen	OrangeRed	Tan
Chartreuse	FloralWhite	LightSkyBlue	Orchid	Teal
Chocolate	ForestGreen	LightSlateGray	PaleGoldenrod	Thistle
Coral	Fuchsia	LightSteelBlue	PaleGreen	Tomato
CornflowerBlue	Gainsboro	LightYellow	PaleTurquoise	Transparent
Cornsilk	GhostWhite	Lime	PaleVioletRed	Turquoise
Crimson	Gold	LimeGreen	PapayaWhip	Violet
Cyan	Goldenrod	Linen	PeachPuff	Wheat
DarkBlue	Gray	Magenta	Peru	White
DarkCyan	Green	Maroon	Pink	WhiteSmoke
DarkGoldenrod	GreenYellow	MediumAquamarine	Plum	Yellow
DarkGray	Honeydew	MediumBlue	PowderBlue	YellowGreen
DarkGreen	HotPink	MediumOrchid	Purple	
DarkKhaki	IndianRed	MediumPurple	Red	
DarkMagenta	Indigo	MediumSeaGreen	RosyBrown	
DarkOliveGreen	Ivory	MediumSlateBlue	RoyalBlue	

FIGURE 2.14   Predefined colors in the Color class

color determines the overall color. For example, high values of red and green combined with a low level of blue results in a shade of yellow.

In C#, a programmer uses the `Color` class, which is part of the Visual Studio package, to define and manage colors. Each object of the `Color` class represents a single color. These may be custom colors or one of a large set of predefined colors. Figure 2.14 lists the predefined colors of the `Color` class. Note that all of these predefined colors are static members, meaning that they can be accessed without having to create a `Color` object.

The `Color` class also contains methods to define and manage colors. For example, you can create a color using a specific amount of red, green, and blue. Alternately, you can obtain the RGB value from an existing color, as well as the hue, saturation, and brightness (HSB). For more information, look up Color Members in the help system.

2.9 YOUR FIRST GUI PROGRAM

This section walks you through the process of creating your first GUI program. You will create a simple blank form and study the code created for you by Visual Studio. Then, you will create an event handler so that you can draw some simple graphics and text on the form.

Open Visual Studio and select File/New/Project. The New Project dialog box appears, as shown in Figure 2.15. To create an interactive program with dialog boxes, text fields, graphics, and the like, click the Windows Application icon under Templates, select the appropriate

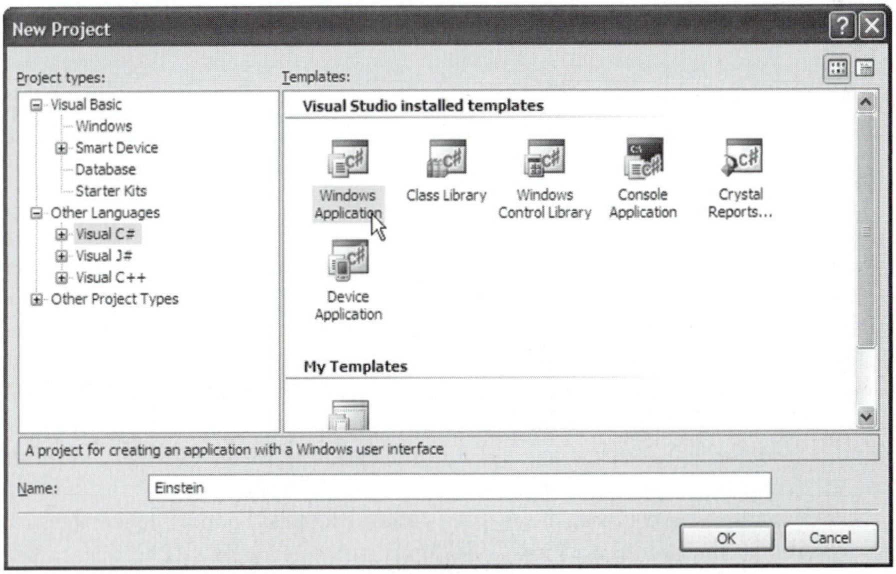

FIGURE 2.15   Creating a Windows application

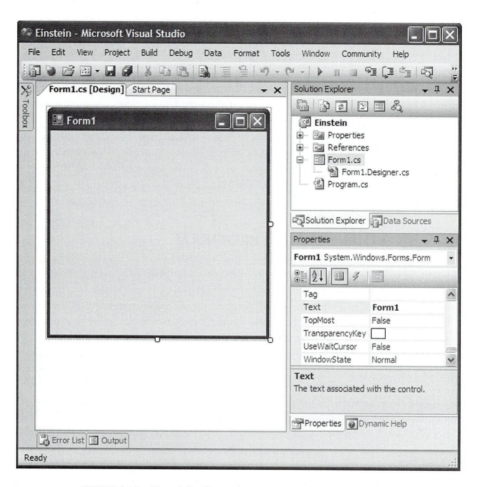

FIGURE 2.16 Visual Studio with Einstein Windows application

directory (Location), and then type a name for your application. For purposes of this exercise, use the name Einstein.

Next, click OK. Visual Studio creates a blank form upon which you can build your application, as shown in Figure 2.16.

For this example, you will use a few simple tools to draw some lines and text on this form. First, widen the form to about 3 inches to make room for your drawing. To widen the form, place the mouse cursor over the small square box on the middle-right side of the form. Click and drag to the right until the form is about 3 inches wide.

Now, let us see what code has already been created by Visual Studio. To view the code, right-click on the form and select View Code. At this time, the file Form1.cs is opened with several lines of code created by Visual Studio, as shown below:

```
using System;
using System.Collections.Generic;
using System.ComponentModel;
using System.Data;
using System.Drawing;
using System.Text;
using System.Windows.Forms;

namespace Einstein
{
  public partial class Form1 : Form
  {
    public Form1()
    {
      InitializeComponent();
    }
  }
}
```

Analysis of System Generated Code for Windows Applications

In the discussion that follows, we are going to outline all the code that Visual Studio has filled in when you created the application. This information is only given in outline form and it is not essential that you grasp the concepts at this time. We only present the material because it will help you focus on the part of the application you are going to write.

First of all, we need to look at all the files that Visual Studio has created for us. To start, go to the Explorer window and click the + sign in front of Form1.cs (see Figure 2.16 above). This reveals a file called `Form1.Designer.cs`. This file is used by the designer to store all of your work as you build your GUI on the form. The content and format of this is controlled by Visual Studio and should NOT be modified by you at any time.

Note that Visual Studio has also created the file `Program.cs`. In a sense, this is the console portion of your application, containing the **static void** Main() line. This file contains the entry point to the application and has just a few lines of code to start the application. You can open this file if you like to see the generated code but do not change anything in the file.

When the application is compiled, the file `Form1.Designer.cs` is combined with the file `Form1.cs` into a single class file. Thus both of these files contain the words **partial class** indicating that each file is incomplete without at least one more file. You do not need to understand the mechanism of partial classes at this time. For now, we will only concern ourselves with an analysis of `Form1.cs`.

Let us begin with the seven lines labeled **using** at the top of the form. Under the hood, Visual Studio has a massive amount of services that you can choose to use when creating windows applications. These services are packaged together in what are called *Name Spaces* such as Drawing, Forms, Data, etc. To simplify your access to these services and to minimize typing, Visual Studio has assumed that you will be using a certain subset of these services (namespaces) in your windows application. You should not remove any of these lines as you may break some of the code that Visual Studio has supplied.

Adding to the Program

You are now ready to write the code to draw some items on the form when the application runs. To draw on the form, you need to create an event handler. (Remember, nothing happens in a Windows application unless an event occurs.) The event we are going to handle is the Paint event, which occurs any time that any portion of the form needs to be redrawn. For example, if you switch windows so that a portion of the form is hidden, the Paint event occurs. Also, when the form is first drawn on the screen, the Paint event occurs when the form is again uncovered.

To create a Paint event handler, first display the form by selecting the Form1.cs [Design] tab, located at the top of the drawing area. Next, find the Properties window (usually located in the lower-right corner of the screen). It should look something like Figure 2.17.

To create an event handler, click the lightning bolt icon at the top of the Properties window. This prompts the display of all the possible events that can be handled for the form. Next, click the AZ icon to show all events in alphabetical order, and then scroll down until you see the Paint event (see Figure 2.18). To create the event handler, double-click in the empty box to the right of the word Paint. This will create an empty event handler, as shown below:

```
private void Form1_Paint(object sender,
            System.Windows.Forms.PaintEventArgs e)
   {
      |
   }
```

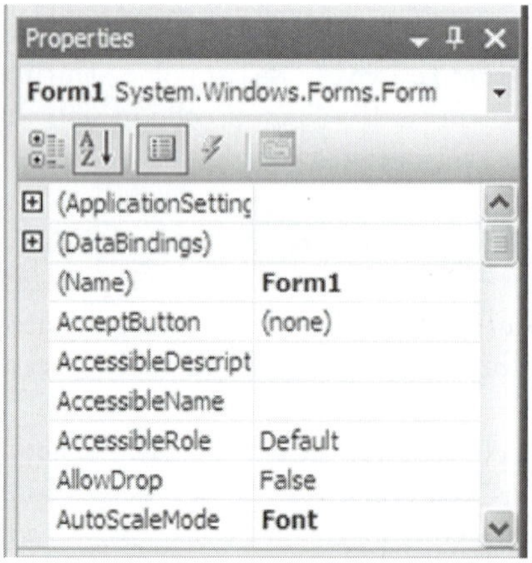

FIGURE 2.17   Form1 properties

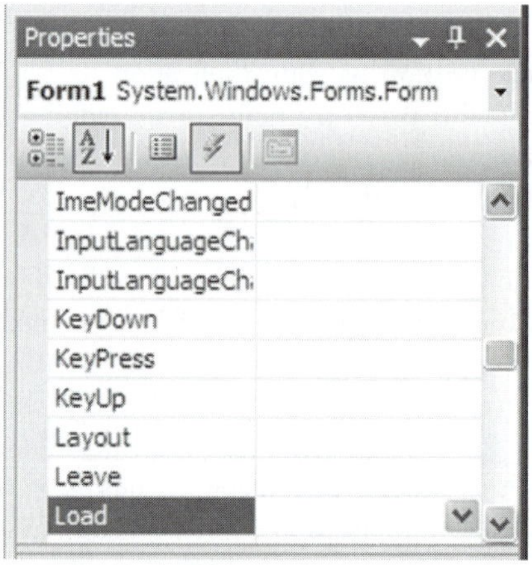

FIGURE 2.18   Form1 events

All that remains is to type the lines that will draw your figure on the form. Complete the program by adding the following lines between the braces of the `Paint` method:

```
Pen pen = Pens.Black;
Font font = new Font("Times New Roman", 12, FontStyle.Regular);
Brush brush = new SolidBrush(Color.Black);
Graphics g = e.Graphics;
g.DrawRectangle(pen, 50, 50, 40, 40);     // Square
g.DrawRectangle(pen, 60, 80, 225, 30);    // rectangle
g.DrawEllipse  (pen, 75, 65, 20, 20);     // circle
g.DrawLine     (pen, 35, 60, 100, 120);   // line
g.DrawString   ("Out of clutter, find simplicity.", font,
                   brush, 110, 55);
g.DrawString   ("-- Albert Einstein", font, brush, 130, 85);
```

The completed program is shown below without the automatic comments.

Listing 2.10

```
//***************************************************************
//   Einstein.cs          C#:  Ken Culp
//
//   Demonstrates a basic windows application using a single form.
//   The form was created using the IDE and all code is in paint.
//***************************************************************
using System;
using System.Drawing;
using System.Windows.Forms;

namespace Einstein
{
  public partial class Einstein : Form
  {
    public Einstein()
    {
      InitializeComponent();
    }

    private void Form1_Paint(object sender, PaintEventArgs e)
    {
      Pen pen = Pens.Black;
      Font font = new Font("Times New Roman", 12,
        FontStyle.Regular);
      Brush brush = new SolidBrush(Color.Black);
      Graphics g = e.Graphics;
      g.DrawRectangle(pen, 50, 50, 40, 40);    // Square
```

Listing 2.10   continued

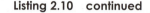

```
        g.DrawRectangle(pen, 60, 80, 225, 30);    // rectangle
        g.DrawEllipse(pen, 75, 65, 20, 20);    // circle
        g.DrawLine(pen, 35, 60, 100, 120);    // line
        g.DrawString("Out of clutter, find simplicity.",
          font, brush, 110, 55);
        g.DrawString("-- Albert Einstein", font, brush, 130, 85);
      }
    }
  }
```

Display

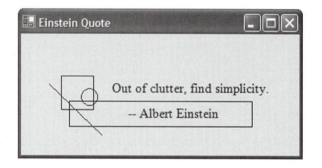

Analysis of the Einstein Application

Examine the line that starts with `public partial class Einstein`. As we noted previously, all C# applications are a class. Here, however, the class defining our form "extends" the `Form` class (this will be explained in Chapter 4). More precisely, form applications use the facilities of the `System.Windows.Forms.Form` class, which is a subset of the Forms library. By starting at this point, we have already gained a lot of functionality. This will become clearer in later chapters.

For now, we will just allow Visual Studio to handle all of this work for us. Visual Studio uses the object-oriented concept of inheritance, which we discussed in Chapter 1 and will explore in more detail later in the book. Note that form classes must also be declared as `public`.

The `Paint` method is one of several Windows event handlers that have particular significance. It is invoked automatically whenever the graphic elements of the form need to be painted to the screen, such as when the form is first run, when another window that was covering it is moved, or when the form itself is moved.

Note that the `Paint` method includes a `PaintEventArgs` object. This object includes a variety of tools, the most important of which is the `Graphics` object. The `Graphics` object is fetched by using the event argument passed to `Paint`. A `Graphics` object defines a particular `graphics context` with which we can interact. The graphics context passed into our `Paint` method represents the drawing surface of the form (excluding the banner). Each graphics context has its own coordinate system, as previously described. In later examples, we will have multiple components, each with its own graphics context.

A `Graphics` object allows us to draw various shapes using methods such as `DrawRectangle`, `DrawEllipse`, `DrawLine`, and `DrawString`. The parameters passed to the drawing methods specify the coordinates and sizes of the shapes to be drawn. We explore these and other methods that draw shapes in the next section.

2.10   DRAWING SHAPES

The C# class libraries provide many classes that let us present and manipulate graphical information. The `Graphics` class is a fundamental part of drawing on the Windows controls.

The `Graphics` Class

The `Graphics` class is defined in the `C#` package. It contains various methods that allow us to draw shapes, including lines, rectangles, and ovals. Figure 2.19 lists some of the fundamental drawing methods of the `Graphics` class. Note that these methods also let us draw circles and squares, which are just specific types of ovals and rectangles, respectively. We discuss additional drawing methods of the `Graphics` class in Chapter 7.

The methods of the `Graphics` class allow us to specify whether we want a shape filled or unfilled. An unfilled shape shows only the outline of the shape and is otherwise transparent (you can see any underlying graphics). A filled shape is solid between its boundaries and covers any underlying graphics.

All of these methods rely on the C# coordinate system, which we discussed earlier in this chapter. Recall that point (`0,0`) is in the upper-left corner, such that x values get larger as we move to the right, and y values get larger as we move down. Any shapes drawn at coordinates that are outside the visible area will not be seen.

> **Key Concept**
>
> Most shapes can be drawn filled (opaque) or unfilled (as an outline).

Many of the `Graphics` drawing methods are self-explanatory, but some require a little more discussion. Note, for instance, that an ellipse drawn by the `DrawEllipse` method is defined by the coordinate of the upper-left corner and dimensions that specify the width and height of a `bounding rectangle`. Shapes with curves, such as ellipses, are often defined by a rectangle that encompasses their perimeters. Figure 2.20 depicts a bounding rectangle for an ellipse.

An arc can be thought of as a segment of an ellipse. To draw an arc, we specify the ellipse of which the arc is a part and the portion of the ellipse in which we're interested. The starting point of the arc is defined by the `start angle` and the ending point of the arc is defined by the `sweep angle`. The

> **Key Concept**
>
> An arc is a segment of an ellipse beginning at a specific start angle and extending for a distance specified by the sweep angle in a clockwise direction.

`public void DrawEllipse(Pen pen,`
`  int x, int y, int width, int height);`
`public void DrawEllipse(Pen pen,`
`  float x, float y,`
`  float width, float height);`
	Draws an ellipse defined by a bounding rectangle specified by a pair of coordinates, a height, and a width.

`public void DrawLine(Pen pen,`
`  int x1, int y1, x2, int y2);`
`public void DrawLine(Pen pen,`
`  float x1, float y1, float x2, float y2);`
	Draws a line connecting the two points specified by coordinate pairs.

`public void DrawRectangle(Pen pen,`
`  int x, int y, int width, int height);`
`public void DrawRectangle(Pen pen,`
`  float x, float y,`
`  float width, float height);`
	Draws a rectangle specified by a coordinate pair, a width, and a height.

`public void DrawString(string s,`
`  Font font, Brush brush,`
`  float x, float y);`
	Draws the specified text string at the specified location with the specified Brush and Font objects.

`public void FillEllipse(Brush brush,`
`  int x, int y, int width, int height);`
`public void FillEllipse(Brush brush,`
`  float x, float y,`
`  float width, float height);`
	Fills the interior of an ellipse defined by a bounding rectangle specified by a pair of coordinates, a width, and a height.

`public void FillPath(Brush brush,` `  GraphicsPath path);`	Fills the interior of a GraphicsPath object.

`public void FillPie(Brush brush,`
`  int x, int y, int width, int height,`
`  int startAngle, int sweepAngle);`
`public void FillPie(Brush brush,`
`  float x, float y,`
`  float width, float height,`
`  float startAngle, float sweepAngle);`
	Fills the interior of a pie section defined by an ellipse specified by a pair of coordinates, a width, and a height and two radial lines.

`public void FillRectangle(Brush brush,`
`  int x, int y, int width, int height);`
`public void FillRectangle(Brush brush,`
`  float x, float y,`
`  float width, float height);`
	Fills the interior of a rectangle specified by a pair of coordinates, a width, and a height.

FIGURE 2.19 Some methods of the `Graphics` class

sweep angle does not indicate where the arc ends, but rather its range. The start angle and the sweep angle are measured in degrees, counterclockwise from the x-axis. The origin for the start angle is an imaginary horizontal line passing through the center of the oval and can be referred to as 0°, as shown in Figure 2.21.

Every graphics object (like the Form) has a current foreground color called ForeColor that is used whenever shapes or strings are drawn. Every surface that can be drawn on also has a background color called BackColor. You can view these properties and set them with the Visual Studio IDE by showing the form object and viewing the Properties window. (Note that if events are shown in the Properties window, click the small rectangle that resembles a report, to the right of the AZ button, to view properties.)

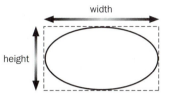

FIGURE 2.20   An ellipse and its bounding rectangle

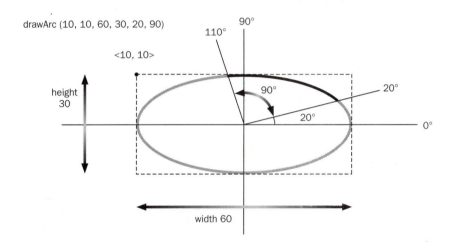

FIGURE 2.21   An arc defined by an ellipse, a start angle, and a sweep angle

The foreground and background colors can also be modified in code in any event handler. Since your Windows application is built from (extends) a standard form, the `ForeColor` and `BackColor` values can be modified by simply referencing the name, as in `BackColor = Color.Cyan`. However, to reduce confusion and to show that you are modifying these values on the form, you should use the word `this`, as shown here:

```
this.BackColor = Color.Cyan;
```

Listing 2.11 shows a program called `Snowman`. It uses various drawing and color methods to draw a winter scene featuring a snowman. Review the code carefully to note how each shape is drawn to create the overall picture.

Note that the snowman figure is based on two constant values called `MID` and `TOP`, which define the midpoint of the snowman (left to right) and the top of the snowman's head. The entire snowman figure is drawn relative to these values. Using constants like these makes it easier to create the snowman and to make modifications later. For example, to shift the snowman to the right or left in our picture, only one constant declaration would have to change.

Listing 2.11

```
//****************************************************************
//  Snowman.cs            C#:  Ken Culp
//
//  Demonstrates basic drawing methods and the use of color.
//****************************************************************
using System;
using System.Collections.Generic;
using System.ComponentModel;
using System.Data;
using System.Drawing;
using System.Text;
using System.Windows.Forms;

namespace Snowman
{
  public partial class Snowman : Form
  {
    public Snowman()
    {
      InitializeComponent();
    }

    private void Snowman_Paint(object sender, PaintEventArgs e)
    {
      const int MID = 150;
      const int TOP = 50;

      this.BackColor = Color.Cyan;            // Background color
      this.Width = 310;                       // Width (optional)
      this.Height = 260;                      // Height (optional)
      this.Text = "Simple Graphics Snowman";  // Title (optional)

      // Pens and brushes: pens for draws; brushes for fills
      Pen blue = new Pen(Color.Blue);
      Pen yellow = new Pen(Color.Yellow);
      Pen white = new Pen(Color.White);
      Pen black = new Pen(Color.Black);
      Brush brWhite = white.Brush;
      Brush brBlack = black.Brush;
      Graphics g = e.Graphics; // Get graphics took kit

      // Draw snowman
      g.DrawRectangle(blue, 0, 175, 300, 50);        // sky
      g.DrawEllipse(yellow, -40, -40, 80, 80);       // sun
      g.FillEllipse(brWhite, MID-20, TOP+40, 40);    // head
      g.FillEllipse(brWhite, MID-35, TOP+35, 70, 50); // top
      g.FillEllipse(brWhite, MID-50, TOP+80, 100, 60); // bot.
```

Listing 2.11   continued

```
        g.FillEllipse(brBlack, MID-10, TOP+10, 5, 5);       // l. eye
        g.FillEllipse(brBlack, MID+5, TOP+10, 5, 5);        // r. eye
        g.DrawArc(black, MID-10, TOP+20, 20, 10, -190, -160); // (:
        // Arms
        g.DrawLine(black, MID-25, TOP+60, MID-50, TOP+40);
        g.DrawLine(black, MID+25, TOP+60, MID+55, TOP+60);
        // Hat: Brim, top
        g.DrawLine(black, MID-20, TOP+5, MID+20, TOP+5);
        g.FillRectangle(brBlack, MID-15, TOP-20, 30, 25);
    }
  }
}
```

Display

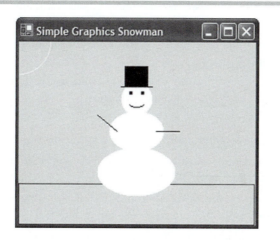

Summary of Key Concepts

> The `Write` and `WriteLine` methods represent two services provided by the `Console.Out` object.

> An escape sequence can be used to represent a character that would otherwise cause compilation problems.

> A variable is a name for a memory location used to hold a value of a particular data type.

> Accessing data leaves it intact in memory, but an assignment statement overwrites the old data.

> Constants hold a particular value for the duration of their existence.

> C# has two kinds of numeric values: integer and floating point. There are eight integer data types and two floating point data types.

> C# supports several character encoding methods, including the 16-bit Unicode (UTF-16) character set to represent character data.

> Expressions are combinations of operators and operands used to perform a calculation.

> C# follows a well-defined set of precedence rules that governs the order in which operators will be evaluated in an expression.

> Narrowing conversions should be avoided because they can lose information.

> Graphical data is represented by dividing it into many small pieces called pixels.

> The C# coordinate system has the origin in the upper-left corner and all visible coordinates are positive.

> Colors are represented in C# using an RGB value-three values that represent the contributions of the primary colors red, green, and blue.

> Most shapes can be drawn filled (opaque) or unfilled (as an outline).

> An arc is a segment of an ellipse beginning at a specific start angle and extending for a distance specified by the sweep angle in a clockwise direction.

Self-Review Questions

2.1   What is primitive data? How are primitive data types different from objects?

2.2   What is a string literal?

2.3   What is the difference between the `Write` and `WriteLine` methods?

2.4   What is a parameter?

2.5   What is an escape sequence? Give some examples.

2.6   What is a variable declaration?

2.7   How many values can be stored in an integer variable?

2.8   What are the eight integer data types in C#? How are they different?

2.9   What is a character set?

2.10 What is operator precedence?

2.11 What is the result of 19%5 when evaluated in a C# expression? Explain.

2.12 What is the result of 13/4 when evaluated in a C# expression? Explain.

2.13 Why are widening conversions safer than narrowing conversions?

2.14 How can a black and white picture be represented using 1's and 0's?

2.15 What is the difference between a console application and a Windows application?

Exercises

2.1   Explain the following programming statement in terms of objects and the services they provide:

```
Console.Out.WriteLine ("I gotta be me!");
```

2.2   What output is produced by the following code fragment? Explain.

```
Console.Out.Write ("Here we go!");
Console.Out.WriteLine ("12345");
Console.Out.Write ("Test this if you are not sure.");
Console.Out.Write ("Another.");
Console.Out.WriteLine ();
Console.Out.WriteLine ("All done.");
```

2.3   What is wrong with the following program statement? How can it be fixed?

```
Console.Out.WriteLine ("To be or not to be, that
is the question.");
```

2.4   What output is produced by the following statement? Explain.

```
Console.Out.WriteLine ("50 plus 25 is " + 50 + 25);
```

2.5   What is the output produced by the following statement? Explain.

```
Console.Out.WriteLine ("He thrusts his fists\n\tagainst" +
    " the post\nand still insists\n\the sees the \"ghost\"");
```

2.6   Given the following declarations, what result is stored in each of the listed assignment statements?

```
int iResult, num1 = 25, num2 = 40, num3 = 17, num4 = 5;
double fResult, val1 = 17.0, val2 = 12.78;
```

a. iResult = num1 / num4;

b. fResult = num1 / num4;

c. iResult = num3 / num4;

d. fResult = num3 / num4;

e. fResult = val1 / num4;

f. fResult = val1 / val2;

g. iResult = num1 / num2;

h. fResult = (**double**) num1 / num2;

i. fResult = num1 / (**double**) num2;

j. fResult = (**double**) (num1 / num2);

k. iResult = (**int**) (val1 / num4);

l. fResult = (**int**) (val1 / num4);

m. fResult = (**int**) ((**double**) num1 / num2);

n. iResult = num3 % num4;

o. iResult = num 2 % num3;

p. iResult = num3 % num2;

q. iResult = num2 % num4;

2.7 For each of the following expressions, indicate the order in which the operators will be evaluated by writing a number beneath each operator.

a. a - b - c - d

b. a - b + c - d

c. a + b / c / d

d. a + b / c * d

e. a / b * c * d

f. a % b / c * d

g. a % b % c % d

h. a - (b - c) - d

i. (a - (b - c)) - d

j. a - ((b - c) - d)

k. a % (b % c) * d * e

l. a + (b - c) * d - e

```
m. (a + b) * c + d * e
n. (a + b) * (c / d) % e
```

2.8   Describe how to create an empty console application and an empty Windows application in Visual Studio.

2.9   Compare and contrast a traditional coordinate system and the coordinate system used by C# graphical components.

2.10   How many bits are needed to store a color picture that is 400 pixels wide and 250 pixels high? Assume color is represented using the RGB technique described in this chapter and that no special compression is done.

2.11   Assuming you have a `Graphics` object called `page`, write a statement that will draw a line from point (20, 30) to point (50, 60).

2.12   Assuming you have a `Graphics` object called `page`, write a statement that will draw a rectangle with height 70 and width 35, such that its upper-left corner is at point (10, 15).

2.13   Assuming you have a `Graphics` object called `page`, write a statement that will draw a circle `centered` on point (50, 50) with a radius of 20 pixels.

2.14   The following lines of code draw the eyes of the snowman in the `Snowman` form. The eyes seem centered on the face when drawn, but the first parameters of each call are not equally offset from the midpoint. Explain.

```
g.FillEllipse(brBlack, MID-10, TOP+10, 5, 5);   // left eye
g.FillEllipse(brBlack, MID+5,  TOP+10, 5, 5);   // right eye
```

2.15   Write four different program statements that increment the value of an integer variable `total`.

Programming Projects

2.1   Create a revised version of the `Lincoln` application from Chapter 1 such that quotes appear around the quotation.

2.2   Write an application that reads three integers and prints their average.

2.3   Write an application that reads two floating point numbers and prints their sum, difference, and product.

2.4   Create a revised version of the `TempConverter` application to convert from Fahrenheit to Celsius. Read the Fahrenheit temperature from the user.

2.5   Write an application that converts miles to kilometers. (One mile equals 1.60935 kilometers.) Read the miles value from the user as a floating point value.

2.6   Write an application that reads values representing a time duration in hours, minutes, and seconds, and then prints the equivalent total number of seconds. (For example, 1 hour, 28 minutes, and 42 seconds is equivalent to 5322 seconds.)

2.7   Create a revised version of the previous project that reverses the computation. That is, read a value representing a number of seconds, then print the equivalent amount of time as a combination of hours, minutes, and seconds. (For example, 9999 seconds is equivalent to 2 hours, 46 minutes, and 39 seconds.)

2.8   Write an application that determines the value of the coins in a jar and prints the total in dollars and cents. Read integer values that represent the number of quarters, dimes, nickels, and pennies. `myTotal.ToString("c")` will convert the float or double value `myTotal` to a currency format for printing.

2.9   Create a revised version of the `Snowman` form with the following modifications:

   > Add two red buttons to the upper torso.

   > Make the snowman frown instead of smile.

   > Move the sun to the upper-right corner of the picture.

   > Display your name in the upper-left corner of the picture.

   > Shift the entire snowman 20 pixels to the right.

2.10 Write a Windows application that writes your name in the center of the form using the `DrawString` method. Experiment with various font sizes and styles.

2.11 Write a Windows application that draws the Big Dipper. Add some extra stars in the night sky (black background).

2.12 Write a Windows application that draws some balloons tied to strings. Make the balloons various colors.

2.13 Write a Windows application that draws the Olympic logo. The circles in the logo should be colored, from left to right, blue, yellow, black, green, and red.

2.14 Write a Windows application that draws a house with a door (and doorknob), windows, and a chimney. Add some smoke coming out of the chimney and some clouds in the sky.

2.15 Write a Windows application that displays a business card of your own design. Include both graphics and text.

2.16 Write a Windows application that displays your name in shadow text by drawing your name in black, then drawing it again slightly offset in a lighter color.

2.17 Write a Windows application that shows a pie chart with eight equal slices, all colored differently.

Answers to Self-Review Questions

2.1   Primitive data includes basic values such as numbers or characters. Objects are more complex entities that usually contain primitive data that helps define them.

2.2   A string literal is a sequence of characters delimited by double quotes.

2.3   Both the `Write` and `WriteLine` methods of the `Console.Out` object write a string of characters to the monitor screen. The difference is that, after printing the characters, the `WriteLine` performs a carriage return so that whatever is printed next appears on the next line. The `Write` method allows subsequent output to appear on the same line.

2.4   A parameter is data that is passed into a method when it is invoked. The method usually uses that data to accomplish the service that it provides. For example, the parameter to the `WriteLine` method indicates what characters should be printed. The two numeric operands to the `Math.Pow` method are the operands to the power function that is computed and returned.

2.5   An escape sequence is a series of characters that begins with the backslash (\) and that implies that the following characters should be treated in some special way. Examples: \n represents the newline character, \t represents the tab character, and \" represents the quotation character (as opposed to using it to terminate a string).

2.6   A variable declaration establishes the name of a variable and the type of data that it can contain. A declaration may also have an optional initialization, which gives the variable an initial value.

2.7   An integer variable can store only one value at a time. When a new value is assigned to it, the old one is overwritten and lost.

2.8   The eight integer data types in C# are **sbyte**, **byte**, **short**, **ushort**, **int**, **uint**, **long**, and **ulong**. They differ in whether or not they can take negative values (signed) and by how much memory space is allocated for each, which determines how large a number they can hold.

2.9   A character set is a list of characters in a particular order. A character set defines the valid characters that a particular type of computer or programming language will support. C# uses the Unicode character set.

2.10   Operator precedence is the set of rules that dictates the order in which operators are evaluated in an expression.

2.11   The result of 19%5 in a C# expression is 4. The remainder operator % returns the remainder after dividing the second operand into the first. Five goes into 19 three times, with 4 left over.

2.12   The result of 13/4 in a C# expression is 3 (not 3.25). The result is an integer because both operands are integers. Therefore, the / operator performs integer division, and the fractional part of the result is truncated.

2.13 A widening conversion tends to go from a small data value, in terms of the amount of space used to store it, to a larger one. A narrowing conversion does the opposite. Information is more likely to be lost in a narrowing conversion, which is why narrowing conversions are considered to be less safe than widening ones.

2.14 A black and white picture can be drawn using a series of dots, called pixels. Pixels that correspond to a value of 0 are displayed in white and pixels that correspond to a value of 1 are displayed in black. By using thousands of pixels, a realistic black and white photo can be produced on a computer screen.

2.15 A console application interacts with the user at the keyboard by writing lines of data to the screen and reading data values back, normally one value at a time. A console application is called a procedural program, because it controls the user. Conversely, a Windows application includes graphical characters, and the user controls the application, being able in many cases to have the program do multiple things at once.

Using Classes and Objects

3

CHAPTER OBJECTIVES

> Discuss the creation of objects and the use of object reference variables.

> Explore the services provided by the `String` class.

> Describe how the C# standard class library is organized into namespaces.

> Explore the services provided by the `Random` and `Math` classes.

> Discuss ways to format output using the `ToString()` method.

> Introduce enumerated types.

> Introduce components and containers used in graphical user interfaces.

> Describe a label component and the use of images.

This chapter further explores the use of predefined classes and the objects we can create from them. Using classes and objects for the services they provide is a fundamental part of object-oriented software, and sets the stage for writing classes of our own. In this chapter, we use classes and objects to manipulate character strings, produce random numbers, perform complex calculations, and format output. This chapter also introduces the concept of an enumerated type, which is a special kind of class in C#. In the Windows Track of this chapter, we lay the foundation for developing GUIs for our programs, and discuss how to display images.

3.1   CREATING OBJECTS

At the end of Chapter 1 we presented an overview of object-oriented concepts, including the basic relationship between classes and objects. Then, in Chapter 2, in addition to discussing primitive data, we provided some examples of using objects for the services they provide. This chapter explores these ideas further.

In previous examples, we've used the `WriteLine` method many times. As we mentioned in Chapter 2, the `WriteLine` method is a service provided by the `Console.Out` object, which represents the standard output stream. To be more precise, the identifier `Out` is an object variable that is stored in the `Console` class. It has been predefined and set up for us as part of the C# standard class library. We can simply use it.

Let's carefully examine the idea of creating an object. In C#, a variable name represents either a primitive value or an object. Like variables that hold primitive types, a variable that refers to an object must be declared. The class used to define an object can be thought of as the type of an object. The declarations of object variables have a similar structure to the declarations of primitive variables.

Overview of Strings

As noted in Chapter 2, the C# type `string` is really an intrinsic or primitive data type because it can be created with a simple variable initialization without the word new. However, C# also includes a class called `String`, which is really an alias of the `string` keyword; in fact, the two can always be used interchangeably. In our code examples, we will use the keyword `string`, but if you look up `string` in the online documentation, it refers to the `String` class. This is not a contradiction, because internally C# represents all primitive types as classes.

C# also supports another structure for maintaining strings called the `StringBuilder` class. It is a lot like `string` except that you use it to build a string in code, particularly when a lot of pieces will be concatenated.

Every time text is appended to a `string` object (or its alias, `String`), the system creates a new string that contains the concatenation of both strings, and then discards and garbage-collects the original string. This is a fairly slow operation, particularly when a large number of concatenations are performed. For this reason, C# includes another class, called `StringBuilder`, which leaves room for additional information to be appended to the string so that appends can happen in place without creating a new string. Therefore, `StringBuilder` is *much* more efficient than `string` when performing appends. Furthermore, if you have some idea about the maximum length that you need when building a string in code, you can allocate that when you are creating the `StringBuilder` object. In the examples that follow, we will use both `string` and `StringBuilder` items so that you can begin to see the differences.

Now let's turn our attention to the creation of objects and the distinction between primitive data types and objects. Consider the following two declarations:

```
int num;
StringBuilder name;
```

The first declaration uses a primitive data type to create a variable, num, that holds an integer value. The second declaration creates a variable that is an object of type StringBuilder. An object variable doesn't hold the data itself; it holds the address of where the data has been stored by the system. Thus, name is an address of an object where num contains the data itself. To understand the difference, consider an analogy to the U.S. postal system. If you know someone's street address, you can find their house. However, the address is not the house itself, it is only the "address" of the house. Thus, the contents of an object are stored somewhere else (called the *heap*) separate from the variable itself.

Initially, neither of the two variables declared above contains any data. We say they are *uninitialized,* which can be depicted as follows:

As we pointed out in Chapter 2, it is always important to make sure a variable is initialized before using it. For an object variable, that means we must make sure it refers to a valid object prior to using it. In most situations the compiler will issue an error if you attempt to use a variable before initializing it.

An object variable can also be set to null, which is a reserved word in C#. A null reference specifically indicates that a variable does not refer to an object. Using the postal system analogy, you might say that the address is blank on the envelope.

Note that, although we've declared a StringBuilder reference variable, no StringBuilder object actually exists yet. The act of creating an object using the new operator is called *instantiation.* An object is said to be an *instance* of a particular class. To instantiate an object, we can use the new operator, which returns the address of the new object. The following two assignment statements give values to the two of the variables declared above:

```
num = 42;
name = new StringBuilder("James Gosling");
```

After the new operator creates the object, a *constructor* is invoked to help set it up initially. A constructor is a special method that has the same name as the class. In this example, the parameter to the constructor is a string literal that specifies the characters that the string object will hold. After these assignments are executed, the variables can be depicted as:

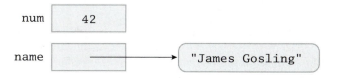

Since an object reference variable holds the address of the object, it can be thought of as a *pointer* to the location in memory where the object is held. We could show the numeric address, but the actual address value is irrelevant—what's important is that the variable refers to a particular object.

After an object has been instantiated, we use the *dot operator* to access its methods. We've used the dot operator many times already, such as in calls to `Console.Out.WriteLine`. The dot operator is appended directly after the object reference, followed by the method being invoked. For example, to use the `Length` property defined in the `StringBuilder` class, we can use the dot operator on the `name` reference variable:

```
count = name.Length;
```

Visual Studio greatly simplifies your editing process when using the dot notation with an object. For example, the object name above is of type `StringBuilder`. When you type the word **name** and then press the period (dot) key, you are presented with a list of all methods and properties associated with the class `StringBuilder` (see Figure 3.1). Microsoft calls this feature *IntelliSense*. Click Help/Search and type **IntelliSense** to see additional details.

As shown in Figure 3.1, `Length` is a property of `name` and has a value that can be examined. Properties are identified in the IntelliSense menu by the icon of a small box with a finger pointing to it. The other items listed for name in Figure 3.1 are the tools associated with it, which are called *methods*. Methods perform some kind of service associated with the class. For example, the first method listed for `name` is `Append`. `Append` is a method that requires additional data, called parameters, that it converts to a string of characters and adds to whatever is already in `name`. `Append` then returns the data as a `StringBuilder` object, which is the concatenation of what was in the string before plus what was added. In general, meth-

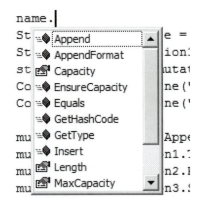

FIGURE 3.1   IntelliSense showing methods and properties for `StringBuilder`

ods can require any number of parameters (including none) and can, optionally, return some type of information.

For the string `"James Gosling"`, the `Length` property returns 13, which includes the space between the first and last names. Some methods do not return a value. Other `string` and `StringBuilder` methods are discussed in the next section.

The act of declaring the object reference variable and creating the object itself can be combined into one step by initializing the variable in the declaration, just as we do with primitive types:

```
StringBuilder title = new StringBuilder(
   "C# Software Solutions");
```

As previously stated, the `string` type is a primitive type, so you never need to use the word new. Simply declare the variable to be of type `string` and give it a value. C# defines string literals delimited by double quotation marks, as we've seen in various examples. This is a shortcut notation. Whenever a string literal appears, a `string` object is created automatically. Here is how to declare a variable of type `string`:

```
string city = "London";
```

That is, for `string` objects, the explicit use of the new operator and the call to the constructor can be eliminated. On the other hand, `StringBuilder` is an object and does require the new operator, as previously shown.

Aliases

Because an object reference variable stores an address, a programmer must be careful when managing objects. First, let's review the effect of assignment on primitive values. Suppose we have two integer variables, num1, initialized to 5, and num2, initialized to 12:

In the following assignment statement, a copy of the value that is stored in num1 is stored in num2:

```
num2 = num1;
```

The original value of 12 in num2 is overwritten by the value 5. The variables num1 and num2 still refer to different locations in memory, and both of those locations now contain the value 5:

num1   5

num2   5

Now consider the following object declarations:

```
StringBuilder x = new StringBuilder("ABC");
StringBuilder y = new StringBuilder("DEF");
Console.Out.WriteLine("Step 1: X="+x+"   Y="+y);
```

As with the numbers, the references x and y refer to two different StringBuilder objects:

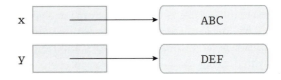

Now suppose the following assignment statement is executed, copying the value in x into y:

```
y = x;
```

This assignment works in the same way as the integer assignment—a copy of the value of x is stored in y. But remember, object variables hold the address of an object, and it is the address that gets copied. Originally, the two references referred to different objects. After the assignment, both x and y contain the same address and therefore refer to the same object:

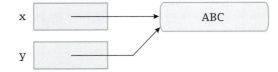

The x and y reference variables are now *aliases* of each other because they are two names that refer to the same object. All references to the object originally referenced by x are now gone; that object cannot be used again in the program. Assume x and y are assigned as shown above. Then consider the following code segment:

```
Console.Out.WriteLine("Before: X="+x+"   Y="+y);
y = x;
x.Append("XYZ");
Console.Out.WriteLine(" After: X="+x+" Y="+y);
```

In this code segment, we modified x by appending the letters "XYZ" to it, but we made no change to y. If we run this code, we see the following output:

```
Before: X=ABC  Y=DEF
 After: X=ABCXYZ Y=ABCXYZ
```

Note that both x and y now reflect the change made to x. Thus, y now points to the same data as x and they are different addresses that point to the same place in memory.

One important implication of aliases is that when we use one reference to change an object, it is also changed for the other reference because there is really only one object. Aliases can produce undesirable effects unless they are managed carefully. As a final thought, let us again note that although string is a class, it is treated as an intrinsic function. Therefore when we write string1 = string2 this is a value copy and there are still two separate string objects although they would now have the same contents.

> **Key Concept**
>
> Multiple reference variables can refer to the same object, and a change to any one variable is reflected in all variables because they point to the same place.

All interaction with an object occurs through a reference variable, so we can use an object only if we have a reference to it. When all references to an object are lost (perhaps by reassignment), that object can no longer contribute to the program. The program can no longer invoke its methods or use its variables. At this point the object is called *garbage* because it serves no useful purpose.

C# performs *automatic garbage collection.* When the last reference to an object is lost, the object becomes a candidate for garbage collection. Occasionally, behind the scenes, the C# environment executes a method that "collects" all the objects marked for garbage collection and returns their memory to the system for future use. The programmer does not have to worry about explicitly reclaiming memory that has become garbage.

3.2   String AND StringBuilder CLASS DETAILS

Let's examine the string and StringBuilder classes in more detail. Figure 3.2 lists the more useful methods of the String class.

Once a string object is created, its value cannot be lengthened or shortened, nor can any of its characters change. Thus we say that a string object is *immutable.* However, several methods in the string class return new string objects that are the result of modifying the original string's value.

Note that some of the string methods refer to the *index* of a particular character. A character in a string can be specified by its position, or index, in the string. The index of the first character in a string is zero, the index of the next character is one, and so on. Therefore, in the string "Hello", the index of the character 'H' is zero and the character at index four is 'o'.

Due to the immutability of strings and the inefficiencies associated with concatenating strings, C# includes the StringBuilder class. StringBuilder supports many of the same methods and properties as the String class, and, in many cases, their use in code will appear quite similar. Figure 3.3 lists some of the constructors and members of the StringBuilder class.

Public Fields	
Empty	This read-only field represents the empty string which is used in compares: if (myString ==String.Empty) {…}

Public Properties	
Length	Gets the number of characters in this instance.

Public Methods	
Compare	Compares two different String objects.
Compare to	Compares this instance with a specified object.
Concat	Concatenates one or more instances of String, or the String representations of the values of one or more instances of Object.
Copy	Creates a new instance of String with the same value as a specified String.
CopyTo	Copies a specified number of characters from a specified position in this instance to a specified position in an array of Unicode characters.
EndsWith	Determines whether the end of this instance matches the specified String.
Format	Replaces each format item in a specified String with the text equivalent of a corresponding object's value.
IndexOf	Returns the offset of the first occurrence of the given string in this instance.
IndexOfAny	Returns the index of the first place in the string that any character in a specified array of Unicode characters occurs.
Insert	Inserts a specified String at a specified index position in this instance.
Join	Concatenates a separator String between each element of a String array, producing one concatenated string.
LastIndexOf	Reports the index position of the last occurrence of a specified Unicode character or String within this instance.
LastIndexOfAny	Reports the index position of the last occurrence in this instance of one or more characters specified in a Unicode array.
PadLeft	Right-aligns the characters in this instance, padding on the left with spaces or a specified Unicode character for a specified total length.
PadRight	Left-aligns the characters in this string, padding on the right with spaces or a specified Unicode character, for a specified total length
Remove	Deletes a specified number of characters from this instance, beginning at a specified position.

FIGURE 3.2   Some String class members (*continues*)

Replace	Replaces all occurances of a specified Unicode character or `String` in this instance with another specified Unicode character or `String`.
Split	Identifies the substrings in this instance that are delimited by one or more characters specified in an array, then places the substrings into a `String` array.
StartsWith	Determines whether the beginning of this instance matches the specified `String`.
Substring	Retrieves a substring from this instance.
ToCharArray	Copies the characters in this instance to a Unicode character array.
ToLower	Returns a copy of this `String` in lowercase.
ToString	Converts the value of this instance to a `String`.
ToUpper	Returns a copy of this `String` in uppercase.
Trim	Removes all occurrences of a set of specified characters from the beginning and end of this instance.
TrimEnd	Removes all occurrences of a set of characters specified in an array from the end of this instance.
TrimStart	Removes all occurrences of a set of characters specified in an array from the beginning of this instance.

Public Operators and Indexers	
= =	Returns `true` if the strings have the same value (contents) and `false` otherwise.
!=	Returns `false` if the strings have the same value (contents) and `true` if the contents are different.
[ ]	Returns the character at the specified index. Index from 0.

FIGURE 3.2 (*continued*)   Some `String` class members

Before we review specific examples of the `String` and `StringBuilder` classes in use, let's take a quick look at how to move between each class and consider some general comments on how to use each. First of all, `string` is generally much easier because it can be initialized with an equal sign (no `new`) and can be appended to by using the + or += sign. By comparison, `StringBuilder` requires the use of a constructor and an `Append` method to create or modify the string contents. However, both classes support the ability to index into the individual characters into the string, and both support inserting or deleting characters in the middle of the string. Also, since `StringBuilder` has a `ToString` method, you can use a `StringBuilder` object any place you need the string contents. Thus, the use of

Public Constructors	
public **StringBuilder**();	Constructs empty StringBuilder with default capacity.
public **StringBuilder**(int)	Constructs empty StringBuilder object with the specified capacity.
public **StringBuilder**(int, int)	Constructs empty StringBuilder object with the specified capacity and maximum capacity.
public **StringBuilder**(string)	Constructs StringBuilder with specified initial string.
public **StringBuilder**(string, int)	Constructs StringBuilder with specified initial string of specified capacity.

Public Properties	
Capacity	Gets or sets the maximum number of characters that can be contained in the memory allocated by the current instance.
Length	Gets or sets the length of this instance.
MaxCapacity	Gets the maximum capacity of this instance.

Public Methods	
Append	Appends the string representation of a specified object to the end of this instance.
AppendFormat	Appends a formatted string, which contains zero or more format specifications, to this instance. Each format specification is replaced by the string representation of a corresponding object argument.
EnsureCapacity	Ensures that the capacity of this instance of StringBuilder is at least the specified value.
Equals	Returns a value indicating whether this instance is equal to a specified object.
Insert	Inserts the string representation of a specified object into this instance at a specified character position.
Remove	Removes the specified range of characters from this instance.
Replace	Replaces all occurrences of a specified character or string in this instance with another specified character or string.
ToString	Overridden. Converts a StringBuilder to a String.

Public Operators and Indexers	
[ ]	Returns the character at the specified index. Index from 0.

FIGURE 3.3   StringBuilder class members

StringBuilder is mainly limited to those cases where you need to append many pieces to make up a string.

The last step is to show how you would convert between each type. To make a StringBuilder object from a string object, use the StringBuilder constructor that takes a string. To create a string object from a StringBuilder, use the ToString method. These are illustrated below:

```
StringBuilder myStringBuilder = new StringBuilder(myString);
string myString = myStringBuilder.ToString();
```

Several string and StringBuilder methods are exercised in the program shown in Listing 3.1. As you examine the StringMutation program, keep in mind that this is not a single string object changing its data; this program creates four separate string type objects using various methods of the string and StringBuilder classes. Originally, the phrase object is set up.

After printing the original phrase and its length, the Append method is executed to create a new StringBuilder object referenced by the variable mutation1:

Listing 3.1

```
//*****************************************************************
// StringMutation.cs          C#:   Ken Culp
// Demonstrates the use of the string and StringBuilder classes
//*****************************************************************
using System;
using System.Text;

namespace StringMutation
{
  class StringMutation
  {
    static void Main(string[] args)
    {
      StringBuilder phrase =
        new StringBuilder("Change is inevitable");
      StringBuilder mutation1;
      string mutation2, mutation3, mutation4;
      Console.Out.WriteLine("Original String: \""
        + phrase + "\"");
      Console.Out.WriteLine("Length of String: "
        + phrase.Length);

      mutation1 = phrase.Append(
        ", except from vending machines.");
      mutation2 = mutation1.ToString().ToUpper();
      mutation3 = mutation2.Replace("E", "X");
      mutation4 = mutation3.Substring(3, 30);
```

Listing 3.1   continued

```
        // Print each mutated string
        Console.Out.WriteLine("Mutation #1: " + mutation1);
        Console.Out.WriteLine("Mutation #2: " + mutation2);
        Console.Out.WriteLine("Mutation #3: " + mutation3);
        Console.Out.WriteLine("Mutation #4: " + mutation4);

        Console.Out.WriteLine("Mutated length: "
          + mutation4.Length);
        Console.In.ReadLine();
      }
    }
  }
```

Output

```
Original String: "Change is inevitable"
Length of String: 20
Mutation #1: Change is inevitable, except from vending machines.
Mutation #2: CHANGE IS INEVITABLE, EXCEPT FROM VENDING MACHINES.
Mutation #3: CHANGX IS INXVITABLX, XXCXPT FROM VXNDING MACHINXS.
Mutation #4: NGX IS INXVITABLX, XXCXPT FROM
Mutated length: 30
```

The `ToUpper` method is executed on the `mutation1` object, and the resulting string is stored in `string` variable `mutation2`.

Notice that the `Length` is a property and `Append` is a method that are accessed from the `phrase` object. Also, the `ToString().ToUpper` method is executed on the `mutation1` object. The `StringBuilder` object does not include a `ToUpper()` method but it does support a `ToString()` method. Therefore, we first convert `mutation1` to a string using `ToString` and then change that result to uppercase by using the `ToUpper()` method.

> ### Key Concept
>
> Usually a method is executed on a particular object, which affects the results.

Any method of the `string` or `StringBuilder` class can be executed on any object, but for any given invocation, a method is executed on a particular object. The results of executing `ToString().ToUpper()` on `mutation1` would be very different than the results of executing `ToString().ToUpper()` on `phrase`. Remember, each object has its own state, which often affects the results of method calls.

The `string` object variables `mutation3` and `mutation4` are initialized by the calls to `mutation2.Replace` and `mutation3.Substring`, respectively. Finally, note that both `phrase` and `mutation1` are referenced inside a `Console.Out.WriteLine` method and that these values are printing as strings. This functions because `StringBuilder` supports a `ToString` method, which is automatically invoked any time there is a need for something of type `string`.

3.3   .NET ARCHITECTURE AND BASE CLASS LIBRARIES

.NET (pronounced "dot net") is a complete *framework* for building a wide variety of applications for both a Windows platform and for Web delivery (.ASP). In this section, we present a brief overview of .NET, particularly the base class libraries as contained in the .NET architecture.

When you execute a program with the F5 key in Visual Studio, the following sequence of events occurs (see Figure 3.4 for details). The source code is compiled into Microsoft intermediate language (IL), which is then submitted to the .NET engine for execution. In order for the engine to execute the program, it has to also load every external service that your program has requested. These services are in the form of class references to either .NET-supplied libraries or user libraries that you have created.

As shown in Figure 3.4, these external libraries may be written in a variety of languages. This is not important, because at the IL level, all languages are generally compatible (with the exception of some unsigned data types). Also, the IL program being constructed is still machine independent at this point.

Once all of these external class libraries have been loaded, the combined IL executable program is presented to the *Just In Time* (JIT) compiler. The JIT compiler (which is platform specific) compiles the program into machine-dependent code for execution.

This architecture is very efficient in both space and speed of execution. Space is saved because the generated IL for the C# program is relatively small and the class libraries can be

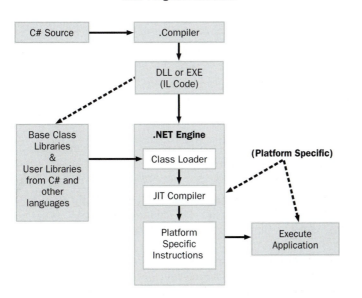

FIGURE 3.4   .NET program execution

shared across a large number of programs. Speed efficiency is realized because the program is compiled rather than interpreted. Specifically, IL is not interpreted one line at a time as it is in some languages, such as Java. This can be very important when the program is in a loop (see Chapter 5) and executing a sequence of lines over and over.

Base Class Libraries

As mentioned previously, the .NET Framework comes with a large number of libraries to simplify and accelerate the development cycle. These libraries were designed to make your job easier, eliminating the need to "reinvent the wheel." There is a good chance that if you need some particular kind of service, such as a data-conversion tool or a graphics tool, or some special kind of object on a form, it is already in the library. Using a tool that is already available is far better than writing your own version, so you should have a general familiarity with the libraries provided by .NET.

To simplify finding services, Microsoft groups related types (services) under one umbrella called a *Namespace*. For example, all text-based services are grouped in the `Text` Namespace. Microsoft then extended this grouping concept by allowing Namespaces to be grouped under other Namespaces. Finally, the most commonly accessed Namespaces are grouped under the `System` Namespace. Figure 3.5 summarizes the more frequently used portions of the `System` Namespace. For additional details, search help in Visual Studio for ".NET Framework class library."

The `using` Declaration

When Visual Studio creates an application (either a console application or a Windows application), it adds several lines to the top of the program that start with the word `using`. For simple applications, these references are sufficient to write your program. Note that without these `using` declarations, you could still access the services in the Namespaces but you would fully qualify the reference. For example, the following code segments were extracted from the `StringMutation` example in Listing 3.1:

```
using System.Text;
    . . .
StringBuilder phrase = new StringBuilder(
  "Change is inevitable");
StringBuilder mutation1;
```

Because we have a `using` line in the program, we can access the `StringBuilder` class. However, if we eliminated the `using` line, we could still reference the `StringBuilder` class as shown below but we would have to type a lot more:

```
System.Text.StringBuilder phrase =
    new System.Text.StringBuilder("Change is inevitable");
System.Text.StringBuilder mutation1;
```

System	Contains fundamental classes and base classes that define commonly used value and reference data types, events and event handlers, interfaces, attributes, and processing exceptions.
System.Collections	Contains interfaces and classes for various collections of objects, such as lists, queues, bit arrays, hash tables and dictionaries.
System.Data	Contains classes for ADO.NET architecture.
System.Data.Common	Contains classes for the .NET Framework data providers.
System.Drawing	Provides access to GDI+ basic graphics functionality.
System.Drawing.Design	Contains classes that extend design-time user interface logic and drawing. Create custom toolbox items, type-specific value editors, or type converters that can convert values between certain types.
System.Drawing.Drawing2D	Provides advanced two-dimensional and vector graphics functionality, gradient brushes, the `Matrix` class (used to define geometric transforms), and the `GraphicsPath` class.
System.Drawing.Printing	Provides print-related services. Printing is covered in Chapter 11.
System.IO	Provides synchronous and asynchronous reading and writing on data streams and files.
System.Net	Provides a simple programming interface for many of the protocols used on networks today.
System.Reflection	Contains classes for analyzing internal program structures.
System.Security	Contains the underlying .NET Framework security system, including base classes for permissions.
System.Text	Contains classes representing ASCII, Unicode, UTF-7, and UTF-8 character encodings; abstract base classes for converting blocks of characters to and from blocks of bytes.
System.Threading	Contains classes that enable multithreaded programming.
System.Web	Supplies classes and interfaces that enable browser-server communication.

FIGURE 3.5   Most Common .NET Namespace

If you are using several types in one Namespace, including the `using` line will greatly reduce typing. However, if you are referencing only one item in the Namespace, you may omit the `using` declaration and use a fully qualified class name, as we did for `StringBuilder` above.

If two classes from two different Namespaces have the same class name, `using` declarations will not suffice because the compiler won't be able to figure out which class is being referenced in the flow of the code. When such situations arise, which is rare, the fully qualified names should be used in the code.

3.4 THE Random CLASS

The need for random numbers occurs frequently when writing software. Games often use a random number to represent the roll of a die or the shuffle of a deck of cards. A flight simulator may use random numbers to determine how often a simulated flight has engine trouble. A program designed to help high school students prepare for the SAT may use random numbers to choose the next question to ask.

The Random class, which is part of the System Namespace, represents a *pseudorandom number generator*. A random number generator picks a number at random out of a range of values. A program that serves this role is technically pseudorandom, because a program has no means to actually pick a number randomly. A pseudorandom number generator performs a series of complicated calculations, based on an initial *seed value*, and produces a number. Though they are technically not random (because they are calculated), the values produced by a pseudorandom number generator usually appear random, at least random enough for most situations.

> **Key Concept**
>
> A pseudorandom number generator performs a complex calculation to create the illusion of randomness.

Figure 3.6 lists some of the methods of the Random class. The nextInt method can be called with no parameters, or we can pass it a single integer value. The version that takes no parameters generates a random number across the entire range of int values, including negative numbers. Usually, though, we need a random number within a more specific range. For instance, to simulate the roll of a die, we might want a random number in the range of 1 to 6. The nextInt method returns a value that's in the range from 0 to one less than its parameter. For example, if we pass in 100, we'll get a return value that is greater than or equal to 0 and less than or equal to 99.

Constructors:
`public Random();`
`public Random(int Seed);`
	Initializes a new instance of the Random class, using the specified seed value (if any). A good seed to use is `DateTime.Now.Millisecond` as this will be a random number based on when the program is run.

`public virtual int Next(` `    int maxValue);`	Returns a nonnegative random number less than the specified maximum.
`public virtual double` `    NextDouble();`	Returns a random number between 0.0 and 1.0.
`protected virtual double` `    Sample();`	Returns a random number between 0.0 and 1.0.

FIGURE 3.6   Some constructors and methods of the Random class

Note that the value that we pass to the nextInt method is also the number of possible values we can get in return. We can shift the range as needed by adding or subtracting the proper amount. To get a random number in the range 1 to 6, we can call nextInt(6) to get a value from 0 to 5, and then add 1.

The nextFloat method of the Random class returns a float value that is greater than or equal to 0.0 and less than 1.0. If desired, we can use multiplication to scale the result, cast it into an int value to truncate the fractional part, and then shift the range as we do with integers.

The program shown in Listing 3.2 produces several random numbers in various ranges.

Listing 3.2

```
//**************************************************************
//   RandomNumbers.cs            C#:   Ken Culp
//
//   Demonstrates the creation of pseudo-random numbers using the
//   Random class.
//**************************************************************
using System;

namespace RandomNumbers
{
  class RandomNum
  {
    static void Main(string[] args)
    {
      System.Random generator =
        new Random(DateTime.Now.Millisecond);
      int num1;
      double num2;

      num1 = generator.Next();
      Console.Out.WriteLine("A random integer: " + num1);

      num1 = generator.Next(10);
      Console.Out.WriteLine("From 0 to 9: " + num1);

      num1 = generator.Next(10) + 1;
      Console.Out.WriteLine("From 1 to 10: " + num1);

      num1 = generator.Next(15) + 20;
      Console.Out.WriteLine("From 15 to 34: " + num1);

      num1 = generator.Next(20) - 10;
      Console.Out.WriteLine("From -10 to 9: " + num1);
```

Listing 3.2 continued

```
        num2 = generator.NextDouble();
        Console.Out.WriteLine("A random double (between 0-1): "
          + num2);

        Console.In.ReadLine(); // Wait for enter key
      }
    }
}
```

Output

```
A random integer: 1773351873
From 0 to 9: 8
From 1 to 10: 6
From 20 to 34: 20
From -10 to 9: -6
A random float (between 0-1): 0.71058085
From 1 to 6: 3
```

3.5 THE Math CLASS

The Math class provides a large number of basic mathematical functions that are often helpful in making calculations. The Math class is defined in the System Namespace of the C#
standard class library. Figure 3.7 lists several of its methods. To find additional information
on how to use each of these members, search the help file for "Math Members" and then
click on the links as needed.

All the methods in the Math class are *static methods* (also called *class methods*), which
means they can be invoked through the name of the class in which they are
defined, without having to instantiate an object of the class first. Static methods are discussed further in Chapter 6.

> **Key Concept**
>
> All methods of the Math class are static, meaning they are invoked through the class name.

The methods of the Math class return values, which can be used in expressions as needed. For example, the following statement computes the absolute
value of the number stored in total, adds it to the value of count raised to
the fourth power, and stores the result in the variable value:

```
value = Math.abs(total) + Math.pow(count, 4);
```

Note that you can pass an integer value to a method that accepts a double parameter.
This is a form of assignment conversion, which was discussed in Chapter 2.

E	Represents natural logarithmic base, specified by the constant, e.
PI	Represents the ratio of the circumference of a circle to its diameter, specified by the constant, π.
Abs	Overloaded. Returns the absolute value of a specified number.
Acos	Returns the angle whose cosine is the specified number.
Asin	Returns the angle whose sine is the specified number.
Atan	Returns the angle whose tangent is the specified number.
Ceiling	Returns the smallest whole number greater than or equal to the specified number.
Cos	Returns the cosine of the specified angle.
Cosh	Returns the hyperbolic cosine of the specified angle.
DivRem	Overloaded. Returns the quotient of two numbers, also passing the remainder as an output parameter.
Exp	Returns e raised to the specified power.
Floor	Returns the largest whole number less than or equal to the specified number.
IEEERemainder	Returns the remainder resulting from the division of a specified number by another specified number.
Log	Overloaded. Returns the logarithm of a specified number
Log10	Returns the base 10 logarithm of a specified number.
Max	Overloaded. Returns the larger of two specified numbers.
Min	Overloaded. Returns the smaller of two numbers.
Pow	Returns a specified number raised to the specified power.
Round	Overloaded. Returns the number nearest the specified value.
Sign	Overloaded. Returns a value indicating the sign of a number.
Sin	Returns the sine of the specified angle.
Sinh	Returns the hyperbolic sine of the specified angle.
Sqrt	Returns the square root of a specified number.
Tan	Returns the tangent of the specified angle.
Tanh	Returns the hyperbolic tangent of the specified angle.

FIGURE 3.7   Some methods of the Math class

The Quadratic program, shown in Listing 3.3, uses the Math class to compute the roots of a quadratic equation (where y equals zero). Recall that a quadratic equation has the following general form:

$$y = ax^2 + bx + c$$

Listing 3.3

```
//***************************************************************
//  Quadratic.cs          C#:   Ken Culp
//
//  Demonstrates the use of the Math class  to perform a
//   calculation based on user input.
//***************************************************************
using System;

namespace Quadratic
{
  class QuadraticEquation
  {
    static void Main(string[] args)
    {
      int a, b, c;   // ax^2 + bx + c
      double discriminant, root1, root2;

      Console.Out.Write("Enter the coefficient of x squared: ");
      a = int.Parse(Console.In.ReadLine());

      Console.Out.Write("Enter the coefficient of x: ");
      b = int.Parse(Console.In.ReadLine());

      Console.Out.Write("Enter the constant: ");
      c = int.Parse(Console.In.ReadLine());

      // Use the quadratic formula to compute the roots.
      // Assume a positive discriminant.

      discriminant = Math.Pow(b, 2) - (4 * a * c);
      root1 = ((-1 * b) + Math.Sqrt(discriminant)) / (2 * a);
      root2 = ((-1 * b) - Math.Sqrt(discriminant)) / (2 * a);

      Console.Out.WriteLine("Root #1: " + root1);
      Console.Out.WriteLine("Root #2: " + root2);

      Console.In.ReadLine(); // Wait for enter key
    }
  }
}
```

Listing 3.3   continued

Output

```
Enter the coefficient of x squared: 3
Enter the coefficient of x: 8
Enter the constant: 4
Root #1: -0.6666666666666666
Root #2: -2.
```

The Quadratic program reads values that represent the coefficients in a quadratic equation (a, b, and c), and then evaluates the quadratic formula to determine the roots of the equation. The quadratic formula is: .

Note that this program assumes that the discriminant (the value under the square root) is positive. If it's not, the results will not be a valid number, which C# represents as NAN (representing Not A Number). In Chapter 5 we will see how we can handle this type of situation gracefully.

3.6   FORMATTING OUTPUT

Formatting output in C# can be simplified by taking advantage of the fact that even primitive data types are classes. All C# classes support a ToString method, but date and numeric types support a ToString method that can handle special formatting. These special ToString methods can take parameters that control how the output is to appear. You can control such things as showing the currency symbol, using commas to separate every three digits in large numbers, parentheses or minus signs, the number of places shown to the right of the decimal, the number of significant positions shown to the left of a decimal, the date format used, etc.

Standard Numeric Formatting

The most common formatting takes place with integers and floating point numbers. Floating point numbers are particularly important because these have can have a decimal point and have a fractional part of the number. Figure 3.8 lists the standard parameters that can be passed to ToString for decimal numbers. Each of these would be evoked as follows:

```
myDouble.ToString(formatSpecifier);
```

For example, to print root1 as a string that includes a currency symbol, the following would be used:

```
Console.Out.Writeline("Root1: " + root1.ToString("C"));
```

The format specifier given to a `ToString` method takes the form of a letter, as listed in Figure 3.8, followed by an optional precision specifier. The length option specifies how long the converted number will be in the output. For example, if `x` contained 11.825, `x.ToString("F2")` would be the string `"11.83"`, which is our number rounded up to two decimal digits.

Format Specifier	Name	Description
C or c	Currency	The number is converted to a string that represents a currency amount. The conversion is controlled by the currency format information of the `NumberFormatInfo` object used to format the number. The precision specifier indicates the desired number of decimal places. If the precision specifier is omitted, the default currency precision given by the `NumberFormatInfo` is used
D or d	Decimal	This format is supported for integral types only. The number is converted to a string of decimal digits (0–9), prefixed by a minus sign if the number is negative. The precision specifier indicates the minimum number of digits desired in the resulting string. If required, the number is padded with zeros to its left to produce the number of digits given by the precision specifier.
E or e	Scientific (exponential)	The number is converted to a string of the form `"–d.ddd...E+ddd"` or `"–d.ddd...e+ddd"`, where each d indicates a digit (0–9). The string starts with a minus sign if the number is negative. One digit always precedes the decimal point. The precision specifier indicates the desired number of digits after the decimal point. If the precision specifier is omitted, a default of six digits after the decimal point is used. The case of the format specifier indicates whether to prefix the exponent with an E or an e. The exponent always consists of a plus or minus sign and a minimum of three digits. The exponent is padded with zeros to meet this minimum, if required.
F or f	Fixed-point	The number is converted to a string of the form `"–ddd.ddd..."` where each d indicates a digit (0–9). The string starts with a minus sign if the number is negative. The precision specifier indicates the desired number of decimal places. If the precision specifier is omitted, the default numeric precision given by the `NumberFormatInfo` is used.
G or g	General	The number is converted to the most compact of either fixed-point or scientific notation, depending on the type of the number and whether a precision specifier is present. If the precision specifier is omitted or zero, the type of the number determines the default precision, as indicated by the following list: • **Byte** or **SByte**: 3 • **Int16** or **UInt16**: 5 • **Int32** or **UInt32**: 10 • **Int64** or **UInt64**: 19 • **Single**: 7 • **Double**: 15 • **Decimal**: 29 Fixed-point notation is used if the exponent that would result from expressing the number in scientific notation is greater than –5 and less than the precision specifier; otherwise, scientific notation is used. The result contains a decimal point if required and trailing zeros are omitted. If the precision specifier is present and the number of significant digits in the result exceeds the specified precision, then the excess trailing digits are removed by rounding. If scientific notation is used, the exponent in the result is prefixed with E if the format specifier is G, or e if the format specifier is g. The exception to the preceding rule is if the number is a **Decimal** and the precision specifier is omitted. In that case, fixed-point notation is always used and trailing zeros are preserved.

FIGURE 3.8   Standard numeric format strings (*continues*)

Format Specifier	Name	Description
N or n	Number	The number is converted to a string of the form `"-d,ddd,ddd.ddd..."`, where each d indicates a digit (0–9). The string starts with a minus sign if the number is negative. Thousand separators are inserted between each group of three digits to the left of the decimal point. The precision specifier indicates the desired number of decimal places. If the precision specifier is omitted, the default numeric precision given by the `NumberFormatInfo` is used.
P or p	Percent	The number is converted to a string that represents a percent as defined by the `NumberFormatInfo.PercentNegativePattern` property or the `NumberFormatInfo.PercentPositivePattern` property. If the number is negative, the string produced is defined by `PercentNegativePattern` and starts with a minus sign. The converted number is multiplied by 100 in order to be presented as a percentage. The precision specifier indicates the desired number of decimal places. If the precision specifier is omitted, the default numeric precision given by `NumberFormatInfo` is used.
R or r	Round-trip	The round-trip specifier guarantees that a numeric value converted to a string will be parsed back into the same numeric value. When a numeric value is formatted using this specifier, it is first tested using the general format, with 15 spaces of precision for a **Double** and 7 spaces of precision for a **Single**. If the value is successfully parsed back to the same numeric value, it is formatted using the general format specifier. However, if the value is not successfully parsed back to the same numeric value, then the value is formatted using 17 digits of precision for a **Double** and 9 digits of precision for a **Single**. Although a precision specifier can be appended to the round-trip format specifier, it is ignored. Round trips are given precedence over precision when using this specifier. This format is supported by floating point types only.
X or x	Hexadecimal	The number is converted to a string of hexadecimal digits. The case of the format specifier indicates whether to use uppercase or lowercase characters for the hexadecimal digits greater than 9. For example, use X to produce `"ABCDEF"`, and x to produce `"abcdef"`. The precision specifier indicates the minimum number of digits desired in the resulting string. If required, the number is padded with zeros to its left to produce the number of digits given by the precision specifier. This format is supported for integral types only.

FIGURE 3.8 (*continued*)   Standard numeric format strings

The `Purchase` program shown in Listing 3.4 uses both types of formatters. It reads in a sales transaction and computes the final price, including tax.

Listing 3.4

```
//****************************************************************
//  Purchase.cs          C#:  Ken Culp
//
//  Demonstrates ToString conversions for number formatting.
//****************************************************************
using System;

namespace Purchase
{
  class Purchase
  {
```

Listing 3.4 continued

```csharp
    //---------------------------------------------------------------
    // Calculates the final price of a purchased item using
    // values entered by the user.
    //---------------------------------------------------------------
    static void Main(string[] args)
    {
      const double TAX_RATE = 0.06; // 6% Sales Tax

      int quantity;
      double subtotal, tax, totalCost, unitPrice;

      Console.Out.Write("Enter the quantity: ");
      quantity = int.Parse(Console.In.ReadLine());

      Console.Out.Write("Enter the unit price: ");
      unitPrice = double.Parse(Console.In.ReadLine());

      subtotal = quantity * unitPrice;
      tax = subtotal * TAX_RATE;
      totalCost = subtotal + tax;

      // Print output with appropriate formatting
      Console.Out.WriteLine("Subtotal: "
        + subtotal.ToString("C"));
      Console.Out.WriteLine("     Tax: " + tax.ToString("C") +
        " at " + TAX_RATE.ToString("P"));
      Console.Out.WriteLine("   Total: "
        + totalCost.ToString("C"));

      // Print using Composite Formatting
      string fmt = "Subtotal: {0,8:c}\n     Tax: {1,8:c}" +
                                   "\n   Total: {2,8:c}";
      Console.Out.WriteLine(fmt, subtotal, tax, totalCost);

      Console.In.ReadLine(); // Wait for enter key
    }
  }
}
```

Output

```
Enter the quantity: 5
Enter the unit price: 3.87
Subtotal: $19.35
     Tax: $1.16 at 6.00 %
   Total: $20.51
```

Custom Numeric Formatting

When the standard formats in the preceding section do not meet your needs, you can create custom formats that will be passed as strings to the `ToString` method. Figure 3.9 lists how special characters are used in the format specifier string to control formatting.

Numeric-to-string conversions can also include a different format for when the number is positive, negative, or zero. These are illustrated below in some example custom numeric conversions taken from the Visual Studio help files. To experiment with these, create a simple console application that requests the number and the format specifier string as separate values and then prints the results.

```
string format = "$#,##0.00;($#,##0.00);Zero"
double MyPos = 19.95, MyNeg = -19.95, MyZero = 0.0;
string MyString = MyPos.ToString(format);
// In the U.S. English culture, MyString has the value: $19.95.

MyString = MyNeg.ToString(format);
// In the U.S. English culture, MyString has the value:
// ($19.95).
// The minus sign is omitted by default.

MyString = MyZero.ToString(format);
// In the U.S. English culture, MyString has the value: Zero.
```

These string conversions can also include characters that will be imbedded into a number as it is converted. For example, the first conversion below takes a floating point number and builds a telephone number complete with parentheses for the area code and a dash between the numbers:

```
double myDouble = 1234567890;
String myString = myDouble.ToString( "(###) ### - ####" );
// The value of myString is "(123) 456 - 7890".
```

This same technique could be used to format a long social security number into the standard 3-2-4 layout:

```
long mySSN = 111223333;
string sSSN = mySSN.ToString( "###-##-####" );
// The string sSSN contains "111-22-3333"
```

Finally, we can also include special characters like the newline or tab using the backslash and the proper escape code:

```
int  MyInt = 42;
MyString = MyInt.ToString( "My Number \n= #" );
```

```
// In the U.S. English culture, MyString has the value:
// "My Number
// = 42".
```

Format Character	Name	Description
0	Zero placeholder	If the value being formatted has a digit in the position where the 0 appears in the format string, then that digit is copied to the result string. The position of the leftmost 0 before the decimal point and the position of the rightmost 0 after the decimal point determine the range of digits that is always present in the result string. The `"00"` specifier causes the value to be rounded to the nearest digit preceding the decimal, where rounding away from zero is always used. For example, formatting 34.5 with `"00"` would result in the value 35.
#	Digit placeholder	If the value being formatted has a digit in the position where the # appears in the format string, then that digit is copied to the result string. Otherwise, nothing is stored in that position in the result string. Note that this specifier never displays the 0 character if it is not a significant digit, even if 0 is the only digit in the string. It will display the 0 character if it is a significant digit in the number being displayed. The `"##"` format string causes the value to be rounded to the nearest digit preceding the decimal, where rounding away from zero is always used. For example, formatting 34.5 with `"##"` would result in the value 35.
.	Decimal point	The first . character in the format string determines the location of the decimal separator in the formatted value; any additional . characters are ignored. The actual character used as the decimal separator is determined by the `NumberDecimalSeparator` property of the `NumberFormatInfo` that controls formatting.
,	Thousand separator and number scaling	The , character serves two purposes. First, if the format string contains a , character between two digit placeholders (0 or #) and to the left of the decimal point, if one is present, then the output will have thousand separators inserted between each group of three digits to the left of the decimal separator. The actual character used as the decimal separator in the result string is determined by the `NumberGroupSeparator` property of the current `NumberFormatInfo` that controls formatting. Second, if the format string contains one or more , characters immediately to the left of the decimal point, then the number will be divided by the number of , characters multiplied by 1000 before it is formatted. For example, the format string `"0,,"` will represent 100 million as simply 100. Use of the , character to indicate scaling does not include thousand separators in the formatted number. Thus, to scale a number by 1 million and insert thousand separators, you would use the format string `"#,##0,,"`.
%	Percentage placeholder	The presence of a % character in a format string causes a number to be multiplied by 100 before it is formatted. The appropriate symbol is inserted in the number itself at the location where the % appears in the format string. The percent character used is dependent on the current `NumberFormatInfo` class.
E0 E+0 E−0 e0 e+0 e−0	Scientific notation	If any of the strings `"E"`, `"E+"`, `"E−"`, `"e"`, `"e+"`, or `"e−"` is present in the format string and is followed immediately by at least one 0 character, then the number is formatted using scientific notation with an E or e inserted between the number and the exponent. The number of 0 characters following the scientific notation indicator determines the minimum number of digits to output for the exponent. The `"E+"` and `"e+"` formats indicate that a sign character (plus or minus) should always precede the exponent. The `"E"`, `"E−"`, `"e"`, or `"e−"` format indicates that a sign character should only precede negative exponents.

FIGURE 3.9 Custom numeric formats (*continues*)

Format Character	Name	Description
\	Escape character	In C# and the Managed Extensions for C++, the backslash character causes the next character in the format string to be interpreted as an escape sequence. It is used with traditional formatting sequences like \n (new line). In some languages, the escape character itself must be preceded by an escape character when used as a literal. Otherwise, the compiler interprets the character as an escape sequence. Use the string "\\" to display \. Note that this escape character is not supported in Visual Basic; however, `ControlChars` provides the same functionality.
'ABC' "ABC"	Literal string	Characters enclosed in single or double quotes are copied to the result string literally, and do not affect formatting.
;	Section separator	The ; character is used to separate sections for positive, negative, and zero numbers in the format string.
Other	All other characters	All other characters are copied to the result string as literals in the position in which they appear.

FIGURE 3.9 (*continued*)   Custom numeric formats

Composite Formatting

Several methods will take a string format object followed by a series of objects and use those objects to fill spots in the string. Thus the string would mark placeholders for numbers, dates, strings, and the like and specify how they are to be formatted. This string would then be followed by a variable list of parameters that will be used.

Methods that support composite formatting are `string.Format`, `Console.Out.Write` (or `WriteLine`), and some implementations of `TextWriter.WriteLine`. The following are a few examples, after which is an explanation of how the process works:

```
string subtotalLine = string.Format(
   "Subtotal:\t{0,8:c}", subtotal);
Console.Out.WriteLine(subtotalLine);
Console.Out.WriteLine("Subtotal:\t{0,8:c}", subtotal);
```

The first example uses the `Format` method from the `string` object to create a new string that has the subtotal value placed in the string. In both cases, the output to the console would look as shown here:

```
Subtotal:        $19.35
```

The extra space between the label and the value is a result of the tab requested and the way the number is formatted. We will cover this shortly. In the previous examples, we illustrated formatting one number into a form, but we can format several. Consider the following code segment:

```
int x = 123;
int y = 231;
Console.Out.WriteLine("Coordinate: ({0}, {1})", x, y);
```

This code would generate the following output:

```
Coordinate: (123, 231)
```

By now you have started to guess some of the principles involved in formatting. Let's take a look at the general form of the format for the placeholder for the object:

```
{index[,alignment][:formatString]}
```

We start the placeholder with the open brace and follow it with an index number as to which of the subsequent parameters is to be placed in this location, with 0 being the first. This is followed by an optional alignment field shown with brackets. Note that the brackets are used to illustrate the syntax only and are not part of the syntax!

The alignment field is a signed numeric constant indicating the preferred length of the number. If the number will fit, the field will be padded with spaces. Padding will occur on the left (right justified) for positive alignment and on the right (left justified) for negative alignment.

After the optional alignment field comes an optional format specification. To specify a format, follow the index number or the alignment number (if used) by a colon and then the string format from Figure 3.8 or Figure 3.9.

This format specification, as already noted, is optional. However, if it is not specified, the general form ("G") from Figure 3.8 is used.

Finish the format specification with a closing brace. Then repeat this process for each object to be included in the format string. Remember, both `string.Format` and `Console.Out.WriteLine` support the format specification followed by a variable length of parameters. In our first examples, we formatted only one value. In the second example, we formatted three.

Let's modify our `Purchase` program and replace all the `WriteLine` calls with a single format string and a single `WriteLine` call:

```
string fmt "Subtotal: (0,8:c)\n+
         "    Tax  (1,8:c)\n" +
         "   Total  (2,8:c)";
Console.Out.WriteLine(fmt, subtotal, tax, totalCost);
```

First let's say a word about the format string. We used blanks to make each of the words "Subtotal", "Tax", and "Total" eight characters long. Then we specified each placeholder as eight characters wide with right justification (positive alignment number). We then specified a currency type, which will give us our currency symbol, and two digits to the right of the decimal. Finally, we placed a newline character after each part of the data. This format string produces the following output:

```
Subtotal:    $19.35
     Tax:     $1.16
   Total:    $20.51
```

The decimal points are nicely aligned and all the data was written in one step. As a final note, remember that the format specification for each item in the list comes from the above two tables. You can include dates, numbers, or even strings in the list.

Listing 3.5

```csharp
//****************************************************************
//  CircleStats.cs          C#:  Ken Culp
//
//  Demonstrates custom formatting of numeric data.
//****************************************************************
using System;

namespace CircleStats
{
  class CircleStats
  {
    //-----------------------------------------------------------
    // Calculates the area and circumference of a circle given
    // its radius.
    //-----------------------------------------------------------
    static void Main(string[] args)
    {
      int radius;
      double area, circumference;

      Console.Out.Write("Enter the circle's radius: ");
      radius = int.Parse(Console.In.ReadLine());

      area = Math.PI * Math.Pow(radius, 2);
      circumference = 2 * Math.PI * radius;

      // Round the output to three decimal places
      Console.Out.WriteLine("The circle's area 1: "
        + area.ToString("0.###"));
      Console.Out.WriteLine("The circle's area 2: "
        + area.ToString("0.000"));
      Console.Out.WriteLine("The circle's circumference: "
        + circumference.ToString("0.###"));
```

Listing 3.5 continued

```
        Console.Out.WriteLine(area.ToString("F2"));

        Console.In.ReadLine(); // Wait for enter key
    }
  }
}
```

Output

```
Enter the circle's radius: 5
The circle's area 1: 78.54
The circle's area 2: 78.540
The circle's circumference: 31.416
```

Note that the area was printed out in two ways, one formatted with `"0.###"` and the other formatted with `"0.000"`. The difference is that the # character outputs a digit only if that digit in not zero. However, the 0 character always outputs a digit. If the data was accurate to three decimal places, then `"0.000"` should be used so that three digits always appear to the right of the decimal.

3.7 ENUMERATED TYPES

C# enables us to define an enumerated type, which we can then use as the type of a variable when it is declared. An enumerated type establishes all possible values of a variable of that type by listing, or enumerating, them. The values are identifiers, and can be anything desired.

> **Key Concept**
>
> Enumerated types are type-safe, ensuring that invalid values will not be used.

For example, the following declaration defines an enumerated type called `Season` whose possible values are `winter`, `spring`, `summer`, and `fall`:

```
enum Season {winter, spring, summer, fall}
```

There is no limit to the number of values that you can list for an enumerated type. Once the type is defined, a variable can be declared of that type:

```
Season time;
```

The variable `time` is now restricted in the values it can take on. It can hold one of the four `Season` values, but nothing else. C# enumerated types are considered to be *type-safe*, meaning that any attempt to use a value other than one of the enumerated values will result in a compile-time error.

The values are accessed through the name of the type. For example:

```
time = Season.spring;
```

Enumerated types can be quite helpful in situations in which you have a relatively small number of distinct values that a variable can assume. For example, suppose we wanted to represent the various letter grades a student could earn. We might declare the following enumerated type:

```
enum Grade {A, B, C, D, F}
```

Any initialized variable that holds a `Grade` is guaranteed to have one of those valid grades. That's better than using a simple character or string variable to represent the grade, which could take on any value.

Suppose we also wanted to represent plus and minus grades, such as A- and B+. We couldn't use A- or B+ as values, because they are not valid identifiers (the characters – and + cannot be part of an identifier in C#). However, the same values could be represented using the identifiers `Aminus`, `Bplus`, etc.

Internally, each value in an enumerated type is stored as an integer, which is referred to as its *ordinal value*. The first value in an enumerated type has an ordinal value of 0, the second one has an ordinal value of 1, the third one 3, and so on. The ordinal values are used internally only. You cannot assign a numeric value to an enumerated type, even if it corresponds to a valid ordinal value.

An enumerated type is a special kind of class, and the variables of an enumerated type are object variables. As such, there are a few methods associated with all enumerated types, but the only one normally accessed is the `ToString` method. `ToString` returns the character string, which is the name assigned to the variable. In our seasons example, `ToString` would return `winter`, `spring`, etc. If, however, you want the numeric offset in the list of values (0, 1, ...), then the enum object has to be typecast to an integer.

Listing 3.6 shows a program called `IceCream` that declares an enumerated type and exercises some of its methods. Because enumerated types are special types of classes, they are not defined within a method. They can be defined either at the class level (within the class but outside a method), as in this example, or at the outermost level.

Listing 3.6

```
//**************************************************************
//   IceCream.cs          C#:   Ken Culp
//
//   Demonstrates the use of enumerated types.
//**************************************************************
using System;

namespace IceCream
```

Listing 3.6   continued

```
{
  class IceCream
  {
    enum Flavor
    {
      vanilla, chocolate, strawbery, fudgeRipple,
      coffee, rockyRoad, mintChocolateChip, cookieDough
    }
    //------------------------------------------------------------
    // Creates and uses variables of the Flavor type.
    //------------------------------------------------------------
    static void Main(string[] args)
    {
      Flavor cone1, cone2, cone3;

      cone1 = Flavor.rockyRoad;
      cone2 = Flavor.chocolate;

      Console.Out.WriteLine("cone1   value: " + cone1);
      Console.Out.WriteLine("cone1 ordinal: " + (int)cone1);
      Console.Out.WriteLine();

      Console.Out.WriteLine("cone2   value: " + cone2);
      Console.Out.WriteLine("cone2 ordinal: " + (int)cone2);
      Console.Out.WriteLine();

      cone3 = cone1;
      Console.Out.WriteLine("cone3   value: " + cone3);
      Console.Out.WriteLine("cone3 ordinal: " + (int)cone3);

      Console.In.ReadLine(); // Wait for enter key
    }
  }
}
```

Output

```
cone1   value: rockyRoad
cone1 ordinal: 5
cone2   value: chocolate
cone2 ordinal: 1
cone3   value: rockyRoad
cone3 ordinal: 5
```

We explore enumerated types further in Chapter 6.

3.8 COMPONENTS AND CONTAINERS

In the Windows Track sections of Chapter 2, we introduced the C# capabilities to draw shapes using the `Graphics` and `Color` classes from the C# base class library. We also defined the concept of a Windows application, which includes a graphical user interface (GUI).

Most of the example programs we've looked at so far have been console applications. More specifically, they have been *command-line applications,* which interact with the user only through simple text prompts. A C# application can have graphical components as well. Throughout the rest of the book, the Windows Track sections at the end of each chapter will explore the capabilities of C# and the Visual Studio IDE to create programs with GUIs. In this chapter we review the form as the basis for all graphics-based applications.

Forms

When a new Windows application is created in Visual Studio (see the end of Chapter 2), Visual Studio creates an empty platform upon which to place graphical objects. This platform is called a *form* and is the basic unit upon which all GUI programs are built under Visual Studio (see Figure 3.10 and the `Snowman` example in Chapter 2).

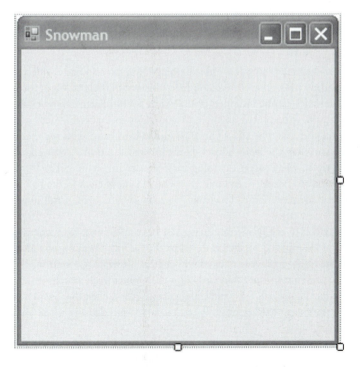

FIGURE 3.10　Blank form

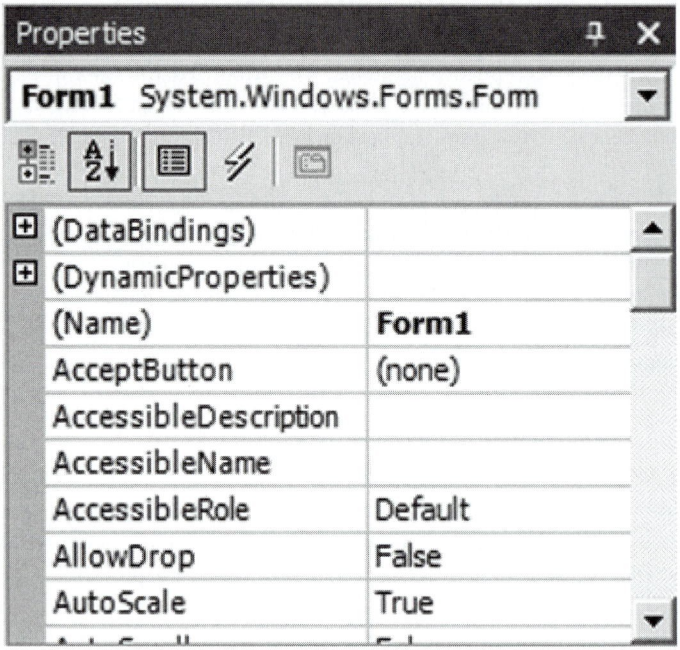

FIGURE 3.11   Form properties

In addition to being a place for graphical objects, a form also has a wide variety of characteristics, including the background color, title, size, width, height, border styles, etc. Most of these characteristics can be modified using Visual Studio Form Designer so that changes appear at an instant visually. For example, if you want to make the form wider, place the mouse cursor on the square at the right edge of the form until you see the double arrow, and then click and drag the right border to the desired location. Other characteristics can be edited directly in the Properties dialog box, shown in Figure 3.11. If you wanted to change the name from Form1 to MyForm, you would simply click in the box to the right of (Name) and type the new name. To change the title of the form, scroll down to the Text entry and type a new title.

Some of the fields in the Properties dialog box have additional help when you try to edit the contents. For example, if you scroll down to the BackColor property and double-click in the field to the right, you are presented with a small down-arrow button. If you click this button, you are presented with a standard color dialog box from which you can modify the colors, as shown in Figure 3.12. If you want a custom color, click the Custom tab. Similarly, if you click on the field FormBorderStyle, Visual Studio displays a box with all possible settings.

Thus, it is quite simple to make most of your cosmetic changes to the form using the Form Designer. Making changes to properties in the Form Designer are considered "design time" changes. However, it is possible to change these properties at run time as well. In the

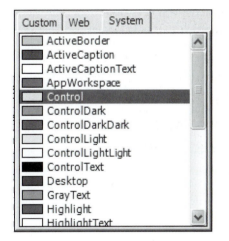

FIGURE 3.12   Color property dialog box

`Snowman` example of Chapter 2, we changed the title of the form using the following line of code:

```
this.Text = "Simple Graphics Snowman";  // Set Form title
```

Here, the word `this` refers to the current form (or class); that is, the form that is currently being displayed. Therefore, the title of the `Snowman` form is changed from Snowman, as it was entered into the Form Designer, to Simple Graphics Snowman.

Loading Forms

When you create a new windows application in Visual Studio, three C# files are added to your application: `Program.cs`, `Form1.cs`, and `Form1.Designer.cs`. You will normally only be editing the file `Form1.cs`. You must *never* edit the `.Designer` file as it contains all your changes made through the designer. If you manually edit the file, the designer might be unable to open it and you could end up having to start over.

The `Program.cs` file contains there executable lines of code as shown below. It is the last line (`Application.Run`) that actually starts the GUI . You will see this line of code in some of our examples later in the book where we create a Windows Forms application directly without using the designer. The name on the `Run` line must match the name of the class name in your form C# file or your application will not run.

```
Application.EnableVisualStyles();
Application.SetCompatibleTextRenderingDefault(false);
Application.Run(new Form1());
```

Note, however, that you can also load forms from code within a form. For example, say you want to display a copyright notice before loading your main form. If your copyright form is named `Copyright`, you could use the two lines below to the Load event for your main form:

```
Copyright frm = new Copyright();
frm.ShowDialog();
```

The first line creates an object of type `Copyright` and the second line calls the method `ShowDialog` to show the form. `ShowDialog` shows the form on top of any other forms that may be loaded and locks out access to any other form in the application. This is the method used to display *dialog* boxes which obtain some information for the user. The data requested from these dialog boxes is needed from the dialog form before the calling form can continue.

You should begin your edit process by renaming the `Form1.cs` file. However, be sure to end the file with the `.cs` extension. Right click the file name in the Solution Explorer window and select rename. That will rename the form and its references in all three files.

Creating New Forms

To illustrate how to use the Form Designer, we will create a variation of the `Snowman` example in Chapter 2 that starts with a copyright screen. We will use the same `Paint` code as Chapter 2 and the techniques described above for loading a form.

From Visual Studio, open your `Snowman` project from Chapter 2 or create a new `Snowman` project just like it. If you want to create a new `Snowman` project, select File/New/Project, click the Visual C# Projects folder, click the Windows Application icon,

FIGURE 3.13 Snowman Solution Explorer

choose your directory, and name the application **Snowman2**. Create the form and verify that this application works as described in Chapter 2.

Now we are going to add a new form with the copyright information that will appear on top of the snowman scene until the user clicks anywhere on the `Copyright` form.

To create your new form, click Project/Add Windows Form. This opens the Add New Item dialog box with the item type already selected to be form. Type the name **Copyright** where it asks for Name and click Open. This will create a second form and display it in the edit window. This is the form to which we will add text data to describe the copyright. At this time, your Solution Explorer pane should look as shown in Figure 3.13.

Accessing Forms Controls in the Form Designer

To the right of the form is a vertical box labeled Toolbox, as shown in Figure 3.14. Move the mouse over this region of the screen and the complete toolbox will appear, as shown in Figure 3.15. Note that the label Toolbox may not appear. Instead, only the icon of the crossed hammer and wrench may be shown. In either case, move the mouse over the icon:

Figure 3.15 shows a subset of the Windows Forms tools. However, when the Toolbox appears, there are several category tabs to choose from. If Windows Forms is not the banner above the list of tools, click the banner labeled Window Forms. Note that the form must be displayed to access the Form Designer tools. If the form is not open, double-click the form name in the Solution Explorer. If the form is open but the current window is the code window, click the form [Design] tab.

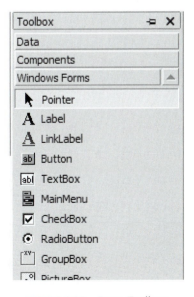

FIGURE 3.14 Toolbox icon   **FIGURE 3.15** Form Toolbox

Placing Controls on the Form

The control we are going to use in this section is the label control. Once we place this control on the form, we will modify its characteristics and contents using the properties window.

The two most common ways to move a control on the form are to 1) double-click on the control on the toolbar, or 2) click and drag the control to the form. When you double-click the control, the control is added to the form in the upper-left corner and is shown with selection tabs, as shown in Figure 3.16. The crossed arrows over the box indicate that the box can be moved by clicking and dragging it to a new location.

Visual Studio gives to every control that is dropped on a form a default name that is based on the type of the control. Thus, this first label control has the name `label1`. Since most label controls are not accessed from code, this name should be fine. Later on, when we are dealing with input controls like buttons and text boxes, we will want a more descriptive label like `LastName`. In the paragraphs that follow, we will use the properties window to modify the content and appearance of this and other labels as we build our `Copyright` form.

In the properties window for the label, scroll down to the property `Text` and type **Copyright 2004 Watson Brothers Inc.** Then, scroll up to the `Font` property and click the plus sign to its left. All the properties associated with the `Font` property are then displayed, as shown in Figure 3.17. Change the Size to 16 and double-click the word Bold. Each time you double-click a True/False property, the value will change between True and False. Double-clicking once will change the property to True, making the text bold.

Now if you look at your text box, all you can read is "Copyrigh," and not even all of that. The problem is that the box is too small to hold the text. Click and drag the lower-right corner tab to expand the box until the complete statement is displayed. Then move the box around until it is centered in the form. Note that your form is also too narrow to allow you to fully expand the box. Grab a corner or edge control of the form and adjust the size. Add additional label boxes and adjust the size of your form until your form appears as

ont	Microsoft Sans Serif, 8.25pt
Name	ab Microsoft Sans Serif
Size	8.25
Unit	Point
Bold	False
GdiCharSet	0
GdiVerticalFont	False
Italic	False
Strikeout	False
Underline	False

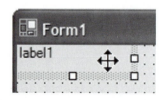

FIGURE 3.16   Label control

FIGURE 3.17   Font properties

FIGURE 3.18   Completed `Copyright` form

shown in Figure 3.18. Feel free to experiment with various font names and styles and foreground colors. Note that if AutoSize is set to true the control will resize to fit the data.

Note that you can control how the text is positioned in the label control. Select the `TextAlign` property to change your labels to centered.

Displaying and Closing the `Copyright` Form

The next step for this project is to display our `Copyright` form on top of the `Snowman` form and force the user to acknowledge the copyright before continuing. We will have the user click anywhere on the `Copyright` form to acknowledge the copyright. To do this, we need to capture a mouse click to have the form go away.

This `Copyright` form could be called a *dialog* form because the user has to acknowledge the form before seeing the main form. Therefore, we want to center the `Copyright` form on the parent form (`Snowman` form). Select the properties for the `Copyright` form and scroll down to `StartPosition` and select `CenterParent`. Although the `Snowman` form will not be shown at all until the copyright is acknowledged (as discussed below), it is always a good practice to have dialog boxes appear in the center of their parent form.

To capture the mouse click on the form, we need to add an event handler to the `Copyright` form. Open the `Copyright` form in Form Designer and click on the event portion of the Properties dialog box (click the lightning bolt icon). Scroll down to `Click` and double-click in the blank space. This will open the code window and create the mouse click handler. Make your click event look like the following:

```
private void Copyright_Click(object sender, System.EventArgs e)
{
  // Close if click on form
  this.Close();              // Close this form
  this.Dispose();            // Delete form
}
```

There are two things to note about the preceding code. First, to close a form, you simply invoke the `Close` method. The use of the word `this` is optional (simply using `Close` would work), but it accentuates the fact that the method is a form-related method. The second thing to note is the `Dispose` method. This is optional, but we are using here since we are finished with the copyright object and will not use it again. `Dispose` tells the system to trash the object.

Displaying the `Copyright` Form and Using the `Load` Event

Our final step to complete our application is to display the `Copyright` form as soon as the `Snowman` application is started. For this purpose, we will use the `Load` event for the form. The `Load` event for a form *occurs only once* and occurs before anything is displayed on the form. We only need to request that the `Copyright` form be displayed as part of the load process for the `Snowman` form.

Thus, our last step is to add an event handler to the `Snowman` form for `Load`. There are a couple of ways to do this. The first is to show the `Snowman` form in the Form Designer, select properties and events, and double-click on `Load`. However, Visual Studio tries to minimize the steps to accomplish any task and thus has established a series of default event handlers for various controls. We will describe the default event handlers for other controls later in the book, but the default event for a form is the `Load` event. Therefore, to create the `Load` event handler, double-click anywhere on the form (but not on any other control). This will create the event handler and display the code. Make your code look like the following:

```
private void Snowman_Load(object sender, System.EventArgs e)
{
  // Show copyright before we start
  Copyright frm = new Copyright();
  frm.ShowDialog();
}
```

We use the `ShowDialog` method because we want to force the user to close the `Copyright` form before they can see the `Snowman` form. At this time, you should test your application.

3.9   DRAWING LINES AND PEN STYLES

In Chapter 2, we drew some simple lines and wrote some text on the screen using a variety of objects, which were not explained in detail. We are going to discuss one of these objects at this time: the pen.

Pens are used in Visual Studio to draw lines and figures and can have a variety of styles. For one thing, lines do not have to be solid; they can be dashed in a variety of ways, such as a series of small dashes, dots only, mixed dots and dashes, or some other custom pattern. Similarly, you can choose how to end each line; you can have rounded ends, square ends, triangular ends, arrowhead ends, etc. This section describes how to create pens and select the drawing options.

Enumerations in Visual Studio

As you learn to program using Visual Studio, you will find that you will be configuring a variety of options on a variety of objects. For each property of an object that has a fixed set of possible settings, Visual Studio defines a class with a variety of static constants that can be used to configure the property.

Thus, configuring the dashed/solid characteristic of a line uses the `DashStyle` enumeration. Similarly, configuring the starting and ending caps on a line uses the `LineCap` enumeration. Study the following lines taken from our `Pens` example below:

```
pen.DashStyle = DashStyle.Solid;
pen.EndCap = LineCap.Round;
```

In the first line, we set the dash style of the line by selecting one of the constant values in the `DashStyle` enumeration. In the second line, we set the cap style of the end of the line to round by using the `LineCap` enumeration. Each entry in an enumeration, as noted previously in this chapter, corresponds to a numeric value. Therefore, we could replace those lines with the following code:

```
pen.DashStyle = 0;
pen.EndCap = 2;
```

Of course, the first set of code is much easier to read. Unless you had memorized the enumeration (who would?), how would you know that setting `EndCap` to 2 would make the end cap round? As you can see, enumerations make the code much more readable and facilitate the coding process. Consider again this line:

```
pen.DashStyle = DashStyle.Solid;
```

Both the property of the pen and the enumeration are called `DashStyle`. This is the Microsoft style. When you type a dot after an object created from a standard C# class and locate the desired property, note the spelling of the property. If there is an enumeration that corresponds to this property, it will have the same name.

In the case of the `EndCap` property shown above, note that there is also a `StartCap` property. Therefore, it was not possible to use a single enumeration for this. Therefore, a more intuitive enumeration of `LineCap` was used. However, all is not lost. Continue and select the desired property and then move the cursor back over the selected property. IntelliSense will then tell you what class that property is, as shown in Figure 3.19.

In Figure 3.19, the start of the line, `System.Drawing.Drawing2D.LineCap`, is the class of the property `Pen.StartCap`. Armed with this information, you would simply type the equal sign and type the word `LineCap` and a dot. IntelliSense would then present you with the choices shown in Figure 3.20.

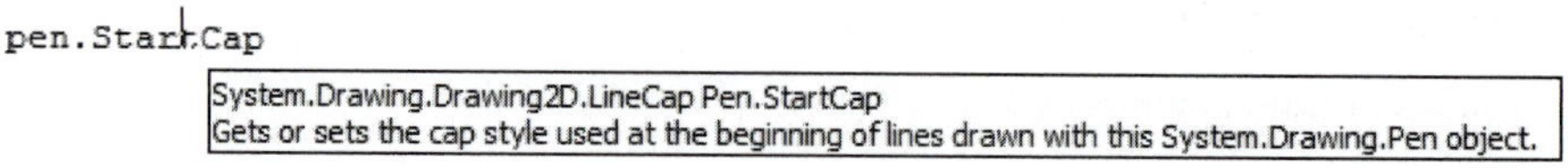

```
pen.StartCap
```

> System.Drawing.Drawing2D.LineCap Pen.StartCap
> Gets or sets the cap style used at the beginning of lines drawn with this System.Drawing.Pen object.

FIGURE 3.19   IntelliSense display of property type

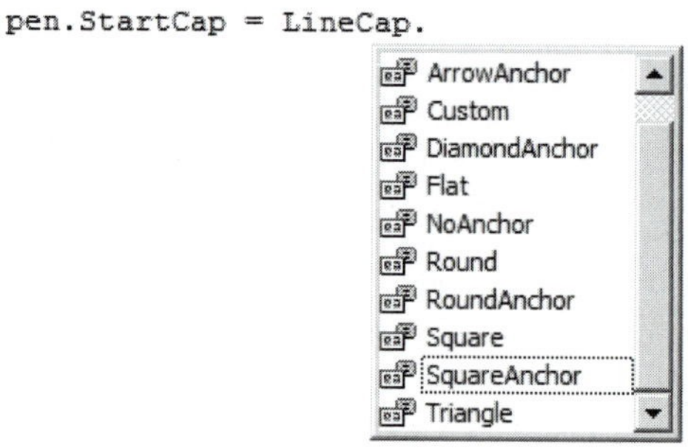

```
pen.StartCap = LineCap.
```

	ArrowAnchor
	Custom
	DiamondAnchor
	Flat
	NoAnchor
	Round
	RoundAnchor
	Square
	SquareAnchor
	Triangle

FIGURE 3.20   `LineCap` enumeration from IntelliSense

Pen Example Program

The example `Pens` program shown in Listing 3.7 uses several of the `LineCap` and `DashStyle` values and shows in the output how each line looks when these styles are used. Not all choices are illustrated, so feel free to try other settings in the program. The `Pens` program uses the `Paint` method, as have previous programs, and manually codes each line type one at a time. A variation of this program will be given in Chapter 7 to show how to use enumerations and the `foreach` construct. To shorten Listing 3.7, we omit showing the code generated by the Form Designer and the `Dispose` method.

Listing 3.7

```csharp
//****************************************************************
//   Pens.cs          C#: Ken Culp
//
//   Demonstrates pen dash styles and pen caps
//****************************************************************
using System;
using System.Collections.Generic;
using System.ComponentModel;
using System.Data;
using System.Drawing.Drawing2D;
using System.Drawing;
using System.Text;
using System.Windows.Forms;

namespace Pens
{
```

Listing 3.7   continued

```csharp
public partial class Pens : Form
{
  public Pens()
  {
    InitializeComponent();
  }

  private void Form1_Paint(object sender, PaintEventArgs e)
  {
    int xpos = 10;                    // Location for text / Line
    int ypos = 10;
    Pen pen = new Pen(Color.Black, 4.0f);
    Graphics g = e.Graphics;
    Brush brush = Brushes.Black;
    Font font =
      new Font("Times New Roman", 12, FontStyle.Bold);

    pen.DashStyle = DashStyle.Solid;
    g.DrawString("Solid:", font, brush, xpos + 85, ypos);
    g.DrawLine(pen, xpos + 80, ypos + 10, xpos, ypos + 10);
    ypos += 20;

    pen.DashStyle = DashStyle.Dash;
    g.DrawString("Dashed:", font, brush, xpos + 85, ypos);
    g.DrawLine(pen, xpos + 80, ypos + 10, xpos, ypos + 10);
    ypos += 20;

    pen.DashStyle = DashStyle.Dot;
    g.DrawString("Dotted:", font, brush, xpos + 85, ypos);
    g.DrawLine(pen, xpos + 80, ypos + 10, xpos, ypos + 10);
    ypos += 20;

    pen.DashStyle = DashStyle.DashDot;
    g.DrawString("Dash Dot:", font, brush, xpos + 85, ypos);
    g.DrawLine(pen, xpos + 80, ypos + 10, xpos, ypos + 10);
    ypos += 20;

    pen.DashStyle = DashStyle.DashDotDot;
    g.DrawString("Dash dot dot:", font, brush, xpos + 85, ypos);
    g.DrawLine(pen, xpos + 80, ypos + 10, xpos, ypos + 10);
    ypos += 20;

    float[] dashPattern = { 2, 1, 2, 3 };  // small, large gap
    pen.DashStyle = DashStyle.Custom;      // -- -- -- --
    pen.DashPattern = dashPattern;
    g.DrawString("Custom (2, 1, 2, 3):",
      font, brush, xpos + 85, ypos);
    g.DrawLine(pen, xpos + 80, ypos + 10, xpos, ypos + 10);
```

Listing 3.7   continued

```
            pen.DashStyle = DashStyle.Solid;
            pen.Width = 10;
            xpos = 300;
            ypos = 10;

            pen.EndCap = LineCap.Flat;
            g.DrawString("Flat/NoAnchor:",
               font, brush, xpos + 85, ypos);
            g.DrawLine(pen, xpos + 80, ypos + 10, xpos, ypos + 10);
            ypos += 20;

            pen.EndCap = LineCap.Triangle;
            g.DrawString("Triangle:", font, brush, xpos + 85, ypos);
            g.DrawLine(pen, xpos + 80, ypos + 10, xpos, ypos + 10);
            ypos += 20;

            pen.EndCap = LineCap.Round;
            g.DrawString("Round:", font, brush, xpos + 85, ypos);
            g.DrawLine(pen, xpos + 80, ypos + 10, xpos, ypos + 10);
            ypos += 20;

            pen.EndCap = LineCap.RoundAnchor;
            g.DrawString("RoundAnchor:", font, brush, xpos + 85, ypos);
            g.DrawLine(pen, xpos + 80, ypos + 10, xpos, ypos + 10);
            ypos += 20;

            pen.EndCap = LineCap.DiamondAnchor;
            g.DrawString("DiamondAnchor:", font, brush, xpos + 85, ypos);
            g.DrawLine(pen, xpos + 80, ypos + 10, xpos, ypos + 10);
            ypos += 20;

            pen.EndCap = LineCap.SquareAnchor;
            g.DrawString("SquareAnchor:",
               font, brush, xpos + 85, ypos);
            g.DrawLine(pen, xpos + 80, ypos + 10, xpos, ypos + 10);
            ypos += 20;
            // Set height to bottom of drawings
            // (this.Height - this.ClientRectangle.Height) is size.
            // Add this to ending ypos and set as new height.
            this.Height =
               (this.Height - this.ClientRectangle.Height) + ypos;
         }
      }
   }
```

Listing 3.7   continued

Output

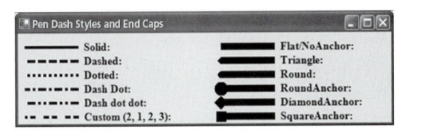

The program uses something called a brush. We will describe brushes in Chapter 4, but for now, just think of it as a way of specifying the color on all methods where it is used. The brush used here is black, but you should change the color to see the effect.

Client Rectangle and Setting Screen Height

Note the last line of the `Paint` method in Listing 3.7. This line sets the height of the window so that the bottom of the window is just past the last line drawn on the screen. A difficulty arises from the fact that the vertical drawing position (`ypos`) is being measured from the top of the graphical area, which starts just below the blue banner line. We want to set the height of the form to be the ending `y` position plus the height of the banner. However, the height of the banner is not immediately available and must be computed.

The canvas upon which the graphical images are being drawn (inside blue borders) is called the client rectangle and is available using the form property `ClientRectangle`. The height of the border, then, is the height of the full window (`this.Height`) minus the height of the `ClientRectangle`. To this value, we add `ypos`.

If you want to ensure that your drawings are not drawn outside the visible area, you can reference the client rectangle for a variety of information.

3.10   IMAGES

Images often play an important role in graphics-based software. C# has the ability to use JPEG and GIF images in various ways. The `Graphics` class contains a `DrawImage` method that allows you to draw the image just as you would draw a shape or character string. An image can also be incorporated into a label component. Let's explore the relationship between images and labels in more detail.

We've seen in previous sections how to drop a label on a form from the Toolbox. If you examine the properties of a label, you find that both text and an image can be assigned to the label. When both are present, how they are displayed is determined by where the text and image are to be positioned on the control. For this discussion, we will be referencing the following properties of the label control:

Text	The text to be displayed
TextAlign	Where the text is to be displayed
Image	The image to be displayed
ImageAlign	Where the image is to be displayed

Label Demo Program

For this exercise, create a new Windows application called LabelDemo and enlarge the form to about 4 inches by 5 inches. Drop three label boxes and drag their corners so that each is about 170 by 100 (check the Size property). Make sure the labels do not overlap. The names of the label controls are unimportant. The completed program is shown in Figure 3.22.

Now we are going to add an image of a devil to each of the label controls. To add the image, double-click the blank to the right of the image property. This displays the Windows Open File dialog box. Open the textbook examples folder, switch to chapter 3, and locate the devil.gif file. Double-click this file. The image is now added to the label. Do this for each label.

Key Concept

A label can contain text, an image, or both.

To adjust the location of the text and the image, we are going to move the image and text using the ImageAlign and TextAlign properties. When you click on the box to the right of one of these properties, Visual Studio displays a graphical image of the possible locations, as shown in Figure 3.21.

Set the text of the three labels to "Devil Left", "Devil Right", and "Devil Above". Next, set the properties as shown in the following table:

Text	TextAlign	ImageAlign
"Devil Above"▯	TopCenter▯	BottomCenter▯
"Devil Right"▯	MiddleLeft▯	MiddleRight▯
"Devil Left"	MiddleRight	MiddleLeft

There is no code to add to this example because all the work was done in the Form Designer. However, each of the properties could have been added in code. For example, you could set the alignment of the text property of label1 at run time. To see how this is done, click the plus sign next to the Windows Form Designer generated code box and look at the end of the code for label1. This is the line of code:

```
this.label1.TextAlign =
System.Drawing.ContentAlignment.MiddleRight;
```

This is an example of another enumeration used to set alignment. In this case, the enumeration is called ContentAlignment. You will frequently find it handy to see how the

FIGURE 3.21   Text and image alignment graphic

Form Designer creates the code and then copy from the Designer to your code and modify to fit your exact needs.

Images can be in a wide variety of formats including BMP, GIF, JPEG, PNG, ICO, EMF, and WMF. When you try to open an image, it will show you all the possible image types.

FIGURE 3.22

Summary of Key Concepts

> The new operator returns a reference to a newly created object.

> Multiple reference variables can refer to the same object, and a change to any one variable is reflected in all variables because they point to the same place.

> Usually a method is executed on a particular object, which affects the results.

> A pseudorandom number generator performs a complex calculation to create the illusion of randomness.

> All methods of the Math class are static, meaning they are invoked through the class name.

> Enumerated types are type-safe, ensuring that invalid values will not be used.

> A label can contain text, an image, or both.

Self-Review Questions

3.1   What does the new operator accomplish?

3.2   What is a C# Namespace?

3.3   Why doesn't the String class have to be specifically imported into our programs?

3.4   What is a class method (also called a static method)?

3.5   What is a null reference?

3.6   What is an alias? How does it relate to garbage collection?

Exercises

3.1   What output is produced by the following code fragment?

```
String m1, m2, m3;
m1 = "Quest for the Holy Grail";
m2 = m1.ToLower();
m3 = m1 + " " + m2;
Console.Out.WriteLine (m3.Replace('h', 'z'));
```

3.2   Write an assignment statement that computes the square root of the sum of num1 and num2 and assigns the result to num3.

3.3   Write a single statement that computes and prints the absolute value of total.

3.4   What is the effect of the following import statement?

```
using System.Windows.Forms
```

3.5   Assuming that a `Random` object called `generator` has been created, what is the range of the result of each of the following expressions?

a. `generator.Next(20)`

b. `generator.Next(8) + 1`

c. `generator.Next(45) + 10`

d. `generator.Next(100) - 50`

3.6   Write code to declare and instantiate an object of the `Random` class (call the object reference variable `rand`). Then write a list of expressions using the `Next` method that generates random numbers in the following specified ranges, including the endpoints:

a. 0 to 10

b. 0 to 500

c. 1 to 10

d. 1 to 500

e. 25 to 50

f. −10 to 15

3.7   Write code statements to print a number with exactly four decimal places (if the last digit is zero, a zero prints).

Programming Projects

3.1   Write an application that reads the `(x,y)` coordinates for two points. Compute the distance between the two points using the following formula:

Distance = $\dfrac{-b \pm \sqrt{b^2 - 4}}{}$

3.2   Write an application that reads the radius of a sphere and prints its volume and surface area. Use the following formulas. Print the output to four decimal places. *r* represents the radius.

Volume = $\frac{4}{3}\pi r^3$

Surface area = $4\pi r^2$

3.3   Write an application that reads the lengths of the sides of a triangle from the user. Compute the area of the triangle using Heron's formula (below), in which *s* represents half of the perimeter of the triangle, and *a*, *b*, and *c* represent the lengths of the three sides. Print the area to three decimal places.

Area = $\sqrt{s(s-a)(s-b)(s-c)}$

3.4   Write an application that creates and prints a random phone number of the form XXX-XXX-XXXX. Include the dashes in the output. Do not let the first three digits contain an 8 or 9 (but don't be more restrictive than that), and make sure that the second set of three digits is not greater than 742. Hint: Think through the easiest way to construct the phone number. Each digit does not have to be determined separately.

3.5   Modify the `LabelDemo` program so that it displays a fourth label, with the text of the label centered above the image.

3.6   Modify the `Snowman` application so that any time you click on the snowman screen, the copyright screen displays again. Display the `Copyright` form with a `ShowDialog` method call and a `Show` method call to see the difference when you try to switch windows between the snowman and the copyright.

Answers to Self-Review Questions

3.1   The `new` operator creates a new instance (an object) of the specified class. The constructor of the class is then invoked to help set up the newly created object.

3.2   A C# namespace is a collection of related classes. The C# standard class library is a group of namespaces that supports common programming tasks.

3.3   The `String` class is part of the language structure, which is automatically available to any C# program. Therefore, no separate `using` declaration is needed.

3.4   A class or static method can be invoked through the name of the class that contains it, such as `Math.Abs`. If a method is not static, it can be executed only through an instance (an object) of the class.

3.5   A null reference is a reference that does not refer to any object. The reserved word `null` can be used to check for null references before following them.

3.6   Two references are aliases of each other if they refer to the same object. Changing the state of the object through one reference changes it for the other because there is actually only one object. An object is marked for garbage collection only when there are no valid references to it.

Writing Classes 4

CHAPTER OBJECTIVES

> Discuss the structure and content of a class definition.

> Establish the concept of object state using instance data.

> Describe the effect of visibility modifiers on methods and data.

> Explore the structure of a method definition, including parameters and return values.

> Discuss the structure and purpose of a constructor.

> Explore the creation of graphical objects.

> Introduce the concepts needed to create an interactive graphical user interface.

> Explore additional Windows controls and drawing utilities.

In Chapter 3 we used classes and objects for the various services they provide. That is, we used the predefined classes in the C# class library that are provided to us to make the process of writing programs easier. In this chapter we address the heart of object-oriented programming: writing our own classes to define our own objects. This chapter explores the basics of class definitions, including the structure of methods and the scope and encapsulation of data. The Windows Track sections of this chapter discuss how to write classes that have graphical representations and introduce the issues necessary to create a truly interactive graphical user interface.

4.1 **ANATOMY OF A CLASS**

In all of our previous examples, we've written a single class containing a single `Main` method. These classes represent small but complete programs. These programs often instantiated objects using predefined classes from the C# class library and used those objects for the services they provide. Those predefined classes are part of the program too, but we never really concern ourselves with them other than to know how to interact with them. We simply trust them to provide the services they promise.

Let's look at another, similar example. The `RollingDice` class shown in Listing 4.1 contains a `Main` method that instantiates two `Die` objects (as in the singular of dice). It then rolls the dice and prints the results. It also calls several other methods provided by the `Die` class, such as the ability to explicitly set and get the current face value of a die. Create the project in Visual Studio with File/New/Project, select console project, and use the name RollingDice.

Before typing the code of Listing 4.1, you will first want to add the Die class and its code as described below. If the Die class is created first, Visual Studio can give you visual cues and reduce your typing of the Main method. For example, to select the Roll method off die1, simply type die1 and dot and the letter "r". This "r" can be either upper or lower case. Once

> **Key Concept**
>
> The heart of object-oriented programming is defining classes that represent objects with well-defined state and behavior.

"r" is typed, the method Roll is highlighted in Intellisense. To accept this method, type the open parenthesis of the method. This will fill in the full Roll name and add the parenthesis. Complete by typing the right parenthesis and semicolon.

Note that classes may be referenced inside classes (more on this later) so to receive the maximum benefit from Intellisense, the classes should be defined from the inside out. That is, from the lowest level class.

Adding Classes to a Project

There are two ways to create a new class as part of an existing project. The first is to select Project/Add Class menu option. The other way is to right click on the project name (**RollingDice**) shown in bold on the next to top line of the Solution Explorer as show below in Figure 4.1 below.

From this menu, select the Add entry to display the Add Menu as shown in Figure 4.2. From this menu, select the bottom entry of Add Class. When this entry is selected or Project/Add Class is selected, Visual Studio displays the Add Item dialog box with the *Class* entry selected. Type the name Die and click the Ok button. This will add a new class for you and display the default code as shown below in Listing 4.1.

Listing 4.1

```
using System;
using System.Collections.Generic;
using System.Text;
namespace RollingDice
```

Listing 4.1   continued

```
{
  class Die
  {
  }
}
```

Visual Studio creates a skeleton class as show above in Listing 4.1. At this time, modify the code so that it matches Listing 4.2 below. Once that is done, save your work (Ctrl/S) and switch back to the main program (`RollingDice.cs`) and type the code as it appears in Listing 4.1. Note how Intellisense now simplifies your work.

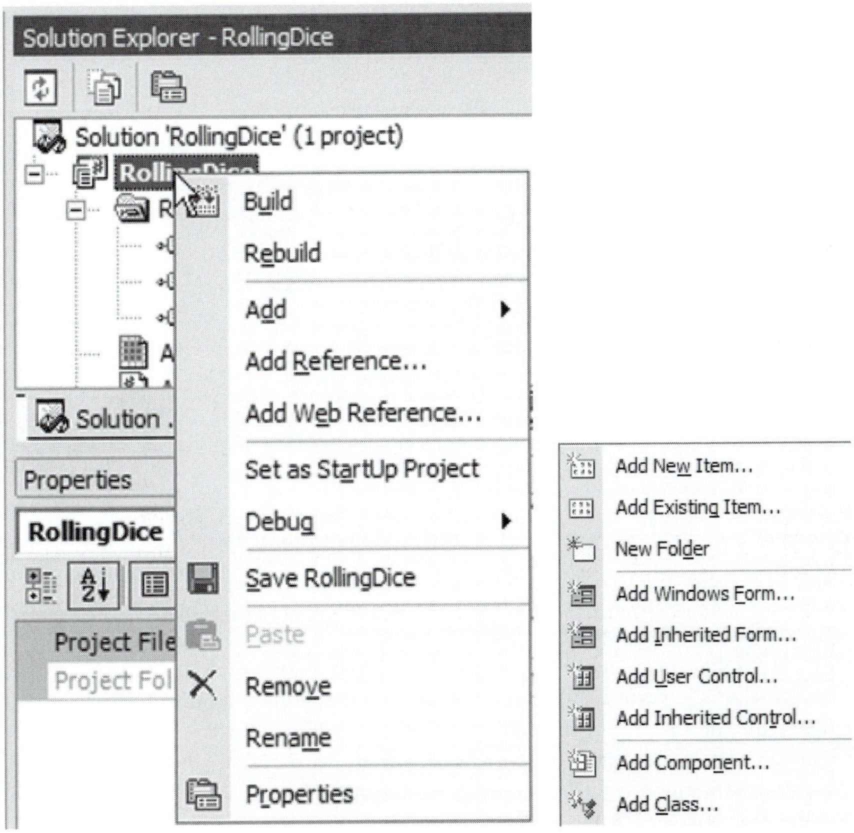

FIGURE 4.1   Modify project context menu   Add to project menu

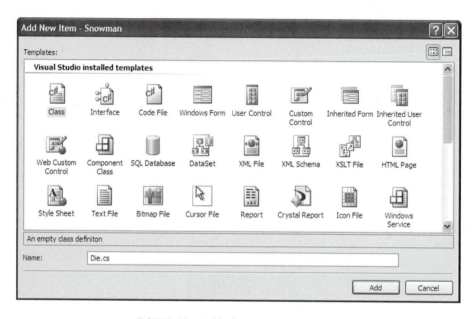

FIGURE 4.2 Add class to project dialog

The primary difference between this example and previous examples is that the Die class is not a predefined part of the C# class library. We have to write the Die class ourselves, defining the services we want Die objects to perform, if this program is to compile and run.

Every class can contain data declarations and method declarations, as depicted in Figure 4.1. The data declarations represent the data that will be stored in each object of the class. The method declarations define the services that those objects will provide. Collectively, the data and methods of a class are called the *members* of a class.

The classes we've written in previous examples follow this model as well, but contain no data at the class level and contain only one method (the main method). We'll continue to define classes like this, such as the RollingDice class, to define the starting point of a program.

True object-oriented programming, however, comes from defining classes that represent objects with well-defined state and behavior. For example, at any given moment a Die object is showing a particular face value, which we could refer to as the state of the die. A Die object also has various methods we can invoke on it, such as the ability to roll the die or get its face value. These methods represent the behavior of a die.

The Die class shown in Listing 4.2 contains two data values: an integer constant (MAX) that represents the maximum face value of the die, and an integer variable (faceValue) that represents the current face value of the die. It also contains a constructor called Die, four regular methods: Roll, SetFaceValue, GetFaceValue, and ToString, and one property FaceValue.

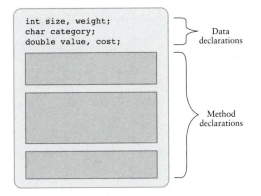

FIGURE 4.3   The members of a class: data and method declarations

Listing 4.2

```
//*************************************************************
//  RollingDice.cs          C#:   Ken Culp
//
//  Demonstrates the creation and use of user-defined classes
//*************************************************************
using System;
namespace RollingDice
{
  class RollingDice
  {
    //-----------------------------------------------------------
    //  Creates two die objects and rolls them several times
    //-----------------------------------------------------------
    static void Main(string[] args)
    {
      Die die1 = new Die();
      Die die2 = new Die();
      int sum;

      die1.Roll();
      die2.Roll();
      Console.Out.WriteLine("Die One: " + die1
        + ", Die Two: " + die2);

      // Accessor and Mutator method of obtaining and
      // modifying object values
      die1.Roll();
      die2.SetFaceValue(4);
      Console.Out.WriteLine("Die One: " + die1
```

Listing 4.2   continued

```
            + ", Die Two: " + die2);
        sum = die1.GetFaceValue() + die2.GetFaceValue();
        Console.Out.WriteLine("Sum 1: " + sum);

        // Property method of obtaining and modifying object values
        die1.Roll();
        die2.FaceValue = 4;
        sum = die1.FaceValue + die2.FaceValue;
        Console.Out.WriteLine("Die One: " + die1
          + ", Die Two: " + die2);
        Console.Out.WriteLine("Sum 2: " + sum);

        // Using number values returned from Roll
        sum = die1.Roll() + die2.Roll();
        Console.Out.WriteLine("Die One: " + die1
          + ", Die Two: " + die2);
        Console.Out.WriteLine("Sum 3: " + sum);

        Console.In.ReadLine();  // Wait for enter key
    }
  }
}
```

Output

```
Die One: 6, Die Two: 6
Die One: 6, Die Two: 4
Sum 1: 10
Die One: 5, Die Two: 4
Sum 2: 9
Die One: 5, Die Two: 6
Sum 3: 11
```

Listing 4.3

```
//****************************************************************
// Die.cs        C#:  Ken Culp
//
// Represents one die (singular of dice) with faces showing
// values between 1 and 6.
//****************************************************************
using System;

namespace RollingDice
{
```

Listing 4.3   continued

```
public class Die
{
  private const int MAX = 6;
  private int faceValue;       // current value on the die
  private Random generator;    // Random number generator

  //-------------------------------------------------------------
  //  Defaults to a six-sided die. Initial face value is 1.
  //-------------------------------------------------------------
  public Die()
  {
    generator = new Random(DateTime.Now.Millisecond);
    faceValue = 1;
  }

  //-------------------------------------------------------------
  //  Rolls the die and returns the result.
  //-------------------------------------------------------------
  public int Roll()
  {
    faceValue = generator.Next(MAX) + 1;
    return faceValue;
  }

  //-------------------------------------------------------------
  //  Property method for fetching and returning the die value.
  //-------------------------------------------------------------
  public int FaceValue
  {
    get
    {
      return faceValue;
    }
    set
    {
      // Validation code would be added here
      faceValue = value;
    }
  }

  //-------------------------------------------------------------
  //  Sets the current die value.
  //-------------------------------------------------------------
  public void SetFaceValue(int face)
  {
    faceValue = face;
  }
```

Listing 4.3   continued

```
    //------------------------------------------------------------
    //  Returns the current die value.
    //------------------------------------------------------------
    public int GetFaceValue()
    {
      return faceValue;
    }


    //------------------------------------------------------------
    //  Returns a string representation of this die
    //------------------------------------------------------------
    public override string ToString()
    {
      return faceValue.ToString();
    }
  }
}
```

You will recall from Chapters 2 and 3 that constructors are special methods that have the same name as the class. The Die constructor gets called when the **new** operator is used to create a new instance of the Die class. The rest of the methods in the Die class define the various services provided by Die objects.

We use a header block of documentation to explain the purpose of each method in the class. This practice is not only crucial for anyone trying to understand the software, it also separates the code visually so that it's easy for the eye to jump from one method to the next while reading the code.

Figure 4.4 lists the methods of the Die class. From this point of view, it looks no different from any other class that we've used in previous examples. The only important difference is that the Die class was not provided for us by the C# standard class library. We wrote it ourselves.

The methods of the Die class include the ability to roll the die, producing a new random face value. The Roll method returns the new face value to the calling method, but you can also get the current face value at any time by using the GetFaceValue method. The SetFaceValue method sets the face value explicitly, as if you had reached over and turned the die to whatever face you wanted. The ToString method of any object gets called automatically whenever you pass the object to a Write or WriteLine method, to obtain a string description of the object to print. Therefore, it's usually a good idea to define a ToString method for most classes. The definitions of these methods have various parts, and we'll dissect them as we proceed through this chapter.

Visual Studio stores each class in its own file. C# allows multiple classes to be stored in one file. If a file contains multiple classes, only one of those classes can be declared using the reserved word **public**. Thus the only time to have more than one class in a file is for a

Die ()	Constructor: Sets the initial face value of the die to 1.
int Roll ()	Rolls the die by setting the face value to a random number in the appropriate range (here, 1 to 6).
SetFaceValue (int face)	Sets the face value of the die to the specified value.
int GetFaceValue ()	Returns the current face value of the die.
override string ToString()	Returns a string representation of the die indicating its current face value.
int FaceValue	Property of type integer that can be used to fetch or modify the face value using an arithmetic replacement statement (=).

FIGURE 4.4   Some methods of the `Die` class

"nested" or internal class. Otherwise, always add one class to a file within the project, as previously described.

Instance Data

Note that in the `Die` class, the constant `MAX` and the variable `faceValue` are declared inside the class, but not inside any method. The location at which a variable is declared defines its *scope,* which is the area within a program in which that variable can be referenced. By being declared at the class level (not within a method), these variables and constants can be referenced in any method of the class.

Attributes such as the variable `faceValue` are called *instance data* because memory space is created for each instance of the class that is created. Each `Die` object has its own `faceValue` variable with its own data space. That's how each `Die` object can have its own state. We see that in the output of the `RollingDice` program: one die has a face value of 5 and the other has a face value of 2. That's possible only because the memory space for the `faceValue` variable is created for each `Die` object.

We can depict this situation as follows:

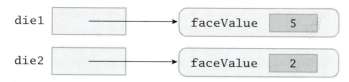

The `die1` and `die2` reference variables point to (that is, contain the address of) their respective `Die` objects. Each object contains a `faceValue` variable with its own memory space. Thus each object can store different values for its instance data.

C# automatically initializes any variables declared at the class level. For example, all variables of numeric types such as **int** and **double** are initialized to zero. However, despite the fact that the language performs this automatic initialization, it is good practice to initialize variables explicitly (usually in a constructor) so that anyone reading the code will clearly understand the intent.

UML Class Diagrams

Throughout this book we use *UML diagrams* to visualize relationships among classes and objects. UML stands for the *Unified Modeling Language,* which has become the most popular notation for representing the design of an object-oriented program.

Several types of UML diagrams exist, each designed to show specific aspects of object-oriented programs. We focus primarily on UML *class diagrams* in this book to show the contents of classes and the relationships among them.

In a UML diagram, each class is represented as a rectangle, possibly containing three sections to show the class name, its attributes (data), and its operations (methods). Figure 4.5 shows a class diagram containing the classes of the RollingDice program.

The arrow connecting the RollingDice and Die classes in Figure 4.5 indicates that a relationship exists between the classes. A dotted line with an open arrowhead indicates that one class *uses* the other wholly by linking methods of the other class. Other types of object-oriented relationships between classes are shown with different types of connecting lines and arrows. We'll discuss these as we explore the appropriate topics in the book.

Keep in mind that UML is not designed specifically for C# programmers. It is intended to be language independent. Therefore, the syntax used in a UML diagram is not necessarily the same as C# syntax. For example, the type of a variable is shown after the variable name, separated by a colon. Return types of methods are shown in the same way.

UML diagrams are versatile. We can include whatever appropriate information is desired, depending on the goal of a particular diagram. We might leave out the data and method sections of a class, for instance, if those details aren't relevant for a particular diagram.

UML diagrams allow us to visualize a program's design. As our programs get larger, made up of more and more classes, these visualizations become increasingly helpful. We will explore new aspects of UML diagrams as the situation dictates.

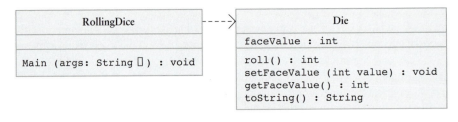

FIGURE 4.5 A UML class diagram showing the classes involved in the RollingDice program

4.2   ENCAPSULATION

We mentioned in our overview of object-oriented concepts in Chapter 1 that an object should be *self-governing*. That is, the instance data of an object should be modified only by that object. For example, the methods of the Die class should be solely responsible for changing the value of the faceValue variable. We should make it difficult, if not impossible, for code outside of a class to "reach in" and change the value of a variable that is declared inside that class. This characteristic is called *encapsulation*.

An object should be encapsulated from the rest of the system. It should interact with other parts of a program only through the specific set of methods that define the services that that object provides. These methods define the *interface* between that object and the program that uses it.

Encapsulation is depicted graphically in Figure 4.6. The code that uses an object, sometimes called the *client* of an object, should not be allowed to access variables directly. The client should call an object's methods, which in turn interact with the data encapsulated within the object. For example, the Main method in the RollingDice program calls the Roll method of the die objects. The Main method should not (and in fact cannot) access the faceValue variable directly.

In C#, we accomplish object encapsulation using *modifiers*. A modifier is a C# reserved word that is used to specify particular characteristics of a programming language construct. In Chapter 2 we discussed the **const** modifier, which is used to declare a constant. C# has several modifiers that can be used in various ways. Some modifiers can be used together, but some combinations are invalid. We discuss various C# modifiers at appropriate points throughout this book, and all of them are summarized in Appendix G.

Visibility Modifiers

Some of the C# modifiers are called *visibility modifiers* because they control access to the members of a class. The reserved words **public** and **private** are visibility modifiers that

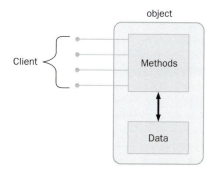

FIGURE 4.6   A client interacting with the methods of an object

can be applied to the variables and methods of a class. If a member of a class has *public visibility*, it can be directly referenced from outside of the object. If a member of a class has *private visibility*, it can be used anywhere inside the class definition but cannot be referenced externally. Two other visibility modifiers, **protected** and **friend**, are relevant only in the context of inheritance. We discuss them in Chapter 8.

Public variables violate encapsulation. They allow code external to the class in which the data is defined to reach in and access or modify the value of the data. Therefore, instance data should be defined with private visibility. Data that is declared as **private** can be accessed only by the methods of the class.

The visibility we apply to a method depends on the purpose of that method. Methods that provide services to the client must be declared with public visibility so that they can be invoked by the client. These methods are sometimes referred to as *service methods*. A **private** method cannot be invoked from outside the class. The only purpose of a **private** method is to help the other methods of the class do their job. Therefore, they are sometimes referred to as *support methods*.

The table in Figure 4.7 summarizes the effects of public and private visibility on both variables and methods.

Giving constants public visibility is generally considered acceptable; although their values can be accessed directly, they cannot be changed, because they were declared using the **const** modifier. Keep in mind that encapsulation means that data values should not be able to be *changed* directly by another part of the code. Because constants, by definition, cannot be changed, the encapsulation issue is largely moot.

UML class diagrams can show the visibility of a class member by preceding it with a particular character. A member with public visibility is preceded by a plus sign (+), and a member with private visibility is preceded by a minus sign (−).

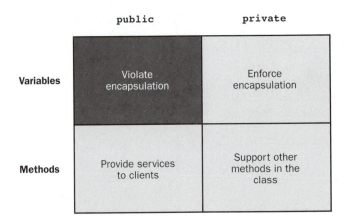

FIGURE 4.7   The effects of public and private visibility

Accessors and Mutators

Because instance data is generally declared with private visibility, a class usually provides services to access and modify data values. A method such as GetFaceValue is called an *accessor method* because it provides read-only access to a particular value. Likewise, a method such as SetFaceValue is called a *mutator method* because it changes a particular value.

Generally, accessor method names have the form GetX, where X is the value to which it provides access. Likewise, mutator method names have the form SetX, where X is the value they are setting. Therefore these types of methods are sometimes referred to as "getters" and "setters."

Some methods may provide accessor and/or mutator capabilities as a side effect of their primary purpose. For example, the Roll method of the Die class changes the faceValue of the die, and returns that new value as well. Note that the code of the Roll method is careful to keep the face value of the die in the valid range (1 to MAX). Service methods must be carefully designed to permit only appropriate access and valid changes.

This points out a flaw in the design of the Die class. Note that there is no restriction on the SetFaceValue method-a client could use it to set the die value to a number such as 20, which is outside the valid range. The code of the SetFaceValue method should allow only valid modifications to the face value of a die. We explore how that kind of control can be accomplished in the next chapter.

For most applications, both the accessor and mutator methods should be replaced by properties, which are covered a bit later in the chapter.

4.3 ANATOMY OF A METHOD

We've seen that a class is composed of data declarations and method declarations. Let's examine method declarations in more detail.

As we stated in Chapter 1, a method is a group of programming language statements that is given a name. A *method declaration* specifies the code that is executed when the method is invoked. Every method in a C# program is part of a particular class.

When a method is called, the flow of control transfers to that method. One by one, the statements of that method are executed. When that method is done, control returns to the location where the call was made and execution continues.

The *called method* (the one that is invoked) might be part of the same class as the *calling method* that invoked it. If the called method is part of the same class, only the method name is needed to invoke it. If it is part of a different class, it is invoked through the name of an object of that other class, as we've seen many times. (Static methods can be accessed with the class name or an object name.) Figure 4.8 shows the flow of execution as methods are called.

We've defined the Main method of a program many times in previous examples. Its definition follows the same syntax as all methods. The header of a method includes the type of

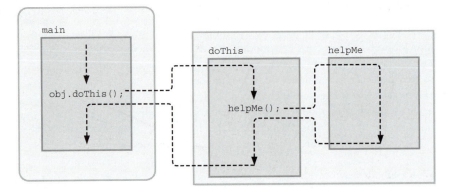

FIGURE 4.8 The flow of control following method invocations

the return value, the method name, and a list of parameters that the method accepts. The statements that make up the body of the method are defined in a block delimited by braces. The rest of this section discusses issues related to method declarations in more detail.

The `return` Statement

The return type specified in the method header can be a primitive type, class name, or the reserved word **void**. When a method does not return any value, **void** is used as the return type, as is always done with the `Main` method. The `SetFaceValue` method of the `Die` class also has a return type of **void**.

> **Key Concept**
>
> The value returned from a method must be consistent with the return type specified in the method header.

A method that returns a value must have a *return statement*. When a **return** statement is executed, control is immediately returned to the statement in the calling method, and processing continues there. A **return** statement consists of the reserved word **return** followed by an expression that dictates the value to be returned. The expression must be consistent with the return type in the method header.

The `GetFaceValue` method of the `Die` class returns an **int** value that represents the current value of the die. The `Roll` method does the same, returning the new value to which `faceValue` was just randomly set. The `ToString` method returns a **string** object.

A method that does not return a value does not usually contain a **return** statement. The method automatically returns to the calling method when the end of the method is reached. Such methods may contain a **return** statement without an expression.

It is usually not good practice to use more than one **return** statement in a method, even though it is possible to do so. In general, a method should have one **return** statement as the last line of the method body, unless that makes the method overly complex.

The value that is returned from a method can be ignored in the calling method. For example, in the `Main` method of the `RollingDice` class, the value that is returned from the `Roll` method is ignored in several calls, while in others the return value is used in a calculation.

Constructors do not have a return type (not even **void**) and therefore cannot have a **return** statement. We discuss constructors in more detail later in this chapter.

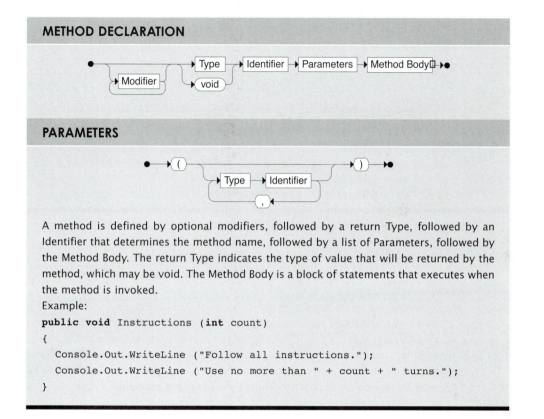

METHOD DECLARATION

PARAMETERS

A method is defined by optional modifiers, followed by a return Type, followed by an Identifier that determines the method name, followed by a list of Parameters, followed by the Method Body. The return Type indicates the type of value that will be returned by the method, which may be void. The Method Body is a block of statements that executes when the method is invoked.

Example:

```
public void Instructions (int count)
{
  Console.Out.WriteLine ("Follow all instructions.");
  Console.Out.WriteLine ("Use no more than " + count + " turns.");
}
```

Parameters

As we defined in Chapter 2, a parameter is a value that is passed into a method when it is invoked. The *parameter list* in the header of a method specifies the types of the values that are passed and the names by which the called method will refer to those values.

> **Key Concept**
>
> When a method is called, the actual parameters are copied into the formal parameters.

The names of the parameters in the header of the method declaration are called *formal parameters.* In an invocation, the values passed into a method are called *actual parameters.* The actual parameters are also called the *arguments* to the method.

A method invocation and definition always give the parameter list in parentheses after the method name. If there are no parameters, an empty set of parentheses is used, as is the case in the `Roll` and `GetFaceValue` methods. The `Die` constructor also takes no parameters, although constructors often do.

The formal parameters are identifiers that serve as variables inside the method and whose initial values come from the actual parameters in the invocation. When a method is called, the value in each actual parameter is copied and stored in the corresponding formal parameter. Actual parameters can be literals, variables, or full expressions. If an expression is used as an actual parameter, it is fully evaluated before the method call and the result is passed as the parameter.

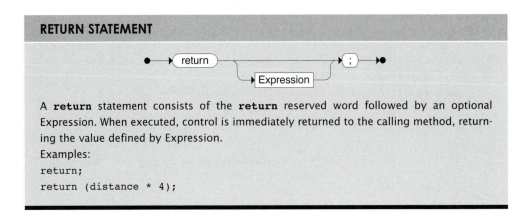

RETURN STATEMENT

A **return** statement consists of the **return** reserved word followed by an optional Expression. When executed, control is immediately returned to the calling method, returning the value defined by Expression.
Examples:
```
return;
return (distance * 4);
```

The only method in the Die class that accepts any parameters is the SetFaceValue method, which accepts a single **int** parameter. The formal parameter name is value. In the Main method, the value of 4 is passed into it as the actual parameter.

The parameter lists in the invocation and the method declaration must match up. That is, the value of the first actual parameter is copied into the first formal parameter, the second actual parameter into the second formal parameter, and so on, as shown in Figure 4.9. The types of the actual parameters must be consistent with the specified types of the formal parameters.

Other details regarding parameter passing are discussed in Chapter 6.

Local Data

As we described earlier in this chapter, the scope of a variable or constant is the part of a program in which a valid reference to that variable can be made. A variable can be declared inside a method, making it *local data* as opposed to instance data. Recall that instance data is declared in a class but not inside any particular method.

Local data has scope limited to only the method in which it is declared. The variable result declared in the ToString method of the Die class is local data. Any reference to result in any other method of the Die class would have caused the compiler to issue an error message. A local variable simply does not exist outside of the method in which it is declared. On the other hand, instance data, declared at the class level, has a scope of the entire class; any method of the class can refer to it.

Because local data and instance data operate at different levels of scope, it's possible to declare a local variable inside a method with the same name as an instance variable declared at the class level. Referring to that name in the method will reference the local version of the variable. This naming practice obviously has the potential to confuse anyone reading the code, so it should be avoided.

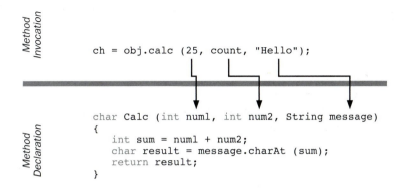
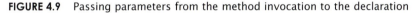

FIGURE 4.9   Passing parameters from the method invocation to the declaration

The formal parameter names in a method header serve as local data for that method. They don't exist until the method is called, and they cease to exist when the method is exited. For example, the formal parameter `value` in the `SetFaceValue` method comes into existence when the method is called and goes out of existence when the method finishes executing.

Bank Account Example

Let's look at another example of a class and its use. The `Transactions` class shown in Listing 4.4 contains a `Main` method that creates a few `Account` objects and invokes their services. To create the application, select File/New/Project and name it **Transactions**. Then, add a class called `Account` and type the code for `Account`. Finally, type the code for Transactions.

The `Account` class, shown in Listing 4.5, represents a basic bank account. It contains instance data representing the account number, the account's current balance, and the name of the account's owner. Note that instance data can be an object reference variable (not just a primitive type), such as the account owner's name, which is a reference to a `String` object. The interest rate for the account is stored as a constant.

The constructor of the `Account` class accepts three parameters that are used to initialize the instance data. The `Deposit` and `Withdraw` methods perform the basic transactions on the account, adjusting the balance based on the parameters. There is also an `AddInterest` method that updates the balance by adding in the interest earned. These methods represent valid ways to change the balance, so a classic mutator such as `SetBalance` is not provided. Instead, the property `Balance` is to be used to set or get the balance.

The status of the three `Account` objects just after they were created in the `Transactions` program could be depicted as follows:

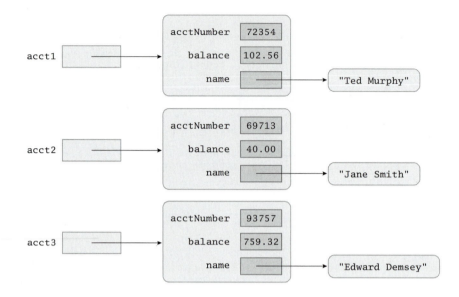

Listing 4.4

```
//****************************************************************
//  Transactions.cs          C#:  Ken Culp
//
//  Driver to exercise the use of multiple Account objects.
//****************************************************************
using System;

namespace Transactions
{
  class Transactions
  {
    //-----------------------------------------------------------
    //  Creates some bank accounts and requests various services.
    //-----------------------------------------------------------
    static void Main(string[] args)
    {
      Account acct1 = new Account("Ted Murphy", 72354, 102.56);
      Account acct2 = new Account("Jane Smith", 69713, 40.00);
      Account acct3 = new Account("Edward Demsey", 93757, 759.32);

      acct1.Deposit(25.85);

      double smithBalance = acct2.Deposit(500.00);
      Console.Out.WriteLine("Smith balance after deposit: " +
        smithBalance);
```

Listing 4.4   continued

```csharp
        Console.Out.WriteLine("Murphy balance after withdrawal: "
          + acct1.Withdraw(430.75, 1.50).ToString("c"));

        acct1.AddInterest();
        acct2.AddInterest();
        acct3.AddInterest();

        Console.Out.WriteLine();
        Console.Out.WriteLine(acct1);
        Console.Out.WriteLine(acct2);
        Console.Out.WriteLine(acct3);

        Console.In.ReadLine();  // Wait for enter key
      }
    }
}
```

Output

```
Smith balance after deposit: 540
Murphy balance after withdrawal: ($303.84)

72354    Ted Murphy       ($314.47)
69713    Jane Smith       $558.90
93757    Edward Demsey    $785.90
```

Listing 4.5

```csharp
//****************************************************************
//  Account.cs              C#:  Ken Culp
//
//  Represents a bank account with basic services such as deposit
//  and withdraw.
//****************************************************************
using System;

namespace Transactions
{
  public class Account
  {

    private const double RATE = 0.035;  // interest rate of 3.5%

    private long acctNumber;
    private double balance;
    private String name;
```

Listing 4.5   continued

```csharp
//----------------------------------------------------------------
//  Sets up the account by defining its owner, account number,
//  and initial balance.
//----------------------------------------------------------------
public Account(String owner, long account, double initial)
{
  name = owner;
  acctNumber = account;
  balance = initial;
}


//----------------------------------------------------------------
//  Validates the transaction, then deposits the specified
//  amount into the account. Returns the new balance.
//----------------------------------------------------------------
public double Deposit(double amount)
{
  balance = balance + amount;
  return balance;
}


//----------------------------------------------------------------
//  Validates the transaction, then withdraws the specified
//  amount from the account. Returns the new balance.
//----------------------------------------------------------------
public double Withdraw(double amount, double fee)
{
  balance = balance - amount - fee;
  return balance;
}


//----------------------------------------------------------------
//  Adds interest to the account and returns the new balance.
//----------------------------------------------------------------
public double AddInterest()
{
  balance += (balance * RATE);
  return balance;
}


//----------------------------------------------------------------
//  Returns a one-line description of the account as a string.
//----------------------------------------------------------------
public override string ToString()
{
  string balanceStr = string.Format("{0:C}", balance);
  return (acctNumber + "\t" + name + "\t" + balanceStr);
}
```

Listing 4.5   continued

```
        //----------------------------------------------------------
        //  Property to get or set Account Number
        //----------------------------------------------------------
        public long AccountNumber
        {
          get { return acctNumber; }
          set { acctNumber = value; }
        }

        //----------------------------------------------------------
        //  Property to get or set Account Balance
        //----------------------------------------------------------
        public double Balance
        {
          get { return balance; }
          set { balance = value; }
        }
    }
}
```

The various methods that update the balance of the account could be more rigorously designed. Checks should be made to ensure that the parameter values are valid, such as preventing the withdrawal of a negative amount (which would essentially be a deposit). This processing is discussed in the next chapter.

4.4   PROPERTIES

For the `Die` class, we showed a way to obtain or modify the face value shown on the die by using an accessor and a mutator, both of which were methods (`GetFaceValue` and `SetFaceValue`). We also illustrated without comment a second technique through what is called a property. We have shown both techniques because both are quite acceptable in C#. We included the accessor/mutator technique because this is how you will see it done in other languages such as Java. In C#, however, the preferred method is to use properties.

Properties give us all the advantages of an accessor or mutator but with much simpler code. Compare the following two pairs of lines of code:

```
die2.SetFaceValue(4);
int x = die2.GetFaceValue();

die2.FaceValue = 4;
int x = die2.FaceValue;
```

The first pair uses methods and must specify the method name and parentheses (plus a value on the Set). The second pair illustrates use of a property where the property name can be used on either side of a replacement statement. This second approach is more logical because it looks just like what we would do to create an integer and initialize it:

```
int x = 8;
```

We mentioned that properties have all the benefits of methods and the convenience of replacement statements. The benefits we were referring to was the ability of methods to validate the input before replacing an internal class variable. For example, we could prevent the employee's last name from being set to nothing or the social security number from being set to zero, etc. Properties give us the ability to perform any amount on computations before accepting a value or returning a value.

Consider again the property code in our Die class:

```
//------------------------------------------------------------
//  Property method for fetching and returning the die value.
//------------------------------------------------------------
public int FaceValue
{
  get
  {
    return faceValue;
  }
  set
  {
    // Validation code would be added here
    faceValue = value;
  }
}
```

From this code, we see that the syntax for a property is the word **public** followed by the type of the property (int here, but it could be any class name) followed by the name of the property *with no parentheses*. Then, we open a brace for the body of the property. This is always followed by a get keyword and an open brace. The get keyword is used when the property appears on the right side of an equal sign and the value of the property is being obtained. Inside the get brace are any number of computations followed by a return of the type specified for the property (an integer in the preceding example). The get method completes with the close brace.

What follows is an optional set keyword, the opening brace, the code, and the closing brace. The set keyword is used when the property appears on the left side of an equal sign and the value of the property is being modified. Here is where you would place validations on the value given on the right side of the equal sign. Note that what was on the right side of the equal sign in the set method is exposed to the property using the keyword value.

In the preceding example, we simply trust the user to give us good data and we set the internal class variable `faceValue` equal to the keyword `value` without any validation.

We mentioned that the `set` portion of a property is optional. If it is not included, the property is "read only," meaning that the value can be read but it cannot be modified. You must specify at least an accessor with the `get` property.

The calling program can then directly access the private data using an equal sign:

```
die2.FaceValue = 4;
sum = die1.FaceValue + die2.FaceValue;
```

When `FaceValue` is referenced in the first line, the property code in Die `set` routine is executed, allowing the class to validate that the value given is in the proper range (more details on this are provided in the next chapter). When this line of code is executed, the keyword `value` will be 4. Thus, `value` can be used in the `set` method to validate the input before using it (excluding values greater than 6 or less than 1). Visual Studio 2005 includes a feature called Refactoring. With this feature you can create a private instance variable and automatically surround it with a public property of the same type. To "Refactor" a variable, right-click on the private variable, left-click Refactor and click Encapsulate field. This adds the property with both a get and set section.

Coding Standards

Coding standards in C# capitalize the first letter of all class methods and properties. Local class variables, by contrast, do not have the first letter capitalized. When a private class variable is exposed by a property, the same name is frequently used, with the property being capitalized and the class variable not. Thus, we have a private integer named `faceValue` and a property named `FaceValue`. This is not a conflict because C# variables are case sensitive. Also, this construct is quite common in C# and improves readability of the code.

4.5   CONSTRUCTORS REVISITED

As we stated in Chapter 2, a constructor is similar to a method that is invoked when an object is instantiated. When we define a class, we usually define a constructor to help us set up the class. In particular, we often use a constructor to initialize the variables associated with each object.

A constructor differs from a regular method in two ways. First, the name of a constructor is the same name as the class. Therefore, the name of the constructor in the `Die` class is `Die`, and the name of the constructor in the `Account` class is `Account`. Second, a constructor cannot return a value and does not have a return type specified in the method header.

A common mistake made by programmers is to put a **void** return type on a constructor. As far as the compiler is concerned, putting any return type on a constructor, even

void, turns it into a regular method that happens to have the same name as the class. As such, it cannot be invoked as a constructor. This leads to error messages that are sometimes difficult to decipher.

Generally, a constructor is used to initialize the newly instantiated object. For instance, the constructor of the Die class sets the face value of the die to 1 initially. The constructor of the Account class sets the values of the instance variables to the values passed in as parameters to the constructor.

We don't have to define a constructor for every class. Visual Studio creates an empty *constructor* for each class added through the Add Item dialog box. This constructor takes no parameters and performs no initialization of class variables. This default constructor is used if we don't provide our own. This default constructor has no effect on the newly created object.

Also, a variety of constructors can be defined for the same class. This might sound fishy since they would all have the same name, that of the class. However, if the signature of the constructor (type and number of parameters) is different from all the others, you can include it.

In the SmilingFace example, the Face class (see Listing 4.7) is used to paint a smiling face at a specific location with a specific face color and smile color. If the default constructor is used (no parameters), the face is yellow with a black smile at location 0, 0. To get a yellow face with a black smile, you would use the second constructor, which includes only the X and Y position. Finally, if you want to specify location and colors, you would use the third constructor.

Debugging: Viewing Contents of Object Variables

In a previous segment on debugging, we discussed how to examine the contents of variables that were primitive data types (numbers and strings). Now we examine how to view the contents of objects while the program is paused at a breakpoint or during single stepping.

Let's begin by stopping our Transactions application after all account adjustments have been made. Set a breakpoint on the Console.Out.WriteLine statement and press F5. It should stop as shown in Figure 4.10.

Now we need to access the Locals window in the lower-left corner of the screen. There will probably be three tabs in that corner, labeled Autos, Locals, and Watch 1. Click the Locals tab and you should see something like what is shown in Figure 4.11. If the Locals tab is not shown, click Debug on the menu, Windows and then Locals.

The Main method defines four local variables, acct1, acct2, acct3, and smithBalance. The first three are objects of type Account and the last is a double. To the left of each of the Account objects is a plus sign. Click the plus sign in front of acct1. When the window is expanded, you should see something similar to what is shown in Figure 4.12.

You now see all the data members of the Account object. Some names appear twice, with an initial lowercase letter indicating the **private** class members (e.g., acctNumber) and an initial uppercase letter indicating **public** properties (e.g., AccountNumber).

You will be happy to find that you can use the Locals window to modify the contents of variables while the program is paused. This could prove very handy, because you could try

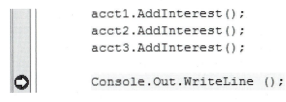

```
            acct1.AddInterest();
            acct2.AddInterest();
            acct3.AddInterest();

            Console.Out.WriteLine ();
```

FIGURE 4.10   Transaction application at a breakpoint

	Value	Type
	{Length=0}	strin
1	{Transactions.Account}	Tran
2	{Transactions.Account}	Tran
3	{Transactions.Account}	Tran
Balance	540.0	doub

os   Locals   Watch 1

FIGURE 4.11   Transaction application Locals window

Locals

Name	Value	Type
args	{Length=0}	string[]
⊟ acct1	{Transactions.Account}	Transactions.Account
System.Object	{Transactions.Account}	System.Object
AccountNumber	72354	long
acctNumber	72354	long
balance	-314.4744	double
Balance	-314.4744	double
name	"Ted Murphy"	string
RATE	0.035	double
⊞ acct2	{Transactions.Account}	Transactions.Account
⊞ acct3	{Transactions.Account}	Transactions.Account
smithBalance	540.0	double

Autos   Locals   Watch 1

FIGURE 4.12   Transaction application Locals window with acct1 expanded

a different value and step through the code again. To change a value, simply click on the value of the variable and change it. In the case of strings, you can double-click on the string value and then change individual letters.

Debugging: Step Into, Step Out, and Step Over

Up to this point, we have been testing applications using the Step Into debug command (F11 or F8). This command corresponds to a single step of the application, executing every line one at a time. Although you can always skip various portions of the application by adding multiple breakpoints, Visual Studio offers another, often more convenient way.

Assume that you have created a method in a class that you have thoroughly tested and know works. When you arrive at the point the method is about to be called, pressing the Step Into key, F11, would take you into the method for single stepping, but you really don't need to test the method again. Instead of using the Step Into key, you can use the Step Over key, F10 or shift+F8. Step Over runs all method code and does not stop until the first line after the method call.

Now assume that you need to test part of a method but are satisfied that the method is going to work okay. Therefore, you really want to return to the caller and continue testing there. Instead of using Step Into a bunch of times to finish the method, simply press the Step Out (Shift+F11 or control+shift+F8) key. This will complete the current method and stop immediately after the method returns.

4.6   USING CLASSES FOR GRAPHICAL IMAGES

Classes are designed to encapsulate all the code associated with a particular function. Thus, we can apply this design to graphical images by placing all the creation and drawing code for an image within the class. Thereafter, the parent would simply ask the graphical image to draw itself at the appropriate time.

In the `SmilingFace` example presented in this section, we create a separate class called `Face` that defines a smiling face of a particular color pattern at a specific location (see discussion of its constructors above). The main form creates three of these smiling faces at three different places on the screen and then paints them in a `Paint` method.

To create the application in Visual Studio, select File/New/Project and create a Windows application named **SmilingFace**. Add a class named `Face` to the project and enter the code as shown in Listing 4.6. Note that this class will draw objects and thus needs access to the `Draw` methods, Colors, Pens, and Brushes. However, when you add a class to a project, Visual Studio does not give you access to these tools by default. Visual Studio only gives you access to the basic functions in the `System` namespace. Therefore, the first line that you should add follows:

```
using System.Drawing;
```

This line gives you access to all the other tools needed to complete the `Face` class. By typing this line first and then typing **Color.**, IntelliSense shows you a list of standard colors. Similarly, when you type **g.** in the `Paint` method, IntelliSense show you a list of all `Graphics` methods.

Once the `Face` class is complete, you need to complete the form logic to create three different faces and paint them. Step one is to create three objects of type `Face` called `face1`, `face2`, and `face3`. Display the code for the form and scroll to near the top. Under the initial brace for the `SmilingFace` class, type the following line:

```
Face face1, face2, face3;
```

Now display the form in the Form Designer, select the events in the Properties dialog box, and scroll down to the `Load` event. Double-click the blank space to the right of the word `Load` and type the code that creates the three faces:

```
face1 = new Face( 10, 10, Color.Yellow, Color.Black);
face2 = new Face(140, 10, Color.Cyan,   Color.Black);
face3 = new Face(270, 10, Color.Red,    Color.Black);
```

This creates a yellow face, a cyan face, and a red face, each with a black smile, at different locations on the screen. All that remains is to have those faces displayed. You want to have the faces painted every time the form's `Paint` event is called. To do this, return to the form designer and create a `Paint` event handler (double-click the `Paint` event in the Properties dialog box). Then type the following code:

```
face1.Paint(e.Graphics);
face2.Paint(e.Graphics);
face3.Paint(e.Graphics);
```

Note that the `Paint` method in the Form knows nothing about what is being done inside the face. It only knows that it wants the face to be painted, so it calls the `Paint` method within the `Face` class, passing to the `Graphics` object the form's `Paint` event that it has received. The completed project is shown in Listings 4.6 and 4.7.

Listing 4.6

```
//*************************************************************
//   SmilingFace.cs              C#: Ken Culp
//
//   Demonstrates use of a class to draw objects on a form.
//   Illustrates multiple constructors.
//*************************************************************
using System;
using System.Collections.Generic;
using System.ComponentModel;
```

Listing 4.6   continued

```csharp
using System.Data;
using System.Drawing;
using System.Text;
using System.Windows.Forms;

namespace SmilingFace
{
  public partial class SmilingFace : Form
  {
    public SmilingFace()
    {
      InitializeComponent();
    }
    Face face1, face2, face3;

    private void SmilingFace_Load(object sender, EventArgs e)
    {
      face1 = new Face(10, 10, Color.Yellow, Color.Black);
      face2 = new Face(140, 10, Color.Cyan, Color.Black);
      face3 = new Face(270, 10, Color.Red, Color.Black);
    }

    private void SmilingFace_Paint(object sender,
      PaintEventArgs e)
    {
      face1.Paint(e.Graphics);
      face2.Paint(e.Graphics);
      face3.Paint(e.Graphics);
    }
  }
}
```

Listing 4.7

```csharp
//****************************************************************
//   Face.cs                    C#: Ken Culp
//
//   Class definition used to draw a smiling face at the specified
//   location with the specified colors.
//****************************************************************
using System;
using System.Collections.Generic;
using System.Text;
using System.Drawing;

namespace SmilingFace
{
```

Listing 4.7   continued

```
class Face
{
  private int x;                   // x & Y on parents surface
  private int y;
  private Color faceCol;   // Color to paint face
  private Color smilCol;   // Color to paint smile
  //----------------------------------------------------------------
  // Three constructors are defined:
  // 1. Default: yellow face, black smile, at 0, 0
  // 2. Yellow face, black smile at given x, y
  // 3. User specified face and smile color, user x, y
  //----------------------------------------------------------------
  public Face()
  {
    x = 0;
    y = 0;
    faceCol = Color.Yellow;
    smilCol = Color.Black;
  }
  public Face(int xPos, int yPos)
  {
    x = xPos;
    y = yPos;
    faceCol = Color.Yellow;
    smilCol = Color.Black;
  }
  public Face(int xPos, int yPos, Color faceColor,
    Color smileColor)
  {
    x = xPos;
    y = yPos;
    faceCol = faceColor;
    smilCol = smileColor;
  }

  //----------------------------------------------------------------
  // Properties to modify display location and colors
  //----------------------------------------------------------------
  public Color FaceColor
  {
    get { return faceCol; }
    set { faceCol = value; }
  }
  public Color SmileColor
  {
    get { return smilCol; }
    set { smilCol = value; }
  }
```

Listing 4.7 continued

```csharp
    public int X
    {
      get { return x; }
      set { x = value; }
    }
    public int Y
    {
      get { return y; }
      set { y = value; }
    }

    //----------------------------------------------------------------
    // Paints face using graphics object passed in using info
    // passed in on constructor or modified by properties.
    //----------------------------------------------------------------
    public void Paint(Graphics g)
    {
      Brush yBrush = new SolidBrush(faceCol);
      Brush bBrush = new SolidBrush(smilCol);
      Pen bPen = new Pen(smilCol, 2);
      Font font = new Font("Times New Roman", 20, FontStyle.Bold);

      g.FillEllipse(yBrush, x, y, 80, 80);               // head
      g.DrawEllipse(bPen, x + 20, y + 30, 15, 7);        // eyes
      g.DrawEllipse(bPen, x + 45, y + 30, 15, 7);        //
      g.FillEllipse(bBrush, x + 25, y + 31, 5, 5);       // pupils
      g.FillEllipse(bBrush, x + 50, y + 31, 5, 5);       //
      g.DrawArc(bPen, x + 20, y + 50, 40, 15, 0, 180); // mouth
    }
  }
}
```

FIGURE 4.13 SmilingFace output

This project clearly demonstrates the benefits of using classes to encapsulate properties (location, color of the face) and methods (`Paint`). As you begin any new project, consider your design and give particular attention to what things are related to what. Group related methods and data into classes as much as possible. This will pay big dividends down the road because your programs will be easier to understand, code, fix, and maintain. This use of classes to group related items together is the foundation for object-oriented programming, frequently called OOP.

4.7   BRUSHES

We briefly mentioned brushes and their use in drawing in Chapter 3. You can see brushes used in the `SmilingFace` example above in a simple way to just create a solid fill. However, there are other types of brushes besides solid brushes. Brushes can also be hatched with lines, filled with bitmap images, or have a gradient. We shall consider each of these brush types in this section.

First of all, let us return to our solid brush and a couple of ways to create the brush. First, the brush can be created from any `Color` object using the `SolidBrush` object using either syntax as shown below:

```
Brush myBrush = new SolidBrush(Color.Black);

SolidBrush myBrush = new SolidBrush(Color.Black);
```

The brush would be created as a black brush and would fill any figure with black. In the first line, the object is of type `Brush`, and in the second line, the object is of the type `SolidBrush`. The distinction in not important at this time except to note that `SolidBrush` is a class derived from the class `Brush` and the class `Brush` cannot be instantiated (cannot issue a new command). You will likely see both versions of the syntax if you examine code from other people.

Another way to create a brush is from an existing `Pen` object, as follows, in which case `myBrush` will be a solid brush with the same color as the `Pen` object:

```
Brush myBrush = myPen.Brush;
```

Hatch Brushes

Now let us examine an entirely different class of brush, the hatched brush. This is a brush that fills an object with the main color and draws lines on the surface. These lines can run diagonally, vertically, horizontally, or exist in a cross-hatch fashion. The syntax for creating one of these brushes is as follows:

```
HatchBrush hb = new HatchBrush(
   HatchStyle.Cross, Color.White, Color.Black);
```

Here, the style of hatching is chosen via the first parameter in the constructor. This first parameter is an enumeration with a variety of options, as shown in Figure 4.14. Note that there are many more members of the `HatchStyle` enumeration, which you can display by pressing the Page Down and Page Up keys in the application. For instructions on using `DrawingEnum`, open the application and press F1.

You may should this utility to see the various `HatchStyle` options (as well as `LineCaps`, described in Chapter 3, and `LinearGradientMode`, covered in the following section). You may also want to view the code, but it uses some capabilities of C# that have not been covered yet.

Gradient Brushes

You can also create brushes that continuously change from one color to another over a specified range. You can specify a specific angle for the gradient, either from an enumeration or directly. The syntax for creating the `LinearGradientBrush` is shown below:

```
using System.Drawing.Drawing2D;
 . . . .
LinearGradientBrush gradientBrush = new
  LinearGradientBrush(rectangle,
Color.Red, Color.Blue, LinearGradientMode.ForwardDiagonal);
LinearGradientBrush gradientBrush = new
  LinearGradientBrush(rectangle,
    Color.Red, Color.Blue, angle);
 . . . .
g.FillRectangle(gradientBrush, xPos, yPos, width, height);
```

The first line exposes a library to our class. This library is where the gradient brushes are defined and is required unless you want to use a fully qualified name. The second line creates a gradient brush by using the enumeration `LinearGradientBrush`, for which there are currently four entries, as shown in Figure 4.15 (also from the `DrawingEnum` application described in the preceding section).

The third line of code above creates a gradient brush where the angle is specified. Note that both constructors for the brush take as the first parameter a `Rectangle` object. A `Rectangle` is an object with basically four values: `X`, `Y`, `Width`, and `Height`. The `X` and `Y` values specify the location of the rectangle and are not used here. The `Width` and `Height` values are used to control the range over which the gradient is to be shown. If this rectangle is the same size as the area being drawn, then there will be only one transition across the object.

Both constructors also take two `Color` objects that specify the two colors to be used for the gradient (red and blue in our example above). There are other constructors that take other parameters giving more control of the effect. You will want to experiment with different settings.

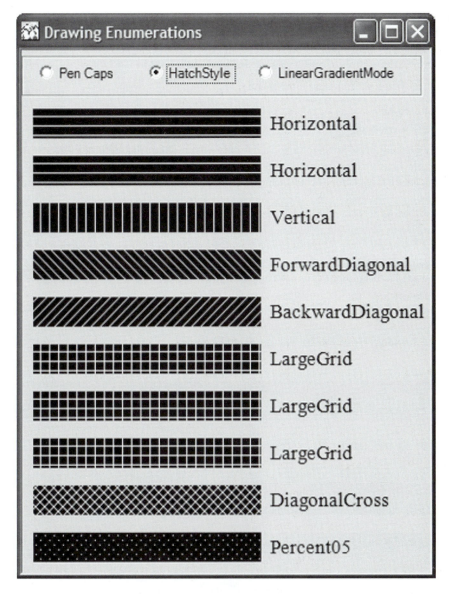

FIGURE 4.14   `HatchStyle` enumeration

4.8   GRAPHICAL USER INTERFACES

In Chapters 2 and 3 we introduced a few key components that are helpful in the design of graphics-based programs. What we need now is true user interaction, which is the heart of a graphical user interface (GUI). This section introduces the concepts needed to create interactive GUI-based programs. It lays the groundwork for all GUI discussions throughout the book.

At least three kinds of objects are needed to create a GUI in C#:

> Windows controls (components)

> events

> event handlers

As we mentioned in Chapter 3, a GUI *control* is an object that defines a screen element to display information or allow the user to interact with a program in a certain way. Examples of GUI components include push buttons, text fields, labels, scroll bars, and menus.

An *event* is an object that represents some occurrence in which we may be interested. Often, events correspond to user actions, such as pressing a mouse button or typing a key on the keyboard. Most GUI components generate events to indicate a user action related to that component. For example, a button component will generate an event to indicate that the button has been pushed. A program that is oriented around a GUI, responding to events from the user, is called *event-driven.*

An *event handler* is code that "waits" for an event to occur and responds in some way when it does. We must carefully establish the relationships among the handler, the event it listens for, and the control that will generate the event.

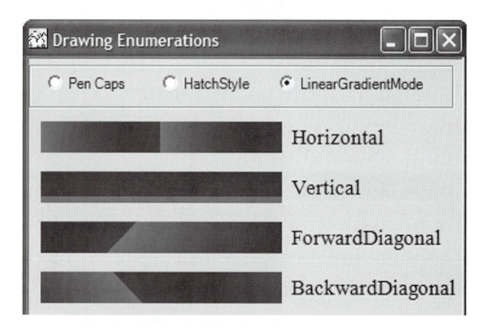

FIGURE 4.15 `LinearGradientMode` enumeration

For now, we will use controls and events that are predefined by classes in the C# library. We will tailor the behavior of the components, but their basic roles have been established. We will, however, write event handlers to perform whatever actions we desire when events occur. In a subsequent chapter, we will explore briefly how to create our own user controls.

Specifically, to create a program that uses a GUI, we must:

> instantiate and set up the necessary controls

> implement handlers that define what happens when particular events occur

> establish the relationship between the handlers and the controls that generate the events of interest

> **Key Concept**
>
> A GUI is made up of controls, events that represent user actions, and event handlers that respond to those events.

In some respects, once you have a basic understanding of event-driven programming, the rest is just detail. There are many types of components you can use that produce many types of events that you may want to acknowledge. But they all work in the same basic way. They all have the same core relationships to one another.

The following sections introduce some more components and present examples of GUI-based programs that allow true user interaction.

4.9   BUTTONS

The `PushCounter` program shown in Listing 4.8 presents the user with a single push button (labeled "`Push Me!`"). Each time the button is pushed, a counter is updated and displayed. Use the following instructions to create the application.

Select File/New/Project and Windows Application. Name the project **PushCounter**, select the desired directory in which to store it, and click OK. Now that the form is displayed, move the cursor over the Toolbox and drop a button onto the form, making the button about 1 inch wide by dragging the right edge tab. In the Properties dialog box, define the following properties:

Name: btnPush
Text: &Push Me

Next, drop a text box on the form, name it **lblPushes**, and set the text to "`Pushes: 0`" (no pushes yet). All that remains is to "handle" the mouse press event.

As we mentioned in Chapter 3, some Visual Studio controls have a default event. For buttons, the default event is the mouse `Click` event. This allows you to create the event handler by simply double-clicking on the button in the Form Designer. This will switch to the code view with a default event handler created for you. Remember, you may also add the event handler by selecting events (lightning bolt icon) in the Properties dialog box, scrolling to the `Click` event, and double-clicking in the blank to the right.

Add the following two lines of code to the `Click` handler:

```
pushes++;      // These are the only two lines added to click!
lblPushes.Text = "Pushes: " + pushes.ToString();
```

Finally, add a private class variable to keep track of the number of clicks. Scroll to the top of the file and add the following line as the first line after the open brace for the class definition:

```
private int pushes = 0;        // Counter for pushes
```

Test your application. Your complete code should resemble that shown in Listing 4.8.

Listing 4.8

```csharp
//*****************************************************************
//   PushCounter.cs         C#: Ken Culp
//
//   Demonstrates a graphical user interface created by:
//      1. dragging a button to the form
//      2. Dragging a text box to the form
//      3. Sizing the form
//      4. Creating button logic by double clicking the button
//*****************************************************************
using System;
using System.Collections.Generic;
using System.ComponentModel;
using System.Data;
using System.Drawing;
using System.Text;
using System.Windows.Forms;

namespace PushCounter
{
  public partial class PushCounter : Form
  {
    public PushCounter()
    {
      InitializeComponent();
    }

    private int pushes = 0;          // Counter for pushes

    private void btnPush_Click(object sender, EventArgs e)
    {
      // Only two lines needed to count click:
      pushes++;
      lblPushes.Text = "Pushes: " + pushes.ToString();
    }
  }
}
```

Listing 4.8   continued

Display

Now that we have created a button, let's take a brief look at some of the other properties that can be set for buttons. As with labels (see LabelDemo in Chapter 3), you can modify the font size, style, color, etc. You can also place graphical images on the button, just like in a label box, and set the alignment in the same way. There are also other events that you can add to the button to add special effects (such as highlighting when the mouse passes over). For more information on buttons, check the help files in Visual Studio.

The only event of interest in this program occurs when the button is pushed. To respond to the event, we must create an event handler for that event, so we must write the code that represents the handler.

A Button generates a Click event when it is pushed. Therefore, the code we wrote was a Click event handler.

Finding Code in Your Source File

Note that the code for all event handlers for a form is usually part of the form on which the event handlers are defined. These handlers will frequently use the services of external objects, but all the code for all handlers will be in the single source file associated with the form.

This structure can sometimes lead to a very cluttered Class file. Therefore, Visual Studio gives you several ways of rapidly locating a particular piece of code. The first way is to go directly from the Designer to a specific piece of code. For example, suppose you want to edit the Click event code for our push button in the previous example. Simply go to the Designer and double-click on the button (default event is Click).

Similarly, if you have created event handlers for non-default events, you can go to the properties window for the control, scroll to the event, and double-click on the event name, which will take you back to the handler created previously.

The third and more general way is to use the explorer buttons at the top of the code file. In the top-right window at the top of the code file, click the drop-down arrow. For our PushCounter example, you would see the display shown in Figure 4.16.

In Figure 4.16, all methods and class members are shown in this list because this is a small form with only two controls. For larger forms, the list would have a vertical scroll bar. Also in the list in Figure 4.16, note that there are two kinds of entries. The first is marked by what looks like a purple book. This corresponds to a method. For example, our `Click` event handler is so listed (`btnPush_Click`). Class members such as our push counter `pushes` is shown with a small green box. To show the definition of methods or members, just click on one of the items in the list.

Review this example carefully, noting how it accomplishes the three key steps to creating an interactive GUI-based program. It creates and sets up the GUI components, creates the appropriate handler for the event of interest, and sets up the relationship between the handler and the component that will generate the event.

Adding Event Handlers Manually

Up to this point, we have been using Visual Studio to add the skeleton event handlers for us so that all we have to do is type the code. In case you might be wondering if this is the only way, it is not. You can manually type the code for the event handler and then add it to the control in Visual Studio, or you can even add the handler to the control in code. Let's explore just writing the code manually and assigning it in Visual Studio.

For a mouse click, you must create a method in the `Form` class that looks like the following:

```
private void myButtonClickHandler(object sender,
   System.EventArgs e)
```

You can give your method any name you want but you must specify precisely two parameters with the types shown above. When referring to methods, we say that specification for the number and type of parameters is the *signature* for the method. For Visual Studio to recognize your event handler, it must match the signature for that event handler. Note that the different events may require a different signature for their handler. The one above is for a mouse click. More information on creating events and writing your own event handlers is available in Chapter 10.

Once the method has been created, you can add the method to the event for the desired control by using the properties window. Go to the Form Designer, click once on the button, select events in the properties window, and scroll to the desired event (in this case, the `Click` event). Click the drop-down arrow to the right of the event name and Visual Studio will show you all methods that match the appropriate signature, as shown in Figure 4.17 (in which only one method is available, `btnPush_Click`). If the signature has an error (missing parameter or wrong type), your method will not be listed. This technique allows the same event handler code to be used for the same event for other controls. For example the `TextChanged` event for several `TextBoxes` could use the same handler to validate user input.

Using code to connect the handler to the control is beyond the scope of this book. If you would like to see how it is done, click the plus sign and expand the Windows Form Designer code and look for the following line:

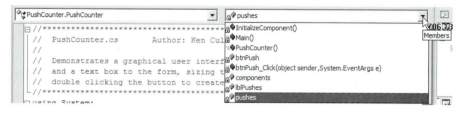

FIGURE 4.16   Finding code in the `Class` file

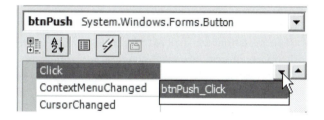

FIGURE 4.17   Selecting event handlers in the Form Designer

```
this.btnPush.Click +=
   new System.EventHandler(this.btnPush_Click);
```

Accept and Cancel Buttons

Another handy feature of Visual Studio is that it enables you to assign special handling to certain buttons. One such handling is to have the Enter key correspond to pressing one of your buttons. This corresponds to what is called the `AcceptButton` in the Form properties. This button, frequently labeled OK, normally corresponds to the user indicating that everything is okay and that they are finished with the form.

Another special handling is to have the Esc key correspond to a button on the screen (usually an Exit button). This button usually means to discard changes. This is called the `CancelButton` in the Form properties.

To set up either of these two features, select the form in the Designer (click on the form away from any control). Then, in the properties window, find the `AcceptButton` and `CancelButton` properties. To make the appropriate association, click the drop-down arrow in the blank space to the right of `AcceptButton` or `CancelButton` and then select the desired button from the list of buttons shown.

4.10   TEXT FIELDS

Let's look at another example that uses another component: a text field. The Fahrenheit program shown in Listing 4.9 presents a GUI that includes a text field into which the user can type a Fahrenheit temperature. When the user presses the Enter (or Return) key, the Convert button is activated and the equivalent Celsius temperature is displayed.

To create the application, select File/New/Project, select Windows Application, and name the project **Fahrenheit**. Make the form about 3.5 inches wide and 1.5 inches high. Add two labels, as shown in the sample output, to label the input Enter Fahrenheit Temperature and label the result Temperature in Celsius. Set the TextAlign property to MiddleRight on both of these labels. Align the right edges of the labels either by visually moving them (they will snap to grid points) or by using Format/Align/Rights.

Add a text box to the form from the Toolbox. Set the TextAlign property to Right and the font size to 10. Name the text box **txtFahrenheit**. Position this text box exactly aligned to the right of the Fahrenheit label. You can do this visually or by selecting Format/Align/Bottoms.

Add a label box to the form and name it **lblCelsius**. Set the TextAlign property to MiddleRight and the font size to 10. Also on this label, set the BorderStyle property to Fixed3D. This last setting places a three-dimensional box around the result field. Align this result box to the right of the Celsius label.

Add two buttons to the form under the labels (see sample output in Listing 4.9). Set the Text property for the first to "&Convert" and its name to btnConvert. Set the Text property for the second to "E&xit" and its name to btnExit. Next, click somewhere in an empty part of the form and examine the properties window. Scroll to the AcceptButton property and set it to btnConvert. This will make the Enter key do the conversion for you. Also, set the CancelButton property for the form to btnExit. This will make the Esc key terminate the application.

Our last step is to add the code to the Convert button and the Exit button. Double-click the Convert button and type the following:

```
double fahrenheitTemp = Double.Parse(txtFahrenheit.Text);
double celsiusTemp = (fahrenheitTemp - 32) * 5 / 9;
lblCelsius.Text = celsiusTemp.ToString("0.00");
txtFahrenheit.Text = fahrenheitTemp.ToString("0.00");
```

Line one of the code takes the input from the text box and converts it to a double-precision floating number. If you type an invalid number here (like letters), the program will terminate with an exception. We will describe exception handling in Chapter 10.

Line two of the code calculates Celsius temperature from the Fahrenheit temperature. Line three writes that value to our output label, converting it to a figure with two places to the right of the decimal.

Line four is not strictly necessary. All it is doing is reformatting the Fahrenheit temperature you typed in to have two places to the right of the decimal so that the numbers will have the same format.

Finally, we have to add the code to the Exit button. Double-click the Exit button in the Designer and type **`this.Close();`**. This will cause the form to close and the application to exit. Your code should look like Listing 4.9.

Listing 4.9

```
//****************************************************************
//  Fahrenheit.cs        C#: Ken Culp
//
//  Demonstrates the use of text fields.  It also shows how to
//  use AcceptButton and CancelButton properties of the form.
//****************************************************************
using System;
using System.Collections.Generic;
using System.ComponentModel;
using System.Data;
using System.Drawing;
using System.Text;
using System.Windows.Forms;

namespace Fahrenheit
{
  public partial class Fahrenheit : Form
  {
    public Fahrenheit()
    {
      InitializeComponent();
    }

    private void btnConvert_Click(object sender, EventArgs e)
    {
      double fahrenheitTemp = Double.Parse(txtFahrenheit.Text);
      double celsiusTemp = (fahrenheitTemp - 32) * 5 / 9;
      lblCelsius.Text = celsiusTemp.ToString("0.00");
      txtFahrenheit.Text = fahrenheitTemp.ToString("0.00");
    }

    private void btnExit_Click(object sender, EventArgs e)
    {
      this.Close();
    }
  }
}
```

Listing 4.9 continued

Output:

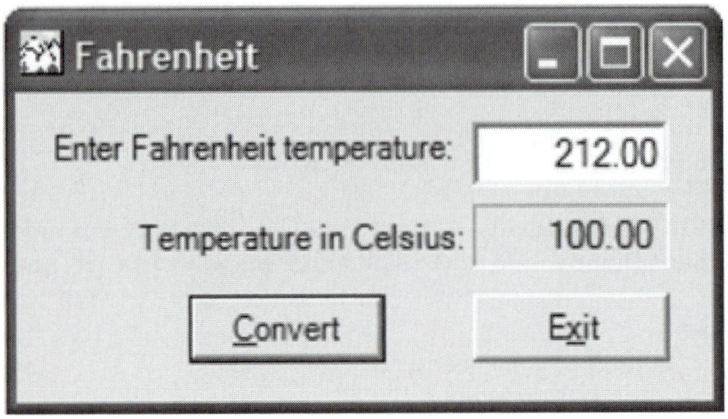

Note that since there is only one input text field, we want the cursor to always be put into that field. If it does not, then other controls were added to the form before the `TextBox`. To fix this, see Section 4.11. This makes our application very easy to use because we simply type a temperature in Fahrenheit and press the Enter key. This activates the Convert button, which displays our result and returns the cursor to the input field.

However, to convert another temperature, you will find that you first have to erase what is there before typing a new value. An easier way is to have all the text in the input field flagged as selected so that when the first character of the new value is typed, the previous value is erased. You have probably seen this capability in word processors, so let's see how we do it in Visual Studio.

Cursor Control and Selecting Portions of Text Boxes in Code

Text selection is the process of highlighting portions of text within an input control like a text box. You can use a mouse and click and drag across a few letters in a document and then press Delete or type something new over them. The same capability from code in Visual Studio uses the two properties `SelectionStart` and `SelectionLength`. These controls also allow us to control the location of the cursor in a text field.

The `Text` property of every control is an object of type `string`. This means that you can index into the string to locate specific letters or patterns in the string. In C#, this indexing always starts at zero, meaning the first character of a string is at location 0. Thus, setting `SelectionStart` to zero will start the selection at the left side of the string.

C# `string` objects also have a property called `Length`. This is the length of the string. Since string indexing starts at location 0, the last character of the string would be at offset `Length - 1`. For example, a three-character string would have letters at offsets 0, 1, and 2. The reason for using this 0-based indexing will be become clearer in Chapter 7 when we discuss arrays.

If you set `SelectionLength` to 0, you can use the `SelectionStart` property to control the location of the cursor. If `SelectionLength` and `SelectionStart` are both 0, then the cursor will be at the left edge of the text. If `SelectionStart` is set to the `Length` property of the `Text` property, the cursor will be after the last character. If `SelectionStart` is set to `Length-1`, the cursor would be just before the last character. For example, assume that you have a text box with the contents "0123456789" and set `SelectionStart` to 3 and `SelectionLength` to 0. Then, the cursor would be between the 2 and 3 and no characters would be highlighted. Another way to think about this is that the cursor is moved to position 3, which is past three characters (0, 1, and 2).

Setting `SelectionLength` to a non-zero value will highlight (blue background usually) the number of characters specified starting at `SelectionStart`. It will then place the cursor at the end of the selected portion. For example, assume that you have a text box with the contents "0123456789" and set `SelectionStart` to 3 and `SelectionLength` to 2. Then, the characters 3 and 4 would be highlighted and the cursor would be between the 4 and 5.

Warning: Using invalid values for `SelectionStart` and `SelectionLength` can cause errors. For example, a negative value for either of these causes an exception. However, if you use a very large number (larger than the length of the string) for either `SelectionStart` or `SelectionLength`, Visual Studio just assumes that you want the cursor to be past the right end of the string. You should not, however, take advantage of this but rather should always use valid values.

Note that if the user drags a mouse across some portion of a text box, `SelectionStart` and `SelectionLength` will be set for you. You can always find out in code if something has been highlighted in a text box by testing `SelectionLength`, which will be greater than 0 if something is selected. We will discuss testing values in the next chapter.

Once some portion of text is highlighted by the user of code, you can directly address it using the property `SelectedText`. This property is also a string object and subject to all methods associated with the string object.

Multiline Text Boxes

When you drop a text box on a form from the Toolbox, it defaults to being a simple, one-field type of input box. Text boxes can also take multiple lines of input with optional scroll bars. This type of text box would be used for large pieces of data, such as a memo area or message text for an email (see Programming Project 4.12). To change a text box to multiple lines, change the text box property `Multiline` to **true**. Then you can set the `ScrollBars` property as appropriate.

If `ScrollBars` is set to `None`, the text box will scroll vertically if more information is typed than fits in the box. However, to see data that has scrolled off the screen, the Page Up, Page Down, or arrow keys will have to be used. If `ScrollBars` is set to `Both` or `Vertical`, then the data can be scrolled with the bars.

Control Characters in Text Boxes

The text box, by default, does not allow you to type an Enter (Return) key or a Tab key. The Enter key would, by default, activate the `AcceptButton` button for the form and the Tab key would move the cursor to the next control on the form.

If you want to allow the user to type multiple lines of text separated by the newline character, change the property `AcceptsReturn` to **true**. Then, when the Enter key is pressed, the cursor will move one line down in the text box and the `AcceptButton` handler will not receive an event. Also set the `Multiline` property to **true**.

If you want to allow the user to type a Tab key, change the property `AcceptsTab` to true. Then, when the Tab key is pressed, the text box will show the tab by skipping some space in the line. Also, the cursor will remain in the same text box.

4.11   SETTING TAB STOPS

Similar to when using a typewriter or word processor, tab stops indicate just how far the cursor should move when the Tab key is pressed. Instead of moving a certain number of characters as in a word processor, tab stops on a form determine which control the cursor will move to on a Tab key. There are two steps to configuring tab settings on a form. The first step is to configure the order in which fields are to be selected when the Tab key is pressed. The second step is to set on which fields the cursor is to stop.

You would set the tab order, for example, if you want the cursor to go from the last name field, to the first name field, to the address field, and so on, rather than jumping from the first name field to the OK button, then to the salary field, the phone number field, and so on. Setting tab order is done on the form by selecting View/Tab Order from Visual Studio when the form is displayed. When we select View/Tab Order in our Fahrenheit example, the screen looks as shown in Figure 4.18.

In Figure 4.18, we certainly do not have the best possible order, so we want to click each control on the form in the following order: text box, Convert button, Exit button, temperature output label, followed by the other two labels. It is not technically necessary to set the order for labels and other controls that cannot receive the focus but we do it here for completeness. After making these changes, our screen looks as follows in Figure 4.19.

Once you have the tab order set the way you want it, select View/Tab Order again to turn off the tab editing. (You will be unable to edit the form until tab editing is switched off.)

Now that we have set the tab order, we need to make sure only those fields that need to be moved to on a Tab key are set as "tab stops." Since we set the Exit button to be the `CancelButton` for the form, the Esc key will always exit the form. Therefore, we do not need to stop there. The other label boxes cannot receive the control so they do not need to be changed.

To prevent the cursor stopping at an input control (button, text box, check box, etc.), change that control's `TabStop` property to **false**. In our example, we set

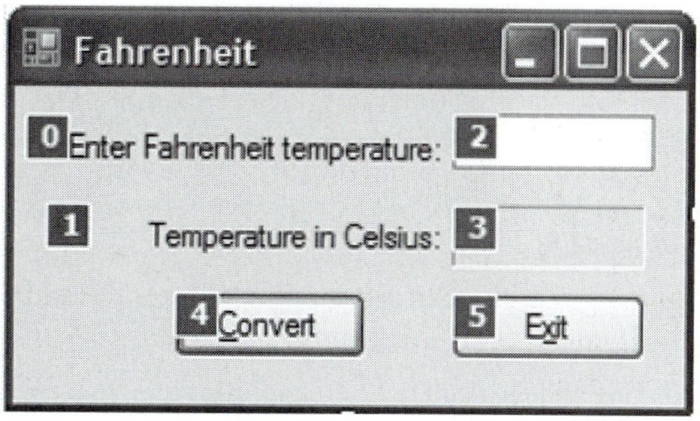

FIGURE 4.18 Tab order before changes

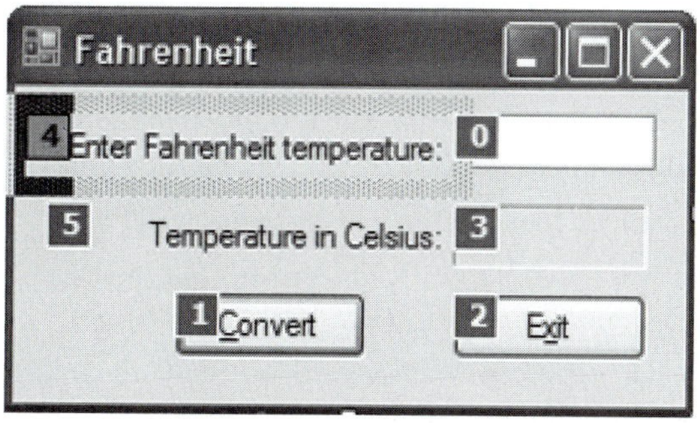

FIGURE 4.19 Tab order after changes

`btnExit.Cancel` to **false**, so our cursor will bounce between the Convert button and the Fahrenheit input box.

Note that by default, all input controls have a `TabStop` property and its value by default (when dropped on a form) is **true**. Also note that labels and other controls that cannot be modified by the user (cannot receive the focus) do not even have a `TabStop` property (it is assumed to be **false**).

Summary of Key Concepts

> The heart of object-oriented programming is defining classes that represent objects with well-defined state and behavior.

> The scope of a variable, which determines where it can be referenced, depends on where it is declared.

> A UML class diagram helps us visualize the contents of and relationships among the classes of a program.

> An object should be encapsulated, guarding its data from inappropriate access.

> Instance variables should be declared with private visibility to promote encapsulation.

> Most objects contain accessor and mutator methods to allow the client to manage data in a controlled manner.

> The value returned from a method must be consistent with the return type specified in the method header.

> When a method is called, the actual parameters are copied into the formal parameters.

> A variable declared in a method is local to that method and cannot be used outside of it.

> A constructor cannot have any return type, even void.

> A GUI is made up of controls, events that represent user actions, and event handlers that respond to those events.

Self-Review Questions

4.1   What is the difference between an object and a class?

4.2   What is the scope of a variable?

4.3   What are UML diagrams designed to do?

4.4   Objects should be self-governing. Explain.

4.5   What is a modifier?

4.6   Describe each of the following:

   a. public method

   b. private method

   c. public variable

   d. private variable

4.7   What does the **return** statement do?

4.8   Explain the difference between an actual parameter and a formal parameter.

4.9   What are constructors used for? How are they defined?

4.10 What is the relationship between an event and a handler?

4.11 Can we add any kind of handler to any component? Explain.

Exercises

4.1   Write a method called `randomInRange` that accepts two integer parameters representing a range. The method should return a random integer in the specified range (inclusive). Assume that the first parameter is greater than the second.

4.2   Write a method called `randomColor` that creates and returns a `Color` object that represents a random color. Recall that a `Color` object can be defined by three integer values between 0 and 255, representing the contributions of red, green, and blue (its RGB value).

4.3   Draw a UML class diagram that shows the relationships among the classes used in the `PushCounter` program.

4.4   Draw a UML class diagram that shows the relationships among the classes used in the `Fahrenheit` program.

Programming Projects

4.1   Design and implement a class called `PairOfDice`, composed of two six-sided `Die` objects. Create a driver class called `BoxCars` with a `Main` method that rolls a `PairOfDice` object 1000 times, counting the number of box cars (two 6s) that occur.

4.2   Using the `PairOfDice` class from Programming Project 4.1, design and implement a class to play a game called Pig. In this game, the user competes against the computer. On each turn, the current player rolls a pair of dice and accumulates points. The goal is to reach 100 points before your opponent does. If, on any turn, the player rolls a 1, all points accumulated for that round are forfeited and control of the dice moves to the other player. If the player rolls two 1's in one turn, the player loses all points accumulated thus far in the game and loses control of the dice. The player may voluntarily turn over the dice after each roll. Therefore, the player must decide to either roll again (be a pig) and risk losing points, or relinquish control of the dice, possibly allowing the other player to win. Implement the computer player such that it always relinquishes the dice after accumulating 20 or more points in any given round.

4.3 Design and implement a class called `Card` that represents a standard playing card. Each card has a suit and a face value. Create a program that deals five random cards.

4.4 Design and implement a class called `Building` that represents a graphical depiction of a building. Allow the parameters to the constructor to specify the building's width and height. Each building should be colored black and contain a few random windows of yellow. Create a program that draws a random skyline of buildings.

4.5 Write a program that displays a graphical seating chart for a dinner party. Create a class called `Diner` (as in one who dines) that stores the person's name, gender, and location at the dinner table. A diner is graphically represented as a circle, color-coded by gender, with the person's name printed in the circle.

4.6 Create a class called `Crayon` that represents one crayon of a particular color and length (height). Design and implement a program that draws a box of crayons.

4.7 Create a class called `Star` that represents a graphical depiction of a star. Let the constructor of the star accept the number of points in the star (4, 5, or 6), the radius of the star, and the center point location. Write a program that draws a sky full of various types of stars. Draw each line of the star yourself and then research the Visual Studio package to see if there is an easier way.

4.8 Modify the `Fahrenheit` program from this chapter so that it has three buttons: "To Fahrenheit", "To Celsius", and "Exit". Change the label for the Fahrenheit temperature to "Enter Temperature:". Modify the converted temperature field label to say either "Fahrenheit Temperature:" or "Celsius Temperature:" depending upon which button is pressed.

4.9 Design and implement an application that displays a button and a label. Every time the button is pushed, the label should display a random number between 1 and 100, inclusive.

4.10 Design and implement an application that presents two buttons and a label to the user. Label the buttons Increment and Decrement, respectively. Display a numeric value (initially 50) using the label. Each time the Increment button is pushed, increment the value displayed. Likewise, each time the Decrement button is pressed, decrement the value displayed.

4.11 Design and implement an application that draws a traffic light and uses a push button to change the state of the light. Pick the new state randomly.

4.12 Develop an application that implements a prototype user interface for composing an email message. The application should have a single window, with a multiline text box for the message body; labeled text fields for the To, Cc, and Bcc address lists and Subject line; and buttons at the top for Send and Attach. Clicking the Attach button should open a new form that asks for a filename and has OK and Cancel buttons. Display the attach form with `ShowDialog` and have either button close the form.

The application does not need to do anything with files selected for attachment, nor does it need to do anything when the Send button is clicked.

Answers to Self-Review Questions

4.1   A class is the blueprint of an object. It defines the variables and methods that will be a part of every object that is instantiated from it. But a class reserves no memory space for variables. Each object has its own data space and therefore its own state.

4.2   The scope of a variable is the area within a program in which the variable can be referenced. An instance variable, declared at the class level, can be referenced in any method of the class. Local variables, including the formal parameters, declared within a particular method, can be referenced only in that method.

4.3   A UML diagram helps us visualize the entities (classes and objects) in a program as well as the relationships among them. UML diagrams are tools that help us capture the design of a program prior to writing it.

4.4   A self-governing object is one that controls the values of its own data. Encapsulated objects, which don't allow an external client to reach in and change their data, are self-governing.

4.5   A modifier is a C# reserved word that can be used in the definition of a variable or method and that specifically defines certain characteristics of its use. For example, by declaring a variable with private visibility, the variable cannot be directly accessed outside of the object in which it is defined.

4.6   The modifiers affect the methods and variables in the following ways:

   a. A **public** method is called a service method for an object because it defines a service that the object provides.

   b. A **private** method is called a support method because it cannot be invoked from outside the object and is used to support the activities of other methods in the class.

   c. A **public** variable is a variable that can be directly accessed and modified by a client. This explicitly violates the principle of encapsulation and therefore should be avoided.

   d. A **private** variable is a variable that can be accessed and modified only from within the class. Variables almost always are declared with private visibility.

4.7   An explicit **return** statement is used to specify the value that is returned from a method. The type of the return value must match the return type specified in the method definition.

4.8   An actual parameter is a value sent to a method when it is invoked. A formal parameter is the corresponding variable in the header of the method declaration; it takes on the value of the actual parameter so that it can be used inside the method.

4.9   Constructors are special methods in an object that are used to initialize the object when it is instantiated. A constructor has the same name as its class, and it does not return a value.

4.10   Events usually represent user actions. An event handler is a method declared in the class definition of the form that performs the appropriate actions for that user action.

4.11   Different controls support a different set of events. To see what events a control supports, open the event portion of the Properties window for that control.

Conditionals and Loops

5

CHAPTER OBJECTIVES

> Define the flow of control through a method.

> Explore boolean expressions that can be used to make decisions.

> Perform basic decision making using `if` and `switch` statements.

> Discuss issues pertaining to the comparison of certain types of data.

> Execute statements repetitively using `while`, `do`, and `for` loops.

> Discuss the concept of an iterator object and use one to read a text file.

> Draw with the aid of conditionals and loops.

> Explore more GUI components and events.

All programming languages have statements that allow you to make decisions to determine what to do next. Some of those statements allow you to repeat a certain activity multiple times. This chapter discusses several such statements, as well as exploring some issues related to comparing data and objects. It includes a discussion of boolean expressions, which form the basis of any decision. The Windows Track sections of this chapter explore new drawing options and several new components and events.

5.1   BOOLEAN EXPRESSIONS

The order in which statements are executed in a running program is called the *flow of control*. Unless otherwise specified, the execution of a program proceeds in a linear fashion. That is, a running program starts at the first programming statement and moves down one statement at a time until the program is complete. A C# application begins executing with the first line of the Main method and proceeds step by step until it gets to the end of the Main method.

Invoking a method alters the flow of control. When a method is called, control jumps to the code defined for that method. When the method completes, control returns to the place in the calling method where the invocation was made and processing continues from there.

> **Key Concept**
>
> Conditionals and loops allow us to control the flow of execution through a method.

Within a given method, we can alter the flow of control through the code by using certain types of programming statements. Statements that control the flow of execution through a method fall into two categories: conditionals and loops.

A *conditional statement* is sometimes called a *selection statement* because it allows us to choose which statement will be executed next. The conditional statements in C# are the **if** statement, the **if-else** statement, and the **switch** statement. These statements allow us to decide which statement to execute next. Each decision is based on a *boolean expression* (also called a *condition*), which is an expression that evaluates to either true or false. The result of the expression determines which statement is executed next.

The following is an example of an **if** statement:

```
if (count > 20)
    Console.Out.WriteLine ("Count exceeded");
```

> **Key Concept**
>
> An **if** statement allows a program to choose whether to execute a particular statement.

The condition in this statement is count > 20. That expression evaluates to a boolean (true or false) result. Either the value stored in count is greater than 20 or it's not. If it is, the Console.Out.WriteLine statement is executed. If it's not, the Console.Out.WriteLine statement is skipped and processing continues with whatever code follows it. The **if** statement and other conditionals are explored in detail in this chapter.

The ability to make decisions like this come up all the time in programming situations. For example, the cost of life insurance might be dependent on whether the insured person is a smoker. If the person smokes, we calculate the cost using a particular formula; if not, we calculate it using another. The role of a conditional statement is to evaluate a boolean condition (whether the person smokes) and then to execute the proper calculation accordingly.

> **Key Concept**
>
> A loop allows a program to execute a statement multiple times.

A *loop*, or *repetition statement*, allows us to execute a programming statement over and over again. Like a conditional, a loop is based on a boolean expression that determines how many times the statement is executed.

For example, suppose we wanted to calculate the grade point average of every student in a class. The calculation is the same for each student; it is just performed on different data. We would set up a loop that repeats the calculation for each student until there are no more students to process.

C# has four types of loop statements: the **while** statement, the **do** statement, the **for** statement, and the **foreach** statement. The **foreach** statement will be introduced here and covered again in Chapter 7 because it is the easiest loop method to use for arrays and is used only for arrays (Chapter 7) and collections (Chapter 12). The rest of these statements will be discussed in the sections that follow. As you will see, each type of loop statement has unique characteristics that distinguish it from the others.

All conditionals and loops are based on boolean expressions, which use equality operators, relational operators, and logical operators to make decisions. Before we discuss the conditional and loop statements, let's explore these operators.

Equality and Relational Operators

The == and != operators are called *equality operators*. They test whether two values are equal or not equal, respectively. Note that the equality operator consists of two equal signs side by side and should not be mistaken for the assignment operator, which uses only one equal sign. If you use the single equal sign in a conditional statement, the compiler will flag an error.

The following **if** statement prints a sentence only if the variables total and sum contain the same value:

```
if (total == sum)
   Console.Out.WriteLine ("total equals sum");
```

Likewise, the following **if** statement prints a sentence only if the variables total and sum do *not* contain the same value:

```
if (total != sum)
   Console.Out.WriteLine ("total does NOT equal sum");
```

C# also has several *relational operators* that let us decide relative ordering between values. Earlier in this section we used the greater than operator (>) to decide if one value was greater than another. We can ask such questions using various operators, depending on the relationship. These include less than (<), greater than or equal to (>=), and less than or equal to (<=). Figure 5.1 lists the C# equality and relational operators.

The equality and relational operators have precedence lower than the arithmetic operators. Therefore, arithmetic operations are evaluated first, followed by equality and relational operations. As always, parentheses can be used to explicitly specify the order of evaluation. In fact, parentheses should be used where they improves the readability of the code.

We'll see more examples of relational operators as we examine conditional and loop statements throughout this chapter.

Logical Operators

In addition to the equality and relational operators, C# has three *logical operators* that produce boolean results. They also take boolean operands. Figure 5.2 lists and describes the logical operators.

The ! operator is used to perform the *logical NOT* operation, which is also called the *logical complement*. The logical complement of a boolean value yields its opposite value. That is, if a boolean variable called found has the value false, then !found is true. Likewise, if found is true, then !found is false. The logical NOT operation does not change the value stored in found.

A logical operation can be described by a *truth table* that lists all possible combinations of values for the variables involved in an expression. Because the logical NOT operator is unary, there are only two possible values for its one operand, true or false. Figure 5.3 shows a truth table that describes the ! operator.

The && operator performs a *logical AND* operation. The result is true if both operands are true, but false otherwise. Compare that to the result of the *logical OR* operator (||), which is true if one or the other or both operands are true, but false otherwise.

The AND and OR operators are both binary operators since each uses two operands. Therefore, there are four possible combinations to consider: both operands are true, both are false, one is true and the other false, and vice versa. Figure 5.4 depicts a truth table that shows both the && and || operators.

Operator	Meaning
==	equal to
!=	not equal to
<	less than
<=	less than or equal to
>	greater than
>=	greater than or equal to

FIGURE 5.1 C# equality and relational operators

Operator	Description	Example	Result
!	logical NOT	! a	true if a is false and false if a is true
&&	logical AND	a && b	true if a and b are both true and false otherwise
||	logical OR	a || b	true if a or b or both are true and false otherwise

FIGURE 5.2 C# logical operators

The logical NOT operator has the highest precedence of the three logical operators, followed by logical AND, then logical OR.

Consider the following **if** statement:

```
if (!done && (count > MAX))
  Console.Out.WriteLine ("Completed.");
```

Under what conditions would the `Console.Out.WriteLine` statement be executed? The value of the boolean variable `done` is either true or false, and the NOT operator reverses that value. The value of `count` is either greater than MAX or it isn't. The truth table in Figure 5.5 breaks down all of the possibilities.

An important characteristic of the `&&` and `||` operators is that they are "short-circuited." That is, if their left operand is sufficient to decide the boolean result of the operation, the right operand is not evaluated. This situation can occur with both operators, but for

a	!a
false	true
true	false

FIGURE 5.3   Truth table describing the logical NOT operator

a	b	a && b	a || b
false	false	false	false
false	true	false	true
true	false	false	true
true	true	true	true

FIGURE 5.4   Truth table describing the logical AND and OR operators

done	count > MAX	!done	!done && (count > MAX)
false	false	true	false
false	true	true	true
true	false	false	false
true	true	false	false

FIGURE 5.5   A truth table for a specific condition

different reasons. If the left operand of the `&&` operator is false, then the result of the operation will be false no matter what the value of the right operand is. Likewise, if the left operand of the `||` operator is true, then the result of the operation is true no matter what the value of the right operand is.

Sometimes you can capitalize on the fact that the operation is short-circuited. For example, the condition in the following **if** statement will not attempt to divide by zero if the left operand is false. If count has the value zero, the left side of the `&&` operation is false; therefore the whole expression is false and the right side is not evaluated.

```
if (count != 0 && total/count > MAX)
   Console.Out.WriteLine ("Testing.");
```

You should consider carefully whether or not to rely on these kinds of subtle programming language characteristics. Not all programming languages work the same way. As we have stressed before, you should always strive to make extremely clear to the reader exactly how the logic of your program works.

5.2   THE **if** STATEMENT

We've used a basic **if** statement in earlier examples in this chapter. Let's now explore it in detail.

An *if statement* consists of the reserved word **if** followed by a boolean expression, followed by a statement. The condition is enclosed in parentheses and must evaluate to true or false. If the condition is true, the statement is executed and processing continues with the next statement. If the condition is false, the statement is skipped and processing continues immediately with the next statement. Figure 5.6 shows this processing.

Consider the following example of an **if** statement:

```
if (total > amount)
   total = total + (amount + 1);
```

In this example, if the value in total is greater than the value in amount, the assignment statement is executed; otherwise the assignment statement is skipped.

Note that the assignment statement in this example is indented under the header line of the **if** statement. This communicates that the assignment statement is part of the **if** statement; it implies that the **if** statement governs whether the assignment statement will be executed. This indentation is extremely important for the human reader, although it is ignored by the compiler.

The example in Listing 5.1 reads the age of the user and then makes a decision as to whether to print a particular sentence based on the age that is entered.

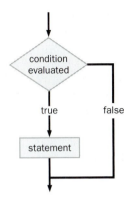

FIGURE 5.6   The logic of an **if** statement

Listing 5.1

```
//****************************************************************
//  Age.cs            C#:   Ken Culp
//
//  Demonstrates the use of an if statement.
//****************************************************************
using System;
using CS1;

namespace Age
{
  class Age
  {
    static void Main(string[] args)
    {
      //---------------------------------------------------------
      //  Reads the user's age and prints comments accordingly.
      //---------------------------------------------------------
      const int MINOR = 21;

      Console.Out.Write("Enter your age: ");
      int age = int.Parse(Console.In.ReadLine());

      Console.Out.WriteLine("You entered: " + age);

      if (age < MINOR)
        Console.Out.WriteLine(
          "Youth is a wonderful thing. Enjoy.");

      Console.Out.WriteLine("Age is a state of mind.");
      Console.In.ReadLine();  // Wait for enter key
    }
  }
}
```

Listing 5.1 continued

Output

```
Enter your age: 40
You entered: 40
Age is a state of mind.
```

The `Age` program echoes the age value that is entered in all cases. If the age is less than the value of the constant `MINOR`, the statement about youth is printed. If the age is equal to or greater than the value of `MINOR`, the `WriteLine` statement is skipped. In either case, the final sentence about age being a state of mind is printed.

Let's look at a few more examples of basic `if` statements. The following `if` statement causes the variable `size` to be set to zero if its current value is greater than or equal to the value in the constant `MAX`:

```
if (size >= MAX)
   size = 0;
```

The condition of the following `if` statement first adds three values together, then compares the result to the value stored in `numBooks`:

```
if (numBooks < stackCount + inventoryCount + duplicateCount)
   reorder = true;
```

If `numBooks` is less than the other three values combined, the boolean variable `reorder` is set to `true`. The addition operations are performed before the less than operator because the arithmetic operators have a higher precedence than the relational operators.

The following `if` statement compares the value returned from a call to `random` to the calculated result of dividing the constant `HIGH` by 5. The odds of this code picking a winner are approximately 1 in 5.

```
if (generator.Next(HIGH) < HIGH / 5)
   Console.Out.WriteLine (
   "You are a randomly selected winner!");
```

The `if-else` Statement

Sometimes we want to do one thing if a condition is true and another thing if that condition is false. We can add an *else clause* to an `if` statement, making it an *if-else statement,* to handle this kind of situation. The following is an example of an `if-else` statement:

```
if (height <= MAX)
   adjustment = 0;
else
   adjustment = MAX - height;
```

---

if STATEMENT

An **if** statement tests the boolean Expression and, if true, executes the first Statement. The optional **else** clause identifies the Statement that should be executed if the Expression is false.

Examples:

```
if (total < 7)
    Console.Out.WriteLine ("Total is less than 7.");

if (firstCh != 'a')
    count++;
else
    count = count / 2;
```

If the condition is true, the first assignment statement is executed; if the condition is false, the second assignment statement is executed. Only one or the other will be executed, because a boolean condition evaluates to either true or false. Note that proper indentation is used again to communicate that the statements are part of the governing **if** statement.

The Wages program shown in Listing 5.2 uses an **if-else** statement to compute the proper payment amount for an employee.

In the Wages program, if an employee works over 40 hours in a week, the payment amount takes into account the overtime hours. An **if-else** statement is used to determine whether the number of hours entered by the user is greater than 40. If it is, the extra hours are paid at a rate one and a half times the normal rate. If there are no overtime hours, the total payment is based simply on the number of hours worked and the standard rate.

> **Key Concept**
>
> An **if-else** statement allows a program to do one thing if a condition is true and another thing if the condition is false.

Listing 5.2

```
//************************************************************
//  Wages.cs          C#:  Ken Culp
//
//  Demonstrates the use of C# I/O classes for keyboard input.
//************************************************************
using System;

namespace Wages
{
```

Listing 5.2 continued

```
class Wages
{
    static void Main(string[] args)
    {
        const double RATE = 8.25d;
        const int STANDARD = 40;

        System.IO.TextReader kbd = Console.In;   // Shortcuts
        System.IO.TextWriter con = Console.Out;
        double pay = 0.0d;

        con.Write("Enter the number of hours worked: ");
        int hours = int.Parse(kbd.ReadLine());

        con.WriteLine();

        // Pay overtime at "time and a half"
        if (hours > STANDARD)
            pay = STANDARD * RATE + (hours - STANDARD) * (RATE * 1.5);
        else
            pay = hours * RATE;

        con.WriteLine("Gross earnings: " + pay.ToString("C"));
        kbd.ReadLine();   // Wait for enter key
    }
}
```

Output

```
Enter the number of hours worked: 46
Gross earnings: $404.25
```

Let's look at another example of an **if-else** statement:

```
if (roster.GetSize() == FULL)
    roster.Expand();
else
    roster.AddName (name);
```

This example makes use of an object called roster. Even without knowing what roster represents, or from what class it was created, we can see that it has at least three methods: GetSize, Expand, and AddName. The condition of the **if** statement calls GetSize and compares the result to the constant FULL. If the condition is true, the Expand method is invoked (apparently to expand the size of the roster). If the roster is not yet full, the variable name is passed as a parameter to the AddName method.

The program in Listing 5.3 instantiates a Coin object, flips the coin by calling the Flip method, then uses an **if-else** statement to determine which of two sentences gets printed based on the result.

The Coin class is shown in Listing 5.4. It stores two integer constants (HEADS and TAILS) that represent the two possible states of the coin, and an instance variable called face that represents the current state of the coin. The Coin constructor initially flips the coin by calling the Flip method, which determines the new state of the coin by randomly choosing a number (either 0 or 1). The IsHeads method returns a boolean value based on the current face value of the coin. The ToString method uses an **if-else** statement to determine which character string to return to describe the coin. The ToString method is automatically called when the myCoin object is passed to Println in the Main method.

We use the Coin class again in later examples in this chapter.

Listing 5.3

```
//****************************************************************
//  CountFlip.cs        C#:   Ken Culp
//
//  Demonstrates the use of an if-else statement.
//****************************************************************
using System;

namespace CoinFlip
{
  class CoinFlip
  {
    //-----------------------------------------------------------
    //  Flips a coin multiple times counting the number of heads
    //  and tails that result.
    //-----------------------------------------------------------
    static void Main(string[] args)
    {
      Coin myCoin = new Coin();  // instantiate the Coin object

      Console.Out.WriteLine(myCoin);
      if (myCoin.isHeads())
        Console.Out.WriteLine("You win.");
      else
        Console.Out.WriteLine("Better luck next time.");

      Console.In.ReadLine();  // Wait for enter key
    }
  }
}
```

Listing 5.3 continued

Output

```
Tails

Better luck next time.
```

Listing 5.4

```csharp
//****************************************************************
//  Coin.cs         C#:  Ken Culp
//
//  Represents a coin with two sides that can be flipped.
//****************************************************************
using System;

namespace CoinLib
{
  public class Coin
  {
    //------------------------------------------------------------
    //  Sets up the coin by flipping it initially.
    //------------------------------------------------------------
    public const int HEADS = 0;
    public const int TAILS = 1;
    private int face;
    private Random generator;

    public Coin()
    {
      generator = new Random(DateTime.Now.Millisecond);
      flip();
    }
    //------------------------------------------------------------
    //  Flips the coin by randomly choosing a face value.
    //------------------------------------------------------------
    public void flip()
    {
      face = generator.Next(2);
    }


    //------------------------------------------------------------
    //  Returns true if the current face of the coin is heads.
    //------------------------------------------------------------
    public bool isHeads()
    {
      return (face == HEADS);
    }
```

Listing 5.4   continued

```
//-------------------------------------------------------------
//  Returns the current face of the coin as a string.
//-------------------------------------------------------------
public override string ToString()
{
  String faceName;

  if (face == HEADS)
    faceName = "Heads";
  else
    faceName = "Tails";

  return faceName;
  }
 }
}
```

Using Block Statements

We may want to do more than one thing as the result of evaluating a boolean condition. In C#, we can replace any single statement with a *block statement*. A block statement is a collection of statements enclosed in braces. We've used these braces many times in previous examples to delimit method and class definitions.

The program called Guessing, shown in Listing 5.5, uses an **if-else** statement in which the statement of the **else** clause is a block statement.

If the guess entered by the user equals the randomly chosen answer, an appropriate acknowledgement is printed. However, if the answer is incorrect, two statements are printed, one that states that the guess is wrong and one that prints the actual answer. A programming project at the end of this chapter expands the concept of this example into the Hi-Lo game.

Note that if the block braces were not used, the sentence stating that the answer is incorrect would be printed if the answer was wrong, but the sentence revealing the correct answer would be printed in all cases. That is, only the first statement would be considered part of the **else** clause.

Remember that indentation means nothing except to the human reader. Statements that are not blocked properly can lead to the programmer making improper assumptions about how the code will execute. For example, the following code is misleading:

```
if (depth > 36.238)
  delta = 100;
else
  Console.Out.WriteLine (
    "WARNING: Delta is being reset to ZERO");
  delta = 0;  // not part of the else clause!
```

The indentation (not to mention the logic of the code) implies that the variable `delta` is reset only when `depth` is less than `36.238`. However, without using a block, the assignment statement that resets `delta` to zero is not governed by the **if-else** statement at all. It is executed in either case, which is clearly not what is intended.

Listing 5.5

```csharp
//************************************************************
//  Guessing.cs          C#:  Ken Culp
//
//  Demonstrates the use of a a block statement in if-else.
//************************************************************
using System;

namespace Guessing
{
  class Guessing
  {
    [STAThread]
    static void Main(string[] args)
    {
      const int MAX = 10;
      int answer, guess;

      System.IO.TextReader kbd = Console.In;    // Shortcuts
      System.IO.TextWriter con = Console.Out;

      Random generator = new Random(DateTime.Now.Millisecond);

      answer = generator.Next(MAX);

      con.Write("I'm thinking of a number between 1 and "
        + MAX.ToString() + ".  Guess what it is: ");
      guess = int.Parse(kbd.ReadLine());

      if (guess == answer)
        con.WriteLine("You got it! Good guessing!");
      else
      {
        con.WriteLine("That is not correct, sorry.");
        con.WriteLine("The number was " + answer.ToString());
      }

      kbd.ReadLine();   // Wait for enter key
    }
  }
}
```

Listing 5.5   continued

Output

```
I'm thinking of a number between 1 and 10. Guess what it is: 7
That is not correct, sorry.
The number was 5
```

A block statement can be used anywhere a single statement is called for in C# syntax. For example, the **if** portion of an **if-else** statement could be a block, or the **else** portion could be a block (as we saw in the Guessing program), or both parts could be block statements. For example:

```
if (boxes != warehouse.getCount())
{
  Console.Out.WriteLine (
    "Inventory and warehouse do NOT match.");
  Console.Out.WriteLine (
    "Beginning inventory process again!");
  boxes = 0;
}
else
{
  Console.Out.WriteLine ("Inventory and warehouse MATCH.");
  warehouse.Ship();
}
```

In this **if-else** statement, the value of boxes is compared to a value obtained by calling the getCount method of the warehouse object (whatever that is). If they do not match exactly, two println statements and an assignment statement are executed. If they do match, a different message is printed and the ship method of warehouse is invoked.

The Conditional Operator

The C# *conditional operator* is similar to an **if-else** statement in some ways. It is a *ternary operator* because it requires three operands. The symbol for the conditional operator is usually written ?:, but it is not like other operators in that the two symbols that make it up are always separated. The following is an example of an expression that contains the conditional operator:

```
(total > MAX) ? total + 1 : total * 2;
```

Preceding the ? is a boolean condition. Following the ? are two expressions separated by the : symbol. The entire conditional expression returns the value of the first expression if the condition is true, and returns the value of the second expression if the condition is false.

Keep in mind that this is an expression that returns a value, and usually we want to do something with that value, such as assign it to a variable:

```
total = (total > MAX) ? total + 1 : total * 2;
```

In many ways, the ?: operator serves like an abbreviated **if-else** statement. The previous statement is functionally equivalent to, but sometimes more convenient than, the following:

```
if (total > MAX)
  total = total + 1;
else
  total = total * 2;
```

Now consider the following declaration:

```
int larger = (num1 > num2) ? num1 : num2;
```

If num1 is greater than num2, the value of num1 is returned and used to initialize the variable larger. If num1 is not greater than num2, the value of num2 is returned and used to initialize larger. Similarly, the following statement prints the smaller of the two values:

```
Console.Out.WriteLine (
  "Smaller: " + ((num1 < num2) ? num1 : num2));
```

The conditional operator is occasionally helpful to evaluate a short condition and return a result. It is not a replacement for an **if-else** statement, however, because the operands to the ?: operator are expressions, not necessarily full statements. Even when the conditional operator is a viable alternative, you should use it sparingly because it is often less readable than an **if-else** statement.

Nested **if** Statements

The statement executed as the result of an **if** statement could be another **if** statement. This situation is called a *nested if.* It allows us to make another decision after determining the results of a previous decision. The program in Listing 5.6, called MinOfThree, uses nested **if** statements to determine the smallest of three integer values entered by the user.

Carefully trace the logic of the MinOfThree program, using various input sets with the minimum value in all three positions, to see how it determines the lowest value. You may wish to experiment with debugging here and just single step the application using the Debug/Step Into button (or F11 key) and watch the flow of the code.

Listing 5.6

```csharp
//***************************************************************
//  MinOfThree.cs           C#:   Ken Culp
//
//  Demonstrates the use of a a block statement in if-else.
//***************************************************************
using System;

namespace MinOfThree
{
  class MinOfThree
  {
    static void Main(string[] args)
    {
      int num1, num2, num3, min = 0;

      System.IO.TextReader kbd = Console.In;          // Shortcuts
      System.IO.TextWriter con = Console.Out;

      con.WriteLine(
        "Enter 3 integers, each followed by the enter key:");

      num1 = int.Parse(kbd.ReadLine());
      num2 = int.Parse(kbd.ReadLine());
      num3 = int.Parse(kbd.ReadLine());

      if (num1 < num2)
        if (num1 < num3)
          min = num1;
        else
          min = num3;
      else
        if (num2 < num3)
          min = num2;
        else
          min = num3;

      con.WriteLine("Minimum value: " + min);

      kbd.ReadLine();   // Wait for enter key
    }
  }
}
```

Listing 5.6 continued

Output

```
Enter three integers:
45
22
69
Minimum value: 22
```

An important situation arises with nested **if** statements. It may seem that an **else** clause after a nested **if** could apply to either **if** statement. For example:

```
if (code == 'R')
  if (height <= 20)
    Console.Out.WriteLine ("Situation Normal");
  else
    Console.Out.WriteLine ("Bravo!");
```

Is the **else** clause matched to the inner **if** statement or the outer **if** statement? The indentation in this example implies that it is part of the inner **if** statement, and that is correct. An **else** clause is always matched to the closest unmatched **if** that preceded it. However, if we're not careful, we can easily mismatch it in our mind and misalign the indentation. This is another reason why accurate, consistent indentation is crucial.

> **Key Concept**
>
> In a nested **if** statement, an **else** clause is matched to the closest unmatched **if**.

Braces can be used to specify the **if** statement to which an **else** clause belongs. For example, if the previous example should have been structured so that the string "Bravo!" is printed if code is not equal to 'R', we could force that relationship (and properly indent) as follows:

```
if (code == 'R')
{
  if (height <= 20)
    Console.Out.WriteLine ("Situation Normal");
}
else
  Console.Out.WriteLine ("Bravo!");
```

By using the block statement in the first **if** statement, we establish that the **else** clause belongs to it.

5.3   COMPARING DATA

When comparing data using boolean expressions, it's important to understand some nuances that arise depending on the type of data being examined. Let's look at a few key situations.

Comparing Floats

An interesting situation occurs when comparing floating point data. Two floating point values are equal, according to the == operator, only if all the binary digits of their underlying representations match. If the compared values are the results of computation, it may be unlikely that they are exactly equal even if they are close enough for the specific situation. Therefore, you should rarely use the equality operator (==) when comparing floating point values.

A better way to check for floating point equality is to compute the absolute value of the difference between the two values and compare the result to some tolerance level. For example, we may choose a tolerance level of 0.00001. If the two floating point values are so close that their difference is less than the tolerance, then we are willing to consider them equal. Comparing two floating point values, f1 and f2, could be accomplished as follows:

```
if (Math.Abs(f1 - f2) < TOLERANCE)
   Console.Out.WriteLine ("Essentially equal.");
```

The value of the constant TOLERANCE should be appropriate for the situation.

Comparing Characters

We know what it means when we say that one number is less than another number, but what does it mean to say one character is less than another character? As we discussed in Chapter 2, characters in C# are based on the Unicode character set, which defines an ordering of all possible characters that can be used. Because the character 'a' comes before the character 'b' in the character set, we can say that 'a' is less than 'b'.

We can use the equality and relational operators on character data. For example, if two character variables ch1 and ch2 hold two characters, we might determine their relative ordering in the Unicode character set with an **if** statement as follows:

```
if (ch1 > ch2)
   Con.WriteLine (ch1 + " is greater than " + ch2);
else
   Con.WriteLine (ch1 + " is NOT greater than " + ch2);
```

The Unicode character set is structured so that all lowercase alphabetic characters ('a' through 'z') are contiguous and in alphabetical order. The same is true of uppercase alphabetic characters ('A' through 'Z') and characters that represent digits ('0' through '9'). The digits precede the uppercase alphabetic

> **Key Concept**
>
> The relative order of characters in C# is defined by the Unicode character set.

characters, which precede the lowercase alphabetic characters. Before, after, and in between these groups are other characters. See the chart in Appendix B for details.

Comparing Objects

The Unicode relationships among characters make it easy to sort characters and strings of characters. If you have a list of names, for instance, you can put them in alphabetical order based on the inherent relationships among characters in the character set.

In object-oriented languages such as C#, the equality relational operator does not normally compare the contents of the object but rather compares whether the two different names indeed point to the same object. That is, the equality operator is true *only* when the names are aliases of each other. It is possible in C# to create your own code for the equality operator (called operator overloads, which are described in Chapter 6). This is particularly true when you create your own objects.

However, some objects in C# are content comparisons just as they are for the primitive types like **int** and **float**. Using the equality and comparison operators with these primitive objects is indeed a value compare, as we have been showing up to this point. If you are familiar with some other object-oriented languages such as Java, you will find that C# takes a different path when it comes to strings. In Java, comparing two objects of type String is *not* a value compare but rather an alias check. In C#, comparing two object of type **string** *is* a value compare. Note the following code:

```
string x = "1234";
string y = "1234";
if (x == y)
  con.WriteLine("Same");
else
  con.WriteLine("Different");
```

> ### Key Concept
>
> The equality operator or the CompareTo method can be used to determine the relative order of strings.

This code would result in the word "Same" being printed. Although two separate objects have been created, they have the same contents, so the comparison says they are the same.

For compatibility (similarity) to Java and other languages, C# also supports a CompareTo method that can be used to compare the contents of two string variables.

Keep in mind that comparing characters and strings is based on the Unicode character set (see Appendix B). This is called a *lexicographic ordering*. If all alphabetic characters are in the same case (upper or lower), the lexicographic ordering will be alphabetic ordering as well. However, when comparing two strings, such as `"able"` and `"Baker"`, the comparison operators or the CompareTo method will conclude that `"Baker"` comes first, because all of the uppercase letters come before all of the lowercase letters in the Unicode character set. A string that is the prefix of another, longer string is considered to precede the longer string. For example, when comparing two strings such as `"horse"` and `"horsefly"`, the CompareTo method will conclude that `"horse"` comes first.

5.4   **THE switch STATEMENT**

Another conditional statement in C# is called the *switch statement,* which causes the executing program to follow one of several paths based on a single value. The *break statement* is also discussed in this section because it is usually used with a **switch** statement.

The **switch** statement evaluates an expression to determine a value and then matches that value with one of several possible *cases.* Each case has statements associated with it. After evaluating the expression, control jumps to the statement associated with the first case that matches the value. Consider the following example:

```
switch (idChar)
{
  case 'A':
    aCount = aCount + 1;
    break;
  case 'B':
    bCount = bCount + 1;
    break;
  case 'C':
    cCount = cCount + 1;
    break;
  default:
    Console.Out.WriteLine (
      "Error in Identification Character.");
}
```

First, the expression is evaluated. In this example, the expression is a simple **char** variable. Execution then transfers to the first statement identified by the case value that matches the result of the expression. Therefore, if idChar contains an 'A', the variable aCount is incremented. If it contains a 'B', the case for 'A' is skipped and processing continues where bCount is incremented.

If no case value matches that of the expression, execution continues with the optional *default case,* indicated by the reserved word **default**. If no default case exists, no statements in the **switch** statement are executed and processing continues with the statement after the **switch** statement. It is often a good idea to include a default case, even if you don't expect it to be executed.

When a **break** statement is encountered, processing jumps to the statement following the **switch** statement. A **break** statement is usually used to break out of each case of a **switch** statement. Without a **break** statement, processing continues into the next case of the **switch**. Therefore, if the **break** statement at the end of the 'A' case in the previous example were not there, both the aCount and bCount variables would be incremented when the idChar contains an 'A'. Usually we want to perform only one case, so a **break** statement is almost always used. Occasionally, though, the "pass through" feature comes in handy.

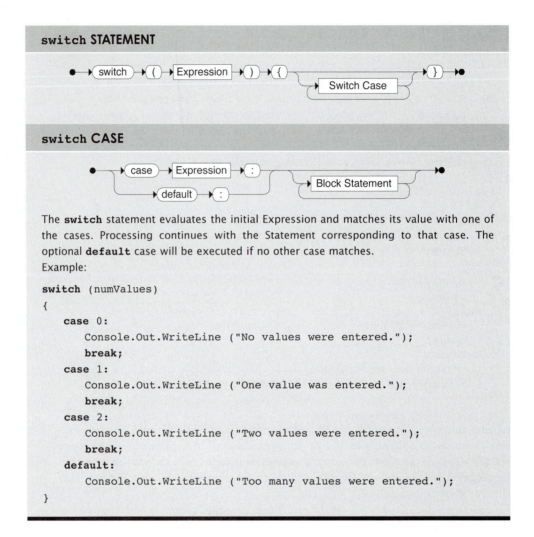

switch STATEMENT

switch CASE

The **switch** statement evaluates the initial Expression and matches its value with one of the cases. Processing continues with the Statement corresponding to that case. The optional **default** case will be executed if no other case matches.
Example:

```
switch (numValues)
{
    case 0:
        Console.Out.WriteLine ("No values were entered.");
        break;
    case 1:
        Console.Out.WriteLine ("One value was entered.");
        break;
    case 2:
        Console.Out.WriteLine ("Two values were entered.");
        break;
    default:
        Console.Out.WriteLine ("Too many values were entered.");
}
```

The expression evaluated at the beginning of a **switch** statement must be an *integral type,* meaning that it is either an **int** or a **char**, or an enumerated type. It cannot evaluate to a **boolean** or floating point value, and even other integer types (**byte**, **short**, and **long**) cannot be used. Furthermore, each case value must be a constant; it cannot be a variable or other expression.

> **Key Concept**
>
> A **break** statement is usually used at the end of each case alternative of a **switch** statement.

Note that the implicit boolean condition of a **switch** statement is based on equality. The expression at the beginning of the statement is compared to each case value to determine which one it equals. A **switch** statement cannot be used to determine other relational operations (such as less than), unless some preliminary processing is done. For example, the GradeReport program in Listing 5.7 prints a comment based on a numeric grade that is entered by the user.

Listing 5.7

```
//*****************************************************************
//  GradeReport.cs            C#:  Ken Culp
//
//  Demonstrates the use of a switch statement.
//*****************************************************************
using System;

namespace GradeReport
{
  class GradeReport
  {
    //------------------------------------------------------------
    //  Reads grade from the user printing appropriate comments.
    //------------------------------------------------------------
    static void Main(string[] args)
    {
      int grade, category;

      System.IO.TextReader kbd = Console.In;          // Shortcuts
      System.IO.TextWriter con = Console.Out;

      con.Write("Enter a numeric grade (0 to 100): ");
      grade = int.Parse(kbd.ReadLine());

      category = grade / 10;
      con.Write("That grade is ");

      switch (category)
      {
        case 10:
          con.WriteLine("a perfect score. Well done.");
          break;
        case 9:
          con.WriteLine("well above average. Excellent.");
          break;
        case 8:
          con.WriteLine("above average. Nice job.");
          break;
        case 7:
          con.WriteLine("average.");
          break;
        case 6:
          con.WriteLine("below average. You should see the");
```

Listing 5.7 continued

```
            con.WriteLine("instructor to clarify the material "
                                    + "presented in class.");
          break;
          default:
            con.WriteLine("not passing.");
            break;
        }
        Console.In.ReadLine();  // Wait for enter key
      }
    }
  }
```

Output

```
Enter a numeric grade (0 to 100): 86
That grade is above average. Nice job.
```

In `GradeReport`, the category of the grade is determined by dividing the grade by 10 using integer division, resulting in an integer value between 0 and 10 (assuming a valid grade is entered). This result is used as the expression of the **switch**, which prints various messages for grades 60 or higher and a default sentence for all other values.

Note that any **switch** statement could be implemented as a set of nested **if** statements. However, nested **if** statements quickly become difficult for a human reader to understand and are error prone to implement and debug. But because a **switch** can evaluate only equality, sometimes nested **if** statements are necessary. It depends on the situation.

5.5 THE while STATEMENT

As we discussed in the introduction of this chapter, a repetition statement (or loop) allows us to execute another statement multiple times. A *while statement* is a loop that evaluates a boolean condition just like an **if** statement does and executes a statement (called the *body* of the loop) if the condition is true. However, unlike the **if** statement, after the body is executed, the condition is evaluated again. If it is still true, the body is executed again. This repetition continues until the condition becomes false; then processing continues with the statement after the body of the **while** loop. Figure 5.7 shows this processing.

The following loop prints the values from 1 to 5. Each iteration through the loop prints one value, then increments the counter.

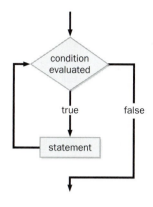

FIGURE 5.7   The logic of a **while** loop

```
while (count <= 5)
{
   Console.Out.WriteLine (count);
   count++;
}
```

Note that the body of the **while** loop is a block containing two statements. The entire block is repeated on each iteration of the loop.

Let's look at another program that uses a **while** loop. The Average program shown in Listing 5.8 reads a series of integer values from the user, sums them up, and computes their average.

---

while STATEMENT

●───▶(while)───▶(( )───▶| Expression |───▶( ))───▶| Statement |───▶●

The **while** loop repeatedly executes the specified Statement as long as the boolean Expression is true. The Expression is evaluated first; therefore, the Statement might not be executed at all. The Expression is evaluated again after each execution of the Statement until the Expression becomes false.

Example:

```
while (total > max)
{
    total = total / 2;
    Console.Out.WriteLine ("Current total: " + total);
}
```

We don't know how many values the user may enter, so we need to have a way to indicate that the user is done entering numbers. In this program, we designate zero to be a *sentinel value* that indicates the end of the input. The **while** loop continues to process input values until the user enters zero. This assumes that zero is not one of the valid numbers that should contribute to the average. A sentinel value must always be outside the normal range of values entered.

Listing 5.8

```
//***********************************************************
//  Average.cs          C#:   Ken Culp
//
//  Demonstrates the use of a while loop, a sentinel value, and
//  a running sum.
//***********************************************************
using System;

namespace Average
{
  class Average
  //-----------------------------------------------------------
  //  Computes the average of the values entered by the user.
  //  The running sum is printed as the numbers are entered.
  //-----------------------------------------------------------
  {
    static void Main(string[] args)
    {
      int sum = 0, num, count = 0;
      double average;

      System.IO.TextReader kbd = Console.In;   // Shortcuts
      System.IO.TextWriter con = Console.Out;

      con.Write("Enter an integer (0 to quit): ");
      num = int.Parse(kbd.ReadLine());

      while (num != 0)  // sentinel num of 0 to terminate loop
      {
        count++;
        sum += num;
        con.WriteLine("The sum so far is " + sum);
        con.Write("Enter an integer (0 to quit): ");
        num = int.Parse(kbd.ReadLine());
      }
      con.WriteLine();
      con.WriteLine("Number of values entered: " + count);

      average = (double)sum / count;
```

Listing 5.8   continued

```
      con.WriteLine("The average is {0:0.000}", average);

      kbd.ReadLine();   // Wait for enter key
    }
  }
}
```

Output

```
Enter an integer (0 to quit): 25
The sum so far is 25
Enter an integer (0 to quit): 164
The sum so far is 189
Enter an integer (0 to quit): -14
The sum so far is 175
Enter an integer (0 to quit): 84
The sum so far is 259
Enter an integer (0 to quit): 12
The sum so far is 271
Enter an integer (0 to quit): -35
The sum so far is 236
Enter an integer (0 to quit): 0

The average is 39.333
```

In the Average program, a variable called sum is used to maintain a *running sum,* which means it is the sum of the values entered thus far. The variable sum is initialized to zero, and each value read is added to and stored back into sum.

We also have to count the number of values that are entered so that after the loop concludes we can divide by the appropriate value to compute the average. Note that the sentinel value is not counted. Consider the unusual situation in which the user immediately enters the sentinel value before entering any valid values. The **if** statement at the end of the program avoids a divide-by-zero error.

Let's examine yet another program that uses a **while** loop. The WinPercentage program shown in Listing 5.9 computes the winning percentage of a sports team based on the number of games won.

Listing 5.9

```
//***************************************************************
//  WinPercentage.cs          C#:  Ken Culp
//
//  Demonstrates the use of a while loop for input validation.
//***************************************************************
```

Listing 5.9   continued

```csharp
using System;

namespace WinPercentage
{
  class WinPercentage
  {
    //-------------------------------------------------------------
    //  Computes the percentage of games won by a team.
    //-------------------------------------------------------------
    static void Main(string[] args)
    {
      const int NUM_GAMES = 12;
      int won;
      double ratio;

      System.IO.TextReader kbd = Console.In;                 // Shortcuts
      System.IO.TextWriter con = Console.Out;

      con.Write("Enter the number of games won (0 to "
                        + NUM_GAMES + "): ");
      won = int.Parse(kbd.ReadLine());

      while (won < 0 || won > NUM_GAMES)
      {
        con.Write("Invalid input. Please reenter: ");
        won = int.Parse(kbd.ReadLine());
      }

      ratio = (double)won / NUM_GAMES;

      con.WriteLine();
      con.WriteLine("Winning percentage: {0:N}%", ratio * 100);

      kbd.ReadLine();  // Wait for enter key
    }
  }
}
```

Output

```
Enter the number of games won (0 to 12): -5
Invalid input. Please reenter: 13
Invalid input. Please reenter: 7

Winning percentage: 58%
```

We use a **while** loop in the WinPercentage program to *validate the input,* meaning we guarantee that the user enters a value that we consider to be valid. In this example, that means that the number of games won must be greater than or equal to zero and less than or equal to the total number of games played. The **while** loop continues to execute, repeatedly prompting the user for valid input, until the entered number is indeed valid.

We generally want our programs to be *robust,* which means that they handle potential problems as elegantly as possible. Validating input data and avoiding errors such as dividing by zero are situations that we should consciously address when designing a program. Loops and conditionals help us recognize and deal with such situations.

Infinite Loops

It is the programmer's responsibility to ensure that the condition of a loop will eventually become false. If it doesn't, the loop body will execute forever, or at least until the program is interrupted. This situation, referred to as an *infinite loop,* is a common mistake.

The following is an example of an infinite loop:

```
int count = 1;
while (count <= 25)   // Warning: this is an infinite loop!
{
   Console.Out.WriteLine (count);
   count = count - 1;
}
```

If you execute this loop, you should be prepared to interrupt it. To stop a program that is caught in a loop, click the square blue box in Visual Studio or select Debut/Stop Debugging from the menu. This will work any time you started the program with the F5 or F11 key.

> **Key Concept**
>
> We must design our programs carefully to avoid infinite loops.

In this example, the initial value of count is 1 and it is decremented in the loop body. The **while** loop will continue as long as count is less than or equal to 25. Because count gets smaller with each iteration, the condition will always be true, or at least until the value of count gets so small that an underflow error occurs. The point is that the logic of the code is clearly wrong.

Let's look at some other examples of infinite loops:

```
int count = 1;
while (count != 50)
   count += 2;
```

In this code fragment, the variable count is initialized to 1 and is moving in a positive direction. However, note that it is being incremented by 2 each time. This loop will never terminate because count will never equal 50. It begins at 1 and then changes to 3, then 5, and so on. Eventually it reaches 49, then changes to 51, then 53, and continues forever.

Now consider the following situation:

```
double num = 1.0;
while (num != 0.0)
    num = num - 0.1;
```

Once again, the value of the loop control variable seems to be moving in the correct direction. And, in fact, it seems like num will eventually take on the value 0.0. However, this loop is infinite (at least on most systems) because num will never have a value *exactly* equal to 0.0. This situation is similar to one we discussed earlier in this chapter when we explored the idea of comparing floating point values in the condition of an **if** statement. Because of the way the values are represented in binary, minute computational errors occur internally, making it problematic to compare two floating point values for equality.

Nested Loops

The body of a loop can contain another loop. This situation is called a *nested loop*. Keep in mind that for each iteration of the outer loop, the inner loop executes completely. Consider the following code fragment. How many times does the string "Here again" get printed?

```
int count1, count2;
count1 = 1;
while (count1 <= 10)
{
  count2 = 1;
  while (count2 <= 50)
  {
    Console.Out.WriteLine ("Here again");
    count2++;
  }
  count1++;
}
```

The WriteLine statement is inside the inner loop. The outer loop executes 10 times, as count1 iterates between 1 and 10. The inner loop executes 50 times, as count2 iterates between 1 and 50. For each iteration of the outer loop, the inner loop executes completely. Therefore, the WriteLine statement is executed 500 times.

As with any loop situation, we must be careful to scrutinize the conditions of the loops and the initializations of variables. Let's consider some small changes to this code. What if the condition of the outer loop were (count1 < 10) instead of (count1 <= 10)? How would that change the total number of lines printed? Well, the outer loop would execute 9 times instead of 10, so the WriteLine statement would be executed 450 times. What if the outer loop were left as it was originally defined, but count2 were initialized to 10 instead of 1 before the inner loop? The inner loop would then execute 40 times instead of 50, so the total number of lines printed would be 400.

Let's look at another example that uses a nested loop. A *palindrome* is a string of characters that reads the same forward or backward. For example, the following strings are palindromes:

> radar

> drab bard

> ab cde xxxx edc ba

> kayak

> deified

> able was I ere I saw elba

Note that some palindromes have an even number of characters, whereas others have an odd number of characters. The `PalindromeTester` program shown in Listing 5.10 tests to see whether a string is a palindrome. The user may test as many strings as desired.

Listing 5.10

```
//************************************************************
//  PalindromeTester.cs        C#:  Ken Culp
//
//  Demonstrates the use of nested while loops.
//************************************************************
using System;

namespace PalindromeTester
{
  class PalindromeTester
  {
    //------------------------------------------------------------
    //  Tests strings to see if they are PalindromeTesters.
    //------------------------------------------------------------
    static void Main(string[] args)
    {
      String str, another = "y";
      int left, right;

      System.IO.TextReader kbd = Console.In;            // Shortcuts
      System.IO.TextWriter con = Console.Out;

      while (another.ToUpper() == "Y") // allows y or Y
      {
        con.WriteLine("Enter a potential Palindrome:");
        str = kbd.ReadLine();

        left = 0;
        right = str.Length - 1;
```

Listing 5.10   continued

```
        while (str[left] == str[right] && left < right)
        {
          left++;
          right--;
        }

        con.WriteLine();

        if (left < right)
          con.WriteLine("String is NOT a Palindrome.");
        else
          con.WriteLine("String IS a Palindrome.");

        con.WriteLine();
        con.Write("Test another PalindromeTester (y/n)? ");
        another = kbd.ReadLine();
      }
    }
  }
}
```

Output

```
Enter a potential palindrome:
radar

That string IS a palindrome.

Test another palindrome (y/n)? y
Enter a potential palindrome:
able was I ere I saw elba

That string IS a palindrome.

Test another palindrome (y/n)? y
Enter a potential palindrome:
abcddcba

That string IS a palindrome.
Test another palindrome (y/n)? y
Enter a potential palindrome:
abracadabra

That string is NOT a palindrome.

Test another palindrome (y/n)? n
```

The code for `PalindromeTester` contains two loops, one inside the other. The outer loop controls how many strings are tested, and the inner loop scans through each string, character by character, until it determines whether the string is a palindrome.

The code for `PalindromeTester` also uses the C# feature that strings can be treated as arrays of characters. We will cover arrays in Chapter 7, so just note here that the syntax `str[5]` is accessing the character in the string located five places from the left. As we have noted previously, all indexing starts with index number 0 being the leftmost character. For example, if the string `str` contains `"abcdefg"`, then `str[5]` is the letter `f` (not the letter `e`).

The variables `left` and `right` store the indices of two characters. They initially indicate the characters on either end of the string. Each iteration of the inner loop compares the two characters indicated by `left` and `right`. We fall out of the inner loop either when the characters don't match, meaning the string is not a palindrome, or when the value of `left` becomes equal to or greater than the value of `right`, which means the entire string has been tested and it is a palindrome.

Also, the following line sets the right pointer to the last character in the string:

```
right = str.Length - 1
```

To understand this, consider the example `"abcdefg"` string previously cited. It has seven characters, numbered from 0 to 6. Therefore, `Length - 1` would be 6, which is the last character.

Note that the following phrases would not be considered palindromes by the current version of the program:

> A man, a plan, a canal, Panama.

> Dennis and Edna sinned.

> Rise to vote, sir.

> Doom an evil deed, liven a mood.

> Go hang a salami; I'm a lasagna hog.

These strings fail our current criteria for a palindrome because of the spaces, punctuation marks, and changes in uppercase and lowercase. However, if these characteristics were removed or ignored, these strings would read the same forward and backward. Consider how the program could be changed to handle these situations. These modifications are included as a programming project at the end of the chapter.

Other Loop Controls

We've seen how the **break** statement can be used to break out of the cases of a **switch** statement. The **break** statement can also be placed in the body of any loop, even though this is usually inappropriate. Its effect on a loop is similar to its effect on a **switch** statement. The execution of the loop is stopped, and the statement following the loop is executed.

It is never necessary to use a **break** statement in a loop. An equivalent loop can always be written without it. Because the **break** statement causes program flow to jump from one place to another, using a **break** in a loop is not good practice. Its use is tolerated in a **switch** statement because an equivalent **switch** statement cannot be written without it. However, you can and should avoid using **break** in a loop.

A *continue statement* has a similar effect on loop processing. The **continue** statement is similar to a **break**, but the loop condition is evaluated again, and the loop body is executed again if it is still true. Like the **break** statement, the **continue** statement can always be avoided in a loop, and for the same reasons it should be.

5.6   THE do STATEMENT

The *do statement* is similar to the **while** statement except that its termination condition is at the end of the loop body. Like the **while** loop, the **do** loop executes the statement in the loop body until the condition becomes false. The condition is written at the end of the loop to indicate that it is not evaluated until the loop body is executed. Note that the body of a **do** loop is always executed at least once. Figure 5.8 shows this processing.

The following code prints the numbers from 1 to 5 using a **do** loop. Compare this code with the similar example earlier in this chapter that uses a **while** loop to accomplish the same task.

```
int count = 0;
do
{
  count++;
  Console.Out.WriteLine (count);
} while (count < 5);
```

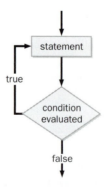

FIGURE 5.8   The logic of a **do** loop

do STATEMENT

The **do** loop repeatedly executes the specified Statement as long as the boolean Expression is true. The Statement is executed at least once, then the Expression is evaluated to determine whether the Statement should be executed again.

Example:

```
do
{
    System.out.print ("Enter a word:");
    word = Keyboard.readString();
    Console.Out.WriteLine (word);
}
while (!word.equals("quit"));
```

Note that the **do** loop begins simply with the reserved word **do**. The body of the **do** loop continues until the *while clause* that contains the boolean condition that determines whether the loop body will be executed again. Sometimes it is difficult to determine whether a line of code that begins with the reserved word **while** is the beginning of a **while** loop or the end of a **do** loop.

Let's look at another example of the **do** loop. The program called ReverseNumber, shown in Listing 5.11, reads an integer from the user and reverses its digits mathematically.

The **do** loop in the ReverseNumber program uses the remainder operation to determine the digit in the 1's position, then adds it into the reversed number, then truncates that digit from the original number using integer division. The **do** loop terminates when we run out of digits to process, which corresponds to the point when the variable number reaches the value zero. Carefully trace the logic of this program with a few examples to see how it works.

> **Key Concept**
>
> A **do** statement executes its loop body at least once.

Listing 5.11

```
//*****************************************************************
//   ReverseNumber.cs          C#:  Ken Culp
//
//   Demonstrates the use of a do/while loop.
//*****************************************************************
using System;
using CS1;

namespace ReverseNumber
{
  class ReverseNumber
```

Listing 5.11   continued

```
{
   //-------------------------------------------------------------
   //  Reverses the digits of an integer mathematically.
   //-------------------------------------------------------------
   static void Main(string[] args)
   {
      int number, lastDigit, reverse = 0;

      Console.Out.Write("Enter a positive integer: ");
      number = Keyboard.readInt();

      do
      {
         lastDigit = number % 10;
         reverse = (reverse * 10) + lastDigit;
         number = number / 10;
      }
      while (number > 0);

      Console.Out.WriteLine("That number reversed is " + reverse);
      Console.In.ReadLine();  // Wait for enter key
   }
}
}
```

Output

```
Enter a positive integer: 2896
That number reversed is 6982
```

If you know you want to perform the body of a loop at least once, then you probably want to use a **do** statement. A **do** loop has many of the same properties as a **while** statement, so it must also be checked for termination conditions to avoid infinite loops.

5.7   THE for STATEMENT

The **while** and the **do** statements are good to use when you don't initially know how many times you want to execute the loop body. The *for statement* is another repetition statement that is particularly well suited for executing the body of a loop a specific number of times that can be determined before the loop is executed.

The following code prints the numbers 1 through 5 using a **for** loop, just as we did using a **while** loop and a **do** loop in previous examples:

```
for (int count=1; count <= 5; count++)
   Console.Out.WriteLine (count);
```

The header of a **for** loop contains three parts separated by semicolons. Before the loop begins, the first part of the header, called the *initialization,* is executed. The second part of the header is the boolean condition, which is evaluated before the loop body (like the **while** loop). If true, the body of the loop is executed, followed by the execution of the third part of the header, which is called the *increment.* Note that the initialization part is executed only once, but the increment part is executed after each iteration of the loop. Figure 5.9 shows this processing.

A **for** loop can be a bit tricky to read until you get used to it. The execution of the code doesn't follow a "top to bottom, left to right" reading. The increment code executes after the body of the loop even though it is in the header.

In this example, the initialization portion of the **for** loop header is used to declare the variable count as well as to give it an initial value. We are not required to declare a variable there, but it is common practice in situations where the variable is not needed outside of the loop. Because count is declared in the **for** loop header, it exists only inside the loop body and cannot be referenced elsewhere. The loop control variable is set up, checked, and modified by the actions in the loop header. It can be referenced inside the loop body, but it should not be modified except by the actions defined in the loop header.

> **Key Concept**
>
> A **for** statement is usually used when a loop will be executed a set number of times.

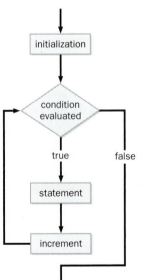

FIGURE 5.9   The logic of a for loop

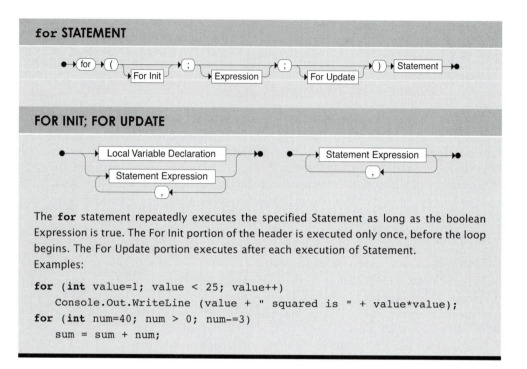

The **for** statement repeatedly executes the specified Statement as long as the boolean Expression is true. The For Init portion of the header is executed only once, before the loop begins. The For Update portion executes after each execution of Statement.
Examples:

```
for (int value=1; value < 25; value++)
    Console.Out.WriteLine (value + " squared is " + value*value);
for (int num=40; num > 0; num-=3)
    sum = sum + num;
```

The increment portion of the **for** loop header, despite its name, could decrement a value rather than increment it. For example, the following loop prints the integer values from 100 down to 1:

```
for (int num = 100; num > 0; num--)
    Console.Out.WriteLine (num);
```

In fact, the increment portion of the **for** loop can perform any calculation, not just a simple increment or decrement. Consider the program shown in Listing 5.12, which prints multiples of a particular value up to a particular limit.

The increment portion of the **for** loop in the Multiples program adds the value entered by the user after each iteration. The number of values printed per line is controlled by counting the values printed and then moving to the next line whenever count is evenly divisible by the PER_LINE constant.

The Stars program in Listing 5.13 shows the use of nested **for** loops. The output is a triangle shape made of asterisk characters. The outer loop executes exactly 10 times. Each iteration of the outer loop prints one line of the output. The inner loop performs a different number of iterations depending on the line value controlled by the outer loop. Each iteration of the inner loop prints one star on the current line. Included in the programming projects at the end of the chapter is one in which you write programs that print variations on this triangle configuration.

Listing 5.12

```
//****************************************************************
//  Multiples.cs          C#:  Ken Culp
//
//  Demonstrates the use of a for loop.
//****************************************************************
using System;
using CS1;

namespace Multiples
{
  class Multiples
  {
    //------------------------------------------------------------
    //  Prints multiples of a user-specified number up to a user-
    //  specified limit.
    //------------------------------------------------------------
    static void Main(string[] args)
    {
      const int PER_LINE = 5;
      int num, limit, mult, count = 0;
      System.IO.TextReader kbd = Console.In;  // Shortcuts
      System.IO.TextWriter con = Console.Out;

      con.Write("Enter a positive value: ");
      num = Keyboard.readInt();

      con.Write("Enter an upper limit: ");
      limit = int.Parse(kbd.ReadLine());

      con.WriteLine();
      con.WriteLine("The multiples of " + num + " between " +
        num + " and " + limit + " (inclusive) are:");

      for (mult = num; mult <= limit; mult += num)
      {
        con.Write(mult + "\t");

        // Print a specific number of values per line of output
        count++;
        if (count % PER_LINE == 0)
          con.WriteLine();
      }
      Console.In.ReadLine();  // Wait for enter key
    }
  }
}
```

Listing 5.12 continued

Output

```
Enter a positive value: 7

Enter an upper limit: 400

The multiples of 7 between 7 and 400 (inclusive) are:
7          14         21         28         35
42         49         56         63         70
77         84         91         98         105
112        119        126        133        140
147        154        161        168        175
182        189        196        203        210
217        224        231        238        245
252        259        266        273        280
287        294        301        308        315
322        329        336        343        350
357        364        371        378        385
392        399
```

Listing 5.13

```
//***************************************************************
//  Stars.cs        C#:  Ken Culp
//
//  Demonstrates the use nested for loops.
//***************************************************************
using System;

namespace Stars
{
  class Stars
  {
    static void Main(string[] args)
    {
      System.IO.TextWriter con = Console.Out; // Shortcut

      const int MAX_ROWS = 10;

      for (int row = 1; row <= MAX_ROWS; row++)
      {
        for (int star = 1; star <= row; star++)
          con.Write("*");
        con.WriteLine();
      }
      Console.In.ReadLine();  // Wait for enter key
    }
  }
}
```

Listing 5.13   continued

Output

```
*
**
***
****
*****
******
*******
********
*********
**********
```

5.8 THE foreach STATEMENT AND AN INTRODUCTION TO ARRAYS

C# includes a very handy tool for processing all the members of a group of items without specifically having to specify the index values as in a **for** loop. This **foreach** syntax is most handy when working with arrays and collections. Although much of Chapter 7 is devoted to discussing arrays and collections, some of the example programs used in this chapter and in Chapter 6 work with arrays, so we need to take a cursory look at arrays now.

As we noted previously, we can look at individual letters of a string by simply specifying the offset of the desired letter as measured from the left edge of the string. Again, this off-set starts with zero. Thus, if the string str contains "abcdefg", then str[5] is the letter f (not the letter e), as previously noted.

This same concept of indexing into a string to examine individual letters can be applied to other types of data. Not only can we have a collection of letters described as a string, but also we can have a collection of other things like integers or floats. We call these collections *arrays*.

The best way to conceptualize an array is to consider a post office with a group of letter boxes. An address will get you to the post office but you need a box number to get your mail. The box number corresponds to the offset into the collection, the array. Thus, our pre-liminary definition of an array is a group of related items that can be located by using some address (an object instance or a variable name) and an offset, which we will call an index.

The following code segment uses a **for** loop to write every character of a sentence to the console:

```
for(int i=0; i<sentence.Length; i++)
{
    Console.Out.WriteLine(sentence[i]);
    // i is offset into string (array)
}
```

This code uses i as the index, which will start at zero and run through Length-1, printing one character to a line. In our post office example, sentence is the address of the post office and i is the box number.

Now, let's look at how much simpler this code is when we use the **foreach** loop.

```
foreach(char c in sentence)
{
    Console.Out.WriteLine(c);
}
```

In this example, **foreach** allows us to skip any loop initialization, and we do not have to specify an index. Recall that a string is a group of letters or **char**'s. This changes the loop initialization from specifying an index and ranges on the index to merely specifying the type of item contained in the collection.

The general form of a **foreach** statement, then, is as follows:

```
foreach(typeOfItemInCollection item in collection) { ...}
```

Thus, the first word inside the parentheses is a primitive data type (**float**, **char**, **string**, **int**, etc.) or a class name. The next word is a variable name that will contain one item at a time from the collection. This variable would be used inside the loop (for example, printed as above). The next item in the syntax is the reserved word **in**. This is followed by the name of the collection (or simply a string, as noted above).

Simple File I/O

To illustrate the **foreach** statement, we will create a simple application that will process an input file and break it down into some pieces. Suppose that we have an input file called urls.inp that contains a list of URLs that we want to process in some way. The following are the first few lines of urls.inp:

```
microsoft.com
msdn.microsoft.com/vcsharp
duke.csc.villanova.edu/lewis/
www.csc.villanova.edu/academics/index.jsp
math.nmu.edu/faculty/faculty.htm
```

The program shown in Listing 5.14 reads the URLs from this file and dissects them to show the various parts of the path. It uses a StreamReader object to read the input file, splits each URL into separate segments (separated by a /), and then prints each segment.

Listing 5.14

```csharp
//*****************************************************************
//  URLDissector.cs          C#:  Ken Culp
//
//  Demonstrates simple looping to read data in a file.  Also
//  shows how to split string data into parts.
//*****************************************************************
using System;
using System.IO;

namespace URLDissector
{
  class URLDissector
  {
    [STAThread]
    static void Main(string[] args)
    {
      string url;
      StreamReader urlStream = new StreamReader("urls.txt");
      TextReader kbd = System.Console.In;   // Shortcuts
      TextWriter con = System.Console.Out;

      url = urlStream.ReadLine();
      while (url != null)
      {
        con.WriteLine("URL: " + url);

        // Print each part of the line
        string[] urlParts = url.Split('/');
        foreach (string urlPart in urlParts)
        {
          con.WriteLine("    " + urlPart);
        }
        url = urlStream.ReadLine();  // Read next line
      }
      kbd.ReadLine();  // Wait for enter key
    }
  }
}
```

There is one **while** loop to control reading a line at a time from the input file. Inside the **while** loop, the line is split into parts, each being a segment of the path. These parts are of type **string** and are substrings of the full path. Thus, we create an array of parts called urlParts using the **string** method Split. Also inside the **while** loop is a **foreach** loop that lists each segment in the line. That is, it lists each item in the urlParts array.

The variable urlPart is defined within the **foreach** loop to be of type **string** and will hold one segment of the line. This variable is written to the console.

If for some reason there is a problem finding or opening the input file, the attempt to create a File object will throw an IOException. (Processing I/O exceptions is discussed further in Chapter 10.)

The body of the outer **while** loop will be executed as long as the url string variable is not empty (**null**)-that is, as long as there is more input in the data file to process, the url string variable is not empty. Each iteration through the loop reads one line (one URL) from the input file and prints it.

The following line defines the collection of URL segments that is created:

```
string[] urlParts = url.Split('/');
```

This creates our collection (array) of items, each of which is of type **string**. We will explain the declaration of arrays in Chapter 7. For now, simply accept that this is the proper way to declare arrays. You might note the similarity between the line above and the declaration of the Main method in the code listing in that Main takes an array of strings as a parameter.

One final thing to note is where the file is opened from. The following open line uses the file name only and no path name ("urls.txt"):

```
StreamReader urlStream = new StreamReader("urls.txt");
```

Thus, the file has to be located in the same directory as where the program runs. When the program is run in debug mode, the executable file is placed in the bin\Debug directory in the application directory. You can open this file in Visual Studio by double-clicking on the file name in the project solution or you can select File/Open/File (press Ctrl+O) from the menu and drill down to the Debug directory and open the file. Real-world applications would use a fully qualified path name, which would have been stored in the registry or an application database. A fully qualified path name might look as follows:

```
string myFileName = "C:\\myDirectory\\mySubDir\\myFile";
```

The backslash is repeated because it denotes that the next character is something special (like a tab or new line). Therefore, to specify a backslash for a Windows path name, you must use the double backslash. Alternately, you can precede the entire string with the @ symbol to have C# ignore special character processing as in:

```
string myfilename = @"C:\myDirectory\mySubDir\myFile";
```

Comparing Loops

The four loop statements (**while**, **do**, **for**, and **foreach**) are functionally equivalent. Any particular loop written using one type of loop can be written using either of the other two loop types. Which type of loop we use depends on the situation.

As we mentioned earlier, the primary difference between a **while** loop and a **do** loop is when the condition is evaluated. If we know we want to execute the loop body at least once, a **do** loop is usually the better choice. The body of a **while** loop, on the other hand, might not be executed at all if the condition is initially false. Therefore, we say that the body of a **while** loop is executed zero or more times, but the body of a **do** loop is executed one or more times.

A **for** loop is like a **while** loop in that the condition is evaluated before the loop body is executed. We generally use a **for** or a **foreach** loop when the number of times we want to iterate through a loop is fixed or can be easily calculated. The **for** loop is preferred when we need to use the index variable somewhere in the loop. However, if the loop only needs to be run for each item in the array, **foreach** will work fine. In many situations, it is simply more convenient to separate the code that sets up and controls the loop iterations inside the **for** loop header from the body of the loop.

Debugging: The Watch Window

In an earlier debugging section, we described the Locals window, which lists all the variables for the currently executing method. If there are a lot of variables, this list could become rather long, making it inconvenient to find a particular variable and requiring constant scrolling. The Watch windows give us a way to select just those variables we want to watch.

Once the program is paused, you can add variables to the Watch window by right-clicking on the variable name and selecting Add Watch. In Figure 5.10, we have added the variables `left`, `right`, and `another`.

In the Watch window, you can make modifications just as you do in the Locals window. Also, of objects are added to the watch list, they can be expanded and modified just like in the Locals window. In other words, the Watch window is the same as the Locals window except you select only those variables that you want to watch.

To remove a variable from the Watch window, right-click anywhere on the line for that variable and select Delete Watch. To delete all variables, right-click in the window, choose Select All, and press the Delete button.

Debugging: The Command Window

We have noted that you can use the Watch or Locals window to view and modify variables. You can also perform these functions, and many others, in the Command window. The commands that you type into the Command window can use variable names from your program, local methods, and system library functions.

The commands are not C# commands but more closely resemble Visual Basic, so for now we will only cover a couple of simple uses for this window. To display the contents of a variable, simply type a question mark (?) followed by the variable name. To change a variable, type the variable name, an equal sign (=), and the new value, and then press Enter. Figure 5.11 shows the string `str` being changed and its new contents being printed.

Notice the banner for the Command window: Command Window–Immediate. The Command window has two modes, Immediate mode and Command mode. When

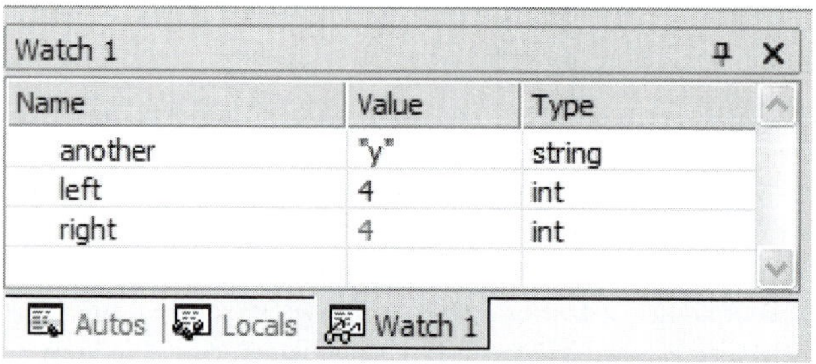

FIGURE 5.10   The Watch window

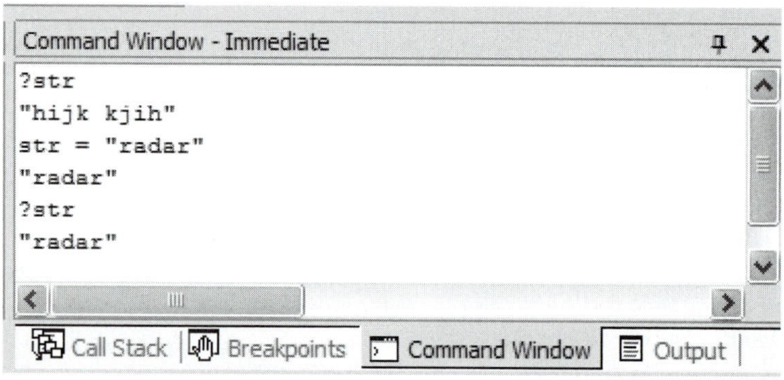

FIGURE 5.11   The Command window

the window is in Command mode, a > prompt character is displayed. In this mode, you cannot access methods off your objects nor reference local variable names. This mode is used to control the format of Visual Studio and will not be needed much in debugging. If the Command window is in Command mode with the prompt, simply type the word **immed** at the prompt to change back to Immediate mode.

If you are in Immediate mode, you can even access library functions. For example, you could write a message to the console by typing **Console.Out.WriteLine("Hello console")**. Note that a semicolon is not used at the end of the line, as would be required for C#. To change from Immediate mode to Command mode, type **>cmd**.

5.9 DRAWING WITH LOOPS AND CONDITIONALS

Conditionals and loops greatly enhance our ability to generate interesting graphics.

The `Bullseye` program shown in Listing 5.15 draws a target. The drawing actually occurs in the `Bullseye_Paint` method. The `Bullseye_Paint` method uses an `if` statement to alternate the colors between black and white.

Listing 5.15

```csharp
//********************************************************************
//  Bullseye.cs          C#:   Ken Culp
//
//  Demonstrates use of conditionals and loops to guide drawing.
//********************************************************************
using System;
using System.Collections.Generic;
using System.ComponentModel;
using System.Data;
using System.Drawing;
using System.Text;
using System.Windows.Forms;

namespace Bullseye
{
  public partial class Bullseye : Form
  {
    public Bullseye()
    {
      InitializeComponent();
    }

    private void Bullseye_Paint(object sender, PaintEventArgs e)
    {
      Graphics page = e.Graphics;
      const int MAX_WIDTH = 300, NUM_RINGS = 5, RING_WIDTH = 25;
      int x = 5, y = 5, diameter;
      Color color = Color.White;   // Color for rings
      Brush brush;
      // Brush for drawing rings
      diameter = MAX_WIDTH;          // Draw largest ring first
      this.BackColor = Color.Cyan; // Set background color

      for (int count = 0; count < NUM_RINGS; count++)
      {
        if (color == Color.Black)    // alternate colors
          color = Color.White;
        else
          color = Color.Black;

        brush = new SolidBrush(color);
        page.FillEllipse(brush, x, y, diameter, diameter);
        diameter -= (2 * RING_WIDTH);  // Move in and paint over
        x += RING_WIDTH;
        y += RING_WIDTH;
      }
      // Draw the red bullseye in the center
```

Listing 5.15   continued

```
        brush = new SolidBrush(Color.Red);
        page.FillEllipse(brush, x, y, diameter, diameter);
      }
    }
  }
```

Note that each ring is actually drawn as a filled circle (an oval of equal width and length). Because we draw the circles on top of each other, the inner circles cover the inner part of the larger circles, creating the ring effect. At the end, a final red circle is drawn for the bull's-eye.

Let's look at another example. Listing 5.16 shows the Boxes class, which draws several randomly sized rectangles in random locations. If the width of a rectangle is below a certain thickness (5 pixels), the box is filled with the color yellow. If the height is less than the same minimal thickness, the box is filled with the color green. Otherwise, the box is drawn, unfilled, in white.

Listing 5.16

```
//*************************************************************
//   Boxes.cs          C#:   Ken Culp
//
//   Demonstrates use of conditionals and loops to guide drawing.
//*************************************************************
using System;
using System.Collections.Generic;
using System.ComponentModel;
using System.Data;
using System.Drawing;
using System.Text;
using System.Windows.Forms;

namespace Boxes
{
  public partial class Boxes : Form
  {
    //-----------------------------------------------------------
    //   Paints boxes of random width/height in a random location.
    //   Narrow or short boxes are highlighted with a fill color.
    //-----------------------------------------------------------
    public Boxes()
    {
      InitializeComponent();
    }
```

Listing 5.16   continued

```
private void Form1_Paint(object sender, PaintEventArgs e)
{
    Graphics page = e.Graphics;
    const int NUM_BOXES = 50, THICKNESS = 5, MAX_SIDE = 50;
    const int MAX_X = 350, MAX_Y = 250;
    int x, y, width, height;

    this.BackColor = Color.Black;   // Form background color
    Random generator = new Random(DateTime.Now.Millisecond);

    for (int count = 0; count < NUM_BOXES; count++)
    {
        x = generator.Next(MAX_X) + 1;
        y = generator.Next(MAX_Y) + 1;
        width = generator.Next(MAX_SIDE) + 1;
        height = generator.Next(MAX_SIDE) + 1;

        if (width <= THICKNESS)   // check for narrow box
        {
            page.FillRectangle(new SolidBrush(Color.Yellow),
                x, y, width, height);
        }
        else
            if (height <= THICKNESS)   // check for short box
            {
                page.FillRectangle(new SolidBrush(Color.Green),
                    x, y, width, height);
            }
            else
            {
                page.DrawRectangle(new Pen(Color.White),
                    x, y, width, height);
            }
    }
}
```

5.10 DETERMINING EVENT SOURCES

In Chapter 4 we began our exploration of creating programs with a truly interactive graphical user interface (GUI). You'll recall that interactive GUIs require that we create event handler objects and set up the relationship between code and the components that generate the events of interest.

Let's look at an example in which one event handler is used to handle events from two different buttons. The program represented by the `LeftRight` class, shown in Listing 5.16, displays a label and two buttons. When the left button is pressed, the label displays the word Left, and when the right button is pressed, the label displays the word Right. When either button is clicked, the event handler will copy the label of the button (Left or Right) to the text box.

To create this application, start with File/New/Project, Windows Application and name it **LeftRight**. Adjust the size of the form to about what you see in the sample output and set the background color of the form to light blue or cyan.

Next, we are going to make the dark blue box for the two buttons. Add a `Panel` control to the bottom of the box and expand it to almost the edges of the form. Set the background color for the panel to dark blue.

Above the panel, add a label that is the same width as the panel and about a quarter-inch high. Clear the `Text` property and give the label the name `labChoice`. Set the `TextAlign` property to `MiddleCenter` and set the font size to 16/bold.

Draw two buttons inside the panel, making them about the size shown. Set the background color to a light gray. Name the left button `btnLeft` and set its text property (label) to `Left`. Set its font size to about 14/bold. Similarly, name the right button `btnRight` and label it `Right`. Now, inside the class toward the end, create the event handler for the click that will be used for both buttons, as shown here:

```
private void Mouse_Click(object sender, System.EventArgs e)
{
  Button btn = (Button) sender;
  labChoice.Text = btn.Text;
}
```

Remember that event handlers must have a precise signature. For mouse events, the method must have two parameters, one of type **object** and the other of type `System.EventArgs`. Otherwise, the next step will not work.

The final step is to assign the event handler to each button. Return to the Designer and click on one of the buttons. In the Properties/Events window, find the `Click` event. Click the drop-down arrow and then click the name of the method we created (`Mouse_Click`). Repeat for the other button. The final result is shown in Listing 5.17.

Listing 5.17

```
//******************************************************************
//  LeftRight.cs          C#:   Ken Culp
//
//  Demonstrates of one event handler for multiple controls and
//  using the button text as result for a label.
//******************************************************************
using System;
```

Listing 5.17   continued

```
using System.Collections.Generic;
using System.ComponentModel;
using System.Data;
using System.Drawing;
using System.Text;
using System.Windows.Forms;

namespace LeftRight
{
  public partial class LeftRight : Form
  {
    public LeftRight()
    {
      InitializeComponent();
    }

    private void ButtonClick(object sender, EventArgs e)
    {
      Button btn = (Button)sender;
      labChoice.Text = btn.Text;
    }
  }
}
```

One final note on how the event handler operates, because it uses a feature that we have not discussed yet. Notice the line that reads `Button btn = (Button)sender`. The `sender` parameter is actually the button that received the event. However, `sender` is not an object of type button which has the `Text` property that we need. Instead, `sender` must be specified as being of type **object** in a properly configured signature for the event handler. Thus, `sender` is really a Button but it appears to be something of type **object**. Therefore, we have to convert its type from **object** to Button before accessing the `Text` property. Thus, `btn` becomes an alias for the button object, but it is of type `Button` so we can now access the `Text` property. This process is called *type casting*.

5.11   DIALOG BOXES

A component called a dialog box can be helpful to assist in GUI processing. A *dialog box* is a graphical window that pops up on top of any currently active window so that the user can interact with it. A dialog box can serve a variety of purposes, such as conveying some information, confirming an action, or allowing the user to enter some information. Usually a dialog box has a solitary purpose, and the user's interaction with it is brief.

In Visual Studio, you can create dialog boxes simply by adding new forms to your project and then requesting those forms to be displayed at the appropriate time. What generally differentiates a standard form as a dialog box is how the box is displayed. Forms to which the user must respond before returning to the previous form are considered dialog boxes. When a response is required, it is called a "modal" display mode.

Visual Studio also includes a standard dialog box that can be used to display a message from the user and then allow them to select from a series of buttons. There is no standard input box for reading one piece of information as some other languages support. Instead, one of the examples below will create a simple dialog box to prompt for the integer and then return the value upon request.

This application will use a variety of new techniques. We are going to create the application as a console application but still use forms for our work. This is a new concept, so think about what is happening as we go. We will describe the steps for creating the application and then show the code. Following that, we will examine the code in detail to learn the steps for creating good dialog boxes.

Start with File/New/Project and Console Application, naming the project **EvenOdd**. Now in order to use Window's Forms, you will need to add a **using** statement for them. You can copy this line from an existing application or just type the following after the line **using** System:

```
using System.Windows.Forms;
```

Select Project/Add Windows Form and name the form **InputBox**. Structure your box as shown in the sample display. Add a label "Enter an Integer:", a `Text` control named `txtInput` for the integer, and two buttons labeled "Cancel" (`Name=btnCancel`) and Ok (`Name=btnOk`). For the form, set the `AcceptButton` property to `btnOk` and the `CancelButton` property to `btnCancel`. Change the form `Text` property to "Input".

Now we need to configure each of the buttons. Select the `Cancel` button and set the property `DialogResult` to `Cancel`. Select the `Ok` button and set its `DialogResult` to `Ok`. We will explain this step a little later.

To complete the configuration for our dialog box, we need some way to get the data back from the box to our main program. Since the text box has a private modifier, we cannot access it directly in the object. Instead, we will create a public property to return the data. Add the following lines of code to the end of the `InputBox` class (after the Form Constructor):

```
public string InputValue
{
  get { return txtInput.Text;  }
  set { txtInput.Text = value; }
}
```

This gives us a public way to access the private `Text` field `txtInput`. Note that we have defined both a **get** and a **set**. The **set** would be used when we want to present the user with a value that can then be modified.

This completes the configuration of our dialog box. Now type the remainder of the code so that your code in `EvenOdd.cs` looks like that shown in Listing 5.18.

Listing 5.18

```csharp
//*************************************************************
//  EvenOdd.cs        C#:   Ken Culp
//
//  Demonstrates how to create dialog boxes and use Window's
//  Forms from a console application.
//*************************************************************
using System;
using System.Collections.Generic;
using System.Text;
using System.Windows.Forms;

namespace EvenOdd
{
  class EvenOdd
  {
    static void Main(string[] args)
    {
      InputBox inputBox = new InputBox();
      DialogResult result;
      string message;
      int num;

      do
      {
        result = inputBox.ShowDialog();
        if (result == DialogResult.OK)
        {
          num = int.Parse(inputBox.InputValue);
          message = "That number is " +
            ((num % 2 == 0) ? "even" : "odd");
          MessageBox.Show(message, "Message",
            MessageBoxButtons.OK, MessageBoxIcon.Information);
          result = MessageBox.Show("Do Another?", "Continue?",
            MessageBoxButtons.YesNo, MessageBoxIcon.Question);
        }
      } while (result == DialogResult.Yes);
    }
  }
}
```

Listing 5.19

```csharp
//*************************************************************
//   InputBox.cs          AC#:   Ken Culp
//
//   Demonstrates a windows form dialog box returning DialogResult
//   values from buttons.
//*************************************************************
using System;
using System.Collections.Generic;
using System.ComponentModel;
using System.Data;
using System.Drawing;
using System.Text;
using System.Windows.Forms;

namespace EvenOdd
{
  public partial class InputBox : Form
  {
    public InputBox()
    {
      InitializeComponent();
    }

    public string InputValue
    {
      get { return txtInput.Text; }
      set { txtInput.Text = value; }
    }
  }
}
```

Output

Listing 5.19   Output continued

Using Dialog Box Results

Now that we have created a dialog box and obtained information from the box, let's analyze what we have done. The first step in our EvenOdd program was to create a variable called result, which stored an indication of which button was pressed. This value was then compared to a set of values in an enumeration called DialogResult. The members of DialogResult correspond to buttons that a user might normally click on a dialog box and include such things as Ok, No, Yes, Cancel, etc. A complete list is shown in Figure 5.12.

Now let's look at how the DialogResult values are passed from the dialog box back to the program that is using the dialog box. The first way is to attach a DialogResult value to a button. We set this appropriately above for Cancel and Ok. What is actually happening under the hood is this: When you click on a button on a form that has a value in DialogResult, the DialogResult property on the button is copied to the DialogResult property on the form and the dialog form automatically closes. Then, the ShowDialog (or Show) method returns this value to the caller. In the code above, the DialogResult value in the button property eventually ended up in the local variable result, which was then compared to the value in the DialogResult enumeration. The value in result was then tested both by our **if** statement and by our **while** statement.

Because what is returned from the Show method is the form's DialogResult property, this value could also be set in code just before the form closes. This would be useful if, during processing, an error was found independent of a specific button being pressed. Similarly, the return result might not be known until some data is examined in code. The following code segment sets the return value to Retry and then closes the form:

```
this.DialogResult = DialogResult.Retry;
this.Close();
```

MessageBox: The System-Supplied Dialog Box

If you examine the code above, you will notice two references to a static method called Show on a Visual Studio library class called MessageBox, a tool for displaying messages to the user and then allowing the user to click an appropriate button.

In addition to being able to specify both the message text and the banner text, several different combinations of buttons can be displayed. Furthermore, you can configure the icon that is displayed. Each of these is controlled by another enumeration as listed below. Also note that you do not have to specify all the various options. Instead, there are a variety of ways to call Show with a different mix of parameters. To see a list of ways to call Show, type the parenthesis after Show and then use the up and down arrows to scroll through the various overloaded methods. Some of these are shown in Figure 5.13.

Result	Meaning or Use
Abort	The user wants to immediately terminate the current action. Usually, the input data is missing or incomplete. This usually bypasses all validations.
Cancel	The user wants to cancel the current action. Like Abort, the input data is probably invalid. This usually accompanies Retry.
Ignore	The system is reporting a possible error and the user has said that it is okay to continue by ignoring the error.
No	The user answered No. A Yes/No question does not normally accompany any input data but may. Validations would depend upon the application.
None	The dialog box is still active and no value for DialogResult is known.
OK	The user claims that all the data is complete and wants to continue.
Retry	The user has seen an error or warning and wants to retry. This is usually after some correction action was taken. Again, this normally accompanies Cancel.
Yes	This is the Yes response to a Yes/No question. As with No, there is usually no data to be validated.

FIGURE 5.12   `DialogResult` enumeration

MessageBox.Show(string message)
   Displays message using no banner and no icon.

MessageBox.Show(string message, string caption)
   Displays message with a caption on the banner bar.

MessageBox.Show(string message, string caption, MessageBoxButtons buttons)
   Displays message with a caption and the specified set of buttons.

MessageBox.Show(string message, string caption, MessageBoxButtons buttons, MessageBoxIcon icon)
   Displays message with a caption, specified buttons, and specified icon.

FIGURE 5.13   Some `MessageBox.Show` method overloads

One of these optional parameters specifies the set of buttons to be displayed, which are shown in Figure 5.14. Some of the choices display one button, some two, and some three. Again, the button clicked is returned as the result of the dialog.

Another enumeration choice is the icon that is displayed on the box. Although you have several icon choices, basically only four different icons can be displayed, as shown in Figure 5.15.

5.12   MORE BUTTON COMPONENTS

Push buttons are only one kind of button that we can use in a C# GUI. Two others are check boxes and radio buttons. Let's look at these in detail.

Check Boxes

A *check box* is a button that can be toggled on or off using the mouse, indicating that a particular boolean condition is set or unset. For example, a check box labeled `Collate` might be used to indicate whether the output of a print job should be collated. Although you might have a group of check boxes indicating a set of options, each check box operates independently. That is, each can be set to on or off and the status of one does not influence the others.

The program in Listing 5.19 displays two check boxes and a label. The check boxes determine whether the text of the label is displayed in bold, italic, both, or neither. Any combination of bold and italic is valid. For example, both check boxes could be checked (on), in which case the text is displayed in both bold and italic. If neither is checked, the text of the label is displayed in a plain style.

Button Option	Meaning
AbortRetryIgnore	Displays three buttons (Abort, Retry, and Ignore).
Ok	The user can only click Ok. This is usually associated with a simple informational message but can be used any place.
OkCancel	The user can click either Ok or Cancel.
RetryCancel	The user can click either Retry or Cancel.
YesNo	The user can click Yes or No.
YesNoCancel	The user has three choices (Yes, No, and Cancel).

FIGURE 5.14   `MessageBoxButtons` enumeration

Icon Choice	Meaning	Icon Displayed
Asterisk	A small bubble with a lowercase i.	
Error	A big red circle with an X on it.	
Exclamation	A yellow triangle with an exclamation.	
Hand	Same as Error.	
Information	Same as Asterisk.	
Question	A small bubble with a question mark.	
Stop	Same as Error.	
Warning	Same as Exclamation.	

FIGURE 5.15 `MessageBoxIcon` enumeration

To create the program select File/New/Project and Windows Application. Design the form as shown below and noted above. Name the bold check box **chkBold** and the italic check box **chkItalic** and label them appropriately. Name the label control **lblSaying**, make it nearly the size of the form, and set the `TextAlign` property to `MiddleCenter`. The font size and style will be set in code.

Now we need to add the event handler to each of the check boxes so that when the user changes the contents of either check box, the format of the label will be changed. The event we need is `CheckedChanged`, which occurs every time the status of the box is changed. Because this is the default handler, we could double-click on the check box to create the control. However, in this case, we want to share the handler across both check boxes. Therefore, we need to manually create the handler as shown in the method `SetStyle` in Listing 5.20.

Once the event handler is defined, go to the Properties/Event window for each check box and set the `CheckedChanged` event to `SetStyle`. Test your application.

This program also uses the `Font` class, which represents a particular *character font.* In general, a `Font` object is defined by the font name, the font style, and the font size. The font family name establishes the general visual characteristics of the characters. We are using the Arial font in this program. Our style of a C# font can be plain, bold, italic, or bold and italic combined. The check boxes in our GUI are set up to change the characteristics of our font style.

The style of a font is selected from the enumeration {Bold, Italic, Regular, Strikeout, Underline}. Multiple styles can be chosen at the same time, but to combine them requires the use of the vertical bar symbol, as in FontStyle.Bold.FontStyle.Italic. The vertical bar is called a "logical or," which will be discussed at a later time. Just remember that if you can use multiple values from an enumeration, list them all separated by the vertical bar.

After a font is created, you can read whether it is bold or not or italic or not but you may not change the values. Thus, it was necessary in our application to use a nested **if** statement to set the combined styles when the font was created.

Listing 5.20

```csharp
//**********************************************************
//   StyleOptions.cs          C#: Ken Culp
//
//   Demonstrates the nested if statements.
//**********************************************************
using System;
using System.Collections.Generic;
using System.ComponentModel;
using System.Data;
using System.Drawing;
using System.Text;
using System.Windows.Forms;

namespace StyleOptions
{
  public partial class StyleOptions : Form
  {
    public StyleOptions()
    {
      InitializeComponent();
    }

    private const int FONT_SIZE = 24;
    private void SetStyle(object sender, EventArgs e)
    {
      // Nested if to set font for text.
      if (chkBold.Checked)
      {
        if (chkItalic.Checked)
          lblSaying.Font = new Font("Arial",
            FONT_SIZE, FontStyle.Bold | FontStyle.Italic);
        else
          lblSaying.Font = new Font("Arial",
            FONT_SIZE, FontStyle.Bold);
      }
```

Listing 5.20 continued

```
        else
        {
          if (chkItalic.Checked)
            lblSaying.Font = new Font("Arial",
              FONT_SIZE, FontStyle.Italic);
          else
            lblSaying.Font = new Font("Arial",
              FONT_SIZE, FontStyle.Regular);
        }

      }
    }
  }
```

FIGURE 5.16 Say it with style output

Note that, given the way the event handler is written in this program, it doesn't matter which check box was clicked to generate the event. Both check boxes are processed by the same handler. It also doesn't matter whether the changed check box was toggled from selected to unselected or vice versa. The state of both check boxes is examined if either is changed.

Also, note how the font is created in the preceding example. The constructor used takes three parameters: a font family name (`"Arial"`), a font size as a **float**, and a `FontStyle` parameter with the enumeration shown above. Because the font size is a floating number, fractional font sizes can be used (like 12.5). There are other constructors as well, including one for which only the font family name and the font size are given. This will create a font with a `FontStyle` of `Regular`.

Radio Buttons

A *radio button* is used with other radio buttons to provide a set of mutually exclusive options. Unlike a check box, a radio button is not particularly useful by itself. It has meaning only when it is used with one or more other radio buttons. Only one option out of the group is valid. At any point in time, one and only one button of the group of radio buttons is selected (on). When a radio button from the group is pushed, the other button in the group that is currently on is automatically toggled off.

The term "radio buttons" comes from the way the buttons worked on an old-fashioned car radio. At any point, one button was pushed to specify the current choice of station; when another was pushed, the current one automatically popped out.

The QuoteOptions program, shown in Listing 5.21, displays a label and a group of radio buttons. The radio buttons determine which quote is displayed in the label. Because only one of the quotes can be displayed at a time, the use of radio buttons is appropriate. For example, if the Comedy radio button is selected, the comedy quote is displayed in the label. If the Philosophy button is then pressed, the Comedy radio button is automatically toggled off and the comedy quote is replaced by a philosophical one.

Create a Windows application named **QuoteOptions** and size the form as shown in Figure 5.17. Next, drop a GroupBox control on the form and make it nearly the same size as the form. Erase the information in the Text property of the group box (so that no label appears). Now, drop three radio buttons into the group box. As we will note below, radio buttons must be located on a group box to function correctly. Name the three radio buttons **radComedy**, **radPhilosophy**, and **radCarpentry**. Add a label control called **labSaying** above the group box, clear any text, center the text, and use a font size of 16 (just like StyleOptions). That almost completes our form design, but before we can finish, we need to fill in some of the code.

Add the three saying variables as shown at the top of the class (see Listing 5.21). Next, we will add an event handler called SetQuote; we will use Visual Studio to create it for us, but we will use our own name instead of the default name that Visual Studio gives us. Open the Event window for the first radio button and type **SetQuote** to the right of the CheckedChanged event and press Enter. Then, type the code as shown in Listing 5.21. This event handler will be assigned to all three radio buttons, so we used a generic and informative name. This handler uses a nested **if** statement to check which message to use and then assigns that message to the Text property of our label control. Note the indenting chosen for the **if** statements. This is an optional format that aligns the conditions being tested and the action associated with each. In this layout, the nested **if** resembles a **case** statement.

Our last step is to return to the Form Designer and select the other two radio button. Set the CheckedChanged event to point to the SetQuote method we created from the first button and then test your application.

Note that, unlike push buttons, both check boxes and radio buttons are *toggle buttons,* meaning that at any time they are either on or off. The difference is in how they are used. Independent options (choose any combination) are controlled with check boxes. Dependent options (choose one of a set) are controlled with radio buttons. If there is only one option to be managed, a check box can be used by itself. As we mentioned earlier, a radio button, on the other hand, makes sense only in conjunction with one or more other radio buttons.

Listing 5.21

```
//***************************************************************
//   QuoteOptions.cs        C#: Ken Culp
//
//   Demonstrates the use radio buttons.
//***************************************************************
using System;
using System.Collections.Generic;
using System.ComponentModel;
using System.Data;
using System.Drawing;
using System.Text;
using System.Windows.Forms;

namespace QuoteOptions
{
  public partial class QuoteOptions : Form
  {
    public QuoteOptions()
    {
      InitializeComponent();
    }

    private string comedyQuote = "Take my wife, please.";
    private string philosophyQuote = "I think, therefore I am.";
    private string carpentryQuote = "Measure twice. Cut once.";

    private void SetQuote(object sender, EventArgs e)
    {
      if (radComedy.Checked)
        labSaying.Text = comedyQuote;
      else if (radPhilosophy.Checked)
        labSaying.Text = philosophyQuote;
      else
        labSaying.Text = carpentryQuote;
    }

    private void QuoteOptions_Load(object sender, EventArgs e)
    {
      // Set up initial message. Note call to event handler above
      SetQuote(sender, e);
    }
  }
}
```

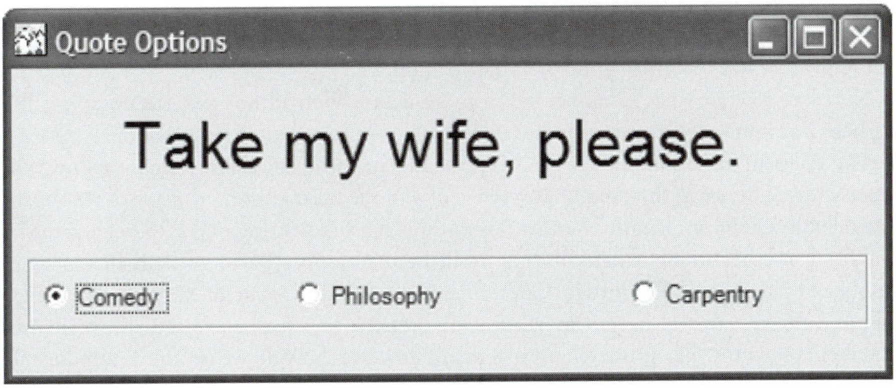

FIGURE 5.17   Quote Options Output

Also note that check boxes and radio buttons produce different types of events. A check box produces an item event and a radio button produces an action event. The use of different event types is related to the differences in button functionality. A check box produces an event when it is selected or deselected, and the listener could make the distinction if desired. A radio button, on the other hand, produces an event only when it is selected (the currently selected button from the group is deselected automatically).

TextBox Validations

It should always be your goal in GUI design to make the user's job as easy as possible. When certain pieces of information are required, the form should indicate that. Also, the user should not be able to proceed if they have not completed required data on the form although it would be okay for them to exit the form.

Now that you have a good understanding of event handlers, we will look at various ways of ensuring that valid data has been entered before certain buttons can be pressed. We also want to look at ways of giving the user a visual cue when they have successfully completed some of the information. This includes automatically moving to the next field when the current field is complete and valid.

This example has three input fields, which are the three parts of a social security number. It also has two buttons, one called Ok and one called Cancel. First, note that you can enter only numbers into the text boxes. Any other characters are simply discarded. Next, note that as you place the third number in the first box, the cursor moves to the second box, and as you place the second number in the second box, the cursor moves to the third box. Finally, note that once you have a complete social security number (3-2-4 form), the Ok button becomes enabled (goes from having shadow text to black text) and the cursor moves to the button. Figure 5.18 shows the form with an incomplete social security number, and Figure 5.19 shows the form with a completed number.

Now let's look at what is happening in more detail. We will not give the complete listing here but rather will cover only the individual event handlers as we go along.

The effect of an automatic tab (moving the cursor from one field to the next) on valid data is created by using the `TextChanged` event and the `MaxLength` property of text boxes. The default maximum length of a text box is the length of a string or 32,767 characters! If you enter another number here, the user will be unable to type more than the specified number of characters. When that number has been typed, the cursor remains at the right edge and the system will beep if more keys are pressed. This feature should always be used when you know the maximum length of a field. However, how do we get the automatic tab?

FIGURE 5.18　Input validation (incomplete)

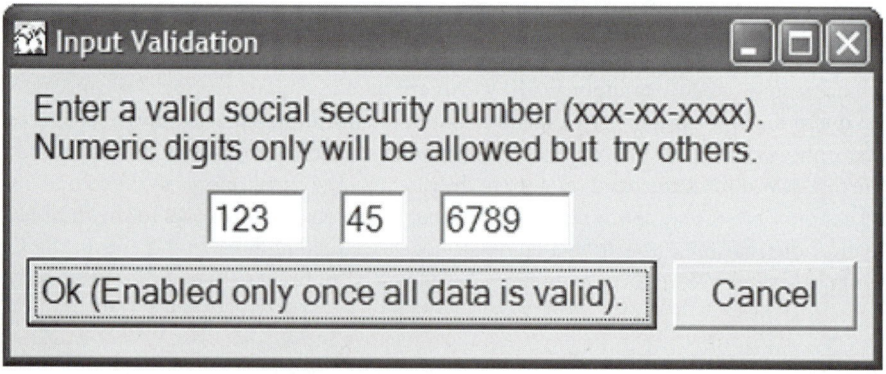

FIGURE 5.19　Input validation (complete)

What we will do is count the characters in a field on each key stroke and, when that number equals the maximum, insert a tab character so that the cursor moves as if the user had pressed the Tab key. Here is a simple event handler that will do just that:

```
private void TextChanged(object sender, System.EventArgs e)
{
   TextBox box = (TextBox) sender;
   int max = box.MaxLength;
   if (box.Text.Length == max) SendKeys.Send("\t");
}
```

Our first step in the event handler is to typecast `sender` to a `TextBox` and then grab the `MaxLength` setting, which we store in `max`. Finally, if the current length of the text box, `Length`, is the same as `max`, we insert a tab key by passing the special escape sequence for tab to the `SendKeys.Send` method. `SendKeys.Send` places characters or a string into the input stream just as if it had come from the keyboard.

This is simple but elegant code that can be added to any form using the `TextChanged` event handler. Because `TextChanged` is the default event for a text box, this event handler to a text box can be created by just double-clicking on the text box.

Now let's examine the complete `TextChanged` event handler for our SSN example. We would like to activate the `Ok` button only if all three parts of the social security number have the right length. Therefore, in the Form Designer, set the `Ok` button to be disabled when the form is loaded (select `Enabled` from properties and set to **false**). Then, once all three parts have a length equal to the maximum, we arm the event key. The following code shows the complete event handler. Note how we aligned each condition and combined them. This vertical alignment improves readability of the code but is optional.

```
private void SsnTextChanged(object sender, EventArgs e)
{
   // Generate tab if field is full
   TextBox box = (TextBox) sender;
   int max = box.MaxLength;
   if (box.Text.Length == max) SendKeys.Send("\t");
   // Arm Ok if all parts are valid
   btnOk.Enabled =
     (txtSSN1.Text.Length == txtSSN1.MaxLength) &&
     (txtSSN2.Text.Length == txtSSN2.MaxLength) &&
     (txtSSN3.Text.Length == txtSSN3.MaxLength);
}
```

Our last job is to keep the user from typing letters into numeric fields. This requires that we handle the `KeyPress` event. `KeyPress` occurs *before* the character is added to the field, which allows us to prevent it from being added. `TextChanged` occurs after the character has been added.

We need to examine the typed character and discard anything not in the range of 0 to 9. However, we must still allow the user to press control characters like the Backspace key, arrow keys, and the like. These keys all map to nondisplayable values that sort below a blank (a space). Thus, we want to reject the key if it is *not* a control character and *is* outside the desired range. This logic translates into the following `KeyPress` handler:

```
private void SsnKeyPress(object sender, KeyPressEventArgs e)
{
    char key = e.KeyChar;
    if ((key >= ' ') && (key < '0' || key > '9'))
        e.Handled = true;
}
```

Here is how to read the **if** statement. Two conditions that must both be true (combined with &&) are surrounded in parentheses. The first condition is that the key is not a control (is a space or greater). The second condition is true if either the key sorts below a '0' or after a '9' (combined with ||). When this condition evaluates to **true**, we set the Handled property on the event argument to **true**. When Handled is set to **true**, the key that was pressed is not passed on to any other handler and thus will not be added to the Text property of the field, thus discarding the key.

Infinite Loops in Event Handlers

It is possible to create an infinite loop in your event handler. If your event handler causes another event of the type it is handling, an infinite loop arises and the program will crash with an error message. The problem is that these loops are not apparent when examining the code, so use caution in coding your event handlers.

One way this happens is to try to change the text of a text box in the `TextChanged` event handler. Your handler finds an error and tries to make changes to the text. This may work if the change will not cause a further text change, but this is generally a dangerous thing to do.

Another way is to try changing the status of a check box or radio button from within the `CheckedChanged` hander. Again, this should be avoided.

Summary of Key Concepts

> Conditionals and loops allow us to control the flow of execution through a method.

> An **if** statement allows a program to choose whether to execute a particular statement.

> A loop allows a program to execute a statement multiple times.

> Logical operators are often used to construct sophisticated conditions.

> Proper indentation is important for human readability; it shows the relationship between one statement and another.

> An **if-else** statement allows a program to do one thing if a condition is true and another thing if the condition is false.

> In a nested **if** statement, an **else** clause is matched to the closest unmatched **if**.

> The relative order of characters in C# is defined by the Unicode character set.

> The equality operator or the CompareTo method can be used to determine the relative order of strings.

> A **break** statement is usually used at the end of each case alternative of a **switch** statement.

> A **while** statement executes the same statement until its condition becomes false.

> We must design our programs carefully to avoid infinite loops.

> A **do** statement executes its loop body at least once.

> A **for** statement is usually used when a loop will be executed a set number of times.

> Radio buttons operate as a group, providing a set of mutually exclusive options.

Self-Review Questions

5.1   What is meant by the flow of control through a program?

5.2   What type of conditions are conditionals and loops based on?

5.3   What are the equality operators? The relational operators?

5.4   What is a nested **if** statement? A nested loop?

5.5   How do block statements help us in the construction of conditionals and loops?

5.6   What happens if a case in a **switch** does not end with a **break** statement?

5.7   What is a truth table?

5.8   How do we compare strings for equality?

5.9   Why must we be careful when comparing floating point values for equality?

5.10   What is an assignment operator?

5.11   What is an infinite loop? Specifically, what causes it?

5.12   Compare and contrast a **while** loop and a **do** loop.

5.13   When would we use a **for** loop instead of a **while** loop?

5.14   What is a dialog box?

5.15   Compare and contrast check boxes and radio buttons.

Exercises

5.1   What happens in the `MinOfThree` program if two or more of the values are equal? If exactly two of the values are equal, does it matter whether the equal values are lower or higher than the third?

5.2   What is wrong with the following code fragment? Rewrite it so that it produces correct output.

```
if (total == MAX)
  if (total < sum)
    Console.Out.WriteLine ("total == MAX and is < sum.");
else
    Console.Out.WriteLine ("total is not equal to MAX");
```

5.3   What is wrong with the following code fragment? Will this code compile if it is part of an otherwise valid program? Explain.

```
if (length = MIN_LENGTH)
    Console.Out.WriteLine ("The length is minimal.");
```

5.4   What output is produced by the following code fragment?

```
int num = 87, max = 25;
if (num >= max*2)
    Console.Out.WriteLine ("apple");
    Console.Out.WriteLine ("orange");
Console.Out.WriteLine ("pear");
```

5.5   What output is produced by the following code fragment?

```
int limit = 100, num1 = 15, num2 = 40;
if (limit <= limit)
{
    if (num1 == num2)
        Console.Out.WriteLine ("lemon");
```

```
      Console.Out.WriteLine ("lime");
   }
   Console.Out.WriteLine ("grape");
```

5.6   Put the following list of strings in lexicographic order as if determined by
      the CompareTo method of the string class. Consult the Unicode chart in
      Appendix B.

```
"fred"
"Ethel"
"?-?-?-?"
"{([])}"
"Lucy"
"ricky"
"book"
"******"
"12345"
"         "
"HEPHALUMP"
"bookkeeper"
"6789"
";+<?"
"^^^^^^^^^^"
"hephalump"
```

5.7   What output is produced by the following code fragment?

```
int num = 0, max = 20;
while (num < max)
{
   Console.Out.WriteLine (num);
   num += 4;
}
```

5.8   What output is produced by the following code fragment?

```
int num = 1, max = 20;
while (num < max)
{
   if (num%2 == 0)
      Console.Out.WriteLine (num);
   num++;
}
```

5.9   What output is produced by the following code fragment?

```
for (int num = 0; num <= 200; num += 2)
   Console.Out.WriteLine (num);
```

5.10 What output is produced by the following code fragment?

```
for(int val = 200; val >= 0; val -= 1)
  if (val % 4 != 0)
     Console.Out.WriteLine (val);
```

5.11 Transform the following **while** loop into an equivalent **do** loop (make sure it produces the same output).

```
int num = 1;
while (num < 20)
{
   num++;
   Console.Out.WriteLine (num);
}
```

5.12 Transform the **while** loop from the previous exercise into an equivalent **for** loop (make sure it produces the same output).

5.13 What is wrong with the following code fragment? What are three distinct ways it could be changed to remove the flaw?

```
count = 50;
while (count >= 0)
{
   Console.Out.WriteLine (count);
   count = count + 1;
}
```

5.14 Write a **while** loop that verifies that the user enters a positive integer value.

5.15 Write a **do** loop that verifies that the user enters an even integer value.

5.16 Write a code fragment that reads and prints integer values entered by a user until a particular sentinel value (stored in SENTINEL) is entered. Do not print the sentinel value.

5.17 Write a **for** loop to print the odd numbers from 1 to 99 (inclusive).

5.18 Write a **for** loop to print the multiples of 3 from 300 down to 3.

5.19 Write a code fragment that reads 10 integer values from the user and prints the highest value entered.

5.20 Write a code fragment that determines and prints the number of times the character 'a' appears in a String object called name.

5.21 Write a code fragment that prints the characters stored in a String object called str backward. Use the **foreach** loop method.

5.22   Write a code fragment that prints every other character in a `String` object called `word` starting with the first character.

5.23   Write a method called `PowersOfTwo` that prints the first 10 powers of 2 (starting with 2). The method takes no parameters and doesn't return anything.

5.24   Write a method called `Alarm` that prints the string `"Alarm!"` multiple times on separate lines. The method should accept an integer parameter that specifies how many times the string is printed. Print an error message if the parameter is less than 1.

5.25   Write a method called `Sum100` that returns the sum of the integers from 1 to 100, inclusive.

5.26   Write a method called `MaxOfTwo` that accepts two integer parameters and returns the larger of the two.

5.27   Write a method called `SumRange` that accepts two integer parameters that represent a range. Issue an error message and return zero if the second parameter is less than the first. Otherwise, the method should return the sum of the integers in that range (inclusive).

5.28   Write a method called `Larger` that accepts two floating point parameters (of type **double**) and returns true if the first parameter is greater than the second, and false otherwise.

5.29   Write a method called `CountA` that accepts a `String` parameter and returns the number of times the character `'A'` is found in the string.

5.30   Write a method called `EvenlyDivisible` that accepts two integer parameters and returns true if the first parameter is evenly divisible by the second, or vice versa, and false otherwise. Return false if either parameter is zero.

5.31   Write a method called `IsAlpha` that accepts a character parameter and returns true if that character is either an uppercase or lowercase alphabetic letter.

5.32   Write a method called `FloatEquals` that accepts three floating point values as parameters. The method should return true if the first two parameters are equal within the tolerance of the third parameter.

5.33   Write a method called `Reverse` that accepts a `string` parameter and returns a string that contains the characters of the parameter in reverse order. Note that there is a method in the `string` class that performs this operation, but for the sake of this exercise, you are expected to write your own.

5.34   Write a method called `IsIsosceles` that accepts three integer parameters that represent the lengths of the sides of a triangle. The method returns true if the triangle is isosceles but not equilateral (meaning that exactly two of the sides have an equal length), and false otherwise.

5.35   Explain what would happen if the radio buttons used in the QuoteOptions program were not organized into a Group object. Modify the program to test your
answer (drop the buttons directly on the form).

Programming Projects

5.1   Design and implement an application that reads an integer value representing a
year from the user. The purpose of the program is to determine if the year is a leap
year (and therefore has 29 days in February) in the Gregorian calendar. A year is a
leap year if it is divisible by 4, unless it is also divisible by 100 but not 400. For
example, the year 2003 is not a leap year, but 2004 is. The year 1900 is not a leap
year because it is divisible by 100, but the year 2000 is a leap year because even
though it is divisible by 100, it is also divisible by 400. Produce an error message
for any input value less than 1582 (the year the Gregorian calendar was adopted).

5.2   Modify the solution to the previous project so that the user can evaluate multiple
years. Allow the user to terminate the program using an appropriate sentinel value.
Validate each input value to ensure that it is greater than or equal to 1582.

5.3   Design and implement an application that reads an integer value and prints the
sum of all even integers between 2 and the input value, inclusive. Print an error
message if the input value is less than 2. Prompt accordingly.

5.4   Design and implement an application that reads a string from the user and prints
it one character per line.

5.5   Design and implement an application that determines and prints the number of
odd, even, and zero digits in an integer value read from the keyboard.

5.6   Design and implement an application that produces a multiplication table, showing the results of multiplying the integers 1 through 12 by themselves.

5.7   Design and implement an application that prints the first few verses of the travel-
ing song "One Hundred Bottles of Beer." Use a loop such that each iteration prints
one verse. Read the number of verses to print from the user. Validate the input.
The following are the first two verses of the song:

100 bottles of beer on the wall
100 bottles of beer
If one of those bottles should happen to fall
99 bottles of beer on the wall
99 bottles of beer on the wall
99 bottles of beer
If one of those bottles should happen to fall
98 bottles of beer on the wall

5.8   Design and implement an application that plays the Hi-Lo guessing game with numbers. The program should pick a random number between 1 and 100 (inclusive), then repeatedly prompt the user to guess the number. On each guess, report to the user that he or she is correct or that the guess is high or low. Continue accepting guesses until the user guesses correctly or chooses to quit. Use a sentinel value to determine whether the user wants to quit. Count the number of guesses and report that value when the user guesses correctly. At the end of each game (by quitting or a correct guess), prompt to determine whether the user wants to play again. Continue playing games until the user chooses to stop.

5.9   Create a modified version of the `PalindromeTester` program so that the spaces, punctuation, and changes in uppercase and lowercase are not considered when determining whether a string is a palindrome. Hint: These issues can be handled in several ways. Think carefully about your design.

5.10 Create modified versions of the `Stars` program to print the following patterns. Create a separate program to produce each pattern. Hint: Parts b, c, and d require several loops, some of which print a specific number of spaces.

```
a. **********    b.          *    c. **********    d.          *
   *********               **       *********              ***
   ********               ***       ********              *****
   *******               ****       *******              *******
   ******               *****       ******              *********
   *****               ******       *****              *********
   ****               *******       ****              *******
   ***               ********       ***              *****
   **               *********       **              ***
   *               **********       *              *
```

5.11 Design and implement an application that prints a table showing a subset of the Unicode characters and their numeric values. Print five number/character pairs per line, separated by tab characters. Print the table for numeric values from 32 (the space character) to 126 (the ~ character), which corresponds to the printable ASCII subset of the Unicode character set. Compare your output to the table in Appendix B. Unlike the table in Appendix B, the values in your table can increase as they go across a row.

5.12 Design and implement an application that reads a string from the user, then determines and prints how many of each lowercase vowel (a, e, i, o, and u) appear in the entire string. Have a separate counter for each vowel. Also count and print the number of non-vowel characters.

5.13 Design and implement an application that plays the Rock-Paper-Scissors game against the computer. When played between two people, each person picks one of three options (usually shown by a hand gesture) at the same time, and a winner is determined. In the game, Rock beats Scissors, Scissors beats Paper, and Paper beats

Rock. The program should randomly choose one of the three options (without revealing it), then prompt for the user's selection. At that point, the program reveals both choices and prints a statement indicating if the user won, the computer won, or if it was a tie. Continue playing until the user chooses to stop, then print the number of user wins, losses, and ties.

5.14 Design and implement an application that prints the verses of the song "The Twelve Days of Christmas," in which each verse adds one line. The first two verses of the song are:

On the 1st day of Christmas my true love gave to me
A partridge in a pear tree.
On the 2nd day of Christmas my true love gave to me
Two turtle doves, and
A partridge in a pear tree.

Use a **switch** statement in a loop to control which lines get printed. Hint: Order the cases carefully and avoid the **break** statement. Use a separate **switch** statement to put the appropriate suffix on the day number (1st, 2nd, 3rd, etc.). The final verse of the song involves all 12 days, as follows:

On the 12th day of Christmas, my true love gave to me
Twelve drummers drumming,
Eleven pipers piping,
Ten lords a leaping,
Nine ladies dancing,
Eight maids a milking,
Seven swans a swimming,
Six geese a laying,
Five golden rings,
Four calling birds,
Three French hens,
Two turtle doves, and
A partridge in a pear tree.

5.15 Design and implement an application that simulates a simple slot machine in which three numbers between 0 and 9 are randomly selected and printed side by side. Print an appropriate statement if all three of the numbers are the same, or if any two of the numbers are the same. Continue playing until the user chooses to stop.

5.16 Design and implement a program that counts the number of integer values in a text input file. Produce a table listing the values you identify as integers from the input file.

5.17 Design and implement a program that draws 20 horizontal, evenly spaced parallel lines of random length.

5.18   Design and implement a program that draws the side view of stair steps from the lower left to the upper right.

5.19   Design and implement a program that draws 100 circles of random color and random diameter in random locations. Ensure that in each case the entire circle appears in the visible area of the window.

5.20   Design and implement a program that draws 10 concentric circles of random radius.

5.21   Design and implement a program that draws a brick wall pattern in which each row of bricks is offset from the row above and below it.

5.22   Design and implement a program that draws a quilt in which a simple pattern is repeated in a grid of squares.

5.23   Modify the previous problem such that it draws a quilt using a separate class called `Pattern` that represents a particular pattern. Allow the constructor of the `Pattern` class to vary some characteristics of the pattern, such as its color scheme. Instantiate two separate `Pattern` objects and incorporate them in a checkerboard layout in the quilt.

5.24   Design and implement a program that draws a simple fence with vertical, equally spaced slats backed by two horizontal support boards. Behind the fence show a simple house in the background. Make sure the house is visible between the slats in the fence.

5.25   Design and implement a program that draws a rainbow. Use tightly spaced concentric arcs to draw each part of the rainbow in a particular color.

5.26   Design and implement a program that draws 20,000 points in random locations within the visible area. Make the points on the left half of the form appear in red and the points on the right half of the panel appear in green. Draw a point by drawing a line with a length of only one pixel.

5.27   Design and implement a program that draws 10 circles of random radius in random locations. Fill in the largest circle in red.

5.28   Design and implement an application that uses dialog boxes to obtain two integer values (one dialog box for each value) and display the sum and product of the values. Use another dialog box to see whether the user wants to process another pair of values.

5.29   Modify the `Die` class from Chapter 4 so that the `SetFaceValue` method does nothing if the parameter is outside of the valid range of values.

5.30   Modify the `Account` class from Chapter 4 so that it performs validity checks on the deposit and withdraw operations. Specifically, don't allow the deposit of a negative number or a withdrawal that exceeds the current balance. Print appropriate error messages if these problems occur.

5.31 Redesign and implement a version of the `PalindromeTester` program so that it uses dialog boxes to obtain the input string, display the results, and prompt to continue.

5.32 Modify the `StyleOptions` program in this chapter to allow the user to specify the size of the font. Use a text field to obtain the size.

5.33 Design and implement a program to process golf scores. The scores of four golfers are stored in a text file. Each line represents one hole, and the file contains 18 lines. Each line contains five values: par for the hole followed by the number of strokes each golfer used on that hole. Determine the winner and produce a table showing how well each golfer did (compared to par).

5.34 Design and implement a program that compares two text input files, line by line, for equality. Print any lines that are not equivalent.

5.35 Design and implement a program that counts the number of punctuation marks in a text input file. Produce a table that shows how many times each symbol occurred.

5.36 Develop a simple tool for calculating basic statistics for a segment of text. The application should have a single window with a multiline text box and a stats box. The stats box should be a panel with a titled border, containing labeled fields that display the number of words in the text box and the average word length, as well as any other statistics that you would like to add. The stats box should also contain a button that, when pressed, recomputes the statistics for the current contents of the text field.

Answers to Self-Review Questions

5.1 The flow of control through a program determines the program statements that will be executed on a given run of the program.

5.2 Each conditional and loop is based on a boolean condition that evaluates to either true or false.

5.3 The equality operators are equal (==) and not equal (!=). The relational operators are less than (<), less than or equal to (<=), greater than (>), and greater than or equal to (>=).

5.4 A nested `if` occurs when the statement inside an `if` or `else` clause is an `if` statement. A nested `if` lets the programmer make a series of decisions. Similarly, a nested loop is a loop within a loop.

5.5 A block statement groups several statements together. We use them to define the body of an `if` statement or loop when we want to do multiple things based on the boolean condition.

5.6   If a case does not end with a **break** statement, processing continues into the statements of the next case. We usually want to use **break** statements in order to jump to the end of the **switch**.

5.7   A truth table is a table that shows all possible results of a boolean expression, given all possible combinations of variables and conditions.

5.8   We compare strings for equality using the `Equals` method of the `string` class, which returns a boolean result. The `CompareTo` method of the `string` class can also be used to compare strings. It returns a positive, 0, or negative integer result depending on the relationship between the two strings.

5.9   Because they are stored internally as binary numbers, comparing floating point values for exact equality will be true only if they are the same bit-by-bit. It's better to use a reasonable tolerance value and consider the difference between the two values.

5.10   An assignment operator combines an operation with assignment. For example, the += operator performs an addition, then stores the value back into the variable on the right-hand side.

5.11   An infinite loop is a repetition statement that never terminates. Specifically, the body of the loop never causes the condition to become false.

5.12   A **while** loop evaluates the condition first. If it is true, it executes the loop body. The **do** loop executes the body first and then evaluates the condition. Therefore, the body of a **while** loop is executed zero or more times, and the body of a **do** loop is executed one or more times.

5.13   A **for** loop is usually used when we know, or can calculate, how many times we want to iterate through the loop body. A **while** loop handles a more generic situation.

5.14   A dialog box is a small window that appears for the purpose of conveying information, confirming an action, or accepting input. Generally, dialog boxes are used in specific situations for brief user interactions.

5.15   Both check boxes and radio buttons show a toggled state: either on or off. However, radio buttons work as a group in which only one can be toggled on at any point in time. Check boxes, on the other hand, represent independent options. They can be used alone or in a set in which any combination of toggled states is valid.

Object-Oriented Design

6

CHAPTER OBJECTIVES

> Establish key issues related to the design of object-oriented software.

> Explore techniques for identifying the classes and objects needed in a program.

> Discuss the relationships among classes.

> Describe the effect of the static modifier on methods and data.

> Discuss the creation of a formal object interface.

> Discuss issues related to the design of methods, including method overloading.

> Explore issues related to the design of graphical user interfaces.

This chapter extends our discussion of the design of object-oriented software. We first focus on the stages of software development and the process of identifying classes and objects in the problem domain. We then discuss various issues that affect the design of a class, including static members, class relationships, and interfaces. We also explore design issues at the method level and introduce the concept of method overloading. A discussion of testing strategies rounds out these issues. In the Windows Track sections of this chapter, we focus on GUI design concepts.

6.1   SOFTWARE DEVELOPMENT ACTIVITIES

Creating software involves much more than just writing code. As the problems you tackle get bigger, and the solutions include more classes, it becomes crucial to carefully think through the design of the software. Any proper software development effort consists of four basic *development activities*:

> > establishing the requirements

> > creating a design

> > implementing the design

> > testing

It would be nice if these activities, in this order, defined a step-by-step approach for developing software. However, although they may seem to be sequential, they are almost never completely linear in reality. They overlap and interact. Let's discuss each development activity briefly.

Software requirements specify *what* a program must accomplish. They indicate the tasks that a program should perform, not how it performs them. Often requirements are expressed in a document called a *functional specification*.

We discussed in Chapter 1 the basic premise that programming is really about problem solving; we create a program to solve a particular problem. Requirements are the clear expression of that problem. Until we truly know what problem we are trying to solve, we can't actually solve it.

The person or group who wants a software product developed (the *client*) will often provide an initial set of requirements. However, these initial requirements are often incomplete, ambiguous, and perhaps even contradictory. The software developer must work with the client to refine the requirements until all key decisions about what the system will do have been addressed.

Requirements often address user interface issues such as output format, screen layouts, and graphical interface components. Essentially, the requirements establish the characteristics that make the program useful for the end user. They may also apply constraints to your program, such as how fast a task must be performed.

A *software design* indicates *how* a program will accomplish its requirements. The design specifies the classes and objects needed in a program and defines how they interact. It also specifies the relationships among the classes. Low-level design issues deal with how individual methods accomplish their tasks.

Key Concept

The effort put into design is both crucial and cost-effective.

A civil engineer would never consider building a bridge without designing it first. The design of software is no less essential. Many problems that occur in software are directly attributable to a lack of good design effort. It has been shown time and again that the effort spent on the design of a program is well worth it, saving both time and money in the long run.

During software design, alternatives need to be considered and explored. Often, the first attempt at a design is not the best solution. Fortunately, changes are relatively easy to make during the design stage.

Implementation is the process of writing the source code that will solve the problem. More precisely, implementation is the act of translating the design into a particular programming language. Too many programmers focus on implementation exclusively when actually it should require the least creativity of all the development activities. The important decisions should be made when establishing the requirements and creating the design.

Testing is the act of ensuring that a program will solve the intended problem given all of the constraints under which it must perform. Testing includes running a program multiple times with various inputs and carefully scrutinizing the results. But it means far more than that. We revisit the issues related to testing in section 6.10.

6.2 IDENTIFYING CLASSES AND OBJECTS

A fundamental part of object-oriented software design is determining the classes that will contribute to the program. We have to carefully consider how we want to represent the various elements that make up the overall solution. These classes determine the objects that we will manage in the system.

One way to identify potential classes is to identify the objects discussed in the program requirements. Objects are generally nouns. You literally may want to scrutinize a problem description, or a functional specification if available, to identify the nouns found in it. For example, Figure 6.1 shows part of a problem description with the nouns circled.

> **Key Concept**
>
> The nouns in a problem description may indicate some of the classes and objects needed in a program.

Of course, not every noun in the problem specification will correspond to a class in your program. This activity is just a starting point that allows you to think about the types of objects a program will manage.

Remember that a class represents a group of objects with similar behavior. A plural noun in the specification, such as products, may indicate the need for a class that represents one of those items, such as `Product`. Even if there is only one of a particular kind of object needed in your system, it may best be represented as a class.

```
The (user) must be allowed to specify each
(product) by its primary (characteristics,)
including its (name) and (product number.) If the
(bar code) does not match the (product,) then an
(error) should be generated to the (message window)
and entered into the (error log.) The (summary
report) of all (transactions) must be structured
as specified in section 7.A.
```

FIGURE 6.1 A partial problem description with the nouns circled

Classes that represent objects should generally be given names that are singular nouns, such as `Coin`, `Student`, and `Message`. A class represents a single item from which we are free to create as many instances as we choose.

Another key decision is whether to represent something as an object or as a primitive attribute of another object. For example, we may initially think that an employee's salary should be represented as an integer, and that may work for much of the system's processing. But upon further reflection we might realize that the salary is based on the person's rank, which has upper and lower salary bounds that must be managed with care. Therefore the final conclusion may be that we'd be better off representing all of that data and the associated behavior as a separate class.

Given the needs of a particular program, we want to strike a good balance between classes that are too general and those that are too specific. For example, it may complicate our design unnecessarily to create a separate class for each type of appliance that exists in a house. It may be sufficient to have a single `Appliance` class, with perhaps a piece of instance data that indicates what type of appliance it is. Then again, it may not be sufficient. It all depends on what the software is going to accomplish.

In addition to classes that represent objects from the problem domain, we likely will need classes that support the work necessary to get the job done. For example, in addition to `Member` objects, we may want a separate class to help us manage all the members of a club.

Keep in mind that when producing a real system, some of the classes we identify during design may already exist. Even if nothing matches exactly, there may be an old class that's similar enough to serve as the basis for our new class. The existing class my be part of the C# standard class library, part of a solution to a problem we've solved previously, or part of a library that can be bought from a third party. These are all examples of software reuse.

Assigning Responsibilities

Part of the process of identifying the classes needed in a program is to assign responsibilities to each class. Each class represents an object with certain behaviors that are defined by the methods of the class. Any activity that the program must accomplish must be represented somewhere in the behaviors of the classes. That is, each class is responsible for carrying out certain activities, and those responsibilities must be assigned as part of designing a program.

The behaviors of a class perform actions that make up the functionality of a program. Thus we generally use verbs for the names of behaviors and the methods that accomplish them.

Sometimes it is challenging to determine which is the best class to carry out a particular responsibility. Consider multiple possibilities. Sometimes such analysis makes you realize that you could benefit from defining another class to shoulder the responsibility.

It's not necessary in the early stages of a design to identify all the methods that a class will contain. It is often sufficient to assign primary responsibilities, and consider how those responsibilities translate to particular methods.

6.3   STATIC CLASS MEMBERS

We've used static methods in various situations in previous examples in the book. Recall that a static method is one that is invoked through its class name, instead of through an object of that class. For example, all the methods of the Math class are static.

Not only can methods be static, but variables can be static as well. We declare static class members using the **static** modifier.

Deciding whether to declare a method or variable as static is a key step in class design. Let's examine the implications of static variables and methods more closely.

Static Variables

So far, we've seen two categories of variables: local variables that are declared inside a method, and instance variables that are declared in a class but not inside a method. The term *instance variable* is used because each instance of the class has its own version of the variable. That is, each object has distinct memory space for each variable so that each object can have a distinct value for that variable.

A *static variable,* which is sometimes called a *class variable,* is shared among all instances of a class. There is only one copy of a static variable for all objects of the class. Therefore, changing the value of a static variable in one object changes it for all of the others. The reserved word **static** is used as a modifier to declare a static variable as follows:

> **Key Concept**
>
> A static variable is shared among all instances of a class.

```
private static int count = 0;
```

Memory space for a static variable is established when the class that contains it is referenced for the first time in a program. A local variable declared within a method cannot be static.

Constants, which are declared using the **const** modifier, are often declared using the **static** modifier. Because the value of constants cannot be changed, there might as well be only one copy of the value across all objects of the class.

Static Methods

In Chapter 2 we briefly introduced the concept of a *static method* (also called a *class method*). Static methods can be invoked through the class name. We don't have to instantiate an object of the class in order to invoke the method. In Chapter 3 (and at the beginning of this section), we noted that all the methods of the Math class are static methods. For example, in the following line of code the Sqrt method is invoked through the Math class name:

```
Console.Out.WriteLine ("Square root of 27: " + Math.Sqrt(27));
```

The methods in the Math class perform basic computations based on values passed as parameters. There is no object state to maintain in these situations; therefore, there is no good reason to force us to create an object in order to request these services.

A method is made static by using the **static** modifier in the method declaration. As we've seen many times, the Main method of a C# program must be declared with the **static** modifier; this is done so that Main can be executed by the interpreter without instantiating an object from the class that contains Main.

Because static methods do not operate in the context of a particular object, they cannot reference instance variables, which exist only in an instance of a class. The compiler will issue an error if a static method attempts to use a nonstatic variable. A static method can, however, reference static variables, because static variables exist independent of specific objects. Therefore, the main method can access only static or local variables.

The program in Listing 6.1 uses a loop to instantiate several objects of the Slogan class, printing each one out in turn. At the end of the program, it invokes a method called GetCount through the class name, which returns the number of Slogan objects that were instantiated in the program.

Listing 6.2 shows the Slogan class. The constructor of Slogan increments a static variable called count, which is initialized to zero when it is declared. Therefore, count serves to keep track of the number of instances of Slogan that are created.

The GetCount method of Slogan is also declared as **static**, which allows it to be invoked through the class name in the Main method. Note that the only data referenced in the GetCount method is the integer variable count, which is static. As a static method, GetCount cannot reference any nonstatic data.

The GetCount method could have been declared without the **static** modifier, but then its invocation in the Main method would have to have been done through an instance of the Slogan class instead of the class itself. Also note that we have created a **static** property called Count, which can also be accessed from the class and not just through an instance.

Listing 6.1

```
//****************************************************************
//   SloganCounter.cs          C#:   Ken Culp
//
//   Demonstrates the use of the static modifier for variables
//   properties, and methods
//****************************************************************
using System;

namespace SloganCounter
{
  class SloganCounter
  {
    static void Main(string[] args)
    {
      Slogan obj;
```

Listing 6.1   continued

```
        obj = new Slogan("Remember the Alamo.");
        Console.Out.WriteLine(Slogan.Count + ": " + obj);

        obj = new Slogan("Don't Worry.  Be Happy.");
        Console.Out.WriteLine(Slogan.Count + ": " + obj);

        obj = new Slogan("Live Free or Die.");
        Console.Out.WriteLine(Slogan.Count + ": " + obj);

        obj = new Slogan("Talk is Cheap.");
        Console.Out.WriteLine(Slogan.Count + ": " + obj);

        obj = new Slogan("Write Once, Run Anywhere");
        Console.Out.WriteLine(Slogan.Count + ": " + obj);

        Console.Out.WriteLine();
        Console.Out.WriteLine("Slogans created: " +
          Slogan.GetCount());

        Console.In.ReadLine();  // Wait for enter key
      }
    }
}
```

Output

```
1: Remember the Alamo.
2: Don't Worry.  Be Happy.
3: Live Free or Die.
4: Talk is Cheap.
5: Write Once, Run Anywhere

Slogans created: 5
```

Listing 6.2

```
//****************************************************************
//  Slogan.cs                C#:  Ken Culp
//
//  Represents a single slogan string.
//****************************************************************
using System;

namespace SloganCounter
{
```

Listing 6.2   continued

```csharp
public class Slogan
{
  private string phrase;
  private static int count = 0;
  //---------------------------------------------------------
  // Constructor:  Sets up the slogan and counts the number of
  // instances created.
  //---------------------------------------------------------
  public Slogan(string str)
  {
    phrase = str;
    count++;
  }

  //---------------------------------------------------------
  // Returns the slogan as a string
  //---------------------------------------------------------
  public override string ToString()
  {
    return phrase;
  }

  //---------------------------------------------------------
  // Static property to obtain the count
  //---------------------------------------------------------
  public static int Count
  {
    get { return count; }
  }

  //---------------------------------------------------------
  // Static method to obtain the count
  //---------------------------------------------------------
  public static int GetCount()
  {
    return count;
  }
}
}
```

6.4 CLASS RELATIONSHIPS

The classes in a software system have various types of relationships to each other. Three of the more common relationships are dependency, aggregation, and inheritance.

We've seen dependency relationships in many examples in which one class "uses" another. This section revisits the dependency relationship and explores the situation where a class depends on itself. We then explore aggregation, in which the objects of one class contain objects of another, creating a "has-a" relationship. Inheritance, which we introduced in Chapter 1, creates an "is-a" relationship between classes. We defer our detailed examination of inheritance until Chapter 8.

Dependency

In many previous examples, we've seen the idea of one class being dependent on another. This means that one class relies on another in some sense. Often the methods of one class will invoke the methods of the other class. This establishes a "uses" relationship.

Generally, if class A uses class B, then one or more methods of class A invoke one or more methods of class B. If an invoked method is static, then A merely references B by name. If the invoked method is not static, then A must have access to a specific instance of class B in order to invoke the method. That is, A must have a reference to an object of class B.

The way in which one object gains access to an object of another class is an important design decision. It occurs when one class instantiates the objects of another, but that's often the basis of an aggregation relationship. The access can also be accomplished by passing one object to another as a method parameter.

In general, we want to minimize the number of dependencies among classes. The less dependent our classes are on each other, the less impact changes and errors will have on the system.

Dependencies Among Objects of the Same Class

In some cases, a class depends on itself. That is, an object of one class interacts with another object of the same class. To accomplish this, a method of the class may accept as a parameter an object of the same class. Designing such a class drives home the idea that a class represents a particular object.

The CompareTo method of the string class is an example of this situation. The method is executed through one String object and is passed another String object as a parameter. For example:

```
if (str1.CompareTo(str2) == 0)
    Console.Out.WriteLine("Strings are the same");
```

The string object executing the method (str1) compares its characters to those of the string object passed as a parameter (str2).

The RationalTester program, shown in Listing 6.3, demonstrates a similar situation. A rational number is a value that can be represented as a ratio of two integers (a fraction). The RationalTester program creates two objects representing rational numbers and then performs various operations on them to produce new rational numbers.

Listing 6.3

```csharp
//****************************************************************
//  RationalTester.cs          C#:  Ken Culp
//
//  Driver to exercise the use of multiple Rational objects.
//****************************************************************
using System;

namespace RationalTester
{
  class RationalTester
  {
    //---------------------------------------------------------------
    //  Creates some rational number objects and performs various
    //  operations on them.
    //---------------------------------------------------------------
    static void Main(string[] args)
    {
      Rational r1 = new Rational(6, 8);
      Rational r2 = new Rational(1, 3);
      Rational r3, r4, r5, r6, r7;

      Console.Out.WriteLine("First rational number: " + r1);
      Console.Out.WriteLine("Second rational number: " + r2);

      if (r1.Equals(r2))
        Console.Out.WriteLine("r1 and r2 are equal.");
      else
        Console.Out.WriteLine("r1 and r2 are NOT equal.");

      r3 = r1.Reciprocal();
      Console.Out.WriteLine("The reciprocal of r1 is: " + r3);

      r4 = r1.Add(r2);
      r5 = r1.Subtract(r2);
      r6 = r1.Multiply(r2);
      r7 = r1.Divide(r2);

      Console.Out.WriteLine("r1 + r2: " + r4);
      Console.Out.WriteLine("r1 - r2: " + r5);
      Console.Out.WriteLine("r1 * r2: " + r6);
      Console.Out.WriteLine("r1 / r2: " + r7);

      Console.In.ReadLine();  // Wait for enter key
    }
  }
}
```

Listing 6.3   continued

Output

```
First rational number: 3/4
Second rational number: 1/3
r1 and r2 are NOT equal.
The reciprocal of r1 is: 4/3
r1 + r2: 13/12
r1 - r2: 5/12
r1 * r2: 1/4
r1 / r2: 9/4
```

The `RationalNumber` class is shown in Listing 6.4. Keep in mind as you examine this class that each object created from the `RationalNumber` class represents a single rational number. The `RationalNumber` class contains various operations on rational numbers, such as addition and subtraction.

The methods of the `RationalNumber` class, such as `Add`, `Subtract`, `Multiply`, and `Divide`, use the `RationalNumber` object that is executing the method as the first (left) operand and use the `RationalNumber` object passed as a parameter as the second (right) operand.

Listing 6.4

```csharp
//*************************************************************
//  Rational.cs        C#:  Ken Culp
//
//  Represents a rational number with numerator and denominator.
//*************************************************************
using System;

namespace RationalTester
{
  public class Rational
  {
    private int numerator, denominator;

    //------------------------------------------------------------
    //  Sets up the rational number by ensuring a nonzero
    //  denominator and making only the numerator signed.
    //------------------------------------------------------------
    public Rational(int numer, int denom)
    {
      if (denom == 0)
        denom = 1;
```

Listing 6.4 continued

```csharp
    // Make the numerator "store" the sign
    if (denom < 0)
    {
      numer = numer * -1;
      denom = denom * -1;
    }

    numerator = numer;
    denominator = denom;

    Reduce();
  }

  //-----------------------------------------------------------
  //  Returns the numerator of this rational number.
  //-----------------------------------------------------------

  /// <summary>
  ///
  /// </summary>
  /// <returns></returns>
  public int GetNumerator() // Documentation on GetNumerator
  {
    return numerator;
  }
  public int Numerator   // Property for numerator
  {
    get { return numerator; }
  }

  //-----------------------------------------------------------
  //  Returns the denominator of this rational number.
  //-----------------------------------------------------------
  public int GetDenominator()
  {
    return denominator;
  }
  public int Denominator   // Property for denominator
  {
    get { return denominator; }
  }

  //-----------------------------------------------------------
  //  Returns the reciprocal of this rational number.
  //-----------------------------------------------------------
  public Rational Reciprocal()
  {
    return new Rational(denominator, numerator);
  }
```

Listing 6.4   continued

```
//-------------------------------------------------------------
//  Adds this rational number to the one passed as a
//  parameter. A common denominator is found by multiplying
//  the individual denominators.
//-------------------------------------------------------------
public Rational Add(Rational op2)
{
   int commonDenominator = denominator * op2.GetDenominator();
   int numerator1 = numerator * op2.GetDenominator();
   int numerator2 = op2.GetNumerator() * denominator;
   int sum = numerator1 + numerator2;

   return new Rational(sum, commonDenominator);
}


//-------------------------------------------------------------
//  Subtracts the rational number passed as a parameter from
//  this rational number.
//-------------------------------------------------------------
public Rational Subtract(Rational op2)
{
   int commonDenominator = denominator * op2.GetDenominator();
   int numerator1 = numerator * op2.GetDenominator();
   int numerator2 = op2.GetNumerator() * denominator;
   int difference = numerator1 - numerator2;

   return new Rational(difference, commonDenominator);
}


//-------------------------------------------------------------
//  Multiplies this rational number by the one passed as a
//  parameter.
//-------------------------------------------------------------
public Rational Multiply(Rational op2)
{
   int numer = numerator * op2.GetNumerator();
   int denom = denominator * op2.GetDenominator();

   return new Rational(numer, denom);
}


//-------------------------------------------------------------
//  Divides this rational number by the one passed as a
//  parameter by multiplying by the reciprocal of the
//  second rational.
//-------------------------------------------------------------
public Rational Divide(Rational op2)
```

Listing 6.4   continued

```csharp
{
   return Multiply(op2.Reciprocal());
}

//-----------------------------------------------------------
//   Determines if this rational number is equal to the one
//   passed as a parameter.  Assumes they are both reduced.
//-----------------------------------------------------------
public bool Equals(Rational op2)
{
   return (numerator == op2.GetNumerator() &&
      denominator == op2.GetDenominator());
}

//-----------------------------------------------------------
//   Returns this rational number as a string.
//-----------------------------------------------------------
public override string ToString()
{
   string result;

   if (numerator == 0)
      result = "0";
   else
      if (denominator == 1)
         result = numerator + "";
      else
         result = numerator + "/" + denominator;

   return result;
}

//-----------------------------------------------------------
//   Reduces this rational number by dividing both numerator
//   and the denominator by their greatest common divisor.
//-----------------------------------------------------------
private void Reduce()
{
   if (numerator != 0)
   {
      int common = Gcd(Math.Abs(numerator), denominator);

      numerator = numerator / common;
      denominator = denominator / common;
   }
}
```

Listing 6.4   continued

```
//------------------------------------------------------------
//  Computes and returns the greatest common divisor of the
//  two positive parameters. Uses Euclid's algorithm.
//------------------------------------------------------------
private int Gcd(int num1, int num2)
{
  while (num1 != num2)
    if (num1 > num2)
      num1 = num1 - num2;
    else
      num2 = num2 - num1;

  return num1;
  }
 }
}
```

Note that some of the methods in the `RationalNumber` class, including `Reduce` and `Gcd`, are declared with private visibility. These methods are `private` because we don't want them executed directly from outside a `RationalNumber` object. They exist only to support the other services of the object.

Aggregation

Some objects are made up of other objects. A car, for instance, is made up of its engine, its chassis, its wheels, and several other parts. Each of these other parts could be considered a separate object. Therefore, we can say that a car is an *aggregation*—it is composed, at least in part, of other objects. Aggregation is sometimes described as a *"has-a" relationship*. For instance, a car has a chassis.

> **Key Concept**
>
> An aggregate object is composed of other objects, forming a has-a relationship.

In the software world, we define an *aggregate object* as any object that contains references to other objects as instance data. For example, an `Account` object contains, among other things, a `string` object that represents the name of the account owner. We sometimes forget that strings are objects, but technically that makes each `Account` object an aggregate object.

Aggregation is a special type of dependency. That is, a class that is defined in part by another class is dependent on that class. The methods of the aggregate object generally invoke the methods of the objects from which it is composed.

Let's consider another example. The program `StudentBody`, shown in Listing 6.5, creates two `Student` objects. Each `Student` object is composed, in part, of two `Address` objects, one for the student's address at school and another for the student's home address. The `main` method does nothing more than create the `Student` objects and print them out. Once again, we are passing objects to the `WriteLine` method, relying on the automatic call to the `ToString` method to create a valid representation of the object that is suitable for printing.

The `Student` class, shown in Listing 6.6, represents a single student. This class would have to be greatly expanded if it were to represent all aspects of a student. We deliberately keep it simple for now so that the object aggregation is clearly shown. The instance data of the `Student` class includes two references to `Address` objects. We refer to those objects in the `ToString` method as we create a string representation of the student. By concatenating an `Address` object to another string, the `ToString` method in `Address` is automatically invoked.

Listing 6.5

```
//*************************************************************
//   StudentBody.cs          C#:   Ken Culp
//
//   Demonstrates the use of an aggregate class.
//*************************************************************
using System;

namespace StudentBody
{
  class StudentBody
  {
    //-------------------------------------------------------------
    //  Creates some Address and Student objects and prints them.
    //-------------------------------------------------------------
    static void Main(string[] args)
    {
      Address school = new Address(
        "800 Lancaster Ave.", "Villanova", "PA", 19085);

      Address jHome = new Address(
        "21 Jump Street", "Lynchburg", "VA", 24551);
      Student john = new Student(
        "John", "Smith", jHome, school);

      Address mHome = new Address(
        "123 Main Street", "Euclid", "OH", 44132);
      Student marsha = new Student(
        "Marsha", "Jones", mHome, school);

      Console.Out.WriteLine(john);
      Console.Out.WriteLine();
      Console.Out.WriteLine(marsha);

      Console.In.ReadLine();   // Wait for enter key
    }
  }
}
```

Listing 6.5 continued

Output

```
John Smith
Home Address:
21 Jump Street
Lynchburg, VA  24551
School Address:
800 Lancaster Ave.
Villanova, PA  19085

Marsha Jones
Home Address:
123 Main Street
Euclid, OH  44132
School Address:
800 Lancaster Ave.
Villanova, PA  19085
```

The Address class is shown in Listing 6.7. It represents a street address. Note that nothing about the Address class indicates that it is part of a Student object. The Address class is kept generic by design and therefore could be used in any situation in which a street address is needed.

The more complex an object, the more likely it will need to be represented as an aggregate object. In UML, aggregation is represented by a connection between two classes, with an open diamond at the end near the class that is the aggregate. Figure 6.2 shows a UML class diagram for the StudentBody program.

Note that in previous UML diagram examples and in Figure 6.2, strings are not represented as separate classes with aggregation relationships, though technically they could be. Strings are so fundamental to programming that often they are represented in a UML diagram as if they were a primitive type.

The this Reference

Before we leave the topic of relationships among classes, we should examine another special reference used in C# programs, called the **this** reference. The word **this** is a reserved word in C#. It allows an object to refer to itself. As we have discussed, a nonstatic method is invoked through (or by) a particular object or class. Inside that method, the **this** reference can be used to refer to the currently executing object.

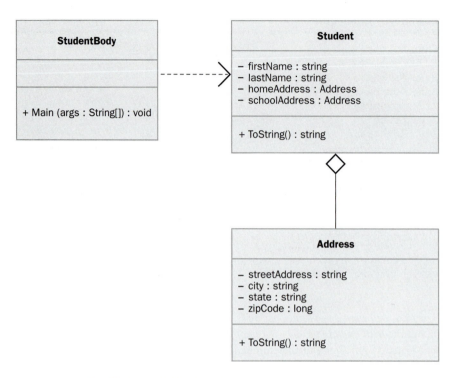

FIGURE 6.2   A UML class diagram showing aggregation

Listing 6.6

```
//*************************************************************
//   Student.cs          C#:   Ken Culp
//
//   Represents a college student.
//*************************************************************
using System;

namespace StudentBody
{
  public class Student
  {
    private string firstName, lastName;
    private Address homeAddress, schoolAddress;

    //-----------------------------------------------------------
    //   Sets up Student object with the specified initial values.
    //-----------------------------------------------------------
    public Student(string first, string last, Address home,
      Address school)
```

Listing 6.6   continued

```
    {
      firstName = first;
      lastName = last;
      homeAddress = home;
      schoolAddress = school;
    }

    //-----------------------------------------------------------
    //  Returns this Student object as a string.
    //-----------------------------------------------------------
    public override string ToString()
    {
      string result;

      result = firstName + " " + lastName + "\n";
      result += "Home Address:\n" + homeAddress + "\n";
      result += "School Address:\n" + schoolAddress;

      return result;
    }
  }
}
```

Listing 6.7

```
//***************************************************************
//  Address.cs        C#:  Ken Culp
//
//  Represents a street address.
//***************************************************************
using System;

namespace StudentBody
{
  public class Address
  {
    private string streetAddress, city, state;
    private long zipCode;

    //-----------------------------------------------------------
    //  Sets up this Address object with the specified data.
    //-----------------------------------------------------------
    public Address(string street, string town,
      string st, long zip)
    {
```

Listing 6.7 continued

```
        streetAddress = street;
        city = town;
        state = st;
        zipCode = zip;
    }

    //-------------------------------------------------------------
    //  Returns this Address object as a string.
    //-------------------------------------------------------------
    public override string ToString()
    {
        string result;

        result = streetAddress + "\n";
        result += city + ", " + state + "   " + zipCode;

        return result;
    }
}
}
```

For example, in a class called ChessPiece there could be a method called Move, which could contain the following line:

```
if (this.position == piece2.position)
    result = false;
```

In this situation, the **this** reference is being used to clarify which position is being referenced. The **this** reference refers to the object through which the method was invoked. So when the following line is used to invoke the method, the **this** reference refers to bishop1:

```
bishop1.Move();
```

However, when another object is used to invoke the method, the **this** reference refers to it. Therefore, when the following invocation is used, the **this** reference in the move method refers to bishop2:

```
bishop2.Move();
```

Often, the **this** reference is used to distinguish the parameters of a constructor from their corresponding instance variables with the same names. For example, the constructor of the Account class was presented in Chapter 4 as follows:

```
public Account (string owner, long account, double initial)
{
  name = owner;
  acctNumber = account;
  balance = initial;
}
```

When writing this constructor, we deliberately came up with different names for the parameters to distinguish them from the instance variables `name`, `acctNumber`, and `balance`. This distinction is arbitrary. The constructor could have been written as follows using the **this** reference:

```
public Account (string name, long acctNumber, double balance)
{
  this.name = name;
  this.acctNumber = acctNumber;
  this.balance = balance;
}
```

In this version of the constructor, the **this** reference specifically refers to the instance variables of the object. The variables on the right-hand side of the assignment statements refer to the formal parameters. This approach eliminates the need to come up with different yet equivalent names. This situation sometimes occurs in other methods but comes up often in constructors.

6.5 INTERFACES

We've used the term "interface" to refer to the set of public methods through which we can interact with an object. That definition is consistent with our use of it in this section, but now we are going to formalize this concept using a particular language construct in C#.

A C# *interface* is a collection of constants and abstract methods. An *abstract method* is a method that does not have an implementation. That is, there is no body of code defined for an abstract method. The header of the method, including its parameter list, is simply followed by a semicolon. An interface cannot be instantiated.

Listing 6.8 shows an interface called `Complexity`. It contains two abstract methods: `SetComplexity` and `GetComplexity`.

Listing 6.8

```
//*************************************************************
//  Complexity.cs          C#:  Ken Culp
//
//  Represents the interface for an object that can be assigned
//  an explicit complexity.
//*************************************************************
using System;

namespace MiniQuiz
{
  public interface Complexity
  {
    void SetComplexity(int complexity);
    int GetComplexity();
  }
}
```

An abstract method can be preceded by the reserved word **abstract**, though in interfaces it usually is not. Methods in interfaces have public visibility by default.

A class *implements* an interface by providing method implementations for each of the abstract methods defined in the interface. A class that implements an interface uses the reserved word **implements** followed by the interface name in the class header. If a class asserts that it implements a particular interface, it must provide a definition for all methods in the interface. The compiler will produce errors if any of the methods in the interface is not given a definition in the class.

The Question class, shown in Listing 6.9, implements the Complexity interface. Both the SetComplexity and GetComplexity methods are implemented. They must be declared with the same signatures as their abstract counterparts in the interface. In the Question class, the methods are defined simply to set or return a numeric value representing the complexity level of the question that the object represents.

Note that the Question class also implements additional methods that are not part of the Complexity interface. Specifically, it defines methods called GetQuestion, GetAnswer, AnswerCorrect, and ToString, which have nothing to do with the interface. The interface guarantees that the class implements certain methods, but it does not restrict it from having others. It is common for a class that implements an interface to have other methods.

Listing 6.9

```csharp
//****************************************************************
//  Question.cs        C#:  Ken Culp
//
//  Represents a question (and its answer).
//****************************************************************
using System;

namespace MiniQuiz
{
  public class Question
  {
    private string question, answer;
    private int complexityLevel;

    //--------------------------------------------------------------
    //  Sets up the question with a default complexity.
    //--------------------------------------------------------------
    public Question(string query, string result)
    {
      question = query;
      answer = result;
      complexityLevel = 1;
    }

    //--------------------------------------------------------------
    //  Sets the complexity level for this question.
    //--------------------------------------------------------------
    public void SetComplexity(int level)
    {
      complexityLevel = level;
    }

    //--------------------------------------------------------------
    //  Returns the complexity level for this question.
    //--------------------------------------------------------------
    public int GetComplexity()
    {
      return complexityLevel;
    }

    //--------------------------------------------------------------
    //  Returns the question.
    //--------------------------------------------------------------
    public string GetQuestion()
    {
      return question;
    }
```

Listing 6.9 continued

```csharp
//-----------------------------------------------------------
//  Returns the answer to this question.
//-----------------------------------------------------------
public string GetAnswer()
{
   return answer;
}


//-----------------------------------------------------------
//  Returns true if the candidate answer matches the answer.
//-----------------------------------------------------------
public bool AnswerCorrect(string candidateAnswer)
{
   return (answer.ToUpper() == candidateAnswer.ToUpper());
}


//-----------------------------------------------------------
//  Returns this question (and its answer) as a string.
//-----------------------------------------------------------
public override string ToString()
{
   return question + "\n" + answer;
}
   }
}
```

Listing 6.10 shows a program called MiniQuiz, which uses some Question objects.

An interface and its relationship to a class that implements it can be shown in a UML class diagram. An interface is represented similarly to a class node except that the designation <<interface>> is inserted above the class name. A dotted arrow with a closed arrowhead is drawn from the class to the interface that it implements. Figure 6.3 shows a UML class diagram for the MiniQuiz program.

Multiple classes can implement the same interface, providing alternative definitions for the methods. For example, we could implement a class called Task that also implements the Complexity interface. In it we could choose to manage the complexity of a task in a different way (though it would still have to implement all the methods of the interface).

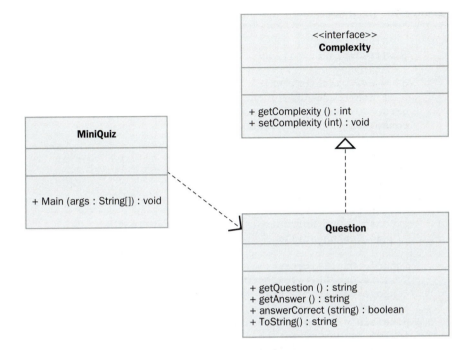

FIGURE 6.3   A UML class diagram for the `MiniQuiz` program

Listing 6.10

```csharp
//****************************************************************
//  MiniQuiz.cs         C#:   Ken Culp
//
//  Demonstrates the use of a class that implements an interface.
//****************************************************************
using System;

namespace MiniQuiz
{
  class MiniQuiz
  //-----------------------------------------------------------
  //  Presents a short quiz.
  //-----------------------------------------------------------
  {
    static void Main(string[] args)
    {
      Question q1, q2;
      string possible;

      q1 = new Question("What is the capital of Jamaica?",
```

Listing 6.10 continued

```
        "Kingston");
    q1.SetComplexity(4);

    q2 = new Question("Which is worse, ignorance or apathy?",
        "I don't know and I don't care");
    q2.SetComplexity(10);
    Console.Out.Write(q1.GetQuestion());
    Console.Out.WriteLine(" (Level: " +
        q1.GetComplexity() + ")");
    possible = Console.In.ReadLine();
    if (q1.AnswerCorrect(possible))
        Console.Out.WriteLine("Correct");
    else
        Console.Out.WriteLine("No, the answer is " +
            q1.GetAnswer());

    Console.Out.WriteLine();
    Console.Out.Write(q2.GetQuestion());
    Console.Out.WriteLine(" (Level: " +
        q2.GetComplexity() + ")");
    possible = Console.In.ReadLine();
    if (q2.AnswerCorrect(possible))
        Console.Out.WriteLine("Correct");
    else
        Console.Out.WriteLine("No, the answer is " +
            q2.GetAnswer());

    Console.In.ReadLine();   // Wait for enter key
    }
  }
}
```

Output

```
What is the capital of Jamaica? (Level: 4)
Kingston
Correct

Which is worse, ignorance or apathy? (Level: 10)
apathy
No, the answer is I don't know and I don't care
```

A class can implement more than one interface. In these cases, the class must provide an implementation for all methods in all interfaces listed. To show that a class implements multiple interfaces, they are listed in the **implements** clause, separated by commas. For example:

```
class ManyThings implements interface1, interface2, interface3
   {
   // contains all methods of all interfaces
   }
```

In addition to, or instead of, abstract methods, an interface can also contain constants, defined using the **const** modifier. When a class implements an interface, it gains access to all the constants defined in it.

The interface construct formally defines the ways in which we can interact with a class. It also serves as a basis for a powerful programming technique called polymorphism, which we discuss in Chapter 9.

The **IComparable** Interface

The C# standard class library contains interfaces as well as classes. The **IComparable** interface, for example, is defined in the C# library. The **IComparable** interface contains only one method, **CompareTo**, which takes an object as a parameter and returns an integer:

```
int CompareTo(object obj) { ...
```

The intention of this interface is to provide a common mechanism for comparing one object to another. One object calls the method and passes another as a parameter, as follows:

```
if (obj1.CompareTo(obj2) < 0)
   Console.Out.WriteLine("obj1 is less than obj2");
```

As specified by the documentation for the interface, the integer that is returned from the **CompareTo** method should be negative if obj1 is less than obj2, 0 if they are equal, and positive if obj1 is greater than obj2. It is up to the designer of each class to decide what it means for one object of that class to be less than, equal to, or greater than another.

In Chapter 5, we mentioned that the **string** class contains a **CompareTo** method that operates in this manner. Now we can clarify that the **string** class has this method because it implements the **IComparable** interface. The **string** class implementation of this method bases the comparison on the lexicographic ordering defined by the Unicode character set.

6.6 METHOD DESIGN

Once you have identified classes and assigned basic responsibilities, the design of each method will determine how exactly the class will define its behaviors. Some methods are straightforward and require little thought. Others are more interesting and require careful planning.

An *algorithm* is a step-by-step process for solving a problem. A recipe is an example of an algorithm. Travel directions are another example of an algorithm. Every method implements an algorithm that determines how that method accomplishes its goals.

An algorithm is often described using *pseudocode,* which is a mixture of code statements and English phrases. Pseudocode provides enough structure to show how the code will operate, without getting bogged down in the syntactic details of a particular programming language or becoming prematurely constrained by the characteristics of particular programming constructs.

This section discusses two important aspects of program design at the method level: method decomposition and the implications of passing objects as parameters.

Method Decomposition

Key Concept

A complex service provided by an object can be decomposed to make use of private support methods.

Occasionally, a service that an object provides is so complicated that it cannot reasonably be implemented using one method. Therefore, we sometimes need to decompose a method into multiple methods to create a more understandable design. As an example, let's examine a program that translates English sentences into Pig Latin.

Pig Latin is a made-up language in which each word of a sentence is modified, in general, by moving the initial sound of the word to the end and adding an "ay" sound. For example, the word *happy* would be written and pronounced *appyhay* and the word *birthday* would become *irthdaybay*. Words that begin with vowels simply have a "yay" sound added on the end, turning the word *enough* into *enoughyay*. Consonant blends such as "ch" and "st" at the beginning of a word are moved to the end together before adding the "ay" sound. Therefore, the word *grapefruit* becomes *apefruitgray*. The `PigLatin` program shown in Listing 6.11 reads one or more sentences, translating each into Pig Latin.

Listing 6.11

```
//****************************************************************
//  PigLatin.cs          C#:  Ken Culp
//
//  Driver to exercise the PigLatinTranslator class.
//****************************************************************
using System;

namespace PigLatin
{
  class PigLatin
```

Listing 6.11   continued

```csharp
  {
    //------------------------------------------------------------
    //  Reads sentences and translates them into Pig Latin.
    //------------------------------------------------------------
    static void Main(string[] args)
    {
      string sentence, result, another;
      PigLatinTranslator translator = new PigLatinTranslator();

      do
      {
        Console.Out.WriteLine();
        Console.Out.WriteLine(
          "Enter a sentence (no punctuation):");
        sentence = Console.In.ReadLine();
        Console.Out.WriteLine();
        result = translator.Translate(sentence);
        Console.Out.WriteLine("That sentence in Pig Latin is:");
        Console.Out.WriteLine(result);

        Console.Out.WriteLine();
        Console.Out.Write("Translate another sentence (y/n)? ");
        another = Console.In.ReadLine();
      }
      while (another.ToLower() == "y");
    }
  }
}
```

Output

```
Enter a sentence (no punctuation):
Do you speak Pig Latin

That sentence in Pig Latin is:
oday ouyay eakspay igpay atinlay

Translate another sentence (y/n)? y

Enter a sentence (no punctuation):
Play it again Sam

That sentence in Pig Latin is:
ayplay ityay againyay amsay

Translate another sentence (y/n)? n
```

The workhorse behind the `PigLatin` program is the `PigLatinTranslator` class, shown in Listing 6.12. The `PigLatinTranslator` class provides one fundamental service, a static method called `Translate`, which accepts a string and translates it into Pig Latin. Note that the `PigLatinTranslator` class does not contain a constructor, because none is needed.

The act of translating an entire sentence into Pig Latin is not trivial. If written in one big method, it would be very long and difficult to follow. A better solution, as implemented in the `PigLatinTranslator` class, is to decompose the `Translate` method and use several other support methods to help with the task.

The `Translate` method uses a `Scanner` object to separate the string into words. Recall that one role of the `Scanner` class (discussed in Chapter 3) is to separate a string into smaller elements called tokens. In this case, the tokens are separated by space characters so we can use the default whitespace delimiters. The `PigLatin` program assumes that no punctuation is included in the input.

The `Translate` method passes each word to the private support method `TranslateWord`. Even the job of translating one word is somewhat involved, so the `TranslateWord` method makes use of two other private methods, `BeginsWithVowel` and `BeginsWithBlend`.

The `BeginsWithVowel` method returns a **bool** value that indicates whether the word passed as a parameter begins with a vowel. Note that instead of checking each vowel separately, the code for this method declares a string that contains all the vowels, and then invokes the `string` method `IndexOf` to determine whether the first character of the word is in the vowel string. If the specified character cannot be found, the `IndexOf` method returns a value of –1.

The `BeginsWithBlend` method also returns a **bool** value. The body of the method contains only a **return** statement with one large expression that makes several calls to the `StartsWith` method of the `String` class. If any of these calls returns true, then the `BeginsWithBlend` method returns true as well.

Note that the `TranslateWord`, `BeginsWithVowel`, and `BeginsWithBlend` methods are all declared with private visibility. They are not intended to provide services directly to clients outside the class. Instead, they exist to help the `Translate` method, which is the only true service method in this class, to do its job. By declaring them with private visibility, they cannot be invoked from outside this class. If the `main` method of the `PigLatin` class were to attempt to invoke the `TranslateWord` method, for instance, the compiler would issue an error message.

Figure 6.4 shows a UML class diagram for the `PigLatin` program. Note the notation showing the visibility of various methods.

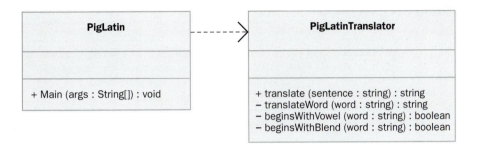

FIGURE 6.4   A UML class diagram for the PigLatin program

Listing 6.12

```
//***************************************************************
//  PigLatinTranslator.cs          C#:   Ken Culp
//
//  Represents a translation system from English to Pig Latin.
//  Demonstrates method decomposition and use of string Split.
//***************************************************************
using System;

namespace PigLatin
{
  public class PigLatinTranslator
  {
    private static string vowels = "aeiou";
    //-----------------------------------------------------------
    //  Translates a sentence of words into Pig Latin.
    //-----------------------------------------------------------
    public string Translate(string sentence)
    {
      string result = "";
      sentence = sentence.ToLower();
      string[] allWords = sentence.Split(' '); // Split words

      foreach (string word in allWords)              // Do every word
      {
        result += TranslateWord(word);
        result += " ";
      }
      return result;
    }
```

Listing 6.12 continued

```csharp
//------------------------------------------------------------
//  Translates one word into Pig Latin. If the word begins
//  with a vowel, the suffix "yay" is appended to the word.
//  Otherwise, the first letter or two are moved to the end
//  of the word, and "ay" is appended.
//------------------------------------------------------------
private string TranslateWord(string word)
{
  string result = "";

  if (BeginsWithVowel(word))
    result = word + "yay";
  else
    if (BeginsWithBlend(word))
      result =
        word.Substring(2) + word.Substring(0, 2) + "ay";
    else
      result = word.Substring(1) + word[0] + "ay";

  return result;
}

//------------------------------------------------------------
//  Determines if the specified word begins with a vowel.
//------------------------------------------------------------
private bool BeginsWithVowel(string word)
{
  char letter = word[0];    // First letter of word
  return (vowels.IndexOf(letter) != -1);
}

//------------------------------------------------------------
//  Determines if the specified word begins with a particular
//  two-character consonant blend.
//------------------------------------------------------------
private bool BeginsWithBlend(string word)
{
  return (word.StartsWith("bl") || word.StartsWith("sc") ||
          word.StartsWith("br") || word.StartsWith("sh") ||
          word.StartsWith("ch") || word.StartsWith("sk") ||
          word.StartsWith("cl") || word.StartsWith("sl") ||
          word.StartsWith("cr") || word.StartsWith("sn") ||
          word.StartsWith("dr") || word.StartsWith("sm") ||
          word.StartsWith("dw") || word.StartsWith("sp") ||
          word.StartsWith("fl") || word.StartsWith("sq") ||
          word.StartsWith("fr") || word.StartsWith("st") ||
          word.StartsWith("gl") || word.StartsWith("sw") ||
          word.StartsWith("gr") || word.StartsWith("th") ||
```

```
                    word.StartsWith("kl") || word.StartsWith("tr") ||
                    word.StartsWith("ph") || word.StartsWith("tw") ||
                    word.StartsWith("pl") || word.StartsWith("wh") ||
                    word.StartsWith("pr") || word.StartsWith("wr"));
      }
   }
}
```

Whenever a method becomes large or complex, we should consider decomposing it into multiple methods to create a more understandable class design. First, however, we must consider how other classes and objects can be defined to create better overall system design. In an object-oriented design, method decomposition must be subordinate to object decomposition.

Method Parameters Revisited

Another important issue related to method design involves the way parameters are passed into a method. By default, in C# all parameters are passed *by value*. That is, the current value of the actual parameter (in the invocation) is copied into the formal parameter in the method header. We mentioned this issue in Chapter 4; let's examine it now in more detail.

Essentially, parameter passing is like an assignment statement, assigning to the formal parameter a copy of the value stored in the actual parameter. This issue must be considered when making changes to a formal parameter inside a method. The formal parameter is a separate copy of the value that is passed in, so any changes made to it have no effect on the actual parameter. After control returns to the calling method, the actual parameter will have the same value as it did before the method was called.

However, when we pass an object to a method, we are actually passing a reference to that object. The value that gets copied is the address of the object. Therefore, the formal parameter and the actual parameter become aliases of each other. If we change the state of the object through the formal parameter reference inside the method, we are changing the object referenced by the actual parameter, because they refer to the same object. On the other hand, if we change the formal parameter reference itself (to make it point to a new object, for instance), we have not changed the fact that the actual parameter still refers to the original object.

The program in Listing 6.13 illustrates the nuances of parameter passing. Carefully trace the processing of this program and note the values that are output. The `ParameterTester` class contains a main method that calls the `ChangeValues` method in a `ParameterModifier` object. Two of the parameters to `ChangeValues` are `Num` objects, each of which simply stores an integer value. The other parameter is a primitive integer value.

Listing 6.14 shows the `ParameterModifier` class, and Listing 6.15 shows the `Num` class. Inside the `ChangeValues` method, a modification is made to each of the three formal parameters: the integer parameter is set to a different value, the value stored in the first `Num` parameter is changed using its `SetValue` method, and a new `Num` object is created and assigned to the second `Num` parameter. These changes are reflected in the output printed at the end of the `ChangeValues` method.

However, note the final values that are printed after returning from the method. The primitive integer was not changed from its original value, because the change was made to a copy inside the method. Likewise, the last parameter still refers to its original object with its original value, because the new Num object created in the method was referred to only by the formal parameter. When the method returned, that formal parameter was destroyed and the Num object it referred to was marked for garbage collection. The only change that is "permanent" is the change made to the state of the second parameter. Figure 6.5 shows the step-by-step processing of this program.

Listing 6.13

```
//*****************************************************************
//   ParameterTester.cs          C#:   Ken Culp
//
//   Demonstrates effects of passing various types of parameters.
//*****************************************************************
using System;

namespace ParameterTester
{
  class ParameterPassing
  {
    //-----------------------------------------------------------
    //  Sets three variables (one primitive and two objects) to
    //  serve as actual parameters to the changeValues method.
    //  Prints their values before and after calling the method.
    //-----------------------------------------------------------
    static void Main(string[] args)
    {
      ParameterModifier modifier = new ParameterModifier();

      int a1 = 111;
      Num a2 = new Num(222);
      Num a3 = new Num(333);

      Console.Out.WriteLine("Before calling changeValues:");
      Console.Out.WriteLine("a1\ta2\ta3");
      Console.Out.WriteLine(a1 + "\t" + a2 + "\t" + a3 + "\n");

      modifier.ChangeValues(a1, a2, a3);

      Console.Out.WriteLine("After calling changeValues:");
      Console.Out.WriteLine("a1\ta2\ta3");
      Console.Out.WriteLine(a1 + "\t" + a2 + "\t" + a3 + "\n");

      Console.In.ReadLine();  // Wait for enter key
    }
  }
}
```

Listing 6.14

```
//******************************************************************
//   ParameterModifier.cs          C#:   Ken Culp
//
//   Demonstrates the effects of changing parameter values.
//******************************************************************

using System;

namespace ParameterTester
{
  public class ParameterModifier
  {
    //-----------------------------------------------------------
    //   Modifies the parameters, printing their values before and
    //   after making the changes.
    //-----------------------------------------------------------
    public void ChangeValues(int f1, Num f2, Num f3)
    {
      Console.Out.WriteLine("Before changing the values:");
      Console.Out.WriteLine("f1\tf2\tf3");
      Console.Out.WriteLine(f1 + "\t" + f2 + "\t" + f3 + "\n");

      f1 = 999;
      f2.SetValue(888);
      f3 = new Num(777);

      Console.Out.WriteLine("After changing the values:");
      Console.Out.WriteLine("f1\tf2\tf3");
      Console.Out.WriteLine(f1 + "\t" + f2 + "\t" + f3 + "\n");

      Console.In.ReadLine();
    }
  }
}
```

Listing 6.15

```
//******************************************************************
//   Num.cs          C#:   Ken Culp
//
//   Represents a single integer as an object.
//******************************************************************
using System;

namespace ParameterTester
{
  public class Num
  {
    private int value;
```

Listing 6.15   continued

```csharp
      //-----------------------------------------------------------
      //  Sets up the new Num object, storing an initial value.
      //-----------------------------------------------------------
      public Num(int update)
      {
        value = update;
      }


      //-----------------------------------------------------------
      //  Sets the stored value to the newly specified value.
      //-----------------------------------------------------------
      public void SetValue(int update)
      {
        value = update;
      }


      //-----------------------------------------------------------
      //  Returns the stored integer value as a string.
      //-----------------------------------------------------------
      public override string ToString()
      {
        return value + "";
      }
   }
}
```

Output

```
Before calling ChangeValues
a1        a2        a3
111       222       333

Before changing the values:
f1        f2        f3
111       222       333

After changing the values:
f1        f2        f3
999       888       777

After calling ChangeValues:
a1        a2        a3
111       888       333
```

STEP 1

Before invoking `changeValues`

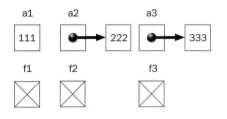

STEP 2

`tester.changeValues (a1, a2, a3);`

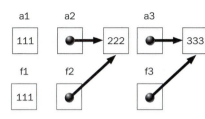

STEP 3

`f1 = 999;`

STEP 4

`f2.setValue (888);`

STEP 5

`f3 = new Num (777);`

STEP 6

After returning from `changeValues`

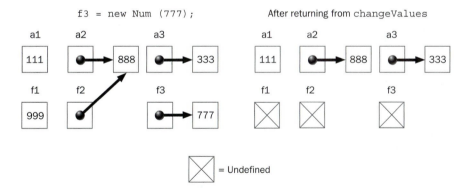

⊠ = Undefined

FIGURE 6.5   Tracing the parameters in the ParameterTester program

The `ref` keyword

As we saw in the preceding discussion, by default, parameters are passed by value. When a parameter is an object, a pointer to that object is passed to the method so that when the method modifies the contents of the passed object, those changes are seen by the caller.

However, when the passed parameter is a primitive type like **int**, then changes made in the called method are made to the copy of the integer, and those changes do not affect the original integer.

However, C# does allow changes to a passed primitive type to be made to the original object. To do this, the called method is not passed a copy of the parameter but rather is passed a pointer to the real parameter. We say that the method is passed a *reference* to the parameter and there is no copy. Note the following syntax change for the ChangeValues method and the way in which that method is called:

```
public void ChangeValues (ref int f1, Num f2, Num f3) {...}
    . . .
modifier.ChangeValues (ref a1, a2, a3);
```

By using the **ref** keyword, we allow the ChangeValues method to change the value of the first parameter. Note the variable a1 is defined and initialized. Second, the **ref** keyword was used in both the method declaration *and* the method invocation.

In this case, the output would look as follows:

```
Before calling ChangeValues
a1        a2        a3
111       222       333

Before changing the values:
f1        f2        f3
111       222       333

After changing the values:
f1        f2        f3
999       888       777

After calling ChangeValues:
a1        a2        a3
999       888       333    NOTE: a1 now shows changes made in method
```

The out keyword

We have seen that methods can return a single value, either a primitive value or a complex object. However, only one object can be returned on the **return** statement, and you will encounter cases in which you want to send back a variety of changed values to the caller. One way is to use the **ref** keyword, as shown in the preceding section. However, using **ref** requires that the caller create an object (or primitive) that is passed to the method for possible modification.

Occasionally, there will be cases where you want a method to return multiple values but the caller does not have a useful value to pass to the method (although you could create one just so that you could pass it to the method with the **ref** keyword). C# gives us another option with the **out** keyword. When a parameter is declared in the method signature as being of type **out**, then the caller need not initialize the parameter but instead can use the returned value after the method completes. Consider the following Add method and its calling syntax in the main program:

```
public void Add(int n1, int n2, out int sum)
{
   sum = n1 + n2;
}
   . . .

int ans;
   . . .
Add(40, 75, out ans);
Console.WriteLine("40 + 75 = {0}", ans);
```

In the preceding code samples, note two things. First, the variable ans is defined in the main program but is not initialized. Second, the **out** keyword is used in both the method declaration *and* the method invocation.

6.7 METHOD OVERLOADING

As we've discussed, when a method is invoked, the flow of control transfers to the code that defines the method. After the method has been executed, control returns to the location of the call, and processing continues.

Often the method name is sufficient to indicate which method is being called by a specific invocation. But in C#, as in other object-oriented languages, you can use the same method name with different parameter lists for multiple methods. This technique is called *method overloading*. It is useful when you need to perform similar methods on different types of data.

> **Key Concept**
>
> The versions of an overloaded method are distinguished by the number, type, and order of their parameters.

The compiler must still be able to associate each invocation to a specific method declaration. If the method name for two or more methods is the same, additional information is used to uniquely identify the version that is being invoked. In C#, a method name can be used for multiple methods as long as the number of parameters, the types of those parameters, and/or the order of the types of parameters is distinct.

For example, we could declare a method called Sum as follows:

```
public int Sum (int num1, int num2)
{
    return num1+num2;
}
```

Then we could declare another method called Sum, within the same class, as follows:

```
public int Sum (int num1, int num2, int num3)
{
    return num1+num2+num3;
}
```

Now, when an invocation is made, the compiler looks at the number of parameters to determine which version of the Sum method to call. For instance, the following invocation will call the second version of the Sum method:

```
sum (25, 69, 13);
```

A method's name, along with the number, type, and order of its parameters, is called the method's *signature*. The compiler uses the complete method signature to *bind* a method invocation to the appropriate definition.

The compiler must be able to examine a method invocation to determine which specific method is being invoked. If you attempt to specify two method names with the same signature, the compiler will issue an appropriate error message and will not create an executable program. There can be no ambiguity.

Note that the return type of a method is not part of the method signature. That is, two overloaded methods cannot differ only by their return type, because the value returned by a method can be ignored by the invocation. The compiler would not be able to distinguish which version of an overloaded method is being referenced in such situations.

The WriteLine method is an example of a method that is overloaded several times, each accepting a single type. The following is a partial list of its various signatures:

> WriteLine (**string** s)

> WriteLine (**int** i)

> WriteLine (**double** d)

> WriteLine (**char** c)

> WriteLine (**bool** b)

The following two lines of code actually invoke different methods that have the same name:

```
Console.Out.WriteLine("Number of students: ");
Console.Out.WriteLine(count);
```

The first line invokes the version of `WriteLine` that accepts a string. The second line, assuming `count` is an integer variable, invokes the version of `WriteLine` that accepts an integer.

We often use a `WriteLine` statement that prints several distinct types, such as:

```
Console.Out.WriteLine("Number of students: " + count);
```

Remember, in this case the plus sign is the string concatenation operator. First, the value in the variable `count` is converted to a string representation, then the two strings are concatenated into one longer string, and finally the definition of `WriteLine` that accepts a single string is invoked.

Constructors can be overloaded, and often are. By providing multiple versions of a constructor, we provide multiple ways to set up an object.

6.8 OPERATOR OVERLOADS IN CLASSES

Primitive data types can easily be compared with the variety of comparison operators like ==, !=, >, and so forth. C# also defines arithmetic on numeric types and uses the plus sign to mean the concatenation of strings. But what can you do with custom classes? We saw that we can use the `CompareTo` method to compare strings (or use the == operator), and we write `CompareTo` methods for our own classes. However, wouldn't it be nice if we could compare our classes with the == or != operators? Also, wouldn't it be convenient if we could define arithmetic operations on our classes?

C# has incorporated the *operator overload* capability of the C++ language into C# to enable us to compare custom classes by using the comparison operators and to define arithmetic for custom classes. Figure 6.6 lists the operators that can be overloaded (defined) in a class.

We now take a look at an example program that overloads several binary operators and the comparison operators. This example uses a class called `Point` that stores two integer (x, y) values for a Cartesian coordinate and then implements all the various overloads and comparison operations.

The comparison operation first examines the x values. If these are different, then the result is based only on x. If x on one point is larger than x on another point, the first point is considered larger. If the x value on one point is smaller, then the point is considered smaller. However, if the x values are the same, then the comparison moves to the y values, and a larger y means a larger point and vice versa. If both x and y are equal, then the objects are considered equal.

Overloading the comparison operators is based on implementing a `CompareTo` method. This is done by implementing the `IComparable` interface, described earlier in the chapter. This `CompareTo` method is used in all the comparison operator overloads.

C# Operator	Definition and Use
`+  -  !  ~  ++  --  true  false`	Unary operators can be overloaded. These take one single parameter and return one value.
`+  -  *  /  %  &  |  ^  <<  >>`	Binary operators can be overloaded. These take two parameters and return one value.
`==  !=  <  >  <=  >=`	Comparison operators can be overloaded but they must be overloaded in pairs (== with !=, < with >, <= with >=).
`public override bool Equals(object o)` `public override int GetHashCode()`	Overrides methods in `System.Object` so that you can implement value comparisons instead of object comparisons. `GetHashCode` must be included to override `Equals`.

FIGURE 6.6   Operators that can be overloaded in C#

Creating Class Libraries

We will use the operator overload example to illustrate how you can create a class (`Point` in this case) and store it in a library for use by other programs. Once the `Point` library is created, it can be used by a variety of other applications. This section explains in detail the steps for creating a class library and then for adding that class library to another project.

To create the `Point` class library, select File/New/Project. In the New Project dialog box, click Class Library under Templates, type the name **Point**, select a directory, and then click OK. The completed form is shown in Figure 6.7.

Type the code as shown in Listing 6.16. Save your file and compile the project using the menu item Build/Build Point.

Listing 6.16

```
//****************************************************************
//  Point.cs            C#:   Ken Culp
//
//  Demonstrates operator overloads and a separate class library.
//  This class maintains (x, y) coordinates and includes
//  comparison operators and arithmetic operators.
//****************************************************************
using System;
```

Listing 6.16 continued

```csharp
namespace DrawTools
{
  public class Point : IComparable
  {
    private int x, y;
    public Point()
    {
      x = 0;
      y = 0;
    }
    public Point(int x, int y)
    {
      this.x = x;
      this.y = y;
    }

    public int X
    {
      get { return x; }
      set { x = value; }
    }
    public int Y
    {
      get { return y; }
      set { y = value; }
    }

    //---------------------------------------------------------
    // Addition of two points
    //---------------------------------------------------------
    public static Point operator +(Point p1, Point p2)
    {
      return new Point(p1.X + p2.X, p1.Y + p2.Y);
    }
    //---------------------------------------------------------
    // Subtraction of two points
    //---------------------------------------------------------
    public static Point operator -(Point p1, Point p2)
    {
      return new Point(p1.X - p2.X, p1.Y - p2.Y);
    }
    //---------------------------------------------------------
    // == Comparison operator (x matches x, y matches y)
    //---------------------------------------------------------
    public override bool Equals(object o)
    {
      Point p = (Point)o;
      return ((x == p.x) && (y == p.y));
```

Listing 6.16 continued

```csharp
        }
        public static bool operator ==(Point p1, Point p2)
        {
            return p1.Equals(p2);
        }
        //---------------------------------------------------------
        // != Comparison operator (x matches x, y matches y)
        //---------------------------------------------------------
        public static bool operator !=(Point p1, Point p2)
        {
            return !p1.Equals(p2);
        }
        //---------------------------------------------------------
        // GetHashCode (required if override Equals)
        //---------------------------------------------------------
        public override int GetHashCode()
        {
            return this.ToString().GetHashCode();
        }

        public override string ToString()
        {
            return "(" + x.ToString() + "," + y.ToString() + ")";
        }

        //---------------------------------------------------------
        // CompareTo: To sort points.  If x value is greater,
        // result is greater regardless of y.  If x values
        // are the same, then check y values.
        //---------------------------------------------------------
        public int CompareTo(object obj)
        {
            Point p = (Point)obj;
            if (this.x > p.X)
                return 1;
            else if (this.x < p.X)
                return -1;
            else  // x values the same
            {
                if (this.y > p.Y)
                    return 1;
                else if (this.y < p.Y)
                    return -1;
                else
                    return 0;
            }
        }
        //---------------------------------------------------------
```

Listing 6.16   continued

```
// < Comparison operator
//------------------------------------------------
public static bool operator <(Point p1, Point p2)
{
  return (p1.CompareTo(p2) < 0);
}
//------------------------------------------------
// > Comparison operator
//------------------------------------------------
public static bool operator >(Point p1, Point p2)
{
  return (p1.CompareTo(p2) > 0);
}
//------------------------------------------------
// <= Comparison operator
//------------------------------------------------
public static bool operator <=(Point p1, Point p2)
{
  return (p1.CompareTo(p2) <= 0);
}
//------------------------------------------------
// >= Comparison operator
//------------------------------------------------
public static bool operator >=(Point p1, Point p2)
{
  return (p1.CompareTo(p2) >= 0);
}
  }
}
```

Now we need to create the main program to test the methods in our Point class. This type of testing is typical during the development cycle. We will talk more about testing shortly, in the "Testing" section.

Create a console application called **OperatorOverload.** Next, right-click the References entry of the Solution Explorer window. This displays the context menu shown in Figure 6.8.

Click Add Reference to open the Add Reference dialog box, shown in Figure 6.9. Click the Projects tab, because you will be accessing your Point project class library.

Click the Browse button, which displays the Windows Open File dialog box. Drill down to the Point application directory, then the bin directory, and finally the Debug directory. In the Debug directory, you will see the file Point.dll listed. Click that file and click the OK button. This takes you back to the Add Reference dialog shown in Figure 6.9, but now your project name is shown in the bottom window. Click OK to add the Point project as a reference to the OperatorOverload project.

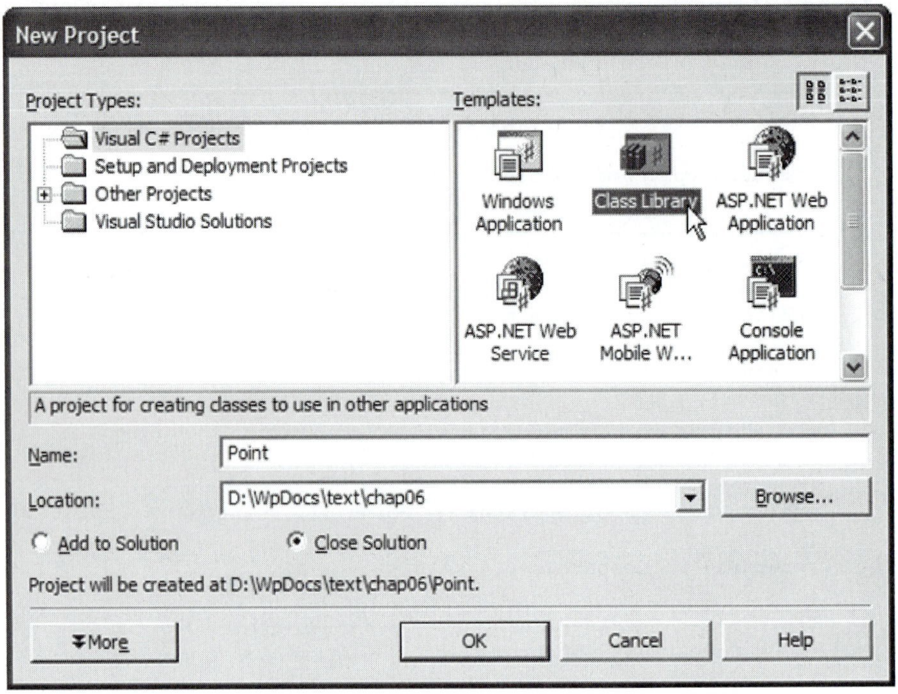

New Project   ✕

Project Types: Templates:

   📁 Visual C# Projects
   📁 Setup and Deployment Projects
  ⊞📁 Other Projects
   📁 Visual Studio Solutions

   📄 Windows   📄 Class Library   📄 ASP.NET Web
   Application   Application

   📄 ASP.NET Web   📄 ASP.NET   📄 Console
   Service   Mobile W...   Application

A project for creating classes to use in other applications

Name: | Point

Location: | D:\WpDocs\text\chap06   ▼ | Browse...

○ Add to Solution   ● Close Solution

Project will be created at D:\WpDocs\text\chap06\Point.

   ⪪More   OK   Cancel   Help

FIGURE 6.7   Creating a class library

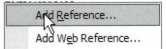

FIGURE 6.8   Adding a reference to a project

The last step to simplify typing the test program is to add a **using** line for the Point library. Recall that the **namespace** used for the Point project was DrawTools. That is the name we need to use on the using statement. Add this line right after the **using** System line. Now type the rest of the code as shown in Listing 6.17.

Note that if you find that you have left something out of your library class, you can go back and edit and rebuild it. Then, when you return to your test project, you will find that the new method or property is defined or that the fixes have been incorporated. Note, however, that if you move the location of the library, you may have to update the reference by deleting it and adding it again.

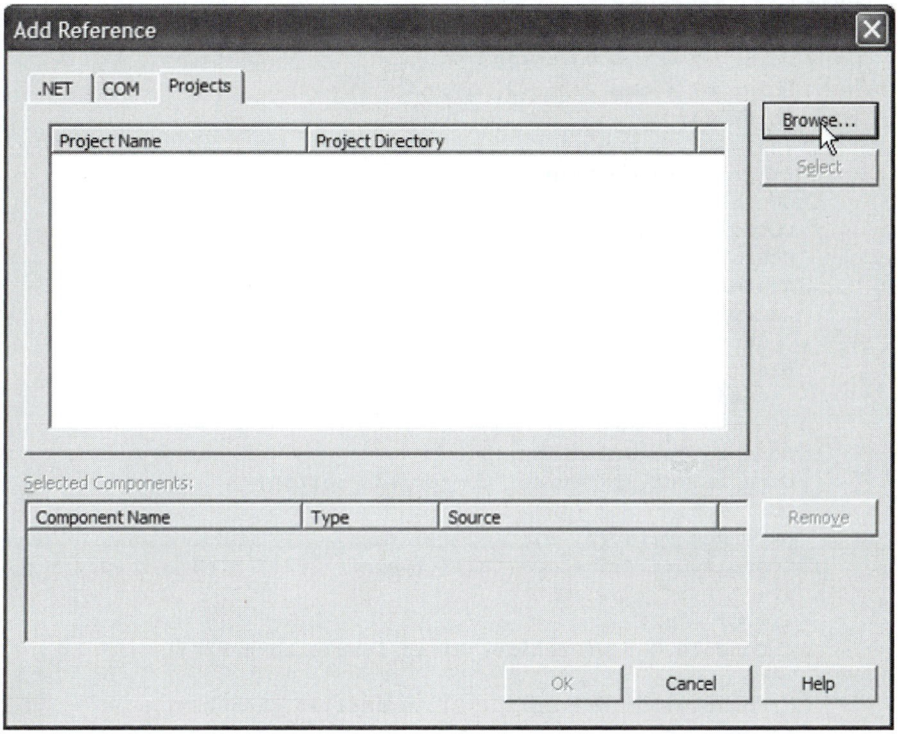

FIGURE 6.9   Selecting a project reference

Listing 6.17

```
//***************************************************************
//  OperatorOverload.cs        C#: Ken Culp
//
//  Demonstrates creating your own comparison and replacement
//  operators for your custom classes.
//***************************************************************
using System;
using System.Diagnostics;
using DrawTools; // Located separately in project Point.

namespace OperatorOverload
{
  class OperatorOverload
  {
    static void Main(string[] args)
    {
      Point p1 = new Point(2, 5);
```

Listing 6.17 continued

```
Point p2 = new Point(20, 50);
Point p3 = new Point(2, 5);
Point p4;

// Write to console
Console.Out.WriteLine("Operator and equality test");
Console.Out.WriteLine("P1:" + p1 + " P2:" + p2 + " P3:" + p3);
Console.Out.WriteLine("P1 + P2: " + (p1 + p2));
Console.Out.WriteLine("P2 - P1: " + (p2 - p1));
if (p1 == p3)
  Console.Out.WriteLine("P1 and P3 are the same");
else
  Console.Out.WriteLine("P1 and P3 are different");

Console.Out.WriteLine();
Console.Out.WriteLine("Comparison tests");
p3.Y = 6;
p4 = new Point(1, 5);
Console.Out.WriteLine("P1:" + p1 + " P2:" + p2 + " P3:" + p3
  + " P4:" + p4);
if (p1 > p2)
  Console.Out.WriteLine("P1 is larger than P2");
else
  Console.Out.WriteLine("P1 is smaller than P2");
if (p1 > p3)
  Console.Out.WriteLine("P1 is larger than P3");
else
  Console.Out.WriteLine("P1 is smaller than P3");
if (p1 < p4)
  Console.Out.WriteLine("P1 is smaller than P4");
else
  Console.Out.WriteLine("P1 is larger than P4");

// Write to Debug window
p1 = new Point(2, 5);
p2 = new Point(20, 50);
p3 = new Point(2, 5);
Debug.WriteLine("Operator and equality test");
Debug.Indent();
Debug.WriteLine("P1:" + p1 + " P2:" + p2 + " P3:" + p3);
Debug.WriteLine("P1 + P2: " + (p1 + p2));
Debug.WriteLine("P2 - P1: " + (p2 - p1));
Debug.WriteLineIf(p1 == p3, "P1 and P3 are the same");
Debug.WriteLineIf(p1 != p3, "P1 and P3 are different");

Debug.WriteLine(" ");
Debug.Unindent();
Debug.WriteLine("Comparison tests");
```

Listing 6.17   continued

```
        Debug.Indent();
        p3.Y = 6;
        p4 = new Point(1, 5);
        Debug.WriteLine("P1:" + p1 + " P2:" + p2 + " P3:" + p3
          + " P4:" + p4);
        Debug.WriteLineIf(p1 > p2, "P1 is larger than P2");
        Debug.WriteLineIf(p1 < p2, "P1 is smaller than P2");
        Debug.WriteLineIf(p1 > p3, "P1 is larger than P3");
        Debug.WriteLineIf(p1 < p3, "P1 is smaller than P3");
        Debug.WriteLineIf(p1 > p4, "P1 is larger than P4");
        Debug.WriteLineIf(p1 < p4, "P1 is smaller than P4");

        Console.In.ReadLine();
    }
  }
}
```

Sample Output

```
Arithmetic operations and equality test
P1:(2,5) P2:(20,50) P3:(2,5)
P1 + P2: (22,55)
P2 - P1: (18,45)
P1 and P3 are the same

Comparison tests
P1:(2,5) P2:(20,50) P3:(2,6) P4:(1,5)
P1 is smaller than P2
P1 is smaller than P3
P1 is larger than P4
```

6.9   OBJECT BROWSER

Visual Studio provides the Object Browser as a tool that you can use to examine the methods and properties of objects within a project. You can also see the parameters associated with a method.

In the previous project, click View/Object Browser. In the tree, click the + sign to the left of Point. Then, if necessary, click the + sign to the left of *DrawTools*. Next, click the word Point and note the list of methods and properties that appears in the right half of the window, as shown in Figure 6.10. You can also view all the classes and methods that make up the core library of all projects. This entry is labeled *mscorlib*. Clicking the + sign to the left of *mscorlib* opens a massive list that you can examine to locate any class or method in that library. We recommend that you experiment using the Object Browser, because it will be of significant help when you need to research the many services offered by C#.

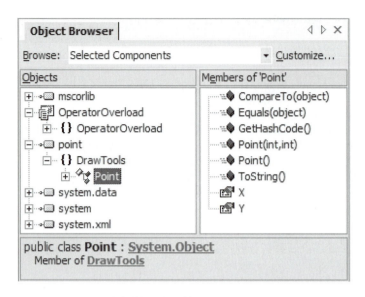

FIGURE 6.10 Object Browser

6.10 TESTING

The term *testing* can be applied in many ways to software development. Testing certainly includes its traditional definition: the act of running a completed program with various inputs to discover problems. But it also includes any evaluation that is performed by human or machine to assess the quality of the evolving system. These evaluations should occur long before a single line of code is written.

The goal of testing is to find errors. By finding errors and fixing them, we improve the quality of our program. It's likely that later on someone else will find any errors that remain hidden during development. The earlier the errors are found, the easier and cheaper they are to fix. Taking the time to uncover problems as early as possible is almost always worth the effort.

> **Key Concept**
>
> Testing a program can never guarantee the absence of errors.

Running a program with specific input and producing the correct results establishes only that the program works for that particular input. As more and more test cases execute without revealing errors, our confidence in the program rises, but we can never really be sure that all errors have been eliminated. There could always be another error still undiscovered. Because of that, it is important to thoroughly test a program in as many ways as possible and with well-designed test cases.

It is possible to prove that a program is correct, but that technique is enormously complex for large systems, and errors can be made in the proof itself. Therefore we generally rely on testing to determine the quality of a program.

After determining that an error exists, we determine the cause of the error and fix it. After a problem is fixed, we should run previous tests again to make sure that while fixing the problem we didn't create another. This technique is called *regression testing*.

Reviews

One technique used to evaluate design or code is called a *review,* which is a meeting in which several people carefully examine a design document or section of code. Presenting our design or code to others causes us to think more carefully about it and permits others to share their suggestions with us. The participants discuss its merits and problems, and create a list of issues that must be addressed. The goal of a review is to identify problems, not to solve them, which usually takes much more time.

A design review should determine whether the requirements are addressed. It should also assess the way the system is decomposed into classes and objects. A code review should determine how faithfully the design satisfies the requirements and how faithfully the implementation represents the design. It should identify any specific problems that would cause the design or the implementation to fail in its responsibilities.

Sometimes a review is called a *walkthrough* because its goal is to step carefully through a document and evaluate each section.

Defect Testing

Since the goal of testing is to find errors, it is often referred to as *defect testing*. With that goal in mind, a good test is one that uncovers any deficiencies in a program. This might seem strange, because we ultimately don't want to have problems in our system. But keep in mind that errors almost certainly exist. Our testing efforts should make every attempt to find them. We want to increase the reliability of our program by finding and fixing the errors that exist, rather than letting users discover them.

> **Key Concept**
>
> A good test is one that uncovers an error.

A *test case* is a set of inputs, user actions, or other initial conditions, and the expected output. A test case should be appropriately documented so that it can be repeated later as needed. Developers often create a complete *test suite,* which is a set of test cases that covers various aspects of the system.

Because programs operate on a large number of possible inputs, it is not feasible to create test cases for all possible input or user actions. Nor is it usually necessary to test every single situation. Two specific test cases may be so similar that they actually do not test unique aspects of the program. To do both would be a wasted effort. We'd rather execute a test case that stresses the program in some new way. Therefore we want to choose our test cases carefully. To that end, let's examine two approaches to defect testing: black-box testing and white-box testing.

> **Key Concept**
>
> It is not feasible to exhaustively test a program for all possible input and user actions.

As the name implies, *black-box testing* treats the thing being tested as a black box. In black-box testing, test cases are developed without regard to the internal workings. Black-box tests are based on inputs and outputs. An entire program can be tested using a black-box technique, in which case the inputs are the user-provided information and user actions such as button clicks. A test case is successful only if the input produces the expected output. A single class can also be tested using a black-box technique, which focuses on the system interface (its public methods) of the class. Certain parameters are passed in, producing certain results. Black-box test cases are often derived directly from the requirements of the system or from the stated purpose of a method.

The input data for a black-box test case is often selected by defining equivalence categories. An *equivalence category* is a collection of inputs that are expected to produce similar outputs. Generally, if a method will work for one value in the equivalence category, we have every reason to believe it will work for the others. For example, the input to a method that computes the square root of an integer can be divided into two equivalence categories: nonnegative integers and negative integers. If it works appropriately for one nonnegative value, it will likely work for all nonnegative values. Likewise, if it works appropriately for one negative value, it will likely work for all negative values.

Equivalence categories have defined boundaries. Because all values of an equivalence category essentially test the same features of a program, only one test case inside the equivalence boundary is needed. However, because programming often produces "off by one" errors, the values on and around the boundary should be tested exhaustively. For an integer boundary, a good test suite would include at least the exact value of the boundary, the boundary minus 1, and the boundary plus 1. Test cases that use these cases, plus at least one from within the general field of the category, should be defined.

Let's look at an example. Consider a method whose purpose is to validate that a particular integer value is in the range 0 to 99, inclusive. There are three equivalence categories in this case: values below 0, values in the range of 0 to 99, and values above 99. Black-box testing dictates that we use test values that surround and fall on the boundaries, as well as some general values from the equivalence categories. Therefore, a set of black-box test cases for this situation might be: -500, -1, 0, 1, 50, 98, 99, 100, and 500.

White-box testing, also known as *glass-box testing*, exercises the internal structure and implementation of a method. A white-box test case is based on the logic of the code. The goal is to ensure that every path through a program is executed at least once. A white-box test maps the possible paths through the code and ensures that the test cases cause every path to be executed. This type of testing is often called *statement coverage*.

Paths through code are controlled by various control flow statements that use conditional expressions, such as **if** statements. In order to have every path through the program executed at least once, the input data values for the test cases need to control the values for the conditional expressions. The input data of one or more test cases should cause the condition of an **if** statement to evaluate to **true** in at least one case and to **false** in at least one case. Covering both true and false values in an **if** statement guarantees that both paths through the **if** statement will be executed. Similar situations can be created for loops and other constructs.

In both black-box and white-box testing, the expected output for each test should be established prior to running the test. It's too easy to be persuaded that the results of a test are appropriate if you haven't first carefully determined what the results should be.

Debugging: Module-Level Testing and Changing Program Order

We have illustrated a variety of applications that use breakpoints or single-stepping. This section covers a few more tools available in Visual Studio for testing and bug killing.

Isolating to an Individual Module

Your first line of defense is to see that the code flow is correct. This can be done by using the single-step features or by using breakpoints. To start at this level, write down the details of the test case that is failing, write down how the program control should flow from module to module, and then set breakpoints at the top of each of these modules. Start the application and submit the test case. This should take you to the first breakpoint. Press F5 (run) and ensure that it gets to the next breakpoint.

If the flow does not go according to your plans, then go back to the module that failed to keep up with the correct sequence and step through the major sections of that module. The idea is to use a search pattern that is designed to narrow down the problem area quickly without having to single-step the entire program.

At the module level, check the paths through the conditional branches (**if** statements, **while** loops). Again, move to smaller and smaller chunks of code to isolate the area containing the error.

Modifying Program Order and Rerunning a Segment of Code

Sometimes during your testing, you find that the data was wrong. We indicated in Chapters 4 and 5 that you can use the Locals window or a Watch window to modify the values in variables and objects. But what do you do after you change the data? How do you back up and try again without having to stop the program, recompile, and run to this point again? The answer is that you can modify the current execution point. The execution point is indicated in the source listing by a large arrow, as shown in Figure 6.11.

The yellow arrow shows the next line of code to be executed. To change the point of execution, click and drag the yellow arrow up or down to the desired point. In Figure 6.12, the current point of execution is being dragged up to the initialization of variable a2. If the mouse button were released at this point, the yellow bar and yellow arrow would be two lines higher. Note that Visual Studio 2005 allows you to modify the code within the method you are currently executing when you are stopped at a breakpoint. Then the modified code can be executed.

Debugging: Tracing Problems and the Output Window

Although we have illustrated how to examine variables when a program is halted, sometimes there is just too many different things we need to view, or we need to view the data too many times. You will find this particularly true when diagnosing problems with loops and lots of conditional paths or when implementing complex code segments.

As an alternative, you can create a report that lists a variety of intermediate results and the form of local variables and organize these in some kind of tabular form. When testing a loop, you might write one line (or lines) of data per trip through the loop. This tracing technique will prove invaluable in isolating the problem.

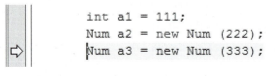

```
int a1 = 111;
Num a2 = new Num (222);
Num a3 = new Num (333);
```

FIGURE 6.11 Current point of execution

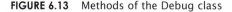

```
int a1 = 111;
Num a2 = new Num (222);
Num a3 = new Num (333);
```

FIGURE 6.12 Changing point of execution

```
public static void Write(string message );
   Writes a text message to the Output window without a new line.

public static void WriteLine(string message );
   Writes a text message to the Output window with a new line.

public static void WriteIf(bool condition,string message );
   Writes a text message to the Output window without a new line if condition is true.

public static void WriteLine(string message );
   Writes a text message to the Output window with a new line if condition is true.

public static void Indent();
   Indents the next set of writes one IndentSize.

public static void Unindent();
   Backs up the next set of writes one IndentSize.

public static int IndentSize;
   Property to set or get the indent size in spaces.
```

FIGURE 6.13 Methods of the Debug class

For example, suppose that the *CompareTo* method of our Point class is failing to find the correct result. You might insert a message at the top of *CompareTo* that lists the x and y values of each point. Then you might write a message in each path through the messy **if** statement.

If you are writing a console application, that diagnostic information could be sent to the console itself and would be interspersed with the normal input and output of the application. In most cases, this would be fine, because the diagnostic information would be removed once the program is operating correctly. At other times, however, you will want to not clutter up the regular console I/O. Also, when you are writing a windows form application, there is usually no console window.

This is where the `System.Diagnostic` namespace and the Output window come into play. The `System.Diagnostic` namespace has a wide variety of methods for diagnosing the program using program control. You can print messages, force the program to break (stop) when a particular condition is encountered, print the stack frame, and lots, lots more. For now, we cover only a few topics. However, to use any of these features, you must add a **using** line for `System.Diagnostics`.

The Output Window

Messages can be written to the Output window using the **static** methods of the *Debug* class (see Figure 6.13).

When the *OperatorOverload* main routine was modified to use the Output window, the code looks as follows, with the Output window shown after it:

```
// Write to Output window
p1 = new Point( 2,  5);
p2 = new Point(20, 50);
p3 = new Point( 2,  5);
Debug.WriteLine("Arithmetic operations and equality test");
Debug.Indent();
Debug.WriteLine("P1:" + p1 + " P2:" + p2 + " P3:" + p3);
Debug.WriteLine("P1 + P2: " + (p1 + p2));
Debug.WriteLine("P2 - P1: " + (p2 - p1));
Debug.WriteLineIf(p1 == p3, "P1 and P3 are the same");
Debug.WriteLineIf(p1 != p3, "P1 and P3 are different");
Debug.WriteLine(" ");
Debug.Unindent();
Debug.WriteLine("Comparison tests");
Debug.Indent();
p3.Y = 6;
p4 = new Point(1, 5);
Debug.WriteLine(
   "P1:" + p1 + " P2:" + p2 + " P3:" + p3 + " P4:" + p4);
Debug.WriteLineIf(p1 > p2, "P1 is larger than P2");
Debug.WriteLineIf(p1 < p2, "P1 is smaller than P2");
Debug.WriteLineIf(p1 > p3, "P1 is larger than P3");
Debug.WriteLineIf(p1 < p3, "P1 is smaller than P3");
Debug.WriteLineIf(p1 > p4, "P1 is larger than P4");
Debug.WriteLineIf(p1 < p4, "P1 is smaller than P4");
```

Output:

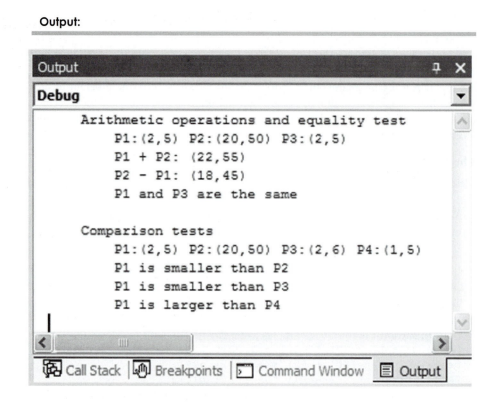

```
Output                                                    ⊥  ✕

Debug                                                         ▼

        Arithmetic operations and equality test
            P1:(2,5)  P2:(20,50)  P3:(2,5)
            P1 + P2:  (22,55)
            P2 - P1:  (18,45)
            P1 and P3 are the same

        Comparison tests
            P1:(2,5)  P2:(20,50)  P3:(2,6)  P4:(1,5)
            P1 is smaller than P2
            P1 is smaller than P3
            P1 is larger than P4


  ◄          ▥                                     ►

   🔲 Call Stack | 🔲 Breakpoints | 🔲 Command Window | 🔲 Output
```

Forcing a Break in Code

Another useful feature of the *System.Diagnostic* namespace is the ability to force the application to stop when a condition exists. For example, suppose that you are testing a loop, and two values inside the loop are never supposed to be equal but somehow they are. You can set up the program to run until those values are equal. The syntax would look as follows (again, you need to add the `System.Diagnostic` namespace to the application to call `Break`):

```
if ( value1 == value2)
    Debugger.Break();
```

6.11 GUI DESIGN

As we focus on the details that allow us to create GUIs, we may sometimes lose sight of the big picture. As we continue to explore GUI construction, we should keep in mind that our goal is to solve a problem. Specifically, we want to create software that is useful. Knowing the details of components, events, and other language elements gives us the tools to put GUIs together, but we must guide that knowledge with the following fundamental ideas of good GUI design:

> Know the user.

> Prevent user errors.

> Optimize user abilities.

> Be consistent.

The software designer must understand the user's needs and potential activities in order to develop an interface that will serve that user well. Keep in mind that, to the user, the interface *is* the software. It is the only way the user interacts with the system. As such, the interface must satisfy the user's needs.

Whenever possible, we should design interfaces so that the user can make as few mistakes as possible. In many situations, we have the flexibility to choose one of several components to accomplish a specific task. We should always try to choose components that will prevent inappropriate actions and avoid invalid input. For example, if an input value must be one of a set of particular values, we should use components that allow the user to make only a valid choice (see the `InputValidation` example in Chapter 5). That is, constraining the user to a few valid choices with, for instance, a set of radio buttons is better than allowing the user to type arbitrary and possibly invalid data into a text field. We cover additional components appropriate for specific situations in this chapter.

Not all users are alike. Some are more adept than others at using a particular GUI or using GUI components in general. We shouldn't design with only the lowest common denominator in mind. For example, we should provide shortcuts whenever reasonable. That is, in addition to providing a normal series of actions that allows a user to accomplish a task, we should also provide redundant ways to accomplish the same task. Using keyboard shortcuts (mnemonics) is a good example. Sometimes these additional mechanisms are less intuitive, but they may be faster for the experienced user.

Finally, consistency is important when dealing with large systems or multiple systems in a common environment. Users become familiar with a particular organization or color scheme; these should not be changed arbitrarily.

6.12 PANELS AND PICTURE BOXES

Up to this point, we have been doing all of our drawing on the client area of the form. However, many controls can be used for drawing including panels, picture boxes, and buttons. Also, some controls can serve as a host for other controls. This section briefly looks at these controls and how to add them.

Panels

As you read in Chapter 5, we can place controls in a group box rather than directly on the form. We used the group box for radio buttons because radio buttons function as a unit and need to be grouped. Visual Studio also supports another control that can serve as a repository for other controls: a panel.

The advantage of using panels is that they can be treated as a group, allowing all the controls on the panel to be hidden or shown in a single instruction (property `Visible` changed). Also, you can arrange a group of controls on a panel in the designer and then move the panel to a new location, without affecting the arrangement of the controls on the panel.

Panels are almost identical to group boxes because both host other controls and can be shown or hidden as a unit. The question, then, is how they differ. One difference is that panels do not have a `Text` property whereas group boxes do. The primary difference, however, is that panel controls also support scroll bars, thus allowing you to place more controls on the panel than can be viewed at any one time. When a portion of included controls is not visible, setting the property `AutoScroll` to **true** and adjusting the margins and size will display scroll bars. We do not illustrate that capability here, but you should be able to figure it out by playing with the properties.

Picture Boxes

A picture box is primarily used as a drawing surface or a place to show images. However, since the picture box is a control, you can also do hit testing and capture events (like `Click`, `MouseOver`, etc.).

Drawing on Controls

All of the drawing tools that can be used on the form can be used on most of the controls, including panels, group boxes, buttons, radio buttons, check boxes, and picture boxes. Our next application illustrates the techniques by building upon our `Boxes` example from Chapter 5. That application will draw a group of boxes in various styles on several controls. Due to space limitations, we do not include the detailed steps for creating the application, but we will analyze the important parts for setting up event handlers and painting on the controls. The application includes the following controls:

Control Name	Description and Use
panel1	Contains one button (unused) and has a background color of red.
pictureBox1	Covers up an unused button, which is demonstrated when Hide is clicked below the picture box. The background color is blue.
groupBox1	Contains two unused radio buttons.
btnToPaint	An unused button that we will paint on.
btnHidePanel	Used to hide the panel, which also hides the one unused button and the two radio buttons that are on it.
btnHidePic	Used to hide the picture button reveling the unused button behind it. Note that the button must be "below" the picture box for the picture box to cover it up. Control order is changed by right-clicking a control and moving it up or down in the order.
btnRedraw	Causes all controls to be repainted. This is described next.

Now let's turn to the painting method used. We extracted the paint method from the Chapter 5 Boxes application and made it into a method that takes four parameters:

```
private void PaintBoxes(Graphics g, int boxCount, int maxSide,
                        Color boxColor)
```

The first parameter is a graphic object, which will be copied from the control during the control's paint method (see below). The next parameter, boxCount, is a count of the number of boxes to draw. The third parameter, maxSide, is the maximum length of a side of the box. The last parameter is the color of the box.

We have to implement a paint method for every control that is to be painted. We do this by clicking the paint event for each control and calling our PaintBoxes method from the preceding code. For example, the following code shows the paint method that draws on our button. This call requests 15 black boxes with a maximum side of 30 pixels.

```
private void btnToPaint_Paint(object sender, PaintEventArgs e)
{
   PaintBoxes(e.Graphics, 15, 30, Color.Black);
}
```

A similar paint method is added for groupBox1, pictureBox1, and panel1. Thus, every time the control is to be redrawn, our PaintBoxes method will be called. This paint event occurs any time something covers up the control or when the Invalidate method is called for the control. Thus, our last step is to add the code for btnRedraw.

We have two choices for causing all controls to redraw. We can either call the Invalidate method for every control (as in pictureBox1.Invalidate) or we can have the form do the work for us. The Invalidate event for the form takes an optional parameter that when set to **true** will cause all controls on the form to be repainted. The complete code for the btnRedraw click handler is as follows:

```
private void btnRedraw_Click(object sender, System.EventArgs e)
{
    this.Invalidate(true);
    // Calling Invalidate for the form with a parameter of
    // true causes Invalidate to be called for all controls on
    // the form.
    // Thus, this single call replaces all of the following:
    //    panel1.Invalidate();
    //    pictureBox1.Invalidate();
    //    groupBox1.Invalidate();
    //    btnToPaint.Invalidate();
}
```

Note that if you only need a couple of controls to repaint, it would be better to enumerate them as shown in the commented code rather than to have all controls repaint. Repainting a limited number of controls would always be faster than repainting all of them. If you called `Invalidate` for the form but did not use the **true** parameter, then nothing would change on the controls.

Please note what happens when you draw graphical images on a control and what happens to text labels and other controls positioned on that control. When you draw on the panel and group box controls, none of the box lines pass through any of the controls contained therein. Thus you could load images, draw figures, write text, or whatever to create a fancy background for the panel or group box, but the controls are not disturbed. However, box lines pass right through the button label and the group box label. This may not be the result that you desire.

Test the application and click the Hide button to see the results. Note that hiding the picture box reveals a button that was hidden below. Visual Studio allows multiple controls to be placed in the same place. This creates a stack of controls, where the first one placed normally is at the bottom of the list. However, you can modify this order by right-clicking a control and selecting Send to Back or Send to Front. In our case, the button was added first and then the picture box, so the picture box is on top, covering up the button until the picture box was hidden.

You could use this hide feature for some slick GUI design in which you add a group of controls to a form and then cover this group with a panel with controls. To switch between sets of controls, simply hide the panel. To make this completely transparent, ensure that the `BorderStyle` property is set to `None` on the panel. The complete code, excluding Designer code, is shown in Listing 6.18.

Listing 6.18

```csharp
//****************************************************************
//  Boxes.cs        C#: Ken Culp
//
//  Demonstrates the use of panels and picture boxes and drawing
//  on each of those surfaces as well as drawing on a group box.
//****************************************************************
using System;
using System.Collections.Generic;
using System.ComponentModel;
using System.Data;
using System.Drawing;
using System.Text;
using System.Windows.Forms;

namespace Boxes
{
  public partial class Boxes : Form
  {
    //---------------------------------------------------------
    //  Paints boxes of random width/height in a random location.
    //  Narrow or short boxes are highlighted with a fill color.
    //---------------------------------------------------------
    public Boxes()
    {
      InitializeComponent();
    }
    Random generator;
    const int THICKNESS = 5, MAX_SIDE = 50;

    private void Boxes_Load(object sender, EventArgs e)
    {
      generator = new Random(DateTime.Now.Millisecond);
    }

    private void PaintBoxes(Graphics g, int boxCount,
      int maxSide, Color boxColor)
    {
      int maxX = (int)g.VisibleClipBounds.Width;
      int maxY = (int)g.VisibleClipBounds.Height;
      int x, y, width, height;

      for (int count = 0; count < boxCount; count++)
      {
        x = generator.Next(maxX) + 1;
        y = generator.Next(maxY) + 1;
        width = generator.Next(maxSide) + 1;
        height = generator.Next(maxSide) + 1;
```

Listing 6.18   continued

```csharp
      if (width <= THICKNESS)   // check for narrow box
      {
        g.FillRectangle(new SolidBrush(Color.Yellow),
          x, y, width, height);
      }
      else
        if (height <= THICKNESS)   // check for short box
        {
          g.FillRectangle(new SolidBrush(Color.Green),
            x, y, width, height);
        }
        else
        {
          g.DrawRectangle(new Pen(boxColor),
            x, y, width, height);
        }
   }
}
private void panel1_Paint(object sender, PaintEventArgs e)
{
  PaintBoxes(e.Graphics, 25, 50, Color.White);
}

private void pictureBox1_Paint(object sender,
  PaintEventArgs e)
{
  PaintBoxes(e.Graphics, 25, 50, Color.White);
}

private void btnHidePanel_Click(object sender,
  System.EventArgs e)
{
  panel1.Visible = !panel1.Visible;
  if (panel1.Visible)
    btnHidePanel.Text = "Hide";
  else
    btnHidePanel.Text = "Show";
}

private void btnHidePic_Click(object sender,
  System.EventArgs e)
{
  pictureBox1.Visible = !pictureBox1.Visible;
  if (pictureBox1.Visible)
    btnHidePic.Text = "Hide";
  else
    btnHidePic.Text = "Show";
```

Listing 6.18   continued

```
    }

    private void btnToPaint_Paint(object sender,
      PaintEventArgs e)
    {
      PaintBoxes(e.Graphics, 15, 30, Color.Black);
    }

    private void groupBox1_Paint(object sender, PaintEventArgs e)
    {
      PaintBoxes(e.Graphics, 15, 30, Color.Blue);
    }

    private void btnRedraw_Click(object sender,
      System.EventArgs e)
    {
      this.Invalidate(true);
      // Setting Invalidate on the form to true casues Invalidate
      // to be called for all controls on the form.  Thus this
      // single call replaces all of the following:
      //    panel1.Invalidate();
      //    pictureBox1.Invalidate();
      //    groupBox1.Invalidate();
      //    btnToPaint.Invalidate();
    }

  }
}
```

6.13 TAB CONTROLS

Sometimes you have so much related information that you cannot conveniently fit it all on one form, and popping up dialog boxes would make the application cumbersome. One solution is the tab control, which allows the form to be extended like tabs in a card catalog. You can name each tab, and add as many tabs as you need (although five or so would tend to be a practical maximum). Reiterating, tab controls are usually used to group related information.

The tab control does need not to fill the entire form. For example, in an employee data screen, you might have the employee's name, department, and employee identification always shown at the top of the form. Below that would be the tab control with one tab for demographics (address, phone, etc.), another for insurance, another for tax deductions, and so on. Also, below the tab control, you might want some buttons to be always visible, for such things as scrolling and exiting the form.

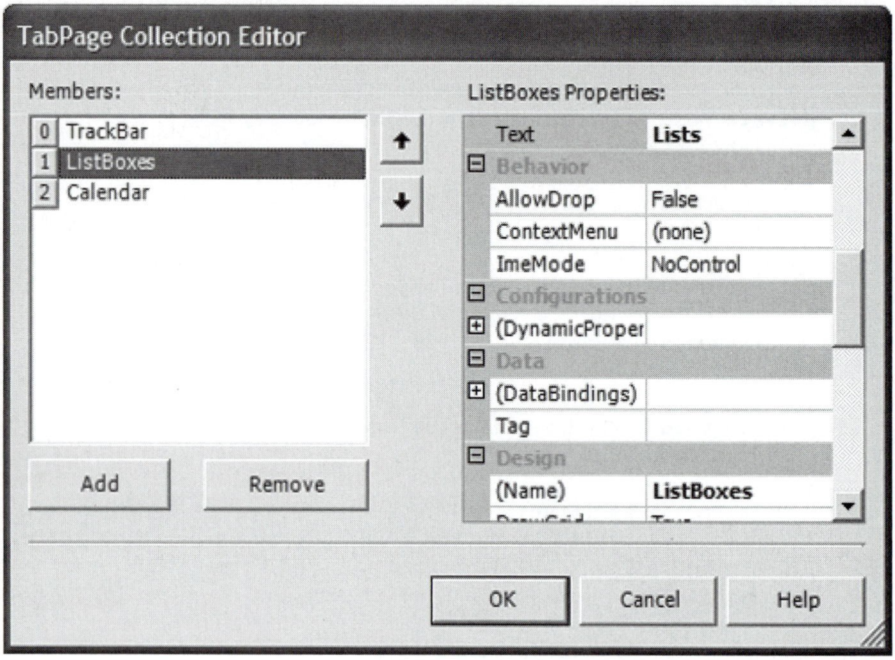

FIGURE 6.14   TabPage Collection Editor

To add a tab control to the form, drag the control from the tool box and set its size appropriately. At this point, the control has no tabs defined. To add tabs, access the Tab Page collection by clicking the button to the right of the `TabPages` property, which displays the TabPage Collection Editor dialog box, shown in Figure 6.14.

In this dialog box, click Add to add each tab. Set the `Text` property to the desired label you want on the tab and give the tab a useful name. In most cases, this is all you need to set for the tab. You may, however, change such things as the foreground and background colors, border styles, image background, etc.

After you add each tab, you can drop controls on it as needed. These controls are visible to the form code just as if they were added to the form, so naming and formatting the controls is the same as for placing them on the form.

An example of a tab control is given in Chapter 10 along with some more advanced controls.

Summary of Key Concepts

> The effort put into design is both crucial and cost-effective.

> The nouns in a problem description may indicate some of the classes and objects needed in a program.

> A static variable is shared among all instances of a class.

> An aggregate object is composed of other objects, forming a has-a relationship.

> An interface is a collection of abstract methods and therefore cannot be instantiated.

> A complex service provided by an object can be decomposed to make use of private support methods.

> The versions of an overloaded method are distinguished by the number, type, and order of their parameters.

> Testing a program can never guarantee the absence of errors.

> A good test is one that uncovers an error.

> It is not feasible to exhaustively test a program for all possible input and user actions.

> The design of any GUI should adhere to basic guidelines regarding consistency and usability.

Self-Review Questions

6.1   Name the four basic activities that are involved in a software development process.

6.2   How are overloaded methods distinguished from each other?

6.3   What is method decomposition?

6.4   Explain how a class can have an association with itself.

6.5   What is an aggregate object?

6.6   What does the **this** reference refer to?

6.7   How are objects passed as parameters?

6.8   What is the difference between a static variable and an instance variable?

6.9   What is the difference between a class and an interface?

6.10 What general guidelines for GUI design are presented in this chapter?

6.11 What are the advantages of overloading operators?

6.12 How do you create your own class library?

6.13 How do you reference a class library created in another project.

6.14 What is the purpose of the Object Browser?

6.15 How would you view the contents of a public variable or property within an object when the program is at a breakpoint?

6.16 How do you force a control to be repainted?

Exercises

6.1   Write a method called `Average` that accepts two integer parameters and returns their average as a floating point value.

6.2   Overload the `Average` method of Exercise 6.1 such that if three integers are provided as parameters, the method returns the average of all three.

6.3   Overload the `Average` method of Exercise 6.1 to accept four integer parameters and return their average.

6.4   Write a method called `MultiConcat` that takes a `string` and an integer as parameters. Return a `string` that consists of the string parameter concatenated with itself `count` times, where `count` is the integer parameter. For example, if the parameter values are `"hi"` and 4, the return value is `"hihihihi"`. Return the original string if the integer parameter is less than 2.

6.5   Overload the `MultiConcat` method from Exercise 6.4 such that if the integer parameter is not provided, the method returns the string concatenated with itself. For example, if the parameter is `"test"`, the return value is `"testtest"`.

6.6   Write a method called `DrawCircle` that draws a circle based on the method's parameters: a `Graphics` object through which to draw the circle, two integer values representing the (x, y) coordinates of the center of the circle, another integer that represents the circle's radius, and a `Color` object that defines the circle's color. The method does not return anything.

6.7   Overload the `DrawCircle` method of Exercise 6.6 such that if the `Color` parameter is not provided, the circle's color will default to black.

6.8   Overload the `DrawCircle` method of Exercise 6.6 such that if the radius is not provided, a random radius in the range 10 to 100 (inclusive) will be used.

6.9   Overload the `DrawCircle` method of Exercise 6.6 such that if both the color and the radius of the circle are not provided, the color will default to red and the radius will default to 40.

6.10 Discuss the manner in which C# passes parameters to a method. Is this technique consistent between primitive types and objects? Explain.

6.11 Explain why a static method cannot refer to an instance variable.

6.12 Can a class implement two interfaces that each contain the same method signature? Explain.

6.13 Create an interface called `Visible` that includes two methods: `MakeVisible` and `MakeInvisible`. Both methods should take no parameters and should return a **bool** result. Describe how a class might implement this interface.

6.14 Draw a UML class diagram that shows the relationships among the elements of Exercise 6.13.

6.15 Create an interface called `VCR` that has methods that represent the standard operations on a video cassette recorder (play, stop, etc.). Define the method signatures any way you desire. Describe how a class might implement this interface.

6.16 Draw a UML class diagram that shows the relationships among the elements of Exercise 6.15.

6.17 Write an operator overload for `++` in the `Point` class. The method should increment both the `x` and `y` values.

6.18 Use the Object Browser to list all the overloaded methods for `DrawLine` in the `Graphics` class.

Programming Projects

6.1 Modify the `Account` class from Chapter 4 so that it also permits an account to be opened with just a name and an account number, assuming an initial balance of zero. Modify the `Main` method of the `Transactions` class to demonstrate this new capability.

6.2 Modify the `Student` class presented in this chapter as follows. Each student object should also contain the scores for three tests. Provide a constructor that sets all instance values based on parameter values. Overload the constructor such that each test score is assumed to be initially zero. Provide a method called `SetTestScore` that accepts two parameters: the test number (1 through 3) and the score. Also provide a method called `GetTestScore` that accepts the test number and returns the appropriate score. Provide a method called `Average` that computes and returns the average test score for this student. Modify the `ToString` method such that the test scores and average are included in the description of the student. Modify the driver class `Main` method to exercise the new `Student` methods.

6.3 Design and implement a class called `Course` that represents a course taken at a school. A course object should keep track of up to five students, as represented by the modified `Student` class from the previous programming project. The constructor of the `Course` class should accept only the name of the course. Provide a method called `AddStudent` that accepts one `Student` parameter (the `Course` object should keep track of how many valid students have been added to the course). Provide a method called `average` that computes and returns the average of all students' test score averages. Provide a method called `Roll` that prints the names of all students in the course. Create a driver class with a `Main` method that creates a course, adds several students, prints a roll, and prints the overall course test average.

6.4 Modify the `RationalNumber` class so that it implements the `IComparable` interface. To perform the comparison, compute an equivalent floating point value from the numerator and denominator for both `Rational` objects, then compare them using a tolerance value of 0.0001. Write a main driver to test your modifications.

6.5 Design a C# interface called `Priority` that includes two methods: `SetPriority` and `GetPriority`. The interface should define a way to establish numeric priority among a set of objects. Design and implement a class called `Task` that represents a task (such as on a to-do list) that implements the `Priority` interface. Create a driver class to exercise some `Task` objects.

6.6 Modify the `Task` class from Programming Project 6.5 so that it also implements the `Complexity` interface defined in this chapter. Modify the driver class to show these new features of `Task` objects.

6.7 Modify the `Task` class from Programming Projects 6.5 and 6.6 so that it also implements the `IComparable` interface from the C# standard class library. Implement the interface such that the tasks are ranked by priority. Create a driver class whose main method shows these new features of `Task` objects.

6.8 Design a C# interface called `Lockable` that includes the following methods: `SetKey`, `Lock`, `Unlock`, and `Locked`. The `SetKey`, `Lock`, and `Unlock` methods take an integer parameter that represents the key. The `SetKey` method establishes the key. The `Lock` and `Unlock` methods lock and unlock the object, but only if the key passed in is correct. The `Locked` method returns a boolean that indicates whether or not the object is locked. A `Lockable` object represents an object whose regular methods are protected: if the object is locked, the methods cannot be invoked; if it is unlocked, they can be invoked. Redesign and implement a version of the `Coin` class from Chapter 5 so that it is `Lockable`.

6.9 Redesign and implement a version of the `Account` class from Chapter 4 so that it is `Lockable` as defined by Programming Project 6.8.

6.10 Redesign and implement a version of the `PigLatin` program so that it uses a GUI. Accept the sentence using a text field and display the results using a label.

6.11 Modify the `CoinFlip` program and place the `Coin` class in its own project. Compile and then add the `Coin` library to the `CoinFlip` project, removing the local class definition.

6.12 Modify the `QuoteOptions` program from Chapter 5 to change its visual appearance. Present the radio buttons in a vertical column with a surrounding border to the left of the quote label.

6.13 Design and implement a program that displays a numeric keypad that might appear on a phone. Above the keypad buttons, show a label that displays the numbers as they are picked. To the right of the keypad buttons, include another button to clear the display. Use a panel for the buttons, giving them a nice background color and a border.

6.14 Design and implement an application that helps a pizza restaurant take orders. Use a tabbed control for different categories of food (pizza, beverages, special items). Collect information about quantity and size. Display the cost of the order as information is gathered. Use appropriate components for collecting the various kinds of information.

6.15 Code the ++ operator overload mentioned in Exercise 6.17 and code the -- operator as well. Test your changes.

6.16 See if you can dig out of the documentation how to write an image to a panel. Locate an image from the Internet and load it onto the panel. Add controls to the panel and see how it appears. Hint: Use a constructor for the `Image` class to create the image and `DrawImage` to draw it. You can start at the `Boxes` example for this program.

Answers to Self-Review Questions

6.1 The four basic activities in software development are requirements analysis (deciding what the program should do), design (deciding how to do it), implementation (writing the solution in source code), and testing (validating the implementation).

6.2 Overloaded methods are distinguished by having a unique signature, which includes the number, order, and type of the parameters. The return type is not part of the signature.

6.3 Method decomposition is the process of dividing a complex method into several support methods to get the job done. This simplifies and facilitates the design of the program.

6.4 A method executed through an object might take as a parameter another object created from the same class. For example, the `CompareTo` method of the `string` class is executed through one `String` object and takes another `String` object as a parameter.

6.5 An aggregate object is an object that has other objects as instance data. That is, an aggregate object is one that is made up of other objects.

6.6 The **this** reference always refers to the currently executing object. A non-static method of a class is written generically for all objects of the class, but it is invoked through a particular object. The **this** reference, therefore, refers to the object through which that method is currently being executed.

6.7 Objects are passed to methods by copying the reference to the object (its address). Therefore the actual and formal parameters of a method become aliases of each other.

6.8 Memory space for an instance variable is created for each object that is instantiated from a class. A static variable is shared among all objects of a class.

6.9 A class can be instantiated; an interface cannot. An interface contains a set of abstract methods for which a class provides the implementation.

6.10 The general guidelines for GUI design include: know the needs and characteristics of the user, prevent user errors when possible, optimize user abilities by providing shortcuts and other redundant means to accomplish a task, and be consistent in GUI layout and coloring schemes.

6.11 Overloading an operator allows for simpler syntax for comparing objects or for performing arithmetic on the objects. Objects could be added together, for example.

6.12 Open a new project of type Class Library.

6.13 Right-click the references in the Solution Explorer and select Add Reference. Select the Projects tab in the Add Reference dialog box and find your project. Add the reference. Finally, add a `using` statement for the namespace of the class library.

6.14 The Object Browser allows properties and methods of classes to be examined.

6.15 In the Autos window, click the + sign to the left of the object name and drill down until you find the desired variable.

6.16 Force a repaint by calling `Invalidate(true)` for the form or call `Invalidate` for the individual controls.

Arrays

7

CHAPTER OBJECTIVES

> Define and use arrays for basic data organization.

> Discuss bounds checking and techniques for managing capacity.

> Discuss the issues related to arrays as objects and arrays of objects.

> Explore the use of command-line arguments.

> Describe the syntax and use of variable-length parameter lists.

> Discuss the creation and use of multidimensional arrays.

> Examine the `ArrayList` class and its generic parameter.

> Explore mouse and keyboard events.

In our programming efforts, we often want to organize objects or primitive data in a form that is easy to access and modify. This chapter introduces arrays, which are programming constructs that group data into lists. Arrays are a fundamental component of most high-level languages. We also explore the `ArrayList` class in the C# standard class library, which provides capabilities similar to arrays, with additional features. In the Graphics Track sections of this chapter, we explore methods that let us draw complex multisided figures, and examine the events generated by the mouse and the keyboard.

7.1 ARRAY ELEMENTS

An array is a simple but powerful programming language construct used to group and organize data. When writing a program that manages a large amount of information, such as a list of 100 names, it is not practical to declare separate variables for each piece of data. Arrays solve this problem by letting us declare one variable that can hold multiple, individually accessible values.

An array is a list of values. Each value is stored at a specific, numbered position in the array. The number corresponding to each position is called an *index* or a *subscript*. Figure 7.1 shows an array of integers and the indexes that correspond to each position. The array is called `height`; it contains integers that represent several peoples' heights in inches.

> **Key Concept**
>
> An array of size *N* is indexed from 0 to *N*-1.

In C#, array indexes always begin at zero. Therefore the value stored at index 5 is actually the sixth value in the array. The array shown in Figure 7.1 has 11 values, indexed from 0 to 10.

To access a value in an array, we use the name of the array followed by the index in square brackets. For example, the following expression refers to the ninth value in the array `height`:

```
height[8]
```

According to Figure 7.1, `height[8]` (pronounced height-sub-eight) contains the value 79. Don't confuse the value of the index, in this case 8, with the value stored in the array at that index, in this case 79.

The expression `height[8]` refers to a single integer stored at a particular memory location. It can be used wherever an integer variable can be used. Therefore you can assign a

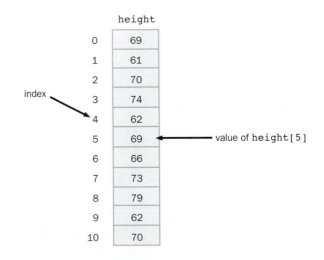

FIGURE 7.1 An array called height containing integer values

value to it, use it in calculations, print its value, and so on. Furthermore, because array indexes are integers, you can use integer expressions to specify the index used to access an array. These concepts are demonstrated in the following lines of code:

```
height[2] = 72;
height[count] = feet * 12;
average = (height[0] + height[1] + height[2]) / 3;
System.out.println ("The middle value is " + height[MAX/2]);
pick = height[rand.nextInt(11)];
```

7.2   DECLARING AND USING ARRAYS

In C#, arrays are objects. To create an array, the reference to the array must be declared. The array must then be instantiated using the new operator, which allocates memory space to store values. The following code represents the declaration for the array shown in Figure 7.1:

> **Key Concept**
>
> In C#, an array is an object that must be instantiated.

```
int[] height = new int[11];
```

The variable `height` is declared to be an array of integers whose type is written as `int[]`. All values stored in an array have the same type (or are at least compatible). For example, we can create an array that can hold integers or an array that can hold strings, but not an array that can hold both integers and strings. An array can be set up to hold any primitive type or any object (class) type. A value stored in an array is sometimes called an *array element*, and the type of values that an array holds is called the *element type* of the array.

Note that the type of the array variable (**int**[]) does not include the size of the array. The instantiation of `height`, using the **new** operator, reserves the memory space to store 11 integers indexed from 0 to 10. Once an array is declared to be a certain size, the number of values it can hold cannot be changed.

The example shown in Listing 7.1 creates an array called `list` that can hold 15 integers, which it loads with successive increments of 10. It then changes the value of the sixth element in the array (at index 5). Finally, it prints all values stored in the array.

Listing 7.1

```
//********************************************************
//  BasicArray.cs          C#:  Ken Culp
//
//  Demonstrates basic array declaration and use.
//********************************************************
using System;
```

Listing 7.1 continued

```
namespace BasicArray
{
  class BasicArray
  {
    const int LIMIT = 15;
    const int MULTIPLE = 10;

    //----------------------------------------------------------
    //  Creates an array, fills it with various integer
    //  values, modifies one value, then prints them out.
    //----------------------------------------------------------
    static void Main(string[] args)
    {
      int[] list = new int[LIMIT];

      // Initialize the array values
      for (int index = 0; index < LIMIT; index++)
        list[index] = index * MULTIPLE;
      list[5] = 999;  // change one array value

      for (int index = 0; index < LIMIT; index++)
        Console.Out.Write(list[index] + "  ");
      Console.Out.WriteLine();

      // Same output using the foreach syntax
      foreach (int x in list)
        Console.Out.Write(x + "  ");
      Console.Out.WriteLine();

      Console.In.ReadLine();  // Wait for enter key
    }
  }
}
```

Output

```
0  10  20  30  40  999  60  70  80  90  100  110  120  130  140
```

Figure 7.2 shows the array as it changes during the execution of the `BasicArray` program. It is often convenient to use **for** loops when handling arrays, because the number of positions in the array is constant. Note that a constant called `LIMIT` is used in several places in the `BasicArray` program. This constant is used to declare the size of the array and to control the **for** loop that initializes the array values.

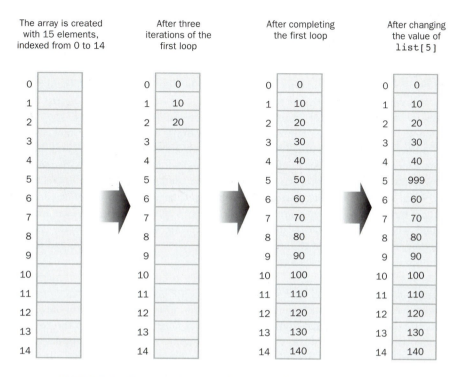

FIGURE 7.2   The array list as it changes in the BasicArray program

The iterator version of the **for** loop is used to print the values in the array. Recall from Chapter 5 that this version of the **for** loop extracts each value in the specified iterator. Every C# array is an iterator, so this type of loop can be used whenever we want to process every element stored in an array.

The square brackets used to indicate the index of an array are treated as an operator in C#. Therefore, just like the + operator or the <= operator, the index operator ([ ]) has a precedence relative to the other C# operators that determines when it is executed. It has the highest precedence of all C# operators.

Bounds Checking

The index operator performs automatic *bounds checking*, which ensures that the index is in range for the array being referenced. Whenever a reference to an array element is made, the index must be greater than or equal to zero and less than the size of the array. For example, suppose an array called prices is created with 25 elements. The valid indexes for the array are from 0 to 24. Whenever a reference is made to a particular element in the array (such as prices[count]), the value of the index is checked. If it is in the valid range of indexes for the array

> **Key Concept**
>
> Bounds checking ensures that an index used to refer to an array element is in range.

(0 to 24), the reference is carried out. If the index is not valid, an exception called `ArrayIndexOutOfBoundsException` is thrown.

Of course, in our programs we'll want to perform our own bounds checking. That is, we'll want to be careful to remain within the bounds of the array and process every element we intend to. Because array indexes begin at zero and go up to one less than the size of the array, it is easy to create *off-by-one errors* in a program, which are problems created by processing all but one element or by attempting to index one element too many.

One way to check for the bounds of an array is to use the `length` constant, which is held in the array object and stores the size of the array. It is a public constant and therefore can be referenced directly. For example, after the single-dimensioned array `prices` is created with 25 elements, the property `prices.Length` contains the value 25. Its value is set once, when the array is first created, and cannot be changed (the property has no corresponding **Set** method). The `Length` property, which is an integral part of each array, can be used when the array size is needed without having to create a separate constant. Remember that the length of the array is the number of elements it can hold, and thus the maximum index of an array is `Length-1`.

Let's look at another example. The program shown in Listing 7.2 reads 10 integers into an array called `numbers`, and then prints them in reverse order.

Note that in the `ReverseOrder` program, the array `numbers` is declared to have 10 elements and therefore is indexed from 0 to 9. The index range is controlled in the **for** loops by using the `Length` field of the array object. You should carefully set the initial value of loop control variables and the conditions that terminate loops to guarantee that all intended elements are processed and only valid indexes are used to reference an array element.

The `LetterCount` example, shown in Listing 7.3, uses two arrays and a `String` object. The array called `upper` is used to store the number of times each uppercase alphabetic letter is found in the string. The array called `lower` serves the same purpose for lowercase letters.

Because there are 26 letters in the English alphabet, both the `upper` and `lower` arrays are declared with 26 elements. Each element contains an integer that is initially zero by default. The `for` loop scans through the string one character at a time. The appropriate counter in the appropriate array is incremented for each character found in the string.

Both of the counter arrays are indexed from 0 to 25. We have to map each character to a counter. A logical way to do this is to use `upper[0]` to count the number of `'A'` characters found, `upper[1]` to count the number of `'B'` characters found, and so on. Likewise, `lower[0]` is used to count `'a'` characters, `lower[1]` is used to count `'b'` characters, and so on. A separate variable called `other` is used to count any nonalphabetic characters that are encountered.

Listing 7.2

```
//*************************************************************
//  ReverseOrder.cs        C#:  Ken Culp
//
//  Demonstrates array index processing.
//*************************************************************
```

Listing 7.2   continued

```
using System;
using CS1;

namespace ReverseOrder
{
  class ReverseOrder
  //------------------------------------------------------------
  //  Reads a list of numbers from the user, storing them in an
  //  array, then prints them in the opposite order.
  //------------------------------------------------------------
  {
    static void Main(string[] args)
    {
      double[] numbers = new double[10];

      Console.Out.WriteLine("The size of the array: " +
        numbers.GetLength(0));

      for (int index = 0; index < numbers.Length; index++)
      {
        Console.Out.Write("Enter number " + (index + 1) + ": ");
        numbers[index] = Keyboard.readDouble();
      }

      Console.Out.WriteLine("The numbers in reverse order:");

      for (int index = numbers.Length - 1; index >= 0; index--)
        Console.Out.Write(numbers[index] + "   ");

      Console.Out.WriteLine();

      Console.In.ReadLine();   // Wait for enter key
    }
  }
}
```

Output

```
The size of the array: 10
Enter number 1: 18.36
Enter number 2: 48.9
Enter number 3: 53.5
Enter number 4: 29.06
Enter number 5: 72.404
Enter number 6: 34.8
Enter number 7: 63.41
Enter number 8: 45.55
```

Listing 7.2   continued

```
Enter number 9: 69.0
Enter number 10: 99.18
The numbers in reverse order:
99.18   69.0   45.55   63.41   34.8   72.404   29.06   53.5   48.9   18.36
```

Listing 7.3

```csharp
//*****************************************************************
//  LetterCount.cs          C#:  Ken Culp
//
//  Demonstrates the relationship between arrays and strings.
//*****************************************************************
using System;
using CS1;

namespace LetterCount
{
  class LetterCount
  {
    //-------------------------------------------------------------
    //  Reads a sentence from the user and counts the number of
    //  uppercase and lowercase letters contained in it.
    //-------------------------------------------------------------
    static void Main(string[] args)
    {
      const int NUMCHARS = 26;

      int[] upper = new int[NUMCHARS];
      int[] lower = new int[NUMCHARS];

      char current;   // the current character being processed
      int other = 0;  // counter for non-alphabetics

      Console.Out.WriteLine("Enter a sentence:");
      string line = Keyboard.readString();

      // Count the number of each letter occurence
      for (int ch = 0; ch < line.Length; ch++)
      {
        current = line[ch];
        if (current >= 'A' && current <= 'Z')
          upper[current - 'A']++;
        else
          if (current >= 'a' && current <= 'z')
            lower[current - 'a']++;
          else
            other++;
      }
```

Listing 7.3   continued

```
    //  Print the results
    Console.Out.WriteLine();
    for (int letter = 0; letter < upper.Length; letter++)
    {
      Console.Out.Write((char)(letter + 'A'));
      Console.Out.Write(": " + upper[letter]);
      Console.Out.Write("\t\t" + (char)(letter + 'a'));
      Console.Out.WriteLine(": " + lower[letter]);
    }

    Console.Out.WriteLine();
    Console.Out.WriteLine("Non-alphabetic characters: " +
      other);

    Console.In.ReadLine();  // Wait for enter key
    }
  }
}
```

Output

```
Enter a sentence:
In Casablanca, Humphrey Bogart never says "Play it again, Sam."

A: 0            a: 10
B: 1            b: 1
C: 1            c: 1
D: 0            d: 0
E: 0            e: 3
F: 0            f: 0
G: 0            g: 2
H: 1            h: 1
I: 1            i: 2
J: 0            j: 0
K: 0            k: 0
L: 0            l: 2
M: 0            m: 2
N: 0            n: 4
O: 0            o: 1
P: 1            p: 1
Q: 0            q: 0
R: 0            r: 3
S: 1            s: 3
T: 0            t: 2
U: 0            u: 1
V: 0            v: 1
```

Listing 7.3   continued

```
W: 0            w: 0
X: 0            x: 0
Y: 0            y: 3
Z: 0            z: 0

Non-alphabetic characters: 14
```

Note that to determine if a character is an uppercase letter, we used the boolean expression (current >= 'A' && current <= 'Z'). A similar expression is used for determining the lowercase letters. We could have used the static methods IsUpper and IsLower in the Char class to make these determinations, but chose not to in this example to drive home the point that because characters are based on the Unicode character set, they have a specific numeric value and order that we can use in our programming.

We use the current character to calculate which index in the array to reference. We have to be careful when calculating an index to ensure that it remains within the bounds of the array and matches to the correct element. Remember that in the Unicode character set the uppercase and lowercase alphabetic letters are continuous and in order (see Appendix C). Therefore, taking the numeric value of an uppercase letter such as 'E' (which is 69) and subtracting the numeric value of the character 'A' (which is 65) yields 4, which is the correct index for the counter of the character 'E'. Note that nowhere in the program do we actually need to know the specific numeric values for each letter.

Initializer Lists

You can use an *initializer list* to instantiate an array and provide the initial values for the elements of the array. It is essentially the same idea as initializing a variable of a primitive data type in its declaration except that an array requires several values.

The items in an initializer list are separated by commas and delimited by braces ({}). When an initializer list is used, the **new** operator is not used. The size of the array is determined by the number of items in the initializer list. For example, the following declaration instantiates the array scores as an array of eight integers, indexed from 0 to 7 with the specified initial values:

```
int[] scores = {87, 98, 69, 87, 65, 76, 99, 83};
```

Key Concept

An initializer list can be used to instantiate an array object instead of using the new operator.

An initializer list can be used only when an array is first declared.

The type of each value in an initializer list must match the type of the array elements. Let's look at another example:

```
char[] vowels = {'A', 'E', 'I', 'O', 'U'};
```

In this case, the variable `vowels` is declared to be an array of five characters, and the initializer list contains character literals.

The program shown in Listing 7.4 demonstrates the use of an initializer list to instantiate an array.

Arrays as Parameters

An entire array can be passed as a parameter to a method. Because an array is an object, when an entire array is passed as a parameter, a copy of the reference to the original array is passed. We discussed this issue as it applies to all objects in Chapter 6.

A method that receives an array as a parameter can permanently change an element of the array because it is referring to the original element value. The method cannot permanently change the reference to the array itself because a copy of the original reference is sent to the method. These rules are consistent with the rules that govern any object type.

An element of an array can be passed to a method as well. If the element type is a primitive type, a copy of the value is passed. If that element is a reference to an object, a copy of the object reference is passed. As always, the impact of changes made to a parameter inside the method depends on the type of the parameter. We discuss arrays of objects further in the next section.

Listing 7.4

```
//*************************************************************
//   Primes.cs        C#:   Ken Culp
//
//   Demonstrates the use of an initializer list for an array.
//*************************************************************
using System;

namespace Primes
{
  class Primes
  {
    //-----------------------------------------------------------
    //   Stores some prime numbers in an array and prints them.
    //-----------------------------------------------------------
    public static void Main(string[] args)
    {
      int[] primeNums = { 2, 3, 5, 7, 11, 13, 17, 19 };

      Console.Out.WriteLine("Array length: " + primeNums.Length);

      Console.Out.WriteLine("The first few prime numbers are:");

      for (int scan = 0; scan < primeNums.Length; scan++)
        Console.Out.Write(primeNums[scan] + "   ");
```

Listing 7.4 continued

```
    Console.Out.WriteLine();

    Console.In.ReadLine();  // Wait for enter key
   }
  }
}
```

Output

```
Array length: 8
The first few prime numbers are:
3   5   7   11   13   17   19
```

7.3 ARRAYS OF OBJECTS

In the previous examples in this chapter, we used arrays to store primitive types such as integers and characters. Arrays can also store references to objects as elements. Fairly complex information management structures can be created using only arrays and other objects. For example, an array could contain objects, and each of those objects could consist of several variables and the methods that use them. Those variables could themselves be arrays, and so on. The design of a program should capitalize on the ability to combine these constructs to create the most appropriate representation for the information.

Keep in mind that the array itself is an object. So it would be appropriate to picture an array of int values called `weight` as follows:

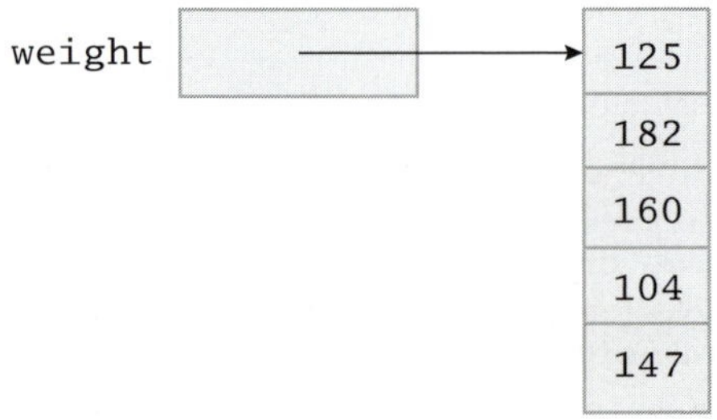

weight → 125
          182
          160
          104
          147

When we store objects in an array, each element is a separate object. That is, an array of objects is really an array of object references. Consider the following declaration:

string[] words = **new string**[5];

The variable `words` is an array of references to `String` objects. The `new` operator in the declaration instantiates the array and reserves space for five `String` references. This declaration does not create any `string` objects; it merely creates an array that holds references to `string` objects. Initially, the array looks like this:

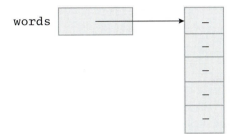

After a few `string` objects are created and put in the array, it might look like this:

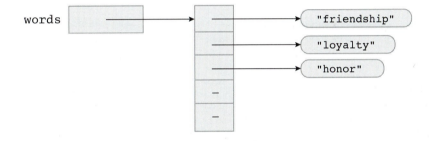

The `words` array is an object, and each character string it holds is its own object. Each object contained in an array has to be instantiated separately.

Keep in mind that `string` objects can be represented as string literals. So the following declaration creates an array called `verbs` and uses an initializer list to populate it with several `string` objects, each instantiated using a string literal:

```
string[] verbs = {"play", "work", "eat", "sleep"};
```

The program called `GradeRange` shown in Listing 7.5 creates an array of `Grade` objects, then prints them. The `Grade` objects are created using several `new` operators in the initialization list of the array.

The `Grade` class is shown in Listing 7.6. Each `Grade` object represents a letter grade for a school course and includes a numerical lower bound. The values for the grade name and lower bound can be set using the `Grade` constructor, or using appropriate mutator methods. Accessor methods are also defined, as is a `ToString` method to return a string representation of the grade. The `ToString` method is automatically invoked when the grades are printed in the `Main` method.

Listing 7.5

```
//*****************************************************************
//  GradeRange.cs          C#:  Ken Culp
//
//  Demonstrates the use of an array of objects.
//*****************************************************************
using System;

namespace GradeRange
{
  class GradeRange
  {
    //----------------------------------------------------------
    //  Stores the possible grades with their numeric lowest
    //  value, then prints them out.
    //----------------------------------------------------------
    public static void Main(string[] args)
    {
      Grade[] grades = {
          new Grade("A",  95), new Grade("A-", 90),
          new Grade("B+", 87), new Grade("B", 85),
          new Grade("B-", 80), new Grade("C+", 77),
          new Grade("C",  75), new Grade("C-", 70),
          new Grade("D+", 67), new Grade("D", 65),
          new Grade("D-", 60), new Grade("F",  0)
          };

      foreach (Grade letterGrade in grades)
        Console.Out.WriteLine(letterGrade);

      Console.In.ReadLine();  // Wait for enter key
    }
  }
}
```

Output

```
A        95
A-       90
B+       87
B        85
B-       80
C+       77
C        75
C-       70
```

Listing 7.5   continued

```
D+         67
D          65
D-         60
F           0
```

Listing 7.6

```csharp
//****************************************************************
//  Grade.cs                C#:  Ken Culp
//
//  Demonstrates a school grade.
//****************************************************************
using System;

namespace GradeRange
{
  public class Grade
  {
    private string name;
    private int lowerBound;
    //------------------------------------------------------------
    // Constructor: Sets up this Grade object with the specified
    // grade name and numeric lower bound
    //------------------------------------------------------------
    public Grade(string grade, int cutoff)
    {
      name = grade;
      lowerBound = cutoff;
    }
    //------------------------------------------------------------
    // Returns a string representation of this grade
    //------------------------------------------------------------
    public override string ToString()
    {
      return name + "\t" + lowerBound.ToString();
    }
    //------------------------------------------------------------
    // Name Property
    //------------------------------------------------------------
    public string Name
    {
      get { return name; }
      set { name = value; }
    }
```

Listing 7.6   continued

```
    //--------------------------------------------------------------
    // LowerBound Property
    //--------------------------------------------------------------
    public int LowerBound
    {
      get { return lowerBound; }
      set { lowerBound = value; }
    }
  }
}
```

Let's look at another example. Listing 7.7 shows the Tunes class, which contains a Main method that creates, modifies, and examines a compact disc (CD) collection. Each CD added to the collection is specified by its title, artist, purchase price, and number of tracks.

Listing 7.8 shows the CDCollection class. It contains an array of CD objects representing the collection. It maintains a count of the CDs in the collection and their combined value. It also keeps track of the current size of the collection array so that a larger array can be created if too many CDs are added to the collection.

The collection array is instantiated in the CDCollection constructor. Every time a CD is added to the collection (using the AddCD method), a new CD object is created and a reference to it is stored in the collection array.

Each time a CD is added to the collection, we check to see whether we have reached the current capacity of the collection array. If we didn't perform this check, an exception would eventually be thrown when we try to store a new CD object at an invalid index. If the current capacity has been reached, the private IncreaseSize method is invoked, which first creates an array that is twice as big as the current collection array. Each CD in the existing collection is then copied into the new array. Finally, the collection reference is set to the larger array. Using this technique, we theoretically never run out of room in our CD collection. The user of the CDCollection object (the Main method) never has to worry about running out of space because it's all handled internally.

Listing 7.7

```
//****************************************************************
//  Tunes.cs          C#:  Ken Culp
//
//  Driver for demonstrating the use of an array of objects.
//****************************************************************
using System;

namespace Tunes
{
  class Tunes
```

Listing 7.7   continued

```
  {
    //-------------------------------------------------------------
    //  Creates a CDCollection object and adds some CDs to it.
    //  Prints reports on the status of the collection.
    //-------------------------------------------------------------
    public static void Main(string[] args)
    {
      CDCollection music = new CDCollection();

      music.AddCd("Storm Front", "Billy Joel", 14.95, 10);
      music.AddCd("Come On Over", "Shania Twain", 14.95, 16);
      music.AddCd("Soundtrack", "Les Miserables", 17.95, 33);
      music.AddCd("Graceland", "Paul Simon", 13.90, 11);

      Console.Out.WriteLine(music);

      music.AddCd("Double Live", "Garth Brooks", 19.99, 26);
      music.AddCd("Greatest Hits", "Jimmy Buffet", 15.95, 13);

      Console.Out.WriteLine(music);

      Console.In.ReadLine();   // Wait for enter key
    }
  }
}
```

Output

```
~~~~~~~~~~~~~~~~~~~~~~~~~~~~~~~~~~~~~~~~~~~
My CD Collection

Number of CDs: 4
Total cost: $61.75
Average cost: $15.44

CD List:

$14.95   10      Storm Front     Billy Joel
$14.95   16      Come On Over    Shania Twain
$17.95   33      Soundtrack      Les Miserables
$13.90   11      Graceland       Paul Simon
~~~~~~~~~~~~~~~~~~~~~~~~~~~~~~~~~~~~~~~~~~~
My CD Collection

Number of CDs: 6
Total cost: $97.69
Average cost: $16.28
```

Listing 7.7 continued

```
CD List:

$14.95   10       Storm Front      Billy Joel
$14.95   16       Come On Over     Shania Twain
$17.95   33       Soundtrack       Les Miserables
$13.90   11       Graceland        Paul Simon
$19.99   26       Double Live      Garth Brooks
$15.95   13       Greatest Hits    Jimmy Buffet
```

Listing 7.8

```csharp
//*****************************************************************
//   CDCollection.cs          C#:  Ken Culp
//
//   Represents a collection of compact discs.
//*****************************************************************
using System;

namespace Tunes
{
  public class CDCollection
  {
    private CD[] collection;
    private int count;
    private double totalCost;

    //-------------------------------------------------------------
    //   Creates an initially empty collection.
    //-------------------------------------------------------------
    public CDCollection()
    {
      collection = new CD[100];
      count = 0;
      totalCost = 0.0;
    }

    //-------------------------------------------------------------
    //   Adds a CD to the collection, increasing the size of the
    //   collection if necessary.
    //-------------------------------------------------------------
    public void AddCd(string title, string artist, double cost,
      int tracks)
    {
      if (count == collection.GetLength(0))
        IncreaseSize();
```

Listing 7.8   continued

```
            collection[count] = new CD(title, artist, cost, tracks);
            totalCost += cost;
            count++;

        }

        //---------------------------------------------------------------
        //  Returns a report describing the CD collection.
        //---------------------------------------------------------------
        public override string ToString()
        {
            string costStr = string.Format("{0:C}", totalCost);
            string avgStr = string.Format("{0:C}", totalCost / count);
            string report =
                "&&&&&&&&&&&&&&&&&&&&&&&&&&&&&&&&&&&&&&&&&&\n";
            report += "My CD Collection\n\n";

            report += "Number of CDs: " + count + "\n";
            report += "    Total cost: " + costStr + "\n";
            report += " Average cost: " + avgStr;

            report += "\n\nCD List:\n\n";


            for (int cd = 0; cd < count; cd++)
                report += collection[cd].ToString() + "\n";

            return report;
        }

        //---------------------------------------------------------------
        //  Doubles the size of the collection by creating a larger
        //  array and copying the existing collection into it.
        //---------------------------------------------------------------
        private void IncreaseSize()
        {
            CD[] temp = new CD[collection.GetLength(0) * 2];

            for (int cd = 0; cd < collection.GetLength(0); cd++)
                temp[cd] = collection[cd];

            collection = temp;
        }
    }
}
```

Figure 7.3 shows a UML class diagram of the Tunes program. Recall that the open diamond indicates aggregation. The cardinality of the relationship is also noted: a CDCollection object contains zero or more CD objects.

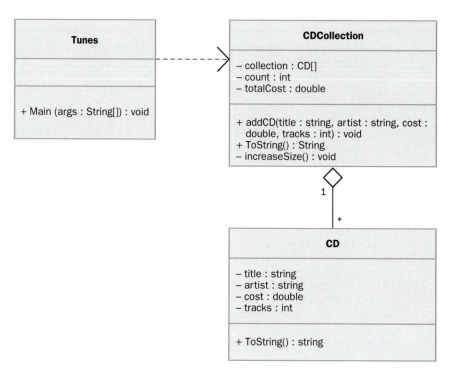

FIGURE 7.3 A UML class diagram of the Tunes program

The `ToString` method of the `CDCollection` class returns an entire report summarizing the collection. The report is created, in part, using calls to the `ToString` method of each `CD` object stored in the collection. Listing 7.9 shows the `CD` class.

Listing 7.9

```
//***************************************************************
//  CD.cs          C#:   Ken Culp
//
//  Represents a compact disc.
//***************************************************************

using System;

namespace Tunes
{
  public class CD
  {
    private string title, artist;
    private double cost;
```

Listing 7.9   continued

```csharp
   private int tracks;

   //---------------------------------------------------------
   //  Creates a new CD with the specified information.
   //---------------------------------------------------------
   public CD(string name, string singer, double price,
     int numTracks)
   {
     title = name;
     artist = singer;
     cost = price;
     tracks = numTracks;
   }

   //---------------------------------------------------------
   //  Returns a description of this CD.
   //---------------------------------------------------------
   public override string ToString()
   {
     string description;
     string costStr = string.Format("{0:C}", cost);

     description = costStr + "\t" + tracks + "\t";
     description += title + "\t" + artist;

     return description;
   }
  }
}
```

7.4   COMMAND-LINE ARGUMENTS

The formal parameter to the Main method of a C# application is always an array of string objects. We've ignored that parameter in previous examples, but now we can discuss how it might occasionally be useful.

The C# run-time environment invokes the Main method when an application is submitted to the interpreter. The String[] parameter, which we typically call args, represents *command-line arguments* that are provided when the interpreter is invoked. Any extra information on the command line when the interpreter is invoked is stored in the args array for use by the program. This technique is another way to provide input to a program.

> **Key Concept**
>
> Command-line arguments are stored in an array of String objects and are passed to the Main method.

When creating console commands from Visual Studio, you are not generally at a DOS command prompt. Instead, Visual Studio opens a command window for you only as long as the application is running. That is the reason we put a Console.In.ReadLine method at the bottom of each console program. However, you need to be at a command prompt in the directory where the program is loaded in order to test command-line arguments.

Visual Studio creates the executable (.exe) file in the directory `bin\Debug` under the project directory. You will need to open a DOS command prompt in that directory to test the program provided. You can configure a shortcut to this process to create a command prompt in the project directory as described in the section "Setting Up Command Prompt" in the *Visual Studio Installation Guide,* given in Appendix D.

The program shown in Listing 7.10 uses command-line arguments to print a name tag. It assumes the first argument represents some type of greeting and the second argument represents a person's name.

If two strings are not provided on the command line for the `NameTag` program, the `args` array will not contain enough (if any) elements, and the references in the program will cause an `ArrayIndexOutOfBoundsException` to be thrown. To prevent the exception, you can add an `if` test that verifies that two parameters were included on the command line. If extra information is included on the command line, it will be stored in the `args` array but ignored by the program.

Listing 7.10

```
//************************************************************
//   NameTag.cs          C#:   Ken Culp
//
//   Demonstrates the use of command-line arguments.
//************************************************************
using System;

namespace NameTag
{
  class NameTag
  {
    //------------------------------------------------------------
    //  Prints a simple name tag using a greeting and a name that
    //  is specified by the user.
    //------------------------------------------------------------
    public static void Main(string[] args)
    {
      if (args.Length < 2)// Make sure parameters present
        Console.Out.WriteLine("Usage:  <Greeting> <Name>");
      else
      {
        Console.Out.WriteLine();
        Console.Out.WriteLine("     " + args[0]);
        Console.Out.WriteLine("My name is " + args[1]);
        Console.Out.WriteLine();
      }
      Console.In.ReadLine();
    }
  }
}
```

Listing 7.10 continued

Output

```
...bin\Debug> NameTag Howdy John

    Howdy
My name is John

...bin\Debug > NameTag Hello Bill

    Hello
My name is Bill
```

Remember that the parameter to the `Main` method is always an array of `string` objects. If you want numeric information to be input as a command-line argument, the program has to convert it from its string representation.

You also should be aware that in some program development environments, a command line is not used to submit a program to the interpreter. In such situations, the command-line information can be specified in some other way. Consult the documentation for these specifics if necessary.

7.5 VARIABLE-LENGTH PARAMETER LISTS

Suppose we wanted to design a method that processed a different amount of data from one invocation to the next. For example, let's design a method called `Average` that accepts a few integer values and returns their average. In one invocation of the method, we might pass in three integers to average:

> **Key Concept**
>
> A C# method can be defined to accept a varying number of parameters.

```
mean1 = Average(42, 69, 37);
```

In another invocation of the same method, we might pass in seven integers to average:

```
mean2 = Average(35, 43, 93, 23, 40, 21, 75);
```

To accomplish this we could define overloaded versions of the `average` method, but that would require that we know the maximum number of parameters there might be and create a separate version of the method for each possibility. Alternatively, we could define the method to accept an array of integers, which could be of different sizes for each call. But that would require packaging the integers into an array in the calling method and passing in one parameter.

C# provides a way to define methods that accept variable-length parameter lists. By using some special syntax in the formal parameter list of the method, we can define the method to accept any number of parameters. The parameters are automatically put into an array for easy processing in the method. For example, the average method could be written as follows:

```
public double Average (params int[] list)
{
  double result = 0.0;

  if (list.Length := 0)
  {
    int sum = 0;
    foreach (int num in list)
      sum += num;
    result = (double)sum / list.Length;
  }
  return result;
}
```

Note the way in which the formal parameters are defined. The **params** keyword indicates that the method accepts a variable number of parameters. In this case, the method accepts any number of **int** parameters, which it automatically puts into an array called list. In the method, we process the array normally.

We can now pass any number of int parameters to the average method, including none at all. That's why we check to see if the length of the array is zero before we compute the average. Note that several of the Console.Out.WriteLine methods use this technique to take a format string followed by a variable number of parameters.

The type of the multiple parameters can be any primitive or object type. For example, the following method accepts and prints multiple Grade objects (we defined the Grade class earlier in this chapter):

```
public void printGrades (params Grade[] grades)
{
  foreach(Grade letterGrade in grades)
    Console.Out.WriteLine (letterGrade);
}
```

A method that accepts a variable number of parameters can also accept other parameters. For example, the following method accepts an **int**, a String object, and then a variable number of **double** values that will be stored in an array called nums:

```
public void test (int count, string name, params double[] nums)
{
  // whatever
}
```

The varying parameters must come last in the formal arguments. A single method cannot accept two sets of varying parameters.

Constructors can also be set up to accept a varying number of parameters. The program shown in Listing 7.11 creates two `Family` objects, passing a varying number of strings (representing the family member names) into the `Family` constructor.

Listing 7.11

```
//***************************************************************
//  VariableParameters.cs          C#:  Ken Culp
//
//  Demonstrates the use of a variable-length parameter list.
//***************************************************************
using System;

namespace VariableParameters
{
  class VariableParameters
  {
    [STAThread]
    static void Main(string[] args)
    {
      Family lewis = new Family("John", "sharon",
        "justin", "Kayla");
      Family camden = new Family("Stephen", "Annie",
        "matt", "Mary", "Simon", "Lucy", "Ruthie",
        "Sam", "David");

      Console.Out.WriteLine(lewis);
      Console.Out.WriteLine();
      Console.Out.WriteLine(camden);

      Console.In.ReadLine();  // Wait for enter key
    }
  }
}
```

Output

```
John
Sharon
Justin
Kayla

Stephen
Annie
Matt
Mary
Simon
```

Listing 7.11   continued

```
Lucy
Ruthie
Sam
David
```

The `Family` class is shown in Listing 7.12. The constructor simply stores a reference to the array parameter until it is needed. By using a variable-length parameter list for the constructor, we make it easy to create a family of any size.

Listing 7.12

```csharp
//****************************************************************
//  Family.cs          C#:   Ken Culp
//
//  Demonstrates the use of a variable-length parameter list.
//****************************************************************
using System;

namespace VariableParameters
{
  public class Family
  {
    //------------------------------------------------------------
    // Constructor:  Sets up this family by storing the
    // (possibly multiple) names passed in as parameters
    //------------------------------------------------------------
    private string[] members;
    public Family(params string[] names)
    {
      members = names;
    }

    //------------------------------------------------------------
    //  Returns a string representation of this family.
    //------------------------------------------------------------
    public override string ToString()
    {
      string result = "";
      foreach (string name in members)
        result += name + "\n";

      return result;
    }
  }
}
```

7.6   TWO-DIMENSIONAL ARRAYS

The arrays we've examined so far have all been *one-dimensional arrays* in the sense that they represent a simple list of values. As the name implies, a *two-dimensional array* has values in two dimensions, which are often thought of as the rows and columns of a table. Figure 7.4 graphically compares a one-dimensional array with a two-dimensional array. We must use two indexes to refer to a value in a two-dimensional array, one specifying the row and another the column.

Brackets are used to represent each dimension in the array. Therefore the type of a two-dimensional array that stores integers is **int**[,]. C# manages the internal indexing for you and maintains the data as a single structure.

The `TwoDArray` program shown in Listing 7.13 instantiates a two-dimensional array of integers. As with one-dimensional arrays, the size of the dimensions is specified when the array is created. The size of the dimensions can be different.

Nested `for` loops are used in the `TwoDArray` program to load the array with values and also to print those values in a table format. Carefully trace the processing to see how the nested loops eventually visit each element in the two-dimensional array. Note that the outer loops are governed by `table.GetLength(0)`, which represents the number of rows, and the inner loops are governed by `table.GetLength(1)`, which represents the number of columns in that row. For any array with more than one dimension, the `GetLength` method must be used to find the length of any given dimension. The parameter passed to `GetLength` is the number of the index, starting with 0. Index 0 is the first index, index 1 the second, and so on.

Note that the `Length` property is still available, but it returns the total number of elements in the array. When there is only one dimension, `Length` and `GetLength(0)` return the same value, so we used this shorter version in earlier code segments. Whenever you need to know how many elements are in a particular dimension, it is far safer to use `GetLength` (even if there is only one dimension). Therefore, get in the habit of using `GetLength`.

As with one-dimensional arrays, an initializer list can be used to instantiate a two-dimensional array, where each element is itself an array initializer list. This technique is used in the `SodaSurvey` program, which is shown in Listing 7.14.

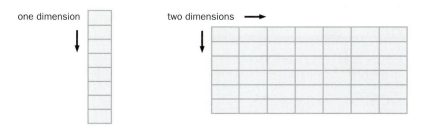

FIGURE 7.4   A one-dimensional array and a two-dimensional array

Listing 7.13

```csharp
//***************************************************************
//   TwoDArray.cs          C#:   Ken Culp
//
//   Demonstrates the use of a two-dimensional array.
//***************************************************************
using System;

namespace TwoDArray
{
  class TwoDArray
  {
    //-----------------------------------------------------------
    //   Creates a 2D array of integers, fills it with increasing
    //   integer values, then prints them out.
    //-----------------------------------------------------------
    public static void Main(string[] args)
    {
      int[,] table = new int[5, 10];

      // Load the table with values
      for (int row = 0; row < table.GetLength(0); row++)
        for (int col = 0; col < table.GetLength(1); col++)
          table[row, col] = row * 10 + col;

      // Print the table
      for (int row = 0; row < table.GetLength(0); row++)
      {
        for (int col = 0; col < table.GetLength(1); col++)
          Console.Out.Write(table[row, col] + "\t");
        Console.Out.WriteLine();
      }

      Console.In.ReadLine;  // Wait for enter key
    }
  }
}
```

Output

0	1	2	3	4	5	6	7	8	9
10	11	12	13	14	15	16	17	18	19
20	21	22	23	24	25	26	27	28	29
30	31	32	33	34	35	36	37	38	39
40	41	42	43	44	45	46	47	48	49

Listing 7.14

```
//*****************************************************************
//  SodaSurvey.cs          C#:  Ken Culp
//
//  Demonstrates the use of a two-dimensional array.
//*****************************************************************
using System;
using System.Collections;

namespace SodaSurvey
{
  class SodaSurvey
  {
    //-----------------------------------------------------------
    //  Determines and prints the average of each row (soda) and
    //  each column (respondent) of the survey scores.
    //-----------------------------------------------------------
    public static void Main(string[] args)
    {
      int[,] scores = new int[,]
        { {3, 4, 5, 2, 1, 4, 3, 2, 4, 4},
          {2, 4, 3, 4, 3, 3, 2, 1, 2, 2},
          {3, 5, 4, 5, 5, 3, 2, 5, 5, 5},
          {1, 1, 1, 3, 1, 2, 1, 3, 2, 4} };

      int SODAS = scores.GetLength(0);
      int PEOPLE = scores.GetLength(1);

      int[] sodaSum = new int[SODAS];
      int[] personSum = new int[PEOPLE];

      for (int soda = 0; soda < SODAS; soda++)
        for (int person = 0; person < PEOPLE; person++)
        {
          sodaSum[soda] += scores[soda, person];
          personSum[person] += scores[soda, person];
        }

      Console.Out.WriteLine("Averages:\n");
      for (int soda = 0; soda < SODAS; soda++)
        Console.Out.WriteLine("Soda #" + (soda + 1) + ": " +
          string.Format("{0:0.#}", (float)sodaSum[soda]/PEOPLE));

      Console.Out.WriteLine();
      for (int person = 0; person < PEOPLE; person++)
        Console.Out.WriteLine("Person #" + (person + 1) + ": " +
```

Listing 7.14   continued

```
            string.Format("{0:0.#}",
            (float)personSum[person] / SODAS));
        Console.In.ReadLine();  // Wait for enter key
    }
  }
}
```

Output

```
Averages:

Soda #1: 3.2
Soda #2: 2.6
Soda #3: 4.2
Soda #4: 1.9

Person #1: 2.2
Person #2: 3.5
Person #3: 3.2
Person #4: 3.5
Person #5: 2.5
Person #6: 3
Person #7: 2
Person #8: 2.8
Person #9: 3.2
Person #10: 3.8
```

Suppose a soda manufacturer held a taste test for four new flavors to see how people liked them. The manufacturer got 10 people to try each new flavor and asked them to give each flavor a score from 1 to 5, where 1 equals poor and 5 equals excellent. The two-dimensional array called scores in the SodaSurvey program stores the results of that survey. Each row corresponds to a soda and each column in that row corresponds to the person who tasted it. More generally, each row holds the responses that all testers gave for one particular soda flavor, and each column holds the responses of one person for all sodas.

The SodaSurvey program computes and prints the average responses for each soda and for each respondent. The sums of each soda and person are first stored in one-dimensional arrays of integers. Then the averages are computed and printed.

Multidimensional Arrays

An array can have one, two, three, or even more dimensions. Any array with more than one dimension is called a *multidimensional array*.

It's fairly easy to picture a two-dimensional array as a table. A three-dimensional array could be drawn as a cube. However, once you are past three dimensions, multidimensional arrays might seem hard to visualize. Yet, consider that each subsequent dimension is simply a subdivision of the previous one. It is often best to think of larger multidimensional arrays in this way.

For example, suppose we wanted to store the number of students attending universities across the United States, broken down in a meaningful way. We might represent it as a four-dimensional array of integers. The first dimension represents the state. The second dimension represents the universities in each state. The third dimension represents the colleges in each university. Finally, the fourth dimension represents departments in each college. The value stored at each location is the number of students in one particular department. Figure 7.5 shows these subdivisions.

Two-dimensional arrays are fairly common. However, you should be cautious when deciding whether to create multidimensional arrays in a program. When dealing with large amounts of data that is managed at multiple levels, additional information and the methods needed to manage that information will probably be required. It is far more likely, for instance, that in the previous example, each state would be represented by an object, which may contain, among other things, an array to store information about each university, and so on.

There is one other important characteristic of C# arrays to consider. As we established previously, C# directly supports multidimensional arrays. However, it also possible to create arrays of arrays, by specifying that the type of one dimension of an array is not a primitive type or a class but rather an array. Those arrays would themselves contain references to other arrays. This layering can continue for as many dimensions as required. When this technique is used, the arrays in any one dimension could be of different lengths. These are sometimes called *ragged* or *jagged arrays*. For example, the number of elements in each row of a two-dimensional array may not be the same. In such situations, make sure that the arrays are managed appropriately.

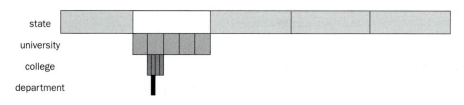

state

university

college

department

FIGURE 7.5   Visualization of a four-dimensional array

7.7   THE `ArrayList` CLASS

The `ArrayList` class is part of C#'s library package in the `System.Collections` namespace. It provides a service similar to an array in that it can store a list of values and reference them by an index. However, whereas an array remains a fixed size throughout its existence, an `ArrayList` object dynamically grows and shrinks as needed. A data element can be inserted into or removed from any location (index) of an `ArrayList` object with a single method invocation.

Since the `ArrayList` class is part of the `Collections` namespace, a **using** line is required to access the class. `ArrayList` is part of a group of classes that serves to organize and manage other objects. We discuss collection classes further in Chapter 12.

Unless we specify otherwise, an `ArrayList` is not declared to store a particular type. That is, an `ArrayList` object stores a list of references to the `Object` class, which means that any type of object can be added to an `ArrayList`. Figure 7.6 lists several methods of the `ArrayList` class.

The program shown in Listing 7.15 instantiates an `ArrayList` called `band`. The method `Add` is used to add several `string` objects to the `ArrayList` in a specific order. Then, one particular string is deleted and another is inserted at a particular index. As with any other object, the `ToString` method of the `ArrayList` class is automatically called whenever it is sent to the `WriteLine` method.

Note that when an element from an `ArrayList` is deleted, the list of elements "collapses" so that the indexes are kept continuous for the remaining elements. Likewise, when an element is inserted at a particular point, the indexes of the other elements are adjusted accordingly.

Specifying an `ArrayList` Element Type

The methods of the `ArrayList` class are designed to accept references to the `Object` class as parameters, thus allowing a reference to any kind of object to be passed to it. Thus, by default, an array can store any type of object. Note that an implication of this implementation is that a member of `ArrayList`, found by indexing into it, is an `Object` reference. In order to retrieve a specific object from the `ArrayList`, the returned object must be cast to its original class. However, in our case, we are using that object reference as a string that automatically calls that object's `ToString` method. We discuss the `Object` class and its relationship to other classes in Chapter 8.

Public Constructors	
public **ArrayList**();	Initializes a new instance of the `ArrayList` class.
public **ArrayList**(int *capacity*);	Initializes a new instance of the `ArrayList` class for the specified capacity.
public **ArrayList**(ICollection c);	Initializes a new instance of the `ArrayList` class that contains elements copied from the specified collection and that has the same initial capacity as the number of elements copied.

Public Properties	
Capacity	Gets or sets the number of elements that the `ArrayList` can contain.
Count	Gets the number of elements actually contained in the `ArrayList`.
Item	Gets or sets the element at the specified index. In C#, this property is the indexer for the `ArrayList` class.

Public Methods	
Adapter	Creates an `ArrayList` wrapper for a specific `IList`.
Add	Adds an object to the end of the `ArrayList`.
AddRange	Adds the elements of an ICollection to the end of the `ArrayList`.
BinarySearch	Overloaded. Uses a binary search algorithm to locate a specific element in the sorted `ArrayList` or a portion of it.
Clear	Removes all elements from the `ArrayList`.
Clone	Creates a shallow copy of the `ArrayList`.
Contains	Determines whether an element is in the `ArrayList`.
CopyTo	Overloaded. Copies the `ArrayList` or a portion of it to a one-dimensional array.
Equals	Overloaded. Determines whether two `Object` instances are equal.
GetRange	Returns an `ArrayList` that represents a subset of the elements in the source `ArrayList`.
IndexOf	Overloaded. Returns the zero-based index of the first occurrence of a value in the `ArrayList` or in a portion of it.
Insert	Inserts an element into the `ArrayList` at the specified index.

FIGURE 7.6   Some members of the ArrayList class

InsertRange	Inserts the elements of a collection into the `ArrayList` at the specified index.
LastIndexOf	Overloaded. Returns the zero-based index of the last occurrence of a value in the `ArrayList` or in a portion of it.
Remove	Removes the first occurrence of a specific object from the `ArrayList`.
RemoveAt	Removes the element at the specified index of the `ArrayList`.
RemoveRange	Removes a range of elements from the `ArrayList`.
Repeat	Returns an `ArrayList` whose elements are copies of the specified value.
Reverse	Overloaded. Reverses the order of the elements in the `ArrayList` or a portion of it.
SetRange	Copies the elements of a collection over a range of elements in the `ArrayList`.
Sort	Overloaded. Sorts the elements in the `ArrayList` or a portion of it.
ToArray	Overloaded. Copies the elements of the `ArrayList` to a new array.
ToString	Returns a string that represents the current `Object`.
TrimToSize	Sets the capacity to the actual number of elements in the `ArrayList`.

FIGURE 7.6 (*continued*) Some members of the ArrayList class

Listing 7.15

```
//*************************************************************
//  Beatles.cs        C#:  Ken Culp
//
//  Demonstrates the use of a ArrayList object and overriding
//  a member of a system class.
//*************************************************************
using System;
using System.Collections;

namespace Beatles
{
  //------------------------------------------------------------
  // Override just the ToString member of ArrayList
  //------------------------------------------------------------
```

Listing 7.15   continued

```csharp
public class Band : ArrayList
{
  public override string ToString()
  {
    string ret = "[";
    for (int i = 0; i < this.Count; i++)
    {
      if (i > 0) ret += ", ";
      ret += this[i];
    }
    return ret + "]";
  }
}
class Beatles
{
  //-------------------------------------------------------------
  //  Stores and modifies a list of band members.
  //-------------------------------------------------------------
  public static void Main(string[] args)
  {
    Band band = new Band();

    band.Add("Paul");
    band.Add("Pete");
    band.Add("John");
    band.Add("George");

    Console.Out.WriteLine(band);

    int location = band.IndexOf("Pete");
    band.RemoveAt(location);

    Console.Out.WriteLine(band);
    Console.Out.WriteLine("At index 1: " + band[1]);

    band.Insert(2, "Ringo");

    Console.Out.WriteLine(band);
    Console.Out.WriteLine("Size of the band: " + band.Count);

    Console.In.ReadLine();  // Wait for enter key
  }
}
}
```

Output

```
[Paul, Pete, John, George]
[Paul, John, George]
```

Listing 7.15   continued

```
At index 1: John
[Paul, John, Ringo, George]
Size of the band: 4
```

Direct your attention to the internal class `Band` located at the top of the listing. This class was defined because the default method `ToString` in `ArrayList` did not give us any information about the contents of the array (it only gives the type of the object). By creating our own class that extends `ArrayList` (just as interfaces are extended), we can modify existing members of the `ArrayList` class. This process is called *overriding* and thus the method declaration `public override string ToString()` is used. Thus we would say that we *derived* our `Band` class from `ArrayList`. Deriving classes from other classes is covered in Chapter 8.

`ArrayList` Efficiency

The `ArrayList` class is implemented, as you might imagine, using an array. That is, the `ArrayList` object stores an array of `Object` references. The methods provided by the class manipulate that array so that the indexes remain continuous as elements are added and removed.

When an `ArrayList` object is instantiated, the internal array is created with an initial capacity that defines the number of references it can currently handle. Elements can be added to the list without needing to allocate more memory until it reaches this capacity. When required, the capacity is expanded to accommodate the new need. We performed a similar operation in the `Tunes` program earlier in this chapter.

When an element is inserted into an `ArrayList`, all the elements at higher indexes are copied into their new locations to make room for the new element. Figure 7.7 illustrates this process. Similar processing occurs when an element is removed from an `ArrayList`, except that the items are shifted in the other direction, closing the gap created by the deleted element to keep the indexes continuous. If several elements are inserted or deleted, this copying is repeated many times over.

If, in general, elements are added to or removed from the end of an `ArrayList`, it's efficiency is not affected. But if elements are added to and/or removed from the front part of

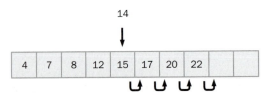

FIGURE 7.7   Inserting an element into an ArrayList object

a long `ArrayList`, a huge amount of element copying will occur. An `ArrayList`, with its dynamic characteristics, is a useful abstraction of an array, but the abstraction masks some underlying activity that can be fairly inefficient, depending on how it is used.

`ArrayList` is a very useful tool when dealing with small amounts of data, and the extensive list of methods will greatly reduce the effort to write simple applications. In our example, we showed how to add elements in order (to the end of the list) and how to insert or delete elements at specific locations in the list. However, you can also insert or extract groups of elements, convert the list to a regular array, and much, much more. You will find that you can frequently save coding time on short projects by using library classes like `ArrayList`.

7.8   THE foreach LOOP

We indicated in Chapter 5 that the easiest way to index through all elements of an array is with the **foreach** loop. The **foreach** loop is handy because you do not have to know how many elements are in the loop; the loop mechanism automatically selects each element in the array in order.

The syntax for the **foreach** statement is as follows:

```
foreach (varType varName in arrayName) {
    statements using varName }
```

The first thing you notice about the syntax is that there is no initialization or limit checking. Instead, you specify the type of the object in the array, give it a temporary name (varName here), and specify the name of the array (arrayName here). The variable type might be a primitive type like **int** or **float**, or it might be a class name like `Coin`.

The variable type need not precisely match the type of the array. For example, `ArrayList` returns items of type **object** even though we stored objects of type `Coin`. We can then specify type to be `Coin`. In the following example, assume that we have several coins in an `ArrayList` object called `coinArray` and we want to print whether each is heads of not. The first example uses the **foreach** syntax and the second uses the regular **for** syntax.

```
foreach (Coin theCoin in coinArray)
  {
    Console.Out.WriteLine("Is Heads: " + theCoin.IsHeads);
  }
```

In the preceding example, the variable `theCoin` is of type `Coin` so there is no need to typecast. This would work as long as the elements in the `ArrayList` are really something of type `Coin`. If something other than `Coin` were found, the system would throw an exception indicating an invalid type conversion.

If we had used a regular `for` loop, the syntax would have been as follows:

```
for (int index=0; index<coinArray.GetLength(0); index++)
  {
    Console.Out.WriteLine("Is Heads: " + ((
      Coin) coinArray[index]).IsHeads);
  }
```

Clearly, in this example the **foreach** syntax is much easier to use. However, there will be times when you need to know the index of the entry in the array as we have in the following example. In this case, the regular **for** statement would be preferred. However, even when using **foreach**, it is always possible to find out which index the current item is by using the `ArrayList.IndexOf` method, passing the variable (`theCoin`) from the **foreach** statement:

```
int index = coinArray.IndexOf(theCoin);
```

As a final note, the variable used in the **foreach** statement only has scope within the brackets for the statement. This is the same as indexing variables declared in a regular **for** statement.

7.9   POLYGONS AND POLYLINES

Arrays are helpful when drawing complex shapes. In fact, many of the drawing methods require arrays for their parameters. A polygon, for example, is a multisided shape that is defined in C# using a series of (x, y) points that indicate the vertices of the polygon. Arrays are often used to store the list of coordinates.

Our drawing efforts so far have used simple x and y coordinates plus lengths and widths. Visual Studio, however, has several classes that will simplify our drawing effort. For example, we can draw a rectangle by passing one structure instead of four points. Also, with arrays of these structures, you can draw multiple structures (lines, rectangles, ellipses) in one step. Before we look at some of these drawing methods in detail, let's review these new structures.

The `Point` and `PointF` Classes

The `Point` class has two internal integer data members corresponding to the x and y coordinates of the point. These are exposed using two integer public properties X and Y. The `ToString` method returns a string in the form `"{X=23,Y=15}"`. The class also overloads the `Equals` method so that equality of two different `Point` objects that represent the same x and y coordinates can be tested with = =.

The `PointF` class is the same as the `Point` class except that the coordinates are type **float** instead of **int**. The `ToString` method returns decimal values as in

"{X=23.5,Y=15.2}". PointF is used when you need to specify fractional values. This is most often used when you are using drawing units other than pixels (inch, millimeter, etc.).

Note how we declared the array of points in Rocket. We were able to use the array initializer, but to specify each (x, y) coordinate, we had to use the **new** Point construct and specify the x and y values. These values could also have been added in code, as shown here:

```
private Point[] flame = new Point[11];
    . . .
flame[3].X = 130;
flame[3].Y = 125;
```

The Size and SizeF Classes

The Size class has two internal integer data members corresponding to the width and height of an object. These are exposed using two integer public properties Width and Height. The ToString method returns a string in the form "{Width=125, Height=150}". The class also overloads the Equals method so that equality of two different Size objects that represent the same width and height can be tested with = =.

Like PointF, the SizeF class accepts values of type **float**. The ToString method returns decimal values, as in "{Width=125.6, Height=150.3}". SizeF is used when you need to specify fractional values. Note that Size and SizeF values can be specified with an array initializer or in code just as shown for Point.

The Rectangle and RectangleF Classes

Rectangles are specified by the location of the upper-left corner of the rectangle plus a width and a height. Thus, a rectangle combines values of a Point and a Size class. Internally, four integer data members represent the upper-left (x, y) corner of the box and the width and height. These values are exposed using four integer public properties: X, Y, Width, and Height. However, there are four other very handy public (but read-only) properties that represent the edges of the rectangle: Left, Right, Top, and Bottom. Since these properties are read-only, you cannot modify them directly.

The ToString method returns "{X=125,Y=150,Width=200,Height=300}". The class also overloads the Equals method so that equality of two different Rectangle objects that represent the same size rectangle at the same location can be tested with = =.

Like PointF, the RectangleF class accepts values of type **float**. The ToString method returns decimal values for the various parameters. Again, RectangleF is used when you need to specify fractional values. Note that Rectangle and RectangleF values can be specified with an array initializer or in code.

Using ArrayList for Size, Point, and Rectangle

Sometimes you do not know how many points, sizes, or rectangles are going to be needed when the program first starts. For example, suppose you are creating a paint application in which the user adds points interactively on a canvas. Declaring an array and having to resize it all the time would be a great nuisance. For this reason, you can use the `ArrayList` class to store the points instead.

The following code segment illustrates how you could define the points and then draw a rectangular window. Note that by using the `ArrayList.Add` method to add the points, we add the points as they occur. Then, when we want to display them, we do not need to know how many points are in the list.

```
brush = new SolidBrush(Color.Gray);
ArrayList window = new ArrayList();
window.Add(new Point( 95, 45));
window.Add(new Point(105, 45));
window.Add(new Point(110, 70));
window.Add(new Point( 90, 70));
Point[] winArray = (Point[]) window.ToArray(typeof(Point));
page.FillPolygon (brush, winArray);
```

Drawing with `Point`, `PointF`, `Rectangle`, `RectangleF`, and `Arrays`

Figure 7.8 lists several variations of drawing methods that we have seen previously plus several new methods that take arrays. The method specification lists the types of parameters required for each. The methods that are variations use `Point` and `Rectangle` structures to replace a series of points being passed. Another method, `DrawRectangles`, simply provides an easy way to specify multiple rectangles and draw them in one call. The `DrawLines` and `DrawBeziers` build a different type of structure altogether.

You draw polygons similarly to how you draw rectangles and ovals. Like these other shapes, a polygon can be drawn filled or unfilled. The methods used to draw a polygon are called `DrawPolygon` and `FillPolygon`. Both of these methods are overloaded as shown in Figure 7.8. The version we will demonstrate here uses arrays of points to define the polygon.

In the version that uses arrays, the `DrawPolygon` and `FillPolygon` methods take two parameters. The first parameter for `FillPolygon` is a `Brush` (color and hatch) and the first for `DrawPolygon` is a `Pen` (color, thickness, dash style). The second parameter for both methods is an array of points representing the x and y coordinates of those points. The second parameter represents the (x, y) coordinates of the vertices of the polygons.

A polygon is always closed. A line segment is always drawn from the last point in the list to the first point in the list.

To draw a series of lines, an array of points is used, just like for a polygon. However, the method `DrawLines` does not connect the last point back to the first. Also, since we are drawing lines, the method takes a `Pen` object (color, thickness, dash pattern) followed by the array of points.

The program shown in Listing 7.16 uses polygons to draw a rocket. In the `RocketPanel` class, shown in Listing 7.17, the array called `rocket` defines the points of the polygon that make up the main body of the rocket. The first point in the array is the

Method	Description
`public void DrawLine(Pen, Point, Point);` `public void DrawLine(Pen, PointF, PointF);`	Draws line between the two points
`public void DrawLines(Pen, Point[]);` `public void DrawLines(Pen, PointF[]);`	Draws lines connecting each point to the next but not closing the last point back to the first
`public void DrawRectangle(Pen, Rectangle);` `public void DrawRectangle(Pen, RectangleF);`	Draws a rectangle
`public void DrawRectangles(Pen, Rectangle[]);` `public void DrawRectangles(Pen, RectangleF[]);`	Draws all rectangles in the array
`public void DrawEllipse(Pen, Rectangle);` `public void DrawEllipse(Pen, RectangleF);`	Draws ellipse inside bounding rectangle
`public void DrawPolygon(Pen, Point[]);` `public void DrawPolygon(Pen, PointF[]);`	Like `DrawLines` except connects the last point to the first

`public void DrawClosedCurve(Pen, Point[]);`
`public void DrawClosedCurve(Pen, PointF[]);`
`public void DrawClosedCurve(Pen, Point[],`
`  float, FillMode);`
`public void DrawClosedCurve(Pen, PointF[],`
`  float, FillMode);`
	Draws closed cardinal spline using optional tension and fill mode

`public void DrawBezier(Pen, Point, Point,` `Point, Point);`	Draws a Bézier spline defined by four Point structures
`public void DrawBeziers(Pen, Point[]);` `public void DrawBeziers(Pen, PointF[]);`	Draws a series of Bézier splines from the array of Point structures
`public void FillRectangle(Brush, Rectangle);` `public void FillRectangle(Brush, RectangleF);`	Fills specified rectangle
`public void FillRectangles(Brush, Rectangle[]);` `public void FillRectangles(Brush, RectangleF[]);`	Fills specified rectangles
`public void FillEllipse(Brush, Rectangle);` `public void FillEllipse(Brush, RectangleF);`	Fills ellipse inside bounding rectangle
`public void FillClosedCurve(Brush, Point);` `public void FillClosedCurve(Brush, PointF);`	Fills interior of closed cardinal spline

FIGURE 7.8   New drawing methods using Points and Rectangles

upper tip of the rocket, and the points progress clockwise from there. The window array specifies the points for the polygon that form the window in the rocket. Both the rocket and the window are drawn as filled polygons.

The flame array defines the points of the lines that are used to create the image of flame shooting out of the tail of the rocket. Because it is drawn using DrawLines, and not a DrawPolygon, the flame is not closed or filled.

Before we move on, let's make a few observations about this example. First, the points will be in the list in the order in which they are added, because each call to Add places the object at the end of the list. However, if you wanted to use an alternate ordering or if you decided you wanted to remove a point in our fictitious editor, you would simply call the appropriate method on ArrayList.

The conversion from ArrayList to an array of Point is not so obvious and requires a little explanation. The ArrayList.ToArray method has two overloads. The first overload takes no parameters but returns an array of Object, which does not help us much. The second overload takes as a parameter the type of an object. Anywhere in Visual Studio that an argument lists a parameter of the type System.Type, you use the **typeof** keyword and a class name (such as Point, used here).

When this version of ToArray is called, it builds the return array in the type we require. However, the ToArray method is of type System.Array and not an array of points. Therefore, the last part of the process of extracting an array of points is to *typecast* the return type from System.Array to Point[]. Although this looks complicated, just keep track of this example and use it for other types of objects stored in ArrayList (PointF, Size, Rectangle, etc.).

Listing 7.16

```
//***********************************************************************
//   Rocket.cs               C#:   Ken Culp
//
//   Demonstrates filling polygons and drawing arrays of lines.
//***********************************************************************
using System;
using System.Collections.Generic;
using System.ComponentModel;
using System.Data;
using System.Drawing;
using System.Text;
using System.Windows.Forms;

namespace Rocket
{
  public partial class Rocket : Form
  {
    private const int SCREEN_WIDTH = 200;
    private const int SCREEN_HEIGHT = 240;
```

Listing 7.16   continued

```
//------------------------------------------------------------
//  Define points using array initializer technique.
//------------------------------------------------------------
private Point[] rocket =
   {new Point(100,  15), new Point(120,  40),
    new Point(120, 115), new Point(130, 125),
    new Point(130, 150), new Point( 70, 150),
    new Point( 70, 125), new Point( 80, 115),
    new Point( 80,  40)                        };

private Point[] window =
   { new Point( 95,  45), new Point(105, 45),
     new Point(110,  70), new Point( 90, 70) };

private Point[] flame =
   { new Point( 70, 155), new Point( 70, 170),
     new Point( 75, 165), new Point( 80, 190),
     new Point( 90, 170), new Point(100, 175),
     new Point(110, 160), new Point(115, 185),
     new Point(120, 160), new Point(130, 175),
     new Point(130, 155)                        };

//------------------------------------------------------------
//  Constructor.
//------------------------------------------------------------
public Rocket()
{
  InitializeComponent();
}

private void Rocket_Load(object sender, System.EventArgs e)
{
  this.BackColor = Color.Black;
  this.Size = new Size(SCREEN_WIDTH, SCREEN_HEIGHT);
}

private void Rocket_Paint(object sender, PaintEventArgs e)
{
  Graphics page = e.Graphics;

  Brush brush = new SolidBrush(Color.Cyan);
  page.FillPolygon(brush, rocket);

  brush = new SolidBrush(Color.Gray);
  page.FillPolygon(brush, window);
  //    The following code illustrates how to use ArrayList
  //    to add points one at a time and then draw them all.
  //      ArrayList window = new ArrayList();
```

Listing 7.16   continued

```
//      window.Add(new Point( 95,  45));
//      window.Add(new Point(105,  45));
//      window.Add(new Point(110,  70));
//      window.Add(new Point( 90,  70));
//      Point[] winArray =
//        (Point[]) window.ToArray(typeof(Point));
//      page.FillPolygon (brush, winArray);

    Pen pen = new Pen(Color.Red);
    page.DrawLines(pen, flame);
  }
 }
}
```

Output

7.10   MOUSE EVENTS

Let's examine the events that are generated when using a mouse. Logically, we can divide these events into two categories: *click* events and *motion* events. The table in Figure 7.9 defines these events.

When you click the mouse button over a C# GUI component, three events are generated: one when the mouse button is pushed down (MouseDown) and two when it is let up

(`MouseUp` and `Click`). A mouse click is defined as pressing and releasing the mouse button in the same location. If you press the mouse button down, move the mouse, and then release the mouse button, a mouse-clicked event is not generated.

A component generates a `MouseEnter` event when the mouse pointer passes into its graphical space. Likewise, it generates a `MouseLeave` event when the mouse pointer leaves its graphical space.

Mouse motion events, as the name implies, occur while the mouse is in motion. The `MouseMove` event indicates simply that the mouse is in motion.

The various drag events are generated when the user has pressed the mouse button down and moved the mouse without releasing the button. Mouse motion events are generated many times, very quickly, while the mouse is in motion. Note that the keyboard is examined during drag to capture whether the Alt, Shift, or Ctrl key is pressed. This data is included in the mouse event object.

In a specific situation, we may care about only one or two mouse events. What events we handle depends on what we are trying to accomplish.

Mouse event handlers differ slightly in their signatures in that different mouse events have three different types of objects they can return as the second parameter of the event handler. Figure 7.9 shows the different mouse events and the type of event they return. Figure 7.10 details the members of `MouseEventArgs`, and Figure 7.11 details the members of `DragEventArgs`. The public methods are derived from `System.Object` and are the same for all event types. Therefore, they are listed in the first table only.

`EventArgs` has no properties; it has only the standard methods from `Object`, as shown in Figure 7.10. Therefore, such handlers only need to know when the event occurs; there is no real data to convey to the handler.

The `Dots` program shown in Listing 7.17 responds to one mouse event. Specifically, it draws a green dot at the location of the mouse pointer whenever the mouse button is pressed.

Listing 7.17

```
//*****************************************************************
//  Dots.cs                        C#:   Ken Culp
//
//  Demonstrates mouse events and drawing on a panel.
//  Created using Visual Studio Toolbox.
//*****************************************************************
using System;
using System.Collections;
using System.Drawing;
using System.Windows.Forms;

namespace Dots
{
```

Listing 7.17   continued

```csharp
public partial class Dots : Form
{
  public Dots()
  {
    InitializeComponent();
  }
  // User defined items
  const int RADIUS = 6;
  ArrayList pointList;
  Brush brush;
  Font font;

  private void Dots_Load(object sender, System.EventArgs e)
  {
    pointList = new ArrayList();
    brush = new SolidBrush(Color.Cyan);
    font = new Font("Times New Roman", 14);
  }

  private void Dots_MouseUp(object sender, MouseEventArgs e)
  {
    Point p = new Point(e.X, e.Y);
    if (e.Y > 20) pointList.Add(p); // No points on top of Count
    this.Invalidate();
  }

  private void Dots_Paint(object sender, PaintEventArgs e)
  {
    Graphics page = e.Graphics;
    page.Clear(Color.Black);
    foreach (Point dot in pointList)
      page.FillEllipse(
        brush, dot.X, dot.Y, RADIUS * 2, RADIUS * 2);
        page.DrawString(
      "Count: " + pointList.Count, font, brush, 5, 5);
  }

}
}
```

Listing 7.17   continued

Output

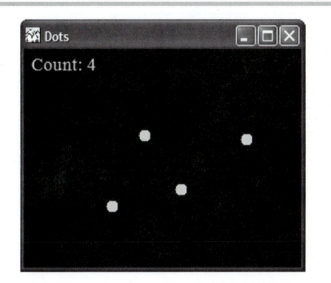

The Dots class keeps track of a list of Point objects that represent all the locations at which the user has clicked the mouse. Each time the panel is painted, all the points stored in the list are drawn.

The list of Point objects is maintained as an ArrayList object. To draw the points, we use a **foreach** loop to iterate over all the points stored in the list. Because ArrayList stores items of type Object, we specify the type of dot on the **foreach** line to be type Point. This allows us to access the (x, y) coordinates without having to typecast to point.

The handler for the MouseUp event is invoked each time the user releases the mouse button while it is over the form. We could have used the Click event just as well and would have obtained exactly the same result.

A mouse event always occurs at some point in two-dimensional space, and the object that represents that event keeps track of that location. In a mouse handler, we can get and use that point whenever we need it. In the Dots program, each time the Dots_MouseUp method is called, the location of the event is obtained using the X and Y properties of the MouseEventArgs object e. From those two values, we create a new point that is stored in the ArrayList. To force a repaint on the form, Invalidate is called.

Let's look at an example that responds to two mouse-oriented events. The RubberLines program, shown in Listing 7.18, draws a line between two points. The first point is determined by the location at which the mouse is first pressed down. The second point changes as the mouse is dragged while the mouse button is held down. When the button is released, the line remains fixed between the first and second points. When the mouse button is pressed again, a new line is started.

Mouse Event	Description	Event Type
MouseEnter	The mouse has just moved over the control.	EventArgs
MouseMove	The mouse has moved to a new location over the control.	MouseEventArgs
MouseHover	The mouse is over the control.	EventArgs
MouseDown	A mouse button was pressed but not necessarily released yet.	MouseEventArgs
MouseWheel	The wheel button on the mouse was moved.	MouseEventArgs
MouseUp	The mouse button was released.	MouseEventArgs
Click	A mouse button was clicked (pressed and released). OnClick, MouseDown, and MouseUp also occur.	EventArgs
DoubleClick	The control was double-clicked. Some controls support DoubleClick (forms, picture boxes, panels, labels, text boxes) and others do not (buttons, check boxes, radio buttons).	EventArgs
MouseLeave	The mouse has just moved away from the control.	EventArgs
DragEnter	Drag has just started.	DragEventArgs
DragOver	Drag is in progress and the mouse is over a control.	DragEventArgs
DragLeave	Drag is in progress and the mouse has just left the control.	EventArgs
DragDrop	Drag was in progress and the mouse button was released over the control.	DragEventArgs

FIGURE 7.9 Mouse events and mouse motion events

In the programming projects at the end of this chapter, you will be asked to change the program to store the lines. Because a line consists of a beginning point and an ending point, you will need four separate integer values (or two Point objects) for each line. One option to store four integers is to use a Rectangle object. The X and Y values could be used for the starting point of the line (the coordinate of the mouse when the button is pressed). Then you could use the Rectangle object's Width and Length values to store the ending point X and Y coordinates, respectively. Another choice would be to add to the project your own class that stores four private integer values (x1, y1, x2, y2) with public properties to expose them.

The form on which the lines are drawn is represented by the RubberLinesForm class, shown in Listing 7.18. Because we need to recognize both a mouse-pressed event and a mouse-dragged event, we need handlers that respond to both mouse button events and

Public Properties	
Button	Gets which mouse button was pressed.
Clicks	Gets the number of times the mouse button was pressed and released.
Delta	Gets a signed count of the number of detents the mouse wheel has rotated. A *detent* is one notch of the mouse wheel.
X	Gets the *x* coordinate of the mouse.
Y	Gets the *y* coordinate of the mouse.

Public Methods	
Equals	Overloaded. Determines whether two Object instances are equal.
GetHashCode	Serves as a hash function for a particular type, suitable for use in hashing algorithms and data structures like a hash table.
GetType	Gets the `Type` of the current instance.
ToString	Returns a `String` that represents the current `Object.`

FIGURE 7.10   MouseEventArgs members

Public Properties	
AllowedEffect	Gets which drag-and-drop operations are allowed by the originator (or source) of the drag event.
Data	Gets the `IDataObject` that contains the data associated with this event.
Effect	Gets or sets the target drop effect in a drag-and-drop operation.
KeyState	Gets the current state of the Shift, Ctrl, and Alt keys, as well as the state of the mouse buttons.
X	Gets the *x* coordinate of the mouse pointer, in screen coordinates.
Y	Gets the *y* coordinate of the mouse pointer, in screen coordinates.

FIGURE 7.11   DragEventArgs members

mouse motion events. To handle dragging, we use three mouse event handlers in our code. The first, MouseIsDown, begins a new line by saving the initial starting point of the line in X and Y of our curLine object and sets dragInProgress to **true**. Next, MouseIsMoved stores the current position of the ending point in Width and Length but leaves dragging alone. Finally, `MouseIsUp` stores the current line in the array and sets `dragInProgress` to **false**.

Our `PaintLines` method checks if `dragInProgress` is **true** and, if so, paints the current line. Note that both `MouseIsMoved` and `MouseIsUp` handlers force a paint by calling `Invalidate`.

Listing 7.18

```
//*****************************************************************
//   RubberLinesForm.cs        C#: Ken Culp
//
//   Draws lines on a form with mouse events (down, up, move).
//   Lines are stored in an ArrayList as Rectangle structures
//   which takes 4 integers (X, Y, Height, Width). Height/Width
//   are used for the end point X and Y.
//*****************************************************************
using System;
using System.Collections;
using System.Drawing;
using System.Windows.Forms;

namespace RubberLines
{
  public class RubberLinesForm : Form
  {
    Pen pen;
    Rectangle curLine;
    bool dragInProgress;
    //-----------------------------------------------------------
    //  Constructor:  Builds the form manually in code
    //-----------------------------------------------------------
    public RubberLinesForm()
    {
      this.AutoScaleBaseSize = new System.Drawing.Size(5, 13);
      this.ClientSize = new System.Drawing.Size(292, 266);
      this.Name = "RubberLinesForm";
      this.Icon = new Icon(@"..\..\Creative.ico");
      this.Text = "Rubber Lines";
      this.BackColor = Color.Black;
      this.MouseUp += new MouseEventHandler(this.MouseIsUp);
      this.MouseDown += new MouseEventHandler(this.MouseIsDown);
      this.MouseMove += new MouseEventHandler(this.MouseIsMoved);
      this.Paint += new PaintEventHandler(this.PaintLines);
      dragInProgress = false;
      pen = new Pen(Color.Cyan, 2);
      curLine = new Rectangle(0, 0, 0, 0);
    }
```

Listing 7.18   continued

```
//-------------------------------------------------------
//   MouseDown.
//-------------------------------------------------------
private void MouseIsDown(object sender, MouseEventArgs e)
{
  dragInProgress = true;   // Now dragging
  curLine.X = e.X;              // Save starting point
  curLine.Y = e.Y;
}
private void MouseIsUp(object sender, MouseEventArgs e)
{
  if (dragInProgress)
  {
    curLine.Width = e.X;   // Save ending point
    curLine.Height = e.Y;
  }
  dragInProgress = false;    // Done dragging
  Invalidate();                  // Repaint
}

//-------------------------------------------------------
//   MouseMoved.
//-------------------------------------------------------
private void MouseIsMoved(object sender, MouseEventArgs e)
{
  if (dragInProgress)
  {
    curLine.Width = e.X;   // Save ending point current
    curLine.Height = e.Y;
    Invalidate();
  }
}

//-------------------------------------------------------
//   Paint.
//-------------------------------------------------------
private void PaintLines(object sender, PaintEventArgs e)
{
  Graphics page = e.Graphics;
  // Paint current line
  page.DrawLine(pen, curLine.X, curLine.Y,
    curLine.Width, curLine.Height);
}
  }
}
```

Listing 7.18   continued

Display

This application was not created by using the Form Designer. Instead, the code was created manually, by adding the code for each event handler and then adding the handler to the form. Note that our class extends Form. Therefore, our class includes all the methods and events that forms support. The Form class has defined handlers for all the events, so we need to assign handlers only to the events that we need to handle.

Remember that the signature for an event handler is very specific, so generally it is simpler to use the Form Designer to create handlers. You can always come back later and clean up the code created by the Form Designer. However, if you want to add your own handlers, the syntax uses the increment notation, the += notation. The logic behind this comes from the fact that there can be many handlers all looking at the same event. Thus, you are "incrementing" the number of handlers when you add a handler. The following are the relevant lines:

```
MouseUp    += new MouseEventHandler(this.MouseIsUp);
MouseDown  += new MouseEventHandler(this.MouseIsDown);
MouseMove  += new MouseEventHandler(this.MouseIsMoved);
Paint      += new PaintEventHandler(this.PaintLines);
```

7.11   KEY EVENTS

A *key event* is generated when a keyboard key is pressed. Key events allow a program to respond immediately to the user while he or she is typing or pressing other keyboard keys such as the arrow keys. If key events are being processed, the program can respond as soon as the key is pressed; there is no need to wait for the Enter key to be pressed or for some other component (like a button) to be activated.

The `Direction` program, shown in Listing 7.19, responds to key events. An image of an arrow is displayed and the image moves across the screen as the arrow keys are pressed. Actually, four different images are used, one for the arrow pointing in each of the primary directions (up, down, right, and left).

To create the application, create a Windows application, make the background color on the form black, and create a label box about 1/2-inch square in the center named `label1`. In the `label1` properties, select the `Image` property and click the button to the right. Select the image file named `arrowDown.gif`. On the form, set the property `KeyPreview` to `true` and add a handler for the `KeyUp` event. Complete the code as shown in Listing 7.19.

The `DirectionPanel` class, shown in Listing 7.19, represents the panel on which the arrow image is displayed. The constructor loads the four arrow images, one of which is always considered to be the current image (the one displayed). The current image is set based on the arrow key that was most recently pressed. For example, if the up arrow is pressed, the image with the arrow pointing up is displayed. If an arrow key is continually pressed, the appropriate image "moves" in the appropriate direction.

Listing 7.19

```
//****************************************************************
//   Direction.cs          C#:   Ken Culp
//
//   Demonstrates the use of key events and loading image files.
//****************************************************************
using System;
using System.Drawing;
using System.Windows.Forms;
using System.IO;

namespace Direction
{
  public partial class Direction : Form
  {
    private Image[] images;
    private int imgX = 110, imgY = 110;     // Upper left corner
    private const int JUMP = 10;            // Amount to move

    public Direction()
    {
      InitializeComponent();
      images = new Image[4];
      images[0] = Image.FromFile(@"..\..\arrowUp.gif");
      images[1] = Image.FromFile(@"..\..\arrowDown.gif");
      images[2] = Image.FromFile(@"..\..\arrowLeft.gif");
      images[3] = Image.FromFile(@"..\..\arrowRight.gif");
      label1.Location = new Point(imgX, imgY);
    }
```

Listing 7.19 continued

```csharp
private void Direction_KeyUp(object sender, KeyEventArgs e)
{
  switch (e.KeyCode)
  {
    case Keys.Up: label1.Image = images[0]; MoveI(0, -JUMP);
    break;
    case Keys.Down: label1.Image = images[1]; MoveI(0, +JUMP);
    break;
    case Keys.Left: label1.Image = images[2]; MoveI(-JUMP, 0);
    break;
    case Keys.Right: label1.Image = images[3]; MoveI(+JUMP, 0);
    break;
    case Keys.X: this.Close(); break;
  }
  e.Handled = true;
}

private void MoveI(int xDir, int yDir)
{
  // Moves cursor but limits to client rectangle.
  int maxX = ClientRectangle.Width - label1.Size.Width;
  int maxY = ClientRectangle.Height - label1.Size.Height;
  imgX += xDir;
  imgY += yDir;
  label1.Location = new Point(imgX, imgY);
}
}
}
```

Display

Now let's study the code. The arrow images are managed as an array of Image objects. Each element of the array is created separately using the static FromFile method of the Image class. The FromFile method requires a path name to the file, unless the images are in the same directory as the executable file.

We used a relative path file specification that works as follows. The executable file is in the bin\Debug directory under the project directory. The images are stored in the project directory, which is two levels up from the Debug directory. Thus, we use the ..\ syntax twice to move back up from the executable directory.

Finally, note that we included the backslash character without duplicating it. C# allows strings to be preceded with the @ sign, which indicates to ignore escape sequences and take the string exactly as specified. You will find this syntax handy when entering path names.

In this example, the image is drawn automatically every time the location of the label is moved. Two things happen on a key press. First, the direction of the arrow is determined and the image for the label is changed to that new image. Second, the label is moved in the direction specified.

Now let's examine how we find out what key is pressed when we enter the Direction_KeyUp handler. A KeyDown or KeyUp handler is passed an argument of type KeyEventArgs. Figure 7.12 lists the various properties and methods of the KeyEventArgs class. In our case, we used the KeyCode property, which can be compared to the Keys enumeration to determine which key was pressed. A switch statement was used for each key that we need to process.

Note also the line in the KeyUp handler that reads e.Handled = **true**. This line keeps the key from also being passed to other handlers. This is not really necessary here but normally is done any time you actually handle the key. Technically, we should have set Handled to true only when the key is something we are looking for.

Public Properties	
Alt	Gets a value indicating whether the Alt key was pressed.
Control	Gets a value indicating whether the Ctrl key was pressed.
Handled	Gets or sets a value indicating whether the event was handled.
KeyCode	Gets the keyboard code for a KeyDown or KeyUp event.
KeyData	Gets the key data for a KeyDown or KeyUp event.
KeyValue	Gets the keyboard value for a KeyDown or KeyUp event.
Modifiers	Gets the modifier flags for a KeyDown or KeyUp event. This indicates which combination of modifier keys (Ctrl, Shift, and Alt) was pressed.
Shift	Gets a value indicating whether the Shift key was pressed.

FIGURE 7.12 KeyEventArgs members

Public Properties	
Handled	Gets or sets a value indicating whether the KeyPress event was handled
KeyChar	Gets the character corresponding to the key pressed

FIGURE 7.13 KeyPressEventArgs members

Key events fire in the order KeyDown, KeyUp, and KeyPress, and, just as MouseDown and MouseUp occur before Click, KeyDown and KeyUp occur before KeyPress. The handler for KeyPress returns an event of type KeyPressEventArgs. The public members of KeyPressEventArgs are listed in Figure 7.13. KeyPress events differ significantly from the KeyDown and KeyUp events in that you cannot obtain the keyboard values for Alt and Ctrl keys nor can you get at any system keys. Nor can you use the Keys enumeration. Instead, KeyPress is designed to use the actual key character. Recall the editing techniques that we used on the social security number in the InputValidation example of Chapter 5; we used the KeyPress button because we wanted to trash anything that was not a number.

Key events fire whenever a key is pressed, but most systems enable the concept of *key repetition*. That is, when a key is pressed and held down, it's as if that key is being pressed repeatedly and quickly. Key events are generated in the same way. In the Direction program, the user can hold down an arrow key and watch the image move across the screen quickly.

The component that generates key events is the one that currently has the *keyboard focus*. Usually the keyboard focus is held by the primary "active" component. A component usually gets the keyboard focus when the user clicks on it with the mouse.

The Direction program sets no boundaries for the arrow image, so it can be moved out of the visible window, then moved back in if desired. You could add code to the listener to stop the image when it reaches one of the window boundaries. This modification is left as a programming project.

7.12 FORM SPECIAL EVENTS

We have already seen examples in which we placed code in an event handler for the Load event. The Load event occurs just before the form is loaded and before anything is displayed on the screen and can be used to initialize values in the form that are not appropriate in the class constructor. In this section, we elaborate a little more on the Load event and cover a variety of other events that can occur on a form. The most useful of these events are listed in Figure 7.14.

Of course, the form control also supports a wide variety of other events for keyboard and mouse operation as well as others that record changes to the status of various properties of the form (like EnableChanged). You can research these by clicking Help/Index, typing **Form**, and selecting events.

Event	Description
`Activated`	The form is activated in code or by the user. Incorporates any data that has been changed since the form was not active.
`Closed`	The form is closed and no longer displayed. Cleans up resources allocated when the form was loaded.
`Closing`	The form is closing but does not have to close. Gives the user a chance to not close the form.
`Deactivate`	The form loses focus and is not the active form.
`Load`	Occurs before a form is displayed for the first time. Performs initializations here and allocates resources.
`Paint`	The control is redrawn.
`Resize`	The control is resized.
`HelpRequested`	The user pressed the Help button (usually F1).

FIGURE 7.14 Some form events

The events listed in Figure 7.14 are handy when action needs to be taken when the status of the form is changed or when the user switches windows. First, we look at the `Load`, `Activated`, `Closing`, and `Closed` events, which can only occur in the order given. As noted in Figure 7.14, `Load` occurs when the form is first loaded and before anything is displayed on the screen. The `Load` event will occur only once during the life of the form and should be used for appropriate initializations. For example, you might open a database or create connections to some remote resource.

The `Activated` event occurs any time the form becomes the topmost window, so that the user can interact with the form. If the user switches to a word processor and then returns to a form, the `Activated` event fires. Use `Activated` when you may need to change some information in the form based on what the user might have done in another window.

The `Deactivate` event is the opposite of the `Activated` event. This event fires when the form is no longer the active form.

The `Closing` event can occur in any one of several ways:

> The user clicks the small **X** in the upper-right corner of the form

> The form code calls the `Close` method

> The user types Alt/F4

> The user uses Task Manager or another program to kill the form

When `Closing` occurs, all the form data is still intact and the form does not have to close. Note the signature of the handler for the `Closing` event:

```
private void ClosingHandler(object sender,
    System.ComponentModel.CancelEventArgs e)
```

The handler is passed a parameter of type `CancelEventArgs`. This parameter includes a property named `Cancel`, which will have a default value of `false` (close, don't cancel) upon entry to the handler. If this value is set to `true`, the form will not close upon exit from the form. The following code would prompt the user if they were sure they wanted to close the form:

```
private void ClosingHandler(object sender,
  System.ComponentModel.CancelEventArgs e)
  {
    DialogResult result = MessageBox.Show("Close Form?",
                         "Sure?", MessageBoxButtons.YesNo,
                         MessageBoxIcon.Question);
    e.Cancel = (result == DialogResult.No);
  }
```

If the user answers "No" (they are not sure they want to exit), `Cancel` is set to `true` and the form will not close.

The `Closed` event occurs after the form is closed (no longer visible) but before the object is disposed of. There is no recovery (cancel) possible at this point. The `Closed` event is used to clean up the resources allocated by the form during the `Load` event. If we had opened a database or created connections, we would close them in this event handler.

The `Paint` event occurs every time any portion of the form becomes invalid. For example, it occurs when the form is completely or partially covered up by another window. `Paint` also occurs when the `Invalidate` method is called for the form. We have created various `Paint` handlers for the form in previous examples.

The `Resize` event occurs when the user manually changes the size of the form or the form size is changed in code. Use this event to move images or controls on the form to match the new size.

The `HelpRequested` event signals that the user has requested help from the application, usually by pressing the F1 key. At this time, you can pop up an informational form, open a web page, or activate a help application.

Summary of Key Concepts

> An array of size N is indexed from 0 to $N–1$.

> In C#, an array is an object that must be instantiated.

> Bounds checking ensures that an index used to refer to an array element is in range.

> An initializer list can be used to instantiate an array object instead of using the `new` operator.

> Instantiating an array of objects reserves room to store references only. The objects that are stored in each element must be instantiated separately.

> Command-line arguments are stored in an array of `string` objects and are passed to the `Main` method.

> A C# method can be defined to accept a varying number of parameters.

> Using an array with more than two dimensions is rare in an object-oriented system.

> An `ArrayList` object is similar to an array, but it dynamically changes size as needed, and elements can be inserted and removed to/from the end or to/from specific locations.

> Moving the mouse and clicking the mouse button generate events to which a program can respond.

> Rubberbanding is the graphical effect caused when a shape seems to expand as the mouse is dragged.

> Key events allow a program to respond immediately to the user pressing keyboard keys.

Self-Review Questions

7.1   Explain the concept of array bounds checking. What happens when a C# array is indexed with an invalid value?

7.2   Describe the process of creating an array. When is memory allocated for the array?

7.3   What is an off-by-one error? How does it relate to arrays?

7.4   What does an array initializer list accomplish?

7.5   Can an entire array be passed as a parameter? How is this accomplished?

7.6   How is an array of objects created?

7.7   What is a command-line argument?

7.8   What are parallel arrays?

7.9   How are multidimensional arrays implemented in C#?

7.10 What are the advantages of using an `ArrayList` object as opposed to an array? What are the disadvantages?

Exercises

7.1 Which of the following are valid declarations? Which instantiate an array object? Explain your answers.

```
int primes = {2, 3, 4, 5, 7, 11};

float elapsedTimes[] = {11.47, 12.04, 11.72, 13.88};

int[] scores = int[30];

int[] primes = new {2,3,5,7,11};

int[] scores = new int[30];

char grades[] = {'a', 'b', 'c', 'd', 'f'};

char[] grades = new char[];
```

7.2 Describe five programs that are difficult to implement without using arrays.

7.3 Describe what problem occurs in the following code. What modifications should be made to it to eliminate the problem?

```
int[] numbers = {3, 2, 3, 6, 9, 10, 12, 32, 3, 12, 6};

for (int count = 1; count <= numbers.length; count++)
    Console.Out.WriteLine (numbers[count]);
```

7.4 Write an array declaration and any necessary supporting classes to represent the following statements:

a. students' names for a class of 25 students

b. students' test grades for a class of 40 students

c. credit-card transactions that contain a transaction number, a merchant name, and a charge

d. students' names for a class and homework grades for each student

e. for each employee of the L&L International Corporation: the employee number, hire date, and the amount of the last five raises

7.5 Write a method called `SumArray` that accepts an array of floating point values and returns the sum of the values stored in the array.

7.6 Write a method called `SwitchThem` that accepts two integer arrays as parameters and switches the contents of the arrays. Take into account that the arrays may be of different sizes.

7.7   Describe a program for which you would use the `ArrayList` class instead of arrays to implement choices. Describe a program for which you would use arrays instead of the `ArrayList` class. Explain your choices.

7.8   The `Dots` program handles a mouse-pressed event to draw a dot. How would the program behave differently if it handled a mouse-released event instead? A mouse-clicked event?

7.9   Create a UML class diagram for the `Direction` program.

Programming Projects

7.1   Design and implement an application that reads an arbitrary number of integers that are in the range 0 to 50 inclusive and counts how many occurrences of each are entered. After all input has been processed, print all of the values (with the number of occurrences) that were entered one or more times.

7.2   Modify the program from Programming Project 7.1 so that it works for numbers in the range between –25 and 25.

7.3   Design and implement an application that creates a histogram that allows you to visually inspect the frequency distribution of a set of values. The program should read in an arbitrary number of integers that are in the range 1 to 100 inclusive; then, produce a chart similar to the one below that indicates how many input values fell in the range 1 to 10, 11 to 20, and so on. Print one asterisk for each value entered.

```
1   -  10  | *****
11  -  20  | **
21  -  30  | ******************
31  -  40  |
41  -  50  | ***
51  -  60  | ********
61  -  70  | **
71  -  80  | *****
81  -  90  | *******
91  - 100  | *********
```

7.4   The lines in the histogram in Programming Project 7.3 will be too long if you enter a large number of values. Modify the program so that it prints an asterisk for every five values in each category. Ignore leftovers. For example, if a category has 17 values, print three asterisks in that row. If a category has 4 values, do not print any asterisks in that row.

7.5   Design and implement an application that computes and prints the mean and standard deviation of a list of integers x_1 through x_n. Assume that there will be no more than 50 input values. Compute both the mean and standard deviation as floating point values, using the following formulas:

$$\text{mean} = \frac{\sum\limits_{i=1}^{n} x_i}{n} \qquad\qquad sd = \sqrt{\frac{\sum\limits_{i=1}^{n} (x_i - \text{mean})^2}{n-1}}$$

7.6   The L&L Bank can handle up to 30 customers who have savings accounts. Design and implement a program that manages the accounts. Keep track of key information and allow each customer to make deposits and withdrawals. Produce appropriate error messages for invalid transactions. Hint: you may want to base your accounts on the `Account` class from Chapter 4. Also provide a method to add 3 percent interest to all accounts whenever the method is invoked.

7.7   The programming projects of Chapter 4 discussed a `Card` class that represents a standard playing card. Create a class called `DeckOfCards` that stores 52 objects of the `Card` class. Include methods to shuffle the deck, deal a card, and report the number of cards left in the deck. The `Shuffle` method should assume a full deck. Create a driver class with a `Main` method that deals each card from a shuffled deck, printing each card as it is dealt.

7.8   Design and implement an application that reads a sequence of up to 25 pairs of names and postal (ZIP) codes for individuals. Store the data in an object designed to store a first name (string), last name (string), and postal code (integer). Assume that each line of input will contain two strings followed by an integer value, each separated by a tab character. Read the entire line into one string variable and then use `String.Split` to separate the values and store them as needed. Finally, sort the list of objects by increasing postal code and print the sorted list in an appropriate format to the screen. Write a `CompareTo` method for your class for the sorting.

7.9   Modify the program you created in Programming Project 7.8 to accomplish the following:

> Support the storing of additional user information: street address (String), city (String), state (String), and 10 digit phone number (integer, contains area code and does not include special characters such as (,), or -).

> Store the data in an `ArrayList` object.

7.10   Use the `Question` class from Chapter 6 to define a `Quiz` class. A quiz can be composed of up to 25 questions. Define the `Add` method of the `Quiz` class to add a question to a quiz. Define the `GiveQuiz` method of the `Quiz` class to present each question in turn to the user, accept an answer for each one, and keep track of the results. Define a class called `QuizTime` with a `Main` method that populates a quiz, presents it, and prints the final results.

7.11 Modify your answer to Programming Project 7.10 so that the complexity level of the questions given in the quiz is taken into account. Overload the `GiveQuiz` method so that it accepts two integer parameters that specify the minimum and maximum complexity levels for the quiz questions and only presents questions in that complexity range. Modify the `Main` method to demonstrate this feature.

7.12 Design a class that represents a star with a specified radius and color. Use a filled polygon to draw the star. Design and implement a program that draws 10 stars of random radius in random locations.

7.13 Design a class that represents the visual representation of a car. Use arrays of points and appropriate drawing tools to draw the car in any graphics context and at any location. Create a main driver to display the car.

7.14 Modify the `QuoteOptions` program from Chapter 5 so that it provides three additional quote options. Use an array to store all of the quote strings.

7.15 Design and implement a program that draws 20 circles, with the radius and location of each circle determined at random. If a circle does not overlap any other circle, draw that circle in black. If a circle overlaps one or more other circles, draw it in cyan. Use an array to store a representation of each circle, then determine the color of each circle. Two circles overlap if the distance between their center points is less than the sum of their radii.

7.16 Design and implement a program that draws a checkerboard with five red and eight black checkers on it in various locations. Store the checkerboard as a two-dimensional array.

7.17 Modify the program from Programming Project 7.16 so that the program determines whether any black checkers can jump any red checkers. Under the checkerboard, print (using `DrawString`) the row and column position of all black checkers that have possible jumps.

7.18 Modify the `RubberLines` program from this chapter so that it shows all of the lines drawn. Show only the final lines (from initial mouse press to mouse release), not the intermediate lines drawn to show the rubberbanding effect. That is, store the line only on mouse up. Hint: Keep track of a list of objects that represent the lines, similar to how the `Dots` program kept track of multiple dots. The cleanest solution is to create your own class to store the end points of the lines as described in the text.

7.19 Design and implement a program that counts the number of times the mouse has been clicked. Display that number in the center of the form window.

7.20 Design and implement an application that creates a polygon shape dynamically using mouse clicks. Each mouse click adds a new line segment from the previous point. Include a button below the drawing area to clear the current polygon and begin another. Draw the polygon but do not fill it.

7.21 Design and implement an application that draws a circle using a rubberbanding technique. The circle size is determined by a mouse drag. Use the original mouse click location as a fixed center point. Compute the distance between the current location of the mouse pointer and the center point to determine the current radius of the circle.

7.22 Design and implement an application that serves as a mouse odometer, continually displaying how far, in pixels, the mouse has moved (while it is over the program window). Display the current odometer value using a label. Hint: Use the mouse movement event to determine the current position, and compare it to the last position of the mouse. Use the distance formula to see how far the mouse has traveled, and add that to a running total distance.

7.23 Design and implement a program whose background changes color depending on where the mouse pointer is located. If the mouse pointer is on the left half of the form, display red; if it is on the right half, display green.

7.24 Design and implement a class that represents a spaceship, which can be drawn (side view) in any particular location. Create a program that displays the spaceship so that it follows the movement of the mouse. When the mouse button is pressed down, have a laser beam shoot out of the front of the spaceship (one continuous beam, not a moving projectile) until the mouse button is released.

7.25 Design and implement a program that helps a hospital analyze the flow of patients through the emergency room. A text input file contains integers that represent the number of patients that entered the emergency room during each hour of each day for four weeks. Read the information and store it in a three-dimensional array (hours, days, weeks). Then analyze it to compare the total number of patients per week, per day, and per hour. Display the results of the analysis.

7.26 Modify the `Direction` program from this chapter so that the image is not allowed to move out of the visible area of the panel. Ignore any key event that would cause that to happen. Hint: Use the width and height of the label box along with the height and width of the `ClientRectangle` to determine the maximum and minimum movement in any direction.

7.27 Modify the `Direction` program from this chapter so that, in addition to responding to the arrow keys, it also responds to four other keys that move the image in diagonal directions. When the `'t'` key is pressed, move the image up and to the left. Likewise, use `'u'` to move up and right, `'g'` to move down and left, and `'j'` to move down and right. Do not move the image if it has reached a window boundary.

7.28 Modify the `RubberLines` program from Programming Project 7.18. Add two panels side by side on the form and have the line draw on one panel only. Thus you will have to keep two sets of lines. Add a button below each panel to erase that panel. Hint: Handle the mouse events at the panel and not at the form. Use a complete set of mouse handlers (down/up/move) for each panel.

7.29 Modify the `RubberLines` program so that you share corresponding mouse handlers by both panels (down handler set to handle events on both panels, etc.). You will have to use the first parameter to the handler (`sender`) to determine the caller. Typecast `sender` to type `Panel` and then check the `Name` property.

Answers to Self-Review Questions

7.1 Whenever a reference is made to a particular array element, the index operator (the brackets that enclose the subscript) ensures that the value of the index is greater than or equal to zero and less than the size of the array. If it is not within the valid range, an `ArrayIndexOutOfBoundsException` is thrown.

7.2 Arrays are objects. Therefore, as with all objects, to create an array we first create a reference to the array (its name). We then instantiate the array itself, which reserves memory space to store the array elements. The only difference between a regular object instantiation and an array instantiation is the bracket syntax.

7.3 An off-by-one error occurs when a program's logic exceeds the boundary of an array (or similar structure) by one. These errors include forgetting to process a boundary element as well as attempting to process a nonexistent element. Array processing is susceptible to off-by-one errors because their indexes begin at zero and run to one less than the size of the array.

7.4 An array initializer list is used in the declaration of an array to set up the initial values of its elements. An initializer list instantiates the array object, so the **new** operator is needed.

7.5 An entire array can be passed as a parameter. Specifically, because an array is an object, a reference to the array is passed to the method. Any changes made to the array elements will be reflected outside of the method.

7.6 An array of objects is really an array of object references. The array itself must be instantiated, and the objects that are stored in the array must be created separately.

7.7 A command-line argument is data that is included on the command line when the interpreter is invoked to execute the program. Command-line arguments are another way to provide input to a program. They are accessed using the array of strings that is passed into the `Main` method as a parameter.

7.8 Parallel arrays are two or more arrays whose corresponding elements are related in some way. Because parallel arrays can easily get out of synch if not managed carefully, it is often better to create a single array of objects that encapsulate the related elements.

7.9 A multidimensional array is implemented in C# either by specifying multiple dimensions or as an array of array objects. The arrays that are elements of the outer array could also contain arrays as elements. This nesting process could continue for as many levels as needed, creating jagged arrays.

7.10 An `ArrayList` keeps the indexes of its objects continuous as they are added and removed, and an `ArrayList` dynamically increases its capacity as needed. In addition, an `ArrayList` is implemented so that it stores references to the `Object` class, which allows any object to be stored in it. A disadvantage of the `ArrayList` class is that it copies a significant amount of data in order to insert and delete elements, and this process is inefficient.

Group Project

In this project you will create a tic-tac-toe game as either a console application or a Windows application. The project will use a two-dimensional array to store the plays for each player.

General (Windows or Console)

A 3 by 3 array of integers will be used to keep track of plays. If the integer value in one cell is a +1, then player 1 has played in that cell. If the value is -1, player 2 has played in that cell. If the value is 0, the cell is available.

A win is then indicated by a total of +3 or -3 in any horizontal or vertical direction or in either of the two diagonals. A "cat" game is indicated by no cell having a 0 value and no player winning. You should keep a counter of available cells and reduce the count on each legal play. Reset this counter on a new game.

Add a method that checks for a win and returns an integer value (1 = player 1 wins; –1 = player 2 wins; 0 = no winner). This method should use **for** loops and index into the game array.

Windows Application

Create a form with 9 square "game" buttons arranged in a 3 by 3 arrangement. Set the text of each button to blank at the start of the game (cell is available). When a player plays in that cell, set the text to X or O as appropriate. Make the font for these buttons about 24 in size, bold, and with the text alignment set to center in both directions. Enable all buttons in the Designer.

Add two more buttons for New Game and Exit. New Game clears the text on all the game buttons, enables all game buttons, and sets the matrix to all zeros. For simplicity, create an array of buttons in the form constructor (to use a loop to enable all buttons).

Use only one event handler for all the game buttons. Use the `Tag` property of each button to store an indication of which button is pressed. One example would be an integer value of 0 to 8. Then the row number is quotient of the integer division of the button number and 3 and the column number is the remainder of this division. Take this number and update the text of the button (X or O) and the game matrix.

Check for a win and cat game on each game button click. Pop up a win message on a win. Also, when a game button is clicked, disable that button so that another play cannot be made there.

Add two label boxes that show the number of wins for each player and the cat. Update these at the end of each game.

Console Application

Prompt the user for their play as two integers (row, column). Indicate which player is playing at that moment. Also, print the current game state after each play:

```
 X | O | X
---+---+---
   | O |
---+---+---
   |   |
```

The game should validate whether a valid position is specified and, if one is not specified, disallow the play and reprint the game status. Check a win and cat game on each play and print a message as appropriate.

After a win or cat game, ask whether the players want to play another game. Count wins for each player and the cat. At the end of the game, print these results.

Inheritance

CHAPTER OBJECTIVES

> Explore the derivation of new classes from existing ones.

> Define the concept and purpose of method overriding.

> Discuss the design of class hierarchies.

> Discuss the issue of visibility as it relates to inheritance.

> Explore the ability to derive one interface from another.

> Discuss object-oriented design in the context of inheritance.

> Describe the inheritance structure for GUI components.

> Explore the overriding of event handlers.

> Discuss the extension of GUI components.

This chapter explains inheritance, a fundamental technique for organizing and creating classes. It is a simple but powerful idea that influences the way we design object-oriented software and enhances our ability to reuse classes in other situations and programs. In this chapter we explore the technique for creating subclasses and class hierarchies, and we discuss a technique for overriding the definition of an inherited method. We examine the **protected** modifier and discuss the effect all visibility modifiers have on inherited attributes and methods. Finally, we discuss how inheritance affects various issues related to graphical user interfaces (GUIs) in C#.

8.1 CREATING SUBCLASSES

In our introduction to object-oriented concepts in Chapter 1 we presented the analogy that a class is to an object what a blueprint is to a house. In subsequent chapters we've reinforced that idea, writing classes that define a set of similar objects. A class establishes the characteristics and behaviors of an object but reserves no memory space for variables (unless those variables are declared as **static**). Classes are the plan, and objects are the embodiment of that plan.

Many houses can be created from the same blueprint. They are essentially the same house in different locations with different people living in them. Now suppose you want a house that is similar to another but with some different or additional features. You want to start with the same basic blueprint but modify it to suit new, slightly different needs. Many housing developments are created this way. The houses in the development have the same core layout, but they have unique features. For instance, they might all be split-level homes with the same basic room configuration, but some may have a fireplace or full basement while others do not, or an upgraded gourmet kitchen instead of the standard version.

It's likely that the housing developer commissioned a master architect to create a single blueprint to establish the basic design of all houses in the development, and then a series of new blueprints that include variations designed to appeal to different buyers. The act of creating the series of blueprints is simplified because they all begin with the same underlying structure, while the variations give them unique characteristics that may be important to the prospective owners.

> **Key Concept**
>
> Inheritance is the process of deriving a new class from an existing one.

Creating a new blueprint that is based on an existing blueprint is analogous to the object-oriented concept of *inheritance,* which is the process in which a new class is derived from an existing one. Inheritance is a powerful software development technique and a defining characteristic of object-oriented programming.

Via inheritance, the new class automatically contains the variables and methods in the original class. Then, to tailor the class as needed, the programmer can add new variables and methods to the derived class or modify the inherited ones.

> **Key Concept**
>
> One purpose of inheritance is to reuse existing software.

In general, new classes can be created via inheritance faster, easier, and cheaper than by writing them from scratch. Inheritance is one way to support the idea of *software reuse.* By using existing software components to create new ones, we capitalize on the effort that went into the design, implementation, and testing of the existing software.

Keep in mind that the word *class* comes from the idea of classifying groups of objects with similar characteristics. Classification schemes often use levels of classes that relate to each other. For example, all mammals share certain characteristics: they are warm-blooded, have hair, and bear live offspring. Now consider a subset of mammals, such as horses. All horses are mammals and have all the characteristics of mammals, but they also have unique features that make them different from other mammals such as dogs.

If we translate this idea into software terms, an existing class called `Mammal` would have certain variables and methods that describe the state and behavior of mammals. A `Horse` class could be derived from the existing `Mammal` class, automatically inheriting the variables and methods contained in `Mammal`. The `Horse` class can refer to the inherited variables and methods as if they had been declared locally in that class. New variables and methods can then be added to the derived class to distinguish a horse from other mammals.

The original class that is used to derive a new one is called the *parent class, superclass,* or *base class.* The derived class is called a *child class,* or *subclass.* C# uses the colon (:) to indicate that a new class is being derived from an existing class. In the following example, `Dictionary` is being derived from `Book`:

```
public class Dictionary : Book
```

The process of inheritance should establish an *is-a relationship* between two classes. That is, the child class should be a more specific version of the parent. For example, a horse is a mammal. Not all mammals are horses, but all horses are mammals. For any class X that is derived from class Y, you should be able to say that "X is a Y." If such a statement doesn't make sense, then that relationship is probably not an appropriate use of inheritance.

> **Key Concept**
>
> Inheritance creates an is-a relationship between the parent and child classes.

Let's look at an example. The program shown in Listing 8.1 instantiates an object of class `Dictionary`, which is derived from a class called `Book`. In the `Main` method, three methods are invoked through the `Dictionary` object: two that were declared locally in the `Dictionary` class and one that was inherited from the `Book` class.

The `Book` class (see Listing 8.2) is used to derive the `Dictionary` class (see Listing 8.3) using the colon in the header of `Dictionary`. The `Dictionary` class automatically inherits the `PageCount` property, as well as the `pages` variable. It is as if the `PageCount` property and the `pages` variable were declared inside the `Dictionary` class. Note that, in the `Dictionary` class, the `ComputeRatio` method explicitly references the `pages` variable, even though the variable is declared in the `Book` class.

Listing 8.1

```
//*************************************************************
//  Words.cs          C#:  Ken Culp
//
//  Demonstrates the use of an inherited method.
//*************************************************************
using System;

namespace Words
{
  class Words
  {
    //-----------------------------------------------------------
    //  Instantiates a derived class and invokes its inherited
    //  and local methods.
    //-----------------------------------------------------------
```

Listing 8.1 continued

```csharp
public static void Main(string[] args)
{
  Dictionary webster = new Dictionary();

  Console.Out.WriteLine("Number of pages: " +
    webster.PageCount);
  Console.Out.WriteLine("Number of definitions: " +
    webster.DefinitionCount);
  Console.Out.WriteLine("Definitions per page: {0:0.0}",
    webster.ComputeRatio());

  Console.In.ReadLine();   // Wait for enter key
}
  }
}
```

Output

```
Number of pages: 1500
Number of definitions: 52500
Definitions per page: 35.0
```

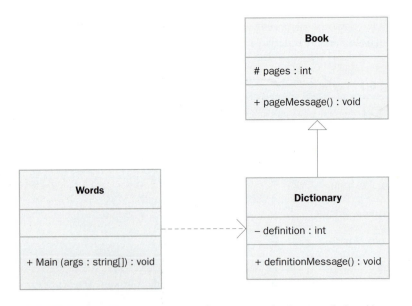

FIGURE 8.1 A UML class diagram showing an inheritance relationship

Also note that although the `Book` class is needed to create the definition of `Dictionary`, no `Book` object is ever instantiated in the program. An instance of a child class does not rely on an instance of the parent class.

Inheritance is a one-way street. The `Book` class cannot use variables or methods that are declared explicitly in the `Dictionary` class. For instance, if we created an object from the `Book` class, it could not be used to invoke the `SetDefinitions` method. This restriction makes sense because a child class is a more specific version of the parent class. A dictionary has pages because all books have pages; but although a dictionary has definitions, not all books do.

Listing 8.2

```
//****************************************************************
//  Book.cs         C#:  Ken Culp
//
//  Represents a book. Used as the parent of a derived class to
//  demonstrate inheritance.
//****************************************************************
using System;

namespace Words
{
  public class Book
  {
    protected int pages = 1500;
    //----------------------------------------------------------
    //  Public access to number of pages
    //----------------------------------------------------------
    public int PageCount
    {
      get { return pages; }
      set { pages = value; }
    }
  }
}
```

Inheritance relationships are often represented in UML class diagrams. Figure 8.1 shows the inheritance relationship between the `Book` and `Dictionary` classes. An arrow with an open arrowhead is used to show inheritance in a UML diagram, with the arrow pointing from the child class to the parent class.

Listing 8.3

```
//*****************************************************************
//  Dictionary.cs         C#: Ken Culp
//
//  Represents a dictionary, which is a book. Used to demonstrate
//  inheritance.
//*****************************************************************
using System;

namespace Words
{
  public class Dictionary : Book
  {
    private int definitions = 52500;

    //---------------------------------------------------------
    //  Public access to number of definitions
    //---------------------------------------------------------
    public int DefinitionCount
    {
      get { return definitions; }
      set { definitions = value; }
    }

    //---------------------------------------------------------
    //  Computes the number of definitions per page
    //---------------------------------------------------------
    public double ComputeRatio()
    {
      return (double)definitions / (double)pages;
    }
  }
}
```

The protected Modifier

As we've seen in previous chapters, visibility modifiers are used to control access to the members of a class. This effect extends into the process of inheritance as well. Any public method or variable in a parent class can be explicitly referenced by name in the child class, and through objects of that child class. On the other hand, private methods and variables of the parent class cannot be referenced in the child class or through an object of the child class.

However, if we declare a variable with public visibility so that a derived class can inherit it, we violate the principle of encapsulation. Therefore, C# provides a third visibility modifier: **protected**. Note that the variable pages is declared with protected visibility in the Book class. When a variable or method is declared with protected visibility, a derived class will inherit it, retaining some of its encapsulation properties. The encapsulation with protected visibility is not as tight as it would be if the variable or method were declared private, but it is better than if it were declared public. Specifically, a variable or method declared with protected visibility may be accessed by any class in the same package. The relationships among all C# modifiers are explained completely in Appendix G.

> **Key Concept**
>
> Protected visibility provides the best possible encapsulation while still permitting inheritance.

In a UML diagram, protected visibility can be indicated by preceding the protected member with a hash mark (#). The `pages` variable of the `Book` class has this annotation in Figure 8.1.

Each variable or method retains the effect of its original visibility modifier. For example, the `PagesCount` property is still considered to be public in its inherited form in the `Dictionary` class.

Let's be clear about our terms. All methods and variables, even those declared with private visibility, are inherited by the child class. That is, their definitions exist and memory space is reserved for the variables. It's just that they can't be referenced by name. This issue is explored in more detail in Section 8.4.

Constructors, however, are not inherited. Constructors are special methods that are used to set up a particular type of object, so it doesn't make sense for a class called `Dictionary` to have a constructor called `Book`. But you can imagine that a child class may want to refer to the constructor of the parent class, which is one of the reasons for the **base** reference, described next.

The base Reference

The reserved word **base** can be used in a class to refer to its parent class. Using the **base** reference, we can access a parent's members. Like the **this** reference, what the word **base** refers to depends on the class in which it is used.

One use of the `base` reference is to invoke a parent's constructor. Let's look at an example. Listing 8.4 shows a modification of the original `Words` program from Listing 8.1. Similar to the original version, we use a class called `Book2` (see Listing 8.5) as the parent of the derived class `Dictionary2` (see Listing 8.6). However, unlike earlier versions of these classes, `Book2` and `Dictionary2` have explicit constructors used to initialize their instance variables. The output of the `Words2` program is the same as it is for the original `Words` program.

> **Key Concept**
>
> A parent's constructor can be invoked using the base reference.

The `Dictionary2` constructor takes two integer values as parameters, representing the number of pages and definitions in the book. Because the `Book2` class already has a constructor that performs the work to set up the parts of the dictionary that were inherited, we rely on that constructor to do that work. However, since the constructor is not inherited, we cannot invoke it directly, so we use the **base** reference to get to it in the parent class. The `Dictionary2` constructor then proceeds to initialize its `definitions` variable.

Listing 8.4

```
//*****************************************************************
//  Words2.cs          C#:  Ken Culp
//
//  Demonstrates the use of the super reference.
//*****************************************************************
using System;

namespace Words2
{
  public class Words2
  {
    //-----------------------------------------------------------
    //  Instantiates a derived class and invokes its inherited
    //  and local methods.
    //-----------------------------------------------------------
    public static void Main(string[] args)
    {
      Dictionary2 webster = new Dictionary2(1500, 52500);

      Console.Out.WriteLine("Number of pages: " +
        webster.PageCount);
      Console.Out.WriteLine("Number of definitions: " +
        webster.DefinitionCount);
      Console.Out.WriteLine("Definitions per page: {0:0.0}",
        webster.ComputeRatio());

      Console.In.ReadLine();  // Wait for enter key
    }
  }
}
```

Output

```
Number of pages: 1500
Number of definitions: 52500
Definitions per page: 35.0
```

Listing 8.5

```
//*****************************************************************
//  Book2.cs          C#:  Ken Culp
//
//  Represents a book. Used as the parent of a derived class to
//  demonstrate inheritance and the use of the super reference.
//*****************************************************************
```

Listing 8.5   continued

```csharp
using System;

namespace Words2
{
  public class Book2
  {
    protected int pages;

    //---------------------------------------------------------
    //  Sets up the book with the specified number of pages.
    //---------------------------------------------------------
    public Book2(int numPages)
    {
      pages = numPages;
    }

    //---------------------------------------------------------
    //  Public access to number of pages
    //---------------------------------------------------------
    public int PageCount
    {
      get { return pages; }
      set { pages = value; }
    }
  }
}
```

Listing 8.6

```csharp
//****************************************************************
//  Dictionary2.cs        C#:  Ken Culp
//
//  Represents a dictionary, which is a book. Used to demonstrate
//  the use of the super reference.
//****************************************************************
using System;

namespace Words2
{
  public class Dictionary2 : Book2
  {
    private int definitions;

    //---------------------------------------------------------
    //  Sets up the dictionary with the specified number of pages
    //  (maintained by the Book parent class) and definitions.
    //---------------------------------------------------------
```

Listing 8.6   continued

```csharp
    public Dictionary2(int numPages, int numDefinitions)
      :
      base(numPages)
    {
      definitions = numDefinitions;
    }

    //------------------------------------------------------------
    //  Public access to number of definitions
    //------------------------------------------------------------
    public int DefinitionCount
    {
      get { return definitions; }
      set { definitions = value; }
    }

    //------------------------------------------------------------
    //  Computes the number of definitions per page
    //------------------------------------------------------------
    public double ComputeRatio()
    {
      return (double)definitions / (double)pages;
    }
  }
}
```

In this case, it would have been just as easy to set the pages variable explicitly in the Dictionary2 constructor instead of using **base** to call the Book2 constructor. However, it is good practice to let each class "take care of itself." If we choose to change the way that the Book2 constructor sets up its pages variable, we would also have to remember to make that change in Dictionary2. By using the **base** reference, a change made in Book2 is automatically reflected in Dictionary2.

A child's constructor is responsible for calling its parent's constructor. Generally, the declaration line of a constructor should use the **base** reference call to a constructor of the parent class. If no such call exists, C# automatically makes a call to the **base** constructor at the beginning of the constructor. This rule ensures that a parent class initializes its variables before the child class constructor begins to execute. Using the **base** reference to invoke a parent's constructor can be done only in the child's constructor, and if included it must be the first line of the constructor.

The base reference can also be used to reference other variables and methods defined in the parent's class. We use this technique in later sections of this chapter.

Multiple Inheritance

C#'s approach to inheritance is called *single inheritance*. This term means that a derived class can have only one parent. Some object-oriented languages allow a child class to have multiple parents. This approach is called *multiple inheritance* and is occasionally useful for describing objects that are in between two categories or classes. For example, suppose we have a class `Car` and a class `Truck` and want to create a new class called `PickupTruck`. A pickup truck is somewhat like a car and somewhat like a truck. With single inheritance, we must decide whether it is better to derive the new class from `Car` or `Truck`. With multiple inheritance, it can be derived from both, as shown in Figure 8.2.

Multiple inheritance works well in some situations, but it comes with a price. What if both `Truck` and `Car` have methods with the same name? Which method would `PickupTruck` inherit? The answer to this question is complex, and it depends on the rules of the language that supports multiple inheritance.

> **Key Concept**
>
> A child class can override (redefine) the parent's definition of an inherited method.

The designers of the C# language explicitly decided not to support multiple inheritance. Instead, we can rely on interfaces to provide the best features of multiple inheritance, without the added complexity. Although a C# class can be derived from only one parent class, it can implement multiple interfaces. Therefore, we can interact with a particular class in specific ways while inheriting the core information from one parent class.

8.2 OVERRIDING METHODS

When a child class defines a method with the same name and signature as a method in the parent class, we say that the child's version *overrides* the parent's version in favor of its own. The need for overriding occurs often in inheritance situations.

The program in Listing 8.7 provides a simple demonstration of method overriding in C#. The `Messages` class contains a `Main` method that instantiates two objects: one from class `Thought` and one from class `Advice`. The `Thought` class is the parent of the `Advice` class.

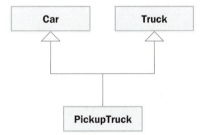

FIGURE 8.2 A UML class diagram showing multiple inheritance

Both the Thought class (see Listing 8.8) and the Advice class (see Listing 8.9) contain a definition for a method called Message. The version of Message defined in the Thought class is inherited by Advice, but Advice overrides it with an alternative version. The new version of the method prints out an entirely different message and then invokes the parent's version of the Message method using the **base** reference.

There are two ways that methods can be overridden:

> The base class specifically authorizes the derived class to override its method. Considered a cooperative approach, this technique is shown in the example in Listing 8.7. To allow a derived class to override a method, you must precede the method type specification with the word **virtual**, as in class Thought. Then, the derived class must precede the method type with the keyword **overrides**, as in the Advice class. If you specify **virtual** in the base class and forget **overrides** in the derived class, the compiler will issue a warning. If you do not specify **virtual** in the base class and use **overrides** in the derived class, the compiler issues an error.

> The base class does not authorize overriding, by not specifying virtual. In this case, the only way that you can use a method with the same name and signature as one in the derived class is to precede the method type with the word **new**. In other words, if we left off the **virtual** on Thought's Message method, then the Advice class would have to declare the Message method as follows:

```
public new void Message() { . . . }
```

Sometimes, a derived class wants to override a method from the base class and then prevent any other classes derived from them from overriding the same method. For example, we could modify the Advice class so that no class derived from Advice could override the Message method. The **sealed** keyword "seals" the method in that class so that derived classes cannot use it. Here is how the modified Message method in Advice would appear:

```
public sealed overrides void Message() { . . . }
```

Listing 8.7

```
//**************************************************************
//  Messages.cs         C#:   Ken Culp
//
//  Demonstrates the use of an overridden method.
//**************************************************************
using System;

namespace Messages
{
  public class Messages
  {
```

Listing 8.7   continued

```
    //----------------------------------------------------------
    //  Instantiates 2 objects, invoking the message method in each
    //----------------------------------------------------------
    public static void Main(string[] args)
    {
      Thought parked = new Thought();
      Advice dates = new Advice();

      parked.Message();

      dates.Message();   // overridden

      Console.In.ReadLine();   // Wait for enter key
    }
  }
}
```

Output

```
I feel like I'm diagonally parked in a parallel universe.
Warning: Dates in calendar are closer than they appear.
I feel like I'm diagonally parked in a parallel universe.
```

The object that is used to invoke a method determines which version of the method is actually executed. When Message is invoked using the parked object in the Main method, the Thought version of Message is executed. When Message is invoked using the dates object, the Advice version of Message is executed.

Listing 8.8

```
//**************************************************************
//  Thought.cs        C#:   Ken Culp
//
//  Represents a stray thought. Used as the parent of a derived
//  class to demonstrate the use of an overridden method.
//**************************************************************
using System;

namespace Messages
{
  public class Thought
  {
    //----------------------------------------------------------
    //  Prints a message.
```

Listing 8.8   continued

```
    //----------------------------------------------------------------
    public virtual void Message()
    {
      Console.Out.WriteLine("I feel like I'm diagonally " +
        "parked in a parallel universe.");

      Console.Out.WriteLine();
    }
  }
}
```

Method overloading is a key element in object-oriented design. It allows two objects that are related by inheritance to use the same naming conventions for methods that accomplish the same general task in different ways. Overloading becomes even more important when it comes to polymorphism, which is discussed in Chapter 9.

Shadowing Variables

It is possible, although strongly discouraged, for a child class to declare a variable with the same name as one that is inherited from the parent. Note the distinction between redeclaring a variable and simply giving an inherited variable a particular value. If a variable of the same name is declared in a child class, it is called a *shadow variable*. It is similar in concept to the process of overriding methods but creates confusing subtleties.

Listing 8.9

```
//****************************************************************
//  Advice.cs          C#:  Ken Culp
//
//  Represents a piece of advice. Used to demonstrate the use of
//  an overridden method.
//****************************************************************
using System;

namespace Messages
{
  public class Advice : Thought
  {
    //----------------------------------------------------------------
    //  Prints message. This method overrides parent's version.
    //  It also invokes parent's version explicitly using base.
    //----------------------------------------------------------------
    public override void Message()
    {
```

Listing 8.9   continued

```
        Console.Out.WriteLine("Warning: Dates in calendar are " +
            "closer than they appear.");

        Console.Out.WriteLine();

        base.Message();

    }
  }
}
```

Because an inherited variable is already available to the child class, there is usually no good reason to redeclare it. Someone reading code with a shadowed variable will find two different declarations that seem to apply to a variable used in the child class. This confusion causes problems and serves no useful purpose. A redeclaration of a particular variable name could change its type, but that is usually unnecessary. In general, you should avoid shadowing variables.

8.3   CLASS HIERARCHIES

A child class derived from one parent can be the parent of its own child class. Furthermore, multiple classes can be derived from a single parent. Therefore, inheritance relationships often develop into *class hierarchies*. The diagram in Figure 8.3 shows a class hierarchy that includes the inheritance relationship between the `Mammal` and `Horse` classes.

There is no limit to the number of children a class can have or to the number of levels to which a class hierarchy can extend. Two children of the same parent are called *siblings*. Although siblings share the characteristics passed on by their common parent, they are not related by inheritance, because one is not used to derive the other.

In class hierarchies, common features should be kept as high in the hierarchy as reasonably possible. That way, the only characteristics explicitly established in a child class are those that make the class distinct from its parent and from its siblings. This approach maximizes the potential to reuse classes. It also facilitates maintenance activities, because when changes are made to the parent, they are automatically reflected in the descendents. Always remember to maintain the is-a relationship when building class hierarchies.

The inheritance mechanism is transitive. That is, a parent passes along a trait to a child class, and that child class passes it along to its children, and so on. An inherited feature might have originated in the immediate parent or possibly several levels higher in a more distant ancestor class.

> **Key Concept**
>
> The child of one class can be the parent of one or more other classes, creating a class hierarchy.

There is no single best hierarchy organization for all situations. The decisions you make when you are designing a class hierarchy restrict and guide more detailed design decisions and implementation options, so you must make them carefully.

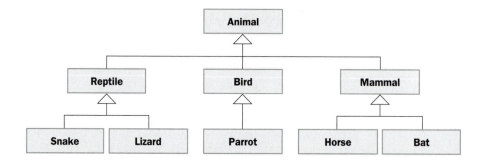

FIGURE 8.3   A UML class diagram showing a class hierarchy

Earlier in this chapter we discussed a class hierarchy that organized animals by their major biological classifications, such as `Mammal`, `Bird`, and `Reptile`. However, in a different situation, the same animals might logically be organized in a different way. For example, as shown in Figure 8.4, the class hierarchy might be organized around a function of the animals, such as their ability to fly. In this case, a `Parrot` class and a `Bat` class would be siblings derived from a general `FlyingAnimal` class. This class hierarchy is as valid and reasonable as the original one. The needs of the programs that use the classes will determine which is best for the particular situation.

The `Object` Class

In C#, all classes are derived ultimately from the **object** class (the name **object** is an alias for `Object` and either may be used). If a class definition doesn't use a colon to derive itself explicitly from another class, then that class is automatically derived from the `Object` class by default. Therefore, the following two class definitions are equivalent:

```
class Thing
{
   // whatever
}
```

and

```
class Thing : Object
{
   // whatever
}
```

Because all classes are derived from `Object`, all public methods of `Object` are inherited by every C# class. They can be invoked through any object created in any C# program.

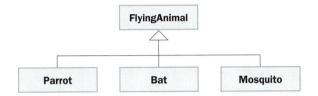

FIGURE 8.4   An alternative hierarchy for organizing animals

The Object class is defined in the mscorlib package of the C# standard class library. Figure 8.5 lists some of the methods of the Object class.

> **Key Concept**
>
> All C# classes are derived, directly or indirectly, from the Object class.

As it turns out, we've been using Object methods quite often in our examples. The ToString method, for instance, is defined in the Object class, so the ToString method can be called on any object. As we've seen several times, when a WriteLine method is called with an object parameter, ToString is called to determine what to print.

Therefore, when we define a ToString method in a class, we are actually overriding an inherited definition and must provide the **overrides** keyword. The definition for ToString provided by the Object class returns a string containing the object's class name followed by a numeric value that is unique for that object. Usually, we override the Object version of ToString to fit our own needs. The String class has overridden the ToString method so that it returns its stored string value.

> **Key Concept**
>
> The ToString and Equals methods are inherited by every class in every C# program.

We are also overriding an inherited method when we define an Equals method for a class. As we've discussed previously, the purpose of the Equals method is to determine whether two objects are equal, meaning that they have identical nonstatic members. The definition of the Equals method provided by the Object class returns true if the two object references actually contain precisely the same data. The ReferenceEquals method, on the other hand, checks whether the two values refer to the same object (that is, whether they are aliases). This distinction is extremely important, particularly if you have experience with other object-oriented languages like Java where the Equals method is an alias check.

Classes often override the inherited definition of the Equals method in favor of a more appropriate definition. However, in most cases, Equals or ReferenceEquals serves the purpose for your classes.

Abstract Classes

An *abstract class* represents a generic concept in a class hierarchy. An abstract class cannot be instantiated and usually contains one or more *abstract methods,* which have no definition. We discussed abstract methods in Chapter 6, in which they were used to define a C# interface. An abstract class is similar to an interface in some ways. However, unlike interfaces, an abstract class can contain methods that are not abstract. It can also contain data declarations other than constants.

> **Key Concept**
>
> An abstract class cannot be instantiated. It represents a concept upon which other classes can build their definitions.

Public Methods	
Equals	Determines whether two `Object` instances are equal (have exactly the same nonstatic members).
GetHashCode	Serves as a hash function for a particular type, suitable for use in hashing algorithms and data structures like a hash table.
GetType	Gets the type of the current instance.
ReferenceEquals	Determines whether the specified `Object` instances are the same instance (aliases of each other).
ToString	Returns a string that represents the current `Object`. This is usually the object type.

Protected Methods	
Finalize	Allows an `Object` to attempt to free resources and perform other cleanup operations before the `Object` is reclaimed by garbage collection. In C#, finalizers are expressed using destructor syntax.
MemberwiseClone	Creates a shallow copy of the current `Object`. A shallow copy copies all nonstatic members of the object and is a useful way to create duplicates of an object (and not aliases).

FIGURE 8.5   Some methods of the Object class

A class is declared as abstract by including the **abstract** modifier in the class header. Any class that contains one or more abstract methods must be declared as abstract. In abstract classes (unlike interfaces) the **abstract** modifier must be applied to each abstract method. A class declared as abstract does not have to contain abstract methods.

Abstract classes serve as placeholders in a class hierarchy. As the name implies, an abstract class represents an abstract entity that is usually insufficiently defined to be useful by itself. Instead, an abstract class may contain a partial description that is inherited by all of its descendants in the class hierarchy. Its children, which are more specific, fill in the gaps.

Consider the class hierarchy shown in Figure 8.6. The `Vehicle` class at the top of the hierarchy may be too generic for a particular application. Therefore we may choose to implement it as an abstract class. In UML diagram, abstract class names are shown in italic.

Concepts that apply to all vehicles can be represented in the `Vehicle` class and are inherited by its descendants. That way, each of its descendants doesn't have to define the same concept redundantly (and perhaps inconsistently). For example, we may say that all vehicles have a particular speed. Therefore we declare a `speed` variable in the `Vehicle` class, and all specific vehicles below it in the hierarchy automatically have that variable because of inheritance. Any change we make to the representation of the speed of a vehicle is automatically reflected in all descendant classes. Similarly, we may declare an abstract method called `FuelConsumption`, whose purpose is to calculate how quickly fuel is being consumed by a particular vehicle. The details of the `FuelConsumption` method must be defined by each type of vehicle, but the `Vehicle` class establishes that all vehicles consume fuel and provides a consistent way to compute that value.

Some concepts don't apply to all vehicles, so we wouldn't represent those concepts at the `Vehicle` level. For instance, we wouldn't include a variable called `numberOfWheels` in the `Vehicle` class, because not all vehicles have wheels. The child classes for which wheels are appropriate can add that concept at the appropriate level in the hierarchy.

There are no restrictions as to where in a class hierarchy an abstract class can be defined. Usually they are located at the upper levels of a class hierarchy. However, it is possible to derive an abstract class from a non-abstract parent.

Usually, a child of an abstract class provides a specific definition for an abstract method inherited from its parent. Note that this is just a specific case of overriding a method, giving a different definition than the one the parent provides. If a child of an abstract class does not give a definition for every abstract method that it inherits from its parent, then the child class is also considered abstract.

> **Key Concept**
>
> A class derived from an abstract parent must override all of its parent's abstract methods, or the derived class will also be considered abstract.

Note that it would be a contradiction for an abstract method to be modified as **static** because a static method can be invoked using the class name without declaring an object of the class. Because abstract methods have no implementation, an abstract static method would make no sense.

Choosing which classes and methods to make abstract is an important part of the design process. You should make such choices only after careful consideration. By using abstract classes wisely, you can create flexible, extensible software designs.

Interface Hierarchies

The concept of inheritance can be applied to interfaces as well as classes. That is, one interface can be derived from another interface. These relationships can form an *interface hierarchy*, which is similar to a class hierarchy. Inheritance relationships between interfaces are shown in UML diagrams using the same connection (an arrow with an open arrowhead) as they are with classes.

> **Key Concept**
>
> Inheritance can be applied to interfaces so that one interface can be derived from another.

When a parent interface is used to derive a child interface, the child inherits all abstract methods and constants of the parent. Any class that implements the child interface must

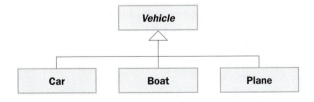

FIGURE 8.6   A vehicle class hierarchy

implement all the methods. There are no visibility issues when dealing with inheritance between interfaces (as there are with protected and private members of a class) because all members of an interface are public.

Class hierarchies and interface hierarchies do not overlap. That is, an interface cannot be used to derive a class, and a class cannot be used to derive an interface. A class and an interface interact only when a class is designed to implement a particular interface.

8.4   VISIBILITY

> **Key Concept**
>
> Private members are inherited by the child class, but cannot be referenced directly by name. They may be used indirectly, however.

As we discussed earlier in this chapter, all variables and methods, even private members, that are defined in a parent class are inherited by a child class. They exist for an object of a derived class, even though they can't be referenced directly. They can, however, be referenced indirectly.

Let's look at an example that demonstrates this situation. The program shown in Listing 8.10 contains a `Main` method that instantiates a `Pizza` object and invokes a method to determine how many calories the pizza has per serving due to its fat content.

The `FoodItem` class shown in Listing 8.11 represents a generic type of food. The constructor of `FoodItem` accepts the number of grams of fat and the number of servings of that food. The `Calories` method returns the number of calories due to fat, which the `CaloriesPerServing` method invokes to help compute the number of fat calories per serving.

The `Pizza` class, shown in Listing 8.12, is derived from the `FoodItem` class, but it adds no special functionality or data. Its constructor calls the constructor of `FoodItem` using the **base** reference, asserting that there are eight servings per pizza.

The `Pizza` object called `special` in the `Main` method is used to invoke the method `CaloriesPerServing`, which is defined as a public method of `FoodItem`. Note that `CaloriesPerServing` calls `Calories`, which is declared with private visibility. Furthermore, `Calories` references the variable `fatGrams` and the constant `CALORIES_PER_GRAM`, which are also declared with private visibility.

Listing 8.10

```
//***************************************************************
//   FoodAnalyzer.cs          C#:  Ken Culp
//
//   Demonstrates indirect referencing through inheritance.
//***************************************************************

using System;

namespace FoodAnalyzer
{
```

Listing 8.10   continued

```csharp
public class FoodAnalyzer
{
  //-------------------------------------------------------------
  //  Instantiates a Pizza object and prints its calories per
  //  serving.
  //-------------------------------------------------------------
  public static void Main(string[] args)
  {
    Pizza special = new Pizza(275);

    Console.Out.WriteLine("Calories per serving: " +
      special.CaloriesPerServing());

    Console.In.ReadLine();  // Wait for enter key
  }
}
}
```

Output

```
Calories per serving: 309
```

Even though the Pizza class cannot explicitly reference Calories, fatGrams, or CALORIES_PER_GRAM, they are available for use indirectly when the Pizza object needs them. A Pizza object cannot be used to invoke the Calories method, but it can call a method that can. Note that a FoodItem object was never created or needed.

Listing 8.11

```csharp
//***************************************************************
//  FoodItem.cs          C#:  Ken Culp
//
//  Represents an item of food. Used as the parent of a
//  derived class to demonstrate indirect referencing
//  through inheritance.
//***************************************************************
using System;

namespace FoodAnalyzer
{
  public class FoodItem
  {
    const int CALORIES_PER_GRAM = 9;
    private int fatGrams;
```

Listing 8.11 continued

```
    protected int servings;

    //------------------------------------------------------------
    //  Sets up this food item with the specified number of fat
    //  grams and number of servings.
    //------------------------------------------------------------
    public FoodItem(int numFatGrams, int numServings)
    {
      fatGrams = numFatGrams;
      servings = numServings;
    }

    //------------------------------------------------------------
    //  Computes and returns the number of calories in this food
    //  item due to fat.
    //------------------------------------------------------------
    private int Calories()
    {
      return fatGrams * CALORIES_PER_GRAM;
    }

    //------------------------------------------------------------
    //  Computes and returns fat calories per serving.
    //------------------------------------------------------------

    public int CaloriesPerServing()
    {
      return (Calories() / servings);
    }
  }
}
```

Listing 8.12

```
//****************************************************************
//  Pizza.cs        C#:  Ken Culp
//
//  Represents a pizza, which is a food item. Used to demonstrate
//  indirect referencing through inheritance.
//****************************************************************
using System;

namespace FoodAnalyzer
{
  public sealed class Pizza : FoodItem
  {
```

Listing 8.12   continued

```
    //-----------------------------------------------------------
    //  Sets up a pizza with the specified amount of fat (assumes
    //  eight servings).
    //-----------------------------------------------------------
    public Pizza(int fatGrams)
      : base(fatGrams, 8)
    {
    }
  }
}
```

8.5   DESIGNING FOR INHERITANCE

As a major characteristic of object-oriented software, inheritance must be carefully and specifically addressed during software design. A little thought about inheritance relationships can lead to a far more elegant design, which pays huge dividends in the long term.

Throughout this chapter, several design issues have been addressed in the discussion of the nuts and bolts of inheritance in C#. The following list summarizes some of the inheritance issues that you should keep in mind during the program design stage:

> Every derivation should be an is-a relationship. The child should be a more specific version of the parent.

> Design a class hierarchy to capitalize on reuse, and potential reuse in the future.

> As classes and objects are identified in the problem domain, find their commonality. Push common features as high in the class hierarchy as appropriate for consistency and ease of maintenance.

> Override methods as appropriate to tailor or change the functionality of a child.

> Add new variables to the child class as needed, but don't shadow (redefine) any inherited variables.

> Allow each class to manage its own data. Therefore, use the **base** reference to invoke a parent's constructor and to call overridden versions of methods if appropriate.

> Use interfaces to create a class that serves multiple roles (simulating multiple inheritance).

> Design a class hierarchy to fit the needs of the application, with attention to how it may be useful in the future.

Key Concept

Software design must carefully and specifically address inheritance.

> Even if there are no current uses for them, override general methods such as `ToString` and `Equals` appropriately in child classes so that the inherited versions don't cause unintentional problems later.

> Use abstract classes to specify a common class interface for the concrete classes lower in the hierarchy.

> Use visibility modifiers carefully to provide the needed access in derived classes without violating encapsulation.

Restricting Inheritance

We showed how the **sealed** modifier can be used on an overridden method declaration to prevent inheritance of the single method. However, sealed can also be applied to a class specification, forever locking it to further derivation. To prevent a class from being used to derive other classes, use the sealed keyword in the class declaration.

The **sealed** modifier can also be applied to an entire class. A sealed class cannot be extended at all. Consider the following declaration:

```
public sealed class Standards
{
  // whatever
}
```

Given this declaration, the `Standards` class cannot be used with the `:` clause in another class declaration. The compiler will generate an error message in such a case. The `Standards` class can be used normally, but it cannot be the parent of another class.

Key Concept

The sealed modifier can be used to restrict inheritance to methods or to classes.

Using the **sealed** modifier to restrict inheritance abilities is a key design decision. It should be done in situations in which a child class could possibly be used to change functionality that you, as the designer, specifically want to be handled a certain way. This issue comes up again in the discussion of polymorphism in Chapter 9.

8.6   THE COMPONENT CLASS HIERARCHY

All of the C# classes that define GUI components are part of a class hierarchy, shown in part in Figure 8.7. Almost all C# GUI components are derived from the `System.Windows` `.Forms.Control` class, which is part of the `System.Windows.Forms` namespace, which defines how most all components work in general. `Control` itself is derived from the `System.ComponentModel.Component` class.

As you examine Figure 8.7, you will also see that events and the event handlers are located in two places. The first group, the simpler events, are derived from `System.EventHandler`. Other event handlers derive from `System.Windows.Forms` `.MouseEventHandler`. Furthermore, many of the controls implement various interfaces and draw method signatures from them.

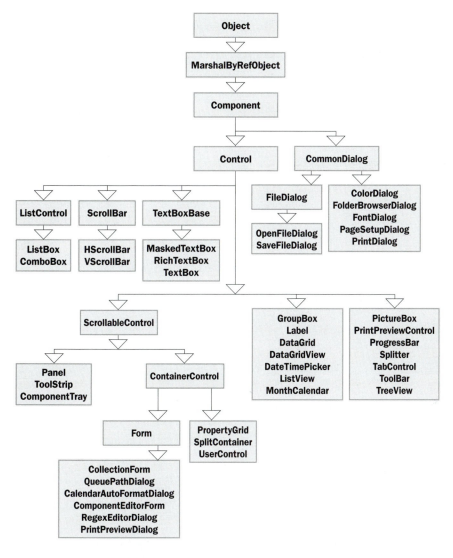

FIGURE 8.7   Windows Forms Component Hierarchy

As this creates a rather complex structure, the best way to explore the hierarchy is with the Object Browser. While you are editing a form-based application, select View/Object Browser. Then select the `System.Windows.Forms` section of the Object Browser and expand it by clicking the plus signs. Figure 8.8 shows an excerpt of a portion of the Object Browser showing some of the methods associated with the `Control` class.

In Figure 8.8, we see that the method `Invalidate` of the `Control` class takes no parameters or can take one boolean parameter. If you wanted additional details on the `Invalidate` method that took the boolean value, click once on the method name. The bottom portion of the Object Browser

Key Concept

The classes that represent C# GUI components are organized into a class hierarchy.

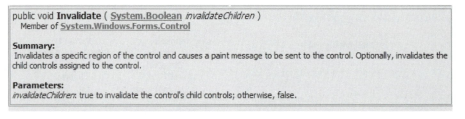

FIGURE 8.8   Object Browser viewing Windows components

public void **Invalidate** (<u>System.Boolean</u> *invalidateChildren*)
   Member of <u>System.Windows.Forms.Control</u>

Summary:
Invalidates a specific region of the control and causes a paint message to be sent to the control. Optionally, invalidates the child controls assigned to the control.

Parameters:
invalidateChildren: true to invalidate the control's child controls; otherwise, false.

FIGURE 8.9   Object Browser viewing Invalidate method

window would then look like Figure 8.9. We have used this method for forms in previous exercises.

In Figure 8.7, note that the `Form` class that is used to create all forms is derived from a class called `ControlContainer`, which is derived from `ScrollableControl`, which is derived from `Control`, which is derived from `System.ComponentModel.Component`. Each of these classes has methods that can be used when you derive your class from `System.Windows.Forms.Form`. Use the Object Browser to see what methods are available if you need to know how to use the method or to know what parameters are supplied. On the other hand, if you know how to use the method but just do not remember its exact name, simply click on the dot after the **this** keyword in a form and use IntelliSense to list the members for you.

   OVERRIDING EVENT HANDLERS

Key Concept

A listener class can be created by deriving it from an event adapter class.

In previous applications, we derived our application class from `System.Windows.Forms.Form`. Then to create event handlers, we simply double-clicked on the event in the properties window to create the event handler. This used the += syntax to add a handler to the event. However, a default event handler is defined for all events in the various parent classes of the controls and for the form.

Thus, an alternative technique is to simply override these methods as they are defined with the keyword **virtual**. Again, when overriding a **virtual** method, it is necessary to use the keyword **overrides**.

The program shown in Listing 8.13 displays a simple form as would be created in a text editor. Whenever the mouse button is clicked over the panel, a line is drawn from the location of the mouse pointer to the center of the panel. The distance that line represents in pixels is displayed.

Listing 8.13

```csharp
//***************************************************************
//  OffCenter.cs        C#: Ken Culp
//
//  Overrides event handlers (begin with word On...) in Form
//  class.  For some handlers, the base event handler must be
//  called as noted.
//
//  This program was created directly in an editor and not using
//  the form designer.
//***************************************************************
using System;
using System.Windows.Forms;
using System.Drawing;

namespace OffCenter
{
  public class OffCenter : Form
  {
    int width, height;
    Point center, current;
    Pen pen;
    Font font;
    Brush brush;

    public OffCenter()
    {
      this.BackColor = Color.Yellow;
      this.Text = "Off Center";
      this.ClientSize = new System.Drawing.Size(292, 266);
      this.Icon = new Icon(@"..\..\Creative.ico");
      this.Name = "OffCenter";
      this.StartPosition =
        System.Windows.Forms.FormStartPosition.CenterScreen;
      pen = new Pen(Color.Black, 1);
      font = new Font("Times New Roman", 10);
```

Listing 8.13 continued

```csharp
      brush = new SolidBrush(Color.Black);
      OnResize(new System.EventArgs());
    }
    //--------------------------------------------------------------
    //  If the form is resized, recompute the screen center.
    //--------------------------------------------------------------
    protected override void OnResize(EventArgs e)
    {
      base.OnResize(e);    // Allow base to first do its thing
      width = this.ClientRectangle.Width;
      height = this.ClientRectangle.Height;
      center = new Point(ClientRectangle.Left + width / 2,
                         ClientRectangle.Top + height / 2);
      current = center;
      Invalidate();
    }
    //--------------------------------------------------------------
    //  If the mouse is moved, update the current position.
    //--------------------------------------------------------------
    protected override void OnMouseUp(MouseEventArgs e)
    {
      // No need to call base.OnMouseMove nothing else needed
      current.X = e.X;
      current.Y = e.Y;
      Invalidate();
    }
    //--------------------------------------------------------------
    //  Override Paint method.
    //--------------------------------------------------------------
    protected override void OnPaint(PaintEventArgs e)
    {
      base.OnPaint(e);   // Allow base to paint all else
      Graphics page = e.Graphics;// Fetch graphics tool kit
      page.DrawEllipse(pen, center.X - 3, center.Y - 3, 6, 6);

      // draw line only if cursor is not in the center
      if (center.X != current.X || center.Y != current.Y)
        page.DrawLine(pen, current, center);

      // compute length of line
      double dX2 = (center.X - current.X) * (center.X - current.X);
      double dY2 = (center.Y - current.Y) * (center.Y - current.Y);
      double distance = Math.Sqrt(dX2 + dY2);
      page.DrawString(string.Format("Distance: {0:0.0#}",
        distance), font, brush, 5, 5);
    }
  }
}
```

Display

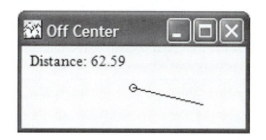

Although a skeleton form was created in the designer, we will set up the form manually. We change the form banner by setting the `Text` property, initialize the `Icon` property by pointing to the file in the application directory, and we set the `BackColor` property. The icon is set using one of the constructors for a new icon that takes a file name. When you modify the icon directly in a designer, it will place the icon in a *Resource* file and load it from there. Resource files are beyond the scope of this book.

Instead of creating the handler as we always did, we override the `OnMouseUp` event handler defined for the form itself. We chose `OnMouseUp` since the second parameter of the `OnClick` method is of type `EventArgs` which does not include the x and y coordinates of the mouse. `OnMouseUp` has a parameter of type `MouseEventArgs` that includes the mouse coordinates.

When we create the event handler in the Form Designer (use the += syntax), we <u>add</u> a handler to the list. The handler thus added is just one of possibly many handlers that will be called on the event. However, when we override the base class' method, we are overriding the main handler. Therefore, if there is processing that is done in the base class that needs to be executed, we must explicitly call that method using the **base** keyword and the same method name and passing the parameter received (see first line of `OnPaint` method in the listing).

Calling the base method was necessary in the `OnPaint` method and the `OnResize` handler (see below) because there may be processing needed there. However, in the `OnMouseUp` method, we did not call the base method because we took all the action necessary when the mouse button was released.

Note that the form can be resized and the program continues to work correctly. If you drag the edges of the form, the `Resize` event occurs. In the listing above, we override the `OnResize` event to handle this event. We then compute a new width and height and a new center of the form. Then we set the current mouse position to the center of the form so no line is drawn and invalidate the form. You should study carefully the computations in `OnResize`.

Because of inheritance, we now have a choice when it comes to creating event handlers. We can add the handler to the list or we can override the base class handler. This is a design decision that should be considered carefully. The best technique depends on the situation.

As a final note, the MouseWheel event is not exposed on many controls but the OnMouseWheel event can be overridden. Thus to access the MouseWheel event, override the method.

Note that the form can be resized and the program will continue to work correctly. If you drag the edges of the form, the `Resize` event occurs. In Listing 8.13, we override the `OnResize` event to handle this event. We then compute a new width and height and a new center of the form. Then we set the current mouse position to the center of the form so no line is drawn, which would invalidate the form. You should study carefully the computations in `OnResize`.

Because of inheritance, we now have a choice when it comes to creating event handlers. We can add the handler to the list or we can override the base class handler. This is a design decision that should be considered carefully. The best technique depends on the situation.

As a final note, the `MouseWheel` event is not exposed on many controls but the `OnMouseWheel` method can be overridden. Thus, to access the `MouseWheel` event, override the method.

8.8 EXTENDING GUI COMPONENTS

There are a couple of fairly straightforward ways to extend window controls. The easiest way is to simply derive a class from the control and then add that control to your project and to your form. The other way is to create a custom control that consists of a variety of other controls. In this section, we discuss each method and then give a single example of both.

The first question you might ask is why you would derive a class from a C#-defined control class. Consider the `TextBox` control that supports an integer property called `MaxLength`. What if you wanted to add a `MinLength` property and then return a `Valid` boolean indicating whether the text length is between these two values? You would need another property (`MinLength`) and handlers to set `Valid` when data was entered into the text box.

Another reason to override system GUI classes is to add your own data to the control. You could add a variety of descriptive information that you could use from code or from the designer. For example, you could add a `Color` variable and public property to the `Button` class, which would be initialized during design time. Then, when the button is clicked, you use the stored color property for a paint operation.

The other way to extend user controls is through the User Control editing capability of Visual Studio. A user control would ordinarily be a collection of various controls that are used repeatedly. In the example in Listing 8.15, we use three separate text boxes to make up a social security number (see the `InputValidation` example in Chapter 5). We then add to this custom control a `Valid` property that indicates whether the number is in a valid format and a `Text` property for setting or reading the social security number.

It is possible to even create your own named events that can be used from the designer and handled in your application. The explanation of how to do this is fairly complicated and beyond the scope of this text.

To demonstrate these concepts, we are going to walk through the steps to create a library with two custom controls (the `TextBox` control with a minimum length) and the SSN control. Then we will create a test project that will use only the SSN control.

Select File/New/Project, select Class Library under Templates in the New Project dialog box, and name the library **SsnControls**. This creates a class definition file for `Class1`, but we will not use that. Right-click References and select Add Reference. This displays a list of libraries in the Add Reference dialog box. Select the .NET tab and double-click `System.Windows.Forms.dll` and `System.Drawing.dll`. Both of these libraries should be listed in the bottom window. Click OK. Now we can use Windows functions for this library.

Now we need to create our variation of the `TextBox` control that supports `MinLength`. Right-click the project name in the explorer window, select Add User Control, and name the control **TextBoxMin**. Open the code and change the base class from `UserControl` to `TextBox`. Compile the application (Build/Build). Add the `minLength` integer private member and the `MinLength` property plus the `Valid` property, making your code look like Listing 8.14. Build what you have so far and remove any errors.

Listing 8.14

```
//****************************************************************
//  TextBoxMin.cs        C#: Ken Culp
//
//  Extends the TextBox class by adding a MinLength property and
//  a Valid property that is true when the text length is between
//  minimum and maximum.
//****************************************************************
using System;
using System.Collections;
using System.ComponentModel;
using System.Drawing;
using System.Data;
using System.Windows.Forms;

namespace SsnControls
{
  public class TextBoxMin : System.Windows.Forms.TextBox
  {
    private int minLength;   // The minimum length

    //------------------------------------------------------------
    //  Constructor: Not really needed
    //------------------------------------------------------------
    public TextBoxMin()
    {
    }
```

Listing 8.14   continued

```
//------------------------------------------------------------
//  MinLength property.  No validation on set.
//------------------------------------------------------------
public int MinLength
{
  get { return minLength; }
  set { minLength = value; }
}

//------------------------------------------------------------
//  Valid property.  True if text length between min and max
//------------------------------------------------------------
public bool Valid
{
  get
  {
    // Return true if min larger than max.
    if (this.MinLength > this.MaxLength) return true;
    int len = this.Text.Length;
    // Return true if length between min and max
    return (this.MinLength <= len && len <= this.MaxLength);
  }
}
  }
 }
}
```

Our next step is to create the social security number control using the `TextBoxMin` control the we just created. Right-click again on the Project, an select Add/Add User Control. Name your control **SSN**. This opens something that looks sort of like a form but does not have a banner line. This is a drawing surface upon which you will drop your new text box.

In the designer, select the tool box and then select the My User Controls tab. Our new `TextBoxMin` control should be there. Double-click the control or otherwise add the control to the form. Name the control **txtSSN1**, set `MinLength` to 3, and set `MaxLength` to 3. Delete the data in the `Text` property.

Add two more `TextBoxMin` controls with the names **txtSSN2** and **txtSSN3**. The minimum and maximum length of `txtSSN2` should be 2 and the minimum and maximum length of `txtSSN3` should be 4. Adjust your text box sizes so that your SSN user control looks like that shown in Figure 8.10.

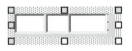

FIGURE 8.10   SSN user control design

Now we need to code the remaining portion of the SSN control properties. We used an array called `boxes` to conveniently access the three parts of the SSN. The creation and setup of that array is done in the constructor. The `Valid` property then uses this array and the `Valid` property of the `TextBoxMin` control we created previously. The `Valid` property is read-only because only the `get` method is specified.

The `Text` property includes both a `get` method and a `set` method. The `get` returns the concatenated strings of the three text boxes. The `set` splits the input string using `MinLength` (which in our case is the same as `MaxLength`). Note that preceding the method is what is called a method attribute:

```
[Browsable(true)]
```

This property causes the public property that you have added to your custom control to be visible during form design. That is, after dragging your SSN control to the form, you can enter a default social security number into the `Text` property. You should use this attribute for all properties that you want exposed to the design phase.

Delete the file `Class1`, because it is not used, and then compile your final code, which should look similar to Listing 8.15.

Listing 8.15

```csharp
//****************************************************************
//   SSN.cs         C#: Ken Culp
//
//   User control with three TextBoxMin boxes where MinLength and
//   MaxLength are both set to 3,2,4 respectively.
//   The Valid property that is true when all 3 parts of the SSN
//   match the specified length.  Text property sets/gets the SSN.
//****************************************************************
using System;
using System.Collections;
using System.ComponentModel;
using System.Windows.Forms;

namespace SsnControls
{
  public class SSN : System.Windows.Forms.UserControl
  {
    private SsnControls.TextBoxMin txtSSN1;
    private SsnControls.TextBoxMin txtSSN2;
    private SsnControls.TextBoxMin txtSSN3;
    private System.ComponentModel.Container components = null;
    private TextBoxMin[] boxes;
```

Listing 8.15 continued

```
//-------------------------------------------------------------
//  Constructor:  Calls form setup; creates list of all boxes
//-------------------------------------------------------------
public SSN()
{
  InitializeComponent();
  boxes = new TextBoxMin[3];
  boxes[0] = txtSSN1;
  boxes[1] = txtSSN2;
  boxes[2] = txtSSN3;
}

protected override void Dispose(bool disposing)
{
  if (disposing)
  {
    if (components != null)
    {
      components.Dispose();
    }
  }
  base.Dispose(disposing);
}

┌─────────────────────────────────────┐
│  Component Designer generated code   │
└─────────────────────────────────────┘


//-------------------------------------------------------------
//  Valid: Property is false unless all parts exactly filled.
//-------------------------------------------------------------
[Browsable(true)]
public bool Valid
{
  get
  {
    bool ok = true;
    foreach (TextBoxMin b in boxes)
    {
      int len = b.Text.Length;
      ok &= (b.Valid);
    }
    return ok;
  }
}

//-------------------------------------------------------------
//  Value: The SSN as an integer value
//-------------------------------------------------------------
```

Listing 8.15   continued

```csharp
[Browsable(true)]
public long Value
{
  get
  {
    long val;
    try
    {
      val = long.Parse(Text);
      return val;
    }
    catch (FormatException err)
    {
      return 0;
    }
  }
  set
  {
    string ssn = value.ToString();
    Text = ssn;
  }
}


//-----------------------------------------------------------
//  Text: The SSN as a string of 9 digits
//-----------------------------------------------------------
[Browsable(true)]
public override string Text
{
  get
  {
    string ret = "";
    foreach (TextBoxMin b in boxes)
      ret += b.Text;
    return ret;
  }
  set
  {
    string val = value;
    // Make sure not passed non-numeric values.
    for (int i = 0; i < val.Length; i++)
      if (val[i] < '0' || val[i] > '9') return;
    // Spread value across text boxes
    foreach (TextBoxMin b in boxes)
    {
      int len = b.MinLength;
      if (val.Length >= len)
```

Listing 8.15   continued

```
            { // Have at least enough for this field
              b.Text = val.Substring(0, len);
              val = val.Substring(len);
            }
            else
            { // Not enough to fill. Use all & done
              b.Text = val;
              val = "";
            }
        }
    }
}


//-------------------------------------------------------------
//  SsnKeyPress:   Trashes all characters except numbers
//-------------------------------------------------------------
private void SsnKeyPress(object sender, KeyPressEventArgs e)
{
    char key = e.KeyChar;
    if ((key >= ' ') && (key < '0' || key > '9')) e.Handled =
                                                  true;

}


//-------------------------------------------------------------
//  SsnTextChanged: Shared TextChanged handler; generates
//  autotab
//-------------------------------------------------------------
private void SsnTextChanged(object sender, EventArgs e)
{
    // Generate tab if field is full
    TextBox box = (TextBox)sender;
    int max = box.MaxLength;
    if (box.Text.Length == max) SendKeys.Send("\t");
}


//-------------------------------------------------------------
//  SsnOnEnter: Moves cursor to start and highlights all
//-------------------------------------------------------------
private void SsnOnEnter(object sender, System.EventArgs e)
{
    TextBox b = (TextBox)sender;
    b.SelectionStart = 0;
    b.SelectionLength = b.Text.Length;
    }
  }
}
```

Our final task is to create a test program. Select File/New/Project and then select Windows Application. In your tool box, select the My User Controls tab and right-click in the blank space. Select Add/Remove items. When the dialog box is displayed, click the Browse button. Find the `SsnControls` project we created previously, and then the bin directory, and then the Debug directory. Double-click the `SsnControls.dll` file. This will add your new controls to your tool box.

Add an event handler for the `Enter` event for each text box to select all the text in the box. To create the handler, select the first text box, select the `Enter` event in the properties window, type the method name **SsnOnEnter**, and press the Enter key.

Drag the SSN control to the form and then add a button. Take the default name of ssn1 but name your button **btnOk**. Add a label so that your form looks like the completed output. Double-click the button and add the code shown in Listing 8.16.

Note that you can use the `Text` property of your custom control at design time. If you type a social security number there, it will appear in the designer and be available at run time.

Test your application.

Listing 8.16

```
//****************************************************************
//  SsnTest.cs        C#:  Ken Culp
//
//  Tests the Social Security Number control.  In order to create
//  the form, you will have to add the SSN control created in the
//  SSN project to your toolbox.  Right-click and select Choose
//  Items. Browse to SSN project, bin, and Release; click on
//  SSN.dll.  Then drop the new control on the form.
//****************************************************************
using System;
using System.Collections.Generic;
using System.ComponentModel;
using System.Data;
using System.Drawing;
using System.Text;
using System.Windows.Forms;

namespace SsnTest
{
  public partial class SsnTest : Form
  {
    public SsnTest()
    {
      InitializeComponent();
    }
```

Listing 8.16 continued

```
private void btnGetSSN_Click(object sender,
  System.EventArgs e)
{
  int ssn = int.Parse(ssn1.Text);
  MessageBox.Show("SSN: " + ssn.ToString("###-##-####") +
    "\nValid: " + ssn1.Valid);
}

private void SsnTest_Closing(object sender,
  System.ComponentModel.CancelEventArgs e)
{
  DialogResult result = MessageBox.Show("Close Form?",
    "Sure?", MessageBoxButtons.YesNo, MessageBoxIcon.Question);
  e.Cancel = (result == DialogResult.No);
}
  }
}
```

Output

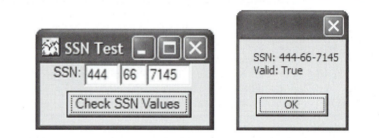

Note that we have included a variation of this example in Chapter 10 under the discussion of events.

8.9 THE Timer CLASS

A *timer* object, created from the Timer class of the System.Timers package, can be thought of as a GUI component. However, unlike other components, it does not have a visual representation that appears on the screen. Instead, as the name implies, it helps us manage an activity over time.

A timer object generates an action event at regular intervals. To perform an animation, we set up a timer to generate an action event periodically, and then update the animation graphics in the listener. Some of the methods and properties of the Timer class are shown in Figure 8.11.

The program shown in Listing 8.17 displays the image of a smiling face that seems to glide across the program window at an angle, bouncing off of the window edges.

The constructor of the ReboundPanel class creates a Timer object, using no parameters. Then, all the properties and events are configured in code, including the delay in milliseconds and the event handler that handles the events of the timer. The class constructor also sets up the initial position for the image and the

> **Key Concept**
>
> A Timer object generates action events at regular intervals and can be used to control an animation.

Public Constructors	
public Timer();	Creates a new timer with all the values set to their default values.
public Timer(double interval);	Creates a new timer with the interval set by the constructor and rest to default values.

Public Properties	
AutoReset	Controls whether the Elapsed event occurs every time the specified interval elapses or only after the first time it elapses.
Enabled	Gets or sets an indicator of whether the Timer should raise the Elapsed event.
Interval	Gets or sets the interval after which the Elapsed event will fire.

Public Methods	
Close	Releases the resources used by the Timer.
Start	Starts raising the Elapsed event by setting Enabled to **true.**
Stop	Stops raising the Elapsed event by setting Enabled to **false.**
ToString	Returns a String that represents the current object.

Public Events	
Tick	Occurs when the interval elapses.

FIGURE 8.11   Some methods of the System.Timers.Timer class

number of pixels it will move, in both the vertical and horizontal directions, each time the image is redrawn.

The `TimerTick` method (the tick event handler) updates the current *x* and *y* coordinate values, and then checks to see if those values cause the image to "run into" the edge of the client space. If so, the movement is adjusted so that the image will make future moves in the opposite direction horizontally, vertically, or both. Note that this calculation takes the image size into account.

The speed of the animation in this program is a function of two factors: the pause between the action events and the distance the image is shifted each time. In this example, the timer is set to generate an action event every 20 milliseconds, and the image is shifted 3 pixels each time it is updated. You can experiment with these values to change the speed of the animation. The goal should be to create an illusion of movement that is pleasing to the eye.

The smiling face graphic is placed upon a label (`label1`) for motion around the screen. The `FromFile` static method from the `Image` class is called to add the image to the label. `FromFile` takes a fully qualified path name. Since the program runs from the `bin\Debug` directory under the project directory, we use a relative path to open the image, which is stored in the project directory. Again, we used the @ sign so that we could use the simpler syntax.

The face is drawn on the client rectangle. Therefore, when the form is resized, the ball will move around in the new rectangle. Rapidly resizing the box can trap the face at the bottom of the screen. This would be considered a bug, so see if you can trap the ball and then find the bug. (Hint: arm the resize event for the form and reposition the ball.)

The `Timer` class we are using is in the `System.Timers` class, which is included if you have a **using** for `System`. Although this is the `Timer` class you should use, there is also a different `Timer` class associated with threads (threads are beyond the scope of this book).

Listing 8.17

```
//***********************************************************
//  Rebound.cs          C#:   Ken Culp
//
//  Demonstrates animation and the Timer class. The position
//  of a graphic is changed on every timer event.
//
//  This application was generated by first creating a
//  console application.  Then the ReboundForm class was
//  added above the Rebound class created for the console
//  application.  For the program to run, you must add
//  the references below and the two using statements.
//    System.Drawing
//    System.Windows.Forms
//***********************************************************
```

Listing 8.17   continued

```
using System;
using System.IO;
using System.Windows.Forms; // Added for forms operations
using System.Drawing;       // Added for drawing operations

namespace Rebound
{
  public class ReboundForm : Form
  {
    private const int WIDTH = 500, HEIGHT = 400;
    private const int IMAGE_SIZE = 35;
    private const int DELAY = 20;
    private Label label1;
    private Timer timer;
    private int imgX, imgY, moveX = 3, moveY = 3;

    public ReboundForm()
    {
      // timer
      timer = new Timer();
      timer.Interval = DELAY;
      timer.Enabled = true;
      timer.Tick += new EventHandler(TimerTick);
      // label1
      label1 = new Label();
      label1.Image = Image.FromFile(@"..\..\happyFace.gif");
      label1.Location = new Point(112, 104);
      label1.Size =
        new System.Drawing.Size(IMAGE_SIZE, IMAGE_SIZE);
      label1.TabIndex = 0;
      label1.Text = "";
      // Form
      this.Width = WIDTH;
      this.Height = HEIGHT;
      this.AutoScaleBaseSize = new Size(5, 13);
      this.Controls.AddRange(new Control[] { label1 });
      this.Text = "Rebound";
      this.Icon = new Icon(@"..\..\Creative.ico");
    }

    private void TimerTick(object sender, EventArgs e)
    {
      int maxX = ClientRectangle.Width - label1.Size.Width;
      int maxY = ClientRectangle.Height - label1.Size.Height;
      imgX += moveX;
      imgY += moveY;
```

Listing 8.17   continued

```
      // Produce bounce by changing sign of step at wall (x or y)
      if (imgX < 0 || imgX > maxX) moveX *= -1;  // Change x?
      if (imgY < 0 || imgY > maxY) moveY *= -1;  // Change y?
      label1.Location = new Point(imgX, imgY);
    }
  }
  class Rebound
  {
    static void Main(string[] args)
    {
      Application.Run(new ReboundForm());
    }
  }
}
```

Display

Summary of Key Concepts

> Inheritance is the process of deriving a new class from an existing one.

> One purpose of inheritance is to reuse existing software.

> Inheritance creates an is-a relationship between the parent and child classes.

> Protected visibility provides the best possible encapsulation while still permitting inheritance.

> A parent's constructor can be invoked using the **base** reference.

> A child class can override (redefine) the parent's definition of an inherited method.

> The child of one class can be the parent of one or more other classes, creating a class hierarchy.

> Common features should be located as high in a class hierarchy as reasonably possible.

> All C# classes are derived, directly or indirectly, from the object class.

> The ToString and Equals methods are inherited by every class in every C# program.

> An abstract class cannot be instantiated. It represents a concept upon which other classes can build their definitions.

> A class derived from an abstract parent must override all of its parent's abstract methods, or the derived class will also be considered abstract.

> Inheritance can be applied to interfaces so that one interface can be derived from another.

> Private members are inherited by the child class, but cannot be referenced directly by name. They may be used indirectly, however.

> Software design must carefully and specifically address inheritance.

> The **sealed** modifier can be used to restrict inheritance to methods or to classes.

> The classes that represent C# GUI components are organized into a class hierarchy.

> A listener class can be created by extending an event handler.

> A Timer object generates action events at regular intervals and can be used to control an animation.

Self-Review Questions

8.1 Describe the relationship between a parent class and a child class.

8.2 How does inheritance support software reuse?

8.3   What relationship should every class derivation represent?

8.4   Why would a child class override one or more of the methods of its parent class?

8.5   Why is the **base** reference important to a child class?

8.6   What is the significance of the `object` class?

8.7   What is the role of an abstract class?

8.8   Are all members of a parent class inherited by the child? Explain.

8.9   What is an interface hierarchy?

8.10 What does a `Timer` object do?

Exercises

8.1   Draw a UML class diagram showing an inheritance hierarchy containing classes that represent different types of clocks. Show the variables and method names for two of these classes.

8.2   Show an alternative diagram for the hierarchy in Exercise 8.1. Explain why it may be a better or worse approach than the original.

8.3   Experiment with a simple derivation relationship between two classes. Put `WriteLine` statements in constructors of both the parent and child classes. Do not explicitly call the constructor of the parent in the child. What happens? Why? Change the child's constructor to explicitly call the constructor of the parent. Now what happens?

Programming Projects

8.1   Design and implement a class called `MonetaryCoin` that is derived from the `Coin` class presented in Chapter 5. Store a value in the monetary coin that represents its value and add a property that returns its value. Create a `Main` driver class to instantiate and compute the sum of several `MonetaryCoin` objects. Demonstrate that a monetary coin inherits its parent's ability to be flipped.

8.2   Design and implement a set of classes that defines the employees of a hospital: doctor, nurse, administrator, surgeon, receptionist, janitor, and so on. Include methods in each class that are named according to the services provided by that person and that print an appropriate message. Create a `Main` driver class to instantiate and exercise several of the classes.

8.3   Design and implement a set of classes that defines various types of reading material: books, novels, magazines, technical journals, textbooks, and so on. Include data values that describe various attributes of the material, such as the number of pages and the names of the primary characters. Include methods that are named appropriately for each class and that print an appropriate message. Create a `Main` driver class to instantiate and exercise several of the classes.

8.4   Design and implement a set of classes that keeps track of various sports statistics. Have each low-level class represent a specific sport. Tailor the services of the classes to the sport in question, and move common attributes to the higher-level classes as appropriate. Create a `Main` driver class to instantiate and exercise several of the classes.

8.5   Design and implement a set of classes that keeps track of demographic information about a set of people, such as age, nationality, occupation, income, and so on. Design each class to focus on a particular aspect of data collection. Create a `Main` driver class to instantiate and exercise several of the classes.

8.6   Modify the `Rebound` program from this chapter such that when the mouse button is clicked the animation stops, and when it is clicked again the animation resumes.

8.7   Modify the `Rebound` program from this chapter so that when the form is clicked, another face is added. Add the face at the mouse location (make sure it is in the client rectangle). Use an `ArrayList` to store the faces. Choose a random speed (step distance) for each face. Clear all faces when the spacebar is pressed.

8.8   Modify Programming Project 8.7 so that mouse clicks remove a face if the mouse was over that face. If the mouse is not over the face, a new face is added. Use the `Remove` or `RemoveAt` method of `ArrayList` to remove the faces.

8.9   Design and implement an application that displays an animation of a car (side view) moving across the screen from left to right. Create a `Car` class that represents the car (or use one that was created for a programming project in Chapter 7).

8.10   Design and implement an application that displays an animation of a horizontal line segment moving across the screen, eventually passing across a vertical line. As the vertical line is passed, the horizontal line should change color. The change of color should occur while the horizontal line crosses the vertical one; therefore, while crossing, the horizontal line will be two different colors.

8.11   Design and implement an application that plays a game called Catch-the-Creature. Use an image to represent the creature. Have the creature appear at a random location for a random duration, then disappear and reappear somewhere else. The goal is to "catch" the creature by pressing the mouse button while the mouse pointer is on the creature image. Create a separate class to represent the creature, and include in it a method that determines if the location of the mouse click corresponds to the current location of the creature. Display a count of the number of times the creature is caught.

8.12   Design and implement an application that works as a stopwatch. Include a display that shows the time (in seconds) as it increments. Include buttons that allow the user to start and stop the time and reset the display to zero. Arrange the components to present a nice interface.

8.13 Design and implement a set of classes that defines a series of three-dimensional geometric shapes. For each shape, store fundamental data about its size and provide methods to access and modify its data. In addition, provide appropriate methods to compute each shape's circumference, area, and volume. In your design, consider how shapes are related and thus where inheritance can be implemented. Create a main driver class to instantiate several shapes of differing types and exercise the behavior you provided.

8.14 Design and implement a set of classes that defines various types of electronics equipment (computers, cell phones, pagers, digital cameras, etc.). Include data values that describe various attributes of the electronics, such as the weight, cost, power usage, and the names of the manufacturers. Include methods that are named appropriately for each class and that print an appropriate message. Create a main driver class to instantiate and exercise several of the classes.

8.15 Design and implement a set of classes that defines various courses in your curriculum. Include information about each course, such as the title, number, description, and department that teaches the course. Consider the categories of classes that comprise your curriculum when designing your inheritance structure. Create a main driver class to instantiate and exercise several of the classes.

Answers to Self-Review Questions

8.1 A child class is derived from a parent class by using inheritance. The methods and variables of the parent class automatically become a part of the child class, subject to the rules of the visibility modifiers used to declare them.

8.2 Because a new class can be derived from an existing class, the characteristics of the parent class can be reused without the error-prone process of copying and modifying code.

8.3 Each inheritance derivation should represent an is-a relationship: the child *is-a* more specific version of the parent. If this relationship does not hold, then inheritance is being used improperly.

8.4 A child class may prefer its own definition of a method in favor of the definition provided for it by its parent. In this case, the child overrides (redefines) the parent's definition with its own.

8.5 The **base** reference can be used to call the parent's constructor, which cannot be invoked directly by name. It can also be used to invoke the parent's version of an overridden method.

8.6   All classes in C# are derived, directly or indirectly, from the `object` class. Therefore, all public methods of the `object` class, such as `Equals` and `ToString`, are available to every object.

8.7   An abstract class is a representation of a general concept. Common characteristics and method signatures can be defined in an abstract class so that they are inherited by child classes derived from it.

8.8   A class member is not inherited if it has private visibility, meaning that it cannot be referenced by name in the child class. However, such members do exist for the child and can be referenced indirectly.

8.9   A new interface can be derived from an existing interface by using inheritance, just as a new class can be derived from an existing class.

8.10 An object created from the `Timer` class produces an action event at regular intervals. It can be used to control the speed of an animation.

Group Project

Plot the equation `y = sin(x)/x` on the client area of a form. The vertical scale for the equation, `y`, will range between –1 and +1. Let a y value of +1 correspond to the top of the client area and a y value of –1 correspond to the bottom of the client area. Use x values from –10 to +10 so that an x value of -10 is at the left of the client area and a value of +10 is at the right. Draw both the vertical and horizontal axes and label values along these axes.

Note that when x is zero, `sin(x)` is also zero, so the computation would yield 0 divided by 0, which is undefined. However, mathematical methods show that when x is 0, `sin(x)/x` equals 1. Therefore, use a specific condition to substitute the value 1 when x is 0 in this case.

The complexity of this problem comes from scaling. The client area will take horizontal values from 0 to `ClientRectangle.Width`, and `Width` is expressed in pixels, typically in the hundreds of pixels. Similarly, the vertical scale ranges downward from 0 to `ClientRectangle.Height`. You will want to place the center of your Cartesian coordinate system for the graph in the center of the client rectangle, meaning that -10 for x would correspond to 0 pixels and +10 would correspond to `ClientRectangle.Width`. Similar computations exist for the vertical axis.

The first step is to create an abstract class called `PlotBase` that handles all the drawing configuration values and the coordinate conversions. This class will then be extended for each formula you will draw. It has the properties and methods listed in Figure 8.12.

The next step is to create the class `SinXdivX` that implements `PlotBase` and implement the `Y` method. Remember that this method will have to handle the computation when x is zero. `SinXdivX` should also have its own constructor that overrides the values of `MinX` (–10), `MaxX` (+10), `MinY` (–1), and `MaxY` (+1).

Now create the form `DrawForm` that will do the actual drawing. For this form, create a custom constructor that takes an object of the type `PlotBase`. Save this object in a local class variable in the form. The form would be called as follows:

```
SinXdivX formula = new SinXdivX();
DrawForm drawForm = new DrawForm(formula);
drawForm.ShowDialog();
```

To draw the graph, we implement the `Paint` event for the form. In `Paint`, use a `for` loop that ranges x from `MinX` to `MaxX` in `Step` steps. Compute y for the first point (x = `MinX`) and then draw a line `LineWidth` wide from that point to the next point using `LineColor`. Then draw a line to each new point from the preceding point. Start with `Step`

Property	
`public float MinX`	Minimum x value on plot. Set to −5 in the constructor.
`public float MaxX`	Maximum x value on plot. Set to +5 in the constructor.
`public float MinY`	Minimum y value on plot. Set to −5 in the constructor.
`public float MaxY`	Maximum y value on plot. Set to +5 in the constructor.
`public float Step`	The amount to increment x from one point to the next. Set to 0.05 in the constructor.
`public float Width`	The width of the drawing area in pixels. Used for the `CartToDraw` methods.
`public float Height`	The height of the drawing area in pixels.
`public Color LineColor`	The line color. Set to a default of black in the constructor.
`public int LineWidth`	The pixel thickness of the line. Set to 1 in the constructor.
Methods	
`public PointF CartToDraw(` `    PointF cartesianPoint);`	Takes a `PointF` point structure in (x, y) coordinates and returns a `PointF` structure in pixel drawing coordinates. This computation is based on `MinX`, `MaxX`, `MinY`, `MaxY`, `Width`, and `Height`.
`public abstract float Y(` `    float x);`	The formula being plotted. It returns a y value for a given x value. It is abstract here because it will be implemented in each class that extends this class.

FIGURE 8.12   Methods and properties of PlotBase

of 0.05 and, once the graph is working, try different values for Step. Step should be obtained from your class the minimum and maximum value for x as well. Define these values as constants in your class.

Add an event handler for the Resize event and choose a FormBorderStyle of Sizable so that the form can be resized. When the form is resized, repaint the graph using the entire client area but with the new values from ClientRectangle.

Once this graph is working, derive a new class from PlotBase and plot

```
y = (x-1)(x-2)(x-3),
```

overriding values in the constructor to use an x scale ranging from 0 to 4 and a y scale that ranges from –4 to +4. Note that the equation will return values that will be off the scale vertically (y larger than +4 and smaller than –4), so these values should not be plotted. If you want, you can add a way in your form to draw both equations at the same time using different color lines. Again, experiment with different values of Step.

Polymorphism

9

CHAPTER OBJECTIVES

> Define polymorphism and explore its benefits.

> Discuss the concept of dynamic binding.

> Use inheritance relationships to create polymorphic references.

> Use interfaces to create polymorphic references.

> Explore sorting and searching using polymorphic implementations.

> Discuss object-oriented design in the context of polymorphism.

> Discuss the processing of events as an example of polymorphism.

> Examine more GUI components.

This chapter discusses polymorphism, another fundamental principle of object-oriented software. We first explore the concept of binding and discuss how it relates to polymorphism. Then we examine how polymorphic references can be accomplished using either inheritance or interfaces. Design issues related to polymorphism are examined. The Windows Track of this chapter discusses how event processing in a graphical user interface is an example of polymorphism. We also examine several new GUI components.

9.1 LATE BINDING

Often, the type of a reference variable matches the class of the object to which it refers exactly. For example, consider the following reference:

```
ChessPiece bishop;
```

The `bishop` variable may be used to point to an object that is created by instantiating the `ChessPiece` class. However, it doesn't have to. The variable type and the object it refers to must be compatible, but their types need not be exactly the same. The relationship between a reference variable and the object it refers to is more flexible than that.

> **Key Concept**
>
> A polymorphic reference can refer to different types of objects over time.

The term *polymorphism* can be defined as "having many forms." A *polymorphic reference* is a reference variable that can refer to different types of objects at different points in time. The specific method invoked through a polymorphic reference can change from one invocation to the next.

Consider the following line of code:

```
obj.DoIt();
```

If the reference `obj` is polymorphic, it can refer to different types of objects at different times. So if that line of code is in a loop, or if it's in a method that is called more than once, that line of code could call a different version of the `DoIt` method each time it is invoked.

At some point, the commitment is made to execute certain code to carry out a method invocation. This commitment is referred to as *binding* a method invocation to a method definition. In many situations, the binding of a method invocation to a method definition can occur at compile time. For polymorphic references, however, the decision cannot be made until run time. The method definition that is used is based on the object that is being referred to by the reference variable at that moment. This deferred commitment is called *late binding* or *dynamic binding*. It is less efficient than binding at compile time because the decision must be made during the execution of the program. This overhead is generally acceptable in light of the flexibility that a polymorphic reference provides.

> **Key Concept**
>
> The binding of a method invocation to its definition is performed at run time for a polymorphic reference.

We can create a polymorphic reference in C# in two ways: using inheritance and using interfaces. Let's look at each in turn.

9.2 POLYMORPHISM VIA INHERITANCE

When we declare a reference variable using a particular class name, it can be used to refer to any object of that class. In addition, it can also refer to any object of any class that is related to its declared type by inheritance. For example, if the class `Mammal` is the parent of the class `Horse`, then a `Mammal` reference can be used to refer to any object of class `Horse`. This ability is shown in the following code segment:

```
Mammal pet;
Horse secretariat = new Horse();
pet = secretariat;  // a valid assignment
```

The reverse operation, assigning the `Mammal` object to a `Horse` reference, can also be done but it requires an explicit cast. Assigning a reference in this direction is generally less useful and more likely to cause problems because although a horse has all the functionality of a mammal (because a horse *is-a* mammal), the reverse is not necessarily true.

This relationship works throughout a class hierarchy. If the `Mammal` class were derived from a class called `Animal`, the following assignment would also be valid:

```
Animal creature = new Horse();
```

> **Key Concept**
>
> A reference variable can refer to any object created from any class related to it by inheritance.

Carrying this to the limit, an `Object` reference can be used to refer to any object, because ultimately all classes are descendants of the `Object` class. An `ArrayList`, for example, uses polymorphism in that it is designed to hold `Object` references. That's why an `ArrayList` can be used to store any kind of object. In fact, a particular `ArrayList` can be used to hold several different types of objects at one time because, by inheritance, they are all `Object` objects.

The reference variable `creature` can be polymorphic because, at any point in time, it can refer to an `Animal` object, a `Mammal` object, or a `Horse` object. Suppose that all three of these classes have a method called `Move` that is implemented in different ways (because the child class overrode the definition it inherited). The following invocation calls the `Move` method, but the particular version of the method it calls is determined at run time:

```
creature.Move();
```

When this line is executed, if `creature` currently refers to an `Animal` object, the `Move` method of the `Animal` class is invoked. Likewise, if `creature` currently refers to a `Mammal` object, the `Mammal` version of `Move` is invoked; likewise if it currently refers to a `Horse` object.

> **Key Concept**
>
> The type of the object, not the type of the reference, is used to determine which version of a method to invoke.

Of course, since `Animal` and `Mammal` represent general concepts, they may be defined as abstract classes. This situation does not eliminate the ability to have polymorphic references. Suppose the `Move` method in the `Mammal` class is abstract, and is given unique definitions in the `Horse`, `Dog`, and `Whale` classes (all derived from `Mammal`). A `Mammal` reference variable can be used to refer to any objects created from any of the `Horse`, `Dog`, and `Whale` classes, and can be used to execute the `Move` method on any of them.

Let's look at another situation. Consider the class hierarchy shown in Figure 9.1. The classes in it represent various types of employees that might be employed at a particular company. Let's explore an example that uses this hierarchy to pay a set of employees of various types.

Listing 9.1   continued

```
Social Security Number: 987-65-4321
Paid: 1246.15
------------------------------------
Name: Woody
Address: 789 Off Rocker
Phone: 555-0000
Social Security Number: 010-20-3040
Paid: 1169.23
------------------------------------
Name: Diane
Address: 678 Fifth Ave.
Phone: 555-0690
Social Security Number: 958-47-3625
Current hours: 40
Paid: 422.0
------------------------------------
Name: Norm
Address: 987 Suds Blvd.
Phone: 555-8374
Thanks!
------------------------------------
Name: Cliff
Address: 321 Duds Lane
Phone: 555-7282
Thanks!
------------------------------------
```

Listing 9.2

```csharp
//********************************************************************
//   Staff.cs          C#:   Ken Culp
//
//   Represents the personnel staff of a particular business.
//********************************************************************
using System;

namespace Firm
{
  public class Staff
  {
    private StaffMember[] staffList;

    //---------------------------------------------------------------
    //   Sets up the list of staff members.
    //---------------------------------------------------------------
    public Staff()
```

Listing 9.2   continued

```
    {
      staffList = new StaffMember[6];

      staffList[0] = new Executive("Sam", "123 Main Line",
        "555-0469", "123-45-6789", 2423.07);

      staffList[1] = new Employee("Carla", "456 Off Line",
        "555-0101", "987-65-4321", 1246.15);
      staffList[2] = new Employee("Woody", "789 Off Rocker",
        "555-0000", "010-20-3040", 1169.23);

      staffList[3] = new Hourly("Diane", "678 Fifth Ave.",
        "555-0690", "958-47-3625", 10.55);

      staffList[4] = new Volunteer("Norm", "987 Suds Blvd.",
        "555-8374");
      staffList[5] = new Volunteer("Cliff", "321 Duds Lane",
        "555-7282");

      ((Executive)staffList[0]).awardBonus(500.00);

      ((Hourly)staffList[3]).addHours(40);
    }

    //-------------------------------------------------------------
    //  Pays all staff members.
    //-------------------------------------------------------------
    public void Payday()
    {
      double amount;
      for (int count = 0; count < staffList.GetLength(0); count++)
      {
        Console.Out.WriteLine(staffList[count]);
        amount = staffList[count].Pay();  // polymorphic
        if (amount == 0.0)
          Console.Out.WriteLine("Thanks!");
        else
          Console.Out.WriteLine("Paid: " + amount);
        Console.Out.WriteLine(
          "----------------------------------");
      }
    }
  }
}
```

Listing 9.3

```
//**************************************************************
//  StaffMember.cs          C#:   Ken Culp
//
//  Represents a generic staff member.
//**************************************************************
using System;

namespace Firm
{

  abstract public class StaffMember
  {
    protected string name;
    protected string address;
    protected string phone;

    //------------------------------------------------------------
    //  Sets up a staff member using the specified information.
    //------------------------------------------------------------
    public StaffMember(string eName, string eAddress,
      string ePhone)
    {
      name = eName;
      address = eAddress;
      phone = ePhone;
    }

    //------------------------------------------------------------
    //  Returns a string including basic employee information.
    //------------------------------------------------------------
    public override string ToString()
    {
      string result = "Name:    " + name + "\n";
      result += "Address: " + address + "\n";
      result += "Phone:   " + phone;
      return result;
    }

    //------------------------------------------------------------
    //  Derived classes must define the pay method for each type
    //  of employee.
    //------------------------------------------------------------
    public abstract double Pay();
  }
}
```

The StaffMember class contains a ToString method to return the information managed by the StaffMember class. It also contains an abstract method called Pay, which takes no parameters and returns a value of type **double**. At the generic StaffMember level, it would be inappropriate to give a definition for this method. However, the descendants of StaffMember each provide their own specific definition for Pay. By defining Pay abstractly in StaffMember, the Payday method of Staff can polymorphically pay each employee.

This is the essence of polymorphism. Each class knows best how it should handle a specific behavior, in this case paying an employee. Yet in one sense it's all the same behavior-the employee is getting paid. Polymorphism lets us treat similar objects in consistent but unique ways.

The Volunteer class, shown in Listing 9.4, represents a person that is not compensated monetarily for his or her work. We keep track only of a volunteer's basic information, which is passed into the constructor of Volunteer, which in turn passes it to the StaffMember constructor using the **base** reference. The Pay method of Volunteer simply returns a zero pay value. If Pay had not been overridden, the Volunteer class would have been considered abstract and could not have been instantiated.

Note that when a volunteer gets "paid" in the Payday method of Staff, a simple expression of thanks is printed. In all other situations, where the pay value is greater than zero, the payment itself is printed.

The Employee class, shown in Listing 9.5, represents an employee that gets paid at a particular rate each pay period. The pay rate, as well as the employee's social security number, is passed along with the other basic information to the Employee constructor. The basic information is passed to the constructor of StaffMember using the **super** reference.

The ToString method of Employee is overridden to concatenate the additional information that Employee manages to the information returned by the parent's version of ToString, which is called using the **base** reference. The Pay method of an Employee simply returns the pay rate for that employee.

The Executive class, shown in Listing 9.6, represents an employee that may earn a bonus in addition to his or her normal pay rate. The Executive class is derived from Employee and therefore inherits from both StaffMember and Employee. The constructor of Executive passes along its information to the Employee constructor and sets the executive bonus to zero.

A bonus is awarded to an executive using the AwardBonus method. This method is called in the Payday method in Staff for the only executive that is part of the staffList array. Note that the generic StaffMember reference must be cast into an Executive reference to invoke the AwardBonus method (which doesn't exist for a StaffMember).

Listing 9.4

```csharp
//***********************************************************
//  Volunteer.cs          C#:  Ken Culp
//
//  Represents a staff member that works as a volunteer.
//***********************************************************
using System;

namespace Firm
{
  public class Volunteer : StaffMember
  {
    //-------------------------------------------------------
    //  Sets up a volunteer using the specified information.
    //-------------------------------------------------------
    public Volunteer(string eName, string eAddress, string ePhone)
      : base(eName, eAddress, ePhone)
    {
      // Do nothing
    }

    //-------------------------------------------------------
    //  Returns a zero pay value for this volunteer.
    //-------------------------------------------------------
    public override double Pay()
    {
      return 0.0;
    }
  }
}
```

The Executive class overrides the Pay method so that it first determines the payment as it would for any employee, and then adds the bonus. The Pay method of the Employee class is invoked using **base** to obtain the normal payment amount. This technique is better than using just the payRate variable, because if we choose to change how Employee objects get paid, the change will automatically be reflected in Executive. After the bonus is awarded, it is reset to zero.

The Hourly class, shown in Listing 9.7, represents an employee whose pay rate is applied on an hourly basis. It keeps track of the number of hours worked in the current pay period, which can be modified by calls to the AddHours method. This method is called from the Payday method of Staff. The Pay method of Hourly determines the payment based on the number of hours worked, and then resets the hours to zero.

Listing 9.5

```csharp
//****************************************************************
//   Employee.cs          C#:  Ken Culp
//
//   Represents a general paid employee.
//****************************************************************
using System;

namespace Firm
{
  public class Employee : StaffMember
  {
    protected string socialSecurityNumber;
    protected double payRate;

    //--------------------------------------------------------------
    //   Sets up an employee with the specified information.
    //--------------------------------------------------------------
    public Employee(string eName, string eAddress, string ePhone,
      string socSecNumber, double rate)
      : base(eName, eAddress, ePhone)
    {
      socialSecurityNumber = socSecNumber;
      payRate = rate;
    }

    //--------------------------------------------------------------
    //   Returns information about an employee as a string.
    //--------------------------------------------------------------
    public override string ToString()
    {
      string result = base.ToString();

      result += "\nSocial Security Number: " +
        socialSecurityNumber;

      return result;
    }

    //--------------------------------------------------------------
    //   Returns the pay rate for this employee.
    //--------------------------------------------------------------
    public override double Pay()
    {
      return payRate;
    }
  }
}
```

Listing 9.6

```csharp
//************************************************************
//  Executive.cs        C#:  Ken Culp
//
//  Represents an executive staff member, who can earn a bonus.
//************************************************************
using System;

namespace Firm
{
  public class Executive : Employee
  {
    private double bonus;

    //------------------------------------------------------------
    //  Sets up an executive with the specified information.
    //------------------------------------------------------------
    public Executive(string eName, string eAddress,
      string ePhone, string socSecNumber, double rate)
      : base(eName, eAddress, ePhone, socSecNumber, rate)
    {
      bonus = 0;  // bonus has yet to be awarded
    }

    //------------------------------------------------------------
    //  Awards the specified bonus to this executive.
    //------------------------------------------------------------
    public void awardBonus(double execBonus)
    {
      bonus = execBonus;
    }

    //------------------------------------------------------------
    //  Computes and returns the pay for an executive, which is
    //  the regular employee payment plus a one-time bonus.
    //------------------------------------------------------------
    public new double Pay()
    {
      double payment = base.Pay() + bonus;
      bonus = 0;
      return payment;
    }
  }
}
```

Listing 9.7

```csharp
//****************************************************************
//  Hourly.cs          C#:   Ken Culp
//
//  Represents an employee that gets paid by the hour.
//****************************************************************
using System;

namespace Firm
{
  public class Hourly : Employee
  {
    private int hoursWorked;

    //-------------------------------------------------------------
    //  Sets up this hourly employee using specified information.
    //-------------------------------------------------------------
    public Hourly(string eName, string eAddress, string ePhone,
      string socSecNumber, double rate)
      : base(eName, eAddress, ePhone, socSecNumber, rate)
    {
      hoursWorked = 0;
    }

    //-------------------------------------------------------------
    //  Adds the specified number of hours to this employee's
    //  accumulated hours.
    //-------------------------------------------------------------
    public void addHours(int moreHours)
    {
      hoursWorked += moreHours;
    }

    //-------------------------------------------------------------
    //  Computes and returns the pay for this hourly employee.
    //-------------------------------------------------------------
    public new double Pay()
    {
      double payment = payRate * hoursWorked;
      hoursWorked = 0;
      return payment;
    }

    //-------------------------------------------------------------
    //  Returns info about this hourly employee as a string.
    //-------------------------------------------------------------
    public string toString()
    {
```

Listing 9.7 continued

```
        string result = base.ToString();
        result += "\nCurrent hours: " + hoursWorked;
        return result;
    }
  }
}
```

9.3 POLYMORPHISM VIA INTERFACES

Now let's examine how we can create polymorphic references using interfaces. As we've seen many times, a class name can be used to declare the type of an object reference variable. Similarly, an interface name can be used as the type of a reference variable as well. An interface reference variable can be used to refer to any object of any class that implements that interface.

Suppose we declare an interface called Speaker as follows:

```
public interface Speaker
{
    public void Speak();
    public void Announce (string str);
}
```

The interface name, Speaker, can now be used to declare an object reference variable:

```
Speaker current;
```

The reference variable, current, can be used to refer to any object of any class that implements the Speaker interface. For example, if we define a class called Philosopher such that it implements the Speaker interface, we can then assign a Philosopher object to a Speaker reference as follows:

```
current = new Philosopher();
```

This assignment is valid because a Philosopher is a Speaker. In this sense the relationship between a class and its interface is the same as the relationship between a child class and its parent. It is an is-a relationship. And that relationship forms the basis of the polymorphism.

The flexibility of an interface reference allows us to create polymorphic references. As we saw earlier in this chapter, using inheritance, we can create a polymorphic reference that can refer to any one of a set of objects as long as they are related by inheritance. Using interfaces, we can create similar polymorphic references among objects that implement the same interface.

For example, if we create a class called `Dog` that also implements the `Speaker` interface, it can be assigned to a `Speaker` reference variable as well. The same reference variable, in fact, can at one point refer to a `Philosopher` object and then later refer to a `Dog` object. The following lines of code illustrate this:

```
Speaker guest;
guest = new Philosopher();
guest.Speak();
guest = new Dog();
guest.Speak();
```

In this code, the first time the `Speak` method is called, it invokes the `Speak` method defined in the `Philosopher` class. The second time it is called, it invokes the `Speak` method of the `Dog` class. As with polymorphic references via inheritance, it is not the type of the reference that determines which method gets invoked; it is based on the type of the object that the reference points to at the moment of invocation.

Note that when we are using an interface reference variable, we can invoke only the methods defined in the interface, even if the object it refers to has other methods to which it can respond. For example, suppose the `Philosopher` class also defined a public method called `Pontificate`. The second line of the following code would generate a compiler error, even though the object can in fact respond to the `Pontificate` method:

```
Speaker special = new Philosopher();
special.Pontificate();  // generates a compiler error
```

The problem is that the compiler can determine only that the object is a `Speaker`, and therefore can guarantee only that the object can respond to the `Speak` and `Announce` methods. Because the reference variable `special` could refer to a `Dog` object (which cannot pontificate), it does not allow the invocation. If we know in a particular situation that such an invocation is valid, we can cast the object into the appropriate reference so that the compiler will accept it, as follows:

```
((Philosopher)special).pontificate();
```

As we can with polymorphic references based in inheritance, an interface name can be used as the type of a method parameter. In such situations, any object of any class that implements the interface can be passed into the method. For example, the following method takes a `Speaker` object as a parameter. Therefore, both a `Dog` object and a `Philosopher` object can be passed into it in separate invocations.

> **Key Concept**
>
> A parameter to a method can be polymorphic, giving the method flexible control of its arguments.

```
public void sayIt (Speaker current)
{
   current.Speak();
}
```

Using a polymorphic reference as the formal parameter to a method is a powerful technique. It allows the method to control the types of parameters passed into it, yet gives it the flexibility to accept arguments of various types.

9.4 SORTING

Let's examine a problem that lends itself to a polymorphic solution. *Sorting* is the process of arranging a list of items in a well-defined order. For example, you may want to alphabetize a list of names or put a list of survey results into descending numeric order. Many sorting algorithms have been developed and critiqued over the years. In fact, sorting is considered to be a classic area of study in computer science.

This section examines two sorting algorithms: selection sort and insertion sort. Complete coverage of various sorting techniques is beyond the scope of this text. Instead we introduce the topic and establish some of the fundamental ideas involved. We do not delve into a detailed analysis of the algorithms but instead focus on the strategies involved and general characteristics.

Selection Sort

The *selection sort* algorithm sorts a list of values by successively putting particular values in their final, sorted positions. In other words, for each position in the list, the algorithm selects the value that should go in that position and puts it there. Let's consider the problem of putting a list of numeric values into ascending order.

The general strategy of selection sort is as follows: Scan the entire list to find the smallest value. Exchange that value with the value in the first position of the list. Scan the rest of the list (all but the first value) to find the smallest value, and then exchange it with the value in the second position of the list. Scan the rest of the list (all but the first two values) to find the smallest value, and then exchange it with the value in the third position of the list. Continue this process for all but the last position in the list (which will end up containing the largest value). When the process is complete, the list is sorted. Figure 9.2 demonstrates the use of the selection sort algorithm.

Let's look at an example. The program shown in Listing 9.8 uses a selection sort to arrange a list of Contact objects into ascending order.

Listing 9.9 shows the Sorting class. It contains two static sorting algorithms. The PhoneList program uses only the SelectionSort method. The other method is discussed later in this section.

The SelectionSort method accepts an array of IComparable objects to sort. Recall that IComparable is an interface that includes only one method, CompareTo, which is designed to return an integer that is less than zero, equal to zero, or greater than zero if the executing object is less than, equal to, or greater than the object to which it is being compared, respectively.

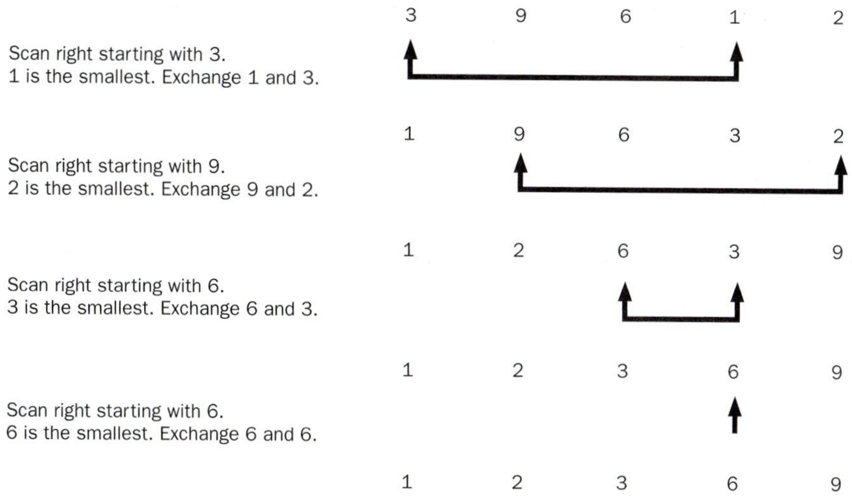

	3	9	6	1	2

Scan right starting with 3.
1 is the smallest. Exchange 1 and 3.

	1	9	6	3	2

Scan right starting with 9.
2 is the smallest. Exchange 9 and 2.

	1	2	6	3	9

Scan right starting with 6.
3 is the smallest. Exchange 6 and 3.

	1	2	3	6	9

Scan right starting with 6.
6 is the smallest. Exchange 6 and 6.

	1	2	3	6	9

FIGURE 9.2   Selection sort processing

Listing 9.8

```
//****************************************************************
//  PhoneList.cs          C#:  Ken Culp
//
//  Driver for testing a sorting algorithm.
//****************************************************************
using System;

namespace PhoneList
{
  class PhoneList
  {
    [STAThread]
    static void Main(string[] args)
    {
      Contact[] names1 = new Contact[8];
      names1[0] = new Contact("John", "Smith", "610-555-7384");
      names1[1] = new Contact("Sarah", "Barnes", "215-555-3827");
      names1[2] = new Contact("Mark", "Riley", "733-555-2969");
      names1[3] = new Contact("Laura", "Getz", "663-555-3984");
      names1[4] = new Contact("Larry", "Smith", "464-555-3489");
      names1[5] = new Contact("Frank", "Phelps", "322-555-2284");
      names1[6] = new Contact("Mario", "Guzman", "804-555-9066");
      names1[7] = new Contact("Marsha", "Grant", "243-555-2837");

      // Duplicate list for second sort test using object.Clone()
      Contact[] names2 = (Contact[])names1.Clone();
```

Listing 9.8   continued

```
        Console.Out.WriteLine("Selection Sort Results");
        Sorting.SelectionSort(names1);
        foreach (Contact friend in names1)
          Console.Out.WriteLine("\t" + friend);

        Console.Out.WriteLine("Insertion Sort Results");
        // Comment out next line if you want to prove that the
        // original, unsorted list was copied to names2.
        Sorting.InsertionSort(names2);
        foreach (Contact friend in names2)
          Console.Out.WriteLine("\t" + friend);

        Console.In.ReadLine();// Wait for enter key
      }
    }
}
```

Output

```
Selection Sort Results
        Barnes, Sarah     215-555-3827
        Getz, Laura       663-555-3984
        Grant, Marsha     243-555-2837
        Guzman, Mario     804-555-9066
        Phelps, Frank     322-555-2284
        Riley, Mark       733-555-2969
        Smith, John       610-555-7384
        Smith, Larry      464-555-3489
Insertion Sort Results
        Barnes, Sarah     215-555-3827
        Getz, Laura       663-555-3984
        Grant, Marsha     243-555-2837
        Guzman, Mario     804-555-9066
        Phelps, Frank     322-555-2284
        Riley, Mark       733-555-2969
        Smith, John       610-555-7384
        Smith, Larry      464-555-3489
```

Listing 9.9

```
//**********************************************************
//  Sorting.cs          C#:  Ken Culp
//
//  Demonstrates selection sort and insertion sort algorithms.
//**********************************************************
using System;
using System.Collections;
```

Listing 9.9   continued

```
namespace PhoneList
{
  public class Sorting
  {
    //------------------------------------------------------------
    // Sorts the specified array of objects using the selection
    // sort algorithm.
    //------------------------------------------------------------
    public static void SelectionSort(IComparable[] list)
    {
      int min;
      int length = list.GetLength(0);
      IComparable temp;

      for (int index = 0; index < length - 1; index++)
      {
        min = index;
        for (int scan = index + 1; scan < length; scan++)
          if (list[scan].CompareTo(list[min]) < 0)
            min = scan;
        //Swap the values
        temp = list[min];
        list[min] = list[index];
        list[index] = temp;
      }
    }
    //------------------------------------------------------------
    // Sorts the specified array of objects using the insertion
    // sort algorithm.
    //------------------------------------------------------------
    public static void InsertionSort(IComparable[] list)
    {
      int length = list.GetLength(0);

      for (int index = 1; index < length; index++)
      {
        IComparable key = list[index];
        int position = index;
        //Shift larger values to the right
        while (position > 0 &&
          key.CompareTo(list[position - 1]) < 0)
        {
          list[position] = list[position - 1];
          position--;
        }
        list[position] = key;
      }
    }
  }
}
```

Any class that implements the `IComparable` interface must define the `CompareTo` method. Therefore, any such object can be compared to another object to determine their relative order.

The `SelectionSort` method is polymorphic. Note that it doesn't refer to `Contact` objects at all, and yet is used to sort an array of `Contact` objects. The `SelectionSort` method is set up to sort any array of objects, as long as those objects can be compared to determine their order. You can call `SelectionSort` multiple times, passing in arrays of different types of objects, as long as they are `IComparable`.

Each `Contact` object represents a person with a last name, a first name, and a phone number. Listing 9.10 shows the `Contact` class.

The `Contact` class implements the `IComparable` interface and therefore provides a definition of the `CompareTo` method. In this case, the contacts are sorted by last name; if two contacts have the same last name, their first names are used.

The implementation of the `SelectionSort` method uses two **for** loops to sort the array. The outer loop controls the position in the array where the next smallest value will be stored. The inner loop finds the smallest value in the rest of the list by scanning all positions greater than or equal to the index specified by the outer loop. When the smallest value is determined, it is exchanged with the value stored at the index. This exchange is done in three assignment statements by using an extra variable called `temp`. This type of exchange is often called *swapping*.

Note that because this algorithm finds the smallest value during each iteration, the result is an array sorted in ascending order (that is, smallest to largest). The algorithm can easily be changed to put values in descending order by finding the largest value each time.

Note how the `CompareTo` method is implemented in `Contact`. We have two values we wish to sort on: the last name and the first name. We could compare the last names first and then compare the first names only if the last names were the same. This would yield code something like the following:

```
if (lastName.Equals(((Contact)other).LastName))
    return firstName.CompareTo(((Contact)other).firstName);
else
    return lastName.CompareTo(((Contact)other).lastName);
```

We chose a simpler approach by implementing the property `LastFirst`, which returns a string that is the concatenation of the last name, a comma, and a first name. Comparing `LastFirst` for two objects then guarantees to sort the object in order by last name and then first name. Thus, our `CompareTo` method becomes a single line, as shown in Listing 9.10.

Let us reiterate that the `CompareTo` and `Equals` methods are passed a parameter of type `Object` even though the parameter is really something of type `Contact`. Since we want to compare things of type `Contact`, we must typecast the `Object` parameter to type `Contact`. Since we want the reference properties off this typecasted object using the dot notation, we have to put the typecasted parameter in parentheses. Thus, to reference the `lastName` variable from `other` in the methods, we must use the following syntax:

```
((Contact)other).lastName
```

Listing 9.10

```
//***************************************************************
//   Contact.cs              C#:   Ken Culp
//
//   Represents a phone contact.
//***************************************************************
using System;

namespace PhoneList
{
  public class Contact : IComparable
  {
    private string firstName, lastName, phone;

    //---------------------------------------------------------
    // Constructor: Sets up contact with the specified data.
    //---------------------------------------------------------
    public Contact(string first, string last,
      string telephone)
    {
      firstName = first;
      lastName = last;
      phone = telephone;
    }
    //---------------------------------------------------------
    // Returns a description of this contact as a string.
    //---------------------------------------------------------
    public override string ToString()
    {
      return lastName + ", " + firstName + "\t" + phone;
    }
    //---------------------------------------------------------
    // Returns a bool indicating equality of object contents
    //---------------------------------------------------------
    public override bool Equals(object other)
    {
      return (lastName.Equals(((Contact)other).lastName) &&
             firstName.Equals(((Contact)other).firstName));
    }
    //---------------------------------------------------------
    // Returns an integer hash code for this class.
    // (Must override GetHashCode of override Equals.)
    //---------------------------------------------------------
```

Listing 9.10 continued

```
   public override int GetHashCode()
   {
      return LastFirst.GetHashCode();
   }

   //---------------------------------------------------------
   // Returns a bool indicating equality of object contents
   //---------------------------------------------------------
   public int CompareTo(object other)
   {
      return LastFirst.CompareTo(
         ((Contact)other).LastFirst);
   }

   //---------------------------------------------------------
   // Properties to get/set class variables.
   //---------------------------------------------------------
   public string LastName
   {  // Last Name
      get { return lastName; }
      set { lastName = value; }
   }
   public string FirstName
   {  // First Name
      get { return firstName; }
      set { firstName = value; }
   }
   public string LastFirst
   {  // Last, First. Used for CompareTo.  Read Only!
      get { return LastName + ", " + FirstName; }
   }
   public string Telephone
   {  // Telephone
      get { return phone; }
      set { phone = value; }
   }
   }
}
```

Insertion Sort

The Sorting class also contains a method that performs an insertion sort on an array of IComparable objects. If used to sort the array of Contact objects in the PhoneList program, it would produce the same results as the selection sort did. However, the logic used to put the objects in order is different.

The *insertion sort* algorithm sorts a list of values by repetitively inserting a particular value into a subset of the list that has already been sorted. One at a time, each unsorted element is inserted at the appropriate position in that sorted subset until the entire list is in order.

The general strategy of insertion sort is as follows: Begin with a "sorted" list containing only one value. Sort the first two values in the list relative to each other by exchanging them if necessary. Insert the list's third value into the appropriate position relative to the first two (sorted) values. Then insert the fourth value into its proper position relative to the first three values in the list. Each time an insertion is made, the number of values in the sorted subset increases by one. Continue this process until all values are inserted in their proper places, at which point the list is completely sorted.

The insertion process requires that the other values in the array shift to make room for the inserted element. Figure 9.3 demonstrates the behavior of the insertion sort algorithm with integers.

Similar to the selection sort implementation, the InsertionSort method uses a **for** loop for the outside step to sort the array. In the insertion sort, however, the outer loop controls the index in the array of the next value to be inserted. The inner loop uses a **while** loop to compare the current insert value with values stored at lower indexes (which make up a sorted subset of the entire list). If the current insert value is less than the value at position, that value is shifted to the right. Shifting continues until the proper position is opened to accept the insert value. Each iteration of the outer loop adds one more value to the sorted subset of the list, until the entire list is sorted.

The last feature to note in this example is how we created the second array for testing. We used the Clone method of Object, which performs a member-by-member copy of all nonstatic members. This creates a separate object but with identical contents. Clone, however, returns something of type Object, so we had to typecast it back to an array of Contact objects. The relevant line is shown here:

```
Contact[] names2 = (Contact[]) names1.Clone();
```

If you are not convinced that the new array is not just an alias of the now sorted first array, remove the call to InsertionSort and show the results. The original unsorted list will print.

Comparing Sorts

There are various reasons for choosing one sorting algorithm over another, including the algorithm's simplicity, its level of efficiency, and the amount of memory it uses. An algorithm that is easier to understand is also easier to implement and debug. However, often the simplest sorts are the most inefficient. Efficiency is usually considered to be the primary criterion when comparing sorting algorithms. In general, one sorting algorithm is less efficient than another if it performs more comparisons than the other. There are several algorithms that are more efficient than the two we examined, but they are also more complex.

Both selection sort and insertion sort have essentially the same level of efficiency. Both have an outer loop and an inner loop with similar properties, if not purposes. The outer loop is executed once for each value in the list, and the inner loop compares the value in the outer loop with most, if not all, of the values in the rest of the list. Therefore, both algorithms perform approximately n^2 number of comparisons, where n is the number of values in the list. We say that both selection sort and insertion sort are algorithms of *order n^2*. More efficient sorts perform fewer comparisons and are of a smaller order, such as $n \log_2 n$.

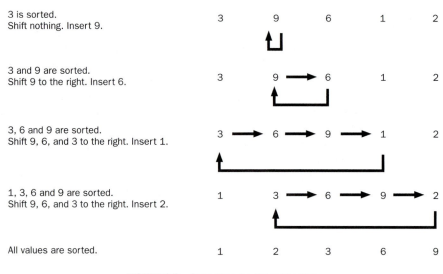

3 is sorted.
Shift nothing. Insert 9.

3 and 9 are sorted.
Shift 9 to the right. Insert 6.

3, 6 and 9 are sorted.
Shift 9, 6, and 3 to the right. Insert 1.

1, 3, 6 and 9 are sorted.
Shift 9, 6, and 3 to the right. Insert 2.

All values are sorted.

FIGURE 9.3   Insertion sort processing

Because both selection sort and insertion sort have the same general efficiency, the choice between them is almost arbitrary. However, there are some additional issues to consider. Selection sort is usually easy to understand and will often suffice in many situations. Further, each value moves exactly once to its final place in the list. That is, although the selection and insertion sorts are equivalent (generally) in the number of comparisons made, selection sort makes fewer swaps.

9.5   SEARCHING

Like sorting, searching for an item is another classic computing problem, and also lends itself to a polymorphic solution. *Searching* is the process of finding a designated *target element* within a group of items. For example, we may need to search for a person named Vito Andolini in a club roster.

The group of items to be searched is sometimes called the *search pool*. The search pool is usually organized into a collection of objects of some kind, such as an array.

Whenever we perform a search, we must consider the possibility that the target is not present in the group. Furthermore, we would like to perform a search efficiently. We don't want to make any more comparisons than we have to.

In this section we examine two search algorithms, linear search and binary search. We explore versatile, polymorphic implementations of these algorithms and compare their efficiency.

Linear Search

If the search pool can be examined one element at a time in any order, one straightforward way to perform the search is to start at the beginning of the list and compare each value in turn to the target element. Eventually, either the target element will be found or we will come to the end of the list and conclude that the target doesn't exist in the group.

This approach is called a *linear search* because it begins at one end and scans the search pool in a linear manner. This process is depicted in Figure 9.4. When items are stored in an array, a linear search is relatively simple.

The program shown in Listing 9.11 is similar to the PhoneList program from the previous section. It begins with the same, unsorted array of Contact objects. It then performs a linear search for a contact and prints the result. Then it calls the SelectionSort method, which was discussed in the previous section, to sort the contacts. It then searches for another contact using a binary search, which is discussed later in this section.

Listing 9.12 shows the Searching class. It contains two static searching algorithms.

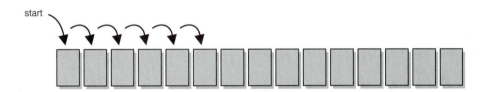

FIGURE 9.4   A linear search

Listing 9.11

```
//*************************************************************
//  PhoneList2.cs        C#:  Ken Culp
//
//  Driver for testing searching algorithms.
//*************************************************************
using System;

namespace PhoneList2
{
  class PhoneList2
  {
    static void Main(string[] args)
    {
      Contact test, found;
      Contact[] names = new Contact[8];

      names[0] = new Contact("John", "Smith", "610-555-7384");
      names[1] = new Contact("Sarah", "Barnes", "215-555-3827");
```

Listing 9.11   continued

```
        names[2] = new Contact("Mark", "Riley", "733-555-2969");
        names[3] = new Contact("Laura", "Getz", "663-555-3984");
        names[4] = new Contact("Larry", "Smith", "464-555-3489");
        names[5] = new Contact("Frank", "Phelps", "322-555-2284");
        names[6] = new Contact("Mario", "Guzman", "804-555-9066");
        names[7] = new Contact("Marsha", "Grant", "243-555-2837");

        test = new Contact("Frank", "Phelps", "322-555-2284");
        found = (Contact)Searching.LinearSearch(names, test);
        if (found != null)
          Console.Out.WriteLine("Found: " + found);
        else
          Console.Out.WriteLine("The contact was not found.");

        Sorting.SelectionSort(names);
        test = new Contact("Mario", "Guzman", "804-555-9066");
        found = (Contact)Searching.BinarySearch(names, test);
        if (found != null)
          Console.Out.WriteLine("Found: " + found);
        else
          Console.Out.WriteLine("The contact was not found.");

        Console.In.ReadLine();// Wait for enter key
      }
    }
}
```

Output

```
Found: Phelps, Frank      322-555-2284
Found: Guzman, Mario      804-555-9066
```

Listing 9.12

```
//****************************************************************
//  Searching.cs          C#:  Ken Culp
//
//  Demonstrates the linear search and binary search algorithms.
//****************************************************************
using System;

namespace PhoneList2
{
  public class Searching
  {
```

Listing 9.12   continued

```
//-----------------------------------------------------------
// Searches specified array of objects for the target using
// a linear search.  Returns a reference to the target object
// from the array if found and null otherwise.
//-----------------------------------------------------------
public static IComparable LinearSearch(IComparable[] list,
  IComparable target)
{
  int index = 0;

  while (!list[index].Equals(target) &&
          index < list.GetLength(0))
    index++;
  if (index < list.GetLength(0))
    return list[index];
  else
    return null;
}


//-----------------------------------------------------------
// Searches specified array of objects for the target using
// a binary search.  Assumes the array is already sorted in
// ascending order when it is passed in.  Returns a reference
// to the target object from the array if found and null
// otherwise.
//-----------------------------------------------------------
public static IComparable BinarySearch(IComparable[] list,
  IComparable target)
{
  int min = 0, max = list.GetLength(0), mid = 0;
  bool found = false;

  while (!found && min <= max)
  {
    mid = (min + max) / 2;
    if (list[mid].Equals(target))
      found = true;
    else
    {
      if (target.CompareTo(list[mid]) < 0)
        max = mid - 1;
      else
        min = mid + 1;
    }
  }
  if (found)
    return list[mid];
```

Listing 9.12 continued

```
        else
            return null;
    }
  }
}
```

In the LinearSearch method, the **while** loop steps through the elements of the array, terminating either when the target is found or the end of the array is reached. After the loop, index will either point to a value found or will be equal to the length of the list (be pointing past the last item). Thus the found condition is determined by comparing index to the length of the list.

Note that we'll have to examine every element before we can conclude that the target doesn't exist in the array. On average, the linear search approach will look through half the data before finding a target that is present in the array.

The LinearSearch method is implemented to process an array of IComparable objects. For this algorithm, however, which relies only on the Equals method, that restriction is not necessary.

Binary Search

If the elements in an array are sorted, in either ascending or descending order, then our approach to searching can be much more efficient than it is using the linear search algorithm. A *binary search* eliminates large parts of the search pool with each comparison by capitalizing on the fact that the search pool is ordered.

Consider the following sorted array of integers:

0	1	2	3	4	5	6	7	8	9	10	11	12	13	14
10	12	18	22	31	34	40	46	59	67	69	72	82	84	98

Suppose we were trying to determine if the number 67 is in this list. Initially, the target might be anywhere in the list, or not at all. That is, at first, all items in the search pool are *viable candidates.*

Instead of starting the search at one end or the other, a binary search begins in the middle of the sorted list. If the target element is not found at that middle element, then the search continues. The middle element of this list is 46, which is not our target, so we must search on. However, since the list is sorted, we know that if 67 is in the list, it will be in the later half of the array. All values at lower indexes are less than 46. Thus, with one comparison, we've taken half of the data out of consideration, and we are left with the following viable candidates:

Viable Candidates

0	1	2	3	4	5	6	7	8	9	10	11	12	13	14
10	12	18	22	31	34	40	46	59	67	69	72	82	84	98

To search the remaining candidates, we once again examine the "middle" element. The middle element is 72, and thus we have still not found the target. But once again, we can eliminate half of the viable candidates-those greater than 72—and we are left with the following:

Viable Candidates

0	1	2	3	4	5	6	7	8	9	10	11	12	13	14
10	12	18	22	31	34	40	46	59	67	69	72	82	84	98

Employing the same approach again, we select the middle element, 67, and find the element we are seeking. If it had not been our target, we would have continued with this process until we either found the value or eliminated all possible data.

With each comparison, a binary search eliminates approximately half of the remaining data to be searched (it also eliminates the middle element as well). That is, a binary search eliminates half of the data with the first comparison, another quarter of the data with the second comparison, another eighth of the data with the third comparison, and so on. The binary search approach is pictured in Figure 9.5.

The `BinarySearch` method from the `Searching` class performs a binary search by looping until the target element is found or until the viable candidates drop to zero. Two integer indexes, `min` and `max`, are used to define the portion of the array that is still considered viable. When `min` becomes greater than `max`, then the viable candidates have been exhausted.

On each iteration of the loop, the midpoint is calculated by dividing the sum of `min` and `max` by two. If there are currently an even number of viable candidates, and thus two "middle" values, this calculation discards the fractional remainder and picks the first of the two.

If the target element is not found, the value of `min` or `max` is modified to eliminate the appropriate half of the viable candidates. Then the search continues.

Comparing Searches

As far as the search algorithms go, there is no doubt that the binary search approach is far more efficient than the linear search. However, the binary search requires that the data be sorted. So once again, the algorithm to choose depends on the situation.

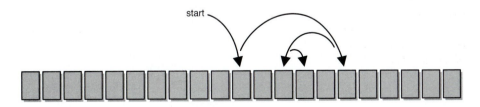

FIGURE 9.5 A binary search

If keeping the data sorted is relatively easy, or if there will be a lot of searching, then using a binary search will likely be more appropriate. On the other hand, a linear search is quite simple to implement and may be the best choice when long-term efficiency is not an issue. If you will never need the list in sorted order except for a one-time search, the cost of sorting first and then using the binary search will be much higher than just using a linear search.

9.6 DESIGNING FOR POLYMORPHISM

We've been evolving the concepts underlying good software design throughout this book. For every aspect of object-oriented software, we should make decisions, consciously and carefully, that lead to well-structured, flexible, and elegant code. We want to define appropriate classes and objects, with proper encapsulation. We want to define appropriate relationships among the classes and objects, including leveraging the powerful aspects of inheritance when possible. Now we can add polymorphism to our set of intellectual tools for thinking about software design.

> **Key Concept**
>
> Polymorphism allows us to apply a consistent approach to inconsistent behaviors.

Polymorphism provides a means to create elegant versatility in our software. It allows us to apply a consistent approach to inconsistent but related behaviors. We should try to find opportunities in our software systems that lend themselves to polymorphic solutions. We should seek them out, actively and deliberately, before we begin to write code.

Whenever you find situations in which different types of objects perform the same type of behavior, there is an opportunity for a polymorphic solution. The more experience you get, the easier it will be to detect such situations. See if you recognize the opportunity for polymorphism in the following situations:

> - Different types of vehicles move in different ways.
> - All business transactions for a company must be logged.
> - All products produced by a company must meet certain quality standards.
> - A hotel needs to plan their remodeling efforts for every room.
> - A casino wants to analyze the profit margin for its games.
> - A dispatcher must schedule moving vans and personnel based on the job size.
> - A drawing program allows the user to draw various shapes.

> **Key Concept**
>
> We should hone our design senses to identify situations that lend themselves to polymorphic solutions.

The common theme in these examples is that the same basic behavior applies to multiple objects, and those behaviors are accomplished differently depending on the specific type of object. Every circle is drawn using the same basic techniques and information, which is different from the information needed and the steps taken to draw a rectangle. Yet both types of shapes get drawn. Different, but similar. Polymorphic.

Once a polymorphic situation is identified, the specifics of the design can be addressed. In particular, should you use inheritance or interfaces as the mechanism to define polymorphic references? The answer to that question lies in the relationships among the different types of objects involved. If those objects can be related naturally by inheritance, with true is-a relationships, then polymorphism via inheritance is probably the way to go. But if the main thing the objects have in common is their need to be processed in a particular way, then perhaps using an interface to create the polymorphic references is the better solution.

9.7 SYSTEM SUPPLIED DIALOG BOXES

Dialog boxes were introduced in Chapter 5 with the `EvenOdd` example, in which we used the Form Designer to create a couple of dialog boxes and then to fetch the data from the dialog boxes (including the `DialogResult` return). Visual Studio also provides us with a set of standardized dialog boxes that we can quickly add to our project, thereby avoiding the necessity of writing our own. These dialog boxes are listed in Figure 9.6 and are also shown on Figure 8.7.

> **Key Concept**
>
> C# includes a variety of system dialog boxes for managing files, fonts, colors, and printing.

System Dialog Box Class	Use
OpenFileDialog	Select an existing file name or type a new file name. Optionally, it can ensure that an existing file is specified. Also supports specification of particular file extensions to display.
SaveFileDialog	Virtually the same as OpenFileDialog except that if you specify an existing file, it warns you and asks whether you want to overwrite the existing file.
FoldersDialog	Select a folder (not a file) or create a new folder.
ColorDialog	Select colors from the system set.
FontDialog	Select a font face, size, and formatting (bold, italic, underline).
PageSetupDialog	Set up page margins, paper size and source, and portrait or landscape mode. You can also access an abbreviated version of PrintDialog.
PrintDialog	Select the printer by name and specify number of copies. Set special features of the printer.

FIGURE 9.6 System dialog boxes

Figure 9.6 lists the system dialog box classes. Each of these classes is derived from `CommonDialog` and inherits all of their members and properties. Then, special properties and methods can be added to each class based on the particular specialization of the box.

The best way to learn how to use these dialog boxes is to open and experiment with the *SystemDialogs* example in Listing 9.13. This example allows you to display each of the system dialog boxes from Figure 9.6; a portion of the information from that dialog box is then presented on the screen. (Listing 9.13 does not include the Form Designer components.)

Listing 9.13

```
//****************************************************************
//  SystemDialogs.cs                C#:  Ken Culp
//
//  Displays the system dialog boxes derived from CommonDialog.
//****************************************************************
using System;
using System.Collections.Generic;
using System.ComponentModel;
using System.Data;
using System.Drawing;
using System.Text;
using System.Windows.Forms;

namespace SystemDialogs
{
  public partial class SystemDialogs : Form
  {
    public SystemDialogs()
    {
      InitializeComponent();
    }

    //-----------------------------------------------------------
    //  btnOpen: Demonstrates OpenFileDialog using image files
    //-----------------------------------------------------------
    private void btnOpen_Click(object sender, System.EventArgs e)
    {
      OpenFileDialog ofd = new OpenFileDialog();
      ofd.CheckFileExists = false;
      ofd.Filter = "All files (*.*)|*.*|Image Files" +
        "(*.BMP;*.JPG;*.GIF)|*.BMP;*.JPG;*.GIF";
      ofd.FilterIndex = 0;
      ofd.Title = "Open Image Type File";
      DialogResult result = ofd.ShowDialog();
      if (result != DialogResult.Cancel && ofd.FileName != "")
        lblFile.Text = "OpenFileDialog.FileName = " +
          ofd.FileName;
```

Listing 9.13   continued

```csharp
}

//------------------------------------------------------------
//  btnSave: Demonstrates SaveFileDialog
//------------------------------------------------------------
private void btnSave_Click(object sender, System.EventArgs e)
{
  // Difference between SaveFileDialog and OpenFileDialog is
  // that SaveFileDialog will prompt if the file exists and
  // ask if the file is to be replaced.
  SaveFileDialog sfd = new SaveFileDialog();
  sfd.Filter = "All files (*.*)|*.*";
  if (sfd.ShowDialog() != DialogResult.Cancel &&
      sfd.FileName != "")
    lblFile.Text = "SaveFileDialog.FileName = " + sfd.FileName;
}

//------------------------------------------------------------
//  btnFolders: Demonstrates FolderBrowserDialog
//------------------------------------------------------------
private void btnFolders_Click(object sender, System.EventArgs e)
{
  FolderBrowserDialog fbd = new FolderBrowserDialog();
  if (fbd.ShowDialog() != DialogResult.Cancel)
    lblFile.Text = "FileBrowserDialog.SelectedPath = " +
      fbd.SelectedPath;
}

//------------------------------------------------------------
//  btnColor: Demonstrates ColorDialog
//------------------------------------------------------------
private void btnColor_Click(object sender, System.EventArgs e)
{
  ColorDialog cdl = new ColorDialog();
  if (cdl.ShowDialog() != DialogResult.Cancel)
    lblFile.ForeColor = cdl.Color;
}

//------------------------------------------------------------
//  btnFont: Demonstrates FontDialog
//------------------------------------------------------------
private void btnFont_Click(object sender, System.EventArgs e)
{
  FontDialog fdl = new FontDialog();
  if (fdl.ShowDialog() != DialogResult.Cancel)
    lblFile.Font = fdl.Font;
}
```

Listing 9.13   continued

```csharp
//-------------------------------------------------------------
//  btnPage: Demonstrates PageSetupDialog
//-------------------------------------------------------------
private void btnPage_Click(object sender, System.EventArgs e)
{
  PageSetupDialog psd = new PageSetupDialog();
  psd.Document = new System.Drawing.Printing.PrintDocument();
  if (psd.ShowDialog() != DialogResult.Cancel)
    lblFile.Text = "Margins (1/100\"): " +
      "L=" + psd.PageSettings.Margins.Left +
      " R=" + psd.PageSettings.Margins.Right +
      " T=" + psd.PageSettings.Margins.Top +
      " B=" + psd.PageSettings.Margins.Bottom;
}


//-------------------------------------------------------------
//  btnPrinter: Demonstrates PrintDialog
//-------------------------------------------------------------
private void btnPrinter_Click(object sender, System.EventArgs e)
{
  PrintDialog pdl = new PrintDialog();
  pdl.Document = new System.Drawing.Printing.PrintDocument();
  if (pdl.ShowDialog() != DialogResult.Cancel)
    lblFile.Text = "PrintDialog.PrinterSettings.PrinterName = "
      + pdl.PrinterSettings.PrinterName;
}


//-------------------------------------------------------------
//  btnExit: Exit program
//-------------------------------------------------------------
private void btnExit_Click(object sender, System.EventArgs e)
{
  this.Close();
}
  }
}
```

Display

Open File Dialog Box (`OpenFileDialog`)

The `OpenFileDialog` class is used to open an existing file or to create a new file. It displays a directory listing similar to the one shown in Figure 9.7. One of the nice features is that it enables you to specify what file types will be included in the directory listing. File types are specified by file extensions and these are grouped into sets with a description and a list of files. The vertical bar (|) character is used to separate groups. Each group also consists of two parts: the description and the list of file extensions. The file extensions must be separated by semicolons.

Another item that can be set on the dialog box is the title on the dialog box as shown Figure 9.7. Also, you can specify a fully qualified path name as `FileName` before calling `ShowDialog`, and that directory will automatically be shown and that file highlighted.

The button clicked by the user is returned in `DialogResult` and the file selected by the user is returned in the property `FileName`. The user can also select a directory and just type a file name rather than select an existing file. Valid files can be checked by setting the `CheckPathExists` or `CheckFileExists` properties. Several other properties and members are also available (see the online help files).

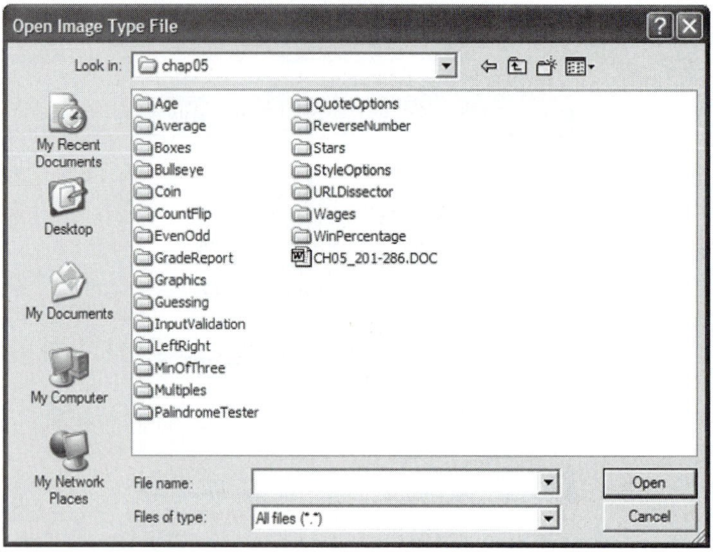

FIGURE 9.7   OpenFileDialog class display

Save File Dialog Box (`SaveFileDialog`)

The `SaveFileDialog` class is almost identical to the `OpenFileDialog` class. The main difference is that, with the `OpenFileDialog` class, if the user selects an existing file, a warning message is issued asking whether the user wants to overwrite the file.

Folder Browser Dialog Box (`FolderBrowserDialog`)

The `FolderBrowserDialog` class allows the user to select a path but not an individual file. The user can also create directories. The dialog box is shown in Figure 9.8. The selected folder path is returned in the `SelectedPath` property.

FIGURE 9.8   FolderBrowserDialog class display

Color Dialog Box (`ColorDialog`)

The `ColorDialog` class allows the user to select from basic colors and to select or create custom colors. The color selected is returned as the `Color` property. The Color dialog box is shown in Figure 9.9.

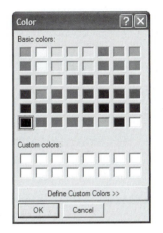

FIGURE 9.9   ColorDialog class display

Font Dialog Box (`FontDialog`)

The `FontDialog` class allows the user to select a font family, font size, and formatting (bold, italic, underline, etc.), as shown in the Font dialog box in Figure 9.10. The selected font is returned in the `Font` property.

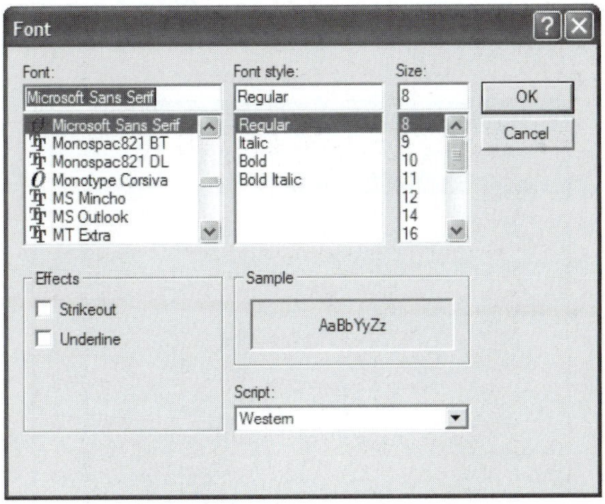

FIGURE 9.10   FontDialog class display

Page Setup Dialog Box (`PageSetupDialog`)

The `PageSetupDialog` class allows the user to select a paper size, a paper source, margins, and (by clicking the Printer button) the printer for a document. The Page Setup dialog box is shown in Figure 9.11. The settings are returned in the `PageSettings` property.

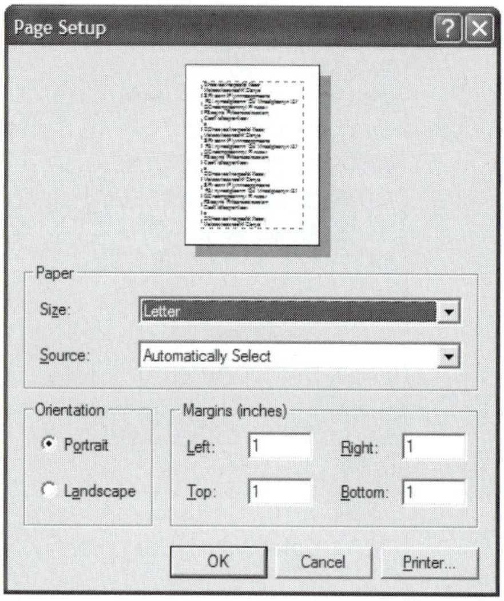

FIGURE 9.11   PageSetupDialog class display

Print Dialog Box (`PrintDialog`)

The `PrintDialog` class allows the user to select a printer and special settings for the printer, as shown in the Print dialog box in Figure 9.12. The settings are returned in the `PrinterSettings` property.

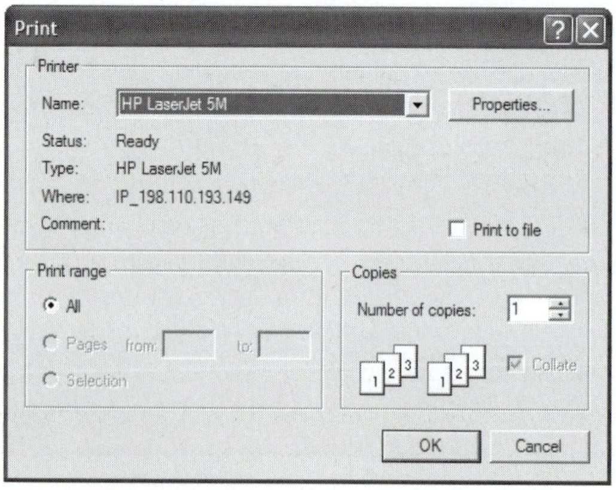

FIGURE 9.12   PrintDialog class display

9.8 SLIDERS AND UP-DOWN COUNTERS

A slider, called a `TrackBar` in C#, is a component that allows the user to specify a numeric value within a bounded range. A slider can be presented either vertically or horizontally, depending upon the setting of the `Orientation` property, and can have optional tick marks and labels indicating the range of values.

A program called `SlideColor` is shown in Listing 9.14. This program presents three sliders and three numeric up-down counters that control the RGB components of a color. The color specified by the values of the sliders is shown in a square that is displayed to the right of the sliders. As the user moves the `TrackBar` control, the color changes and the numeric value of the slider is shown in the `NumericUpDown` control to its right. Similarly, if the user clicks the up and down arrows on the numeric controls or types a value in the field, the color changes and the slider moves to the correct position.

To create the `SlideColor` application, first create a new Windows application from the New Project dialog box. Add a panel control to the right of the form, which will show the color that the user chooses. Leave its default name as `panel1` and set `BackColor` to Black (0,0,0). Add one slider control named `tbrRed` to the form, sizing it as shown in the sample output of Listing 9.14. Set `Minimum` to 0 and `Maximum` to 255 and set `TickFrequency` to 25. Set the `Tag` property to 0.

Next, right-click the control in the designer and click Copy. Right-click over a blank place on the form and then click Paste to copy the red control. Move the copied control to the proper location and call it `tbrGreen`. Set `Tag` to 1. Repeat for `tbrBlue` and set `Tag` to 2. By using this copy technique, it is not necessary to set the `Minimum`, `Maximum`, or `TickFrequency` values, because they were copied from `tbrRed`.

Add a `NumericUpDown` control called `nudRed` to the right of the red slider. Set `Font.Size` to 12, `Minimum` to 0, `Maximum` to 255, and `Tag` to 0. Copy this control to `nudGreen` with a `Tag` of 1 and to `nudBlue` with a `Tag` of 2. Run the application to make sure all the controls look okay. Note that at this point, the sliders move but nothing happens.

Before we add event handlers and the remaining code, let us turn our attention to the `Tag` property that we set for these controls. `Tag` is not used by C#. It is available for your programming convenience and may contain any kind of object. When we typed numbers in the designer, these values were created as strings. You can, if desired, open the Windows Form Designer code and change `Tag` to point to any *existing* object. We, however, can live with the string value because we will just convert it to integer.

We want to use only one event handler for the `TrackBar` control and one event handler for the `NumericUpDown` control. Therefore, we will use `Tag` to store an index so that we can tell in the event handler which control was changed. Although we could use **if** statements and examine the `sender` parameter to see which control caused the event, it is much easier just to grab the value in the `Tag` field off whichever control called the event handler.

In the event handler for the slider, we will update the value in the up/down control. Similarly, in the event handler for the up/down control, we will update the slider. This is potentially a dangerous situation and could cause an infinite loop: slider update up/down, which causes an event to the up/down, which updates the slider and causes an event for the slider, and so on. This turned out to not cause a problem, because when the up/down control is updated from the slider and the up/down control tries to go back and update the slider, the value being placed in the slider is the same as the previous contents and thus no `Scroll` event occurs.

To be absolutely safe, we bracketed the update function with a variable so that when one event handler is updating a value for the other control, it keeps that control from generating an event coming back. However, as previously noted, the program still works if you remove all lines that reference the `updateInProgress` variable.

In each handler, we will use the value in `Tag` as an index to an array of controls of the other type so that the values of the slider and the up/down control are always in sync. These arrays should be defined at the top of the class and initialized immediately after the `InitializeComponent` call in the class constructor.

The default event for the `TrackBar` control is the `Scroll` event, which occurs if the slider is moved. This is the event that we want to handle, so go to the properties/event window for tbrRed, type **TrackBarScroll** as the event handler name, and press the Enter key. Type the code shown in Listing 9.14. Next, select the `tbrGreen` event and add the same handler to it, and then do likewise to `tbrBlue`.

Similarly, select the `ValueChanged` event for nudRed, type **UpDownChanged**, press Enter, and type the code. Add this handler to the other two up/down controls.

Listing 9.14

```
//****************************************************************
//  SlideColor.cs          C#:  Ken Culp
//
//  Demonstrates TrackBar and NumericUpDown controls and how to
//  create colors from the Red/Green/Blue components
//****************************************************************
using System.Drawing;
using System.Windows.Forms;

namespace SlideColor
{
  public partial class SlideColor : Form
  {
    private bool updateInProgress = false;
    private TrackBar[] tbrBars;              // List of TrackBars
    private NumericUpDown[] nudBoxes;    // List of UpDown boxes

    public SlideColor()
    {
      InitializeComponent();
      TrackBar[] tbar = { tbrRed, tbrGreen, tbrBlue };
      tbrBars = tbar;
      NumericUpDown[] nudb = { nudRed, nudGreen, nudBlue };
```

Listing 9.14   continued

```
      nudBoxes = nudb;
    }
    private void TrackBarScroll(object sender, System.EventArgs e)
    {
      if (updateInProgress) return;
      updateInProgress = true;
      TrackBar tb = (TrackBar)sender;
      int index = int.Parse((string)tb.Tag);    // Which changed?
      nudBoxes[index].Value = tb.Value;
      updateInProgress = false;
    }

    private void UpDownChanged(object sender, System.EventArgs e)
    {
      panel1.BackColor =
        Color.FromArgb((int)nudRed.Value, (int)nudGreen.Value,
            (int)nudBlue.Value);
      if (updateInProgress) return;
      updateInProgress = true;
      NumericUpDown ud = (NumericUpDown)sender;
      int index = int.Parse((string)ud.Tag);    // Which changed?
      tbrBars[index].Value = (int)ud.Value;
      updateInProgress = false;
    }
  }
}
```

Output

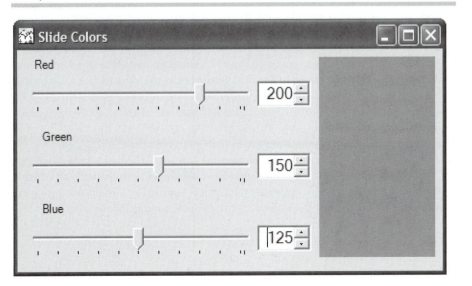

A slider is often a good choice when a large range of values is possible but strictly bounded on both ends. Compared to alternatives such as a text field, sliders convey more information to the user and eliminate input errors.

Numeric up/down controls are also useful when the user sometimes needs to type a specific value or wants to make only minor adjustments to the value.

9.9   SYSTEM REGISTRY OPERATIONS

Microsoft Windows operating systems include a service called the *Registry*. The Registry is a tree-structured database that is used as a repository for application configuration information and system setup data. For example, when you open an application after using it previously, the Registry remembers the settings (such as last edited file) from the last time that you used it.

Most applications on your computer use the Registry to store this class of information. It is used as a persistent database that lives on after the program is terminated and even after the computer is shut down. To keep one application from overwriting information of another application, the Registry database uses a tree structure that allows every application to keep its own information in separate branches of the tree.

At the top of the Registry key are seven predefined branches under which all Registry information must be kept, as shown in Figure 9.13.

Of these seven major branches, you probably use only the bottom two of them. The first, LocalMachine, is used to store information that is readable regardless of which user is logged on to the machine. You could run the program once as one user and then log on as a different user, and the values would still be available to the program. These tend to be system-wide values that need to be stored and include such things as the location of files on disk (which does not change with users).

The other branch that you likely use is CurrentUser. This stores values on a per-user basis. If multiple users are using one machine, you want a program to remember the last file edited by each user and not store one per user. Note that when you change users, the Registry branch CurrentUser points to the new user and returns that user's information. Information that had been stored in CurrentUser prior to changing users is still stored and will again be available when you change back. The name CurrentUser is used as a convenience to programs so that they do not have to figure out where in the Registry data for the current user is located.

As a final thought during this overview, note that CurrentUser and CurrentMachine yield the same result if only one user ever uses the machine. The data would be stored in different places in the Registry but the program would always fetch the same set of values.

Data is stored in the Registry in name/value pairs. A string key is given either a string or numeric value. Each branch in the Registry can contain multiple name/value pairs and/or contain more branches (thus the "tree" nomenclature). Thus, the Registry tree is very similar to the file system directory tree in that directories contain files and/or more directories.

Support for the Registry is provided by the `Win32` library. The first item we need in this library is the `RegistryKey` class. All of our operations require a key of this type. Also in the `Win32` library is the `Registry` class that defines seven keys corresponding to the major branches of the tree (refer to Figure 9.13). To access data in the Registry, we define an object of the `RegistryKey` class and set it equal to one of the branches.

From this point, we use `CreateSubKey` to create a new "subkey" that points to the final branch in the tree where the desired application data is stored. This subkey to the Registry corresponds building a path name to your files are stored are stored on a directory. Once we have this key, we use the methods `GetValue` and `SetValue` to fetch and save name/value pairs.

To illustrate use of the Registry to store information, let's modify the `SlideColor` application to save the color chosen the last time the program was run. To do this, we add two event handlers and a class variable in the form to hold the key to our branch in the tree. The first event is the `Load` event, where we create the key and fetch the previous values (if any). The second event is the `Closed` event that occurs once the form has been closed. In the `Closed` handler, we use the key created in the `Load` event and store the data. In the interest of space, we will review only the modifications made to `SlideColor`. The first is the top of the class file:

```
public class SlideColor : System.Windows.Forms.Form
{
  Microsoft.Win32.RegistryKey rk;  // Define Key type
    . . .
```

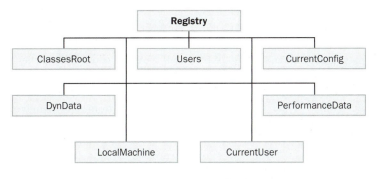

FIGURE 9.13 Registry information.

Now let's take a quick look at the two new event handlers:

```
private void SlideColor_Load(object sender, System.EventArgs e)
{
    // Fetch last used color from the Registry.
    // Use local machine so values persist across users.

    // Create a key to our data
    rk = Microsoft.Win32.Registry.LocalMachine;
    rk = rk.CreateSubKey(@"Software\CSharpText\SlideColor");
    // Fetch stored values
    nudRed.Value =   int.Parse( (string) rk.GetValue("Red",
                     "0"));
    nudGreen.Value = int.Parse( (string) rk.GetValue("Green",
                     "0"));
    nudBlue.Value =  int.Parse( (string) rk.GetValue("Blue",
                     "0"));
}
private void SlideColor_Closed(object sender,
                               System.EventArgs e)
{
    // Save values in the registry
    rk.SetValue("Red",   nudRed.Value);
    rk.SetValue("Green", nudGreen.Value);
    rk.SetValue("Blue",  nudBlue.Value);
}
```

The first executable line of the Load event (rk = Microsoft.Win32.Registry .LocalMachine;) creates a key that points to the main LocalMachine branch. The next line creates and accesses the branch of our data using the CreateSubKey method. Note that a string resembling a path is passed to this method. This method call updates the key in rk to point to the branch containing our data.

This path is relative to the current value in the key or the local machine branch. Also, if the path already exists, no error is obtained and only the key is updated. The first branch of the path passed to CreateSubKey is the word Software; other branches exist, but Software is the branch you should choose for software-related programs.

Continuing down the path, we find a branch designating a major heading. This is usually a manufacturer's name or a major software system from the manufacturer (like Microsoft). In our case, it represents all Registry data related to this book. The last branch of our path is the name of the application. However, for some vendors, there may be several more levels in the tree before you actually get to the last branch. For example, the following is the path to Microsoft Word version 10.0 machine level data:

```
HKEY_LOCAL_MACHINE\Software\Microsoft\Office\10.0\Word
```

The Registry path we have chosen for our `SlideColor` application is as follows:

`HKEY_LOCAL_MACHINE\Software\CSharpText\SlideColor`

Note that the actual path does not show precisely the words `LocalMachine` or `CurrentUser`, which we use with the `Win32` library. Instead, you see `HKEY_LOCAL_MACHINE`. The `HKEY` notation is how the various branches look in the tree, but the `Win32` library exposes those branches using a simpler notation.

These first two lines of the `Load` event create the key to our application data. Then the `Load` event has to retrieve the values. The `GetValue` method is passed the name part of the name/value pair and returns the value. The complexity arises from the fact that the `GetValue` method returns an `Object` and what gets stored by `SetValue` is a `String`. However, we want an integer. So, first we have to typecast the returned object value to a string and then parse it into an integer, which explains the syntax for the last three lines of the `Load` event.

Also note that the `GetValue` method takes two parameters. The first is the key name and the second is the default value that will be returned if the key does not exist in the database. By setting this default to `"0"`, we force the color to be black the first time the program is run.

The `Closed` event handler is much easier to code because it uses the Registry key created in the `Load` event (the instance variable `rk`). All we have to do is call `SetValue` with the name and the value as shown.

Once we have saved values with `SetValue`, we can see those values and others through a library program called Registry Editor (RegEdit for short). RegEdit is considered to be a very dangerous program to use because you can inadvertently mess up your system to the point that it will not boot. However, when all you do is examine values, it can prove useful. We do not have the space to describe its use but Figure 9.14 displays a sample of the screen showing our color values. We expanded each branch until we arrived at `SlideColor` and then double-clicked Blue in the right window. This displayed our value of 255 (which could be edited, but don't).

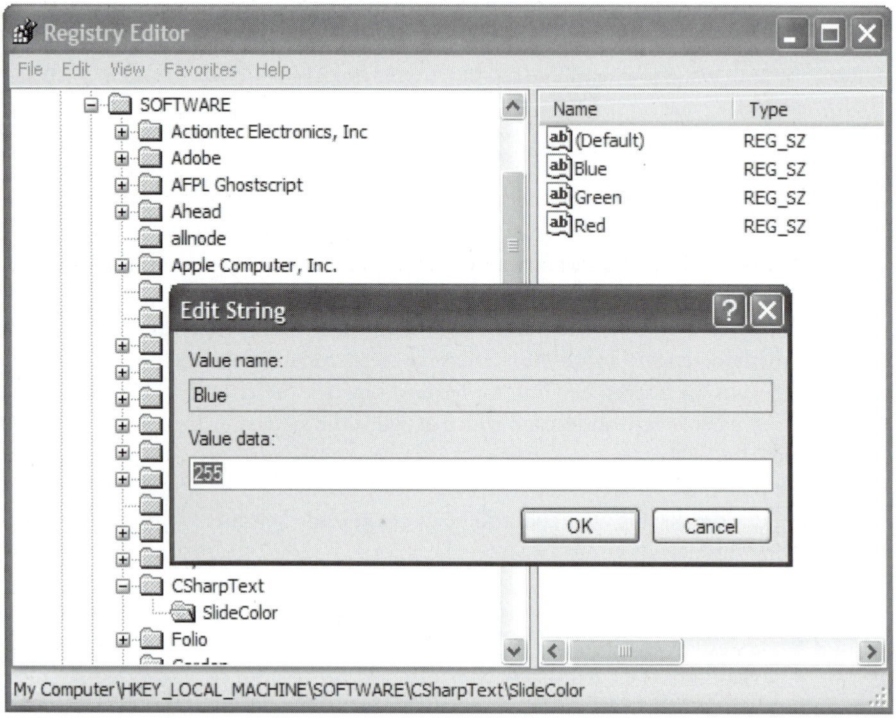

FIGURE 9.14 RegEdit sample screen

Summary of Key Concepts

> A polymorphic reference can refer to different types of objects over time.

> The binding of a method invocation to its definition is performed at run time for a polymorphic reference.

> A reference variable can refer to any object created from any class related to it by inheritance.

> The type of the object, not the type of the reference, is used to determine which version of a method to invoke.

> An interface name can be used to declare an object reference variable.

> An interface reference can refer to any object of any class that implements that interface.

> A parameter to a method can be polymorphic, giving the method flexible control of its arguments.

> Implementing a sort algorithm polymorphically allows it to sort any comparable set of objects.

> Polymorphism allows us to apply a consistent approach to inconsistent behaviors.

> We should hone our design senses to identify situations that lend themselves to polymorphic solutions.

> C# includes a variety of system dialog boxes for managing files, fonts, colors, and printing.

> Sliders and up/down controls allow the user to specify a numeric value within a bounded range.

> The system Registry stores application configuration information in a tree-structured database.

Self-Review Questions

9.1   Which is better: selection sort or insertion sort? Explain.

9.2   What is polymorphism?

9.3   How does inheritance support polymorphism?

9.4   How is overriding related to polymorphism?

9.5   How can polymorphism be accomplished using interfaces?

9.6   What is the `FontDialog` class used for?

9.7   Why is a slider a better choice than a text field in some cases?

Exercises

9.1   Draw and annotate a class hierarchy that represents various types of faculty at a university. Show what characteristics would be represented in the various classes of the hierarchy. Explain how polymorphism could play a role in the process of assigning courses to each faculty member.

9.2   What would happen if the Pay method were not defined as an abstract method in the StaffMember class of the Firm program?

9.3   Draw the containment hierarchy tree for the SlideColors program.

Programming Projects

9.1   Rewrite the Sorting class so that both sorting algorithms put the values in descending order. Create a driver class with a Main method to exercise the modifications.

9.2   Modify the Tunes program from Chapter 7 so that it keeps the CDs sorted by title.

9.3   Design and implement a program that graphically displays the processing of a selection sort. Use bars of various heights to represent the values being sorted. Display the set of bars after each swap. Put a delay in the processing of the sort to give the human observer a chance to see how the order of the values changes.

9.4   Repeat Programming Project 9.3 using an insertion sort.

9.5   Design and implement a program that combines the functionality of the StyleOptions and QuoteOptions programs from Chapter 5. That is, the new program should present the appropriate quote (using radio buttons) whose style can be changed (using check boxes). Also include a slider that regulates the size of the quotation font. Design the containment hierarchy carefully and create a nice interface.

9.6   Design and implement an application that draws the graph of the equation $ax^2 + bx + c$, where the values of a, b, and c are set using three sliders.

Answers to Self-Review Questions

9.1   Selection sort and insertion sort are generally equivalent in efficiency, because they both take about n^2 number of comparisons to sort a list of n numbers. Selection sort, though, generally makes fewer swaps. Several sorting algorithms are more efficient than either of these.

9.2   Polymorphism is the ability of a reference variable to refer to objects of various types at different times. A method invoked through such a reference is bound to different method definitions at different times, depending on the type of the object referenced.

9.3   In C#, a reference variable declared using a parent class can be used to refer to an object of the child class. If both classes contain a method with the same signature, the parent reference can be polymorphic.

9.4   When a child class overrides the definition of a parent's method, two versions of that method exist. If a polymorphic reference is used to invoke the method, the version of the method that is invoked is determined by the type of the object being referred to, not by the type of the reference variable.

9.5   An interface name can be used as the type of a reference. Such a reference variable can refer to any object of any class that implements that interface. Because all classes implement the same interface, they have methods with common signatures, which can be dynamically bound.

9.6   The `FontDialog` class allows the user to specify a font family, a font size, and the font characteristics like bold, underline, etc.

9.7   If in a specific situation user input should be a numeric value from a bounded range, a slider is probably a better choice than a text field. A slider prevents an improper value from being entered and conveys the valid range to the user.

Exceptions

CHAPTER OBJECTIVES

> Discuss the purpose of exceptions.

> Examine exception messages and the call stack trace.

> Examine the `try-catch` statement for handling exceptions.

> Explore the concept of exception propagation.

> Describe the exception class hierarchy in the C# standard class library.

> Explore I/O exceptions and the ability to write text files.

> Create GUIs using mnemonics and tool tips.

> Explore additional GUI components and containers.

Exception handling is an important part of an object-oriented software system. Exceptions represent problems or unusual situations that may occur in a program. C# provides various ways to handle exceptions when they occur. We explore the class hierarchy from the C# standard library used to define exceptions, as well as the ability to define our own exception objects. This chapter also discusses the use of exceptions when dealing with input and output, and examines an example that writes a text file. The Windows Track sections of this chapter explore some special features of Visual Studio components, as well as a few additional components and containers.

10.1 EXCEPTION HANDLING

As we've discussed briefly in other parts of the text, problems that arise in a C# program may generate exceptions or errors. An *exception* is an object that defines an unusual or erroneous situation. An exception is thrown by a program or the run-time environment and can be caught and handled appropriately if desired. An *error* is similar to an exception except that an error generally represents an unrecoverable situation and should not be caught. C# has a predefined set of exceptions and errors that may occur during the execution of a program.

Key Concept

Errors and exceptions are objects that represent unusual or invalid processing.

Problem situations represented by exceptions and errors can have various kinds of root causes. Here are some examples of situations that cause exceptions to be thrown:

> an attempt to divide by zero

> an array index that is out of bounds

> accessing a file that could not be found

> a requested I/O operation that could not be completed normally

> an attempt to use a null reference

> an attempt to execute an operation that violates some kind of security measure

These are just a few examples. There are dozens of others that address very specific situations.

As many of these examples show, an exception can represent a truly erroneous situation. But as the name implies, an exception may simply represent an exceptional situation. That is, an exception may represent a situation that won't occur under usual conditions. Exception handling is set up to be an efficient way to deal with such situations, especially given that they don't happen too often.

We have several options when it comes to dealing with exceptions. A program can be designed to process an exception in one of three ways:

> not handle the exception at all

> handle the exception where it occurs

> handle the exception at another point in the program

We explore each of these approaches in the following sections.

10.2 UNCAUGHT EXCEPTIONS

If a program does not handle the exception at all, it will terminate abnormally and produce a message that describes what exception occurred and where it was produced. The information associated with an exception is often helpful in tracking down the cause of a problem.

Let's look at the output of an exception. The program shown in Listing 10.1 throws an `ArithmeticException` when an invalid arithmetic operation is attempted. In this case, the program attempts to divide by zero.

Because there is no code in this program to handle the exception explicitly, the program must be terminated. The cause of the error will be displayed in one of two ways depending upon how you ran the program. If you ran the program from Visual Studio using the debugger (F5 key), you receive a dialog box that allows you to pause the program (click Break) or let it continue (click Continue). Allowing the program to continue terminates the program after the statement that caused the error. Therefore, the last `WriteLine` statement in the program never executes, because the exception occurs first.

Debugging note: Clicking Break allows you to examine the contents of program variables by moving the cursor over the variable or the Watch or Locals window. However, you cannot change the current position or step through the program after the error. Any attempt to step from the break terminates the program.

Listing 10.1

```csharp
//****************************************************************
//   Zero.cs          C#:   Ken Culp
//
//   Demonstrates an uncaught exception.
//****************************************************************
using System;

namespace Zero
{
  public class Zero
  {
    //-------------------------------------------------------------
    //  Deliberately divides by zero to produce an exception.
    //-------------------------------------------------------------
    public static void Main(string[] args)
    {
      int numerator = 10;
      int denominator = 0;

      Console.Out.WriteLine(numerator / denominator);

      Console.Out.WriteLine("This text will not be printed.");

      Console.In.ReadLine();   // Wait for enter key
    }
  }
}
```

Listing 10.1   continued

Output

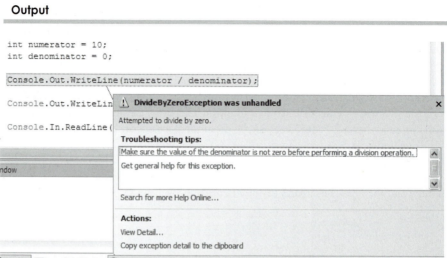

```
int numerator = 10;
int denominator = 0;

Console.Out.WriteLine(numerator / denominator);
```

The preceding dialog box describes and points to the cause of the error, and the yellow cursor will be on the offending line of code in Visual Studio. The first line of the exception output indicates which exception was thrown and provides some information about why it was thrown. The additional information may also prove useful.

If the program was run from the command prompt, you will receive a text message similar to the following:

```
Unhandled Exception: System.DivideByZeroException:
    Attempted to divide by zero.
  at Zero.Zero.Main(String[] args) in
    e:\samples\chap10\zero\zero.cs:line 21
```

This message identifies the class name of the exception, describes the cause, and then gives the location of the error, down to the line number. If there had been a series of methods, one calling the other, a trace back would have been shown indicating who called whom and at what line numbers. This stack trace is also available in Visual Studio when the program is run with the debugger. Select the Call Trace window or request the Call Trace window by typing >Debug.CallStack in the immediate window.

All of the preceding information and more is available through the properties of the exception that is shown. We examine the exception object in the next section.

10.3 THE try-catch STATEMENT

Let's now examine how we catch and handle an exception when it is thrown. The *try-catch statement* identifies a block of statements that may throw an exception. A *catch clause*, which follows a **try** block, defines how a particular kind of exception is handled. A **try** block can have several **catch** clauses associated with it. Each **catch** clause is called an *exception handler.*

When a **try** statement is executed, the statements in the **try** block are executed. If no exception is thrown during the execution of the **try** block, processing continues with the statement following the **try** statement (after all of the **catch** clauses). This situation is the normal execution flow and should occur most of the time.

Key Concept

Each **catch** clause handles a particular kind of exception that may be thrown within the **try** block.

If an exception is thrown at any point during the execution of the **try** block, control is immediately transferred to the appropriate catch handler if it is present. That is, control transfers to the first **catch** clause whose exception class corresponds to the

Try STATEMENT

Try Statement

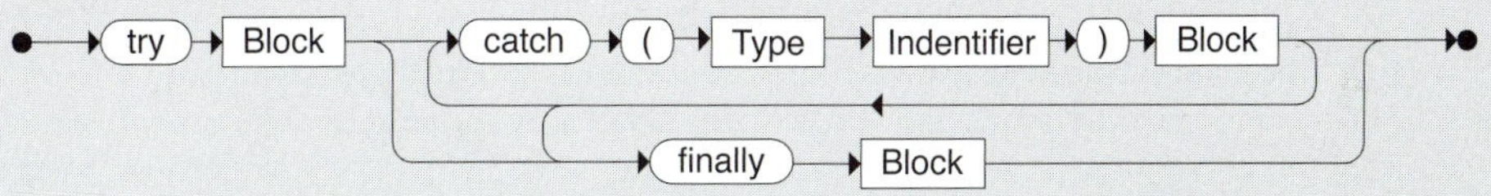

A **try** statement contains a block of code followed by one or more **catch** clauses. If an exception occurs in the **try** block, the code of the corresponding **catch** clause is executed. The **finally** clause, if present, is executed no matter how the **try** block is exited.

Example:

```
try
{
   Console.Out.WriteLine(int.parseInt(numString));
}
catch (NumberFormatException exception)
{
   Console.Out.WriteLine("Caught an exception.");
}
finally
{
   Console.Out.WriteLine("Done.");
}
```

class of the exception that was thrown. After executing the statements in the **catch** clause, control transfers to the statement after the entire **try-catch** statement.

Let's look at an example. Suppose a hypothetical company uses codes to represent its various products. A product code includes, among other information, a character in the tenth position that represents the zone from which that product was made, and a four-digit integer in positions 4 through 7 that represents the district in which it will be sold. Due to some reorganization, products from zone R are banned from being sold in districts with a designation of 2000 or higher. The program shown in Listing 10.2 reads product codes from the user and counts the number of banned codes entered.

The programming statements in the **try** block attempt to pull out the zone and district information, and then determine whether it represents a banned product code. If there is any problem extracting the zone and district information, the product code is considered to be invalid and is not processed further. For example, an IndexOutOfRangeException could be thrown by the Substring methods. Furthermore, a FormatException could be thrown by the Parse method if the Substring does not contain a valid integer. A particular message is printed depending on which exception is thrown. In either case, since the exception is caught and handled, processing continues normally.

Listing 10.2

```csharp
//**********************************************************
//   ProductCodes.cs        C#:   Ken Culp
//
//   Demonstrates the use of a try-catch block and handling
//   multiple exceptions from the same try-catch block.
//**********************************************************
using System;

namespace ProductCodes
{
  public class ProductCodes
  {
    //-------------------------------------------------------------
    //  Counts the number of product codes that are entered with
    //  a zone of R and and district greater than 2000.
    //-------------------------------------------------------------
    public static void Main(string[] args)
    {
      string code;
      char zone;
      int district, valid = 0, banned = 0;


      Console.Out.Write("Enter product code (XXX to quit): ");
      code = Console.In.ReadLine();
```

Listing 10.2   continued

```
      while (code != "XXX")
      {
        try
        {
          zone = code[9];
          district = int.Parse(code.Substring(3, 4));
          valid++;
          if (zone == 'R' && district > 2000)
            banned++;
        }
        catch (IndexOutOfRangeException exception)
        {
          Console.Out.WriteLine("Improper code length: " +
            code);
        }
        catch (FormatException exception)
        {
          Console.Out.WriteLine("District is not numeric: " +
            code);
        }

        Console.Out.Write("Enter product code (XXX to quit): ");
        code = Console.In.ReadLine();
      }

      Console.Out.WriteLine("# of valid codes entered: " +
        valid);
      Console.Out.WriteLine("# of banned codes entered: " +
        banned);

      Console.In.ReadLine();  // Wait for enter key
    }
  }
}
```

Output

```
Enter product code (XXX to quit): TRV2475A5R-14
Enter product code (XXX to quit): TRD1704A7R-12
Enter product code (XXX to quit): TRL2k74A5R-11
District is not numeric: TRL2k74A5R-11
Enter product code (XXX to quit): TRQ2949A6M-04
Enter product code (XXX to quit): TRV2105A2
Improper code length: TRV2105A2
Enter product code (XXX to quit): TRQ2778A7R-19
Enter product code (XXX to quit): XXX
# of valid codes entered: 4
# of banned codes entered: 2
```

Note that, for each code examined, the integer `valid` is incremented only if no exception is thrown. If an exception is thrown, control transfers immediately to the appropriate `catch` clause. Likewise, the zone and district are tested by the `if` statement only if no exception is thrown.

The `finally` Clause

A `try-catch` statement can have an optional *finally clause*. The `finally` clause defines a section of code that is executed no matter how the `try` block is exited. Most often, a `finally` clause is used to manage resources or to guarantee that particular parts of an algorithm are executed.

If no exception is generated, the statements in the `finally` clause are executed after the `try` block is complete. If an exception is generated in the `try` block, control first transfers to the appropriate `catch` clause. After executing the exception-handling code, control transfers to the `finally` clause and its statements are executed. A `finally` clause, if present, must be listed following the `catch` clauses.

Note that a `try` block does not need to have a `catch` clause, but in such a case would require a `finally` clause . If there are no `catch` clauses, a `finally` clause must be used or a compiler error will be issued.

10.4   EXCEPTION PROPAGATION

If an exception is not caught and handled where it occurs, control is immediately returned to the method that invoked the method that produced the exception. We can design our software so that the exception is caught and handled at this outer level. If it isn't caught there, control returns to the method that called it. This process is called *propagating the exception*. This propagation continues until the exception is caught and handled or until it is passed out of the `Main` method, which terminates the program and produces an exception message. To catch an exception at an outer level, the method that produces the exception must be invoked inside a `try` block that has `catch` clauses to handle it.

The `Propagation` program shown in Listing 10.3 succinctly demonstrates the process of exception propagation. The `Main` method invokes method `Level1` in the `ExceptionScope` class (see Listing 10.4), which invokes `Level2`, which invokes `Level3`, which produces an exception. Method `Level3` does not catch and handle the exception, so control is transferred back to `Level2`. The `Level2` method does not catch and handle the exception either, so control is transferred back to `Level1`. Because the invocation of `Level2` is made inside a `try` block (in method `Level1`), the exception is caught and handled at that point.

Note that the output does not include the messages indicating that the methods `Level3` and `Level2` are ending. These `WriteLine` statements are never executed, because an exception occurred and has not yet been caught.

However, after method `Level1` handles the exception, processing continues normally from that point, printing the messages indicating that method `Level1` and the program are ending.

Note also that the **catch** clause that handles the exception uses the `Message` property and `StackTrace` property to output that information. The stack trace shows the methods that were called when the exception occurred. The sample output for Listing 10.3 was reformatted for easier reading.

Listing 10.3

```
//*************************************************************
//  Propagation.cs        C#:  Ken Culp
//
//  Demonstrates exception propagation.
//*************************************************************
using System;

namespace Propagation
{

  public class Propagation
  {
    //------------------------------------------------------------
    //  Invokes level1 method to begin the exception demonstation
    //------------------------------------------------------------
    static public void Main(string[] args)
    {
      ExceptionScope demo = new ExceptionScope();

      Console.Out.WriteLine("Program beginning.");
      demo.Level1();
      Console.Out.WriteLine("Program ending.");

      Console.In.ReadLine();   // Wait for enter key
    }
  }
}
```

Output

```
Program beginning.
Level 1 beginning.
Level 2 beginning.
Level 3 beginning.

The exception message is: Attempted to divide by zero.
```

Listing 10.3   continued

```
The call stack trace:
    at Propagation.ExceptionScope.Level3()
      in d:\text\chap10\propagation\exceptionscope.cs:line 57
    at Propagation.ExceptionScope.Level2()
      in d:\text\chap10\propagation\exceptionscope.cs:line 44
    at Propagation.ExceptionScope.Level1()
      in d:\text\chap10\propagation\exceptionscope.cs:line 22
Level 1 ending.
Program ending.
```

Listing 10.4

```csharp
//*************************************************************
//  ExceptionScope.cs          C#:  Ken Culp
//
//  Demonstrates exception propagation.
//*************************************************************
using System;

namespace Propagation
{
  public class ExceptionScope
  {
    //-----------------------------------------------------------
    //  Catches & handles the exception that is thrown in Level3.
    //-----------------------------------------------------------
    public void Level1()
    {
      Console.Out.WriteLine("Level 1 beginning.");

      try
      {
        Level2();
      }
      catch (DivideByZeroException problem)
      {
        Console.Out.WriteLine();
        Console.Out.WriteLine("The exception message is: " +
          problem.Message);
        Console.Out.WriteLine();
        Console.Out.WriteLine("The call stack trace:" +
          problem.StackTrace);
        Console.Out.WriteLine();
      }
```

Listing 10.4   continued

```
      Console.Out.WriteLine("Level 1 ending.");
   }

   //-----------------------------------------------------------
   //  Serves as an intermediate level. The exception propagates
   //  through this method back to Level1.
   //-----------------------------------------------------------
   public void Level2()
   {
      Console.Out.WriteLine("Level 2 beginning.");
      Level3();
      Console.Out.WriteLine("Level 2 ending.");
   }

   //-----------------------------------------------------------
   //  Performs a calculation to produce an exception. It is not
   //  caught and handled at this level.
   //-----------------------------------------------------------
   public void Level3()
   {
      int numerator = 10, denominator = 0;

      Console.Out.WriteLine("Level 3 beginning.");
      int result = numerator / denominator;
      Console.Out.WriteLine("Level 3 ending.");
   }
  }
}
```

A programmer must pick the most appropriate level at which to catch and handle an exception. There is no single best answer as to how to do this. It depends on the situation and the design of the system. Sometimes the right approach will be not to catch an exception at all and let the program terminate.

10.5   THE EXCEPTION CLASS HIERARCHY

The classes that define various exceptions are related by inheritance, creating a class hierarchy that is shown in part in Figure 10.1. This information was extracted from Table 1 of the article "Introduction to Exception Handling in Visual Basic .NET," by Cat Francis of the Microsoft Visual Studio Team.

The Exception class is defined in the System namespace and is the parent to all the other Exception classes. Many types of exceptions are derived from the Exception class, and these classes also have many children.

Exception Class	Thrown when	Derived Classes
ArgumentException	One or more of the arguments provided to a method is not valid	ArgumentNullException ArgumentOutOfRangeException ComponentModel.InvalidEnum ArgumentException DuplicateWaitObjectException
ArithmeticException	Errors occur in an arithmetic, casting, or conversion operation	DivideByZeroException NotFiniteNumberException OverflowException
ArrayTypeMismatchException	Attempt made to store an element of the wrong type within an array	None
BadImageFormatException	File image of a DLL or executable program is invalid	None
Configuration. ConfigurationException	An error occurs in a configuration setting	None
Configuration. Install.InstallException	An error occurs during the commit, rollback, or uninstall phase of an installation	None
ContextMarshalException	Attempt to marshal an object across a context boundary fails	None
Drawing. Printing.InvalidPrinterException	Attempt made to access a printer using invaild printer settings	None
FormatException	The format of an argument does not meet the parameter specifications of the invoked method	Net.CookieException Reflection.CustomAttribute FormatException UriFormatException
IndexOutofRangeException	Attempt made to access an element of an array with an index that is outside the bounds of the array	None
InvalidCastException	Invalid casting or explicit conversion	None
IO.InternalBufferOverflowException	The internal buffer overflows	None

FIGURE 10.1   Part of the Error and Exception class hierarchy (*continues*)

Exception Class	Thrown when	Derived Classes

`IO.IOException`	An I/O error occurs	`IO.DirectoryNotFoundException`
		`IO.EndOfStreamException`
		`IO.FileLoadException`
		`IO.FileNotFoundException`
		`IO.PathTooLongException`

`NullReferenceException`	Attempt to dereference a null object reference	None
`OutOfMemoryException`	Not enough memory to complete the execution of a program	None
`RankException`	Array with the wrong number of dimensions is passed to a method	None
`Resources.MissingManifest` `ResourceException`	Main assembly does not contain the resources for the neutral culture, but they are required because of a missing appropriate satellite assembly	None
`Runtime.` `  Serialization.SerializationException`	An error occurs during serialization or deserialization	None
`StackOverflowException`	Overflow of the execution stack due to too many pending method calls	None
`Threading.` `  SynchronizationLockException`	A synchronized method is invoked from an unsynchronized block of code	None
`Threading.ThreadAbortException`	Call made to the `Abort` method	None
`Threading.ThreadInterruptedException`	Thread interrupted while in a `WaitSleepJoin` state	None
`Threading.ThreadStateException`	Thread in an invalid `ThreadState` for the method call	None

FIGURE 10.1 (continued)   Part of the Error and Exception class hierarchy

We can define our own exceptions by deriving a new class from `Exception` or one of its descendants. The class we choose as the parent depends on what situation or condition the new exception represents.

The program in Listing 10.5 instantiates an exception object and throws it. The exception is created from the `OutOfRangeException` class, which is shown in Listing 10.6.

Note that this exception is not part of the C# standard class library. It was created to represent the situation in which a value is outside a particular valid range.

After reading in an input value, the `Main` method evaluates it to see whether it is in the valid range. If it is not, the *throw statement* is executed. A **throw** statement is used to begin exception propagation. Because the `Main` method does not catch and handle the exception, the program will terminate if the exception is thrown, printing the message associated with the exception.

We create the `OutOfRangeException` class by extending the `Exception` class. Often, a new exception is nothing more than what you see in this example: an extension of some existing exception class that stores a particular message describing the situation it represents. The important point is that the class is ultimately a descendant of the `Exception` class, which gives it the ability to be thrown using a **throw** statement.

Listing 10.5

```csharp
//****************************************************************
//   CreatingExceptions.cs        C#:   Ken Culp
//
//   Demonstrates ability to define an exception via inheritance.
//****************************************************************
using System;
using CS1;

namespace CreatingExceptions
{
  public class CreatingExceptions
  {
    //-------------------------------------------------------------
    //   Creates an exception object and possibly throws it.
    //-------------------------------------------------------------
    public static void Main(string[] args)
    {
      const int MIN = 25, MAX = 40;

      Console.Out.Write("Enter an integer value between " + MIN +
        " and " + MAX + ", inclusive: ");
      int value = Keyboard.readInt();

      //   Determines if the exception should be thrown
      if (value < MIN || value > MAX)
      {
```

Listing 10.5   continued

```
        OutOfRangeException problem =
          new OutOfRangeException("Input value is out of range.");
        throw problem;
      }
      Console.Out.WriteLine("End of main method.");   // never here
      Console.In.ReadLine();
    }
  }
}
```

Output

```
Enter an integer value between 25 and 40, inclusive: 69

Unhandled Exception:
  CreatingExceptions.OutOfRangeException: Input value is out of
      range.
  at CreatingExceptions.CreatingExceptions.Main(String[] args)
  in d:\text\chap10\creatingexceptions\creatingexceptions.cs:
      line 30
    d:\WpDocs\text\chap10\CreatingExceptions\bin\Debug>
```

Listing 10.6

```
//**************************************************************
//  OutOfRangeException.cs        C#:  Ken Culp
//
//  Represents an exceptional condition in which a value is
//  out of some particular range.
//**************************************************************
using System;

namespace CreatingExceptions
{
  public class OutOfRangeException : Exception
  {
    //-----------------------------------------------------------
    //  Sets up the exception object with a particular message.
    //-----------------------------------------------------------
    public OutOfRangeException(string message)
      : base(message)
    {
      // Everything done by Base Class
    }
  }
}
```

The type of situation handled by this program, in which a value is out of range, does not need to be represented as an exception. We've previously handled such situations using conditionals or loops. Whether you handle a situation using an exception or whether you take care of it in the normal flow of your program is an important design decision.

Figure 10.2 lists some of the properties and methods of the `Exception` class. Exceptions are derived from this class and inherit all of these members.

10.6 I/O EXCEPTIONS

Processing input and output is a task that often produces unforeseeable situations, leading to exceptions being thrown. Let's explore some I/O issues and the problems that may arise.

A *stream* is an ordered sequence of bytes. The term stream comes from the analogy that as we read and write information, the data flows from a source to a destination (or *sink*) as water flows down a stream. The source of the information is like a spring filling the stream, and the destination is like a cave into which the stream flows.

> **Key Concept**
>
> A stream is a sequence of bytes; it can be used as a source of input or a destination for output.

In a program, we treat a stream as either an *input stream,* from which we read information, or as an *output stream,* to which we write information. That is, a program serves either as the spring filling the stream or as the cave receiving the stream. A program can deal with multiple input and output streams at one time. A particular store of data, such as a file, can serve either as an input stream or as an output stream to a program, but it generally cannot be both at the same time.

There are three streams that are referred to as the *standard I/O streams.* They are listed in Figure 10.3. The `System` class contains three object reference variables (`in`, `out`, and `err`) that represent the three standard I/O streams. These references are declared as both public and static, which allows them to be accessed directly through the `System` class.

We've been using the standard output stream, with calls to `Console.Out.WriteLine` for instance, in examples throughout this book. We've also used the standard input stream to read interactively from the user.

> **Key Concept**
>
> Three public reference variables in the `System` class represent the standard I/O streams.

The standard I/O streams, by default, represent particular I/O devices. `Console.In` typically represents keyboard input, whereas `Console.Out` and `Console.Error` typically represent a particular window on the monitor screen. The `Console.Out` and `Console.Error` streams write output to the same window by default (usually the one in which the program was executed), though they could be set up to write to different places. The `Console.Error` stream is usually where error messages are sent.

In addition to the standard input streams, the `System.IO` package of the C# class library provides many classes that let us define streams with particular characteristics. Some of the classes deal with files, others with memory, and others with strings. Some classes assume that the data they handle consists of characters, whereas others assume the data consists of raw bytes of binary information. Some classes provide the means to manipulate the data in the stream in some way, such as buffering the information or numbering it. By combining

Public Constructors	

`public Exception();`
`public Exception(string);`
`public Exception(string,`
`    Exception);`
	Creates a new instance of the `Exception` class with an optional string message and an optional inner exception.

Public Properties	
`HelpLink`	Used to link to a help file.
`InnerException`	Returns the `Exception` that caused the current exception.
`Message`	Gets a string message that describes the current exception.
`Source`	Gets or sets the name of the application or the object that causes the error.
`StackTrace`	Gets a string representation of the stack frame when the exception was thrown.
`TargetSite`	Gets the method that throws the current exception.

Public Methods	
`public virtual Exception` `    GetBaseException();`	When overridden in a derived class, this returns the `Exception` that is the root cause of one or more subsequent exceptions.
`ToString()`	Creates and returns a string representation of the current exception, including much of the other available information.

FIGURE 10.2   Exception class members

Standard I/O Stream	Description
`Console.In`	Standard input stream
`Console.Out`	Standard output stream
`Console.Error`	Standard error stream (output for error messages that can be redirected to a file)

FIGURE 10.3   Standard I/O streams

classes in appropriate ways, we can create objects that represent a stream of information that has the exact characteristics we want for a particular situation.

The broad topic of C# I/O, and the sheer number of classes in the `System.IO` package, prohibits us from covering it in detail in this book. Our focus for the moment is on I/O exceptions.

Many operations performed by I/O classes can potentially throw an `IOException`. The `IOException` class is the parent of several exception classes that represent problems when trying to perform I/O (refer to Figure 10.1).

Because I/O often deals with external resources, many problems can arise in programs that attempt to perform I/O operations. For example, a file from which we want to read might not exist; when we attempt to open the file, an exception will be thrown because that file can't be found. In general, we should try to design programs to be as robust as possible when dealing with potential problems.

> **Key Concept**
>
> The C# class library contains many classes for defining I/O streams with various characteristics.

We've seen in previous examples how we can use the `Scanner` class to read and process input read from a text file. Now let's explore an example that writes data to a text output file. Writing output to a text file requires simply that we use the appropriate classes to create the output stream, and then call the appropriate methods to write the data.

Listing 10.7

```csharp
//****************************************************************
//   TestData.cs         C#:   Ken Culp
//
//   Demonstrates the use of a character file output stream.
//****************************************************************
using System;
using System.IO;

namespace TestData
{
  public class TestData
  {
    //--------------------------------------------------------------
    //   Creates file of test data that consists of ten lines each
    //   containing ten integer values in the range 10 to 99.
    //--------------------------------------------------------------
    public static void Main(string[] args)
    {
      const int MAX = 10;
      int value;

      // Relative path places the file in the Solution (project)
      // directory (up two directories from bin\Debug).
      string file = @"..\..\test.dat";
```

Listing 10.7   continued

```
        Random rand = new Random(DateTime.Now.Millisecond);
        StreamWriter outFile = new StreamWriter(file);

        for (int line = 1; line <= MAX; line++)
        {
          for (int num = 1; num <= MAX; num++)
          {
            value = rand.Next(90) + 10;
            outFile.Write(value + "    ");
          }
          outFile.WriteLine();
        }
        outFile.Close();
        Console.Out.WriteLine("Output file has been created: " +
          file);

        Console.In.ReadLine();  // Wait for enter key
      }
    }
}
```

Output

```
Output file has been created: ..\..\test.dat
```

Suppose we want to test a program we are writing, but don't have the real data available. We could write a program that generates a test data file that contains random values. The program shown in Listing 10.7 generates a file that contains random integer values within a particular range. It also writes one line of standard output, confirming that the data file has been written.

The StreamWriter class represents a text output file, but has minimal method support for manipulating data. System.IO is an object of the TextWriter class, which provides Write and WriteLine methods.

Note that in the TestData program, we have eliminated explicit exception handling. That is, if something goes wrong, we simply allow the program to terminate, instead of specifically catching and handling the problem. For each program, we must carefully consider how best to handle the exceptions that may be thrown. This requirement is especially important when dealing with I/O, which is fraught with potential problems that cannot always be foreseen.

The TestData program uses nested **for** loops to compute random values and write them to the output file. After all values are printed, the file is closed. Output files must be closed explicitly to ensure that the data is retained. In general, it is good practice to close all file streams explicitly when they are no longer needed.

The data that is contained in the file `test.dat` after the `TestData` program is run might look like this:

```
85  90  93  15  82  79  52  71  70  98
74  57  41  66  22  16  67  65  24  84
86  61  91  79  18  81  64  41  68  81
98  47  28  40  69  10  85  82  64  41
23  61  27  10  59  89  88  26  24  76
33  89  73  36  54  91  42  73  95  58
19  41  18  14  63  80  96  30  17  28
24  37  40  64  94  23  98  10  78  50
89  28  64  54  59  23  61  15  80  88
51  28  44  48  73  21  41  52  35  38
```

10.7 GENERATING CUSTOM EVENTS

An exception is much like an event in that it is an urgent request from an object for attention by the owner of that object. In object-oriented programming, all events take the form of messages, as we have discussed previously. Up to this point, however, we have described how to handle those messages (events) generated by the library packages. In this section, we look at how you can code your classes to generate events. We will modify our SSN control from Chapter 8, which will generate its own event called `SsnChanged` any time something is changed in the SSN. We will look at how our `SsnControls` program generates the event and at how our `SsnTest` program handles it.

Creating the Delegate

Key Concept

Custom events can be created in a class that can be handled in other classes.

The first step in creating an event in code is to define the signature for the event handler. This signature, called a *delegate,* is defined as part of the class generating the event. The relevant code from the upgraded `SsnControls.SSN.cs` file is shown here:

```
//-------------------------------------------------------------
// Define the required signature for the SsnChanged event
// handler. This method is called a delegate.
//-------------------------------------------------------------
public delegate void SsnChangedHandler(SSN caller, bool valid);
```

Defining the Event

The declaration of `SsnChazngedHandler` is not a method declaration, as you can see by the missing braces. Instead, it is the model of the signature that all event handlers must follow if they are to be recognized to handle the event. In a sense, this creates a type specification that must be matched when the handler is added to the object.

The next step is to define the event itself that can be trapped by the owner of the object:

```
//------------------------------------------------------------
// Define the SsnChanged event
//------------------------------------------------------------
public event SsnChangedHandler SsnChanged;
```

Generating the Event

As the user types in any of the text boxes that make up the social security number, we need to generate our `SsnChanged` event. Therefore, in our custom control, we capture the `TextChanged` event for each text box and generate our own event. The following is the line of code in the *TextChanged* event handler that generates the event:

```
SsnChanged(this, Valid);   // THROW CUSTOM EVENT
```

Noting the signature of the delegate, we see that two parameters are required. The first is something of type SSN (the custom control) and the second is a boolean. To the first, we pass the keyword **this**, which is the SSN control. To the second, we pass our `Valid` property.

Note that this declaration of the event specifies that the event is of the type `SsnChangedHandler`, which is our delegate signature for this event. This specification creates the requirement that to add an event to the SSN custom control, that handler must match this signature exactly.

Handling the Event

Next, we need to consume the event by using an object of the type we just created. This is a two-step process: first we define the event handler, and then we add the handler to the object. Therefore, we modify `SsnTest` to create the event handler that matches the signature specified in the delegate. The relevant line of code is shown next. Note that this handler was created automatically from the Form Designer, as we shall describe shortly.

```
private void ssn1_SsnChanged(SsnControls.SSN caller, bool valid)
```

Finally, we add the handler to the object (in this case, our SSN control). The following is the line of code generated by the Form Designer in our revised *SsnTest* application. The name of the control in our test application is *SSN1*.

```
this.ssn1.SsnChanged +=
  new SsnControls.SSN.SsnChangedHandler(this.ssn1_SsnChanged);
```

Compare this method declaration to the delegate and you will see that it exactly matches the relevant parts (the **void** return type and the two parameters of type *SSN* and **bool**). Note that this is actually the second handler being added to the control. We added a dummy handler (a do-nothing method) to the *SSN* class in the constructor for SSN. The relevant code from *SsnControls* is as follows:

```
//------------------------------------------------------------
// Constructor:  Build array of text boxes & define handler
//------------------------------------------------------------
public SSN()
{
  . . .
  this.SsnChanged += new SsnChangedHandler(OnSsnChanged);
}
//------------------------------------------------------------
// Dummy overridable event handler.
//------------------------------------------------------------
public virtual void OnSsnChanged(SSN caller, bool valid) {}
```

Reviewing Event Processing

To summarize, here are the steps that you need to follow to create and handle your own events:

1. Define the signature of the handler with the **public delegate** keywords.

2. Define the event with the **public event** keywords, making the event match the **delegate** type.

3. Create the event in the control in response to other events. Note that any custom event must result from another event, because no code runs in the custom control except in response to an existing event.

4. Create an event handler in the code using the control with the custom event. This handler must match the delegate signature exactly. Alternately, if you have created a custom control, use the Form Designer to create the handler for you by double-clicking the event name in the properties for the control.

5. Add that event handler to the object of the type specified and add appropriate code for the handler.

Before we leave this example, let us enumerate the steps that you can take if you would like to code this application for yourself or modify the version from Chapter 8. First, you must manually add the **delegate** and **event** declarations in *SsnControls*. Next, you need to code the dummy handler and add the code to the constructor, as shown in the preceding section. Then, recompile *SsnControls*.

Now code the changes to *SsnTest*. If you are starting from scratch, follow the steps in Chapter 8 to add a reference to the project. However, you will want to remove the two custom controls from your tool box because they refer to the old version of the control without events. To remove the controls, right-click the control in the tool box and select Delete. Delete both the *TextBoxMin* and *SSN* controls. Then, right-click in a blank space on the My User Controls tab and add the new controls (see Chapter 8). If you skip this step of updating the toolbar, your application will not compile or run.

Delete the SSN control (if you started from the Chapter 8 version) and add it back again. This is necessary to get access to the new version. Now you will be able to see the *SsnChanged* event in the event list in the properties window.

Double-click the *SsnChanged* event and add the code for your handler. The complete code for the revised custom SSN control is shown in Listing 10.8.

Listing 10.8

```
//*****************************************************************
//  SSN.cs        C#:  Ken Culp
//
//  User control with 3 TextBoxMin boxes where MinLength and
//  MaxLength are both set to 3,2,4 respectively.
//  The Valid property that is true when all 3 parts of the SSN
//  match the appropriate length.  Text property sets or get the
//  SSN.  An event is defined called SsnChanged.
//*****************************************************************
using System;
using System.ComponentModel;
using System.Windows.Forms;

namespace SsnControls
{
  public class SSN : System.Windows.Forms.UserControl
  {
    private SsnControls.TextBoxMin txtSSN1;
    private SsnControls.TextBoxMin txtSSN2;
    private SsnControls.TextBoxMin txtSSN3;
    private System.ComponentModel.Container components = null;
    private TextBoxMin[] boxes;

    //-------------------------------------------------------
    // Define the required signature for the SsnChanged
    // event handler.  This method is called a delegage.
    //-------------------------------------------------------
    public delegate void SsnChangedHandler(
      SSN caller, bool valid);
```

Listing 10.8   continued

```csharp
//-----------------------------------------------------
// Define the SsnChanged event
//-----------------------------------------------------
public event SsnChangedHandler SsnChanged;

//-----------------------------------------------------
// Constructor:  Build text box array, define handler
//-----------------------------------------------------
public SSN()
{
  InitializeComponent();
  boxes = new TextBoxMin[3];
  boxes[0] = txtSSN1;
  boxes[1] = txtSSN2;
  boxes[2] = txtSSN3;
  this.SsnChanged += new SsnChangedHandler(OnSsnChanged);
}

//-----------------------------------------------------
// Dummy overridable event handler.
//-----------------------------------------------------
public virtual void OnSsnChanged(SSN caller, bool valid) { }

protected override void Dispose(bool disposing)
{
  if (disposing)
  {
    if (components != null)
    {
      components.Dispose();
    }
  }
  base.Dispose(disposing);
}

#region Component Designer generated code
/// <summary>
/// Required method for Designer support - do not modify
/// the contents of this method with the code editor.
/// </summary>
private void InitializeComponent()
{
  this.txtSSN1 = new SsnControls.TextBoxMin();
  this.txtSSN2 = new SsnControls.TextBoxMin();
  this.txtSSN3 = new SsnControls.TextBoxMin();
  this.SuspendLayout();
  //
  // txtSSN1
  //
```

Listing 10.8   continued

```
this.txtSSN1.Location = new System.Drawing.Point(0, 0);
this.txtSSN1.MaxLength = 3;
this.txtSSN1.MinLength = 3;
this.txtSSN1.Name = "txtSSN1";
this.txtSSN1.Size = new System.Drawing.Size(32, 20);
this.txtSSN1.TabIndex = 0;
this.txtSSN1.TextAlign =
  System.Windows.Forms.HorizontalAlignment.Center;
this.txtSSN1.Enter +=
  new System.EventHandler(this.SsnOnEnter);
this.txtSSN1.KeyPress +=
  new System.Windows.Forms.
  KeyPressEventHandler(this.SsnKeyPress);
this.txtSSN1.TextChanged +=
  new System.EventHandler(this.SsnTextChanged);
//
// txtSSN2
//
this.txtSSN2.Location = new System.Drawing.Point(31, 0);
this.txtSSN2.MaxLength = 2;
this.txtSSN2.MinLength = 2;
this.txtSSN2.Name = "txtSSN2";
this.txtSSN2.Size = new System.Drawing.Size(25, 20);
this.txtSSN2.TabIndex = 1;
this.txtSSN2.TextAlign =
  System.Windows.Forms.HorizontalAlignment.Center;
this.txtSSN2.Enter +=
  new System.EventHandler(this.SsnOnEnter);
this.txtSSN2.KeyPress +=
  new System.Windows.Forms.
  KeyPressEventHandler(this.SsnKeyPress);
this.txtSSN2.TextChanged +=
  new System.EventHandler(this.SsnTextChanged);
//
// txtSSN3
//
this.txtSSN3.Location = new System.Drawing.Point(55, 0);
this.txtSSN3.MaxLength = 4;
this.txtSSN3.MinLength = 4;
this.txtSSN3.Name = "txtSSN3";
this.txtSSN3.Size = new System.Drawing.Size(40, 20);
this.txtSSN3.TabIndex = 2;
this.txtSSN3.TextAlign =
  System.Windows.Forms.HorizontalAlignment.Center;
this.txtSSN3.Enter +=
  new System.EventHandler(this.SsnOnEnter);
this.txtSSN3.KeyPress +=
  new System.Windows.Forms.
  KeyPressEventHandler(this.SsnKeyPress);
```

Listing 10.8   continued

```csharp
        this.txtSSN3.TextChanged +=
          new System.EventHandler(this.SsnTextChanged);
        //
        // SSN
        //
        this.Controls.Add(this.txtSSN3);
        this.Controls.Add(this.txtSSN2);
        this.Controls.Add(this.txtSSN1);
        this.Name = "SSN";
        this.Size = new System.Drawing.Size(104, 24);
        this.ResumeLayout(false);
        this.PerformLayout();

    }
    #endregion

    [Browsable(true)]
    public bool Valid
    {
      get
      {
        bool ok = true;
        foreach (TextBoxMin b in boxes)
        {
          int len = b.Text.Length;
          ok &= (b.Valid);
        }
        return ok;
      }
    }

    [Browsable(true)]
    public long Value
    {
      get
      {
        long val;
        try
        {
          val = long.Parse(Text);
          return val;
        }
        catch (FormatException err)
        {
          return 0;
        }
      }
      set
      {
```

Listing 10.8   continued

```csharp
      string ssn = value.ToString();
      if (value > 0)
        Text = value.ToString();
      else
        Text = "";
    }
  }

  [Browsable(true)]
  public override string Text
  {
    get
    {
      string ret = "";
      foreach (TextBoxMin b in boxes)
        ret += b.Text;
      return ret;
    }
    set
    {
      string val = value;
      // Make sure not passed non-numeric values.
      for (int i = 0; i < val.Length; i++)
        if (val[i] < '0' || val[i] > '9') return;
      // Spread value across text boxes
      foreach (TextBoxMin b in boxes)
      {
        int len = b.MinLength;
        if (val.Length >= len)
        { // Have at least enough for this field
          b.Text = val.Substring(0, len);
          val = val.Substring(len);
        }
        else
        { // Not enough to fill. Use all & done
          b.Text = val;
          val = "";
        }
      }
    }
  }

  private void SsnKeyPress(object sender, KeyPressEventArgs e)
  {
    char key = e.KeyChar;
    if ((key >= ' ') && (key < '0' || key > '9'))
      e.Handled = true;
  }
```

Listing 10.8   continued

```
    private void SsnTextChanged(object sender, EventArgs e)
    {
      // Generate tab if field is full
      TextBox box = (TextBox)sender;
      int max = box.MaxLength;
      if (box.Text.Length == max) SendKeys.Send("\t");
      SsnChanged(this, Valid);  // THROW CUSTOM EVENT
    }

    private void SsnOnEnter(object sender, System.EventArgs e)
    {
      TextBox b = (TextBox)sender;
      b.SelectionStart = 0;
      b.SelectionLength = b.Text.Length;
    }


  }
}
```

The code for the revised *Ssn Test* example is shown in Listing 10.9. Note that we modified the application to give a continuous feedback as characters were typed in the SSN control. Therefore, we removed the Display button and replaced it with an Ok button to terminate the application. Ok is not armed until a valid SSN is supplied.

Listing 10.9

```
//-------------------------------------------------------------
//  SsnTest.cs        C#:  Ken Culp
//
//  Tests the Social Security Number control using events.
//*************************************************************
using System;
using System.Windows.Forms;

namespace SsnTest
{
  public class SsnTest : System.Windows.Forms.Form
  {
    private System.Windows.Forms.Label label1;
    private System.Windows.Forms.Button btnOk;
    private System.Windows.Forms.Label label2;
    private System.Windows.Forms.Label labText;
    private System.Windows.Forms.Label label3;
    private System.Windows.Forms.Label labValid;
```

Listing 10.9   continued

```csharp
private SsnControls.SSN ssn1;
private System.ComponentModel.Container components = null;

public SsnTest()
{
  InitializeComponent();
}

protected override void Dispose(bool disposing)
{
  if (disposing)
  {
    if (components != null)
    {
      components.Dispose();
    }
  }
  base.Dispose(disposing);
}
```

```
Form Designer generated code
```

```csharp
static void Main()
{
  Application.Run(new SsnTest());
}

private void btnOk_Click(object sender, System.EventArgs e)
{
  this.Close();
}

private void ssn1_SsnChanged(
  SsnControls.SSN caller, bool valid)
{
  labText.Text = ssn1.Text;
  labValid.Text = ssn1.Valid.ToString();
  btnOk.Enabled = valid; // Ok only enabled on valid data
}

}
}
```

Output

SSN Test | _ □ ✕
SSN: 123 | 45 |

Text: 12345

Valid: False

Ok

SSN Test | _ □ ✕
SSN: 123 | 45 | 6789

Text: 123456789

Valid: True

Ok

10.8 TOOL TIPS AND MNEMONICS

Key Concept

Tool tips and mnemonics can enhance the functionality of a graphical user interface.

Let's take a look at some special features that can be used with any Windows form application. Appropriate use of these features will enhance the user interface and facilitate the use of your forms. This section describes the use of tool tips and mnemonics, as well as how to disable components. These features are demonstrated using an example.

Tool Tips

Any form control can be assigned a *tool tip,* which is a short line of text that will appear when the cursor is rested momentarily on top of the component. Tool tips are usually used to inform the user about the component, such as the purpose of a button.

To define a tool tip, you first drag a `ToolTip` control, shown in Figure 10.4, from the toolbar to the form. The `ToolTip` control can be placed anywhere on the form because it does not really reside on the form. Instead, a definition is added to the source file and the icon shows up in a newly opened region below the form, as shown in Figure 10.5.

Once there is a `ToolTip` control on the form, you can add the text for a tool tip to each control on the form in the Properties window. That is, after you add the `ToolTip` control

FIGURE 10.4 ToolTip on the form

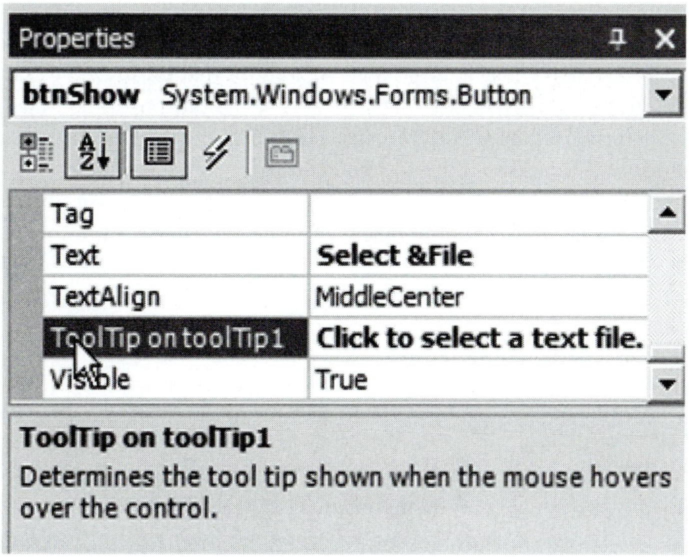

FIGURE 10.5   ToolTip entry in Properties window

to the form, the Properties window includes a new property called ToolTip on *xxx*, where *xxx* is the name you gave to the `ToolTip` control (`toolTip1` by default), as shown in Figure 10.5. Although this new property appears in the Form Designer, that is only a matter of convenience; it is not really a property. In other words, you cannot access the message text typed in the Form Designer by using the name of the control. Instead, you have to use the `SetToolTip` method from the `ToolTip` object, passing the name of the control to change along with the new tool tip. For example, the following line of code changes our tool tip on `btnShow`:

```
toolTip1.SetToolTip(btnShow, "Now you have a new tip.");
```

When the button is displayed, it appears normally. When the user rolls the mouse pointer over the button, hovering there momentarily, the tool tip text pops up. When the user moves the mouse pointer off of the button, the tool tip text disappears.

Mnemonics

A *mnemonic* is a character that allows the user to push a button, move the cursor to a particular text box, or make a menu choice using the keyboard instead of the mouse. For example, when a mnemonic has been defined for a button, the user can hold down the Alt key and press the mnemonic character to activate the button. Using a mnemonic to activate the button causes the system to behave just as it would if the user had used the mouse to press the button. Using a mnemonic on a label causes the focus to move to the next control in the tab order that is capable of receiving focus (usually a text box).

A mnemonic character is set in the Text property on a label, on a button or a menu item. To establish the mnemonic, modify the `Text` property and place the ampersand (&) character in front of the letter that is to be used to activate that button. For example, if our `btnShow` button had a text label of "`Show &File`", the button would appear when the application is running as Show File, with the letter F underlined. When the user presses Alt-F, the button is activated as if the user had clicked it with the mouse.

Because the label for a button can be changed in code, the mnemonic character can also be changed. If we were to execute the following line of code, the button would appear as Show File:

```
btnShow.Text = "&Show File";
```

Disabling Components

Key Concept

Components should be disabled when their use is inappropriate.

Disabling components is a good idea when users should not be allowed to use the functionality of a component. The grayed-out appearance of the disabled component is an indication that using the component is inappropriate (and, in fact, impossible) at the current time. Disabled components not only convey to the user which actions are appropriate and which aren't, they also prevent erroneous situations from occurring. To disable and enable components, we change the `Enabled` property of the component to indicate whether the component should be disabled (**false**) or enabled (**true**). For example:

```
btnShow.Enabled = false;
```

Let's look at an example that uses tool tips, mnemonics, and disabled components. The program in Listing 10.10 presents the image of a light bulb and provides a button to turn on the light bulb and a button to turn off the light bulb.

Listing 10.10

```
//**********************************************************
//  LightBulb.cs              C#:  Ken Culp
//
//  Demonstrates enabling buttons appropriately as well as how
//  to change tool tips in code.  Also shows how to change the
//  value of a tooltip.
//**********************************************************
using System;
using System.Collections.Generic;
using System.ComponentModel;
using System.Data;
```

Listing 10.10   continued

```csharp
using System.Drawing;
using System.Text;
using System.Windows.Forms;

namespace LightBulb
{
  public partial class LightBulb : Form
  {
    public LightBulb()
    {
      InitializeComponent();
    }

    private void btnOn_Click(object sender, System.EventArgs e)
    {
      label1.Image = Image.FromFile(@"..\..\lightBulbOn.gif");
      btnOff.Enabled = true;
      btnOn.Enabled = false;
    }

    private void btnOff_Click(object sender, System.EventArgs e)
    {
      label1.Image = Image.FromFile(@"..\..\lightBulbOff.gif");
      btnOn.Enabled = true;
      btnOff.Enabled = false;
    }

    private void btnChange_Click(object sender,
      System.EventArgs e)
    {
      toolTip1.SetToolTip(btnOn, "New on tip: read caption!");
      toolTip1.SetToolTip(btnOff, "New off tip: read caption!");
    }

    private void btnExit_Click(object sender, System.EventArgs e)
    {
      this.Close();
    }
  }
}
```

Display

There are actually two images of the light bulb: one showing it turned on and one showing it turned off. These images are brought in as `Image` objects. The `FromFile` static method off `Image` class is used to read the image and assign it to our label.

To create this application, on the form, drop four buttons named `btnOn`, `btnOff`, `btnChange`, and `btnExit`. Drop a label control called `label1` and size it to the width of both buttons. Add a `ToolTip` control to the form and then set the tool tip on each of the buttons. Double-click each button and add the code shown in Listing 10.10.

Note that the mnemonic character used for each button is underlined in the display. When you run the program, the tool tips automatically include an indication of the mnemonic that can be used for the button.

10.9   LIST BOXES AND COMBO BOXES

The *list box* and *combo box* allow the user to select one of several options from a drop-down menu. When the user clicks the drop-down arrow on one of these boxes, a list of options is displayed from which the user can choose. The current choice is displayed in the box.

> ### Key Concept
>
> List boxes and combo boxes provide a drop-down menu of options from which the user may select.

The list box offers a predefined list of items that the user cannot edit; the only action available to the user is to pick an entry from the list. This list can be built in the Form Designer or during code at run time. The combo box includes the functions of the list box but also allows the user to edit the data selected from the list, which makes the combo box significantly more flexible than the list box.

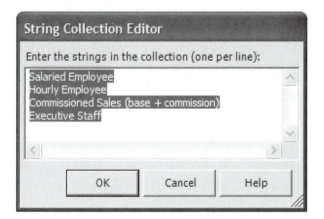

FIGURE 10.6 String Collection Editor dialog box

A list box cannot be edited. Changing the value of a list box can be accomplished only by selecting an item from the list. In a combo box, however, the user can change the value either by selecting an item from the list or by typing a particular value into the combo box area.

The options offered in these boxes can be established in one of two ways. One way is to create the list at design time. The property `Items` on these controls implements a collection (like an array, as discussed in Chapter 12) and can be edited by clicking the small button to the right of the property name. This displays the String Collection Editor dialog box, shown in Figure 10.6.

Simply type each entry, one to a line, and click OK. If you want to add to the list in code, you use the Collection `Add` method, shown next. The method takes a string and will add the item to the end of the list.

```
cmbList.Items.Add(cmbList.Text);
```

If you want to add the item to a specific location in the list, you can use the `Insert` method, which takes an index and the string. Generally, however, the list is built from top to bottom. You can also build the list by calling the `AddRange` method, which takes a variable number of strings and adds them to the end of the list. Collections also support `Remove` and `RemoveAt` methods for deleting unwanted items from the list.

Miscellaneous Controls Example

Listing 10.11 presents an example program, called `Tab`, that illustrates the list and combo boxes as well as calendar controls and date controls. After we describe the application in this section, we refer to it in the following sections.

Our `Tab` application consists of one form with a tab control and three tabs. The first tab shows a variation on our color slider example in Chapter 9. The second tab demonstrates the list and combo boxes. The third tab shows two types of calendar controls for selecting dates. The application also includes a status bar, which shows some of the interactions with the tabs and shows the time of day by using a `Timer` object.

The source to the program (except for the Form Designer code) is shown in Listing 10.11. Open the program and exercise it extensively. Then look at the various controls in the Form Designer and examine their properties, particularly the `Items` property of the list box and combo box.

Listing 10.11

```
//***************************************************************
//  Tab.cs         C#:   Ken Culp
//
//  Miscellaneous controls demonstration program
//***************************************************************
using System;
using System.Data;
using System.Drawing;
using System.Windows.Forms;

namespace Tab
{
  public partial class Tab : Form
  {
    public Tab()
    {
      InitializeComponent();
    }
    //-------------------------------------------------------------
    // mc1:  Computes a contrasting color value from input.
    //-------------------------------------------------------------
    private byte Mc1(byte b)
    {
      if (b < 125) return 255;
      return 0;
    }
    //-------------------------------------------------------------
    // MaxContrast:  Computes a contrasting color from the input.
    //-------------------------------------------------------------
    private Color MaxContrast(Color c)
    {
      return Color.FromArgb(Mc1(c.R), Mc1(c.G), Mc1(c.B));
    }


    //-------------------------------------------------------------
    // drawAll:  Draws all items on form and status bar.
    //-------------------------------------------------------------
    private void DrawAll()
    {
```

Listing 10.11   continued

```csharp
    moCal.SetDate(DateTime.Now);
    labRed.Text = tbarRed.Value.ToString();
    labGreen.Text = tbarGreen.Value.ToString();
    labBlue.Text = tbarBlue.Value.ToString();
    labShow.BackColor = Color.FromArgb(tbarRed.Value,
                                       tbarGreen.Value,
                                       tbarBlue.Value);
    labShow.ForeColor = MaxContrast(labShow.BackColor);
    Invalidate();              // Cause form to repaint
    statusBar1.Invalidate(); // Cause status bar to repaint
}
//-----------------------------------------------------------
// btnExit: punt.
//-----------------------------------------------------------
private void butExit_Click(object sender, EventArgs e)
{
    this.Close();
}
//-----------------------------------------------------------
// lstType.SelectedIndexChanged: Show selected item data
//-----------------------------------------------------------
private void lstType_SelectedIndexChanged(object sender,
    EventArgs e)
{
    int empType = lstType.SelectedIndex;
    labType.Text = "(" + empType.ToString() + ") " +
        lstType.SelectedItem;
}
//-----------------------------------------------------------
// btnAddToList:  Add shown item to list if not duplicate.
//-----------------------------------------------------------
private void butAddToList_Click(object sender, EventArgs e)
{
    if (cmbList.Items.Contains(cmbList.Text))
        MessageBox.Show("Duplicate value");
    else
        cmbList.Items.Add(cmbList.Text);
}
//-----------------------------------------------------------
// moCal.DateChanged: Show date a in label, dtPicker, status.
//-----------------------------------------------------------
private void moCal_DateChanged(object sender,
    DateRangeEventArgs e)
{
    labDateMo.Text = moCal.SelectionStart.Date.ToString();
    dtPicker.Value = moCal.SelectionStart.Date;
    selDate.Text = moCal.SelectionStart.
        Date.ToShortDateString();
```

Listing 10.11 continued

```
  }
  //------------------------------------------------------------------
  // statusBar1.DrawItem: changes BackColor of one item in bar.
  //------------------------------------------------------------------
  private void statusBar1_DrawItem(object sender,
    StatusBarDrawItemEventArgs e)
  {
    // Called for the selColor panel on the status bar
    Graphics g = e.Graphics;
    g.Clear(labShow.BackColor);
  }
  //------------------------------------------------------------------
  // Load:  Set up display and set today's date.
  //------------------------------------------------------------------
  private void TabForm_Load(object sender, System.EventArgs e)
  {
    timer1.Start();
    selPage.Text = "TrackBar";
    DrawAll();
    moCal.TodayDate = DateTime.Now.Date;
  }
  //------------------------------------------------------------------
  // timer1.Tick:  Update date/time in status bar.
  //------------------------------------------------------------------
  private void timer1_Tick(object sender, System.EventArgs e)
  {
    curTime.Text = DateTime.Now.ToLongTimeString();
  }
  //------------------------------------------------------------------
  // dtPicker.ValueChanged:  reflect date to moCal.
  //------------------------------------------------------------------
  private void dtPicker_ValueChanged(object sender, EventArgs e)
  {
    moCal.SetDate(dtPicker.Value);
  }
  //------------------------------------------------------------------
  // tabControl1.Click:  Show currently selected tab name.
  //------------------------------------------------------------------
  private void tabControl1_Click(object sender, EventArgs e)
  {
    selPage.Text = tabControl1.SelectedTab.Text;
    statusBar1.Invalidate();
  }
  //------------------------------------------------------------------
  // TrackBarScroll:  Used for all bars; changes colors.
  //------------------------------------------------------------------
  private void TrackBarScroll(object sender, EventArgs e)
  {
```

Listing 10.11   continued

```
        DrawAll();  // DrawAll uses new values in bars to paint
    }
  }
}
```

Output

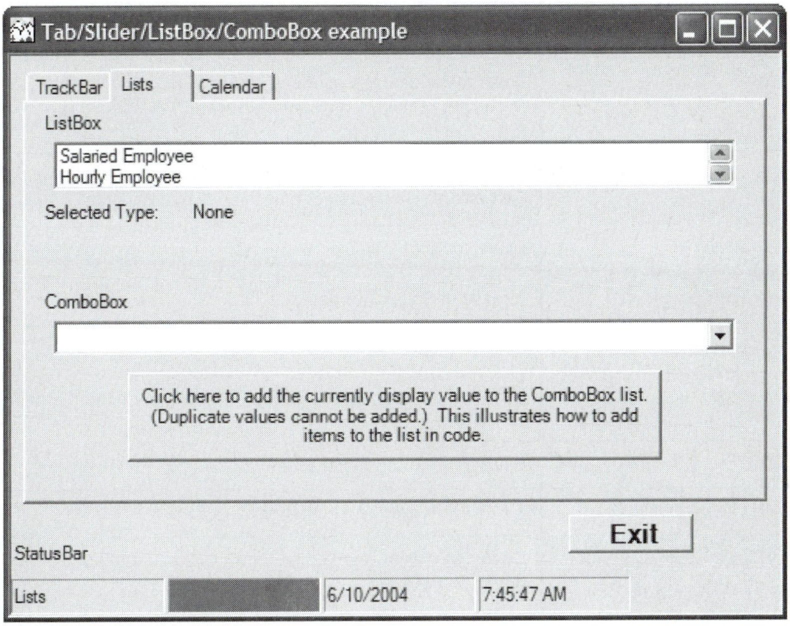

10.10 CALENDAR CONTROLS

Visual Studio has a couple of nice controls to prompt the user for a date. One shows a full calendar and the other shows a box resembling a text box with a drop-down arrow. The first is used when space is available to show the whole month (or more) and the other is used when space is at a premium.

The first, larger control is MonthCalendar. Drop this control on your form and size it as needed to fit around other controls. Give the control a logical name for use in the code. This control allows you to select a range of dates and not just a single date (although you can restrict the user to one day by setting the MaxSelectionCount property). Thus, to access the information, you use the SelectionStart and SelectionEnd properties. Some of the members of the MonthCalendar control are shown in Figure 10.7.

Properties	Description
BoldedDates	An array of DateTime objects to highlight as bold.
CalendarDimensions	Number of rows and columns of months to display (usually 1 by 1).
FirstDayOfWeek	The first day of the week (use Day enumeration).
MaxDate	The last date the user can scroll to. The default is no maximum.
MaxSelectionCount	The maximum number of days that can be selected. Set this to 1 if you want the user to be able to select only 1 day.
MinDate	The earliest date the user can scroll to. The default is no minimum. In many cases, you will want to set this to the current date.
MonthlyBoldedDates	An array of dates to highlight each month. Dates specified as Date/Time objects but only the day of the month is used.
SelectionEnd	Ending date of the selected range.
SelectionRange	A range of dates (two dates).
SelectionStart	Beginning date of the selected range.
ShowToday	If true, shows the current date selected at the bottom of the control.
ShowTodayCircle	Circles the current date (today).
ShowWeekNumbers	If true, numbers the weeks from 1 to 52.
TodayDate	Set or get the day marked as today. One place to set the day is during Form Load.

Methods	
AddAnnuallyBoldedDate	Adds a date to be marked in bold each year.
AddBoldedDate	Adds a single date to be marked in bold.
AddMonthlyBoldedDate	Adds a date to be marked in bold each month.
SetDate	Sets a date as the currently selected date.
SetSelectionRange	Sets the range of selected dates.
ToString	Shows the selected range of dates as a long string.

FIGURE 10.7   MonthCalendar properties (*continues*)

Events	
DateChanged	The date selected has changed.
DateSelected	Occurs when the mouse is used to select a specific date.

FIGURE 10.7 (*continued*)   MonthCalendar properties

In the preceding `Tab` program, we used the default event, `DateChanged`, to catch any changes in the date. The new date was then transferred to the `DateTimePicker` control (see below) and to the status bar. The relevant code from the previous example is shown next. The default event handler was created by double-clicking the control.

```
private void moCal_DateChanged(object sender,
DateRangeEventArgs e)
{
   labDateMo.Text = moCal.SelectionStart.Date.ToString();
   dtPicker.Value = moCal.SelectionStart.Date;
   selDate.Text = moCal.SelectionStart.Date.ToShortDateString();
}
```

We also set the current date in the form `Load` event with this line of code:

```
moCal.TodayDate = DateTime.Now.Date;
```

Now let's take a brief look at the other control, `DateTimePicker`. The control has many of the properties of text boxes including size, font, and colors. Two properties, `MinDate` and `MaxDate`, control the range of dates that can be used and the `Value` property a read/write property for the selected date. Like text boxes, `DateTimePicker` includes all the usual mouse and keyboard events. However, the default event, `ValueChanged`, is the most useful because it indicates when the user has changed the chosen date. Because `ValueChanged` is the default event, double-clicking the control creates the handler for this event. In the Tab program in Listing 10.11, we handle the `ValueChanged` event to transfer the date selected to the `MonthCalendar` control by using the `SetDate` method:

```
private void dtPicker_ValueChanged(object sender, EventArgs e)
{
   moCal.SetDate(dtPicker.Value);
}
```

When the down button at the right of the control is clicked, a month calendar is displayed that is identical to the month calendar shown in the example above. However, the user can type a date (and time) directly into the control without using the month calendar. The format of the display is controlled by the `Format` property. When you want the user to type a date/time, the best format to use is Short. Try various settings for Format to determine the one that works best for you. You can even try Custom, by entering a string in the CustomFormat property (M = month, d = day, y = year, m = minute, h = hour).

10.11 STATUS BAR

The Visual Studio StatusBar control is primarily used as an output device to give the user visual clues and statistics during program execution. The status bar must be located ("docked") at one of the edges of the form, and is usually positioned at the bottom of the form. The number of "panels" and the characteristics of each panel in the status bar are again configured by editing a collection.

To configure a StatusBar control, drop the control on the form and dock it at the desired location. Then, locate the Panels property and click the edit button at the right. This displays the StatusBar Collection Editor, as shown in Figure 10.8. New panels are added by clicking the Add button. For each panel, give it a useful name for access from code, set width, and set the Style property. The normal style to use is Text when you will be adding text information to the panel. In the example shown in Figure 10.8, the Style property is set to OwnerDraw because we want to show the chosen color in the selColor panel. If you want fixed text in the panel, enter that text in the Collection Editor. The Alignment property of a panel can be Left, Right, or Center.

The relevant portions of the preceding example that write to the panels of the StatusBar are listed below. The following line shows the currently selected date and occurs in the DateChanged event of the MonthCalendar:

```
selDate.Text = moCal.SelectionStart.Date.ToShortDateString();
```

Now we will illustrate handling the event that occurs when the current tab is changed on the tab control. The event we want is the Click event. This event occurs when the current tab is changed or when the tab is clicked. To illustrate the change, we copy the name of the selected tab (the Text property) to the status bar panel for listing the tab. Once we change the status bar, we force the status bar to repaint by calling its Invalidate method.

```
private void tabControl1_Click(object sender, EventArgs e)
{
  selPage.Text = tabControl1.SelectedTab.Text;
  statusBar1.Invalidate();
}
```

We need to show the currently chosen color from the color tab in the selColor panel. We use the DrawItem event for the status bar that occurs as each panel is drawn. Note that the selColor panel is the only one set to OwnerDraw, so DrawItem will occur only for the selColor panel. Thus the sender object will be the selColor panel and the Graphics

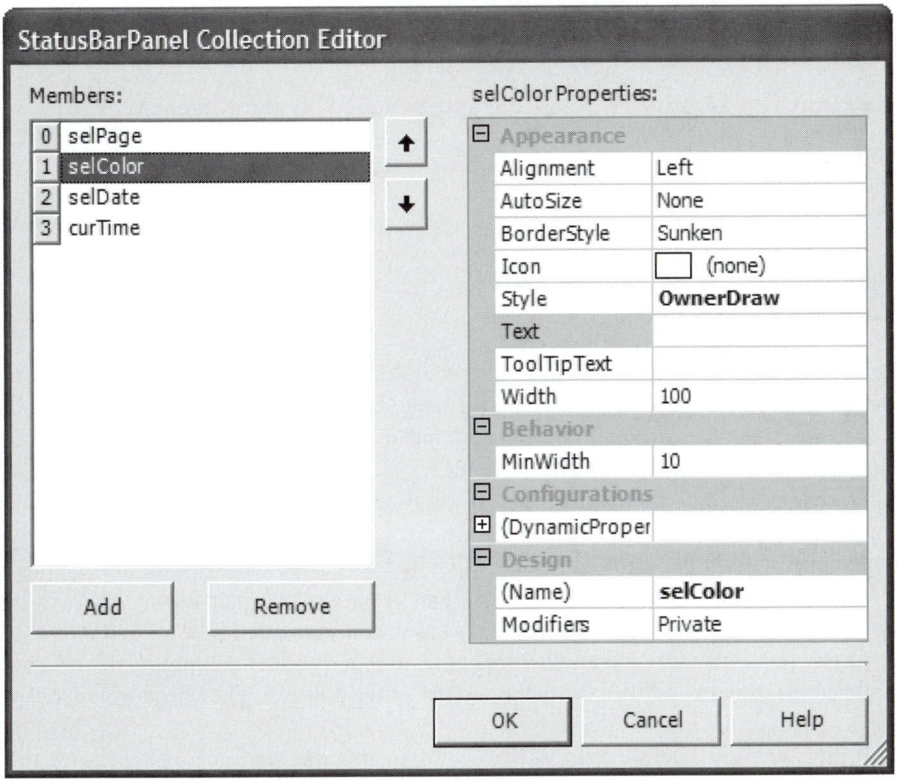

FIGURE 10.8   Collection Editor for status bar

object from the Event arguments is for drawing on the selColor panel. Once we have this Graphics object, all we have to do is clear the background to the appropriate color. The following is the complete code:

```
private void statusBar1_DrawItem(
  object sender, StatusBarDrawItemEventArgs e)
{
  // This is being called for the selColor panel on
  // the status bar
  Graphics g = e.Graphics;
  g.Clear(labShow.BackColor);
}
```

This last panel to draw is for the time. We use the Tick event from the Timer control. This event occurs once every second, because we set the Interval property in the Form Designer to 1000 (Interval takes values in milliseconds). The current time is then written to the curTime panel. Note that the date and time are formatted using a call to the DateTime method ToLongTimeString.

```
private void timer1_Tick(object sender, System.EventArgs e)
{
  curTime.Text = DateTime.Now.ToLongTimeString();
}
```

10.12 MENUS

Complex menus can be added to a form quite quickly using the menu editor of the Form Designer. To add a menu to a form, drag the MenuStrip control to the form and then add menu items using the editor. As you edit each menu item, the properties of that menu item should be updated in the Properties window.

Once you add the MenuStrip control to the form, the form appears as shown in Figure 10.9.

The first step is to type the name of the first menu. Assume that we want the first menu to be the File menu and we want this menu item to be selectable by pressing the Alt+F key combination. Then you type the text (&File) as shown in Figure 10.10.

At this point, you can add another main menu item or a subitem under File. Let's add an Open menu item and then set the properties of that control. The screen would look as shown in Figure 10.11.

If the user clicks File, we really don't need to do anything until the user clicks the submenu item Open. However, if the user clicks the Open item, we need to do something. Therefore, we want to give the event a useful name before we create the event handler. Once we finish typing "&Open", the Properties window for the MenuStrip control would look as shown in Figure 10.12.

In this Properties window, we would want to change the name to something like "*mnuFileOpen*" and probably would want to set the shortcut property to Ctrl+O to match other Windows applications. Another property that some controls might need is the *Checked* property, which, if set to true, places a check mark in front of the item. This check mark is usually toggled on and off each time an item is clicked and would be used for a two-state property like Bold or Italic.

The last step to configure for this menu item is to create the event handler. In the Properties window, select events and double-click the *Click* event. This creates the handler for you.

Since you have named this control, you can make changes to the menu item from code. For example, you could change the label by changing the *Text* property. Alternately, you can switch the *Checked* property. Another useful feature is the ability to disable a menu item or hide it entirely. If a menu item does not make sense in the current context but you still want the user to see the menu entry, set the *Enabled* property to **false**. If you don't even want the menu item to be visible, set the *Visible* property to **false**.

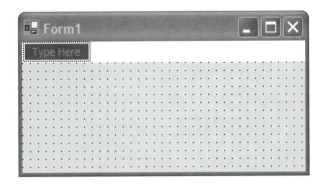

FIGURE 10.9   MainMenu initial screen

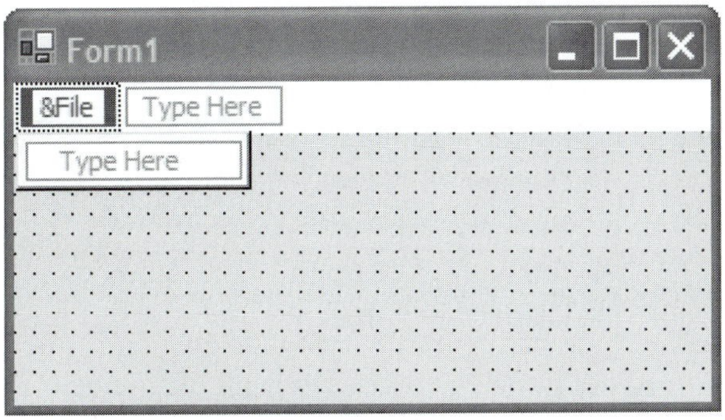

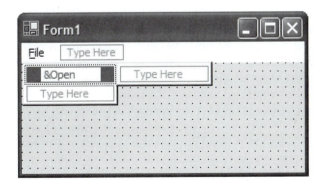

FIGURE 10.10   MainMenu screen with &File

FIGURE 10.11   MainMenu screen with File/Open

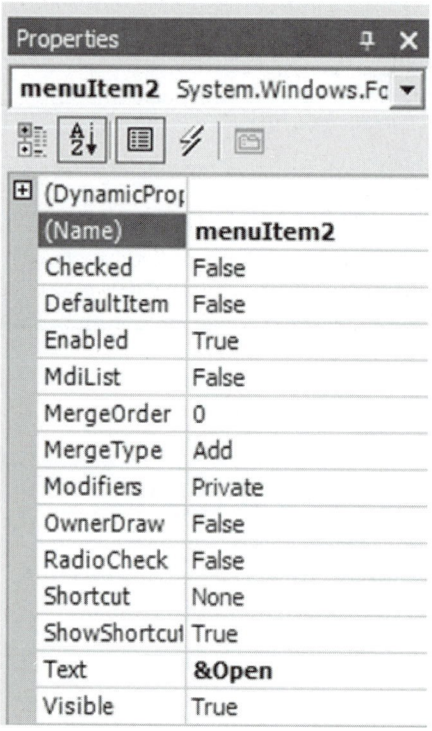

FIGURE 10.12   File/Open menu item properties

You repeat the preceding design process until you have created the complete menu structure and all the event handlers. Also, you can create submenus under submenus and so on to any level. We recommend that you limit this, however, to three levels.

You should get into the practice of naming every menu entry as you go even if you are not currently using it except as a heading for other entries ("menuItem27" is not very useful). This is because there are a variety of events and processing that can be done in code to improve the usability of your application and the overall experience of your user. We, unfortunately, do not have enough space to cover these features.

The next example, the `SerializeTest` program, illustrates the use of menus and introduces our next topic, serialization. In this example, we have an `Employee` class that stores basic demographic information about the employee and a screen that shows the corresponding pieces of information. To this form we add a single top-level menu labeled File with four items (Open, Save, Save As, and Exit). We assigned the standard shortcut keys to these menu items (Ctrl+O, Ctrl+S, Ctrl+A, and Alt+F4, respectively). We also used logical names for the controls of *mnuFileOpen*, *mnuFileSave*, *mnuFileAs*, and *mnuFileExit*.

On File/Save, we will write the contents to disk using serialization (see next section) after prompting for a file name. On subsequent File/Save, we will simply save the data without prompting for the file name. File/Save As will always prompt for a file name before writing the file. We also use the Registry to save the name of the file so that it can be used the next time the program is run and a File/Open is requested.

We are employing validation on the input (method *CheckValid*) whenever the SSN is changed or the first or last name is changed. The SSN must be valid, the last name must be at least three characters long, and the first name must be at least one character long. No other validations are performed.

We created two methods to move the data between the form control and the `Employee` object called *ToScreen* (`Employee` to screen) and *ToRecord* (screen to `Employee`). *ToScreen* is called on File/Open and *ToRecord* is called on File/Save and File/Save As.

The code for the form (less Form Designer code) is shown in Listing 10.12. The code for the `Employee` class that is a part of the solution is shown in Listing 10.13.

Listing 10.12

```csharp
//*************************************************************
//  SerializeTest.cs        C#:  Ken Culp
//
//  Saves and loads employee information to a file using
//  serialization.  Choices are made from a single File menu.
//*************************************************************
using System;
using System.Windows.Forms;
using System.IO;
using System.Runtime.Serialization.Formatters.Binary;

namespace SerializeTest
{
  public partial class SerializeTest : Form
  {
    Microsoft.Win32.RegistryKey rk;
    private string lastFile;
    private Employee employee = new Employee();
    public SerializeTest()
    {
      InitializeComponent();
    }
    //-----------------------------------------------------------
    // Moves data from employee record to controls
    //-----------------------------------------------------------
    private void ToScreen()
    {
      txtLast.Text = employee.Last;
      txtFirst.Text = employee.First;
      txtAddr.Text = employee.Address;
      txtCity.Text = employee.City;
      txtState.Text = employee.State;
```

Listing 10.12 continued

```csharp
    txtZip.Text = employee.ZipCode;
    txtPhone.Text = employee.Phone;
    ssn1.Value = employee.SSN;
  }
  //-------------------------------------------------------------
  // Moves data from screen to employee record
  //-------------------------------------------------------------
  private void ToRecord()
  {
    employee.Last = txtLast.Text;
    employee.First = txtFirst.Text;
    employee.Address = txtAddr.Text;
    employee.City = txtCity.Text;
    employee.State = txtState.Text;
    employee.ZipCode = txtZip.Text;
    employee.Phone = txtPhone.Text;
    employee.SSN = ssn1.Value;
  }
  //-------------------------------------------------------------
  // File/Save menu. If have file name , write else prompt.
  //-------------------------------------------------------------
  private void mnuFileSave_Click(object sender, System.EventArgs e)
  {
    ToRecord();
    if (lastFile == null)
      SaveFile();
    else
      WriteFile(lastFile);
  }
  //-------------------------------------------------------------
  // File/Save As menu. Always prompt for file name.
  //-------------------------------------------------------------
  private void mnuFileAs_Click(object sender, System.EventArgs e)
  {
    ToRecord();
    // File/Save As:  Ask user for file name to use for save.
    SaveFile();
  }
  //-------------------------------------------------------------
  // SaveFile.  Prompts for file name & calls WriteFile
  //-------------------------------------------------------------
  private void SaveFile()
  {
    // Prompte for file name and writes DataSet as XML.
    // Saves the file name in registry and for later use.
    SaveFileDialog dlg = new SaveFileDialog();
    dlg.Filter = "Employee Data (.emx)|*.emx|All Files (*.*)|*.*";
    dlg.FilterIndex = 1;
```

Listing 10.12   continued

```csharp
    dlg.FileName = (string)rk.GetValue("Lastfile");
    DialogResult result = dlg.ShowDialog();
    if (result == DialogResult.OK)
    {
      rk.SetValue("Lastfile", dlg.FileName);
      WriteFile(dlg.FileName);
    }
  }
  //--------------------------------------------------------------
  // WriteFile.  Serialization takes place here.
  //--------------------------------------------------------------
  private void WriteFile(string fileName)
  {
    FileStream fs = new FileStream(fileName,
      FileMode.Create, FileAccess.Write, FileShare.None);
    BinaryFormatter bf = new BinaryFormatter();
    bf.Serialize(fs, employee);
    lastFile = fileName;
    fs.Close();
  }
  //--------------------------------------------------------------
  // File/Open menu. Save last file for next run.
  //--------------------------------------------------------------
  private void mnuFileOpen_Click(object sender,
    System.EventArgs e)
  {
    // File/Open
    OpenFileDialog dlg = new OpenFileDialog();
    dlg.Filter =
      "Employee Database (*.emx)|*.emx|All Files (*.*)|*.*";
    dlg.FilterIndex = 1;
    dlg.FileName = (string)rk.GetValue("Lastfile");
    DialogResult result = dlg.ShowDialog();
    if (result == DialogResult.OK)
    {
      rk.SetValue("Lastfile", dlg.FileName);
      try
      {
        FileStream fs = new FileStream(dlg.FileName,
          FileMode.Open, FileAccess.Read, FileShare.None);
        BinaryFormatter bf = new BinaryFormatter();
        employee = (Employee)bf.Deserialize(fs);
        fs.Close();
        ToScreen();   // Fetch data from record to screen
        CheckValid();
        lastFile = dlg.FileName;
        txtLast.Focus();  // Place cursor on last name field
      }
```

Listing 10.12 continued

```csharp
    catch (Exception err)
    {
      MessageBox.Show("Cannot Read File: " + err.ToString(),
        "Read Error", MessageBoxButtons.OK,
        MessageBoxIcon.Exclamation);
    }
  }
}
//--------------------------------------------------------------
// CheckValid.  Validate First & Last names, SSN
//--------------------------------------------------------------
private void CheckValid()
{
  bool valid = ssn1.Valid &&
               (txtLast.Text.Length > 2) &&
               (txtFirst.Text.Length > 0);
  mnuFileSave.Enabled = valid;
  mnuFileAs.Enabled = valid;
}
//--------------------------------------------------------------
// Generic TextChanged handler used for all fields
//--------------------------------------------------------------
private void EmployeeTextChanged(object sender,
  EventArgs e)
{
  CheckValid();
}
//--------------------------------------------------------------
// SSN changed handler.  Validate all fields.
//--------------------------------------------------------------
private void ssn1_SsnChanged(SsnControls.SSN caller,
  bool valid)
{
  CheckValid();
}
//--------------------------------------------------------------
// Form load.  Create Registry Key
//--------------------------------------------------------------
private void SerializeTest_Load(object sender,
  System.EventArgs e)
{
  rk = Microsoft.Win32.Registry.LocalMachine;
  rk = rk.CreateSubKey(@"Software\CSharpBook\SerializeTest");
}
//--------------------------------------------------------------
// Menu/File/Exit.  We are out of here.
//--------------------------------------------------------------
private void mnuFileExit_Click(object sender,
```

Listing 10.12   continued

```
        System.EventArgs e)
    {
        this.Close();
    }
  }
}
```

Listing 10.13

```
//****************************************************************
//  Employee.cs        C#:  Ken Culp
//
//  Employee information system data class.
//  This class implements IComparable so that sorted lists can be
//  made.  IComparable requires only the method CompareTo be
//  implemented.  Note that properties are used throughout rather
//  than public fields.
//****************************************************************
using System;
using System.Collections;
using System.Runtime.Serialization;

namespace EmployeeLibrary
{
//The following line is required for serialization.
  [Serializable]
  public class Employee : IComparable
  {
    //-------------------------------------------------------------
    //  Employee type enumeration
    //-------------------------------------------------------------
    public enum EmpTypes
    {
      Salaried = 0, Hourly = 1, Sales = 2, Manager = 3
    }

    //-------------------------------------------------------------
    //  Private data members of class exposed below by properites
    //-------------------------------------------------------------
    private static int nextEmpId = 0;
    private string first, last, address, city, state, zip, phone;
    private long ssn;
    private int empId;
    private DateTime dob;    // Date of Birth
    private double salary;// Salary, hourly rate, or base pay
    private double comRate;  // Commission rate (may be unused)
    private double options;  // Option earn rate (may be unused)
```

Listing 10.13   continued

```
private EmpTypes empType;

//------------------------------------------------------------
//  Constructor: Uses the current value of the static member
//    nextEmpId as this employees Id and then increments to
//    the next value.  Since nextEmpId is static, each
//    Employee object created will have a different empId.
//    Many constructors could be added that took different
//    combinatons of values for the private fields above.
//------------------------------------------------------------
public Employee()
{
  empId = ++nextEmpId;
}
//------------------------------------------------------------
//  Public properties exposing the private data members
//------------------------------------------------------------
public string First
{
  get { return first; }
  set { if (value != "") first = value; }
}
public string Last
{
  get { return last; }
  set { if (value != "") last = value; }
}
public string Address
{
  get { return address; }
  set { address = value; }
}
public string City
{
  get { return city; }
  set { city = value; }
}
public string State
{
  get { return state; }
  set { state = value; }
}
public string ZipCode
{
  get { return zip; }
  set { zip = value; }
}
public string Phone
```

Listing 10.13   continued

```csharp
    {
      get { return phone; }
      set { phone = value; }
    }
    public long SSN
    {
      get { return ssn; }
      set { ssn = value; }
    }
    public DateTime DOB
    {
      get { return dob; }
      set { dob = value; }
    }
    public double Salary
    {
      get { return salary; }
      set { salary = value; }
    }
    public double Commission
    {
      get { return comRate; }
      set { comRate = value; }
    }
    public double Options
    {
      get { return options; }
      set { options = value; }
    }
    public EmpTypes EmpType
    {
      get { return empType; }
      set { empType = value; }
    }
    public int CompareTo(object o)
    {
      Employee that = (Employee)o;
      string nameThis = this.last + this.first;
      string nameThat = that.Last + that.First;
      if (nameThis == "") nameThis = " ";
      if (nameThat == "") nameThat = " ";
      return nameThis.ToUpper().CompareTo(nameThat.ToUpper());
    }
    public int ID
    {
      get { return empId; }
    }
  }
}
```

10.13   SERIALIZATION

The entire contents of an object, regardless of how complex, can be written to a file in single, straightforward operations. These objects may contain either primitive members (**int**, **long**, etc.) or pointers or references to other objects. In fact, complete link lists (see Chapter 12) or even trees can be written. This process is called *serialization.*

The first step is to mark the classes that will be included in a serialization step as being "Serializable." This is done by placing the `Serialization` attribute in the source file just before the class file. In the `Employee` class in Listing 10.13, locate these two lines near the top:

```
[Serializable]
public class Employee
```

The first line is the required attribute and it must precede the class specification. However, for this to compile, we need to include a `using` line for `System.Runtime.Serialization`, as shown near the top of the `Employee` class.

All classes referenced during Serialization must be marked as "Serializable." This includes the object passed on the write call and all classes (objects) referenced by that object. For example, if you try to Serialize A, and A references B and C, and C references D, then A, B, C, and D must all have the `[Serializable]` attribute. In our example, if `Employee` references an object of another class, that class would also have to be marked Serializable.

Now let's look at the actual code for reading and writing the Serializable objects. The first step is to add a `using` line to our test form:

```
using System.Runtime.Serialization.Formatters.Binary;
```

The WriteFile method is reproduced here for convenience:

```
//-------------------------------------------------------
// WriteFile.  Serialization takes place here.
//-------------------------------------------------------
private void WriteFile(string fileName)
{
  FileStream fs = new FileStream(fileName,
    FileMode.Create, FileAccess.Write, FileShare.None);
  BinaryFormatter bf = new BinaryFormatter();
  bf.Serialize(fs, employee);
  lastFile = fileName;
  fs.Close();
}
```

The first step is to create a `FileStream` object for writing the file. We specify that the file is to be written, that it is not to be shared, and that if it does not exist, it is to be created. Next, we need a `BinaryFormatter` object to convert the binary data within the object to the form used in the Serialized output file. For more details on binary formatters and other formatters, consult the Visual Studio help files. Using the `BinaryFormatter` object, we simply call the `Serialize` method, passing the `FileStream` object that points to the file on disk and our object. That's it.

Be aware, however, that the `Serialize` method can throw an exception, but that is unlikely to happen because we are creating the file. However, if you specified a file that was already open and tried to Serialize, an exception would be thrown. Therefore, better code would surround this call with a `try-catch` block.

Now let's examine how we would read the data back in. The following are the relevant methods from the File/Open menu item:

```
FileStream fs = new FileStream(dlg.FileName,
  FileMode.Open, FileAccess.Read, FileShare.None);
BinaryFormatter bf = new BinaryFormatter();
employee = (Employee) bf.Deserialize(fs);
fs.Close();
```

The first line again creates a `FileStream` object to read the file. This time, however, we specify read and not shared. Again, we need a `BinaryFormatter` object, but this time we call the `Deserialize` method, passing only the `FileStream` object. The return type of `Deserialize` is an **Object** so this must be typecast back to our `Employee` type.

There are many other capabilities of the Serialization system. We have only scratched the surface, showing you enough that you can add this capability to your code.

10.14 SCROLL PANELS

Sometimes we need to deal with images or information is too large to fit in a reasonable area. In such cases, a tab control is not useful. The panel control is often the best solution to this problem, because it is derived from `ScrollableControl` (see Figure 8.7) and can be scrolled both vertically and horizontally. If you set `AutoScroll` to **true** and adjust the `AutoScrollMargin` and `AutoScrollMinSize` values, you can add more controls that can all be displayed at one time in the area bounded by the panel control.

Start by adding the panel control to the form and sizing it to fit on your form among the other controls. This panel will be a window to a group of controls that can be scrolled into view in the panel by using the scroll bars. Now you can drop controls on to the panel.

As you place controls near the margin of the panel, scroll bars will appear in the Form Designer. Use the scroll bars and position the controls as

Key Concept

A scrolling panel is useful for viewing large objects or large amounts of data.

appropriate. If you place more controls on the panel than can be seen at once, scroll bars will appear when the form is displayed, allowing access to all the controls.

Another use for a scrolling panel is illustrated in Listing 10.14. This presents a form that contains a single panel that mostly fills the form. The panel is used to view an image of a fairly large subway map for Philadelphia and the surrounding areas. A label is added to the panel in the Form Designer to almost fill the panel, and the BorderStyle property is set to Fixed3D. The image is then loaded into an Image object, which is then added to the label. The actual dimensions of the image are used to adjust the dimensions of the label so that the entire image will fit in the label.

Listing 10.14

```csharp
//*************************************************************
//   TransitMap.cs         C#:   Ken Culp
//
//   Demonstrates the use of a scroll panel and accessing the size
//   of an image after loading it.  By setting on the Panel to
//   Fill, the panel will expand to fill the form.  Therefore, a
//   menu item is used to exit rather than a button.
//*************************************************************
using System;
using System.Drawing;
using System.Windows.Forms;

namespace TransitMap
{
  public partial class TransitMap : Form
  {
    Image map;

    public TransitMap()
    {
      InitializeComponent();
    }
    //------------------------------------------------------------
    //   Load: read image from project directory & size label.
    //------------------------------------------------------------
    private void TransitMap_Load(object sender, System.EventArgs e)
    {
      map = Image.FromFile(@"..\..\septa.jpg");
      label1.Size = map.Size;
      label1.Image = map;
    }
    //------------------------------------------------------------
    //   mnuExit: Punt.
    //------------------------------------------------------------
    private void mnuExit_Click(object sender, EventArgs e)
```

Listing 10.14   continued

```
    {
       this.Close();
    }
  }
}
```

Display

As you can see, the code is very small if we exclude the portion created by the Form Designer. The only tricky part of the code is where we resize the label in the form Load event to match the size of the label that we read in. Again note that we used a relative path to access the image file.

10.15 SCROLLING TEXT BOXES

We can also configure a text box to scroll by setting the Multiline property to **true** and the ScrollBars property to **true**. Then, when the text placed in the box cannot all be displayed, the box will be scrolled automatically.

In Listing 10.15, we created a form with a single text box and a button that reads the contents of the text file and copies it to the Text property of the text box. This application is not robust in that only small, text files can be shown. Attempting to show program files or large files may produce unpredictable results.

Listing 10.15

```
//***********************************************************
//  ShowFile.cs          C#:  Ken Culp
//
//  Demonstrates a scrolling text box and simple file I/O.
//  Note that only text files should be viewed.
//***********************************************************
using System;
using System.Drawing;
using System.Windows.Forms;
using System.IO;

namespace ShowFile
{
  public class ShowFile : System.Windows.Forms.Form
  {
    private System.Windows.Forms.TextBox txtShow;
    private System.Windows.Forms.Button butExit;
    private System.Windows.Forms.Button butFont;
    private System.Windows.Forms.Button butColor;
    private System.Windows.Forms.ToolTip toolTip1;
    private System.Windows.Forms.Button btnShow;
    private System.ComponentModel.IContainer components;

    public ShowFile()
    {
      InitializeComponent();
    }
    protected override void Dispose( bool disposing ) . . .

    #region Windows Form Designer generated code
       . . .
    #endregion

    static void Main()
    {
      Application.Run(new ShowFile());
    }

    private void butExit_Click(object sender, System.EventArgs e)
    {
      this.Close();
    }

    private void butShow_Click(object sender, System.EventArgs e)
```

Listing 10.15   continued

```csharp
    {
      DialogResult result;
      StreamReader sr;
      OpenFileDialog dlg = new OpenFileDialog();
      dlg.CheckFileExists = true;
      result = dlg.ShowDialog();
      if (result == DialogResult.OK)
      {
        try
        {
          sr = new StreamReader(dlg.FileName);
          txtShow.Text = sr.ReadToEnd();
          sr.Close();
        }
        catch (IOException err)
        {
          MessageBox.Show("Unable to open file: " +
                            err.ToString());
        }
      }
    }


    private void butColor_Click(object sender, System.EventArgs e)
    {
      DialogResult result;
      ColorDialog dlg = new ColorDialog();
      result = dlg.ShowDialog();
      if (result == DialogResult.OK)
        txtShow.ForeColor = dlg.Color;
    }

    private void butFont_Click(object sender, System.EventArgs e)
    {
      DialogResult result;
      FontDialog dlg = new FontDialog();
      result = dlg.ShowDialog();
      if (result == DialogResult.OK)
        txtShow.Font = dlg.Font;
    }
  }
}
```

Output

10.16 SPLIT PANES

A *split pane* is a form that displays two components separated by a moveable divider bar. Depending on how the form is set up, the two components are displayed either side by side or one on top of the other, as shown in Figure 10.13. In C# we can create a split form using the `Splitter` class in conjunction with a view control like `ListView` or `TreeView`.

The orientation of the split is set using the `Dock` property in the `Splitter` class and the view classes. The `Dock` property is selected from the `System.Windows.Forms.DockStyle` enumeration, as shown in Figure 10.14.

This same `DockStyle` property is used for the `ListView` and `TreeView` controls, which yields the following strategy for building a vertical split form in the Form Designer. First, drop a view control on the form and set its `Dock` property to `Left`. Next, add the `Splitter` control to the form to the right of the first view control and likewise set it to dock at the left. Finally, add a view control to the form to the right of the Splitter and set its `Dock` property to `Fill`. You can also do this process by starting at the right and working left. To build a horizontal split, start at the top (dock at top) and work down, with the last control always set to `Fill`.

> **Key Concept**
>
> A split form displays two components side by side or one on top of the other.

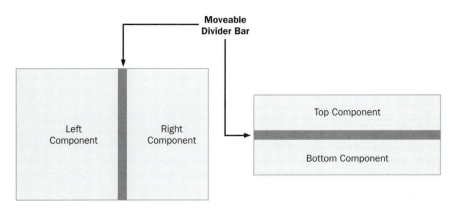

FIGURE 10.13   The configurations of a split pane

Location	Description
Bottom	Dock to the bottom edge of its containing control. This would create a horizontal splitter built up from the bottom of the screen.
Fill	The control's edges are docked to all edges where it is located. The control is automatically sized appropriately.
Left	Dock to the left edge of its containing control. This would create a vertical splitter built up from the left side of the screen.
None	The control is not docked.
Right	Dock to the right edge of its containing control. This would create a vertical splitter built up from the right side of the screen.
Top	Dock to the top edge of its containing control. This would create a horizontal splitter built down from the top of the screen.

FIGURE 10.14   DockStyle enumeration

The location of the divider bar determines how much visible area is devoted to each component in the split pane. You can drag the divider bar across the container area using the mouse. As it moves, the visible space is increased for one component and decreased for the other. The total space allotted for both components changes only if the size of the entire split pane changes.

Also, by setting a DockStyle of Fill, the images will always expand as the form is resized. This is handy because you do not need to handle the Resize event for the form.

In the example program PickImage in Listing 10.16, we create a vertical split with a list of image names on the left in a TreeView control and view of the image on the right in a

`ListView` control. We will first describe how to create the application and then discuss some of features of `TreeView` and `ListView`.

To create the application, first drop a `TreeView` control on the form and set its name to **treeView** and set its `Dock` property to `Left`. When you use the Form Designer to set the dock, you see a graphical image, as shown in Figure 10.15.

Click the desired location (left, right, top, or bottom) to dock to an edge. Click the center for `Fill` or `None` for none. In code, you would use the enumeration.

Now add a `Splitter` control to the form to the right of the `TreeView`, docked left and named `splitter`. Manually set the `Width` of the splitter in the properties window to 4.

Next add a `ListView` control to the form to the right of the `Splitter` named `listView` and set `Dock` to `Fill`. This should complete the layout of the form and it should resemble the sample output shown below except for a populated list and an image.

The next step is to add the image names to the `TreeView` control. A `TreeView` control has a series of nodes in a list. You can also have nodes under nodes, creating a tree structure to any desired level. To manually add the images to our list, select the `TreeView` control and click the button on the `Nodes` property. This displays the `TreeView` collection editor, shown in Figure 10.16.

The editor allows you to add nodes at the root or under a selected existing node (Add Child button). In our example, we add all nodes at the root with the Add Root button. Click Add Root and type the label of each entry until your list matches that in Figure 10.16. Click Add Root repeatedly until all items are in the list and then click OK. Once you click OK, the control will show all the entries on the form.

Now we need to add the code to handle the display of each graphic as the user clicks an item in the list. The first step is to handle the `AfterSelect` event for the `ListView` control. This event occurs after the user clicks an item in the list or uses the arrow keys to navigate the list. `AfterSelect` is the default event, so double-click the `TreeView` control to create the handler. Type the code shown in Listing 10.16. Note that the path name for the image is built up from the `Text` property of the node that was selected. Also, after selecting the image, the form is invalidated so the paint method will fire.

Let's now code the `Paint` method. Create the event handler from the properties/events window for the form (be sure the form is selected). Type the code shown in Listing 10.16 (this will be discussed shortly).

Our last step in creating the application is to select the toucan as our first image. Again, on the form, create the `Load` event handler (double-clicking the banner of the form is the fastest way). Type the code from Listing 10.16. The completed source (except for Form Designer code) is shown in Listing 10.16.

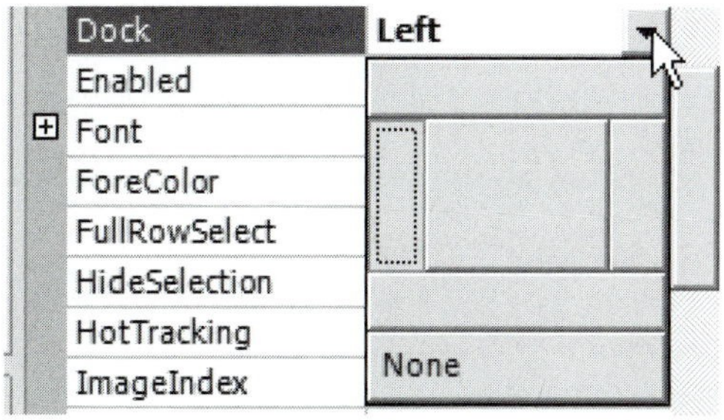

FIGURE 10.15   DockStyle selection in Form Designer

FIGURE 10.16   TreeNode Editor

Listing 10.16

```
//*****************************************************************
//  PickImage.cs              C#:  Ken Culp
//*****************************************************************
using System.Drawing;
using System.Windows.Forms;

namespace PickImage
{
  public partial class PickImage : Form
  {
    Image curImage;

    public PickImage()
    {
      InitializeComponent();
    }
    private void treeView_AfterSelect(object sender,
      TreeViewEventArgs e)
    {
      // Fetch file name from Text property attached to node
      curImage = Image.FromFile(@"..\..\" + e.Node.Text);

      // Force redraw of form.
      this.Invalidate();
    }

    private void PickImage_Load(object sender,
      System.EventArgs e)
    {
      // Start with toucan: Set listView highlight & image.
      Image curImage = Image.FromFile(@"..\..\toucan.gif");
      treeView.SelectedNode = treeView.Nodes[6];
    }

    private void PickImage_Paint(object sender, PaintEventArgs e)
    {
      // There is no paint method for a ListView object.
      // Must create our own Graphics object to paint.
      Graphics g = listView.CreateGraphics();
      g.Clear(Color.White);
      g.DrawImage(curImage, 0, 0);
      // Graphic objects from CreateGraphics should be disposed
      g.Dispose();
    }
  }
}
```

Listing 10.16   continued

Output

In the output example for Listing 10.16, we resized the window vertically to better fit the toucan. If you display the tiger or the world map, all of these images cannot be seen. Simply expand the window to see all of the image.

Before we leave this example, note a few things about how we drew the image in the `ListView` control. The `ListView` control does not generate a `Paint` event nor does it have an overloadable `OnPaint` method. However, we can still paint on the control but we need to manually create a graphics object. Windows controls include a `CreateGraphics()` method that returns an object of type `Graphics` that can be used to draw on the control. We create that `Graphics` object in the form `Paint` event handler and then clear the `ListView` control and paint the image at location 0, 0. Before exiting the `Paint` method, we dispose of the `Graphics` object we created. This is not necessary, because it will eventually be disposed of by the garbage collector, but it is always a good practice.

10.17 OTHER SAMPLE PROGRAMS

These examples illustrate the principles of polymorphism used in this chapter and apply them to Windows-based applications. These applications are summarized in the following table.

Application Name	Description
`Employee`	Single-screen application for creating employees of various types (salaried, sales, hourly, executive). The screen fields are modified based on the employee type and the data is stored by various classes. Data can be saved to disk using the `Serialize` method. Options are selected by using buttons and menus. The data is stored using `ArrayList` structures.
`groupBox1`	Similar in interface to the `Employee` application except that the underlying data is stored using Active Data Objects (ADO). ADO is beyond the scope of this book, but this application is included in case you wish to study ADO applications. The actual file data is stored in an XML file rather than in an SQL-based database.
`EmployeeAdoJet`	Same as `EmployeeADO` except the data is stored in a Microsoft Jet database. Jet databases can be created and viewed using Microsoft Access. A sample database is included in the directory called Demo.mdb.

Summary of Key Concepts

> Errors and exceptions are objects that represent unusual or invalid processing.

> Each **catch** clause handles a particular kind of exception that may be thrown within the **try** block.

> The **finally** clause is executed whether the **try** block is exited normally or because of a thrown exception.

> If an exception is not caught and handled where it occurs, it is propagated to the calling method.

> A programmer must carefully consider how and where exceptions should be handled, if at all.

> A new exception is defined by deriving a new class from the `Exception` class or one of its descendants.

> A stream is a sequence of bytes; it can be used as a source of input or a destination for output.

> Three public reference variables in the `Console` class represent the standard I/O streams.

> The C# library contains many classes for defining I/O streams with various characteristics.

> Custom events can be created in a class that can be handled in other classes.

> Tool tips and mnemonics can enhance the functionality of a graphical user interface.

> Components should be disabled when their use is inappropriate.

> List boxes and combo boxes provide a drop-down menu of options from which the user may select.

> A scrolling panel is useful for viewing large objects or large amounts of data.

> A split form displays two components side by side or one on top of the other.

Self-Review Questions

10.1   In what ways might a thrown exception be handled?

10.2   What is a **catch** phrase?

10.3   What happens if an exception is not caught?

10.4   What is a stream?

10.5   What are the standard I/O streams?

10.6   What is a tool tip?

10.7 What is a mnemonic and how is it used?

10.8 Why might you want to disable a component?

10.9 Describe the use of scroll bars on a scroll panel.

10.10 What is a combo box?

10.11 How does a combo box differ from a list box?

10.12 What is a tab control?

Exercises

10.1 Create a UML class diagram for the ProductCodes program.

10.2 What would happen if the **try** statement were removed from the Level1 method of the ExceptionScope class in the Propagation program?

10.3 What would happen if the **try** statement described in the previous exercise were moved to the Level2 method?

10.4 Draw the containment hierarchy tree for the LightBulb program.

10.5 Draw the containment hierarchy tree for the PickImage program.

Programming Projects

10.1 Design and implement a program that creates an exception class called StringTooLongException, designed to be thrown when a string is discovered that has too many characters in it. In the Main driver of the program, read strings from the user until the user enters "DONE". If a string is entered that has too many characters (say 20), throw the exception. Allow the thrown exception to terminate the program.

10.2 Modify the solution to Programming Project 10.1 such that it catches and handles the exception if it is thrown. Handle the exception by printing an appropriate message, and then continue processing more strings.

10.3 Modify the LightBulb program to change the tool tip for each button to state how many times that button has been clicked.

10.4 Modify the SsnControls application and change the SSN control to create an event called SsnBad that occurs when someone attempts to modify the Text property with nonnumeric data. Currently, the Set method of the Text property just ignores all bad data. Recompile the class library. Next, modify the SsnTest application to handle that event. Note that you will have to delete the SSN control from the tool box and from the form and then re-add the control to the form to get access to your new event. Add a button that tries to set SSN1.Text to "abcdefghi" and then display an error message with `MessageBox.Show` in the event handler, showing that you caught the error.

10.5   Modify the `StyleOptions` program from Chapter 5 so that it uses a split form. Orient the split such that the label is on the top and the style check boxes are on the bottom. Add tool tips to the check boxes to explain their purpose.

10.6   Modify the `PickImage` program so that it presents several additional image options. Open some blank space below the `ListView` and `TreeView` controls and add a button and a text box. When the button is clicked, add the text in the `TextBox` control to the `TreeView` control. Try adding a valid image file name located in the `PickImage` directory and see if you can display it. Use `treeView.Nodes.Add(`**`string`** `newFile)` to add the new file to the list.

10.8   Design and implement an application that performs flashcard testing of simple mathematical problems. Allow the user to pick the category. Repetitively display a problem and get the user's answer. Indicate whether the user's answer is right or wrong for each problem, and display an ongoing score.

Answers to Self-Review Questions

10.1   A thrown exception can be handled in one of three ways: it can be ignored, which will cause a program to terminate; it can be handled where it occurs using a **`try`** statement; or it can be caught and handled higher in the method-calling hierarchy.

10.2   A **`catch`** phrase of a **`try`** statement defines the code that will handle a particular type of exception.

10.3   If an exception is not caught immediately when thrown, it begins to propagate up through the methods that were called to get to the point where it was generated. The exception can be caught and handled at any point during that propagation. If it propagates out of the `Main` method, the program terminates.

10.4   A stream is a sequential series of bytes that serves as a source of input or a destination for output.

10.5   The standard I/O streams in C# are `Console.In`, the standard input stream; `Console.Out`, the standard output stream; and `Console.Error`, the standard error stream. Usually, standard input comes from the keyboard and standard output and error go to a default window on the monitor screen.

10.6   A tool tip is a small amount of text that can be set up to appear when the cursor comes to rest on a component. It usually gives information about that component.

10.7   A mnemonic is a keyboard character that can be used to activate a control, such as a button, as if the user had used the mouse to do so. The user activates a mnemonic by holding down the Alt key and pressing the appropriate character.

10.8 A component should be disabled if it is not a viable option for the user at a given time. This not only prevents user error, but also helps clarify what the current valid actions are.

10.9 A scroll form can have a vertical scroll bar on the right side and/or a horizontal scroll bar along the bottom. The programmer can determine, in either case, whether the scroll bar should always appear, never appear, or appear as needed to be able to view the underlying component.

10.10 A combo box is a component that allows the user to choose from a set of options in a pull-down list. An editable combo box also allows the user to enter a specific value.

10.11 A combo box allows the user to select from a list of entries or type their own value into the box. A list box allows selection from a specific list but does not allow manual entry.

10.12 A tab control allows multiple sections of controls to be added to a form, with each section selected by clicking on a named tab.

Group Project

Create a new application similar to `PickImage` so that it shows on the left side of the screen a hierarchy of files obtained from scanning the directory. In other words, create a simple version of Windows Explorer on the left side of the screen. On the right side, show the contents of the file if it is an image file (.gif, .jpg, .bmp) using the `Paint` method in `PickImage`. If it is a text file (.txt), display the text of the file using the techniques shown in the `ShowFile` example and the `ListView.Items` collection. This is a large project that will require significant research into the `Directory`, `DirectoryInfo`, `File`, and `FileInfo` classes and into some of the finer details of the `TreeView` and `ListView` controls.

As an alternative to displaying the contents of the files, show only directory entries on the left half and all directories and files under the current directory on the right half. You can list the files by name only or list them with an appropriate type of icon.

Recursion

11

CHAPTER OBJECTIVES

> Explain the underlying concepts of recursion.

> Explore examples that promote recursive thinking.

> Examine recursive methods and unravel their processing steps.

> Define infinite recursion and discuss ways to avoid it.

> Explain when recursion should and should not be used.

> Demonstrate the use of recursion to solve problems.

> Explore the use of recursion in graphics-based programs.

> Define the concept of a fractal and its relationship to recursion.

Recursion is a powerful programming technique that provides elegant solutions to certain problems. This chapter provides an introduction to recursive processing. It explains the basic concepts underlying recursion and then explores the use of recursion in programming. Several specific problems are solved using recursion, demonstrating its versatility, simplicity, and elegance.

RECURSIVE THINKING

We've seen many times in previous examples that one method can call another method to accomplish a goal. What we haven't seen yet, however, is that a method can call itself. Recursion is a programming technique in which a method calls itself in order to fulfill its purpose. But before we get into the details of how we use recursion in a program, we need to explore the general concept of recursion. The ability to think recursively is essential to being able to use recursion as a programming technique.

In general, recursion is the process of defining something in terms of itself. For example, consider the following definition of the word decoration:

decoration: *n.* any ornament or adornment used to decorate something

The word *decorate* is used to define the word *decoration.* You may recall your grade school teacher telling you to avoid such recursive definitions when explaining the meaning of a word. However, in many situations, recursion is an appropriate way to express an idea or definition. For example, suppose we wanted to formally define a list of one or more numbers, separated by commas. Such a list can be defined recursively either as a number or as a number followed by a comma followed by a list. This definition can be expressed as follows:

A *List* is a: number

or a: number   comma   List

This recursive definition of *List* defines each of the following lists of numbers:

```
24, 88, 40, 37
96, 43
14, 64, 21, 69, 32, 93, 47, 81, 28, 45, 81, 52, 69
70
```

No matter how long a list is, the recursive definition describes it. A list of one element, such as in the last example, is defined completely by the first (nonrecursive) part of the definition. For any list longer than one element, the recursive part of the definition (the part which refers to itself) is used as many times as necessary until the last element is reached. The last element in the list is always defined by the nonrecursive part of the definition. Figure 11.1 shows how one particular list of numbers corresponds to the recursive definition of *List*.

Infinite Recursion

Note that the definition of *List* contains one option that is recursive and one option that is not. The part of the definition that is not recursive is called the *base case.* If all options had a recursive component, the recursion would never end. For example, if the definition of *List* were simply "a number followed by a comma followed by a *List*," no list could ever end. This problem is called

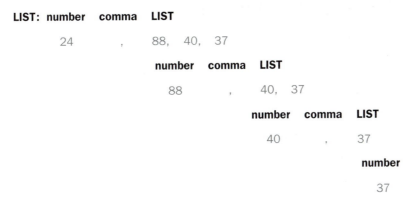

FIGURE 11.1   Tracing the recursive definition of *List*

infinite recursion. It is similar to an infinite loop except that the "loop" occurs in the definition itself.

As in the infinite loop problem, a programmer must be careful to design algorithms so
that they avoid infinite recursion. Any recursive definition must have a base case that does
not result in a recursive option. The base case of the *List* definition is a single number that
is not followed by anything. In other words, when the last number in the list is reached, the
base case option terminates the recursive path.

Recursion in Math

Let's look at an example of recursion in mathematics. The value referred to as *N*! (pronounced *N factorial*) is defined for any positive integer *N* as the product of all integers
between 1 and *N* inclusive. Therefore, 3! is defined as:

```
3!  =  3*2*1  =  6
```

and 5! is defined as:

```
5!  =  5*4*3*2*1  =  120.
```

Mathematical formulas are often expressed recursively. The definition of
N! can be expressed recursively as:

```
1! = 1
N! = N * (N-1)! for N > 1
```

Key Concept

Mathematical problems and formulas
are often expressed recursively.

The base case of this definition is 1!, which is defined as 1. All other values of *N*! (for *N* > 1)
are defined recursively as *N* times the value (*N*–1)!. The recursion is that the factorial function is defined in terms of the factorial function.

Using this definition, 50! is equal to 50 * 49!. And 49! is equal to 49 * 48!. And 48! is equal to 48 * 47!. This process continues until we get to the base case of 1. Because N! is defined only for positive integers, this definition is complete and will always conclude with the base case.

The next section describes how recursion is accomplished in programs.

11.2 RECURSIVE PROGRAMMING

Let's use a simple mathematical operation, albeit highly inefficient to demonstrate the concept of recursive programming. Consider the process of summing the values between 1 and N inclusive, where N is any positive integer. The sum of the values from 1 to N can be expressed as N plus the sum of the values from 1 to $N–1$. That sum can be expressed similarly, as shown in Figure 11.2.

For example, the sum of the values between 1 and 20 is equal to 20 plus the sum of the values between 1 and 19. Continuing this approach, the sum of the values between 1 and 19 is equal to 19 plus the sum of the values between 1 and 18. This may sound like a strange way to think about this problem, but it is a straightforward example that can be used to demonstrate how recursion is programmed.

Key Concept

Each recursive call to a method creates new local variables and parameters.

As we mentioned earlier, in C#, as in many other programming languages, a method can call itself. Each call to the method creates a new environment in which to work. That is, all local variables and parameters are newly defined with their own unique data space every time the method is called. Each parameter is given an initial value based on the new call. Each time a method terminates, processing returns to the method that called it (which may be an earlier invocation of the same method). These rules are no different from those governing any "regular" method invocation.

A recursive solution to the summation problem is defined by the following recursive method called Sum:

```csharp
// This method returns the sum of 1 to num
public int Sum (int num)
{
    int result;
    if (num == 1)
        result = 1;
    else
        result = num + Sum (num-1);
    return result;
}
```

Note that this method essentially embodies our recursive definition that the sum of the numbers between 1 and N is equal to N plus the sum of the numbers between 1 and $N–1$.

$$\sum_{i=1}^{N} i \;=\; N \;+\; \sum_{i=1}^{N-1} i \;=\; N \;+\; N-1 \;+\; \sum_{i=1}^{N-2} i$$

$$=\; N \;+\; N-1 \;+\; N-2 \;+\; \sum_{i=1}^{N-3} i$$

$$\vdots$$

$$=\; N \;+\; N-1 \;+\; N-2 \;+\; \cdots \;+\; 2 \;+\; 1$$

FIGURE 11.2   The sum of the numbers 1 through *N*, defined recursively

The Sum method is recursive because Sum calls itself. The parameter passed to Sum is decremented each time Sum is called until it reaches the base case of 1. Recursive methods invariably contain an **if-else** statement, with one of the branches, usually the first one, representing the base case, as in this example.

Suppose the Main method calls Sum, passing it an initial value of 1, which is stored in the parameter num. Since num is equal to 1, the result of 1 is returned to Main and no recursion occurs.

Now let's trace the execution of the Sum method when it is passed an initial value of 2. Since num does not equal 1, Sum is called again with an argument of num-1, or 1. This is a new call to the method Sum, with a new parameter num and a new local variable result. Since this num is equal to 1 in this invocation, the result of 1 is returned without further recursive calls. Control returns to the first version of Sum that was invoked. The return value of 1 is added to the initial value of num in that call to Sum, which is 2. Therefore, result is assigned the value 3, which is returned to the Main method. The method called from Main correctly calculates the sum of the integers from 1 to 2 and returns the result of 3.

The base case in the summation example is when *N* equals 1, at which point no further recursive calls are made. The recursion begins to fold back into the earlier versions of the Sum method, returning the appropriate value each time. Each return value contributes to the computation of the sum at the higher level. Without the base case, infinite recursion would result. Each call to a method requires additional memory space; therefore, infinite recursion often results in a run-time error indicating that memory has been exhausted.

Trace the Sum function with different initial values of num until this processing becomes familiar. Figure 11.3 illustrates the recursive calls when Main invokes Sum to determine the sum of the integers from 1 to 4. Each box represents a copy of the method as it is invoked, indicating the allocation of space to store the formal parameters and any local variables. Invocations are shown as solid lines, and returns as dotted lines. The return value result is shown at each step. The recursive path is followed completely until the base case is reached; the calls then begin to return their result up through the chain.

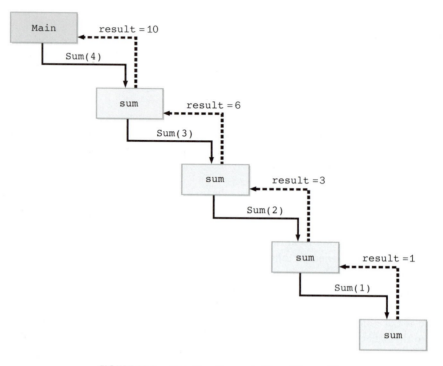

FIGURE 11.3 Iterative Computation of 1 . . . N

Recursion vs. Iteration

Of course, there is a nonrecursive solution to the summation problem we just explored. One way to compute the sum of the numbers between 1 and num inclusive in an iterative manner is as follows:

```
sum = 0;
for (int number = 1; number <= num; number++)
    sum += number;
```

This solution is certainly more straightforward than the recursive version. We used the summation problem to demonstrate recursion because it is simple, not because you would use recursion to solve it under normal conditions. Recursion has the overhead of multiple method invocations and, in this case, presents a much slower and more complicated solution than its iterative counterpart.

A programmer must learn when to use recursion and when not to use it. Determining which approach is best depends on the problem being solved. All problems can be solved in an iterative manner, but in some cases the iterative version is much more complicated. Recursion, for some problems, allows us to create relatively short, elegant programs.

> **Key Concept**
>
> Recursion is the most elegant and appropriate way to solve some problems, but for others it is less intuitive than an iterative solution.

Direct vs. Indirect Recursion

Direct recursion occurs when a method invokes itself, such as when Sum calls Sum. *Indirect recursion* occurs when a method invokes another method, eventually resulting in the original method being invoked again. For example, if method M1 invokes method M2, and M2 invokes method M1, we can say that M1 is indirectly recursive. The amount of indirection could be several levels deep, as when M1 invokes M2, which invokes M3, which invokes M4, which invokes M1. Figure 11.4 depicts a situation with indirect recursion. Method invocations are shown with solid lines, and returns are shown with dotted lines. The entire invocation path is followed, and then the recursion unravels following the return path.

Indirect recursion requires all of the same attention to base cases that direct recursion requires. Furthermore, indirect recursion can be more difficult to trace because of the intervening method calls. Therefore, extra care is warranted when designing or evaluating indirectly recursive methods. Ensure that the indirection is truly necessary and clearly explained in documentation.

11.3   USING RECURSION

Each of the following sections describes a particular recursive problem. For each one, we examine exactly how recursion plays a role in the solution and how a base case is used to terminate the recursion. As you examine these examples, consider how complicated a nonrecursive solution for each problem would be.

Traversing a Maze

Solving a maze involves a great deal of trial and error: following a path, backtracking when you cannot go further, and trying other untried options. Such activities often are handled nicely using recursion. The program shown in Listing 11.1 creates a Maze object and attempts to traverse it.

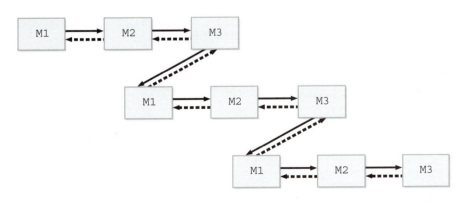

FIGURE 11.4   Indirect recursion

The `Maze` class, shown in Listing 11.2, uses a two-dimensional array of integers to represent the maze. The goal is to move from the top-left corner (the entry point) to the bottom-right corner (the exit point). Initially, a 1 indicates a clear path and a 0 indicates a blocked path. As the maze is solved, these array elements are changed to other values to indicate attempted paths and ultimately a successful path through the maze if one exists.

Listing 11.1

```
//*************************************************************
//  MazeSearch.cs          C#:   Ken Culp
//
//  Demonstrates recursion.
//*************************************************************
using System;

namespace MazeSearch
{

  public class MazeSearch
  {
    //-------------------------------------------------------------
    //  Creates a new maze, prints its original form, attempts to
    //  solve it, and prints out its const form.
    //-------------------------------------------------------------
    public static void Main(String[] args)
    {
      Maze labyrinth = new Maze();

      Console.Out.WriteLine(labyrinth);

      if (labyrinth.Traverse(0, 0))
        Console.Out.WriteLine(
          "The maze was successfully Traversed!");
      else
        Console.Out.WriteLine("There is no possible path.");
      Console.Out.WriteLine(labyrinth);

      Console.In.ReadLine();   // Wait for enter key
    }
  }
}
```

Listing 11.1   continued

Output

```
1110110001111
1011101111001
0000101010100
1110111010111
1010000111001
1011111101111
1000000000000
1111111111111

The maze was successfully traversed!

7770110001111
3077707771001
0000707070300
7770777070333
7070000773003
7077777703333
7000000000000
7777777777777
```

Listing 11.2

```csharp
//****************************************************************
//  Maze.cs          C#:  Ken Culp
//
//  Represents a maze of characters. The goal is to get from the
//  top left corner to the bottom right, following a path of 1s.
//****************************************************************
using System;

namespace MazeSearch
{
  public class Maze
  {
    private const int TRIED = 3;
    private const int PATH = 7;

    private int[,] grid = {
      {1,1,1,0,1,1,0,0,0,1,1,1,1},
      {1,0,1,1,1,0,1,1,1,1,0,0,1},
      {0,0,0,0,1,0,1,0,1,0,1,0,0},
      {1,1,1,0,1,1,1,0,1,0,1,1,1},
      {1,0,1,0,0,0,0,1,1,1,0,0,1},
```

Listing 11.2 continued

```
    {1,0,1,1,1,1,1,1,0,1,1,1,1},
    {1,0,0,0,0,0,0,0,0,0,0,0,0},
    {1,1,1,1,1,1,1,1,1,1,1,1,1} };

//------------------------------------------------------------
//  Attempts to recursively Traverse the maze. Inserts
//  special characters indicating locations that have been
//  tried and that eventually become part of the solution.
//------------------------------------------------------------
public bool Traverse(int row, int column)
{
  bool done = false;

  if (Valid(row, column))
  {
    grid[row, column] = TRIED;  // this cell has been tried

    if (row == grid.GetLength(0) - 1 &&
        column == grid.GetLength(1) - 1)
      done = true;  // the maze is solved
    else
    {
      done = Traverse(row + 1, column);    // down
      if (!done)
        done = Traverse(row, column + 1);  // right
      if (!done)
        done = Traverse(row - 1, column);  // up
      if (!done)
        done = Traverse(row, column - 1);  // left
    }
    if (done)  // this location is part of the const path
      grid[row, column] = PATH;
  }
  return done;
}

//------------------------------------------------------------
//  Determines if a specific location is valid.
//------------------------------------------------------------
private bool Valid(int row, int column)
{
  bool result = false;

  // check if cell is in the bounds of the matrix
  if (row >= 0 && row < grid.GetLength(0) &&
    column >= 0 && column < grid.GetLength(1))
    // check if cell is not blocked and not previously tried
    if (grid[row, column] == 1)
```

Listing 11.2   continued

```
            result = true;
      return result;
   }

   //------------------------------------------------------------
   //  Returns the maze as a string.
   //------------------------------------------------------------
   public override string ToString()
   {
     String result = "\n";

     for (int row = 0; row < grid.GetLength(0); row++)
     {
        for (int column = 0; column < grid.GetLength(1); column++)
          result += grid[row, column] + "";
        result += "\n";
     }
     return result;
   }
  }
 }
```

The only valid moves through the maze are in the four primary directions: down, right, up, and left. No diagonal moves are allowed. In this example, the maze is 8 rows by 13 columns, although the code is designed to handle a maze of any size.

Let's think this through recursively. The maze can be traversed successfully if it can be traversed successfully from position (0, 0). Therefore, the maze can be traversed successfully if it can be traversed successfully from any positions adjacent to (0, 0), namely position (1, 0), position (0, 1), position (–1, 0), or position (0, –1). Picking a potential next step, say (1, 0), we find ourselves in the same type of situation we did before. To successfully traverse the maze from the new current position, we must successfully traverse it from an adjacent position. At any point, some of the adjacent positions may be invalid, may be blocked, or may represent a possible successful path. We continue this process recursively. If the base case, position (7, 12), is reached, the maze has been traversed successfully.

The recursive method in the Maze class is called Traverse. It returns a boolean value that indicates whether a solution was found. First the method determines whether a move to the specified row and column is valid. A move is considered valid if it stays within the grid boundaries and if the grid contains a 1 in that location, indicating that a move in that direction is not blocked. The initial call to Traverse passes in the upper-left location (0, 0).

If the move is valid, the grid entry is changed from a 1 to a 3, marking this location as visited so that later we don't retrace our steps. The Traverse method then determines whether the maze has been completed by having reached the bottom-right location. Therefore, there are actually three possibilities of the base case for this problem that will terminate any particular recursive path:

> > an invalid move because the move is out of bounds

> > an invalid move because the move has been tried before

> > a move that arrives at the final location

If the current location is not the bottom-right corner, we search for a solution in each of the primary directions, if necessary. First, we look down by recursively calling the `Traverse` method and passing in the new location. The logic of the `Traverse` method starts all over again using this new position. A solution is either ultimately found by first attempting to move down from the current location, or it's not found. If it's not found, we try moving right. If that fails, we try up. Finally, if no other direction has yielded a correct path, we try left. If no direction from the current location yields a correct solution, then there is no path from this location, and `Traverse` returns false.

If a solution is found from the current location, the grid entry is changed to a 7. The first 7 is placed in the bottom-right corner. The next 7 is placed in the location that led to the bottom-right corner, and so on until the final 7 is placed in the upper-left corner. Therefore, when the final maze is printed, the 0's still indicate a blocked path, a 1 indicates an open path that was never tried, a 3 indicates a path that was tried but failed to yield a correct solution, and a 7 indicates a part of the final solution of the maze.

Note that there are several opportunities for recursion in each call to the `Traverse` method. Any or all of them might be followed, depending on the maze configuration. Although there may be many paths through the maze, the recursion terminates when a path is found. Carefully trace the execution of this code while following the maze array to see how the recursion solves the problem. Then consider the difficulty of producing a non-recursive solution.

The Towers of Hanoi

The *Towers of Hanoi* puzzle was invented in the 1880s by Edouard Lucas, a French mathematician. It has become a favorite among computer scientists because its solution is an excellent demonstration of recursive elegance.

The puzzle consists of three upright pegs and a set of disks with holes in the middle so that they slide onto the pegs. Each disk has a different diameter. Initially, all the disks are stacked on one peg in order of size such that the largest disk is on the bottom, as shown in Figure 11.5.

The goal of the puzzle is to move all the disks from their original (first) peg to the destination (third) peg. We can use the "extra" peg as a temporary place to put disks, but we must obey the following three rules:

> > We can move only one disk at a time.

> > We cannot place a larger disk on top of a smaller disk.

> > All disks must be on some peg except for the disk in transit between pegs.

These rules imply that we must move smaller disks "out of the way" in order to move a larger disk from one peg to another. Figure 11.6 shows the step-by-step solution for the

FIGURE 11.5   The Towers of Hanoi puzzle

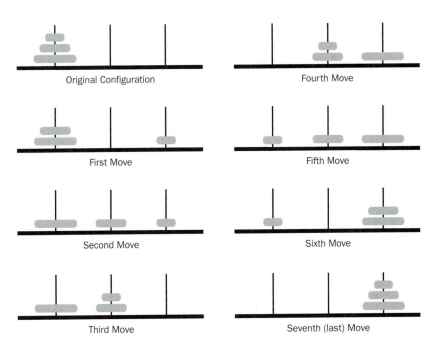

FIGURE 11.6   A solution to the three-disk Towers of Hanoi puzzle

Towers of Hanoi puzzle using three disks. In order to ultimately move all three disks from the first peg to the third peg, we first have to get to the point where the smaller two disks are out of the way on the second peg so that the largest disk can be moved from the first peg to the third peg.

The first three moves shown in Figure 11.6 can be thought of as moving the smaller disks out of the way. The fourth move puts the largest disk in its final place. The last three moves then put the smaller disks to their final place on top of the largest one.

Let's use this idea to form a general strategy. To move a stack of N disks from the original peg to the destination peg:

> Move the topmost *N*–1 disks from the original peg to the extra peg.

> Move the largest disk from the original peg to the destination peg.

> Move the *N*–1 disks from the extra peg to the destination peg.

This strategy lends itself nicely to a recursive solution. The step to move the *N*–1 disks out of the way is the same problem all over again: moving a stack of disks. For this subtask, though, there is one less disk, and our destination peg is what we were originally calling the extra peg. An analogous situation occurs after we've moved the largest disk, and we have to move the original *N*–1 disks again.

The base case for this problem occurs when we want to move a "stack" that consists of only one disk. That step can be accomplished directly and without recursion.

The program in Listing 11.3 creates a TowersOfHanoi object and invokes its Solve method. The output is a step-by-step list of instructions that describes how the disks should be moved to solve the puzzle. This example uses four disks, which is specified by a parameter to the TowersOfHanoi constructor.

The TowersOfHanoi class shown in Listing 11.4 uses the Solve method to make an initial call to MoveTower, the recursive method. The initial call indicates that all the disks should be moved from peg 1 to peg 3, using peg 2 as the extra position.

Listing 11.3

```
//*************************************************************
//   SolveTowers.cs          C#:   Ken Culp
//
//   Demonstrates recursion.
//*************************************************************
using System;

namespace SolveTowers
{

  public class SolveTowers
  {
    //-------------------------------------------------------------
    //   Creates a TowersOfHanoi puzzle and solves it.
    //-------------------------------------------------------------
    public static void Main(String[] args)
    {
      TowersOfHanoi towers = new TowersOfHanoi(4);

      towers.Solve();

      Console.ReadLine();  // Wait for enter key
    }
  }
}
```

Listing 11.3   continued

Output

```
Move one disk from 1 to 2
Move one disk from 1 to 3
Move one disk from 2 to 3
Move one disk from 1 to 2
Move one disk from 3 to 1
Move one disk from 3 to 2
Move one disk from 1 to 2
Move one disk from 1 to 3
Move one disk from 2 to 3
Move one disk from 2 to 1
Move one disk from 3 to 1
Move one disk from 2 to 3
Move one disk from 1 to 2
Move one disk from 1 to 3
Move one disk from 2 to 3
```

Listing 11.4

```csharp
//****************************************************************
//   TowersOfHanoi.cs          C#: Ken Culp
//
//   Represents the classic Towers of Hanoi puzzle.
//****************************************************************
using System;

namespace SolveTowers
{
  public class TowersOfHanoi
  {
    private int totalDisks;
    //------------------------------------------------------------
    //   Sets up the puzzle with the specified number of disks.
    //------------------------------------------------------------
    public TowersOfHanoi(int disks)
    {
      totalDisks = disks;
    }
    //------------------------------------------------------------
    //   Performs initial call to MoveTower to solve the puzzle.
    //   Moves the disks from tower 1 to tower 3 using tower 2.
    //------------------------------------------------------------
```

Listing 11.4   continued

```
public void Solve()
{
   MoveTower(totalDisks, 1, 3, 2);
}
//---------------------------------------------------------------
//  Moves the specified number of disks from one tower to
//  another by moving a subtower of n-1 disks out of the way,
//  moving one disk, then moving the subtower back.
//  Base case of 1 disk.
//---------------------------------------------------------------
private void MoveTower(int numDisks, int start,
   int end, int temp)
{
   if (numDisks == 1)
      MoveOneDisk(start, end);
   else
   {
      MoveTower(numDisks - 1, start, temp, end);
      MoveOneDisk(start, end);
      MoveTower(numDisks - 1, temp, end, start);
   }
}
//---------------------------------------------------------------
//  Prints instructions to move one disk from the specified
//  start tower to the specified end tower.
//---------------------------------------------------------------
private void MoveOneDisk(int start, int end)
{
   Console.Out.WriteLine("Move one disk from " + start +
      " to " + end);
}
   }
}
```

The MoveTower method first considers the base case (a "stack" of one disk). When that occurs, it calls the MoveOneDisk method that prints a single line describing that particular move. If the stack contains more than one disk, we call MoveTower again to get the N–1 disks out of the way, then move the largest disk, and then move the N–1 disks to their final destination with yet another call to MoveTower.

Note that the parameters to MoveTower describing the pegs are switched around as needed to move the partial stacks. This code follows our general strategy and uses the MoveTower method to move all partial stacks. Trace the code carefully for a stack of three disks to understand the processing. Compare the processing steps to Figure 11.6.

Contrary to its short and elegant implementation, the solution to the Towers of Hanoi puzzle is terribly inefficient. To solve the puzzle with a stack of N disks, we have to make 2^N-1 individual disk moves. This situation is an example of *exponential complexity*. As the number of disks increases, the number of required moves increases exponentially.

Legend has it that priests of Brahma are working on this puzzle in a temple at the center of the world. They are using 64 gold disks, moving them between pegs of pure diamond. The downside is that when the priests finish the puzzle, the world will end. The upside is that even if they move one disk every second of every day, it will take them over 584 billion years to complete it. That's with a puzzle of only 64 disks! It is certainly an indication of just how intractable exponential algorithmic complexity is.

> **Key Concept**
>
> The Towers of Hanoi solution has exponential complexity, which is very inefficient. Yet the implementation of the solution is incredibly short and elegant.

11.4   RECURSION IN GRAPHICS

The concept of recursion has several uses in images and graphics. The following section explores some image- and graphics-based recursion examples.

Tiled Pictures

Carefully examine the display for the `TiledPictures` form shown in Listing 11.5. There are actually three unique images among the menagerie. The entire area is divided into four equal quadrants. A picture of the world (with a circle indicating the Himalayan mountain region) is shown in the bottom-right quadrant. The bottom-left quadrant contains a picture of Mt. Everest. In the top-right quadrant is a picture of a mountain goat.

The interesting part of the picture is the top-left quadrant. It contains a copy of the entire collage, including itself. In this smaller version you can see the three simple pictures in their three quadrants. And again, in the top-left corner, the picture is repeated (including itself). This repetition continues for several levels. It is similar to the effect you can create when looking at a mirror in the reflection of another mirror.

This visual effect is created quite easily using recursion. The class constructor for the form initially loads the three images. Note that the constructor also sets the dimensions of the `ClientSize` so that the initial size of the form in the Form Designer does not matter. The `Paint` method then invokes the `DrawPictures` method, which accepts a parameter that defines the size of the area in which pictures are displayed. It draws the three images using the `DrawImage` method, with parameters that scale the picture to the correct size and location. The `DrawPictures` method is then called recursively to draw the upper-left quadrant.

On each invocation, if the drawing area is large enough, the `DrawPictures` method is invoked again, using a smaller drawing area. Eventually, the drawing area becomes so small that the recursive call is not performed. Note that `DrawPictures` assumes the origin (0, 0) coordinate as the relative location of the new images, no matter what their size is.

The base case of the recursion in this problem specifies a minimum size for the drawing area. Because the size is decreased each time, the base case eventually is reached and the recursion stops. This is why the upper-left corner is empty in the smallest version of the collage.

Listing 11.5

```csharp
//****************************************************************
//  TiledPictures.cs          C#:  Ken Culp
//
//  Demonstrates the use of recursion.
//****************************************************************
using System;
using System.Collections.Generic;
using System.ComponentModel;
using System.Data;
using System.Drawing;
using System.Text;
using System.Windows.Forms;

namespace Tiled_Pictures
{
  public partial class TiledPictures : Form
  {
    private Image world, everest, goat;
    private const int CLIENT_WIDTH = 320;
    private const int CLIENT_HEIGHT = 320;
    private const int MIN = 20;   // smallest picture size
    //------------------------------------------------------------
    //  Constructor:  Loads three images and adjust screen size
    //------------------------------------------------------------
    public TiledPictures()
    {
      InitializeComponent();
      world = Image.FromFile(@"..\..\world.gif");
      everest = Image.FromFile(@"..\..\everest.gif");
      goat = Image.FromFile(@"..\..\goat.gif");
      this.ClientSize = new Size(CLIENT_WIDTH, CLIENT_HEIGHT);
    }
    //------------------------------------------------------------
    //  Draws the three images, then calls itself recursively.
    //------------------------------------------------------------
    public void drawPictures(int size, Graphics page)
    {
      page.DrawImage(everest, 0, size / 2, size / 2, size / 2);
      page.DrawImage(goat, size / 2, 0, size / 2, size / 2);
      page.DrawImage(world, size / 2, size / 2, size / 2, size / 2);
```

Listing 11.5   continued

```
      if (size > MIN)
        drawPictures(size / 2, page);
   }
   //-----------------------------------------------------------
   //  Performs the initial call to the drawPictures method.
   //-----------------------------------------------------------
   private void TiledPictures_Paint(object sender,
                                    PaintEventArgs e)
   {
      Graphics page = e.Graphics;
      drawPictures(CLIENT_WIDTH, page);
   }
 }
}
```

Display

Fractals

A *fractal* is a geometric shape that can be made up of the same pattern repeated at different scales and orientations. The nature of a fractal lends itself to a recursive definition. Interest in fractals has grown immensely in recent years, largely due to Benoit Mandelbrot, a Polish mathematician born in 1924. He demonstrated that fractals occur in many places in mathematics and nature. Computers have made fractals much easier to generate and investigate. Over the past quarter century, the bright, interesting images that can be created with fractals have come to be considered as much an art form as a mathematical interest.

One particular example of a fractal is called the *Koch snowflake,* named after Helge von Koch, a Swedish mathematician. It begins with an equilateral triangle, which is considered to be the Koch fractal of order 1. Koch fractals of higher orders are constructed by repeatedly modifying all the line segments in the shape.

To create the next higher-order Koch fractal, each line segment in the shape is modified by replacing its middle third with a sharp protrusion made of two line segments, each having the same length as the replaced part. Relative to the entire shape, the protrusion on any line segment always points outward. Figure 11.7 shows several orders of Koch fractals. As the order increases, the shape begins to look like a snowflake.

The form code shown in Listing 11.6 draws a Koch snowflake of several different orders. The buttons at the top of the form allow the user to increase and decrease the order of the fractal. Each time a button is clicked, the fractal image is redrawn.

Note that the arrow on the mouse buttons changes color when the mouse is moved over the image. This is done by changing the image on each button on `MouseEnter` and `MouseLeave`. Since we need four images, we use an array of images control called `ImageList`. Once dropped on a form, this control appears not on the form but in the area below the form. Choose a useful name for the control, because you will be referencing the control in code. You add images to the control by adding them to the `Images` collection. Then, you reference the images in code by using array notation and an index, as shown in the `MouseEnter` and `MouseLeave` handlers.

The image files are named `increase.gif`, `decrease.gif`, `increasePressed.gif`, and `decreasePressed.gif` and are located in the `KochSnowflake` directory. These

FIGURE 11.7   Several orders of the Koch snowflake

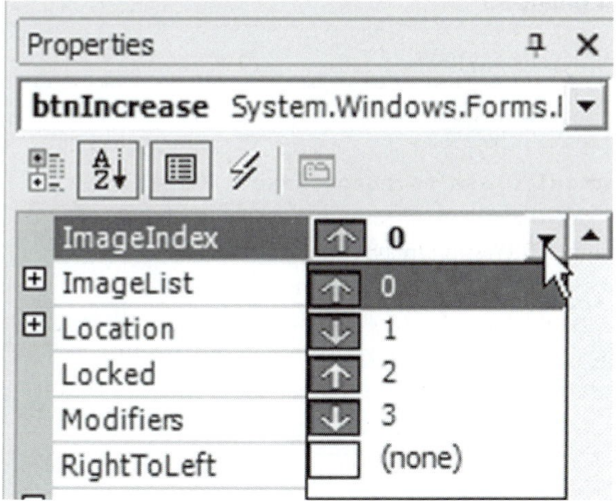

FIGURE 11.8   Selecting from ImageIndex

image files are added to our `ImageList` control named `imgButtons` one at a time in the preceding order, so they will be numbered 0 to 3 in the preceding order.

Once the images have been added to the `ImageList` control, we can use the list to set the initial images for the buttons. Select a button and, in the Properties window, set the `ImageList` property to `imgButtons`. Clicking the drop-down arrow to the right of the `ImageList` property will list all controls of the type `ImageList` so that you can select it without having to type the name.

After setting the `ImageList` property for the button, you now only have to select the correct button from the list. Select the `ImageIndex` property and click the drop-down arrow. You will see all the images in `imgButtons`, as shown in Figure 11.8. Select the desired image from the list.

Listing 11.6

```
//**************************************************************
//  KochSnowflake.cs        C#:  Ken Culp
//
//  Builds a GUI for displaying and changing the Koch Snowflake.
//  Note:  The buttons respond to the mouse being over them.
//         Thus the image for the button is changed when the
//         mouse enters/leaves each button implying 4 images.
//         These were created at design time in an ImageList
//         control and then the handlers index into the list.
//**************************************************************
using System;
using System.Drawing;
```

Listing 11.6   continued

```csharp
using System.Windows.Forms;

namespace KochSnowflake
{
  public partial class KochSnowflake : Form
  {
    private KochPanel fractal;

    public KochSnowflake()
    {
      InitializeComponent();
      fractal = new KochPanel(4);
    }
    //-----------------------------------------------------------
    //  Load:  Show current order
    //-----------------------------------------------------------
    private void KochSnowflake_Load(object sender, EventArgs e)
    {
      lblOrder.Text = "Order: " + fractal.Order.ToString();
    }
    //-----------------------------------------------------------
    //  btnIncrease events: Click, Enter, Leave
    //-----------------------------------------------------------
    private void btnIncrease_Click(object sender, EventArgs e)
    {
      fractal.Order++;
      lblOrder.Text = "Order: " + fractal.Order.ToString();
      picBox.Invalidate();
    }
    private void btnIncrease_MouseEnter(object sender,
      EventArgs e)
    {
      btnIncrease.ImageIndex = 2;
    }
    private void btnIncrease_MouseLeave(object sender,
      EventArgs e)
    {
      btnIncrease.ImageIndex = 0;
    }
    //-----------------------------------------------------------
    //  btnDecrease events: Click, Enter, Leave
    //-----------------------------------------------------------
    private void btnDecrease_Click(object sender, EventArgs e)
    {
      fractal.Order--;
      lblOrder.Text = "Order: " + fractal.Order.ToString();
      picBox.Invalidate();
    }
    private void btnDecrease_MouseEnter(object sender,
      EventArgs e)
```

Listing 11.6   continued

```
  {
    btnDecrease.ImageIndex = 3;
  }
  private void btnDecrease_MouseLeave(object sender,
    EventArgs e)
  {
    btnDecrease.ImageIndex = 1;
  }
  //-----------------------------------------------------------
  //  picBox.Paint:  Draws the fractal
  //-----------------------------------------------------------
  private void picBox_Paint(object sender, PaintEventArgs e)
  {
    fractal.Paint(e.Graphics);
  }
  }
}
```

Display

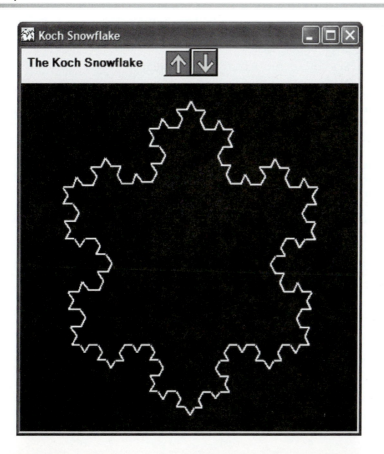

The fractal image is drawn on a canvas defined by the KochPanel class shown in Listing 11.7. The Paint method makes the initial calls to the recursive method DrawFractal. The three calls to DrawFractal in the Paint method represent the original three sides of the equilateral triangle that make up a Koch fractal of order 1.

The variable current represents the order of the fractal to be drawn. Each recursive call to DrawFractal decrements the order by 1. The base case of the recursion occurs when the order of the fractal is 1, which results in a simple line segment between the coordinates specified by the parameters.

Listing 11.7

```csharp
//***************************************************************
//  KochPanel.cs          C#:  Ken Culp
//
//  A drawing surface on which to paint a Koch Snowflake.
//***************************************************************
using System;
using System.Drawing;
using System.Drawing.Drawing2D;

namespace KochSnowflake
{
  public class KochPanel
  {
    private const int PANEL_WIDTH = 400;
    private const int PANEL_HEIGHT = 400;
    private const int MIN_ORDER = 1, MAX_ORDER = 9;
    private const int TOPX = 200, TOPY = 20;
    private const int LEFTX = 60, LEFTY = 300;
    private const int RIGHTX = 340, RIGHTY = 300;

    private double SQ;
    private int current;   // current order
    private Pen drawPen;   // pen for drawing

    //-------------------------------------------------------------
    //  Sets the initial fractal order to the value specified.
    //-------------------------------------------------------------
    public KochPanel(int currentOrder)
    {
      current = currentOrder;
      SQ = Math.Sqrt(3.0) / 6;
      drawPen = new Pen(Color.White, 2);
    }
    //-------------------------------------------------------------
    //  Sets the fractal order to the value specified.
    //-------------------------------------------------------------
```

Listing 11.7   continued

```
public int Order
{
  get { return current; }
  set
  {
    if (MIN_ORDER <= value && value <= MAX_ORDER)
      current = value;
  }
}
//---------------------------------------------------------------
//  Draws the fractal recursively. The base case is order 1
//  for which a simple straight line is drawn. Otherwise
//  three intermediate points are computed, and each line
//  segment is drawn as a fractal.
//---------------------------------------------------------------
public void DrawFractal(int order, int x1, int y1,
      int x5, int y5,
  Graphics page)
{
  int deltaX, deltaY, x2, y2, x3, y3, x4, y4;

  if (order == 1)
    page.DrawLine(drawPen, x1, y1, x5, y5);
  else
  {
    deltaX = x5 - x1;  // distance between end points
    deltaY = y5 - y1;

    x2 = x1 + deltaX / 3;  // one third
    y2 = y1 + deltaY / 3;

    x3 = (int)((x1 + x5) / 2 + SQ * (y1 - y5));  // tip
    y3 = (int)((y1 + y5) / 2 + SQ * (x5 - x1));

    x4 = x1 + deltaX * 2 / 3;  // two thirds
    y4 = y1 + deltaY * 2 / 3;

    DrawFractal(order - 1, x1, y1, x2, y2, page);
    DrawFractal(order - 1, x2, y2, x3, y3, page);
    DrawFractal(order - 1, x3, y3, x4, y4, page);
    DrawFractal(order - 1, x4, y4, x5, y5, page);
  }
}
//---------------------------------------------------------------
//  Performs the initial calls to the DrawFractal method.
//---------------------------------------------------------------
public void Paint(Graphics page)
{
```

Listing 11.7 continued

```
        DrawFractal(current, TOPX, TOPY, LEFTX, LEFTY, page);
        DrawFractal(current, LEFTX, LEFTY, RIGHTX, RIGHTY, page);
        DrawFractal(current, RIGHTX, RIGHTY, TOPX, TOPY, page);
      }
    }
  }
```

If the order of the fractal is higher than 1, three additional points are computed. In conjunction with the parameters, these points form the four line segments of the modified fractal. Figure 11.9 shows the transformation.

Based on the position of the two end points of the original line segment, a point one-third of the way and a point two-thirds of the way between them are computed. The calculation of $<x_3, y_3>$, the point at the tip of the protrusion, is more convoluted and uses a simplifying constant that incorporates multiple geometric relationships. The calculations to determine the three new points actually have nothing to do with the recursive technique used to draw the fractal, so we won't discuss the details of these computations here.

An interesting mathematical feature of a Koch snowflake is that it has an infinite perimeter but a finite area. As the order of the fractal increases, the perimeter grows exponentially larger, with a mathematical limit of infinity. However, a rectangle large enough to surround the second-order fractal for the Koch snowflake is large enough to contain all higher-order fractals. The shape is restricted forever in area, but its perimeter gets infinitely longer.

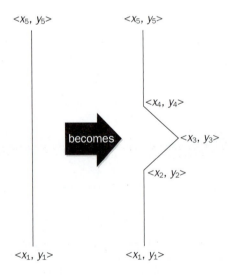

FIGURE 11.9 The transformation of each line segment of a Koch snowflake

11.5   PRINTING

Up to this point, all the drawing we have done has been on Windows controls such as a form or a panel. We now turn our attention to drawing as it relates to printing and generating printed reports. For the most part, printing resembles drawing on the screen in that you use a `Graphics` object and the usual draw methods. However, the physical characteristics of a printer are different from the screen, and event handling has some special considerations. In the sections that follow, we highlight only a small fraction of the details regarding how to print in C#. For more information, show the help files and examine the various controls described here (select the "All Members" entry under the control name in the Index).

The Print Document (`PrintDocument`)

At the heart of printing is the `PrintDocument` class. This class has a fairly large number of members, so Figure 11.10 lists only the most useful.

A `PrintDocument` object can be created in code or can be added directly from the toolbar to the form. When a `PrintDocument` object is added to the form from the tool box, it

PrintDocument Properties	
DocumentName	View or change the document name to display in a print status dialog box or printer queue when the document is printing.
PrinterSettings	View or change the printer to use for this document.

PrintDocument Public Methods	
Print	Starts the document's printing process.
ToString	Provides text information about the document.

PrintDocument Public Events	
BeginPrint	Occurs when the `Print` method is called but before the `PrintPage` event (before the first page of the document prints).
EndPrint	Occurs after the last page of the document has printed.
PrintPage	Occurs when the output to print for the current page is needed. This is the default and most used event.

FIGURE 11.10   Some PrintDocument members

appears at the bottom of the screen and is not actually placed on the form. If you add a document by using the Form Designer, you can configure the properties in the Form Designer as well. One of the properties you will want to configure is `DocumentName`. You will also want to add the handler for the `PrintPage` event. We will describe the actual printing process later in this section.

To print using only the `PrintDocument` requires that after creating the object, you would have a handler for the `PrintPage` event, have completed the `PrinterSettings` property, and start printing by calling the `Print` method. Therefore, to simply print directly to a printer (or to a file), follow these steps:

1. Create the `PrintDocument` object.

2. Add a handler to the `PrintPage` event.

3. Set the `PrinterSettings` property.

4. Call the `Print` method using the document object.

5. Handle the `PrintPage` event.

Printer Settings (`PrinterSettings`)

The `PrintSettings` class includes everything known about the printer, including such things as `PrinterName`, `Copies`, `PaperSources`, and the like. These properties control the printing process.

You can enter all of these properties via code (which would be really tedious) or you can first prompt the user for these values, using the `PageSetupDialog` class, as described in Chapter 9. One of the properties of `PageSetupDialog` is `PrinterSettings`, which would then be copied from the setup dialog to the print document before the `Print` method is called.

Using the Preview Dialog (`PrintPreviewDialog`)

Using the `PrintPreviewDialog`, described in Chapter 9, is by far the easiest way to print, and thus it is the way we use in our example. The preview dialog will request the document be printed and show the document to the user for printing. From that point, the user can scroll through the generated output, change the printer, print, or simply exit.

To use the `PrintPreviewDialog` control, simply drop the control on your form *after* you have added the `PrintDocument` property. Then set the `PrintDocument` property of the control to point to the document already added. Then, when the `Show` or `ShowDialog` method is called from the preview dialog object, the `Print` method for the document is requested and the `PrintPage` event handler generates the output. To print using the dialog, follow these steps:

1. Drop a `PrintDocument` control on the form and give it a name you can recognize (or keep the Form Designer default name).

2. Set `DocumentName` and add a `PrintPage` handler to the document.

3. Drop a `PrintPreviewDialog` control on the form and set the `PrintDocument` property to the name given to the document in Step 1.

4. Call the `Show` or `ShowDialog` method from the `PrintPreviewDialog` control.

The Printed Page

Before we describe how to write the event handler for the `PrintPage` event, we need to describe some of the characteristics of the printed page and how drawing methods address locations on the printed page.

The origin of the coordinates for drawing on a printed page default to the upper-left corner of the page, with positive values being measured to the right and down. The default unit of measure when using a `Graphics` object and the drawing methods on a printed page is 1/100 inch (kind of like pixels for a screen). If the page dimensions (passed to the handler) are 8.5 inches wide by 11 inches high, then x would need to range from 0 to 850 and y from 0 to 1100. To use inches, you can change the coordinate system (not covered here) or multiply each location in inches by 100.

Most printers have resolutions larger than 1/100 of an inch. Therefore, for more precise specification of a position, use floating-point coordinates rather than integers (all methods support integer or floating-point coordinates).

The `PrintPage` Event Handler

The last step for printing is probably the hardest. We can get to this point in a matter of seconds by using the Form Designer and the previously described steps and controls. Now let's look at how we generate a good-looking report.

The signature for the `PrintPage` handler from the example presented in the following section is shown here:

```
private void printDoc_PrintPage(object sender,
    System.Drawing.Printing.PrintPageEventArgs pea)
```

We created the event handler from the Form Designer but changed the second parameter from e to pea, which is more descriptive. The first parameter, sender, is the `PrintDocument` object. The second parameter contains all the information about the printing process, as described in Figure 11.11.

`PrintPageEventArg` includes the `PageSettings` object, which is very useful, as described in Figure 11.12.

The data passed with `PrintPageEventArgs` (see Figure 11.11) allows for very detailed control of the print process. You can ensure printing within bounds, adjust various settings, decide whether to print in color or not, and a lot more.

PrintPageEventArgs Public Properties	
Cancel	View or change a setting saying that the print job should be canceled
Graphics	The Graphics object for printing the page
HasMorePages	View or change whether an additional page should be printed
MarginBounds	View the rectangular area representing the portion of the page inside the margins
PageBounds	View the rectangular area representing the total area of the page
PageSettings	Get the page settings for the current page

FIGURE 11.11   Some PrintPageEventArgs properties

PageSettings Public Properties	
Bounds	View the size of the page, including the page orientation specified by the Landscape property
Color	View or modify whether the page should be printed in color
Landscape	View or modify whether the page should be printed in landscape or portrait orientation (true is landscape)
Margins	View or modify the margins
PaperSize	View or modify the paper size
PaperSource	View or modify the page's paper source (lower tray, etc.)
PrinterResolution	View the printer resolution for the page
PrinterSettings	View or modify the printer settings for the page

FIGURE 11.12   Some PageSettings properties

A Print Example

This section presents a simple printing example that illustrates the techniques described in the previous sections. We will start with the SerializeTest application from Chapter 10 and add a report that shows the data from the dialog box. To create the application, copy the SerializeTest application to a new directory and open it. When we created the example code below, we renamed SerializeTest to PrintTest everywhere it occurred, including the name of the file. Listing 11.8 lists only the code changes associated with printing. The remainder of the code remains the same.

Now, drop a `PrintDocument` control on the form and name it **printDoc**. Drop a `PrintPreviewDialog` control on the form and name it **printDlg**. Set the dialog box `PrintDocument` property to point to `printDoc`.

Next, expand the File menu and add an entry labeled **&Print** with a name of **mnuFilePrint**. Set the `Shortcut` property to `Ctrl/P`. Create a click event handler for the `Click` event for this menu item and type the code shown in Listing 11.8.

Next, add an integer class variable somewhere to the class called `curPage` and define an integer constant called `MAX_PAGES` and set its value to 2. We added our class variables right after the event handler for the menu item so that it would be next to the code that references it.

Finally, add the event handler to the `PrintPage` event for the print document. Type the code as shown in Listing 11.8. In the code, we do not use much of the extensive information passed to the event handler. We use only the left, right, and top margins for printing our report, the `Graphics` object, and the `HasMorePages` property. Note that a quality, multiline report that could span a page would use the bottom margin as well.

Listing 11.8

```
//-------------------------------------------------
//   Menu/File/Print.  Shows print preview dialog
//   Displaying the preview dialog fires the PrintPage
//   event below.
//-------------------------------------------------
private void mnuFilePrint_Click(object sender, System.EventArgs e)
{
  curPage = 1;
  printDlg.Width = 500;
  printDlg.Height = 500;
  printDlg.ShowDialog();
}

private int curPage;   // Current Page Number
const int MAX_PAGES = 2;

private void printDoc_PrintPage(object sender,
  System.Drawing.Printing.PrintPageEventArgs pea)
{
  // The default x and y coordinates during printing are
  // measured in 1/100 of an inch or 1 inch offset
  // would be a value of 100.
  Graphics g = pea.Graphics;

  // Compute margins for our printing.
```

Listing 11.8 continued

```
int left   = pea.MarginBounds.X;                    // Left
int right  = left + pea.MarginBounds.Width;         // Right
int top    = pea.MarginBounds.Top;                  // Top
int center = left + pea.MarginBounds.Width / 2;     // Center

// Create brushes and fonts.
Brush brush = new SolidBrush(Color.Black);
Font ft16B = new Font("Times New Roman", 16, FontStyle.Bold);
Font ft12B = new Font("Times New Roman", 12, FontStyle.Bold);
Font ft12R = new Font("Times New Roman", 12, FontStyle.Regular);

// Create StringAlignment controls.
StringFormat sfLeft   = new StringFormat();
StringFormat sfRight  = new StringFormat();
StringFormat sfCenter = new StringFormat();
sfLeft  .Alignment = StringAlignment.Near;
sfRight .Alignment = StringAlignment.Far;
sfCenter.Alignment = StringAlignment.Center;

// Some data strings for output.
string cityStZip = emp.City + ", " + emp.State +
                   "  " + emp.ZipCode;
string ssn = emp.SSN.ToString("###-##-####");
string curPageS = "Page: " + curPage.ToString();

// Banner 1 inch down, centered in page.  Include page #.
g.DrawString(this.Text, ft16B, brush, center, top, sfCenter);
g.DrawString(curPageS,  ft12B, brush, right,  top, sfRight);

// Labels right justified and values left justified.
int x  = left + 100; // Location for labels/data
int y = 200; // start data 2 inches down

g.DrawString("Last:",     ft12B, brush, x,   y, sfRight);
g.DrawString(emp.Last,    ft12R, brush, x+8, y, sfLeft);
y += 15; // To new line
g.DrawString("First:",    ft12B, brush, x,   y, sfRight);
g.DrawString(emp.First,   ft12R, brush, x+8, y, sfLeft);
y += 15; // To new line
g.DrawString("Address:",  ft12B, brush, x,   y, sfRight);
g.DrawString(emp.Address, ft12R, brush, x+8, y, sfLeft);
y += 15; // To new line
g.DrawString(cityStZip,   ft12R, brush, x+8, y, sfLeft);
y += 15; // To new line
g.DrawString("Phone:",    ft12B, brush, x,   y, sfRight);
g.DrawString(emp.Phone,   ft12R, brush, x+8, y, sfLeft);
y += 15; // To new line
```

Listing 11.8   continued

```
    g.DrawString("SSN:",        ft12B, brush, x,    y, sfRight);
    g.DrawString(ssn,           ft12R, brush, x+8, y, sfLeft);

    // To simulate multipage report, print same data twice
    curPage++;
    pea.HasMorePages = (curPage <= MAX_PAGES);
}
```

Starting the Print Job

Let's examine the code in Listing 11.8 in detail. First, note the simplicity of the event handler for the menu item. All it absolutely had to do was call `dlgPrint.ShowDialog`. We also modified the dimensions of the dialog box so that viewing the document would be a little easier. We also initialized a variable that is used to control a multipage print process. This is quite typical. In most cases, the variable is some pointer to a list of information that gets updated during the print process. Then, when we start a new page, we know where to pick back up in our list of data.

Creating Fonts and Brush

Next, we build three font objects based on font size and the bold property. The large, bold font is used for the report banner, the smaller bold font is used for the data labels, and the normal font is used for the data itself. We also create a black brush.

Justifying Text

The `DrawString` methods have an option to justify the text in any of three ways: `Far`, `Near`, and `Center`. `Far` and `Near` are used rather than "Right" and "Left" because Visual Studio supports alphabets from other countries that can be written right to left (note the `RightToLeft` property on various controls, including text boxes). For our purposes, where we write left to right, `Far` corresponds to right justification and `Near` corresponds to left justification (the default).

String alignment is one of the capabilities of the `StringFormat` class. The features of this class, other than alignment, are beyond the scope of this text. These include text direction (including vertical!), text wrapping in a bounding rectangle, and much, much more. Search the index for `StringFormat` and select the "All Members" category and follow the links from there. For our example, we use only the alignment portion.

Writing the Report

Before writing the report, we format three strings from the employee data. Formatting these is not necessary but improves readability of the code. Once we have these, we begin writing the report by starting with our banner line, which includes a centered title and a right-justified page number.

Now, to keep track of where we are in the report, we use two integers, x for the horizontal offset and y for the vertical. We increment y after every line but x remains constant.

We use *x* for writing the data labels and the data itself. We right-justify the data label at *x* and left-justify the data itself 0.08 inch to the right. This leaves a gap of 0.08 inch between the label and its value.

Multipage Reports

To simulate a multipage report, we write the same data to two different pages using our `curPage` variable above and the `MAX_PAGES` constant created previously. When you reach the exit point from the `PrintPage` handler, you must tell the system if there are more pages (the default is that there are not). This is done by setting the `HasMorePages` property to **true** when there are more pages. We simply evaluate whether or not we have passed the last page and set that value in `HasMorePages`.

When `HasMorePages` is set to true, as soon as the event handler exits, it is called again for the next page. This process is repeated until all pages are done. Thus the `PrintPage` event handler will be called repeatedly until `HasMorePages` is set to **false**. Note, however, that `HasMorePages` is false upon every entry to the event handler. Therefore, to print another page, you must set `HasMorePages` to true before exiting the handler. The .NET system uses these repeated calls to keep track of the split between pages.

Example Summary

Printing at the `Graphics` object level is quite similar to drawing on the screen. However, causing the `PrintPage` event, which corresponds to the `Paint` event for the form, requires a manual program or user intervention. This is accomplished by calling the `Print` method from a `PrintDocument` object or by calling the `Show` or `ShowDialog` method on a `PrintPreviewDialog`. Handling multipage reports also requires keeping a class-level variable to keep track of where you are and use of the `HasMorePages` property. Finally, you can use a `StringFormat` object in your drawing to accomplish a variety of special formatting.

Summary of Key Concepts

> Recursion is a programming technique in which a method calls itself. A key to being able to program recursively is to be able to think recursively.

> Any recursive definition must have a nonrecursive part, called the base case, which permits the recursion to eventually end.

> Mathematical problems and formulas are often expressed recursively.

> Each recursive call to a method creates new local variables and parameters.

> A careful trace of recursive processing can provide insight into the way it is used to solve a problem.

> Recursion is the most elegant and appropriate way to solve some problems, but for others it is less intuitive than an iterative solution.

> The Towers of Hanoi solution has exponential complexity, which is very inefficient. Yet the implementation of the solution is incredibly short and elegant.

> A fractal is a geometric shape that is defined naturally in a recursive manner.

Self-Review Questions

11.1   What is recursion?

11.2   What is infinite recursion?

11.3   When is a base case needed for recursive processing?

11.4   Is recursion necessary?

11.5   When should recursion be avoided?

11.6   What is indirect recursion?

11.7   Explain the general approach to solving the Towers of Hanoi puzzle. How does it relate to recursion?

11.8   What is a fractal? What does it have to do with recursion?

Exercises

11.1   Write a recursive definition of a valid C# identifier (see Chapter 1).

11.2   Write a recursive definition of xy (x raised to the power y), where x and y are integers and $y > 0$.

11.3   Write a recursive definition of $i * j$ (integer multiplication), where $i > 0$. Define the multiplication process in terms of integer addition. For example, $4 * 7$ is equal to 7 added to itself 4 times.

11.4   Write a recursive definition of the Fibonacci numbers. The Fibonacci numbers are a sequence of integers, each of which is the sum of the previous two numbers. The first two numbers in the sequence are 0 and 1. Explain why you would not normally use recursion to solve this problem.

11.5   Modify the method that calculates the sum of the integers between 1 and N shown in this chapter. Have the new version match the following recursive definition: The sum of 1 to N is the sum of 1 to $(N/2)$ plus the sum of $(N/2 + 1)$ to N. Trace your solution using an N of 7.

11.6   Write a recursive method that returns the value of $N!$ (N factorial) using the definition given in this chapter. Explain why you would not normally use recursion to solve this problem.

11.7   Write a recursive method to reverse a string. Explain why you would not normally use recursion to solve this problem.

11.8   Design or generate a new maze for the `MazeSearch` program in this chapter and rerun the program. Explain the processing in terms of your new maze, giving examples of a path that was tried but failed, a path that was never tried, and the ultimate solution.

11.9   Annotate the lines of output of the `SolveTowers` program in this chapter to show the recursive steps.

11.10   Produce a chart showing the number of moves required to solve the Towers of Hanoi puzzle using the following number of disks: 2, 3, 4, 5, 6, 7, 8, 9, 10, 15, 20, and 25.

11.11   How many line segments are used to construct a Koch snowflake of order N? Produce a chart showing the number of line segments that make up a Koch snowflake for orders 1 through 9.

Programming Projects

11.1   Design and implement a recursive version of the `PalindromeTester` program from Chapter 3.

11.2   Design and implement a program that implements Euclid's algorithm for finding the greatest common divisor of two positive integers. The greatest common divisor is the largest integer that divides both values without producing a remainder. An iterative version of this method was part of the `RationalNumber` class presented in Chapter 6. In a class called `DivisorCalc`, define a static method called **Gcd** that accepts two integers, **num1** and **num2**. Create a driver to test your implementation. The recursive algorithm is defined as follows:

> Gcd (num1, num2) is num2 if num2 <= num1 and num2 divides num1

> Gcd (num1, num2) is Gcd (num2, num1) if num1 < num2

> Gcd (num1, num2) is Gcd (num2, num1%num2) otherwise

11.3   Modify the `Maze` class so that it prints out the path of the final solution as it is discovered, without storing it.

11.4   Design and implement a program that traverses a 3D maze.

11.5   Modify the `TiledPictures` program so that the repeated images appear in the lower-right quadrant.

11.6   Design and implement a recursive program that solves the Non-Attacking Queens problem. That is, write a program to determine how eight queens can be positioned on an eight-by-eight chessboard so that none of them is in the same row, column, or diagonal as any other queen. There are no other chess pieces on the board.

11.7   In the language of an alien race, all words take the form of Blurbs. A Blurb is a Whoozit followed by one or more Whatzits. A Whoozit is the character 'x' followed by zero or more 'y's. A Whatzit is a 'q' followed by either a 'z' or a 'd', followed by a Whoozit. Design and implement a recursive program that generates random Blurbs in this alien language.

11.8   Design and implement a recursive program to determine whether a string is a valid Blurb as defined in Programming Project 11.7.

11.9   Design and implement a recursive program to determine and print the Nth line of Pascal's Triangle, as shown below. Each interior value is the sum of the two values above it. *Hint:* Use an array to store the values on each line.

```
                1
              1   1
            1   2   1
          1   3   3   1
        1   4   6   4   1
      1   5  10  10   5   1
    1   6  15  20  15   6   1
  1   7  21  35  35  21   7   1
1   8  28  56  70  56  28   8   1
```

11.10 Design and implement a form that generalizes the `KochSnowflake` program. Allow the user to choose a fractal design from a menu item and to pick the background and drawing colors. The buttons to increase and decrease the order of the fractal will apply to whichever fractal design is chosen. In addition to the Koch snowflake, include a C-curve fractal whose order 1 is a straight line. Each successive order is created by replacing all line segments by two line segments, both half of the size of the original, and which meet at a right angle. Specifically, a C-curve of order N from $<x1, y1>$ to $<x3, y3>$ is replaced by two C-curves from $<x1, y1>$ to $<x2, y2>$ and from $<x2, y2>$ to $<x3, y3>$ where:

> $x2 = (x1 + x3 + y1 - y3) / 2;$

> $y2 = (x3 + y1 + y3 - x1) / 2;$

11.11 Design and implement a graphic version of the Towers of Hanoi puzzle. Allow the user to set the number of disks used in the puzzle. The user should be able to interact with the puzzle in two main ways. The user can move the disks from one peg to another using the mouse, in which case the program should ensure that each move is legal. The user can also watch a solution take place as an animation, with Pause/Resume buttons. Permit the user to control the speed of the animation.

11.12 Write a program that implements a recursive search of a sorted list of strings. Your program should include a recursive method that determines whether or not a given string is present within a sorted array (or, if you choose, an `ArrayList`) by searching successively smaller segments of the list.

Include a test driver that prompts the user for Strings to be searched. The user should enter one string per line, with an empty line indicating the end of the series. After the sorted list of Strings has been entered, the program should prompt the user for a search string. The program should then print a message stating whether or not the search string was found in the list, the total number of strings in the list, and the number of comparisons made while looking for the search string.

11.13 Write a program that prompts the user for a list of cities, where each city has a name and x and y coordinates. After all cities have been entered, the program should use a recursive algorithm to print the length of all possible routes that start at the first city entered, end at the last city entered, and visit every city in the list. For each route, the program should print the name of each city visited, followed by length of the route.

11.14 A Sierpinski Triangle is a fractal formed by drawing a triangle, and then using the midpoints of each side of the triangle to form another triangle. This inner triangle is then removed. The result is three smaller triangles (one at the top and one in each corner) on which the process is repeated. After iteration N, the image will contain 3^N triangles, each of which is similar to the original triangle.

Write a program that implements a recursive algorithm for drawing a Sierpinski Triangle. The user interface for the program should include a `JSlider` that allows the user to select a value for N. The slider should allow the user to pick a value for N between 0 and the maximum possible value of N based on the size of the program window. The maximum slider value should change as appropriate when the window is resized.

11.15   Modify the KochSnowflake program and add a menu. From this menu, include the File menu with Print and Exit as submenus. For printing, use the preview dialog so that you can see the results and optionally print them. A standard printed page is 8.5 inches by 11 inches, or 850 pixels by 1100 pixels. Leave half-inch margins on both sides and center the snowflake in the page.

Answers to Self-Review Questions

11.1   Recursion is a programming technique in which a method calls itself, solving a smaller version of the problem each time, until the terminating condition is reached.

11.2   Infinite recursion occurs when there is no base case that serves as a terminating condition or when the base case is improperly specified. The recursive path is followed forever. In a recursive program, infinite recursion will often result in an error that indicates that available memory has been exhausted.

11.3   A base case is always required to terminate recursion and begin the process of returning through the calling hierarchy. Without the base case, infinite recursion results.

11.4   Recursion is not necessary. Every recursive algorithm can be written in an iterative manner. However, some problem solutions are much more elegant and straightforward when written recursively.

11.5   Avoid recursion when the iterative solution is simpler and more easily understood and programmed. Recursion has the overhead of multiple method calls and is not always intuitive.

11.6   Indirect recursion occurs when a method calls another method, which calls another method, and so on until one of the called methods invokes the original. Indirect recursion is usually more difficult to trace than direct recursion, in which a method calls itself.

11.7   The Towers of Hanoi puzzle of N disks is solved by moving $N-1$ disks out of the way onto an extra peg, moving the largest disk to its destination, then moving the $N-1$ disks from the extra peg to the destination. This solution is inherently recursive because, to move the substack of $N-1$ disks, we can use the same process.

11.8   A fractal is a geometric shape that can comprise multiple versions of the same shape at different scales and different angles of orientation. Recursion can be used to draw the repetitive shapes over and over again.

Group Project

Modify the ShowFile example from Chapter 10 and change the buttons to a menu system. Under the File main menu, add Open, Print, and Exit submenus. Create a second main menu called Format and add Font and Color submenus. When Print is requested, write the selected file to a PrintPreviewDialog control.

Research the MeasureString method of a Font object to determine how much text will fit per line. With this, create your own word wrap by adding one word at a time from the input to a test line until that test line will no longer fit on the current line. Save that last word and use it as the first word of the next line. Also, you will want to start a new line when you encounter a newline character in the input. Be sure to use the font that is selected.

To parse the input, you have to read the input text one line at a time using a ReadLine method. Research System.IO to find the right class to read a text file.

Also, use MeasureString to determine how far to advance vertically. In our example, we advanced a fixed amount, but more accuracy is available from MeasureString. Using the vertical calculation, determine when you have reached the end of the page, so that all pages are printed.

You should only allow files with a .txt extension. Adjust your OpenFileDialog accordingly. If you write binary data to a real printer, most anything can happen. Also, ReadLine will also cause serious problems with binary data.

Collections and Data Structures

12

CHAPTER OBJECTIVES

> Explore the concept of a collection.

> Stress the importance of separating the interface from the implementation.

> Examine the difference between fixed and dynamic implementations.

> Define and use dynamically linked lists.

> Introduce classic linear data structures such as queues and stacks.

> Introduce classic nonlinear data structures such as trees and graphs.

> Discuss the C# Collections API.

Problem solving often requires techniques for organizing and managing information. This chapter explores objects that store information, called collections, as well as various ways to implement them. Many collections have been developed over the years, and some of them have become classics. This chapter explains how collections can be implemented using references to link one object to another.

12.1   COLLECTIONS AND DATA STRUCTURES

We have seen collections many times in the Visual Studio Form Designer. A *collection* is an object that serves as a repository for other objects. It is a generic term that can be applied to many situations, but we usually use it when discussing an object whose specific role is to provide services to add, remove, and otherwise manage the elements that are contained within. For example, the `ArrayList` class (discussed in Chapter 7) represents a collection. It provides methods to add elements to the end of a list or to a particular location in the list based on an index value. It provides methods to remove specific elements as needed.

Some collections maintain their elements in a specific order, while others do not. Some collections are *homogeneous,* meaning that they can contain all of the same type of object; other collections are *heterogeneous,* which means they can contain objects of various types. An `ArrayList` is heterogeneous because it can hold an object of any type. To be more precise, `ArrayList` is a homogeneous collection of type `Object` since it stores `Object` references. This means that it can store any object because of inheritance and polymorphism.

Separating Interface from Implementation

Key Concept

An object, with its well-defined interface, is a perfect mechanism for implementing a collection.

A crucial aspect of collections is that they can be implemented in a variety of ways. That is, the underlying *data structure* that stores the objects can be implemented using various techniques. The `ArrayList` class from the C# standard library, for instance, supports array operations and the collection methods. All operations on an `ArrayList` are accomplished by invoking methods that perform the appropriate operations on the underlying structure, but these operations are transparent to the program.

Objects are perfectly suited for defining collections. An object, by definition, has a well-defined interface whose implementation is hidden in the class. The way in which the data is represented, and the operations that manage the data, is encapsulated inside the object. This type of object is reusable and reliable, because its interaction with the rest of the system is controlled.

12.2   DYNAMIC REPRESENTATIONS

Key Concept

The size of a dynamic data structure grows and shrinks as needed.

An array is only one way in which a list can be represented. Arrays are limited in one sense because they have a fixed size throughout their existence. Sometimes we don't know how big to make an array because we don't know how much information we will store. The `ArrayList` class handles this by creating a larger array and copying everything over whenever necessary. This is not necessarily an efficient implementation.

A *dynamic data structure* is implemented using links. By using references as links between objects, we can create whatever type of structure is appropriate for the situation. If implemented carefully, the structure can be quite efficient to search and modify. Structures created in this way are considered to be dynamic because their size is determined dynamically, as they are used, and not by their declaration.

Dynamic Structures

Recall that the variable used to keep track of an object is actually a reference to the object, meaning that it stores the address of the object. A declaration such as

```
House home = new House ("602 Greenbriar Court");
```

actually accomplishes two things: it declares home to be a reference to a House object, and it instantiates an object of class House. Now consider an object that contains a reference to another object of the same type. For example:

```
class Node
{
   int info;
   Node next;
}
```

Two objects of this class can be instantiated and chained together by having the next reference of one Node object refer to the other Node object. The second object's next reference can refer to a third Node object, and so on, creating a *linked list*. The first node in the list could be referenced using a separate variable. The last node in the list would have a next reference that is **null**, indicating the end of the list. Figure 12.1 depicts this situation.

> **Key Concept**
>
> A dynamically linked list is managed by storing and updating references to objects.

In this example, the information stored in each Node class is a simple integer, but keep in mind that we could define a class to contain any amount of information of any type.

A Dynamically Linked List

The program in Listing 12.1 sets up a list of Magazine objects and then prints the list. The list of magazines is encapsulated inside the MagazineList class, shown in Listing 12.2, and is maintained as a dynamically linked list.

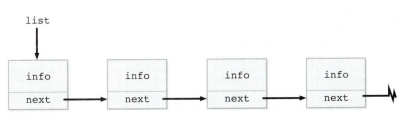

FIGURE 12.1   A linked list

The `MagazineList` class represents the list of magazines. From outside of the class (an external view), we do not focus on how the list is implemented. We don't know, for instance, whether the list of magazines is stored in an array or in a linked list. The `MagazineList` class provides a set of methods that allows the user to maintain the list of books. That set of methods, specifically `Add` and `ToString`, defines the operations of the `MagazineList` class.

The `MagazineList` class uses an inner class called `MagazineNode` to represent a node in the linked list. Each node contains a reference to one magazine and a reference to the next node in the list. Because `MagazineNode` is an inner class, it is reasonable to allow the data values in the class to be public. Therefore, the code in the `MagazineList` class refers to those data values directly.

The `Magazine` class, shown in Listing 12.3, is well encapsulated, with all data declared as `private` and methods provided to accomplish any updates necessary. Note that, because we use a separate class to represent a node in the list, the `Magazine` class itself does not need to contain a link to the next `Magazine` in the list. That allows the `Magazine` class to be free of any issues regarding its containment in a list.

Listing 12.1

```
//**************************************************************
//   MagazineRack.cs          C#:   Ken Culp
//
//   Driver to exercise the MagazineList collection.
//**************************************************************
using System;

namespace MagazineRack
{

  public class MagazineRack
  {
    //-------------------------------------------------------------
    //  Creates a MagazineList object, adds several magazines to
    //  the list, then prints it.
    //-------------------------------------------------------------
    public static void Main(String[] args)
    {
      MagazineList rack = new MagazineList();

      rack.Add(new Magazine("Time"));
      rack.Add(new Magazine("Woodworking Today"));
      rack.Add(new Magazine("Communications of the ACM"));
      rack.Add(new Magazine("House and Garden"));
      rack.Add(new Magazine("GQ"));

      Console.Out.WriteLine(rack);
```

Listing 12.1   continued

```
        Console.In.ReadLine();   // Wait for Enter key
    }
  }
}
```

Output

```
Time
Woodworking Today
Communications of the ACM
House and Garden
```

Other methods could be included in the MagazineList class. For example, in addition to the Add method provided, which always adds a new magazine to the end of the list, another method called Insert could be defined
to add a node anywhere in the list (to keep it sorted, for instance). A parameter to Insert could indicate the value of the node after which the new node
should be inserted. Figure 12.2 shows how the references would be updated
to insert a new node.

> **Key Concept**
>
> Insert and delete operations can
> be implemented by carefully
> manipulating object references.

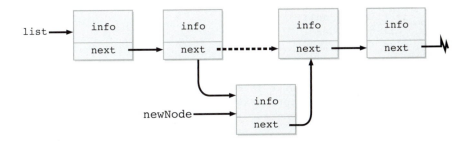

FIGURE 12.2   Inserting a node into the middle of a list

Listing 12.2

```
//****************************************************************
//  MagazineList.cs        C#:  Ken Culp
//
//  Represents a collection of magazines in a single link list
//  with no sorting of data.  For a double-link list with
//  sorting, see the LinkList project in this directory.
//****************************************************************
using System;
```

Listing 12.2   continued

```csharp
namespace MagazineRack
{
  public class MagazineList
  {
    private MagazineNode list;

    //-------------------------------------------------------------
    //  Sets up an initially empty list of magazines.
    //-------------------------------------------------------------
    public MagazineList()
    {
      list = null;
    }

    //-------------------------------------------------------------
    //  Creates a new MagazineNode object and adds it to the end
    //  of the linked list.
    //-------------------------------------------------------------
    public void Add(Magazine mag)
    {

      MagazineNode node = new MagazineNode(mag);
      MagazineNode current;

      if (list == null)
        list = node;
      else
      {
        current = list;
        while (current.next != null)
          current = current.next;
        current.next = node;
      }
    }

    //-------------------------------------------------------------
    //  Returns this list of magazines as a string.
    //-------------------------------------------------------------
    public override String ToString()
    {
      String result = "";

      MagazineNode current = list;

      while (current != null)
      {
        result += current.magazine + "\n";
        current = current.next;
      }
```

Listing 12.2   continued

```csharp
      return result;
   }

   //*************************************************************
   //  An inner class representing a node in the magazine list.
   //  The public variables are accessed via MagazineList class.
   //*************************************************************
   private class MagazineNode
   {
      public Magazine magazine;
      public MagazineNode next;
      //-----------------------------------------------------------
      //  Sets up the node
      //-----------------------------------------------------------
      public MagazineNode(Magazine mag)
      {
         magazine = mag;
         next = null;
      }
   }
}
}
```

Listing 12.3

```csharp
//*************************************************************
//  Magazine.cs        C#:   Ken Culp
//
//  Represents a single magazine.
//*************************************************************
using System;

namespace MagazineRack
{

   public class Magazine
   {
      private String title;

      //-----------------------------------------------------------
      //  Sets up the new magazine with its title.
      //-----------------------------------------------------------
      public Magazine(String newTitle)
      {
         title = newTitle;
      }
```

Listing 12.3 continued

```
//--------------------------------------------------------------
//  Returns this magazine as a string.
//--------------------------------------------------------------
public override String ToString()
{
    return title;
}
    }
}
```

Another operation that would be helpful for a list would be a `Delete` method to remove a particular node. Recall from our discussion in Chapter 3 that by removing all references to an object, it becomes a candidate for garbage collection. Figure 12.3 shows how references would be updated to delete a node from a list. You must take care to accomplish the modifications to the references in the proper order to ensure that other nodes are not lost and that references continue to refer to valid, appropriate nodes in the list.

Other Dynamic List Representations

You can use different list implementations, depending on the specific needs of the program you are designing. For example, in some situations, it may make processing easier to implement a *doubly linked list* in which each node has not only a reference to the next node in the list, but also a reference to the previous node in the list. Our generic `Node` class might be declared as follows:

```
class Node
{
    int info;
    Node next, prev;
}
```

Key Concept

Many variations on the implementation of dynamically linked lists can be defined.

Figure 12.4 shows a doubly linked list. Note that, like a singly linked list, the `next` reference of the last node is **null**. Similarly, the previous node of the first node is **null** since there is no node that comes before the first one. This type of structure makes it easy to move back and forth between nodes in the list, but requires more effort to set up and modify.

Another implementation of a linked list could include a *header node* for the list that has a reference to the front of the list and another reference to the rear of the list. A rear reference makes it easier to add new nodes to the end of the list. The header node could contain other information, such as a count of the number of nodes currently in the list. The declaration of the header node would be similar to the following:

```
class ListHeader
{
    int count;
    Node front, rear;
}
```

Note that the header node is not of the same class as the Node class to which it refers. Figure 12.5 depicts a linked list that is implemented using a header node.

Still other linked list implementations can be created. For instance, the use of a header can be combined with a doubly linked list, or the list can be maintained in sorted order. The implementation should cater to the type of processing that is required. Some extra effort to maintain a more complex data structure may be worthwhile if it makes common operations on the structure more efficient.

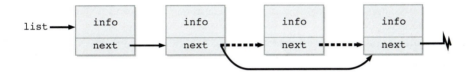

FIGURE 12.3   Deleting a node from a list

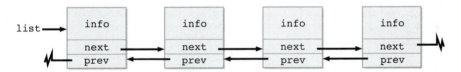

FIGURE 12.4   A doubly linked list

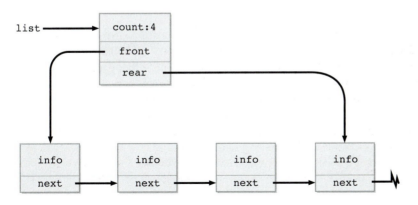

FIGURE 12.5   A list with front and rear references

12.3 LINEAR DATA STRUCTURES

In addition to lists, some data structures have become classic in that they represent important generic situations that commonly occur in computing. Like lists, a queue and a stack are *linear data structures,* meaning that the data they represent is organized in a linear fashion. This section explores some linear data structures in more detail.

Queues

A *queue* is similar to a list except that it has restrictions on the way you put items in and take items out. Specifically, a queue uses *first-in, first-out* (FIFO) processing. That is, the first item put in the list is the first item that comes out of the list. Figure 12.6 depicts the FIFO processing of a queue.

Any waiting line is a queue. Think about a line of people waiting for a teller at a bank. A customer enters the queue at the back and moves forward as earlier customers are serviced. Eventually, each customer comes to the front of the queue to be processed.

Note that the processing of a queue is conceptual. We may speak in terms of people moving forward until they reach the front of the queue, but the reality might be that the front of the queue moves as elements come off. That is, we are not concerned at this point with whether the queue of customers moves toward the teller or remains stationary as the teller moves when customers are serviced.

The Visual Studio library includes a `Queue` class that you can use for your program. Some of the members of this class are shown in Figure 12.7. (Add a using `System.Collections` line).

A queue data structure typically supports at least two methods and one public property:

> `Enqueue` adds an item to the rear of the queue

> `Dequeue` removes an item from the front of the queue

> `Count` returns number of entries in the queue (0 = empty)

In addition to the members of the `Queue` class shown in Figure 12.7, there are several others, some of which derive from `Object`. To list all the members, select Help/Index and type `Queue`. From the `Queue` class, select the "All Members" entry and follow the links from there.

Items go on the queue
at the rear (enqueue)

Items come off the queue
at the front (dequeue)

FIGURE 12.6 A queue data structure

Public Constructors	
`public Queue()`	Creates a new instance of the `Queue` class with the default initial capacity.
`public Queue(ICollection)`	Creates a new instance of the `Queue` class and fills all elements from `ICollection`.
`public Queue(int capacity)`	Creates a new instance of the `Queue` class with the specified capacity or the default capacity, whichever is larger.

Public Properties	
`Count`	Gets the number of elements contained in the `Queue`.

Public Methods	
`public virtual void Clear()`	Removes all objects from the `Queue`.
`public virtual object Clone()`	Creates a shallow copy of the `Queue`.
`public virtual bool Contains(object obj)`	Checks whether the given element is in the `Queue`.
`public virtual void CopyTo(Array array, int index)`	Copies the `Queue` to an existing one-dimensional array, starting at the specified index.
`public virtual object Dequeue()`	Removes and returns the object at the beginning of the `Queue`.
`public virtual void Enqueue(object obj)`	Adds an object to the end of the `Queue`.
`public virtual object Peek()`	Returns the object at the beginning of the `Queue` without removing it.
`public virtual object[] ToArray()`	Returns all `Queue` members as an array.
`public virtual string ToString()`	Returns a string representation of the object.
`public virtual void TrimToSize()`	Sets the capacity to the actual number of elements in the `Queue`.

FIGURE 12.7   Some members of the Queue class

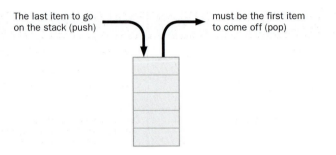

The last item to go
on the stack (push)

must be the first item
to come off (pop)

FIGURE 12.8   A stack data structure

Stacks

A *stack* is similar to a queue except that its elements go on and come off at the same end. The last item to go on a stack is the first item to come off, like a stack of plates in the cupboard or a stack of hay bales in the barn. A stack, therefore, processes information in a *last-in, first-out* (LIFO) manner, as shown in Figure 12.8.

A typical stack ADT includes at least two methods and one public property:

> `Push` pushes an item onto the top of the stack

> `Pop` removes an item from the top of the stack

> `Count` returns number of entries in the stack (0 = empty)

The C# library contains a class called `Stack` that implements a stack data structure. It contains methods that correspond to the standard stack operations, plus a method that searches for a particular object in the stack. Figure 12.9 lists the most commonly used members of the `Stack` class (add a `using System.Collections` line).

The `Stack` class has a `Contains` method that returns a boolean **true** if the item is in the stack or **false** if it is not. This type of searching is not usually considered to be part of the classic stack ADT.

Like `ArrayList` operations, the `Stack` operations operate on `object` references. Because all objects are derived from the `object` class, any object can be pushed onto a stack. If primitive types are to be stored, they must be treated as objects using the corresponding wrapper class.

Let's look at an example that uses a stack to solve a problem. The program in Listing 12.4 accepts a string of characters that represents a secret message. The program decodes and prints the message.

Public Constructors	
`public Stack()`	Creates a new instance of the `Stack` class with the default initial capacity.
`public Stack(ICollection)`	Creates a new instance of the `Stack` class and fills all elements from `ICollection`.
`public Stack(int capacity)`	Creates a new instance of the `Stack` class with the specified capacity or the default capacity, whichever is larger.

Public Properties	
`Count`	Gets the number of elements contained in the `Stack`.

Public Methods	
`public virtual void Clear()`	Removes all objects from the `Stack`.
`public virtual object Clone()`	Creates a shallow copy of the `Stack`.
`public virtual bool Contains( object obj)`	Checks whether the given element is in the `Stack`.
`public virtual void CopyTo( Array array, int index)`	Copies the `Stack` to an existing one-dimensional Array, starting at the specified index.
`public virtual object Peek()`	Returns the object at the top of the `Stack` without removing it.
`public virtual object Pop()`	Removes and returns the object at the top of the `Stack`.
`public virtual void Push( object obj)`	Inserts an object on the top of the `Stack`.
`public virtual object[] ToArray()`	Returns all `Stack` members as an array.
`public virtual string ToString()`	Returns a string representation of the object.

FIGURE 12.9   Some members of the Stack class

Listing 12.4

```
//*************************************************************
//  Decode.cs            C#:   Ken Culp
//
//  Demonstrates the use of the Stack class.
//*************************************************************
using System;
using System.Collections;
using CS1;

namespace Decode
{
  public class Decode
  {
    //-----------------------------------------------------------
    //   Decodes a message by reversing each word in a string.
    //-----------------------------------------------------------
    public static void Main(String[] args)
    {
      Stack word = new Stack();
      String message;
      int index = 0;

      Console.Out.WriteLine("Enter the coded message:");
      message = Keyboard.readString();
      Console.Out.WriteLine("The decoded message is:");

      while (index < message.Length)
      {
        // Push word onto stack
        while (index < message.Length && message[index] != ' ')
        {
          word.Push(message[index]);
          index++;
        }

        // Print word in reverse
        while (word.Count > 0)
          Console.Out.Write(((char)word.Pop()));
        Console.Out.Write(" ");
        index++;
      }

      Console.Out.WriteLine();
      Console.In.ReadLine();  // Wait for enter key
    }
  }
}
```

Listing 12.4   continued

Output

```
Enter the coded message:
artxE eseehc esaelp
The decoded message is:
Extra cheese please
```

A message that has been encoded has each individual word in the message reversed. Words in the message are separated by a single space. The program uses the `Stack` class to push the characters of each word on the stack. When an entire word has been read, each character appears in reverse order as it is popped off the stack and printed.

12.4   NONLINEAR DATA STRUCTURES

Some data structures are considered to be *nonlinear data structures* because their data is not organized linearly. This section examines two types of nonlinear structures: trees and graphs.

Trees

A *tree* is a nonlinear data structure that consists of a *root node* and potentially many levels of additional nodes that form a hierarchy. All nodes other than the root are called *internal nodes*. Nodes that have no children are called *leaf nodes*. Figure 12.10 depicts a tree. Note that we draw a tree "upside down," with the root at the top and the leaves at the bottom.

> **Key Concept**
>
> A tree is a nonlinear data structure that organizes data into a hierarchy.

In a general tree like the one in Figure 12.10, each node could have many child nodes. As we mentioned in Chapter 8, the inheritance relationships among classes can be depicted using a general tree structure.

In a *binary tree,* each node can have no more than two child nodes. Binary trees are useful in various programming situations and usually are easier to implement than general trees. Technically, binary trees are a subset of general trees, but they are so important in the computing world that they usually are thought of as their own data structure.

The operations on trees and binary trees vary, but minimally include adding and removing nodes from the tree or binary tree. Because of their nonlinear nature, trees and binary trees are implemented nicely using references as dynamic links. However, it is possible to implement a tree data structure using a fixed representation such as an array.

Graphs

Like a tree, a *graph* is a nonlinear data structure. Unlike a tree, a graph does not have a primary entry point like the tree's root node. In a graph, a node is linked to another node by

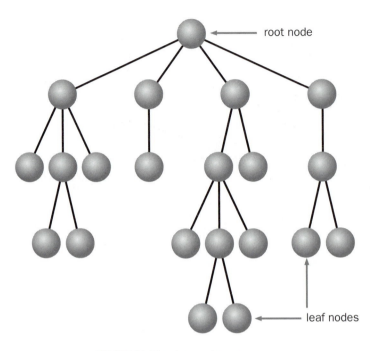

FIGURE 12.10 A tree data structure

a connection called an *edge*. Generally there are no restrictions on the number of edges that can be made between nodes in a graph. Figure 12.11 presents a graph data structure.

Graphs are useful when representing relationships for which linear paths and strict hierarchies do not suffice. For instance, the highway system connecting cities on a map and airline connections between airports are better represented as graphs than by any other data structure discussed so far.

In a general graph, the edges are bidirectional, meaning that the edge connecting nodes A and B can be followed from A to B and also from B to A. In a *directed graph*, or *digraph*, each edge has a specific direction. Figure 12.12 shows a digraph, in which each edge indicates the direction using an arrowhead.

> **Key Concept**
>
> A graph is a nonlinear data structure that connects nodes using generic edges.

A digraph might be used, for instance, to represent airline flights between airports. Unlike highway systems, which are in almost all cases bidirectional, having a flight from one city to another does not necessarily mean there is a corresponding flight going the other way. Or, if there is, we may want to associate different information with it, such as cost.

Like trees, graphs often are implemented using dynamic links, although they can be implemented using arrays as well.

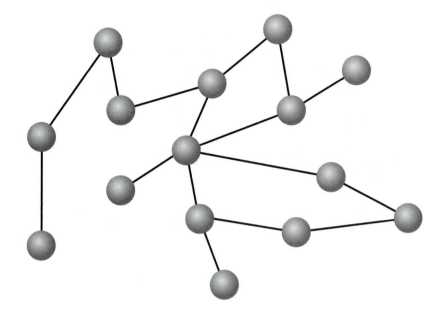

FIGURE 12.11   A graph data structure

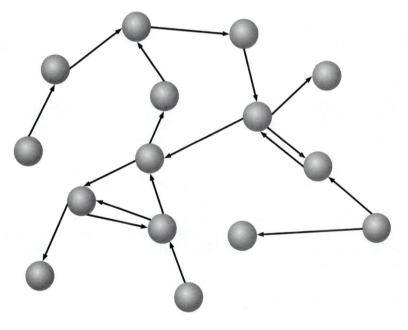

FIGURE 12.12   A directed graph

12.5 C# COLLECTION CLASSES

The C# standard class library contains several classes that represent collections of various types. For those of you who have been implementing Windows applications and forms, you have already seen several collections and collection editors. All of these were built on the underlying collection support included in .Net.

Collection classes can be either generic or specific in nature. The generic solution is to simply create a variable of type `Collection`. When created in this way, the collection stores and retrieves items of type **object** much the same way as `ArrayList` did in Chapter 7. To retrieve information from a generic collection, it is necessary to typecast it back to the type of the object needed (see Chapter 7).

The other solution is to create your own strongly typed collection class by extending the `CollectionBase` abstract class. By extending `CollectionBase`, you can force precise typing on the `Add` method and return the precise type needed in the `Item` property.

`ArrayList`, also discussed in Chapter 7, is derived from `CollectionBase` and includes a custom indexer (see below) so the items in the collection could be accessed as an array. It also includes a Sort method for sorting the data. Some of the members of the `CollectionBase` class are shown below in Figure 12.13.

To illustrate these methods, we took the `Employee` example from Chapter 10 that used `ArrayList` and converted it to use our own collection class. Because the `Employee`

Public Properties	
int **Count**	Gets the number of elements in the collection. Read only.

Public Methods	
public virtual void Clear()	Removes all objects from the collection.
public virtual void RemoveAt(int index)	Removes the object at the specified index from the collection.
public virtual string ToString()	Returns a string representation.

Protected Properties	
protected ArrayList InnerList	Gets an `ArrayList` of elements from the collection.
protected IList List	Gets an `IList` of elements from the collection.

FIGURE 12.13 Some members of the CollectionBase class

application from Chapter 10 is quite extensive, we will highlight the source code modifications in our `Employee` to support our collection class and the segments of the main program that had to deal with the list. Below is a new class that creates a collection of objects of type `Employee`.

Listing 12.5

```
//*********************************************************
//  EmployeeList.cs        C#:  Ken Culp
//
//  Creates a collection object of Employees
//*********************************************************
using System;
using System.Collections;

namespace EmployeeList
  {
  [Serializable]
  public class EmployeeList : System.Collections.CollectionBase
  {
    //------------------------------------------------------
    //  Constructor.  Empty
    //------------------------------------------------------
    public EmployeeList() : base()
    {
    }

    //------------------------------------------------------
    //  IndexOf.  Returns offset in list of a specific Employee
    //------------------------------------------------------
    public int IndexOf(Employee emp)
    {
      return List.IndexOf(emp);
    }

    //------------------------------------------------------
    //  Add.  Adds an employee to the list
    //------------------------------------------------------
    public void Add(Employee emp)
    {
      List.Add(emp);
    }

    //------------------------------------------------------
    //  Remove.  Removes a specific employee from the list
    //------------------------------------------------------
    public void Remove(Employee emp)
```

Listing 12.5   continued

```
  {
    List.Remove(emp);
  }


  //------------------------------------------------------------
  //  Sort.  Just uses Sort method of ArrayList
  //------------------------------------------------------------
  public void Sort()
  {
    InnerList.Sort();
  }


  //------------------------------------------------------------
  //  Custom indexer so list can be addressed as an array
  //------------------------------------------------------------
  public Employee this[int index]
  {
    get
    {
      if (index < 0 || index > List.Count - 1)
        throw new IndexOutOfRangeException("Invalid Index");
      return (Employee)List[index];
    }
    set
    {
      if (index < 0 || index > List.Count - 1)
        throw new IndexOutOfRangeException("Invalid Index");
      List[index] = value;
    }
  }
}
```

Our Add method takes an item of type Employee and adds it to the list. For this, we use the Add method on the protected member of the CollectionsBase called List. This Add method takes an item of type **Object**. Since List is a protected member, it cannot use it directly, which is why we must create our own Add method. So while we are at it, we will ensure that our Add method is passed something of type Employee instead of type **Object** (see Add method above).

The Remove method, similarly, takes the passed parameter of type Employee and calls the protected List method Remove. List.Remove takes a parameter of type **Object**, so we just pass along the Employee object passed in. Again, our Remove method signature ensures that the caller passes something of type Employee and not type **Object**.

We added a Sort method to our custom collection class to support showing our employees in sorted order. CollectionBase also exposes a protected member called InnerList that is of type ArrayList. ArrayList includes a Sort method that will sort members in the list as long as the objects in the list implement the `IComparable` interface (which our `Employee` class implements). Thus sorting is simple, requiring only one line, as shown in Listing 12.5. Note that we cannot call `InnerList.Sort` directly because `InnerList` is a protected member of the `CollectionBase` class.

All that remains is for our custom collection to provide a way for members of the list to be examined in a random order. Thus, we need to make our collection look like an array just like `ArrayList`. Therefore, our last step in building our custom collection class is to create an *indexer*. The next section describes how to create indexers. For now, recognize that the indexer allows us to use the array notation to access individual members in the class. Furthermore, an `Employee` type is returned when indexing into the collection, thereby keeping to our strategy of strict typing.

The principal advantage of implementing our own collection class is for those cases in which we extract data from the collection. We want what returned is something of type `Employee` instead of type **Object** (as returned from `ArrayList`). Our custom indexer returns values of type `Employee`. This greatly simplifies accessing members of the list. Consider the following contrasting lines of code:

```
emp = (Employee)employees[curEmp];        // Before (ArrayList)
emp = employees[curEmp];                  // After (Employee
                                          // collection)

EmpToScr((Employee)employees[curEmp]);    // Before (ArrayList)
EmpToScr(employees[curEmp]);              // After (Employee
                                          // collection)
```

Now, since our list returns objects of the desired type, it is no longer necessary to type-cast from `object` to `Employee`. If we did not want to set up the custom indexer, we could add an `Item` method as shown next. After verifying a valid index, the `Item` method uses the array notation for `List` but typecasts the return back to our employee.

```
public Employee Item(int index)
{
  if (index < 0 || index > List.Count - 1)
    throw new IndexOutOfRangeException("Invalid Index");
  return (Employee)List[index];
}
```

In summary, to simplify creating our own collections, we must implement several methods that are not implemented in the `CollectionBase` class. At a minimum, we must include `Add`, `Remove`, and some way to obtain a specific item in the list that is of the desired type (either an `Item` method or a custom indexer). These methods should be strongly typed and return an item of the appropriate type.

12.6   ADDING CUSTOM INDEXERS TO A CLASS

In addition to being able to overload operators in classes, we can define our own array structure, allowing our classes to appear as arrays. This technique is called a *custom indexer* and can be added to any class for which that would make sense.

The index value used in our previous collection class used an integer index. When using integer indexes, a custom indexer is added to a class with the following syntax:

```
public Employee this[int index]
```

The indexer is marked as **public** and its type is set to the desired type (**Employee** here). The keyword **this** references the current class. After the **this** keyword is an open bracket, followed by the type of the index, an index variable name, the close bracket, and then the method body. Using this syntax allows us to reference the code as shown in the following relevant lines from our **EmployeeList** example:

```
private employeeList Employees;    // The list of employees
   . . .
emp = employees[curEmp];           // Fetch current employee
```

Although we will not give a lot of details, it is interesting to note that the indexer can use an index parameter of some type other than integer! For example, we could search our employees list by last name passed on the indexer. Relevant code would be as shown next. For completeness, such a method would return a **null** if the employee is not found.

```
public Employee this[string lastName]
   . . .
emp = employees["Jones"];          // Fetch employee by last name
```

We could even extend this concept to use two index values. This would allow us to create an indexer that looked up employees by both last and first name:

```
//-----------------------------------------------------------
// Custom indexer to find employee by last/first names.
// First tries for a match on both last and first names.
// Failing that, it tries only a match on last name.
// All comparisons are done in uppercase so match
// occurs regardless of case.
//-----------------------------------------------------------
public Employee this[string last, string first]
{
  get
  {
    if (first.Length > 0)
    {
```

```
    // First try exact match ignoring case
    foreach(Employee emp in List)
      if (emp.Last .ToUpper() == last .ToUpper()
      emp.First.ToUpper() == first.ToUpper())
        return emp;
    return null;

  }
  // Only last given, try to match that
  foreach(Employee emp in List)
    if (emp.Last.ToUpper() == last.ToUpper())
      return emp;

  // If here, never found a match
  return null;

  }
}
```

In the preceding indexer, we take the string name passed in and do a linear search of the list. Clearly, since the list is sorted, we could use a binary search or at least stop once the passed name is larger than the current entry. We skipped the binary search to simplify the code. The code that uses the second (name) indexer to look up employees within the list is as follows:

```
private void mnuFind_Click(object sender, System.EventArgs e)
{
  Find dlg = new Find();
  DialogResult result = dlg.ShowDialog();
   if (result != DialogResult.Cancel)
  {
    Employee emp = Employees[dlg.Last, dlg.First];
    if (emp == null)
      MessageBox.Show("Name not found");
    else
    {
      curEmp = Employees.IndexOf(emp);
      EmpToScr(emp);
    }
  }
}
```

The EmployeeList program handles duplicates by having the Find menu item return the first employee matching the name(s) give. From that point, the user can scroll alphabetically through the list to find other, possibly, matching names.

As you can see, indexers give you a great deal of flexibility in creating your classes. Combining the custom indexer with the `Collection` class enables you to produce a series of typed collections.

You may be wondering why we need custom indexers at all. It would appear that a method with parentheses would work just as well. Indeed, we could write a method like the following that would search the list and return the employee record (or **null** if no match is found):

```
public Employee Find(string last, string first)
```

Clearly, a method would serve just as well. However, the indexer syntax is cleaner and briefer, requiring only a few brackets as opposed to a dot, a method name, and the parameters. The same is true if you need to update the data as follows. You would need a method in either case to replace the indexer syntax.

```
employees[curEmp] = emp;    // Update employee.
```

Summary of Key Concepts

> An object, with its well-defined interface, is a perfect mechanism for implementing a collection.

> The size of a dynamic data structure grows and shrinks as needed.

> A dynamically linked list is managed by storing and updating references to objects.

> Insert and delete operations can be implemented by carefully manipulating object references.

> Many variations on the implementation of dynamically linked lists can be defined.

> A queue is a linear data structure that manages data in a first-in, first-out manner.

> A stack is a linear data structure that manages data in a last-in, first-out manner.

> A tree is a nonlinear data structure that organizes data into a hierarchy.

> A graph is a nonlinear data structure that connects nodes using generic edges.

Self-Review Questions

12.1   What is a collection?

12.2   Why are objects particularly well suited for implementing collections?

12.3   What is a dynamic data structure?

12.4   What is a doubly linked list?

12.5   What is a header node for a linked list?

12.6   How is a queue different from a list?

12.7   What is a stack?

12.8   What is the `Stack` class?

12.9   What do trees and graphs have in common?

12.10   What is `CollectionBase` used for?

Exercises

12.1   Suppose `current` is a reference to a `Node` object and that it currently refers to a specific node in a linked list. Show, in pseudocode, the steps that would delete the node following `current` from the list. Carefully consider the cases in which `current` is referring to the first and last nodes in the list.

12.2   Modify your answer to Exercise 12.1 assuming that the list was set up as a doubly linked list, with both `next` and `prev` references.

12.3 Suppose `current` and `newNode` are references to `Node` objects. Assume `current` currently refers to a specific node in a linked list and `newNode` refers to an unattached `Node` object. Show, in pseudocode, the steps that would insert `newNode` behind `current` in the list. Carefully consider the cases in which `current` is referring to the first and last nodes in the list.

12.4 Modify your answer to Exercise 12.3 assuming that the list was set up as a doubly linked list, with both `next` and `prev` references.

12.5 Would the front and rear references in the header node of a linked list ever refer to the same node? Would they ever both be null? Would one ever be null if the other was not? Explain your answers using examples.

12.6 Show the contents of a queue after the following operations are performed. Assume the queue is initially empty.

```
> -Enqueue (45);

> -Enqueue (12);

> -Enqueue (28);

> -Dequeue();

> -Dequeue();

> -Enqueue (69);

> -Enqueue (27);

> -Enqueue (99);

> -Dequeue();

> -Enqueue (24);

> -Enqueue (85);

> -Enqueue (16);

> -Dequeue();
```

12.7 In terms of the final state of a queue, does it matter how dequeue operations are intermixed with enqueue operations? Does it matter how the enqueue operations are intermixed among themselves? Explain using examples.

12.8 Show the contents of a stack after the following operations are performed. Assume the stack is initially empty.

```
> -Push (45);

> -Push (12);

> -Push (28);

> -Pop();

> -Pop();
```

> -Push (69);

> -Push (27);

> -Push (99);

> -Pop();

> -Push (24);

> -Push (85);

> -Push (16);

> -Pop();

12.9   In terms of the final state of a stack, does it matter how the pop operations are intermixed with the push operations? Does it matter how the push operations are intermixed among themselves? Explain using examples.

12.10   Would a tree data structure be a good choice to represent a family tree that shows lineage? Why or why not? Would a binary tree be a better choice? Why or why not?

12.11   What data structure would be a good choice to represent the links between various Web sites? Give an example.

Programming Projects

12.1   Consistent with the example from Chapter 6, design and implement an application that maintains a collection of compact discs using a linked list. In the `Main` method of the `Driver` class, add various CDs to the collection and print the list when complete.

12.2   Modify the `MagazineRack` program presented in this chapter by adding delete and insert operations into the `MagazineList` class. Have the `Magazine` class implement the `IComparable` interface, and base the processing of the `Insert` method on calls to the `CompareTo` method in the `Magazine` class that determines whether one `Magazine` title comes before another lexicographically. In the `Driver` class, exercise various insertion and deletion operations. Print the list of magazines when complete.

12.3   Design and implement a version of selection sort (from Chapter 9) that operates on a linked list of nodes that each contain an integer.

12.4   Design and implement a version of insertion sort (from Chapter 9) that operates on a linked list of nodes that each contain an integer.

12.5   Design and implement an application that simulates the customers waiting in line at a bank. Use a queue data structure to represent the line. As customers arrive at the bank, customer objects are put in the rear of the queue with an enqueue operation. When the teller is ready to service another customer, the customer object is removed from the front of the queue with a dequeue operation. Randomly determine when new customers arrive at the bank and when current customers are finished at the teller window. Print a message each time an operation occurs during the simulation.

12.6 Modify the solution to the Programming Project 12.5 so that it represents eight tellers and therefore eight customer queues. Have new customers go to the shortest queue. Determine which queue had the shortest waiting time per customer on average.

12.7 Design and implement an application that evaluates a postfix expression that operates on integer operands using the arithmetic operators +, -, *, /, and %. You are already familiar with *infix expressions,* in which an operator is positioned between its two operands. A *postfix expression* puts the operators after its operands. Keep in mind that an operand could be the result of another operation. This eliminates the need for parentheses to force precedence. For example, the following infix expression:

(5 + 2) * (8 - 5)

is equivalent to the following postfix expression:

5 2 + 8 5 - *

The evaluation of a postfix expression is facilitated by using a stack. As you process a postfix expression from left to right, you encounter operands and operators. If you encounter an operand, push it on the stack. If you encounter an operator, pop two operands off the stack, perform the operation, and push the result back on the stack. When you have processed the entire expression, there will be one value on the stack, which is the result of the entire expression.

12.8 Design and implement a program that prompts the user to enter a String and then performs two palindrome tests. The first should use a single stack to test whether the string is a palindrome. The second should use two stacks to test whether the string is a palindrome when capitalization, spaces, punctuation, and other nonalphanumeric characters are ignored. The program should print the results of both tests.

12.9 Design and implement a class named `StringTree`, a binary tree for storing Strings in lexigraphical order. The tree should store values using the following class:

```
class Node {
  public String value;
  public Node left;
  public Node right;
  public Node(String value) {
    this.value = value;
```

```
        this.left = null;
        this.right = null;
    }
}
```

For any `Node` in the tree, a `String` in the `Node` pointed to by the left field should come before the node's string, and a string in the `Node` pointed to by the right field should come after the node's string. For example, if the string "quick" is added to an empty tree, its Node becomes the root of the tree. The node for string "brown" would then be added as quick's left node, and the node for "rabbit" would be added as quick's right node. If the string "a" was then added to the tree, it would be added as the brown's left node.

Your `StringTree` class should include a method for adding Strings, and two methods for printing the results of a depth-first traversal. (A depth-first traversal first prints the values on the left of a given node, then prints the value of the node itself, followed by the values on the right of the node. In this case, the results should be in lexigraphical order.) One depth-first traversal method should use recursion. The other should use a stack and no recursion.

Write a test driver that prompts the user for strings, adding them to a tree. When the user enters a blank line, both traversal methods should be invoked on the tree.

12.10 Design and implement an application to support a moderated question-and-answer session in which audience members submit questions to a queue. The question at the front of the queue may be answered by the speaker or panel, and a list of answered or unanswered questions may be retrieved at any time.

The program should accept the following simple commands: 'Q' will allow an audience member to submit a question, along with their name; 'A' will allow the speaker to enter an answer to the question currently at the top of the queue; 'P' will allow the speaker to pass on a question, moving it from the front of the queue to the end of the queue; 'R' will allow the speaker to mark a question as rejected, removing it from the queue; 'LA' will print a numbered list of answered questions, along with the answers; 'LU' will print a numbered list of unanswered questions; finally, 'X' will print numbered lists of answered and unanswered questions, and then exit the program.

You should create a `Question` class to store each question, its answer, and any other question state information. You must use only the methods in the class that provide queue functionality: remove the first element, append an element to the end, retrieve the queue size, and iterate over the list.

12.11 Design and implement your own `Stack` class and test it with the application given in this chapter. Use an array of objects as the underlying data storage mechanism and expand the array as needed. Start with an initial array size and then expand by 50 percent each time. Include the methods `Push`, `Pop`, and `Peek` and an integer `Count` property as described in the Microsoft package. Also add a boolean `Empty` property that returns **true** when the count is zero and **false** otherwise.

12.12 Design and implement your own Queue class. For a test application, prompt the user for a series of lines of text and then, when an empty (blank) line is entered, echo back every line. Use an array of objects as the underlying data storage mechanism and expand the array as needed. Start with an initial array size and then expand by 50 percent each time. Include the methods Enqueue, Dequeue, and Peek and an integer Count property as described in the Microsoft package. Also add a boolean Empty property that returns **true** when the count is zero and **false** otherwise.

Answers to Self-Review Questions

12.1 A collection is an object whose purpose is to store and organize primitive data or other objects. Some collections represent classic data structures that are helpful in particular problem-solving situations.

12.2 A collection is a group of data and the operations that can be performed on that data. An object is essentially the same thing in that we encapsulate related variables and methods in an object. The object hides the underlying implementation of the collection, separating the interface from the underlying implementation, permitting the implementation to be changed without affecting the interface.

12.3 A dynamic data structure is constructed using references to link various objects together into a particular organization. It is dynamic in that it can grow and shrink as needed. New objects can be added to the structure and obsolete objects can be removed from the structure at run time by adjusting references between objects in the structure.

12.4 Each node in a doubly linked list has references to both the node that comes before it in the list and the node that comes after it in the list. This organization allows for easy movement forward and backward in the list, and simplifies some operations.

12.5 A header node for a linked list is a special node that holds information about the list, such as references to the front and rear of the list and an integer to keep track of how many nodes are currently in the list.

12.6 A queue is a linear data structure like a list but it has more constraints on its use. A general list can be modified by inserting or deleting nodes anywhere in the list, but a queue only adds nodes to one end (enqueue) and takes them off of the other (dequeue). Thus a queue uses a first-in, first-out (FIFO) approach.

12.7 A stack is a linear data structure that adds (pushes) and removes (pops) nodes from one end. It manages information using a last-in, first-out (LIFO) approach.

12.8 The Stack class is defined in the .Net library. It implements a generic stack ADT. The Stack class stores Object references, so the stack can be used to store any kind of object.

12.9   Trees and graphs are both nonlinear data structures, meaning that the data they store is not organized in a linear fashion. Trees create a hierarchy of nodes. The nodes in a graph are connected using general edges.

12.10   The `CollectionBase` class is used to create highly typed collections by implementing the class.

Number Systems A

This appendix contains a detailed introduction to number systems and their underlying characteristics. The particular focus is on the binary number system, its use with computers, and its similarities to other number systems. This introduction also covers conversions between bases.

In our everyday lives, we use the *decimal number system* to represent values, to count, and to perform arithmetic. The decimal system is also referred to as the *base-10 number system*. We use 10 digits (0 through 9) to represent values in the decimal system.

Computers use the *binary number system* to store and manage information. The binary system, also called the *base-2 number system*, has only two digits (0 and 1). Each 0 and 1 is called a *bit*, short for binary digit. A series of bits is called a *binary string*.

There is nothing particularly special about either the binary or decimal systems. Long ago, humans adopted the decimal number system probably because we have 10 fingers on our hands. If humans had 12 fingers, we would probably be using a base-12 number system regularly and find it as easy to deal with as we do the decimal system now. It all depends on what you get used to. As you explore the binary system, it will become more familiar and natural.

Binary is used for computer processing because the devices used to manage and store information are less expensive and more reliable if they have to represent only two possible values. Computers have been made that use the decimal system, but they are not as convenient.

There are an infinite number of number systems, and they all follow the same basic rules. You already know how the binary number system works, but you just might not be aware that you do. It all goes back to the basic rules of arithmetic.

Place Value

In decimal, we represent the values of 0 through 9 using only one digit. To represent any value higher than 9, we must use more than one digit. The position of each digit has a *place value* that indicates the amount it contributes to the overall value. In decimal, we refer to the one's column, the ten's column, the hundred's column, and so on forever.

Each place value is determined by the *base* of the number system, raised to increasing powers as we move from right to left. In the decimal number system, the place value of the digit furthest to the right is 10^0, or 1. The place value of the next digit is 10^1, or 10. The place value of the third digit from the right is 10^2, or 100, and so on. Figure A.1 shows how each digit in a decimal number contributes to the value.

The binary system works the same way except that we exhaust the available digits much sooner. We can represent 0 and 1 with a single bit, but to represent any value higher than 1, we must use multiple bits.

The place values in binary are determined by increasing powers of the base as we move right to left, just as they are in the decimal system. However, in binary, the base value is 2. Therefore the place value of the bit furthest to the right is 2^0, or 1. The place value of the next bit is 2^1, or 2. The place value of the third bit from the right is 2^2, or 4, and so on. Figure A.2 shows a binary number and its place values.

The number 1101 is a valid binary number, but it is also a valid decimal number as well. Sometimes to make it clear which number system is being used, the base value is appended as a subscript to the end of a number. Therefore you can distinguish between 1101_2, which is equivalent to 13 in decimal, and 1101_{10} (one thousand, one hundred and one), which in binary is represented as 10001001101_2.

A number system with base N has N digits (0 through $N-1$). As we have seen, the decimal system has 10 digits (0 through 9), and the binary system has two digits (0 and 1). They all work the same way. For instance, the base-5 number system has five digits (0 to 4).

Note that, in any number system, the place value of the digit furthest to the right is 1, since any base raised to the zero power is 1. Also notice that the value 10, which we refer to as "ten" in the decimal system, always represents the base value in any number system. In base 10, 10 is one 10 and zero 1's. In base 2, 10 is one 2 and zero 1's. In base 5, 10 is one 5 and zero 1's.

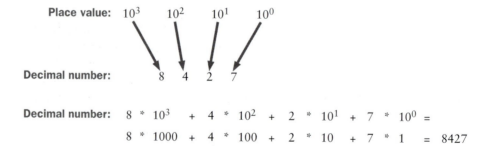

FIGURE A.1 Place values in the decimal system

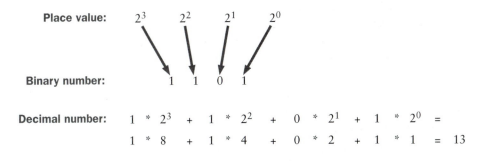

FIGURE A.2 Place values in the binary system

Bases Higher Than 10

Since all number systems with base N have N digits, then base 16 has 16 digits. But what are they? We are used to the digits 0 through 9, but in bases higher than 10, we need a single digit, a single symbol, that represents the decimal value 10. In fact, in *base 16*, which is also called *hexadecimal*, we need digits that represent the decimal values 10 through 15.

For number systems higher than 10, we use alphabetic characters as single digits for values greater than 9. The hexadecimal digits are 0 through F, where 0 through 9 represent the first 10 digits, and A represents the decimal value 10, B represents 11, C represents 12, D represents 13, E represents 14, and F represents 15.

Therefore the number 2A8E is a valid hexadecimal number. The place values are determined as they are for decimal and binary, using increasing powers of the base. So in hexadecimal, the place values are powers of 16. Figure A.3 shows how the place values of the hexadecimal number 2A8E contribute to the overall value.

All number systems with bases greater than 10 use letters as digits. For example, base 12 has the digits 0 through B and base 19 has the digits 0 through I. However, beyond having a different set of digits and a different base, the rules governing each number system are the same.

Keep in mind that when we change number systems, we are simply changing the way we represent values, not the values themselves. If you have 18_{10} pencils, it may be written as 10010 in binary or as 12 in hexadecimal, but it is still the same number of pencils.

Figure A.4 shows the representations of the decimal values 0 through 20 in several bases, including *base 8*, which is also called *octal*. Note that the larger the base, the higher the value that can be represented in a single digit.

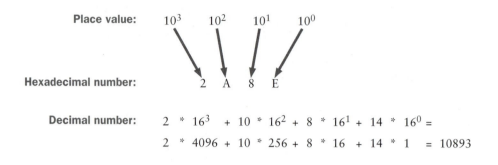

Place value: 10^3 10^2 10^1 10^0

Hexadecimal number: 2   A   8   E

Decimal number: $2 * 16^3 + 10 * 16^2 + 8 * 16^1 + 14 * 16^0 =$

$2 * 4096 + 10 * 256 + 8 * 16 + 14 * 1 = 10893$

FIGURE A.3 Place values in the hexadecimal system

Conversions

We've already seen how a number in another base is converted to decimal by determining the place value of each digit and computing the result. This process can be used to convert any number in any base to its equivalent value in base 10.

Now let's reverse the process, converting a base-10 value to another base. First, find the highest place value in the new number system that is less than or equal to the original value. Then divide the original number by that place value to determine the digit that belongs in that position. The remainder is the value that must be represented in the remaining digit positions. Continue this process, position by position, until the entire value is represented.

For example, Figure A.5 shows the process of converting the decimal value 180 into binary. The highest place value in binary that is less than or equal to 180 is 128 (or 2^7), which is the eighth bit position from the right. Dividing 180 by 128 yields 1 with 52 remaining. Therefore the first bit is 1, and the decimal value 52 must be represented in the remaining seven bits. Dividing 52 by 64, which is the next place value (2^6), yields 0 with 52 remaining. So the second bit is 0. Dividing 52 by 32 yields 1 with 20 remaining. So the third bit is 1 and the remaining five bits must represent the value 20. Dividing 20 by 16 yields 1 with 4 remaining. Dividing 4 by 8 yields 0 with 4 remaining. Dividing 4 by 4 yields 0 with 0 remaining.

Since the number has been completely represented, the rest of the bits are zero. Therefore 180_{10} is equivalent to 10110100 in binary. This can be confirmed by converting the new binary number back to decimal to make sure we get the original value.

This process works to convert any decimal value to any target base. For each target base, the place values and possible digits change. If you start with the correct place value, each division operation will yield a valid digit in the new base.

Binary (base 2)	Octal (base 8)	Decimal (base 10)	Hexadecimal (base 16)
0	0	0	0
1	1	1	1
10	2	2	2
11	3	3	3
100	4	4	4
101	5	5	5
110	6	6	6
111	7	7	7
1000	10	8	8
1001	11	9	9
1010	12	10	A
1011	13	11	B
1100	14	12	C
1101	15	13	D
1110	16	14	E
1111	17	15	F
10000	20	16	10
10001	21	17	11
10010	22	18	12
10011	23	19	13
10100	24	20	14

FIGURE A.4 Counting in various number systems

In the example in Figure A.5, the only digits that could have resulted from each division operation would have been 1 or 0, since we were converting to binary. However, when we are converting to other bases, any valid digit in the new base could result. For example, Figure A.6 shows the process of converting the decimal value 1967 into hexadecimal.

The place value of 256, which is 16^2, is the highest place value less than or equal to the original number, since the next highest place value is 16^3 or 4096. Dividing 1976 by 256 yields 7 with 175 remaining. Dividing 175 by 16 yields 10 with 15 remaining. Remember that 10 in decimal can be represented as the single digit A in hexadecimal. The 15 remaining can be represented as the digit F. Therefore 1967_{10} is equivalent to 7AF in hexadecimal.

Place value	Number	Digit
128	180	1
64	52	0
32	52	1
16	20	1
8	4	0
4	4	1
2	0	0
1	0	0

$$180_{10} = 10110100_2$$

FIGURE A.5 Converting a decimal value into binary

Shortcut Conversions

We have established techniques for converting any value in any base to its equivalent representation in base 10, and from base 10 to any other base. Therefore you can now convert a number in any base to any other base by going through base 10. However, an interesting relationship exists between the bases that are powers of 2, such as binary, octal, and hexadecimal, which allows very quick conversions between them.

To convert from binary to hexadecimal, for instance, you can simply group the bits of the original value into groups of four, starting from the right, then convert each group of four into a single hexadecimal digit. The example in Figure A.7 demonstrates this process.

To go from hexadecimal to binary, we reverse this process, expanding each hexadecimal digit into four binary digits. Note that you may have to add leading zeros to the binary version of each expanded hexadecimal digit if necessary to make four binary digits. Figure A.8 shows the conversion of the hexadecimal value 40C6 to binary.

Why do we section the bits into groups of four when converting from binary to hexadecimal? The shortcut conversions work between binary and any base that is a power of 2. We section the bits into groups of that power. Since $2^4 = 16$, we section the bits in groups of four.

Converting from binary to octal is the same process except that the bits are sectioned into groups of three, since $2^3 = 8$. Likewise, when converting from octal to binary, we expand each octal digit into three bits.

Place value	Number	Digit
256	1967	7
16	175	A
1	15	F

$$1967_{10} = 7AF_{16}$$

FIGURE A.6 Converting a decimal value into hexadecimal

To convert between, say, hexadecimal and octal is now a process of doing two shortcut conversions. First convert from hexadecimal to binary, then take that result and perform a shortcut conversion from binary to octal.

By the way, these types of shortcut conversions can be performed between any base B and any base that is a power of B. For example, conversions between base 3 and base 9 can be accomplished using the shortcut grouping technique, sectioning or expanding digits into groups of two, since $3^2 = 9$.

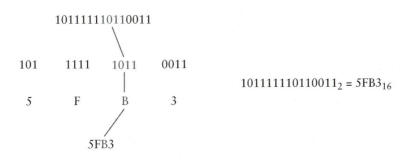

$$101111110110011_2 = 5FB3_{16}$$

FIGURE A.7 Shortcut conversion from binary to hexadecimal

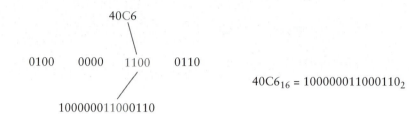

FIGURE A.8 Shortcut conversion from hexadecimal to binary

The Unicode Character Set B

The Java programming language uses the Unicode character set for managing text. A *character set* is simply an ordered list of characters, each corresponding to a particular numeric value. Unicode is an international character set that contains letters, symbols, and ideograms for languages all over the world. Each character is represented as a 16-bit unsigned numeric value. Unicode, therefore, can support over 65,000 unique characters. Only about half of those values have characters assigned to them at this point. The Unicode character set continues to be refined as characters from various languages are included.

Many programming languages still use the ASCII character set. ASCII stands for the American Standard Code for Information Interchange. The 8-bit extended ASCII set is quite small, so the developers of Java opted to use Unicode in order to support international users. However, ASCII is essentially a subset of Unicode, including corresponding numeric values, so programmers used to ASCII should have no problems with Unicode.

Figure B.1 shows a list of commonly used characters and their Unicode numeric values. These characters also happen to be ASCII characters. All of the characters in Figure B.1 are called *printable characters* because they have a symbolic representation that can be displayed on a monitor or printed by a printer. Other characters are called *nonprintable characters* because they have no such symbolic representation. Note that the space character (numeric value 32) is considered a printable character, even though no symbol is printed when it is displayed. Nonprintable characters are sometimes called *control characters* because many of them can be generated by holding down the control key on a keyboard and pressing another key.

The Unicode characters with numeric values 0 through 31 are nonprintable characters. Also, the delete character, with numeric value 127, is a nonprintable character. All of these characters are ASCII characters as well. Many of them have fairly common and well-defined uses, while others are more general. The table in Figure B.2 lists a small sample of the nonprintable characters.

Nonprintable characters are used in many situations to represent special conditions. For example, certain nonprintable characters can be stored in a text document to indicate, among other things, the beginning of a new line. An editor will process these characters by starting the text that follows it on a new line, instead of printing a symbol to the screen. Various types of computer systems use different nonprintable characters to represent particular conditions.

Value	Char	Value	Char	Value	Char	Value	Char	Value	Char
32	space	51	3	70	F	89	Y	108	l
33	!	52	4	71	G	90	Z	109	m
34	"	53	5	72	H	91	[	110	n
35	#	54	6	73	I	92	\	111	o
36	$	55	7	74	J	93	]	112	p
37	%	56	8	75	K	94	^	113	q
38	&	57	9	76	L	95	–	114	r
39	'	58	:	77	M	96	`	115	s
40	(	59	;	78	N	97	a	116	t
41	)	60	<	79	O	98	b	117	u
42	*	61	=	80	P	99	c	118	v
43	+	62	>	81	Q	100	d	119	w
44	'	63	?	82	R	101	e	120	x
45	–	64	@	83	S	102	f	121	y
46	.	65	A	84	T	103	g	122	z
47	/	66	B	85	U	104	h	123	{
48	0	67	C	86	V	105	i	124	l
49	1	68	D	87	W	106	j	125	}
50	2	69	E	88	X	107	k	126	~

FIGURE B.1 A small portion of the Unicode character set

Except for having no visible representation, nonprintable characters are essentially equivalent to printable characters. They can be stored in a Java character variable and be part of a character string. They are stored using 16 bits, can be converted to their numeric value, and can be compared using relational operators.

The first 128 characters of the Unicode character set correspond to the common ASCII character set. The first 256 characters correspond to the ISO-Latin-1 extended ASCII character set. Many operating systems and Web browsers will handle these characters, but they may not be able to print the other Unicode characters.

Value	Character
0	*null*
7	*bell*
8	*backspace*
9	*tab*
10	*line feed*
12	*form feed*
13	*carriage return*
27	*escape*
127	*delete*

FIGURE B.2   Some nonprintable characters in the Unicode character set

Coding Standards, Software Engineering and Related Topics

Created by Ken Culp, Northern Michigan University

THE QUALITY ISSUE

If you are a student new to programming, you will probably find the current topic beyond the scope of the text and perhaps beyond the requirements for passing a class based on this text. However, it has been our experience that learning the concept of quality programming associated with the C# language will improve your skills in the class and better prepare you for any future job that requires programming. In a word, quality counts and in the long run will pay dividends to you and others.

Code with others and yourself in mind

As you program, you should first realize that writing a program is not a one-time event. In fact, you will often return to a program many times as you enhance it and/or make repairs. Furthermore, a significant period of time may have passed from the time you wrote a program until you return to work on it again. This is particularly true today in the world of Object Oriented Programming where the objective is to create reusable code. In this case, you will develop modules that are or will be used by you or others in your organization.

For example, you might create a module (.dll) that handles the creation of a database. Some time in the future, you decide to use that module with some changes for another program. If you open the old program and cannot figure out what it was doing, it might end up being faster to start from scratch.

For this reason, you should always remember as you program that you or someone else may have to read and repair this program. The techniques in this appendix will help you to create quality programs that can be easily understood by you and others and can be modified readily.

Standards

One of the things that made the Internet so successful in such a short period of time were the standards that were established. Everyone and anyone knew what it would take to create web sites and to access these sites. In other words, these set rules facilitate working together, even with people you don't know or with whom you do not even share a common language.

So it is in the programming world of C#. If everyone does similar things in similar ways, I can pick up your program and more easily understand what it is trying to do. Thus, this section will highlight things that, if you do them, will improve the quality of your code, will make it easier for your instructor and others to analyze your code, and make the job of cooperating on projects in teams much easier!

One final note here is appropriate. These are recommendations or suggestions and not hard-and-fast rules. Different companies may publish their own standards that are at variance with these. In fact your instructor may require you to follow some different standards. The standards shown here are those that have generally evolved in industry over the last couple of years and are somewhat unique to both the Visual Studio platform and the C# language.

NAMING CONVENTIONS

Remember that the names you use for variables, methods, method parameters, classes and the like will be used repeadly in your program and frequently appear in *Intellisense* as you type your programs. Therefore, the names you use should clearly indicate the use to which they will apply. Also, by following a fixed style for names, you can more easily identify the type of identifier being used. Here are some specifics.

Definitions

Initial Upper Case: Sometimes called the "Title" case. Set the first letter of in the identifier as uppercase and the first letter of each additional word is capitalized. No underscores are used to separate words but the casing is used to highlight the words. Examples: `ForeColor`, `FontSize`.

Initial Lower Case: Sometimes called the "Camel" case. Set the first word into lower case and follow with the first letter of each subsequent word in upper case. Again, no underscores are used. Examples: `foreColor`, `fontSize`.

All Upper Case: All letters are given in upper case. These are generally reserved for either constants of for words that are only two letters long. Since all letters are in the same case, underscores can be used to separate words. Examples: PI, MIN_GRADE.

Class Naming

All class names should be in initial upper case format without any underscores. Class name should be descriptive and avoid abbreviations unless the name would be too long. For example, `EmployeeInsuranceData` might be abbreviated to `EmpInsData`. Excessive use of abbreviations should be avoided. Thus EIData would not be a recommended replacement for the previous example.

Interface Naming

In general, interfaces should follow the same conventions as classes except that the initial letter should always be a capital I followed by a second capital letter of the word that describes the interface. Example: IComparable, IFormatable. The names should describe the behavior of the interface (the first example above indicates classes that have a CompareTo method among others to facilitate sorting. Classes can start with a capital I but the next letter would not be capitalized as this would be a name reserved for an interface).

Enumerations

Enumerations should follow the Initial Upper Case pattern and avoid use of abbreviations. Use should be clearly indicated from the name. Enumerations should be used where possible to replace a list of constants.

Member Variables

Class Member variables should always be located immediately after the class definition so they can be found quickly. If these member variables are to be wrapped by a Property, then you should prefix the variable name with "m_" as in these examples: m_LastName, m_FirstName. For internally used class variables, use Initial Lower Case as in lastName.

Method Parameters

Method parameters follow the Initial Lower Case pattern and, in general, use descriptive nouns to indicate use. Remember that the name you choose here will appear with *Intellisense* when you type the method name elsewhere. Therefore, you should minimize use of abbreviations.

Methods

Methods should all follow the Initial Upper Case and should generally be composed of verbs. The function should be clear from the name, particularly for public functions as these would appear in *Intellisense*.

Properties

Properties expose hidden member variables (see convention above). Therefore, these use the Initial Upper Case format. Use nouns because variables describe things. The property name would be the same as the member variable without the "m_"as in this example:

```
public class MyClass
{
    string m_LastName;
    ...
    public string LastName
    {
      get { return m_LastName; }
      set { m_LastName = Value;}
    }
    ...
}
```

Local Variables

Local variables should follow the Initial Upper Case pattern and avoid use of abbreviations. Use should be clearly indicated from the name. For example:

```
string lastName;
```

Constants

Constants should always be in All Initial Upper Case pattern and avoid use of abbreviations. Use should be clearly indicated from the name. Also, use underscore to separate words. For example:

```
const Single PI = 3.14159;
const string KEY_FILE = "C:\KEYS\KEYFILE";
```

CODING STANDARDS

The following are general guidelines that should be followed with creating your program.

Structured Programming

In general, you should adhere strictly to the constraints of good structured programming. This means no use of the `continue` statement. Also, the `break` statement should only be used to terminate cases of a `switch` statement. Also, where possible, every method should have only one `return` statement. It is always possible to code around the extra `return` statements. For example:

```
if (txtLast.TextLength < 5)
{
return;
}
  <method code here>
```

Could be replaced with the following:

```
if (txtLast.TextLength >= 5)
{
    <method code here>
}
return;
```

As a final note under Structured Programming, you should avoid use of one-line `if` statements. Go ahead and use the two braces even though there is only one line of code in between. This will improve program readability.

Classes and Packages

Break up your program into smaller parts using separate classes to encapsulate related functions. If you are writing console applications, do not add code to the `main` method but place them in other classes. Also, if only one class is to be imported from a package, use that class by name. If more than one class is to be imported, use the * symbol.

Modifiers

Do not ever declare class variables with the `public` modifier. Instead, mark the variable as `private` and wrap a property around it. Also, do not use modifiers inside an interface. Cleary mark all constants with the `const` directive.

Properties are *nouns*, methods are *verbs*

Properties designate things so should be designated as nouns or nouns with adjectives. Methods, on the other hand, take actions and should be named with verbs.

Method Size

In general, you will find that your programs will be easier to create and maintain if you can limit a method to one or at most two screens worth of code (excluding comments). It is always nice to be able to see an entire method when you switch to full-screen mode. To do this, break out pieces of code within one method and place it in another method, always looking for breaking out that part that might eventually be shared with another piece of code.

Program Structure including use of #Region

Locate related methods together in a class. Then surround the related items with a #Region and #End Region directives. For example:

```
#Region "Employee Payroll Functions"
  public int GiveRaise()
    ...
  public Double ComputeWage(int hours)
    ...
# End Region
```

In the above example, a box with a minus sign would appear in the code that can be used to minimize that portion of the code. This is just like what the complier adds to the "Windows Form Designer Generated Code" when creating a form. In this way, you can minimize large blocks of code and facilitate finding code in the program. For example, in the figure below, the entire form's code has been compressed down using multiple Region blocks. To see any section of the code, the user would click one of the plus signs.

```
⊞ Windows Form Designer generated code

⊞ Class Variables

⊞ Support methods:  Count, DbToForm, FormToDb, ClearFields

⊞ Form Load event: Fills data set; loads cboGenre; shows first row.

⊞ Update Menu Save and Cancel items and support methods (Undelete belov

⊞ Scroll buttons (Next/Previous), scroll methods, Mouse Wheel support

⊞ Code to set record scroll order
```

INTERNAL DOCUMENTATION AND STYLE

Overview

In general, you should have enough comments so that if you were to look at the code some time later, you could remember exactly what was being done. As noted above, think as you code about you or someone else having to come back later and make changes.

Therefore, liberal use of comments in your code is encouraged. Comments are particularly useful when the code is not obvious and when creating complex algorithms. In general, you should comment everything that is not obvious. For example, comments should be included at the beginning of every class, at the beginning of every method, on properties, etc. Here are some specifics:

XML Documentation

C# allows program developers to document their code using XML. In the source code, this appears as lines beginning with /// and that precede 1) a user-defined type such as a class, interface; 2) a member such as a field, property, or method; 3) a namespace. The documentation place there can be processed as comments and placed in a file. For more information, select Help/Index and then type "XML Documentation." Start with the "Tutorial [C#]" entry in the list of topics.

When a new C# class is added to a project, the designer adds an XML class header much like the one below. Place the description of the file (class) between the `<summary>` and `</summary>` tags.

```
/// <summary>
/// Summary description for LinkList.
/// </summary>
```

Replace the default first line (Summary description...) with the first line of the description. Then press enter. Each time you press enter, the editor will create a new line with /// and be ready for more text. When you are done, just backspace over the last set of ///.

Header Blocks

Every source code module should contain a module header. We recommend you use the XML header section as described above because it will then be easy to find and could be exported to an XML documentation file. The documentation should include the author, the date it was created and the purpose of the file. Also, external dependencies can be delineated in this section.

Methods and Parameters

You should include a description of the function of every method. This includes the purpose of the method as well as the use of each of the passed parameters and the return value. Also, if some complex algorithm is being used, that should be described with external documentation references if appropriate.

Inline Comments

Similarly, use comments within the code. These can either be before or between lines of code or placed on the line of code itself. In general, try to keep all of a line visible in the designer code window so avoid long comments at the end of a code line.

However, you need not comment the obvious. For example, the comment on the following would be redundant.

```
index++; // Add one to the index
```

Indentation

Make total use of indentation as C# would format your code. Use as a minimum, two spaces for indentation. However, 3 spaces are better and the Express version of C# installs with a standard of four spaces. Always align the else part of an if-statement with the if part. Be sure beginning and ending braces always remain aligned in the same column (another reason to keep single methods to a page of code).

Also, always place beginning and ending braces on their own line except in very short Property specifications. This facilitates seeing what code is associated with the block as shown below.

```
while (item != null)
{
   s += item.ToString() + " ";
   item = item.next;
}
```

Similarly, readability is improved if each **case** of a **switch** statement is indented your standard indentation amount.

Visual Studio Installation Guide D

Created by Ken Culp, Northern Michigan University

INSTALLING VISUAL STUDIO FROM THE WEB

You can install the Visual Studio package and the associated documentation (MSDN) from the CD with this book or download it from the Internet. To use the CD, insert the CD and follow the steps that come up on your screen. Then skip to the "Starting Visual Studio" section of this appendix. To use the Internet, you'll want to use a high-speed connection. This appendix provides instructions for the most current version of Visual Studio at the time of publication.

To begin the installation process, open the following URL:

http://www.msdn.microsoft.com/vstudio/express

This is Microsoft's web site for downloading the free "Express" versions of Visual Studio. From this site, you would pick the version that most closely matches your requirements. For use with this text, you will need to download the C# version as shown at the right. You may download other products also if you wish to play with them. However, the C# installation will include the documentation and, optionally, the SQL Server Express package (see below).

When you click the *Visual C# 2005 Express Edition,* you are presented with full screen of details. On this screen is a *Download Now* box that resembles the one shown at the right. In that box, click the *Download Now* button.

The download process will not yet begin. Instead, you are given some final warnings about the need to remove any previous versions of Visual Studio <u>2005</u> that may have been installed. This warning is shown below.

For Windows Development

Visual Basic 2005 Express Edition »
Productivity that is ideal for first time or casual Windows programming.

Visual C# 2005 Express Edition »
A great combination of power and productivity for the Windows developer.

Visual C++ 2005 Express Edition »
Horsepower with a finer degree of control than other Express Editions.

Visual J# 2005 Express Edition »
Ideal for those with prior Java-language experience or learning the Java language.

Download Now

Download Now!

1. Uninstall beta versions

Before installing, you **must** uninstall any previous versions of SQL Server 2005, Visual Studio 2005, and the .NET Framework 2.0.

2. Download and install

Download and install Visual C# 2005 Express Edition!!

⬇ Download

Note: Having network issues or need to burn a CD for offline installation? Follow the manual installation instructions.

3. Register

Why register? You'll need to get your registration key. Additionally, you'll get a lot of free stuff including royalty-free images from Corbis, online training from Microsoft Learning, E-books from Microsoft Press and more. Learn more about registration benefits.

Need Help?

Having problems downloading or installing Express? Visit the Support area on this site or the Express Forums for troubleshooting tips and answers to common questions.

In the unlikely event you have been testing Visual Studio 2005 in one of its Beta test versions, you <u>must</u> remove them before the express version is to be installed. If you have installed one of these versions, click the link given in step 1. This will give you two ways to unload these versions: 1) a step-by-step procedure; or 2) a removal program. Take the removal program path and run that program before returning to this screen.

If you have not installed any prior versions of Visual Studio 2005 or you have removed them from your system, click the *Download* link in step 2 above. This displays the download screen for the small (2.80 megabyte) **vcsetup.exe** program as shown at the right.

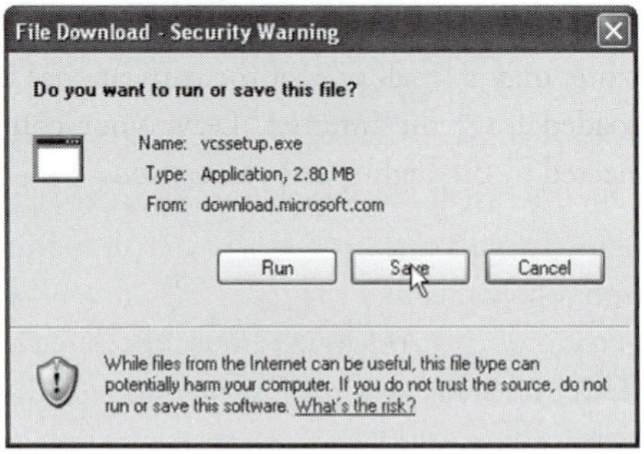

Then run the program. When you select **Save**, the system file save dialog box is shown (see right). For best results, **Save** the program to a separate directory like a "<u>downloads</u>" directory.

Once you click **Save**, the file is downloaded to your hard drive. Once the download completes, you will be given the option to run the program as shown in the figure below.

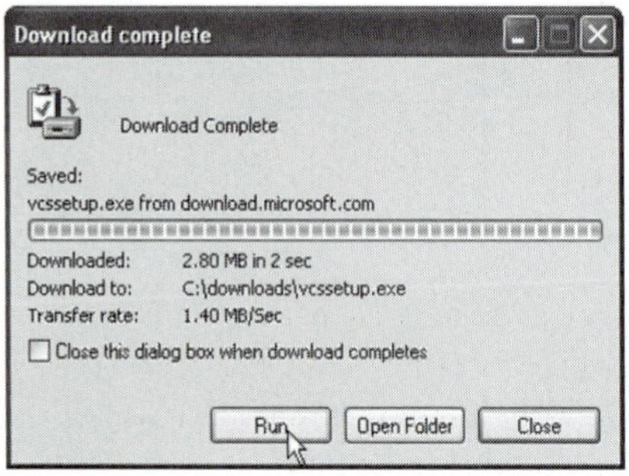

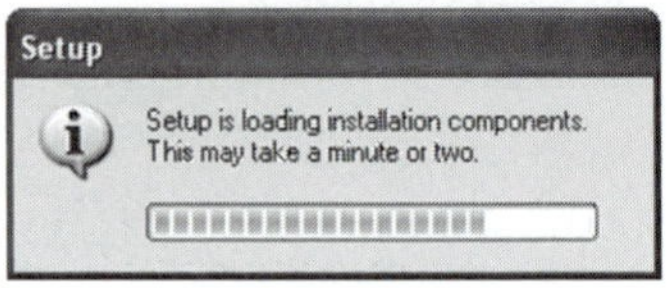

From the **Download Complete** box above, click the **Run** button. This will activate the **Setup Working** dialog box as shown above on the right.

Visual Studio Setup

When this step is complete, the initial welcome screen is displayed as shown at the right. You are asked a question about whether to send Microsoft the results of your installation. In general, you should leave the check in this box and click the **Next** button. **Note:** At this time, only a small part of the software has been downloaded from the internet. Leave your computer connected to the high-speed connection.

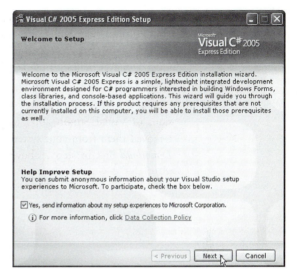

When you click next, you are asked to acknowledge the End User License Agreement from Microsoft as shown below at the left. Read the agreement and click the box marked "**I accept …**" and then click the button labeled **Next.**

At this point, you are presented with some choices as to what packages to install as shown in the figure above at the right. For purposes of this text, you will probably not require the SQL server (unless you wish to play with the **EmployeeAdoSql** example program from Chapter 10). Ask your instructor if you should check this box.

From the **Installation Options** screen, click the **Next** button. This displays the **Destination Folder** option box as shown below on the left. In general, you should just leave the defaults and click the **Install** button. As noted at the bottom of this dialog box, you must remain connected to the internet during the download (see the **Download and Install Progress** box below right).

Once all the software has been downloaded from the internet, the display will change to the box shown at the right. When this box is displayed, you can disconnect from the internet as noted in the box. Note that several items are being installed:

1. **.NET Framework 2.0:** Configures your computer to be able to run programs created with C#.

2. **Visual C# 2005 Express Edition:** The software that allows you to create and run the programs shown in this book.

3. **MSDN 2005 Express Edition:** This is the documentation for C# so you can obtain help during program development.

4. **SQL Server:** Optional database manager.

Once the installation is complete, you will be allowed to register your product **which must be done within 30 days!** Click the Register link on this last screen and supply the information requested. If you do not register at this time, you can start C# and click Help/Register Product at any time during the first 30 days. Also, if you have not registered, a baloon will appear asking you to register each time you start C#.

STARTING VISUAL STUDIO

You can start the program by clicking on the **Start** icon on your desktop, selecting **All Programs** and then clicking **Microsoft Visual C# Express Edition.** This is illustrated below.

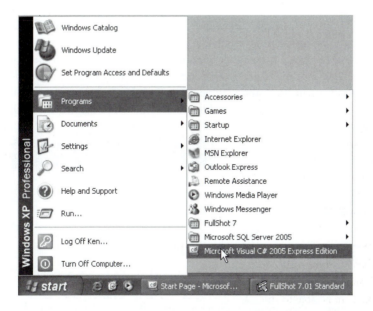

ADDING A VISUAL STUDIO ICON TO YOUR DESKTOP

If you find having to click Start/All Programs/C# over and over, you can simplify the process by adding an icon to your desktop and/or your Quick Lauch area by following these procedures. First, navigate again the Visual Studio C# icon: Click the **Start** icon on your desktop and click **All Programs.** Now, right click the **Microsoft Visual C# Express**

Addition and from the popup window, select **Send To.** Then from the Send To menu, select **Desktop** (**Create Shortcut**). This is illustrated below.

This will create an icon on your desktop that looks like the one shown below at the left. From now on, you can start C# by double-clicking this icon. Also, you can use the quick launch area of the screen by right clicking the Task bar, left clicking properties, and clicking the check box labeled "Show Quick Launch." If you have selected this option, you can drag this new C# icon from the desktop to the task bar quick lauch area (note that the taskbar cannot be locked). This will add the icon to the Quick Launch area as shown below at the right.

SETTING UP COMMAND PROMPT

Console applications can easily be run from Visual Studio by selecting Debug/Start (F5). However, the console window will remain open only as long as the program is running or waiting on input. When the application completes, the console window is closed.

If you wish to test your applications directly by running the .exe file from the command prompt, you can create a tool on the tool bar that will make that job a lot easier. Click Tools/External Tools to display the External Tools dialog. Click the Add button and give the new tool the name "Command P&rompt." Browse to where windows is installed on your machine then to the `system32` directory and then select cmd.exe. For most systems, the "Command" field should contain `C:\WINDOWS\system32\cmd.exe`. Next click the arrow to the right of "Initial Directory" and select Project Directory and then append to the end of the string the letters "\bin\Debug." Leave "Use Output Window" and "Prompt for Arguments" unchecked, check Close on Exit and click OK. The dialog box should look like the following:

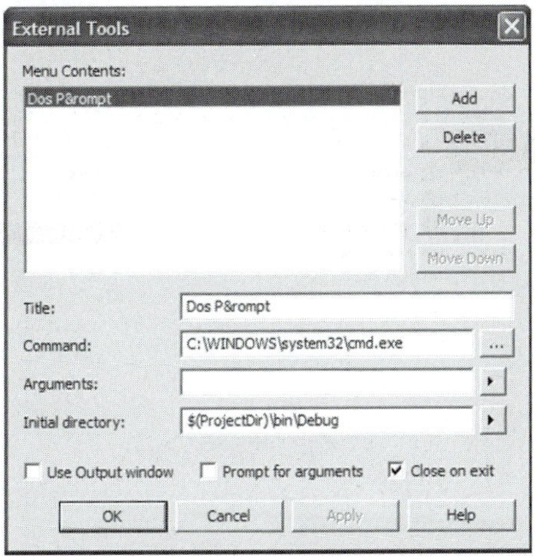

Click OK to save your changes. Now to run the command, select Tools/Command Prompt. This will open a command window in the bin\Debug directory of the selected project. Your Tool menu item should look something like the figure shown below.

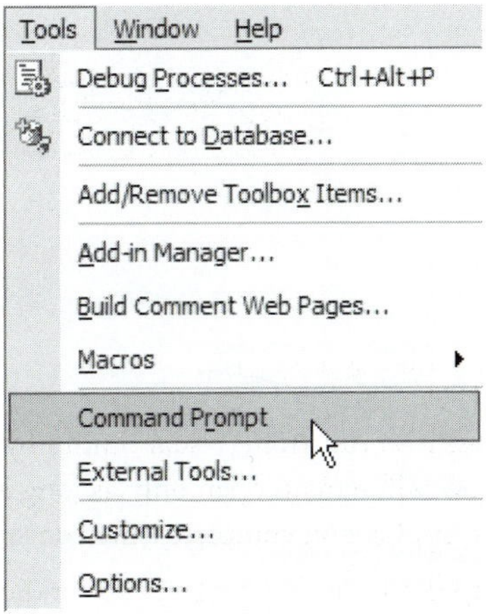

The executable program is usually the project name followed by the .exe extension. Therefore, to execute the program, type the project name plus any optional parameters and press the <enter> key.

Appendices E through G are available at www.aw.com/cssupport under "Author: Lewis."

Index